Writing in the Works

Writing in the Works

THIRD EDITION

Susan Blau
BOSTON UNIVERSITY

Kathryn Burak
BOSTON UNIVERSITY

Australia • Brazil • Japan • Korea • Mexico • Singapore • Spain • United Kingdom • United States

Writing in the Works, Third Edition
Susan Blau, Kathryn Burak

Senior Publisher: Lyn Uhl

Publisher: Monica Eckman

Acquisitions Editor: Margaret Leslie

Senior Development Editor: Leslie Taggart

Development Editor: Lisa Moore

Assistant Editor: Amy Haines

Editorial Assistant: Danielle Warchol

Associate Media Editor: Janine Tangney

Executive Marketing Manager: Stacey Purviance

Marketing Manager: Melissa Holt

Marketing Coordinator: Brittany Blais

Marketing Communications Manager: Courtney Morris

Senior Content Project Manager: Michael Lepera

Senior Art Director: Jill Ort

Senior Print Buyer: Betsy Donaghey

Senior Rights Acquisition Specialist: Dean Dauphinais

Production Service: Integra - Chicago

Text Designer: Bill Reuter

Cover Designer: Bill Reuter

Cover Image: Fusion Series #1936 – Collage on Paper - copyright Cecil Touchon – Courtesy the International Museum of Collage, Assemblage and Construction (collagemuseum.com)

Library of Congress Control Number: 2011928565

ISBN-13: 978-1-111-83460-9

ISBN-10: 1-111-83460-1

Wadsworth
20 Channel Center Street
Boston, MA 02210
USA

Cengage Learning is a leading provider of customized learning solutions with office locations around the globe, including Singapore, the United Kingdom, Australia, Mexico, Brazil and Japan. Locate your local office at **international.cengage.com/region**

Cengage Learning products are represented in Canada by Nelson Education, Ltd.

For your course and learning solutions, visit **www.cengage.com.**

Purchase any of our products at your local college store or at our preferred online store **www.cengagebrain.com.**

Instructors: Please visit **login.cengage.com** and log in to access instructor-specific resources.

Printed in China
2 3 4 5 6 7 15 14 13 12

Brief Contents

Segretain/Getty Images

PART 1: THE WRITER'S CRAFT

Enrique's Journey © 2002 Los Angles Times. Photos by Don Barletti

PART 2: WRITING TO EXPLORE

TAO Images/SuperStock

PART 3: WRITING TO INFORM

PART 4: WRITING TO ANALYZE

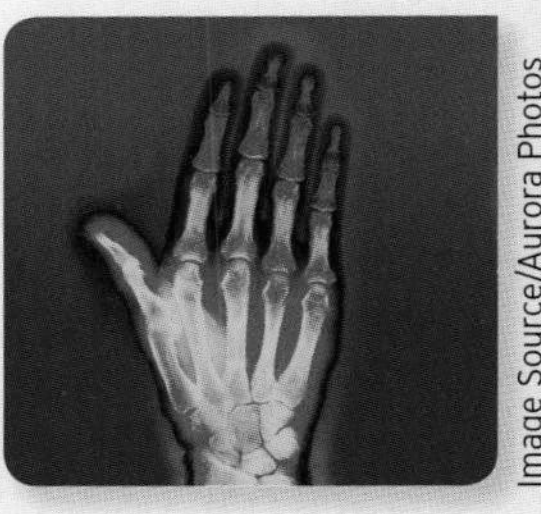
Image Source/Aurora Photos

Luba Lukova

PART 5: WRITING TO ARGUE

Tony Law/Redux Pictures

PART 6: RESEARCH AND DOCUMENTATION

PART 7: GRAMMAR HANDBOOK

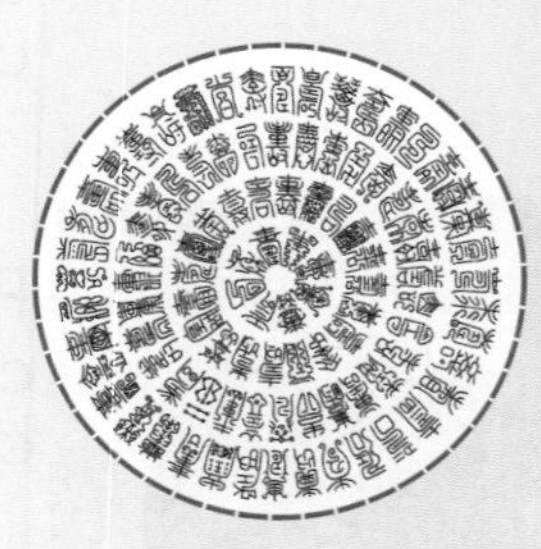

John Lock/Shutterstock.com

Detailed Contents

Part 1: The Writer's Craft

CHAPTER 1: THE RHETORICAL SITUATION WRITERS' CHOICES 2

CHAPTER 2: THE WRITER'S PROCESS 21

CHAPTER 3: COLLABORATION, PEER REVIEW, AND WRITING AS A PUBLIC ACT 45

CHAPTER 4: READING, THINKING, AND WRITING CRITICALLY 65

Part 2: Writing to Explore

CHAPTER 5: WRITING A PERSONAL STATEMENT APPLICATION ESSAYS 95

CHAPTER 6: WRITING A NARRATIVE
MEMOIRS 127

CHAPTER 7: WRITING ABOUT OTHERS PROFILES 171

Part 3: Writing to Inform

CHAPTER 8: WRITING AN EXPOSITION SHORT ARTICLES 215

CHAPTER 9: WRITING A REPORT

Part 4: Writing to Analyze

CHAPTER 10: WRITING AN EVALUATION FILM REVIEWS 279

CHAPTER 11: WRITING A CAUSAL ANALYSIS
LONG RESEARCHED ARTICLES 313

Part 5: Writing to Argue

CHAPTER 14: WRITING FOR YOUR COMMUNITY PROPOSALS 443

Part 6: Research and Documentation

CHAPTER 15: RESEARCH 479

CHAPTER 19: COMMON ERRORS 593

CHAPTER 20: TROUBLE SPOTS FOR NONNATIVE SPEAKERS OF ENGLISH 609

Writing Projects

CHAPTER 1 Write about the Rhetorical Situation. Music Review | Lady Gaga. In three to four paragraphs, summarize the article and apply your understanding to the choices that a writer makes about genre, purpose, audience, voice, media, and design.

CHAPTER 2 Write a Literacy Narrative. Write about when you first became aware of yourself as a literate person, someone who could read and write. A literacy narrative, a form of memoir told in first person, allows a glimpse into how a writer got started, the struggles of writing, or the process of discovering the power of words.

CHAPTER 4 Write a Rhetorical Analysis. Choose a text and write your own rhetorical analysis using the lists of questions in this chapter to guide you through reading and formulating ideas, summarizing, and writing an analytical thesis that explains a pattern you observed or a decision you made about the text.

CHAPTER 5 Write an Application Essay. Target an audience—a job, a scholarship program, or an internship—and write a personal statement that reveals some of your personality, beliefs, and goals in a way that defines your connection to the audience.

CHAPTER 6 Write a Memoir, a true story about some part of your life. Your story can relate a single event or a series of closely linked events. Show a change of mind or heart, a discovery, a confirmation or contradiction of a belief, a disappointment, or a decision.

CHAPTER 7 Write a Profile. At their best, profiles invite the reader into the subject's world. In your profile of a person or group, focus on some specific aspect that is noteworthy. You do not have to admire the people you write about, but you should find their accomplishments, lifestyles, or philosophies interesting and maybe even fascinating to explore.

CHAPTER 8 **Write a Short Article.** Provide a tightly focused and intensely detailed view of something most people don't know about—a remote concept or idea, a new discovery, theory, process, or phenomenon—enlarging it to expand our understanding of that subject. Use multiple sources and compress and combine the details from your research to reveal something new that will surprise your readers.

CHAPTER 9 **Write a Report.** Write a fair, balanced, and concise summary that reports detailed information on an event or trend that has significance for your community. Focus on abstracting the main point from a whole collection of information.

CHAPTER 10 **Write a Film Review.** Evaluate a film by stating your overall opinion—positive, negative, or mixed—and supporting your opinion with evidence. In a film review your evidence will come from an analysis of the film elements: the story, acting, writing, cinematography, soundtrack, or special effects.

CHAPTER 11 **Write a Causal Analysis.** Identify a pattern or trend. Find proof the trend exists in statistics and anecdotes from practitioners and other experts. Those same sources may lead you toward your speculation about why the trend came about and/or what significant effects have been the result. Create a well-reasoned analysis defending your conclusions about what the causes and/or effects of the trend are.

CHAPTER 12 **Write an Argument.** Choose an issue that is current and debatable, one that could be argued from different perspectives. Define your position on the issue, and then find a good opportunity to add to the debate. Your argument should include an informed perspective, moving beyond personal preference and into a logical argument that demonstrates you understand the issue fully by including all sides, not just the position you are defending.

CHAPTER 13 **Create a Visual Argument.** In most advertisements, public service messages included, visuals work in conjunction with words. Find a nonprofit group or organization in your community that offers information or services that could benefit the public. Choose a medium (print, video, alternative). Research accurate and useful information, create images to support that information, and have the words

(Continued)

and images work in concert. Your aim is to serve your community by raising awareness of an issue, initiating a new behavior or attitude, or changing a behavior or attitude.

CHAPTER 14 Write a Proposal. Write a three- to five-page proposal that suggests a fresh way to help solve a local, community, or global public problem. Identify a problem, suggest a feasible solution, and present the benefits of the solution. The purpose of any proposal is to persuade readers to take some action: to donate time or money or to create a program, plan, or public service campaign.

CHAPTER 15 Create an Annotated Bibliography. Create an annotated bibliography, an alphabetized list of sources, put into one of the documentation styles (MLA, APA, or another) that you then notate with summary, evaluation, and/or commentary.

DIY (DO IT YOURSELF) MEDIA AND DESIGN

DIYs in each chapter offer a variation on the assignment that explores issues of media and design for a variety of microgenres.

CHAPTER 5 THE RÉSUMÉ AND APPLICATION LETTER

CHAPTER 6 THE GRAPHIC MEMOIR

CHAPTER 7 ORAL HISTORY: A SPOKEN WORD PROJECT

CHAPTER 8 THE HYBRID ESSAY—WORDS AND PICTURES

CHAPTER 9 WRITING FOR A BLOG: AN INSIDER'S VIEW

CHAPTER 10 A SCENE IN A SCREENPLAY

CHAPTER 11 INFOGRAPHICS—THE VISUAL INFORMATION OF DATA

CHAPTER 12 A FACEBOOK PAGE FOR AN EVENT AROUND AN ISSUE

CHAPTER 13 THE YOUTUBE ADVOCACY VIDEOE

CHAPTER 14 THE POWERPOINT PROPOSAL

Thematic Contents

Personal Experience

The Experience of Others

Media and Popular Culture

Matt Richtel, "Growing Up Digital, Wired for Distraction"
John Pareles, "Lavish Words and the Headwear to Match"
Anthony Kuhn, "For Japanese Women, the Past Is the Latest Fad"
Charles Fishman, "The Scoop on Disney's Dirty Laundry"
Janet Maslin, "Such a Very Long Way from Duvets to Danger"
Roger Ebert, "*Fight Club*"
Ty Burr, "Avatar"
Thomas McCarthy, scene from "The Visitor"
Ryan Conrath (student), "Scorcese Back at Film School, *The Departed*"

Gender, Race, Identity

Caryl Rivers and Rosalind C. Barnett, "The Difference Myth"
Susan Saulny, "Race Remixed: Black? White? Asian? More Americans Choose All of the Above"
Nitya K. Venkataraman (student), "That Other Part"
Lauren Wilcox, "Going with the Grain"
David Brooks, "Gangsta, in French"
Jody Rosen, "David Brooks, Playa Hater: The *New York Times* Columnist Grapples with 'Gangsta Rap'"
Jessica Hollander, "Stopping Teen Dating Violence"
Dana Benjamin, Johanna Mayhew, Alexandra Mayer-Hohdahl, and Peter Myers (students), "Proposal to Help End Slavery in Sudan"
Garland Waller, "Proposal for *The Silent Screams: Court-Ordered Abuse of Children*"
Jenna Livingston, Sarah Bomie Chae, Michael Thill, and Alexandria McManus (students), "South Shore Women's Center PSA"
J.R. Moehringer, "A Hidden and Solitary Soldier"
Thanos Matthai (student), "A Fine Balance: The Life of an Islamic Teenager"
Tess Langan (student), "Looking for Students Like Me"
Anny Chih, "500 Words or Less"

Social Change

Caryl Rivers and Rosalind C. Barnett, "The Difference Myth"
Jessica Polanski (student), "Smoke"
Stephen Budiansky, "Math Lessons for Locavores"
Nitya K. Venkataraman (student), "That Other Part"
Zeyu Xu, Jane Hannaway, and Colin Taylor, "Making a Difference?: The Effects of Teach for America in High School"
Katie Koch (student), "Reading at Grade Level"
Jessica Hollander, "Stopping Teen Dating Violence"

Science and Technology

Writing for Visual Communication

Education

Preface

Are you a writer? Most people would decidedly say no.

Oh, maybe I wrote some school papers, and the occasional letter of application.

That's all? You don't write reports, letters of complaint, recommendations? You don't speak out at public forums or respond to blogs and message boards? Most professional, college-educated people would actually be surprised to find how much they do write.

So, are you a writer?

Well, I write, but I'm not a writer.

Our goal in writing this book is two-fold: First, our aim is to demystify the writing most people are exposed to every day—the kind of writing that informs and teaches and entertains and enlightens. And second, we aim to help train confident, worldly writers—students who see themselves as fluent, capable, and well-prepared to ride the global communication wave: Students who say yes, I am a writer.

Boston University Photography

Authors Kathryn Burak and Susan Blau

We hope, through our approach to writing, that students see not just the relevance of the skills, but also their practicality, that writing is a valuable personal tool. We do want them to understand that it takes effort, but we also allow them to ask why it is worth the effort—why should they want to be writers? To answer that, we make two pacts with student. The first pact we make with our students is that writing well will have value in their lives, particularly as they develop distinct voices through their studies and later in their professional lives. The second is that their writing will have readers.

An Emphasis on Student Writing for Real-World Audiences: The Classroom and Beyond

While the classroom is the first real-world audience a student experiences, we make the point that students can write for audiences beyond the classroom. We start by choosing readings that are high-quality and current, writing that people turn to in order to become informed, educated, entertained, and enlightened. We make these choices because the writing we ask students to do is part of the world they inhabit—or aspire to inhabit—a world where they imagine themselves as players. They learn to write application essays, blogs, memoirs, news stories, film reviews, editorials, and researched magazine articles. They learn the tried-and-true academic writing skills—narration, exposition, analysis, and persuasion—in a context that makes sense and has meaning to them. We reinforce those skills with practice exercises seeded throughout the book, practice exercises that say to the student-writer, bring what you already know about writing and build on that knowledge. The end results are students who enter the stream of ideas with healthy skepticism and confidence, and most importantly, as flexible writers who can adapt the messages to many different audiences.

Teachers who have used this book have seen their students publish their writing in print publications and on Web sites. Students have often been paid for their work (movie reviews, profiles, and news stories, to name a few), and sometimes they have donated their writing to advocacy groups for use in public service. Many of our students have contributed their pieces to this book and can see their classroom work enter the world as worthy examples of student writing in a particular genre. In the end, students have left the course with a portfolio of writing samples—and of accomplishments that have a connection to a bigger, more diverse world that includes—but also goes beyond—the classroom.

An Organization that Reflects a Real-World Writing Process

We have organized each assignment chapter in this book in a way that allows students to gain mastery on their own if they are so inclined. Each writing assignment is broken down into distinct skills that are reinforced by practices placed throughout the chapters. The practices build the skills that students need to complete the longer chapter assignment. Contemporary professional and student writing provide examples for students to read and assimilate, and one reading in each assignment chapter serves as an "anatomy" of that form, with textual notations that show students how the writing skills translate into practice. The new process plans help students organize priorities for each genre.

As teachers guide students through skills and then ask them to put their skills together, students gain a sense of mastery. The goal is to put writing into a process that involves reading, researching, drafting, revising, and peer reviewing and then to let students take charge of their own writing. This kind of process prepares them for writing beyond the classroom in the workplace and in civic life. We stress that the study of writing has its roots in the academic world but that its branches reach well into the world of politics, entertainment, and commerce. And along those lines, the assignments of this book look to the future of writing for a digital world where verbal and visual messages are inseparable. Students of real-world writing must have analytical skills to read images as well as text.

Research Integrated as Part of a Real-World Approach to Writing

The "worldly" approach of this book also means thinking in a new way about research skills and the ways that research has usually been isolated to one or two assignments in writing classes. Professional writing involves research in all writing, and each of the assignment chapters integrates research into the writing task. Students learn what kind of research they need to do even before they can write a memoir or an application essay, and they learn how to research in print, online, and in person.

We offer students all the traditional information about finding, evaluating, and documenting their sources in print media, but we also help them fine-tune their skills in evaluating and documenting new media, including blogs and social media, for their research. We include the most recent documentation guidelines, so students can cite their sources accurately and avoid even the whiff of plagiarism. Plagiarism has become even more pressing a problem in the digital age, and we help students understand the parameters of intellectual property theft so they can avoid committing an act of unintentional plagiarism.

NEW TO THIS EDITION

In this third edition of *Writing in the Works,* we have enlisted colleagues, students, and writing teachers from far and wide to help us reinvent the text to incorporate more ideas about the demands new media will make on our students—while they are in school and when they are out in the world.

New Coverage of the Thesis Statement (The Big Idea)

Ironically, while we were re-examining our real-world approach, we found ourselves reaching back to classical academic writing to consider the importance of the thesis statement in all forms of writing. But in considering how to explain what is arguably the most difficult concept for a writing teacher, we concluded a one-size-fits-all approach doesn't work. Instead, in each chapter, we have a feature that tailors the thesis to purpose.

- Each chapter includes extensive coverage of composing a thesis statement, noting that the structure of a thesis statement can change depending on the genre. This coverage is highlighted in a section called The Big Idea.

New Coverage of the Rhetorical Situation

Drawing on our already distinct emphasis on how important considering audience is for a writer, we refocused our attention on the rhetorical situation.

- New Chapter 1 on The Rhetorical Situation (including audience, purpose, genre, design, visual literacy, and media concerns) features an assignment on analyzing the rhetorical situation of a music review. Each writing assignment includes a section on that genre's rhetorical situation and poses questions for considering the rhetorical situation after each reading.

New DIY (Do/Design It Yourself) Microgenre Variations for Each Writing Project.

After learning the skills involved in writing for a traditional genre, we offer students the option of applying those skills to an alternative, less traditional assignment. The DIYs emphasize design and media.

- DIYs (Do/Design it Yourself) at the end of each chapter highlight a microgenre such as PowerPoints (Proposals), YouTube videos (Public Service Messages), and Facebook pages (Editorials).

OTHER NEW FEATURES IN THIS EDITION

✓ **New design** with new pedagogy and Web support featuring splashy chapter images for the assignments that accompany the opening vignettes.

✓ **"What's to Come"** chapter objectives that preview each chapter's coming attractions.

- ✓ **Process Plan**—a graphic organizer for key elements in each assignment.
- ✓ **New Organization** around Writing to Explore, Inform, Analyze, and Argue that helps students connect the goals they learn for academic writing to real-world writing.
- ✓ **Streamlined Chapter** structure that begins with a Process Plan, a description of the writing project, an Anatomy (annotated essays), an exclusive interview with the author, and a new section on the rhetorical situation for that particular genre.
- ✓ **Literacy Narrative** assignment with walk-through of student paper in Chapter 2, The Writer's Process. Coverage of the rhetorical strategies is now included in this chapter.
- ✓ **Chapter 3, Collaboration, Peer Review, and Writing as a Public Act,** now appears as a separate chapter and continues to include the popular walk-through of one student's writing process and a student's published essay that was written for an assignment (a profile by a student writer on drug addiction and nursing published in a nursing journal).
- ✓ **Rhetorical Analysis** assignment is now included in Chapter 4, Reading, Thinking, and Writing Critically, with an annotated sample from an inspiring new reading, "Hardscrabble Salvation," plus a student's rhetorical analysis.
- ✓ **Social media coverage** in Chapter 9, Writing a Report: News for Print, Web, and Social Media, combines two previous chapters (News Reports and Writing for the Web) and focuses on the important role social media now plays in research and reporting. This chapter also emphasizes the critical skill of summary with special coverage of creating an Abstract.
- ✓ **Enhanced coverage of argument and logical appeals** in Chapter 12, Writing an Argument: Editorials, Commentaries and Blogs and in Chapter 13, Creating a Visual Argument: Public Service Messages.
- ✓ **The annotated bibliography** is a new addition to Chapter 15, Research.
- ✓ **New pedagogy** on writing style. New exercises for each reading have been added that focus on imitating a writer's style.

HALLMARK FEATURES

- ✓ **Real-world approach** emphasizes the genre of each assignment and publication possibilities that further connect writing inside and outside the classroom.
- ✓ **Student writing** is included in each chapter in the readings section and often as the annotated model essay.
- ✓ **Research paths** are included in each chapter to make research part of every writing project.
- ✓ **"Insider" tips** for writing are included from authors who are practicing writers.

- ✓ **Exclusive interviews** with the writers whose essays are printed in the Anatomies are included.
- ✓ **The Writer's Notebook, Peer Review Logs, and Revision Checklists** provide additional prompts to aid in invention, revision, and proofreading.
- ✓ **Mini-assignments** are included in Part 1.
- ✓ **Practices** are provided that coach students through skills related to each genre.
- ✓ **Writer's Notebook** offers a selection of exercises that teachers can use as collaborative and journal writing.
- ✓ **Four-in-one value** (text includes rhetoric, reader, research, and handbook).

THE SUPPLEMENTS PACKAGE

Cengage Learning's English CourseMate
Brings course concepts to life with interactive learning, study, and exam preparation tools that support the printed textbook. CourseMate includes:

- An interactive eBook
- An interactive teaching and learning tools including:

  Quizzes

  Interviews with Professional Writers

  Practice Exercises

  PowerPoints

  Springboards for Writing in Other Genres and more.
- Engagement Tracker, a first-of-its-kind tool that monitors student engagement in the course.

Learn more at www.cengage.com/coursemate.

Enhanced InSite for *Writing in the Works*, 3rd Edition
Insightful, effective writing begins with Enhanced InSite™. From a single, easy-to-navigate site, you can manage the flow of papers online, check for originality, access electronic grade-marking, and conduct peer reviews. Students can also access an interactive eBook, private tutoring options, anti-plagiarism tutorials, and downloadable grammar podcasts. Learn more at www.cengage.com/insite.

Interactive eBook
Students can do all of their reading online or use the eBook as a handy reference while they're completing their online coursework. The eBook includes the full text of the print version and user-friendly navigation, search and highlight tools, and more.

ACKNOWLEDGMENTS

First, our thanks go to our students who bring their enthusiasm to our classrooms, providing insights, criticisms, and ideas about how to make writing instruction useful and interesting. Without them, we would never know what works. We thank our colleagues in the CO201 Writing Program at Boston University, who helped us test our ideas and have generously shared their own ideas for inclusion in this book. We extend gratitude to the teachers who have used the first edition of *Writing in the Works* and who have shared our excitement about the material while offering their encouragement and suggestions. Our families continue to inspire us and support us. And finally, we thank the editorial staff at Cengage Learning, and especially our wonderful and creative editor, Lisa Moore, who has guided us through this massive re-imagining of our book. We are grateful to Lyn Uhl and Monica Eckman for the special interest they have taken in this project; and especially to Leslie Taggart and Margaret Leslie for their support, enthusiasm, and guidance throughout the process; as well as Elizabeth Ramsey for her expert coordination of the reviews and the myriad other ways she kept us going on the new edition; and then to Danielle Warchol who came in at the end and facilitated the journey of the manuscript into production. Michael Lepera, and Angel Chavez have expertly guided this book into its new design and kept their good humor all along the way, even when images needed replacement at the eleventh hour. Finally, a heartfelt thank you to them for this beautiful book.

We would like also to thank the many colleagues all over the country who wrote such thoughtful and useful comments as they reviewed this book, during the development of the first edition, the revision of the second edition, and now for this brand-new third edition:

Andrea L. Beaudin, *Southern Connecticut State University*

Jose M. Blanco, *Miami Dade College*

Mary Ann Bretzlauf, *College of Lake County*

Mark Browning, *Johnson County Community College*

Jo Ann Buck, *Guilford Technical Community College*

Avon Crismore, *Indiana University–Purdue University, Fort Wayne*

Rachel Darabi, *Indiana University–Purdue University, Fort Wayne*

Cherie Post Dargan, *Hawkeye Community College*

Adenike Davidson, *University of Central Florida*

Susan Shibe Davis, *Arizona State University*

Julia K. Ferganchick, *University of Arkansas at Little Rock*

Gregory R. Glau, *Arizona State University*

Jo-Sandra B. Greenberg, *Brookhaven College*

Jack Jacobs, *Auburn University*
Meredith James, *Eastern Connecticut State University*
Millie M. Kidd, *Mount St. Mary's College*
Paul Lehman, *University of Central Oklahoma*
Mitchell R. Lewis, *Elmira College*
JoAnne Liebman Matson, *University of Arkansas at Little Rock*
Alfred J. López, *Florida International University*
Peter Lovenheim, *Rochester Institute of Technology*
James J. McKeown, Jr., *McLennan Community College*
T. Gerard McNamee, *Eastern Oregon University*
Constantina Michalos, *Houston Baptist University*
Kate Mohler, *Mesa Community College*
Cindy Moore, *St. Cloud University*
Ed Moritz, *Indiana University–Purdue University, Fort Wayne*
Marti L. Mundell, *Washington State University*
Charles Naccarato, *Ohio University*
Scott Oates, *University of Wisconsin, Eau Claire*
R. J. Osborne, *Grossmont College*
Victoria Ramirez, *Weber State University*
Gordon Reynolds, *Ferris State University*
Lawrence Roderer, *J. Sargeant Reynolds Community College*
Connie G. Rothwell, *University of North Carolina at Charlotte*
Karin Russell, *Keiser University*
Mark Schaub, *Grand Valley State University*
Steven P. Schneider, *University of Texas, Pan-American*
Ingrid Schreck, *College of Marin*
Joseph M. Schuster, *Webster University*
Arvis Scott, *McLennan Community College*
Rhonda L. Smith, *Jacksonville College*
Howard Tinberg, *Bristol Community College*
Pay Tyrer, *West Texas A&M University*
Xiao Wang, *Broward Community College*

We also owe a debt of gratitude to all our reviewers and particularly to Jared Abraham at Weatherford College and Allyson Jones at Stevens-Haneger College for the early and formative guidance on the new organization of the text as well as for seeing us through every stage of development. In addition, the research section and the addition of the annotated bibliography was improved by their comments and by those of Mark Bagget, Samford University; Dana Brewer, Weatherford College; Michael Lueker, Our Lady of the Lake University; and Dylan Parkhurst, Stephen F. Austin University. The advice of Stevens Amidon, Indiana Purdue University, Fort Wayne; Shauna Gobbel, Northampton Community College; and Amy Stolley, Saint Xavier University all were also instrumental in creating the final organization for each chapter. A thank you for the thoughtful and helpful reviews of *Writing in the Works* goes to:

Jared Abraham, *Weatherford College*

Stephen Amidon, *Indiana Purdue University*

Mark Bagget, *Samford University, Fort Wayne*

Dana Brewer, *Weatherford College*

Aaron Clark, *Brookhaven College*

Brock Dethier, *Utah State University*

Shauna Gobbel, *Northampton Community College*

Ghazala Hasmi, *J. Sargeant Reynolds Community College*

Robert Heaton, *Utah State University*

Vicki Hendricks, *Broward, South Campus*

Michael Lueker, *Our Lady of the Lake Universtiy*

Dylan Parkhurst, *Stephen F. Austin University*

Peter Rand, *Boston University*

Dick Ravin, *Boston University*

Allyson Jones, *Stevens-Haneger College*

Amy Stolley, *Saint Xavier University*

Kristy Wooten, *Catawba Valley Community College*

Susan Blau
Kathryn Burak

How Does *Writing in the Works* Help Students Achieve the WPA Outcomes?

To help instructors and students consider shared goals, this edition incorporates the Council of Writing Program Administrators' (WPA) objectives and outcomes. A complete description of the ways *Writing in the Works* supports the WPA objectives and outcomes follows. On the following pages, each of the five primary outcomes of the WPA Outcomes Statement for First-Year Composition is followed by an explanation and illustration of how—and where—*Writing in the Works* supports that outcome.

1. RHETORICAL KNOWLEDGE

From the WPA Outcomes Statement:

By the end of first-year composition, students should

- Focus on a purpose
- Respond to the needs of different audiences
- Respond appropriately to different kinds of rhetorical situations
- Use conventions of format and structure appropriate to the rhetorical situation
- Adopt appropriate voice, tone, and level of formality
- Understand how genres shape reading and writing
- Write in several genres

How *Writing in the Works* Helps Students Accomplish These Outcomes:

Writing in the Works emphasizes the rhetorical situation, the choices a writer makes in his or her writing and revising, for each writing assignment. It asks students to read critically to understand the rhetorical situation of a variety of texts, and then to write, demonstrating their understanding of their own choices, about voice, purpose, audience, media, and design.

CHAPTER 1, The Rhetorical Situation, teaches students specifically about voice, purpose, audience, media, and design in all their writing.

- Each assignment chapter has a feature called "The Rhetorical Situation," which explores the subtleties of the rhetorical situation for that specific genre.
- Each reading in every assignment chapter asks a targeted question about the rhetorical situation of that reading.
- Writing in the Works' approach is genre-based. Each assignment chapter introduces students to the elements of ten different genres: application essays, memoirs, profiles, short expository articles, news reports, film reviews, causal analysis, editorials (and blogs), proposals, and public service messages.

2. CRITICAL THINKING, READING AND WRITING

From the WPA Outcomes Statement:

By the end of first-year composition, students should

- Use writing and reading for inquiry, learning, thinking, and communicating

- Understand a writing assignment as a series of tasks, including finding, evaluating, analyzing, and synthesizing appropriate primary and secondary sources
- Integrate their own ideas with those of others
- Understand the relationships among language, knowledge, and power

How *Writing in the Works* Helps Students Accomplish These Outcomes:

Writing in the Works integrates critical thinking, reading and writing skills into a variety of activities, including peer-review guidance on critically assessing the work of others and absorbing that assessment into one's own work. Rhetorical appeals, logic, reasoning, and persuasion are presented through both words and images.

- **CHAPTER 4,** Reading, Thinking, and Writing Critically, focuses on incremental skill building: learning how to paraphrase, summarize, annotate, outline, analyze, and synthesize texts, along with using rhetorical appeals, and leads students through the steps of writing a critical analysis.
- These skills are reinforced in many of the following chapters. For example, summary skills are emphasized in Chapter 9, Writing a Report: News for Print, Web, and Social Media; inductive and deductive reasoning are outlined as a strategy for organizing thinking in Chapter 8, Writing Exposition: Short Articles; persuasion is discussed as part of a set of strategies to use in Chapter 5, Writing a Personal Statement: Application Essays.
- Every assignment chapter has an annotated example, called the "anatomy" of that genre that leads students step-by-step through a critical analysis of a that reading. Q&As with the authors of those essays provide additional insight into how writers think about their work.

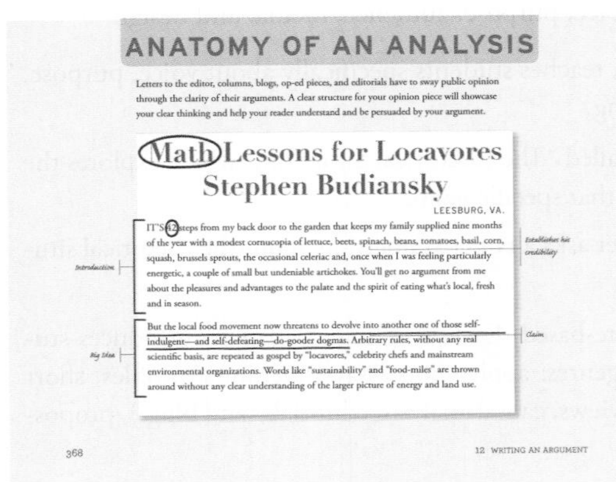

ANATOMY OF AN ANALYSIS

Letters to the editor, columns, blogs, op-ed pieces, and editorials have to sway public opinion through the clarity of their arguments. A clear structure for your opinion piece will showcase your clear thinking and help your reader understand and be persuaded by your argument.

Math Lessons for Locavores
Stephen Budiansky

LEESBURG, VA.

Introduction — IT'S 42 steps from my back door to the garden that keeps my family supplied nine months of the year with a modest cornucopia of lettuce, beets, spinach, beans, tomatoes, basil, corn, squash, brussels sprouts, the occasional celeriac and, once when I was feeling particularly energetic, a couple of small but undeniable artichokes. You'll get no argument from me about the pleasures and advantages to the palate and the spirit of eating what's local, fresh and in season. — Establishes his credibility

Big Idea — But the local food movement now threatens to devolve into another one of those self-indulgent—and self-defeating—do-gooder dogmas. Arbitrary rules, without any real scientific basis, are repeated as gospel by "locavores," celebrity chefs and mainstream environmental organizations. Words like "sustainability" and "food-miles" are thrown around without any clear understanding of the larger picture of energy and land use. — Claim

368 12 WRITING AN ARGUMENT

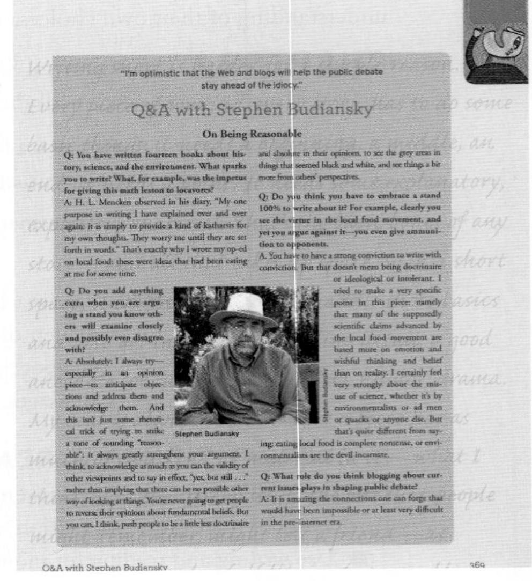

"I'm optimistic that the Web and blogs will help the public debate stay ahead of the idiocy."

Q&A with Stephen Budiansky

On Being Reasonable

Q: You have written fourteen books about history, science, and the environment. What sparks you to write? What, for example, was the impetus for giving this math lesson to locavores?
A: H. L. Mencken observed in his diary, "My one purpose in writing I have explained over and over again: it is simply to provide a kind of katharsis for my own thoughts. They worry me until they are set forth in words." That's exactly why I wrote my op-ed on local food: these were ideas that had been eating at me for some time.

Q: Do you add anything extra when you are arguing a stand you know others will examine closely and possibly even disagree with?
A: Absolutely. I always try—especially in an opinion piece—to anticipate objections and address them and acknowledge them. And this isn't just some rhetorical trick of trying to strike a tone of sounding "reasonable"; it always greatly strengthens your argument, I think, to acknowledge as much as you can the validity of other viewpoints and to say in effect, "yes, but still . . ." rather than implying that there can be no possible other way of looking at things. You're never going to get people to reverse their opinions about fundamental beliefs. But you can, I think, push people to be a little less doctrinaire and absolute in their opinions, to see the grey areas in things that seemed black and white, and see things a bit more from others' perspectives.

Stephen Budiansky

Q: Do you think you have to embrace a stand 100% to write about it? For example, clearly you see the virtue in the local food movement, and yet you argue against it—you even give ammunition to opponents.
A. You have to have a strong conviction to write with conviction. But that doesn't mean being doctrinaire or ideological or intolerant. I tried to make a very specific point in this piece: namely that many of the supposedly scientific claims advanced by the local food movement are based more on emotion and wishful thinking and belief than on reality. I certainly feel very strongly about the misuse of science, whether it's by environmentalists or ad men or quacks or anyone else. But that's quite different from saying: eating local food is complete nonsense, or environmentalists are the devil incarnate.

Q: What role do you think blogging about current issues plays in shaping public debate?
A: It is amazing the connections one can forge that would have been impossible or at least very difficult in the pre-Internet era.

Q&A with Stephen Budiansky 369

- Every chapter asks: How will I focus my writing? As students encounter a new genre with specific audience and aims, they are led through a method of inquiry in generating a genre-specific thesis statement. Students begin to understand the critical role of a focusing statement and that the thesis statement takes on a different form with each genre.
- Students discover the connection between writing and imagery in the Visual Literacy feature in each chapter. These visual literacy exercises make connections to the key elements in the genre and expand student's critical thinking skills.
- *Writing in the Works* approaches argumentation and logical appeals (pathos, logos, and ethos) in three chapters, each one illustrating a different but distinct application of the skills essential to persuasion. Students consider how to use classical appeals in different rhetorical situations when they compose
    1. Editorials
    2. Visual Arguments
    3. Proposals

VISUAL LITERACY: EYEWITNESS ACCOUNTS

BRINGING YOUR READER INTO THE MOMENT WITH PHOTOGRAPHS THAT TELL STORIES

PHOTOGRAPHS—and film and video—make everyone an eyewitness to event. The best examples of photojournalism capture more than just the landscape of that moment, though. They also tell a story with characters and conflict. They make us all eyewitnesses. Read the captions that accompany these news photos and the other photos in this chapter to get the photographers' insights into what they were thinking.

Jonathan Wiggs/Globe Staff/Getty Images

Jonathan Wiggs/Fall River/March 30
We'd had several days of heavy rain in Massachusetts, causing a lot of flooding. Reports were coming in that there was heavy damage in Fall River. The damage was a little difficult for me to find, because streets were blocked off. But I eventually found where several streets had buckled. The neighborhood had just undergone extensive reconstruction of its sewer system and repaving of its streets, so the damage was a particularly cruel blow.

254 9 WRITING A REPORT

NO MORE FISH IN THE SEA?

PROJECT OCEAN

Help us to protect our oceans and change the way we eat.
Find out more and join the campaign at selfridges.com/projectocean

ZSL

SELFRIDGES

Image Courtesy of The Advertising Archives

Writing For Your Community

14

alterfalter/shutterstock.com

PROPOSALS

When you sit down to write, you must have one clear goal in your mind. What is the ONE thing you want your reader [or] funder to remember?

—Garland Waller

A community group in a small town has taken on a project called Teddy Bears on Patrol. The group will provide teddy bears to the local police department. Police officers, in turn, will give the bears to upset or traumatized children who may have been involved in traffic accidents or domestic violence.

A high school student in a suburban community has helped found the Teen Action Board. The group's goal is to address the issue of sexual assault among high school students. With other teens around her state, she has created the See It and Stop It campaign. The campaign's primary focus is using teen peer groups to help recognize and stop behavior that can escalate to date rape.

A young woman who grew up in foster homes has spearheaded a campaign to create the Bridges to Independence program to provide transitional housing for 18-year-olds who are no longer eligible to live in foster homes. These young adults will be able to stay in this safe environment while being mentored in seeking jobs, filling out college applications, and learning independent living skills.

WHAT'S TO COME

All of these projects began when individuals or groups identified problems: children traumatized by violence, the alarming incidence of teen date

443

WPA OUTCOMES CORRELATION

- Each reading in every assignment chapter ends with a list of questions for rhetorical analysis as well as questions for writing and discussion.

3. PROCESSES

From the WPA Outcomes Statement:

By the end of first-year composition, students should

- Be aware that it usually takes multiple drafts to create and complete a successful text
- Develop flexible strategies for generating, revising, editing, and proofreading
- Understand writing as an open process that permits writers to use later invention and re-thinking to revise their work
- Understand the collaborative and social aspects of writing processes
- Learn to critique their own and others' works
- Learn to balance the advantages of relying on others with the responsibility of doing their part
- Use a variety of technologies to address a range of audiences

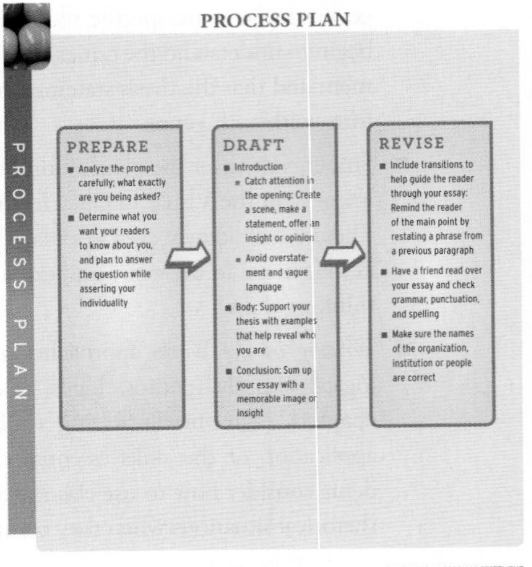

How *Writing in the Works* Helps Students Accomplish These Outcomes:

Writing in the Works bases all writing instruction on process pedagogy.

- **CHAPTER 2,** The Writer's Process, details the interdependent activities of brainstorming, composing, and revising, complete with practice exercises to reinforce the instruction. For example, practice exercises lead students through freewriting, clustering, and outlining activities as possible avenues for idea generation.
- **CHAPTER 3,** Collaboration, Peer Review, and Writing as a Public Act, ties into teaching students about the collaborative and social aspects of writing.
- Each chapter provides students with a graphic process plan that illustrates the activities involved in preparing, composing, and revising for each genre.
- The instruction includes sections on How to Find a Topic, How to View a Subject, and How to Conduct and Interview.
- Research is presented as a brainstorming activity as well as a way to gather evidence to support claims.
- *Writing in the Works* includes thorough instruction on the use of primary as well as secondary sources.

- Practice exercises help "coach" students by isolating individual skills involved in writing a particular genre and build into a repertoire as students progress through each chapter. For example, in building an argument, students are led through the steps of detecting fallacies. In writing a memoir, students explore narrative techniques of internal monologue, how to use dialogue, and the effect of showing rather than telling.

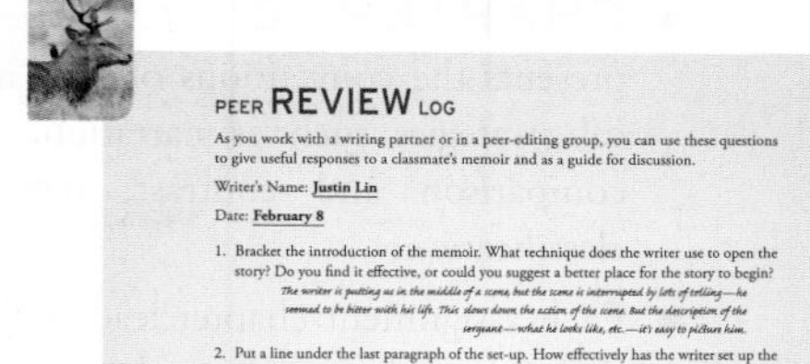

PEER REVIEW LOG

As you work with a writing partner or in a peer-editing group, you can use these questions to give useful responses to a classmate's memoir and as a guide for discussion.

Writer's Name: **Justin Lin**

Date: **February 8**

1. Bracket the introduction of the memoir. What technique does the writer use to open the story? Do you find it effective, or could you suggest a better place for the story to begin?

   The writer is putting us in the middle of a scene, but the scene is interrupted by lots of telling—he seemed to be bitter with his life. This slows down the action of the scene. But the description of the sergeant—what he looks like, etc.—it's easy to picture him.

2. Put a line under the last paragraph of the set-up. How effectively has the writer set up the story? What other information or sensory details might help you better understand the events that follow?

   Not sure I can do this—the whole thing seems like set-up. I think the focus of the story is the night-time beating and how this might have affected the writer, so everything that leads up to that scene seems like set-up, but it's hard to tell.

3. Box a section that presents the setting of the story. What details might make the setting stronger, more vivid, or more specific?

THE RHETORICAL SITUATION: PERSONAL STORIES FOR PUBLIC AUDIENCES

Although memoirs are true stories, memoirists borrow techniques from fiction to make their stories feel personal to a public audience. They create scenes full of narrative detail—scenes that leave footprints in their readers' memories. They explore

The Rhetorical Situation 133

- Writer's Notebook suggestions provide students with brainstorming activities and can be used as starting points for their writing or collaborative activities. For example, a news report can begin with the prompt to find a new trend on campus and research its evolution, then get quotations from "practitioners" and experts to help explain it.
- Peer Review Guidelines in each chapter provide extensive work-in-progress questions for collaborative peer groups.
- Collaborative critical thinking and critical looking practice exercises encourage class discussion.
- Multi-media assignments such as blogs, visual essays, photo essays, and videos are connected to the writing assignments. Students learn to use new technologies as they research and compose text.
- DIY (Do/Design it Yourself) mini-assignments such as resume writing, graphic memoirs, oral histories, Facebook pages, and PowerPoints appear in each genre chapter.

4. KNOWLEDGE OF CONVENTIONS

From the WPA Outcomes Statement:

By the end of first-year composition, students should

- Learn common formats for different kinds of texts
- Develop knowledge of genre conventions ranging from structure and paragraphing to tone and mechanics
- Practice appropriate means of documenting their work
- Control such surface features as syntax, grammar, punctuation, and spelling.

How *Writing in the Works* Helps Students Accomplish These Outcomes:

Writing in the Works provides thorough instruction in the conventions of genre, format, documentation, grammar, and mechanics.

- **CHAPTER 2,** The Writer's Process, presents the conventions of style and rhetorical strategies such as narration, description, comparison and contrast, definition, and classification.
- Each assignment chapter leads off with a section on understanding the conventions of that genre.
- Specific instruction focuses on how to cite primary sources as well as secondary sources in a number of assignment chapters as well as in Chapter 15, Research.
- "The Big Idea" section in each chapter leads students through adapting a thesis statement for different genres.
- **CHAPTER 16,** Documentation, presents MLA and APA documentation styles, teaches students the conventions of academic citation with an emphasis on how to avoid plagiarism, and adds information on the anatomy of an annotated bibliography.
- Four chapters comprise the Grammar Handbook, which teaches the vocabulary of grammar; punctuation; the avoidance of common errors in sentence structure, agreement, pronoun case, verb tense, parallelism, and modification; and the avoidance of trouble spots for nonnative English speakers. Practice exercises reinforce the instruction in each chapter, giving instructors the means to provide a quick check of their students' understanding of the material.

DEVELOPING A WORKING THESIS: THE SPECIFIC FOCUS OF YOUR BIG IDEA

We are using the term "big idea" to mean the overarching concept in a piece of writing. It is the first step in developing your thesis. For example, the big idea of an editorial you might write could be to persuade your administration to use green technology in new buildings on campus.

Once you identify this big idea, you can then refine it and narrow it down to form the specific point you are making. As we said in Chapter 1, this specific point of a piece of writing goes by many names. In a news story it can be the *angle*, in a proposal a *plan*, and in a memoir a *theme*. It can be called an *evaluative thesis* in a review, or an *analytical thesis* in a researched article, or an *argumentative thesis* in an editorial.

Here is an example of how you might narrow your big idea and develop your thesis:

BIG IDEA: PERSUADE THE ADMINISTRATION TO USE GREEN TECHNOLOGY IN NEW BUILDINGS

Argumentative Thesis: Green technology is not only good for our planet but it also will be a cost effective way to heat and cool the new lecture halls.

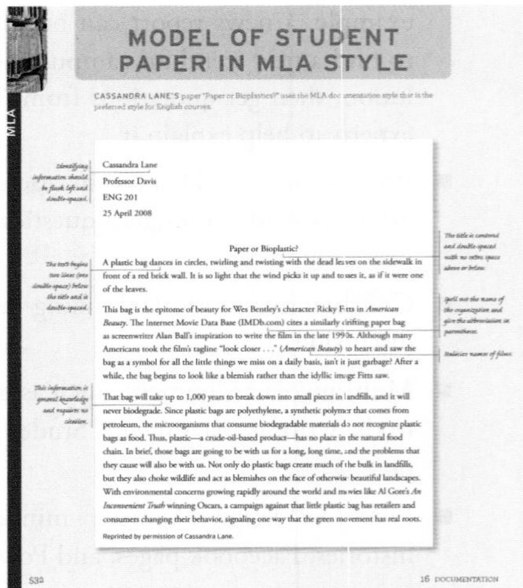

MLA

MODEL OF STUDENT PAPER IN MLA STYLE

CASSANDRA LANE'S paper "Paper or Bioplastics?" uses the MLA documentation style that is the preferred style for English courses.

Identifying information should be flush left and double-spaced.

Cassandra Lane

Professor Davis

ENG 201

25 April 2008

The title is centered and double-spaced with no extra space above or below.

Paper or Bioplastic?

The text begins two lines (one double-space) below the title and is double-spaced.

A plastic bag dances in circles, twirling and twisting with the dead leaves on the sidewalk in front of a red brick wall. It is so light that the wind picks it up and tosses it, as if it were one of the leaves.

Spell out the name of the organization and give the abbreviation in parentheses.

Italicize names of films.

This bag is the epitome of beauty for Wes Bentley's character Ricky Fitts in *American Beauty*. The Internet Movie Data Base (IMDb.com) cites a similarly drifting paper bag as screenwriter Alan Ball's inspiration to write the film in the late 1990s. Although many Americans took the film's tagline "look closer . . ." (*American Beauty*) to heart and saw the bag as a symbol for all the little things we miss on a daily basis, isn't it just garbage? After a while, the bag begins to look like a blemish rather than the idyllic image Fitts saw.

This information is general knowledge and requires no citation.

That bag will take up to 1,000 years to break down into small pieces in landfills, and it will never biodegrade. Since plastic bags are polyethylene, a synthetic polymer that comes from petroleum, the microorganisms that consume biodegradable materials do not recognize plastic bags as food. Thus, plastic—a crude-oil-based product—has no place in the natural food chain. In brief, those bags are going to be with us for a long, long time, and the problems that they cause will also be with us. Not only do plastic bags create much of the bulk in landfills, but they also choke wildlife and act as blemishes on the face of otherwise beautiful landscapes. With environmental concerns growing rapidly around the world and movies like Al Gore's *An Inconvenient Truth* winning Oscars, a campaign against that little plastic bag has retailers and consumers changing their behavior, signaling one way that the green movement has real roots.

Reprinted by permission of Cassandra Lane.

532 16 DOCUMENTATION

5. COMPOSING IN ELECTRONIC ENVIRONMENTS

From the WPA Outcomes Statement:

As has become clear over the last twenty years, writing in the 21st century involves the use of digital technologies for several purposes, from drafting to peer reviewing to editing. Therefore, although the kinds of composing processes and texts expected from students vary across programs and institutions, there are nonetheless common expectations.

By the end of first-year composition, students should:

Use electronic environments for drafting, reviewing, revising, editing, and sharing texts

Locate, evaluate, organize, and use research material collected from electronic sources, including scholarly library databases; other official databases (e.g., federal government databases); and informal electronic networks and internet sources

Understand and exploit the differences in the rhetorical strategies and in the affordances available for both print and electronic composing processes and texts.

How *Writing in the Works* Helps Students Accomplish These Outcomes:

Writing in the Works assignments, practices, and research instruction all integrate electronic environments in their expectations and their instruction. The accompanying Web site creates its own rich electronic environment.

- Research Paths in each chapter help students understand how to use research as an integral part of the writing process.
- The companion Web site allows students to access the readings and their accompanying questions, practice exercises, peer-review logs, and revision checklists online. The companion Web site invites students to engage in interactive, multimodal activities, including working with video and collaborative writing projects.

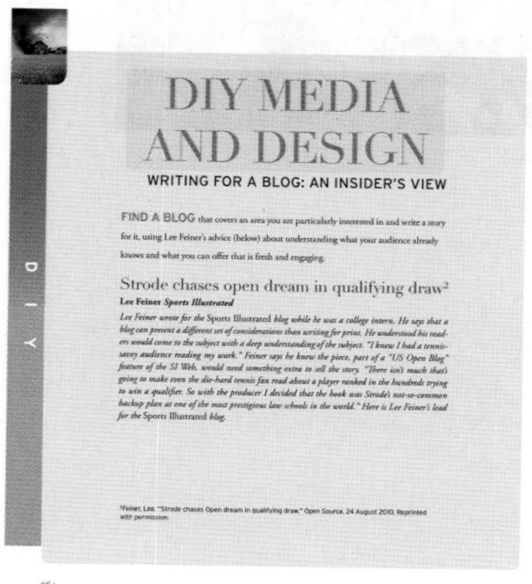

DIY MEDIA AND DESIGN

WRITING FOR A BLOG: AN INSIDER'S VIEW

FIND A BLOG that covers an area you are particularly interested in and write a story for it, using Lee Feiner's advice (below) about understanding what your audience already knows and what you can offer that is fresh and engaging.

Strode chases open dream in qualifying draw[2]

Lee Feiner *Sports Illustrated*

Lee Feiner wrote for the Sports Illustrated *blog while he was a college intern. He says that a blog can present a different set of considerations than writing for print. He understood his readers would come to the subject with a deep understanding of the subject. "I knew I had a tennis-savvy audience reading my work." Feiner says he knew the piece, part of a "US Open Blog" feature of the SI Web, would need something extra to sell the story. "There isn't much that's going to make even the die-hard tennis fan read about a player ranked in the hundreds trying to win a qualifier. So with the producer I decided that the book was Strode's not-so-common backup plan at one of the most prestigious law schools in the world." Here is Lee Feiner's lead for the* Sports Illustrated *blog.*

[2]Feiner, Lee. "Strode chases Open dream in qualifying draw." Open Source. 24 August 2010. Reprinted with permission.

264 9 WRITING A REPORT

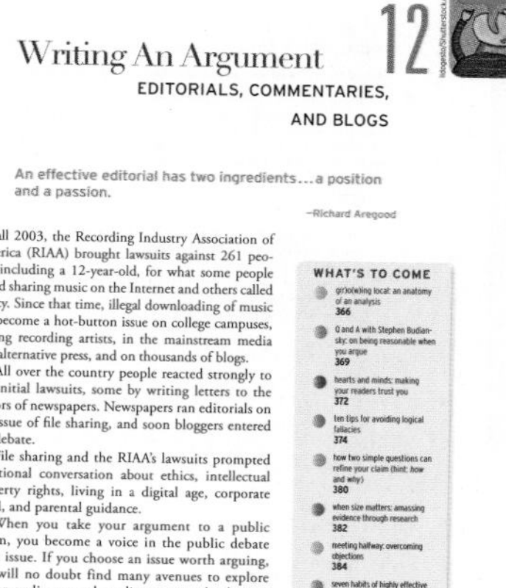

Writing An Argument 12

EDITORIALS, COMMENTARIES, AND BLOGS

An effective editorial has two ingredients...a position and a passion.

—Richard Aregood

In fall 2003, the Recording Industry Association of America (RIAA) brought lawsuits against 261 people, including a 12-year-old, for what some people called sharing music on the Internet and others called piracy. Since that time, illegal downloading of music has become a hot-button issue on college campuses, among recording artists, in the mainstream media and alternative press, and on thousands of blogs.

All over the country people reacted strongly to the initial lawsuits, some by writing letters to the editors of newspapers. Newspapers ran editorials on the issue of file sharing, and soon bloggers entered the debate.

File sharing and the RIAA's lawsuits prompted a national conversation about ethics, intellectual property rights, living in a digital age, corporate greed, and parental guidance.

When you take your argument to a public forum, you become a voice in the public debate of an issue. If you choose an issue worth arguing, you will no doubt find many avenues to explore and an audience ready to listen, to applaud, or to counter your claims.

WHAT'S TO COME

363

- The assignments in the book combine and connect writing for print and writing for electronic media.
- Social media, such as Facebook, Twitter, and YouTube are discussed, analyzed, and integrated into the instruction throughout the assignment chapters.
- Assignments illustrate the importance of how skills can be applied to real-world writing. For example, students can see the relevance of good summary skills in Chapter 9, Writing a Report: News for Print, Web, and Social Media when they post to a news blog or create their own Web page.
- The DIY features in all the assignment chapters allow students to apply the instruction in those genres to a variety of electronic media—video, PowerPoint presentations, and audio projects.

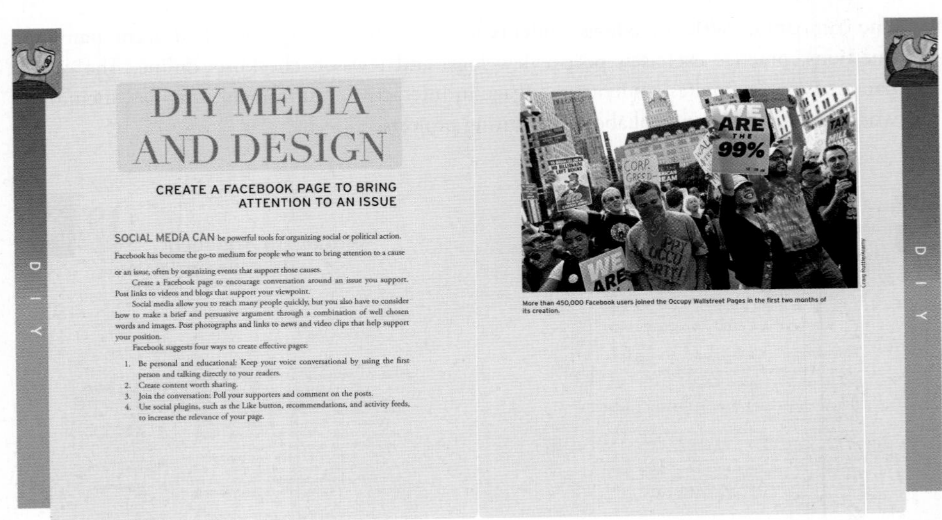

DIY MEDIA AND DESIGN

CREATE A FACEBOOK PAGE TO BRING ATTENTION TO AN ISSUE

SOCIAL MEDIA CAN be powerful tools for organizing social or political action. Facebook has become the go-to medium for people who want to bring attention to a cause or an issue, often by organizing events that support those causes.

Create a Facebook page to encourage conversation around an issue you support. Post links to videos and blogs that support your viewpoint.

Social media allow you to reach many people quickly, but you also have to consider how to make a brief and persuasive argument through a combination of well chosen words and images. Post photographs and links to news and video clips that help support your position.

Facebook suggests four ways to create effective pages:

1. Be personal and educational: Keep your voice conversational by using the first person and talking directly to your readers.
2. Create content worth sharing.
3. Join the conversation: Poll your supporters and comment on the posts.
4. Use social plugins, such as the Like button, recommendations, and activity feeds, to increase the relevance of your page.

More than 450,000 Facebook users joined the Occupy Wallstreet Pages in the first two months of its creation.

Craig Nuttle/Alamy

PART 1

The Writer's Craft

Segretain/Getty Images

Arman Zender/ Shutterstock.com

The Rhetorical Situation 1
WRITERS' CHOICES

Prose is architecture, not interior decoration.

—Ernest Hemingway

Never before has information been so immediate and so accessible. Thanks to wireless and digital technology, information—about the world, our friends, the weather—is always at our fingertips. Practically every day Facebook offers members new applications that allow them to connect with each other in new ways—through pokes, virtual hugs, and vampires bites. Once the domain of the under-21 crowd, Facebook now includes political candidates whose pages are loaded with up-to-the-minute information and pictures, so we can see the gaffes and grimaces of world leaders broadcast 24/7 on YouTube.

The Internet has opened the globe to libraries and museums as well as coffee shop conversations. A sixth grader in Des Moines, Iowa might have access to as much information as a university student at Oxford. We have so much information and so many facts and opinions that at times trying to get an understanding of an issue can be like trying to get a drink of water from a hose turned on full blast. But information alone has little value. Being able to see beyond the packaging, pictures, and music videos that are the companions to most of our daily messages is vital to becoming successful in academics as well as in careers. Those people who navigate the raging stream of information skillfully will be those who can think critically and read discriminately—those able to tell the treachery from the treasure. They will be writers who understand the significance of words and the connections between the words and images of messages.

They will also be the people who understand the myriad of choices writers face each time they sit down to compose. Assume that some bureaucratic mix-up gets you riled. You want to set things right or at the very least vent your pent-up anger. Do you fire off a

WHAT'S TO COME

quick e-mail? Write a 500-word op-ed for the local paper? Send a formal letter of complaint to the head of the company? To decide, you have to consider the rhetorical situation you are in, that is, what you want to communicate and to whom. Maybe the e-mail will suffice to diffuse your anger, but the considered letter of complaint might get you a more considered response. The op-ed will do the best job of broadcasting your concerns to the most people, but it will not necessarily reach the individual who could do something about the problem.

Every time you sit down to write, you have to make these kinds of choices. Each rhetorical situation includes choices about:

- genre: what type of text you are writing
- purpose: what you are trying to accomplish
- audience: whom you are writing for
- voice: how you want to sound
- media and design: how you want your writing to look

CHOOSING THE RIGHT GENRE

A genre is a type of writing—from an informative report to a Facebook posting—and each type of writing requires particular rhetorical moves. Usually, the genre for your classroom writing assignments is already chosen for you. You may be asked to write a memoir or an essay, a report or a review. Each of these genres follows a general pattern and comes with a set of readers' expectations. Readers pick up a film review, for example, to find out a critic's analysis and evaluation of a film—and maybe to get some news about the stars. Within the confines of any genre is room to experiment, to take some risks, to surprise, and even to delight your reader.

But before the delight can happen, you have to do some thinking about the best genre for your purpose. If you have a story to tell about something that happened to you, you could write a memoir or you could choose to write a personal essay. To figure out which is best suited for your purposes, you have to figure out what each offers you as a writer. Both genres, in this case, are nonfiction and autobiographical, but the memoir is narrative in structure. It tells a story that offers insight into some slice of your life. The personal essay is interpretive. You may tell a story but then you expand on it; you philosophize and draw connections and conclusions. You have to decide which genre is the right one for the story you want to tell.

When left to your own devices, you make the choice of genre by analyzing the rhetorical situation. Each of the elements—genre, purpose, audience, voice, design—are interrelated. If you care a great deal about the importance of eating local and organic

PRACTICE 1.1

Collaborative Activity: Identifying Genres and Patterns

1. Choose an area of interest among these three: books, music, and films.
2. For your chosen area, generate as many genres as you can think of for that area. Make the genres as specific as you can, so instead of "fiction" as a genre for books, divide that category into mysteries, romances, science fiction, and so forth.
3. Select three or four of the genres you have identified, and make a list of your expectations for that genre. What patterns do you expect to find in a mystery novel, for example, or a science fiction one?

food, for example, and you want to write about that topic, you have to decide what you are trying to accomplish. If it is to persuade others to your way of thinking, you have to figure out your audience. Whom do you want to persuade? If your intended audience is the fast-food-loving college student, then how do you best reach that audience? What kind of evidence do you have to amass? What kind of voice will help change students' minds? What is the best genre for your purpose and your audience? There is no one right answer. Perhaps you should write an argumentative essay and publish it on your college's Web site. Or, perhaps you should write a spoof or a parody knowing that many unpersuaded students would be better convinced through humor.

You also need to keep up-to-date on how the purpose or readers of genres sometimes change or shift. Blogs, for example, began as informal genres, almost as Web logs (as the name suggests) or diary entries, read by a handful of friends or like-minded people. In time, journalists and experts in a variety of fields began blogging

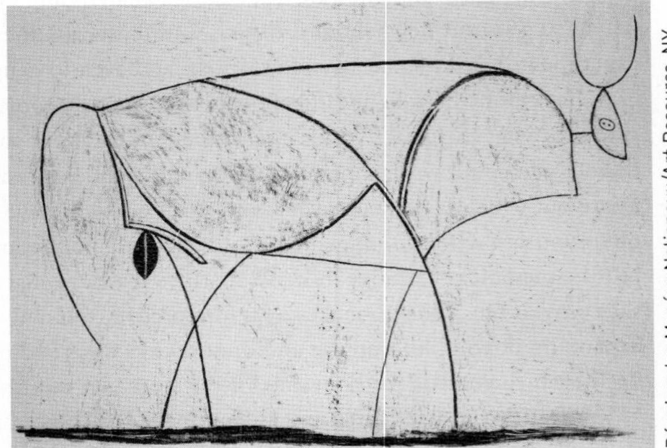

Réunion des Musées Nationaux/Art Resource, NY

Pablo Picasso refined his style in a series of lithographs honing the image to get to the essence of the bull.

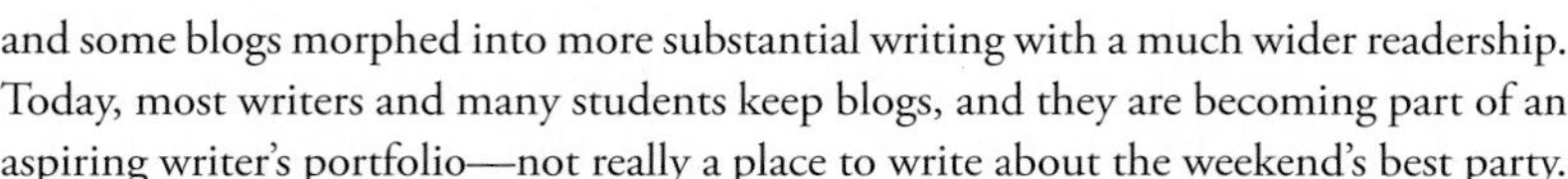

and some blogs morphed into more substantial writing with a much wider readership. Today, most writers and many students keep blogs, and they are becoming part of an aspiring writer's portfolio—not really a place to write about the weekend's best party.

In the following assignments chapters you will learn to write in a variety of genres: application essays, memoirs, news stories, film reviews, editorials, blogs, proposals, public service messages, Web sites, and magazine articles. You will learn the usual patterns used in that genre, and you will learn how to make a writer's choice about which genre best suits your purpose.

IDENTIFYING YOUR PURPOSE

Let's go through the process of figuring out the *purpose* for one typical writing assignment:

> Choose a local issue on your college campus or in your community, or choose a global issue that is in the news and that interests you. Decide what your position is on this issue and argue persuasively for your position in a letter to the editor, a column, a blog, or a guest editorial for a specific newspaper or online news site.

This assignment gives you a great deal of information about the rhetorical situation. Four genres—letter to the editor, a column, a blog, or a guest editorial—are suggested and each has somewhat different requirements and audiences. But, the general purpose of the assignment is clear: you are to "argue persuasively" on a position in the news. Once you identify your topic and your position, you can use that information to figure out what is meaningful to you in that topic and what your specific purpose will be.

Let's say you chose to write about texting and driving, a hot-button topic on your campus. One possible thesis for an editorial that supports a bill outlawing texting while driving might be "Texting while driving endangers the lives of drivers, passengers, and pedestrians and must be outlawed." Your general purpose is "to argue"; your specific purpose is to prove the point that texting while driving endangers people's lives.

THE GENERAL PURPOSE

We have all had the experience of not really knowing what we want to say and noodling around on paper, trying out one idea or sentence after another, trying to figure out what on earth we want to say about a topic. How do you figure out your purpose for an academic assignment or one in the workplace or in your community? Are you going to

- *tell* a story (Writing to Explore)
- *report* on an event (Writing to Inform)
- *review* a book or *analyze* a poem (Writing to Analyze)
- *argue* for building bicycle lanes in city streets or *lobby* for an internship (Writing to Argue)?

PRACTICE 1.2

Identifying Purpose

Below are three typical writing assignments. Identify a general and a specific purpose for each:

1. Choose a campus event to attend. Write a news report suitable for publication in your school paper.
2. Joy Tipping in the *Dallas Morning News* wrote, "TV gurus say the ABC show ["Lost"] has changed the medium and enriched pop culture by cultivating an Internet base of obsessive fans and using new technology to enhance viewers' experiences with snazzy extras such as mini 'mobisodes' for cellphone viewing and content hidden on-screen for hard-core fans." Do you agree?
3. You are irate that cigarette company advertisements target young people and poor people. Write a letter to the American Cancer Society proposing that it pitch its next efforts to keep junior high kids from smoking.

Keep in mind that these purposes are not mutually exclusive. You could certainly write an essay that tells a story about your ability to keep cool under pressure while at the same time analyzing the pressurized situation—all to persuade your reader that you would be the perfect intern in a busy public relations firm.

Under the general headings of exploring, informing, analyzing, and persuading, you can break down your purpose into smaller categories, such as educating, explaining, expressing an emotion—really anything at all that you want to accomplish through your writing.

You can often figure out the purpose of a classroom assignment by looking at its language. Many essay assignments have the purpose embedded in the topic or question asked. If the topic asks you to "support" or "justify," or "argue," you can be certain that the purpose of the paper is for you to take a position on a controversial topic and support it with evidence. If you are asked to "describe," or "illustrate," or "report" your purpose is most likely to inform your reader about a topic. "Explicate" or "review" suggests that you analyze, and "tell a story" or "give an example" often suggests that you explore a situation in more depth.

THE BIG IDEA

Writing can be exploratory or experimental, but if you are writing for a public audience (a teacher, an editor, a producer) take this process of identifying your purpose one step further. You can think of your specific purpose in a piece of writing as the point or the *big idea* you are trying to communicate. Every piece of writing, no matter how long or complicated, is organized around one big idea that is your perspective on your topic, the point you are making in your writing.

Tips about the Big Idea

Each piece of writing has one main big idea.

1. The big idea is not an obvious fact.
2. Because #1 is true, the big idea needs help: explanation, support, defense.
3. Stick to the big idea until the very last word of your writing.

Whatever your purpose, though, you have to know what idea you are trying to communicate. The big idea behind your writing, its overarching concept, provides the focus of your paper. Once you figure out your big idea for a piece of writing, you can then narrow your focus to the specific point you want to make in your writing.

Different genres have different terminology for the big idea. In academic essays, the big idea is called a *thesis*. In stories, it is called the *theme*. In an advertisement the big idea is called a *concept*; in an editorial or other argumentative essay, it is called a *claim*. In analysis or review writing, the big idea is your *interpretation*. Journalists call the big idea in a feature article the *nut graf* or the *bridge graf* (*graf*, being shorthand for *paragraph*).

FAQS ABOUT THE BIG IDEA

Q: Is it always a single sentence?

A: *No, sometimes your big idea takes a paragraph or two. This is especially true in profiles and trend analyses.*

Q: Is it always an opinion?

A: *No, in a short essay, it is factual, but it is a fact that needs some explanation, not something obvious like grass is green.*

Q: Do narratives really have a single big idea?

A: *Well, depending on your interpretation, yes. But then, ten people could watch the same movie and come up with ten interpretations. But, when you are writing a narrative, chances are you have a predominant message or a reason to tell the story—a point that goes beyond the events and into what the events say.*

Q: How could a news story have a big idea?

A: *News stories have angles, ways to decipher the importance of the events. In the angle, we find the big idea. Interestingly, though, since news stories are stories, they share this ability to mean several things depending on the audience. So, a single news event could have, and often does have, several different angles once it is reported. But each of those angles will come in a separate story. One big idea per customer.*

ENGAGING YOUR AUDIENCE

In today's world we are closer to our "audience" than ever before. Facebook posts, blogs, and tweets all let our readers follow our daily lives, read our musings, and get to know us well. But, how do we go through that virtual looking glass and get a sense of who the readers are?

Your readers can be easily bored and distractible. If the blog is not engaging, the next one is only a click away. Magazines can be put down, letters crumpled, or reports put in the "circular file." Your job as a writer is to engage your reader, but first you have to know something about this elusive being.

PRACTICE 1.3

Engaging Your Audience

Create a reader profile for the following writing assignments:

- A film review for an online general interest magazine
- An essay for the "Modern Love" section of the *New York Times*
- A book review for your campus newspaper
- A literary analysis for your American Literature class
- A public service print advertisement for MADD (Mothers Against Drunk Driving)

Understandably, students often write for their professors. After all, the professor will be the first-line reader and evaluator of the work. The problem, of course, is imagining your professor as your only reader limits your range. Think about a broader readership: a world full of potential readers. Who are they? What will draw them to your message? What will make them come back for more?

Think about your audience as the reader of the genre you are writing. News readers want their information delivered in clear, direct language with all the pertinent information summarized quickly in the first paragraph or two. You can think of this reader gulping morning coffee and surfing the Internet. On the other hand, a reader who picks up a memoir or reads a personal essay expects to be riveted by the story of your life and has probably set aside some leisure time to do so. Maybe this reader is tucked up in bed with her e-reader.

You can create this kind of profile of your reader for any assignment you tackle. Thinking about the expectations of the genre, and the purpose of your writing, will help guide you to a sense of your audience. A useful rule of thumb is to think of your reader as "intelligent but ignorant." What this means is that your reader is as smart as if not smarter than you are but does not yet know your take on the topic. Explaining your ideas to this reader keeps you focused and on your toes.

CREATING YOUR VOICE

As you make choices about genre, purpose, and audience you also have to consider your writer's *voice.* You create a voice as you write—a voice that reveals something about who you are and speaks directly to your reader. When you talk, you reveal your personality by the words you choose to use and by your tone of voice, volume, and inflections. You can also use expressions and gestures—body language—to make your points. A raised eyebrow or a dismissive shrug can convey irony or negativity, even if your words are full of praise.

TONE: FORMAL, PERSONAL, LYRICAL, OR PLAINSPOKEN

When you write, you have fewer tools with which to work. You are limited to expressing your attitude through your choice of words and sentence structure—maybe even through punctuation and graphics. Nevertheless, you can still create writing that falls anywhere on the spectrum between sounding formal to sounding chatty, and you can also create a desired *tone.* You can make your writing sound, among other ways, ironic, droll, funny, cutting, serious, cynical, lively, lyrical, dull, or flippant.

Creating your voice is part of the craft of writing. Whenever you write an academic essay, an application for a study-abroad program, or a letter of appeal to raise money for a charity, you make decisions about how you want to sound and how you want your reader to respond to you. You develop an inner ear, a sense of what sounds right and what sounds discordant, the more you write and the more you read.

Of course, you do not have just one voice. You have multiple voices that you use in writing, just as you do in speech, for different audiences. Just as you would probably not curse in the classroom, you would usually not use slang or sloppy writing in an academic essay or a scholarship application.

More to the point, you fit your voice to the assignment's purpose and the conventions of your genre. When writing a film review for your college newspaper, you might appropriately use a humorous voice, one filled with wordplay and puns. On the other hand, when writing an essay or editorial expressing your views on the death penalty, you would probably use a serious, even impassioned voice.

All of these voices are authentic. They are all part of who you are and how you express yourself in different situations. No matter what choices you make as a writer—to use a formal or personal tone, lyrical or plainspoken language—you create your voice through the words you use and the way you structure your sentences. Keep in mind that you control your language; you make conscious choices to use *this* word rather than *that* one, this type of sentence rather than another.

How do you make those decisions? All writers confront these questions of voice. Some genres and some audiences require a certain style, but more often than not, style is more of a writer's choice. You might use a common word like *house* or its more erudite and distant cousin *edifice*. You might use a simple sentence to cement a point, or you might use a lengthy one to create an unbroken series of images. The end product of all these stylistic choices becomes your writer's voice, your personality emerging from the page.

STYLISTIC CHOICES AND THE WRITER'S VOICE: LEWIS THOMAS IN THE LIVES OF A CELL

Even when writing about seemingly dry topics, good writers try to engage their readers. The following passage comes from a book called *The Lives of a Cell* by science writer Lewis Thomas.

> We live in a dancing matrix of viruses; they dart, rather like bees, from organism to organism, from plant to insect to mammal to me and back again, and into the sea, tugging along pieces of this genome, strings of genes from that, transplanting grafts of DNA, passing around heredity as though at a great party.

Thomas is having fun with this writing. He begins with a short, simple assertion but chooses a surprising adjective—*dancing*—to describe the matrix of viruses in which we live. Then, by stringing together the long series of phrases, Thomas makes his sentence seem to dance as well. He plays with language as he plays with sentence length by returning to the dance image at the end of the sentence. He shows the viruses passing around heredity as one might pass around canapés: *as though at a great party.* Here is a writer who has put a great deal of effort into his

PRACTICE 1.4

Defining Voice

Define the voices in the following passages. Support your definition by citing specific examples of vocabulary, sentence structure, or punctuation. If you can, make a guess about the writer's occupation and intended audience. On what evidence do you base your guess? In what kind of publication would you expect to find each of the passages?

1. *Men in Black II* has one moment of goofy, brilliant invention: There is a new alien threat in town, and Agent Jay (Will Smith), seeking help, has to retrieve his partner, Agent Kay (Tommy Lee Jones), who, at the end of the first movie, was neutralized and now works in the Truro, Massachusetts, post office. Got that?
2. The African-American contribution to composition studies—an enormous one—flows from various confluences inside African American intellectual and rhetorical traditions. Free black churches, culturally specific jeremiads, slave narratives, secret schools, black women's clubs, and

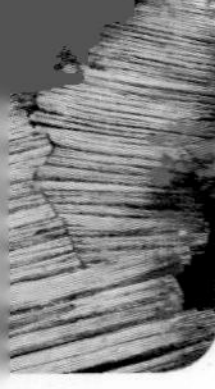

writing, but the result seems effortless. His style is lively, and his voice is engaging. Above all, his writing is crystal clear.

(*Continued*)

black colleges all represent an enriching merger of African-American intellectual and activist concern with writing instruction initiatives.

3. Knit in a breathable pique-stitch from smooth Peruvian combed cotton, these shirts have a weathered softness and a comfortable, broken-in feel you will enjoy right away. Gently sandwashed to mellow the colors and minimize shrinkage.

DECIDING ON MEDIA AND DESIGN: PACKAGING YOUR MESSAGE

You also have to consider how to deliver your message—in what medium and with what design elements. Writing is rarely black words in 12-point type on a white page nowadays. Words often come with music, images that move or stay still and sometimes can be delivered immediately to a cell phone. You definitely have to think about how your message will be read, whether it is on paper or on a screen. Imagine a two-story billboard. Then think about the tiny screen of your cell phone. What is possible to write on each of these spaces is just one part of your thinking about how a message might be delivered to your audience. You need to think about what is customary—what is appropriate.

CONSIDERING YOUR MEDIA

In writing for the business world, as in dressing for the professional world, certain choices are predetermined. You will present information onscreen, perhaps using PowerPoint. You will augment your presentations with film. You will need to think about the size of the words, the typeface or font, the amount of words anyone would want to read on a screen. These are not arbitrary decisions. These elements are not decorations.

The way your message is read will help you choose what you write. There is no escaping the interconnected nature of how a message looks and what it says to specifically targeted readers.

FAQS ABOUT PACKAGES FOR MESSAGES

Q: What if my message takes several forms—a speech that also will appear on the Internet?

A: *Think about what the main delivery system is, because there probably is one. If your main delivery is a YouTube video of a speaker, your writing should conform to the rules for the spoken word: writing short, concrete sentences that work with the breath of the speaker.*

Q: How will I know the best package for my message?

A: *Most of the time, the answer to this is tied up with the outcome you would like to achieve. If you are writing a blog, you want to engage your readers and you want them to come back and read more, later. You will keep brevity in mind, remembering how onscreen readers do not like to scroll too much, for example.*

Q: Should I think about how to incorporate other kinds of media—sound and photographs?

A: *Yes and no. The reality of being a working writer means you enter the stream of writing—and the stream is crowded with messages, each one competing with all the others. But yours should not include media for the sake of it. Remember, this is not about decoration. These choices help carry your message and help make it stronger, but ultimately it is your big idea, the clarity of your message, and the style of your message, that will make or break it. It is important to remember: Sometimes a message can be simply words on a page, billboard, or phone screen.*

Ten Tips for a Clear Writing Style

Writers, whether in the professional or academic world, put a premium on a crisp, direct writing style, a style that communicates ideas clearly, economically, and precisely.

1. **Cut Clutter** Cluttered writing hides your good ideas under unnecessary padding and robs your sentences of their power. You can express the most complex ideas in clear language that helps your reader understand your thinking.

   Wordy: *The students* who won the prizes *will meet the judges* at the conference on the day when they hold the dinner to commemorate their work.

(continued)

Ten Tips for a Clear Writing Style (continued)

Clear: *The prize-winning students will meet the judges at the conference's commemorative dinner.*

2. **Avoid Redundancy** Be alert to the meanings of the words you select. Many people misuse the word *unique*. If you know that *unique* means one of a kind, unrivaled and incomparable, you will not make the common error of qualifying it with *somewhat* or *very*.

   Other redundant expressions:

   Refer ~~back~~
   Repeat ~~again~~
   Free ~~complimentary~~ dinner
   Smiled ~~happily~~
   ~~Tall~~ skyscraper
   ~~End~~ result
   Cooperate ~~together~~
   ~~Basic~~ fundamentals

3. **Limit Qualifiers** Qualifiers (adjectives and adverbs) limit or modify other words, and they also add color and texture to writing. However, some qualifiers—such as *many, somewhat, very, relatively*, and *rather*—do the opposite; they make writing dull. Try reading the following sentence from E.B. White's *The Elements of Style* without the qualifiers *particularly, little, very, rather*, and *pretty*, and see if you agree that these words sap the sentence of its strength.

   > The constant use of the adjective *little* (except to indicate size) is particularly debilitating; we should all try to do a little better, we should all be very watchful of this rule, for it is a rather important one, and we are pretty sure to violate it now and then.

4. **Cut *It is* and *There are* from Your Writing** When possible, take extra care to cut avoid writing or to rewrite sentences beginning with *It is* or *There are*. Known as expletive constructions, these phrases commit two writing sins: they add unnecessary language, and they keep your reader from getting to the point of the sentence.

   Original: *There are two cats sleeping in the bay window.*

   Rewrite: *Two cats sleep in the bay window.*

5. **Use Your Natural Vocabulary** Sometimes writers are tempted to pump some air into flabby prose by inflating their language. Almost always, the result sounds awkward, unnatural, even confusing. When you use your natural vocabulary, words that have meaning and nuance for you,

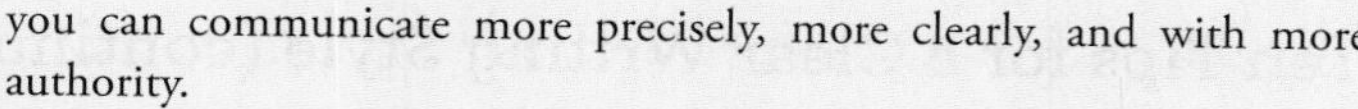

you can communicate more precisely, more clearly, and with more authority.

Pumped up: *The deleterious result of prolixity in writing results in obfuscatory textual material.*

Natural: *Wordiness results in confusing writing.*

6. **Limit Jargon** The business world is notoriously infested with jargon—"I appreciate this opportunity to input that concept from a business effectiveness viewpoint"—but doctors, economists, grammarians, and others also speak to each other in a kind of specialized language. It is tempting for those of us who wish to sound knowledgeable to try out "insider" language, especially when writing a paper for a class in literature, sociology, or psychology—fields that have a specialized vocabulary. Whenever possible, avoid that temptation.

7. **Avoid Euphemism** *Euphemism* is language that covers up the truth—either out of prudery (using *powder room* instead of *bathroom* or *bathroom* instead of *toilet*), sensitivity (using *passed on* instead of *died*), or the desire to sound more respectful or elevated (using *waste disposal personnel* instead of *garbage collectors*). Euphemisms can make your writing sound wordy and pretentious.

8. **Use the Active Voice (Most of the Time)** A sentence is in the active or passive voice depending on whether the subject of the sentence performs or receives the action. In the active voice, the subject is the actor. In the passive voice, the subject receives the action.

   Passive Voice: *The president was elected by the voters in a landslide victory.*

   Active Voice: *Voters elected the president in a landslide victory.*

   Certain genres also call for the passive voice.

   - Lab Report: "*Liquid was poured into the test tube*" and "*Incisions were made.*" *(passive)*

   Readers of lab reports focus on what happened, what actions occurred. Knowing exactly who poured the liquid into the test tube is not important.

   - Newspaper Article: *Three people were injured last night in a house fire. (passive)*

   This sentence places emphasis on the injured people rather than on the fire itself.

(continued)

PRACTICE 1.5

Identifying Active and Passive Voices

Test your understanding of the active and passive voice by identifying the following sentences as active or passive and by rewriting any passive-voice sentences in the active voice.

1. *Saving Private Ryan* was viewed by my entire history class.
2. Super Bowl ads are watched more avidly than the game itself.
3. The New Year's Eve party was attended by the rich and famous.
4. The band played its final set to the audience's loud approval.
5. World War II was won in 1945.
6. World War II ended in 1945.

Ten Tips for a Clear Writing Style (continued)

(You can read more about active and passive voice in the Grammar Refresher, Chapter 17.)

9. **Use Concrete Nouns** Concrete nouns refer to objects, persons, or places that you can perceive with your five senses. (Abstract nouns refer to ideas or concepts—*forgiveness, trust, love.*) Readers remember specifics, not generalities. If a person you are describing sits under a tree, let your readers know if the tree is a redwood or a pine, if it is old and gnarled or a sapling.

A really tall building	A skyscraper
An extremely cheap person	A miser
A lot of good food	A feast

10. **Use Strong Verbs** The verb packs the most punch in a sentence. Strong verbs describe or express action, giving a sentence its energy and power. Weak verbs do the opposite; they deaden sentences.

    Forms of the verb *to be* appear more than any other verb in English sentences. All of the forms of *to be* (*am, is, are, was, were, being, been*), called *state-of-being* or *linking verbs,* show no action.

    Any time you can substitute an active verb for a form of *to be,* you can infuse some liveliness into your sentence.

    Weak: *There was a thief robbing my building.*

    Stronger: *A thief robbed my building.*

    The more precisely you can choose a verb, the clearer your meaning becomes. You can eliminate modifiers if you select a verb with the precise meaning you seek.

    Original: *I looked at the book very carefully.*

    More precise: *I scrutinized the book*

PRACTICE 1.6

Editing for Clarity and Brevity

Revise this passage, changing vague nouns to specific ones and substituting strong verbs for weak ones. Try to eliminate every use of a form of *to be,* even if it means rewriting the sentences.

> There are a lot of people doing research today who are conducting an investigation into how the things in our heads work. The question they are looking to answer is how our brains store stuff. One woman in psychology is focusing on animal studies. Dr. Phyllis Johnson is doing experiments with rats who are running around in confusing places. She is looking to find out how neurological impulses work as these rodents are going through the mazes. A man who is also in psychology, Dr. Louis Young, is working with human subjects who are students at the local college. These subjects will be doing things inside magnetic resonance

DESIGNING YOUR MESSAGE

The nonverbal parts of messages—illustrations and photographs—shape our understanding of a message in the same way that words do. These messages can be completely nonverbal, and if they are well designed, we can "read" them as we would read written language. Nonverbal communication—facial expressions and body language—reveals how much information we understand without language.

Even as babies, before we understood language, our earliest attempts at "reading" were figuring out what to make of the world around us. Babies cry when they look at angry faces but smile when they look at happy faces. Just the drawings of faces can elicit these responses from an infant.

Our understanding of nonverbal messages is as learned as it is instinctive, and this understanding seems deeply imbedded in our perception of information; so deeply imbedded that we do not always understand why we are persuaded by the things we see. But if we slow down the process of perceiving messages—looking and reading—we can understand why some images are so very powerful. Keep in mind that learning to look critically is a skill much like learning to read critically.

Think about an angry note you might write by hand with underlining and all capital letters. (*I DON'T EVER WANT TO SEE YOU AGAIN!*) The medium you use to convey your anger might be a thick Sharpie-brand marker—a good choice for delivering a strong (not to mention waterproof) message.

Now consider the same message written in pink crayon. The words would say one thing literally, but the appearance of the words on paper might connote something else. Small alterations in the way the message looks can add up to big changes in what the message means. Most of the messages you receive daily—and many of the ones you create—are packaged with visual imagery: photographs, illustrations, and even streaming video. As you read through the chapters of this book, you will learn how to decode many types of visual messages and learn to *look critically.* To become better at critical "seeing," you will examine many of the choices designers and artists have made—from the font or typeface choices to the cropping or placement of images on the page or screen. To get started, look at two examples of visual elements in messages—layout and color.

LAYOUT One important visual element is the way that words are placed on the page—also called *layout.* The poet e. e. cummings, for example, encoded meaning into his words through their placement on the page, making a blank canvas out of a blank page and using the space of the page to change, shape, and enhance literal meaning:

l(a
le
af
fa
ll
s)
one
l
iness

(*Continued*)

imaging machines. It is hoped that these things that they do will be providing answers to long-standing questions about stuff we remember.

PRACTICE 1.7

Using Layout to Emphasize Meaning

Use the following sentence to explore how layout could enhance or change the written meaning of the words. Limit yourself to layout choices only. Choose Times Roman or Arial font, up to 20 points in size. Limit your space to an 8 ½ by 11-inch sheet of white paper.

We used to play a game in which we would hold our breaths for as long as we could.

Through cummings's design of his message, the letters look like a leaf falling, and his metaphor for loneliness is clear.

COLOR Color is another important design element. Color has great influence on emotion and, in turn, on perceived meaning. As with all things visual, our associations with color are as instinctive as they are culturally learned. The image of a bride all dressed in white would not have the same meaning if viewed in the Far East, where brides have traditionally worn red. Can you imagine what the neighbors would say in America if a widow wore purple? However, in Thailand, wearing purple would be completely appropriate at a time of mourning. Because color takes on its own character depending on where the viewer lives, Web designers are warned that they need to be aware of the intensity of meaning colors can carry. Shades and hues of colors can convey different meanings to different viewers. As you begin to look at messages in a more critical way, also consider the importance of color.

PRACTICE 1.8

Using Color to Emphasize Meaning

How might this image be used to make a point?

1. First, list all the meanings of the word *red*.
2. Next, list all the meanings associated with the color *green*.
3. Now, think of one product that might be advertised with this image.

DESIGN CHECKLIST The significance of the nonverbal parts of messages is more important than ever now that so much of our communication takes place on video screens. To become an astute reader of the visual, you first need to break down the nonverbal parts of a message into separate elements. Knowing what to look for is key. The following list is a good way to begin "looking" critically.

1. **Look at the individual elements. Without trying to interpret the significance of the visual elements, describe what you see.** You might describe this drawing by Saul Steinberg, on the next page, in these words.

   This is a line drawing of a little girl and a grown-up man. The characters face one another in profile. The drawing is very simple. Coming from the man's mouth is a dark, jagged line. The line starts at his mouth and makes some angular turns and then ends in the air near the girl. The line starting at the girl's mouth is curlicued and forms childish drawings of dogs and houses and flowers, all connected. The man's line is drawn over the girl's. The drawing has a cartoonish look to it.

2. **Look for patterns and make connections.** Carefully observing the details of the drawing might result in this type of description.

   This simple and amusing line drawing shows an adult and a child talking to each other. Your eye is drawn first to the heavy, bold line that represents the words coming out of the adult's mouth. The man seems to speak in a loud, assertive voice, and the subject of his words seems to be abstract, especially when compared with the little girl's words. She talks about all kinds of things—puppies and houses and flowers—all of which seem concrete and playful.

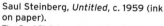

Saul Steinberg, *Untitled*, c. 1959 (ink on paper).
The Saul Steinberg Foundation/Artists Rights Society (ARS), New York

3. **Form an opinion or theory.** You might conclude this way:

   The adult attempts to impress or instruct the child by speaking loudly. Since his line cancels hers out, he has the upper hand. Steinberg's message may be that children have interesting—if not always perfectly logical—things to say, but adults speak with more authority. Steinberg's drawing comments on the puffed-up egos of some adults and their inability to listen to children.

WRITING ABOUT THE RHETORICAL SITUATION

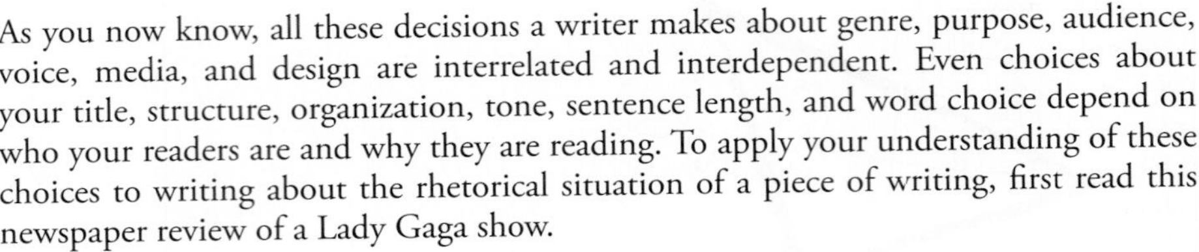

As you now know, all these decisions a writer makes about genre, purpose, audience, voice, media, and design are interrelated and interdependent. Even choices about your title, structure, organization, tone, sentence length, and word choice depend on who your readers are and why they are reading. To apply your understanding of these choices to writing about the rhetorical situation of a piece of writing, first read this newspaper review of a Lady Gaga show.

MUSIC REVIEW | LADY GAGA

Lavish Worlds, and the Headwear to Match[1]

By Jon Pareles

Published: January 21, 2010

http://www.nytimes.com/2010/01/22/arts/music/22gaga.html

WHEN *LADY Gaga* finished her thumping, strobing, razzle-dazzle song-and-dance numbers at *Radio City Music Hall* on Wednesday night, she held her pose and kept the stage lights on, delighting her many camera-wielding fans. Her Monster Ball tour always provided something worth a snapshot: a sci-fi tableau, perhaps, or a skimpy, glittery costume. The more her image gets around, the better Lady Gaga does. "Take my picture!" she urged the audience, in her first of four sold-out shows at Radio City. "I want to be a star."

Newscom

She is. A combination of well-planned outlandishness, media exposure and catchy, stuttering choruses—"pa-pa-pa-pa-paparazzi," "p-p-p-poker face"—has made Lady Gaga a multimillion-selling, Grammy-nominated star in less than a year and a half since the 2008 release of her debut album, "The Fame" (Streamline/Konlive/Cherrytree/Interscope). Stefani Joanne Angelina Germanotta, aka Lady Gaga, sings, writes, dresses and apparently exists to toy with celebrity as performance art, seeing how freaky (in a fascinating way) she can be as she reaches a mass audience.

[1]JON PARELES, "Lavish Worlds, and the Headwear to Match" from http://www.nytimes.com/2010/01/22/arts/music/22gaga.html. Reprinted with the permission of PARS International.

While showpeople like *David Bowie* and *Madonna* established this career path, Lady Gaga is strutting along it with larger-than-life style and, behind that, actual musical gifts. Her voice is strong enough to expose in a cappella singing, and she backed herself up with her own piano playing, sounding like a female *Elton John* when she played (and belted) "Speechless," wearing a huge black-feather shawl.

Her opening acts reflected her two main source genres: R&B from Jason Derülo and glam-rock from Semi Precious Weapons. Lady Gaga's songs are solid, most often pumped up by hefty Eurodisco beats. Between snappy choruses—"Just dance" or "Caught in a bad romance"—her verses sometimes revel in desire, sometimes question it. Newer songs on "The Fame Monster," the expanded 2009 edition of "The Fame," add misgivings and brutal undercurrents to the sex, money and, yes, fame that the original album coveted.

The staging layered more complications onto the songs, placing Lady Gaga in otherwordly realms. She first appeared behind a scrim showing a computerized grid, with a lighted costume that made her more a collection of white dots than a body: a figure in an electronic universe, like a digitized pop star.

No one in pop is more audacious about headwear. Onstage and in photos on video screens, she wore Egyptian-deity golden armor, antlers, a shiny red chauffeur's hat, a spiked black hood and an exoskeletonlike helmet, not to mention bondage-style rings connecting her head to a bar held up by two men. It's hard to say what that had to do with "Paparazzi"—which mingles love, stalking and media awareness—but even when connections were cryptic, the show had its own momentum.

The 10 dancers were rarely a comradely chorus line or a party scene. More often they appeared inhuman with hoods or masks, or made up like animals or ghouls, although that didn't stop Lady Gaga from mimicking a few sexual positions with them. Her stage persona veered from kindly—urging fellow misfits to follow their dreams, announcing that proceeds from her Jan. 24 show would be donated to Haiti relief—to bellicose, at one point taking a gun off her piano and aiming it at the audience, firing sparks to the sound of automatic weaponry. "I'm a free bitch," she declared more than once. Near the end, she ascended in an orb of rotating silver rings, like a disco angel.

The spectacle sustains her, she insisted. "When they ask me why I spent all my money on my show, I tell them, because my fans are sexy," she said. "But the question is: Do you think I'm sexy?" The answer was loudly affirmative. It grew even louder as Lady Gaga went on to compare herself to Tinker Bell, needing applause to live.

QUESTIONS ABOUT THE RHETORICAL SITUATION

1. Considering Genre: What information does this review include? What features cue you in to the fact that this is a review of a performance?
2. Considering Audience: Why would someone read this article? Where was it published? Who would be the typical reader? Does the reader need any special knowledge, vocabulary, or background to understand this review?

3. Considering Purpose: What is the writer's goal in this review? How much information about the performance does the writer provide? What other information does the writer include that suggests his purpose in writing this review?
4. Considering Voice: How would you describe the reviewer's voice? How does the voice reflect both the subject matter and the reasons someone would want to read about this performance?
5. Considering Media and Design: What does the photograph of Lady Gaga reveal about her public image? Look at the way the shot is composed as well as what it contains.

WRITING ABOUT THE RHETORICAL SITUATION

In three to four paragraphs, summarize the article and comment on the writer's choices and how they relate to the specific genre of a music review. In your analysis, include your observations about how carefully the writer considers the audience and the choices the writer makes that reflect an understanding of who the readers are and why they are reading.

The Writer's Process

2

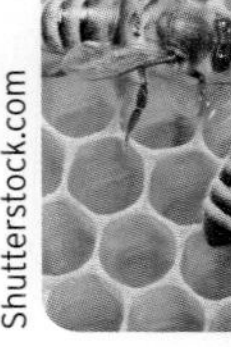
Tischenko Irina/ Shutterstock.com

You can't wait for inspiration. You have to go after it with a club.

—Jack London

THE WRITING PROCESS

For most people, writing is a messy business—not straightforward at all. If you watch a videotape of a writer at work (which writing researchers actually do), you will see more seemingly random activity—and more emotion—than you might expect. Most writers, once they begin to write, jump from task to task. They may start writing and then back up and make a list. They may order their notes and then write a conclusion before writing the paper itself. They may spend an hour on a single paragraph or get the whole paper done in that hour. Writers also stretch, yell, grimace, pace the room, and laugh aloud.

Research also reveals that some writers move in a straight line from stage to stage in the writing process, but many of us do not first brainstorm, then draft, then revise, and then proofread. Instead, writers often move both forward and backward among stages, often revisiting earlier stages before advancing. This process, known as *recursive*, looks more like a circle than a straight line.

As the diagram on page 23 suggests, to move forward you sometimes have to back up and reconsider a key idea, do a little more research, or think for a while about the meaning of a word. You can brainstorm at any part of the process, not just before you write; and while you are brainstorming, you are often also revising by editing out the workable ideas from the impractical ones (*Dumb idea, will not work. . . . Maybe I could go in this direction. . . . That will not support the argument, but I might be able to use it later*). During revision, ideas can surface that redirect the whole paper or generate whole new sections.

One writing student explains her writing process for a literature class this way:

> This past semester when I had to analyze books for my writing class, I would usually first write my introduction with a vague idea of the topic and somehow end the introduction with a thesis. . . . I would usually write that on a Post-It note to put on my computer

WHAT'S TO COME

PRACTICE 2.1

Writing Rituals

1. Describe your own writing rituals. What do you do to get yourself primed for writing?
2. Interview a classmate about his or her writing rituals. Compare your rituals with your classmate's rituals.
3. Observe the writing ritual of someone you know—a friend, family member, or roommate, for example. Watch this person get ready to write. Take notes on your observations. Then interview the person and see if his or her perception matches yours.

"Write about dogs!"

George Booth/Cartoonbank.com

because heaven knows I like to get off topic. Then I would go through the books to be analyzed and pull out the important facts/quotes I wanted to include in my paper. I am a pretty visual person, so I would usually group quotes (etc.) from different books through webs or colored lists.

GETTING STARTED

Sometimes the hardest part of writing is getting started. Most of us have concocted a hundred ways to delay that moment. One person has to clean the room in which she writes; another has to have all his research done, notes organized, and virtual pencils sharpened; yet another works out of chaos, needing a cluttered desk to get started. Once we actually begin writing, other behaviors click in. One person cannot finish a sentence unless every word is spelled correctly and the sentence is grammatically perfect; another types madly, almost randomly, discovering what she means as she writes.

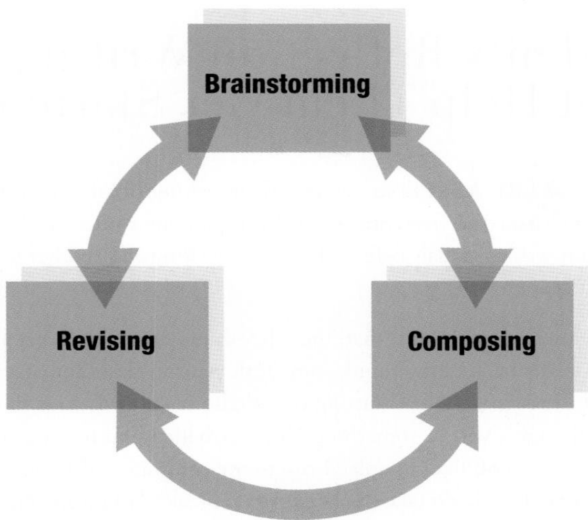

The Writing Process

FINDING YOUR OWN WRITING PROCESS

Ways of jump-starting the writing process are as individual as each writer. A friend tells this story about discovering her own writing process. Sara, a teacher and writer, took a six-month leave from teaching to research and write a series of articles. She woke up on Morning One, feeling enormous relief that she did not have to put on work clothes, gulp down breakfast, and drive twenty miles to her office through rush-hour traffic. A cup of coffee in hand, and still wearing sweats and a T-shirt, she sat down in front of her computer. Nothing. She got up, paced, sat down again. Panic set in. She decided to take the day off and not rush herself.

Day Two mirrored Day One. So did Day Three. By Day Four Sara dreaded getting up, so she lay in bed, trying to figure out the problem. It came to her that she had interrupted her lifelong habit of thinking and planning her day's writing as she showered, dressed, and drove. So she did just that. She showered, dressed, drove for twenty minutes around her neighborhood, got out of her car, reentered her house, took off her coat, sat down at the computer, and began writing.

Driving randomly around your neighborhood or campus may not be the best way for you to start a writing assignment, but most writers have their own rituals, whether they are as simple as having that second cup of coffee or as elaborate as Sara's. Discovering what works for you may be one of the most important first steps to becoming a comfortable and confident writer.

KEEPING A WRITER'S NOTEBOOK

One way to help you get started is to have a place to record random thoughts, overheard dialogue, and ideas that come unbidden in the midst of your daily life. Whether it is an iPad, a black-and-white composition notebook, a reporter's spiral

PRACTICE 2.2

Writing Processes

1. Describe your own writing process. You may want to consider the following questions:
   a. Do you start with an outline or a list?
   b. Do you write the introduction first, or the conclusion?
   c. When do you do your research: before you start, throughout the process, and/or after you have finished a first draft and know where the holes are?
   d. Does this process vary, depending on the assignment? If so, how?
2. Set up a tape recorder next to you as you write an assignment. Record the process aloud as you go, explaining what you are doing as you do it. ("Now I am stuck. I am going back to read the assignment. Taking a break. Just got an idea. Wrote for fifteen minutes straight.") Write a short analysis of your own writing process.
3. Discuss a classmate's writing process with him or her. Use the questions above, or come up with your own questions. How do your writing processes differ? How are they the same?

Three Students Reflect on Writing Rituals that Help Them Get Started

THREE STUDENTS WERE ASKED to describe their writing rituals when they get a writing assignment. When asked to freewrite about this topic, one student realized that she had not thought about writing rituals before. The act of writing allowed her to reflect on her own writing practice.

"I react with a few instinctive ideas (oh, this, that, the other thing) and then forget about it for a few days. Probably in the back of my mind, some little neuron-slash-hamster is running inside the wheel of idea generation, churning out plethoric subconscious thoughts. Eventually one of those thoughts will be something Neanderthalic—I'm not too smart—like "Paper. Thursday. Due," and off like a maniac I run to my computer. Although I claim to write nonstop till it's done, I really do take my fair share of breaks. "Oh, this comma is a good excuse to eat a cookie," or "Oh, that letter *Z* represents the time to check my e-mail," or "Ah, this prose is so poetic I'll play guitar for half an hour." So things take a lot longer than expected, but this keeps my little hamster from getting too tired."

—Nathan Welton (Student), "I react with a few instinctive ideas."

"When I enter my dorm room, I'm never focused on just my paper. I always seem captured by everything else in my room (computer, radio, food, bed . . . everything but the paper). In order to channel my energy to just the paper, I completely clear my desk, giving myself an open, fresh plain on which my thoughts will venture unimpeded. If this fails or the room does not act as a proper studying room, I bring my laptop/books into the lounge in hopes of finding it quiet; if not, I go downstairs to one of many other lounges and begin my work. I guess I have to "clean house" prior to working, as it also cleanses my mind of junk thoughts, off-subject pondering, . . . etc."

—Reprinted by permission of Matt Sato.

"I've never really thought about my writing rituals *per se*. After pondering what my personal rituals are, I would have to say I do just that . . . ponder. When I find out about a writing assignment, I usually start brainstorming immediately. I also seem to become more aware of the subject about which I have to write (i.e., I notice that subject in everyday life; I observe how that subject plays into my life)."

—Reprinted by permission of Arielle Greenleaf.

notepad, or napkins held together with paper clips, almost all writers keep this kind of notebook, also known as a daybook or journal. Blogs also serve as public places to share writing, ideas, tidbits of interesting information or insight.

When you first get an assignment, read it carefully. Record it in your daybook. When you have a writing assignment, the assignment itself may retreat to the back of

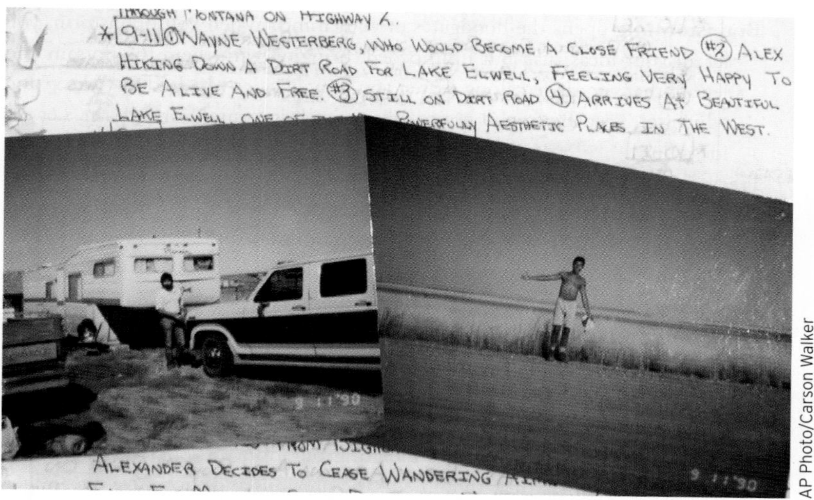

THROUGH MONTANA ON HIGHWAY 2.
*9-11 ① WAYNE WESTERBERG, WHO WOULD BECOME A CLOSE FRIEND #2 ALEX
HIKING DOWN A DIRT ROAD FOR LAKE ELWELL, FEELING VERY HAPPY TO
BE ALIVE AND FREE. #3 STILL ON DIRT ROAD ④ ARRIVES AT BEAUTIFUL
AESTHETIC PLACES IN THE WEST.
ALEXANDER DECIDES TO CEASE WANDERING

AP Photo/Carson Walker

The film and book, Into the Wild, were based on Chris McCandless's notebook

your mind as you go about your daily life. Being aware of what your assignment is can help you on a subconscious level. As you jog or shower or even as you talk with friends or attend a class, you may find yourself thinking about the topic or coming up with an approach or an idea for the assignment. As you come up with ideas, jot them down.

Similarly, you might wake up in the morning with a solution to a knotty writing problem that you were trying to untangle when you went to bed, or perhaps that you were not even consciously thinking about. By giving the matter a rest while you do, you can gain a new perspective. If you keep a notebook by your bedside, you can write a few notes while the ideas are fresh.

Writing an idea inscribes it not only on the paper but also in your mind. Your ideas can incubate in a notebook. When it is time to write, you may find your words flowing more clearly than you had imagined they would because of the activity of your subconscious mind. Writing can also help you retrieve memories of other words you have written, ideas you have formed, passages you have read, or experiences you have had. One idea leads to another. You will discover that the very act of writing can get your creativity flowing. Bringing forth one idea stimulates a series of other ideas, even pulling long-forgotten details from your memory.

TECHNIQUES FOR GETTING UNSTUCK, GETTING STARTED, AND GETTING REFRESHED

If you become blocked, you may want to think about using some brainstorming techniques to get started. Brainstorming is useful when you begin to cast about for topics or ideas about topics, when you want to develop an idea, when you are reading about and researching a topic, and when you need to refresh your thinking.

PRACTICE 2.3

Keeping a Notebook

1. Keep a writer's notebook for two days. Jot down ideas.
   - Dreams or snippets of dreams you remember when you wake
   - Funny or insightful comments made by friends or professors
   - Clever advertisements or tag lines
   - Quotations from your reading
   - Overheard conversations
   - Unusual events from the news or from your own observations
   - Controversies that you hear or read about
   - Original writing: descriptions of people, places, and events that interest you
2. Write about anything that might work well in a piece of writing, but do not use your notebook as merely a log of your activities. Think of it as a collecting place for images, quotations, ideas, and bits of dialogue. Fill at least two pages each day.
3. Write a few paragraphs evaluating the experience of keeping a notebook for these two days.

Brainstorming opens the floodgates of your mind. When you brainstorm, you let all your ideas rush out unimpeded, bringing with them the flotsam and jetsam that get carried along. Later, you can consider which ideas to keep and which to reject. Be careful not to edit yourself in content or in form. Let the ideas flow.

Freewriting is the practice of writing without limitations and without a clear destination, using free association. It is writing to discover meaning. Write freely for a set period of time, such as ten minutes, and write everything you can think of about your topic.

Clustering, also known as *word webbing* or *branching*, can be a powerful brainstorming technique. Writers who are visual thinkers find that clustering helps them find relationships among ideas, allowing them to generate a complex interrelationship of ideas. When you create a word web, you write a keyword in the center of a page, circle the word, and in quick succession write a series of associated words or phrases radiating out from it. Circle each word or phrase, and connect it with a line to the previous and successive one. When you run that string as far as it will go, return to the center, and begin again in another direction. (See cluster map below.)

PRACTICE 2.4

Getting Unstuck: Freewriting

1. Try your hand at freewriting as it is described on this page. If you do not have a topic in mind or an assignment to work with, write about anything you know about: basketball, colonial America, music, global warming, cooking, chaos theory, or civil liberties, perhaps.
2. Read your freewrite. Circle any interesting ideas that might be useful to develop for later writings. Put a box around any phrases or sentences that might be keepers.
3. What was your response to the freewriting? Is it a technique you might find useful? Why or why not?

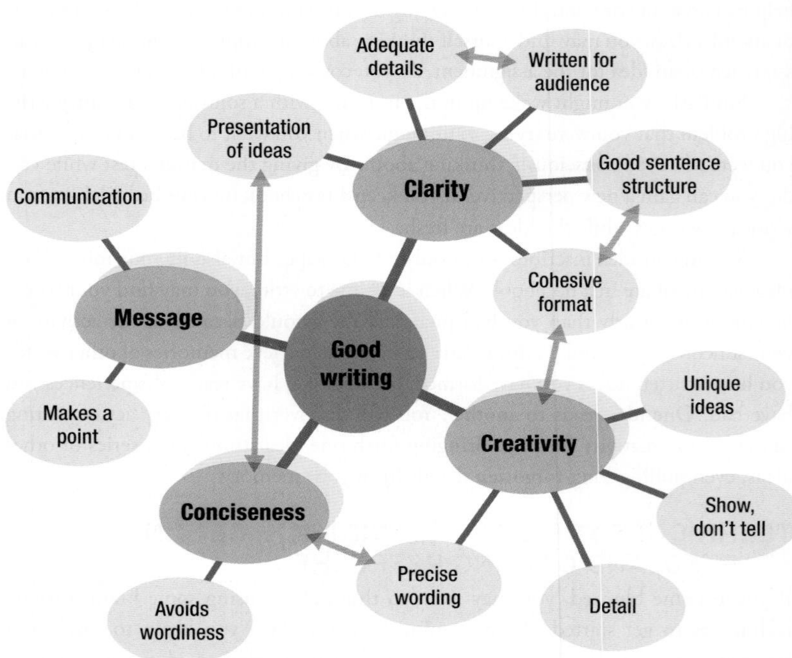

Cluster Map of "Good Writing"

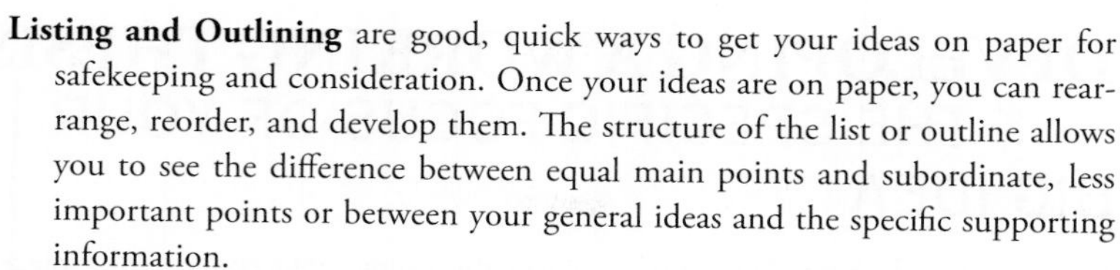

Listing and Outlining are good, quick ways to get your ideas on paper for safekeeping and consideration. Once your ideas are on paper, you can rearrange, reorder, and develop them. The structure of the list or outline allows you to see the difference between equal main points and subordinate, less important points or between your general ideas and the specific supporting information.

Collaborating with a partner or in a group can also be helpful since you can build on each other's knowledge and backgrounds. When you collaborate with others, you have to find language to articulate your ideas, and the feedback you get provides you with fresh perspectives.

PLANNING AND SHAPING

No matter what type of writing assignment, part of the process is doing some research, finding a focus, developing a working thesis, and organizing your material.

CREATING A RESEARCH PATH

You put your foot on the research path when you begin asking questions about your topic and then start finding the answers, which, of course, often leads to more questions. As you continue researching, you may find new avenues to travel, different directions to take, and, in the best of situations, surprising discoveries to make.

There are many ways to begin your research. You can talk to people who know the subject or to friends and classmates, just to start airing your thoughts. You can go online to find information, and you can go to the library and find books and articles on your subject. Read for information and inspiration. Whether you are writing a short or long researched article, a blog, a film script, or a memoir, you can jumpstart your thinking by reading widely and deeply. (For more guidance on a variety of primary and secondary research techniques from conducting an interview to conducting an effective Web search, see Chapter 15, Research.)

Remember to take careful notes on the ideas, quotations, and sources you consult as you gather your information. You can think of your sources as the signposts on your journey. You will need to remember who sent you in what direction, and you do that by giving credit to those whose words you have read, absorbed, or been inspired by. (See Chapter 16 for more on documentation and avoiding plagiarism.) Part of the fun of research lies in becoming knowledgeable about a topic and familiar with the experts, the theories, and the controversies.

You continue on that research path throughout the writing process. You can consult sources as you brainstorm, as you write your first draft, and as you revise. The more you learn about a topic, the more interesting it becomes to you, and the better you can communicate that interest—even intellectual excitement—to your readers.

DEVELOPING A WORKING THESIS: THE SPECIFIC FOCUS OF YOUR BIG IDEA

We are using the term "big idea" to mean the overarching concept in a piece of writing. It is the first step in developing your thesis. For example, the big idea of an editorial you might write could be to persuade your administration to use green technology in new buildings on campus.

Once you identify this big idea, you can then refine it and narrow it down to form the specific point you are making. As we said in Chapter 1, this specific point of a piece of writing goes by many names. In a news story it can be the *angle*; in a proposal a *plan*, and in a memoir a *theme*. It can be called an *evaluative thesis* in a review, or an *analytical thesis* in a researched article, or an *argumentative thesis* in an editorial.

Here is an example of how you might narrow your big idea and develop your thesis:

BIG IDEA: PERSUADE THE ADMINISTRATION TO USE GREEN TECHNOLOGY IN NEW BUILDINGS

Argumentative Thesis: Green technology is not only good for our planet but it also will be a cost effective way to heat and cool the new lecture halls.

No matter what it is called, your specific focus helps you organize your ideas and communicate your thinking to your audience. Your specific focus should be

- Substantive (not self-evident)
- Neither too broad nor too narrow for the scope of the paper
- Supported by evidence (facts, statistics, expert opinion, anecdotes, examples) in the body of your paper
- Engaging to your audience

Often, your thinking will shift as you develop your topic. You may not even discover your true focus until you have explored some side paths. Stay flexible as you draft your paper, and refine or redefine your big idea.

ORGANIZING YOUR MATERIAL

Once you have identified your big idea and homed in on your thesis, consider how best to develop the ideas and support the thesis. An informal list is all some writers need, especially for a short piece of writing. Outlines are useful with more complex

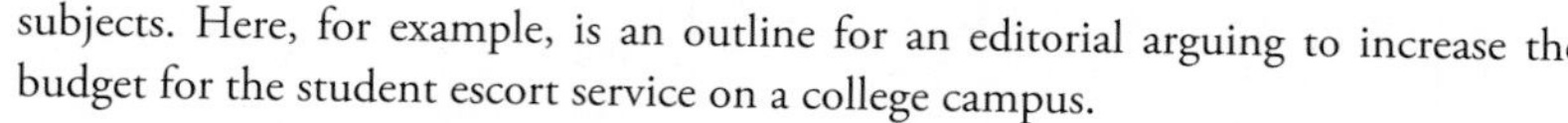

subjects. Here, for example, is an outline for an editorial arguing to increase the budget for the student escort service on a college campus.

Sample Student Outline

I. Thesis: Student escort service is underfunded, a situation that compromises student safety.
II. Other student activities have much larger budgets
    A. Sports
    B. Outdoor club
    C. Debate society
III. The escort service budget is too small
    A. $800 for advertising and staffing
    B. No money to purchase a van or pay for gas
    C. Statement from head of escort service about lack of $$
IV. Student safety is compromised
    A. Anecdote about sophomore girl who reported a stalker
    B. Statement of Chief of Police Perez:"If even one student is frightened on this campus, we have to beef up security." (Personal interview 2/19/11)
V. Call for action: We have to get more funding for the student escort service.
    A. Petition administration
    B. Elect new student government

Outlining also makes good sense and is a powerful organizational strategy—*after* you have written your first draft—as a springboard into revision. Once you have a draft in hand, putting your ideas into outline form allows you to get an overview of how the paper has taken shape so far and to see where you might need to revise. As you line up your main and subordinate points, you can easily see if your points are parallel, if your support is sufficient, and if your ideas proceed logically.

Whether you outline at the beginning, middle, or end of your writing process, make sure you think of the resulting structure as flexible. The outline should open up your thinking, not limit it.

WRITING THE FIRST DRAFT

Your first draft can be messy and experimental, freeform and rough. Get your ideas on paper, and keep the ideas flowing. Try not to edit yourself or think of your worst writing critic peering over your shoulder. The first draft is not the place to worry about grammar, spelling, and style—yet. You will have plenty of time later to revise and edit your paper. In the following excerpt from her instructional book on writing, *bird by bird*, Anne Lamott reassures her readers about how messy a first draft can be.

PRACTICE 2.5

Using Rhetorical Strategies

Practice some of the strategies that you will find starting on page 31 for developing a short article by writing several sentences on one or more of the following topics.

1. Give an example of how it feels to have a learning disability. Illustrate what the person experiences.
2. Write a short description of an unusual ethnic food that most people have not tried.
3. Write a concise narrative of a historical event in your community. Include character, conflict, and drama.
4. Define a term that many people have heard but do not fully understand, such as *encryption*, the *infield fly rule*, or *postmodernism*.
5. Explain the process you go through when you dispute a traffic ticket.
6. Compare and/or contrast two college campuses.

[First Drafts] from *bird by bird*[1]

Anne Lamott

NOW, PRACTICALLY even better news than that of short assignments is the idea of shitty first drafts. All good writers write them. This is how they end up with good second drafts and terrific third drafts. People tend to look at successful writers, writers who are getting their books published and maybe even doing well financially, and think that they sit down at their desks every morning feeling like a million dollars, feeling great about who they are and how much talent they have and what a great story they have to tell; that they take in a few deep breaths, push back their sleeves, roll their necks a few times to get all the cricks out, and dive in, typing fully formed passages as fast as a court reporter. But this is just the fantasy of the uninitiated. I know some very great writers, writers you love who write beautifully and have made a great deal of money, and not one of them sits down routinely feeling wildly enthusiastic and confident. Not one of them writes elegant first drafts. All right, one of them does, but we do not like her very much. We do not think that she has a rich inner life or that God likes her or can even stand her. (Although when I mentioned this to my priest friend Tom, he said you can safely assume you've created God in your own image when it turns out that God hates all the same people you do.)

Very few writers really know what they are doing until they've done it. Nor do they go about their business feeling dewy and thrilled. They do not type a few stiff warm-up sentences and then find themselves bounding along like huskies across the snow. One writer I know tells me that he sits down every morning and says to himself nicely, "It's not like you don't have a choice, because you do—you can either type or kill yourself." We all often feel like we are pulling teeth, even those writers whose prose ends up being the most natural and fluid. The right words and sentences just do not come pouring out like ticker tape most of the time. Now, Muriel Spark is said to have felt that she was taking dictation from God every morning—sitting there, one supposes, plugged into a Dicta-phone, typing away, humming. But this is a very hostile and aggressive position. One might hope for bad things to rain down on a person like this.

For me and most of the other writers I know, writing is not rapturous. In fact, the only way I can get anything written at all is to write really, really shitty first drafts.

The first draft is the child's draft, where you let it all pour out and then let it romp all over the place, knowing that no one is going to see it and that you can shape it later. You just let this childlike part of you channel whatever voices and visions come through and onto the page. If one of the characters wants to say, "Well, so what, Mr. Poopy Pants?," you let her. No one is going to see it. If the kid wants to get into really sentimental, weepy, emotional territory, you let him. Just get it all down on paper, because there may be something great in those six crazy pages that you would never have gotten to by more rational, grown-up means. There may be something in the very last line of the very last paragraph on page six that you just love, that is so beautiful or wild that you now know what you're supposed to be writing about, more or less, or in what direction you might go—but there was no way to get to this without first getting through the first five and a half pages.

[1]Anne Lamott, "Shitty First Drafts," from Bird by Bird: Some Instructions on Writing and Life, copyright © 1994 by Anne Lamott. Used by permission of Pantheon Books, a division of Random House, Inc.

DEVELOPING PARAGRAPHS

Every piece of writing needs an introduction, body, and conclusion as well as an organizing principle—a reason why this paragraph follows that one. A clear organization sets up expectations, even a sense of anticipation, for readers. Your job as a writer is to keep readers interested and moving forward. Ideally, readers should be drawn into your writing by your introduction, and they should keep reading because they are on a well-lit path that leads inevitably to your conclusions

- **Introduction**: The introductory section of a piece of writing should engage the reader and announce the topic. Invite your reader into your piece of writing with a lively voice and a clear focus on your paper's big idea. Expository introductions often explain a topic and can begin with a compelling analogy or metaphor, or offer a fact or statistic. Narrative introductions can create a scene, describe a setting, quote a character in the story, or tell a short anecdote.
- **Body**: The body of your paper is the meaty part. Depending on the genre, here is where you inform, explore, analyze, or argue. Just as the thesis statement announces the topic and focus of your paper, the topic sentence announces—in general terms—the subject of your paragraph. Most paragraphs begin with a clear topic sentence that provides overviews but often needs to be supported by specifics. Lists and outlines are useful at this stage to help you sort your big topic into main points and subordinate points and to make sure you have put your points into the best possible order.
- Co**nclusion**: Conclusions should not be afterthoughts. Their function is to complete your argument or story and to remind the reader of your big idea. The best conclusions present an image, a quotation, or an idea that lingers in the readers' minds. Leave your reader with something to ponder.

USING RHETORICAL STRATEGIES

In the assignment chapters, Chapters 5 through 14, you will see how considerations of purpose, development strategy, and audience will lead you to different organizational patterns. If you were writing about the Grand Canyon, for example, for a science class or a science publication, you might want to explain the *process* of the formation of canyons. For a travel article, you might decide instead to *tell the story* of your trip to the Grand Canyon, explaining the canyon from a visitor's perspective.

You might also combine a number of strategies in a single piece of writing. For an article about the history of jazz, you might define the musical genre in the first paragraph, tell the story of the first jazz performance in the second paragraph, and then compare jazz with other musical genres like the blues, for example, in the third paragraph. What is important is not which pattern you choose but that you build a strong structure for your piece of writing.

Descriptions and examples of some effective rhetorical strategies follow. As you examine each development strategy, think of the strategy as a possible way to develop an entire article as well as a way to develop an individual paragraph:

■ Narration	telling a story
■ Description	creating a picture with words
■ Examples	using specifics to make a point
■ Process analysis	explaining how something is done
■ Comparison and/or contrast	showing similarities and differences
■ Classification	breaking down into parts
■ Causes and/or effect	exploring the reasons why something occurred and/ or discussing its aftereffects
■ Definition	explaining what something is

NARRATION Stories grab readers' attention and can help make an abstract or general point unforgettable. In an article about bar codes, for example, the author includes the following background story as he develops his topic.

> The format for the bar code came to Joe Woodland while he was at the beach in 1949. Woodland, who is now 80, had spent World War II working on the Manhattan Project. After the war, he returned to Drexel University to teach mechanical engineering. While there, a colleague of Woodland's, Bernard Silver, overheard the president of the Food Fair grocery stores appealing to a Drexel dean for help automating the process of grocery checkout. Silver and Woodland started brainstorming ideas.
>
> Several months later, Woodland was vacationing on Miami's South Beach, pondering the problem and considering how Morse code might be used to solve it. Woodland idly stuck his fingers in the sand and pulled them toward him, raking a set of parallel lines that represented a kind of "long form" of dots and dashes. Those lines were the inspiration for the bar-code design that he and Silver ultimately patented.
>
> —Charles Fishman, "Bar None" from "Agenda Items," Fast Company, June 2001, p. 147. Reprinted with permission.

DESCRIPTION Description requires close attention to sensory details: sights, sounds, scents, and textures. In this description of the Queen Anne Victorian, a house style in use between 1870 and 1910, the writer includes enough descriptive details to help you recognize a Queen Anne Victorian-style house when you see one.

> The most popular of the several Victorian styles, it is easily recognized by its turrets, elaborate wrap-around porches, and decorative shingles. Victorian architecture was a romantic rebellion against classical symmetry, so doors, windows, porches, and towers were all deliberately off center. Renewed appreciation of the artisanship of this style has transformed the region's many surviving Queen Annes

PRACTICE 2.6

Using Narration

Choose one of the following topics, and write a narrative paragraph using a brief story from your own or someone else's life to support the topic. Be sure to help your reader by providing clear transitions.

- Allergies
- Books
- Music
- Learning to drive
- Exercise

PRACTICE 2.7

Using Description

Choose one of the following topics, and brainstorm a list of descriptive details using some of your senses: sight, touch, smell, and sound.

- A comfortable room in your home
- An object you can see from where you are now sitting
- A swimming pool
- A computer keyboard
- A teacher, a coach, or a boss

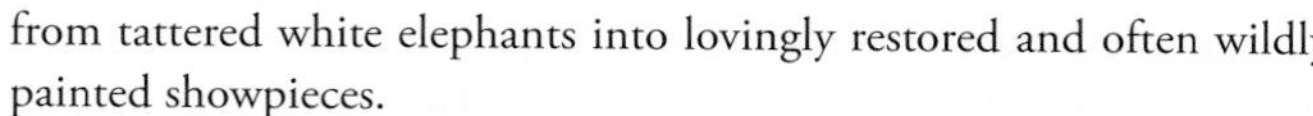

from tattered white elephants into lovingly restored and often wildly painted showpieces.

—Carol Stocker, "House Styles of New England,"• The Boston Globe, Life at Home, June 5, 2003. Reprinted with permission.

EXAMPLES Examples allow you to make your meaning clear and also force you to refine your own thinking. This paragraph about bar codes gives the reader a number of examples about why bar codes are versatile and important.

> The bar code is one of the killer apps of the digital economy. More than a million companies worldwide use the familiar UPC (Universal Product Code) symbol to identify consumer products. But the UPC symbol is just a subset of a much wider world of bar codes that are used for all kinds of identification and inventory control. FedEx, UPS, and the U.S. Postal Service use proprietary bar codes to move mail and parcels. NASA uses bar codes on the back of the heat-resistant tiles of its space shuttles to make sure the right tiles get in the right places. Researchers use tiny bar codes to track bees in and out of hives.

—Charles Fishman, "Bar None" from "Agenda Items," Fast Company, June 2001, p. 147. Reprinted with permission.

PRACTICE 2.8

Using Examples

Develop one of the following topic sentences for a short expository article by giving one or more examples.

- Applying to college is labor intensive.
- Recent films have been innovative (or predictable).
- Small classes allow for more (or less) student participation.
- Large classes create more (or fewer) opportunities for class discussion.
- Contemporary music expresses a variety of emotions.

PROCESS ANALYSIS Process analysis explains how something works (a computer, a grading system, the electoral college), how something was accomplished (the Russian Revolution, the formulation of the AIDS cocktail), or how to do something (organize a walkathon, solve an algebraic equation, dissect a frog or a poem). Gruesome though they may be, autopsies fascinate many people, and in this description of an autopsy, the author's description flows clearly from the first step to the last.

> Most people don't have a To Do list that includes "witness an autopsy"—probably because they think it would be unpleasant. I, on the other hand, have always been intrigued by the procedure. Now that I have observed an autopsy, I can confirm that it's definitely not for the weak of stomach.
>
> For the benefit of readers who are interested, here's what generally happens during a forensic autopsy:
>
> The first step is to photograph the body. Trace evidence such as hair samples and nail scrapings (preserved by paper bags on the hands) are collected, and fingerprints taken. Descriptions of clothing and jewelry are recorded, then the items are removed. The body is laid out on its back on the steel autopsy table, X-rays are taken and then the body is cleaned. The next step is to weigh and measure the body, and note any identifying marks (such as tattoos and scars).
>
> The pathologist makes the first incision: from shoulder to shoulder, then straight down the torso to the pelvis. This is called the "Y" incision (though Dr. Baden says his looks more like a "U" with a tail). This provides easy access to all the internal organs, once the rib cage

PRACTICE 2.9

Using Process Analysis

Write a short paragraph about one of the following processes.

- How to catch a cold
- How to make an airline reservation
- How to set up an e-mail account
- How to diaper a baby
- How to apply to college

is lifted away. Next, internal organs—lungs, liver, stomach, kidneys, etc.—are removed, examined, and weighed. Tissue and fluid samples are taken for microscopic analysis.

The final step, perhaps the most difficult for a layperson to watch, is the examination of the head. An incision is made in the back of the head, from ear to ear, and the skin is brought forward over the face. An electric saw is used to cut through the skull, and the skullcap is removed. The brain is taken out, examined and weighed.

At this point, any organs that will not be needed for additional study are returned to the body cavity. Then the incisions are closed by the autopsy assistant (called the *deiner*), which leaves the body presentable for viewing at a funeral service. (The skull incision can't be seen when the head of the deceased is lying on the casket pillow.)

All samples and evidence are sent for laboratory analysis. When results are available (anywhere from several days to several weeks later), the medical examiner presents his final diagnosis in a written report.

—Noreen P. Browne, "Anatomy of an Autopsy," Biography Magazine (August 2002): 76.

PRACTICE 2.10

Using Comparison and/or Contrast

Assume that you are writing an article explaining the American educational system to someone from another country. Focus on the difference between high school and college or between elementary school and junior high school.

1. List three or four points of similarity and dissimilarity.
2. Develop one paragraph of comparison and/or contrast

COMPARISON AND/OR CONTRAST Showing similarities between and among ideas, people, places, or objects can help readers gain a context or framework in which to learn about the subject. Similarly, by showing how things differ, you can help readers understand a new or an unfamiliar idea.

The two standard ways to organize comparison or contrast are the block format and the point-by-point format. In the *block format,* you present all information about the first item, then move onto the second. In the *point-by-point format,* you alternate discussion of one item with discussion of the second item. In either case, be sure you do not just point out similarities and differences; you also have to interpret them.

In the following excerpt from a short article about American impressionist painters, the comparison and contrast of French and American artists give the reader a deeper understanding and appreciation of the techniques and philosophy of impressionism, showing how each group of artists interpreted the form from its own national perspective:

> American impressionists such as John H. Twachtman, Childe Hassam, Theodore Robinson, and Mary Cassatt were influenced by the French painters in the 1890s and into the early 20th century. Like their French counterparts, they were interested in recreating the sensation of light in nature and used intense colors and a similar dab or fleck brushstroke, but they parted with the French painters' *avant garde* approach to form. The French artists rejected painting as a pictorial record of images and made the details of their subjects dissolve into the painting, leaving the impression of an image rather than a record of an image. American impressionists, on the other hand, took a more conservative approach to representing

the details of figures and form. The American artists were interested in capturing the specific subject, not just in representing the idea of a subject.

—Kate Burak, "American Impressionists"

CLASSIFICATION When you develop your ideas through classification, you divide your information into mutually exclusive classes. The simplest classification system breaks information down into two categories—animals that eat meat and those that do not eat meat, for example. More complex topics break these categories into smaller subdivisions.

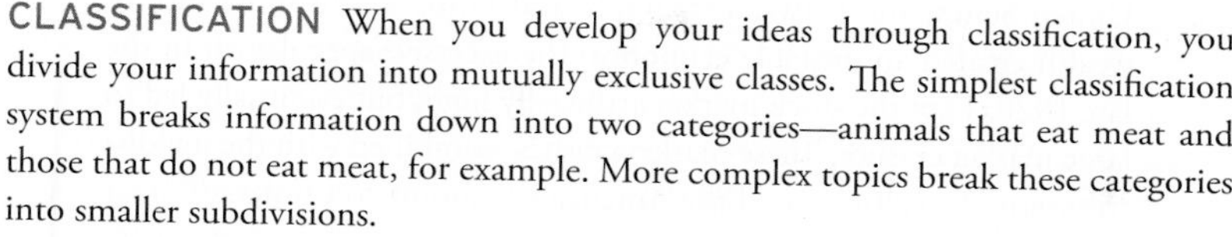

Classification is a useful way to organize large amounts of information and provide an overview of what will follow. For example, in the introduction to *The Fourth Genre*, the writers divide and classify literature into the usual three genres: poetry, drama, and fiction. But their purpose is not to explain these three genres; instead, they use this classification to define a new "fourth genre"—creative nonfiction.

> Creative nonfiction is the fourth genre. This assumption, declared in the title of this book, needs a little explaining. Usually literature has been divided into three major genres or types: poetry, drama, and fiction. Poets, dramatists, and novelists might arrange this trio in a different order, but the idea of three literary genres has, until very recently, dominated introductory courses in literature, generic divisions in literature textbooks, and categories of literature in bookstores. Everything that couldn't be classified in one of these genres or some subgenre belonging to them (epic poetry, horror novels) was classified as "nonfiction," even though, as Jocelyn Bartkevicius points out elsewhere in this collection, they could be classified as "nonpoetry" just as well. Unfortunately, this classification system suggests that everything that is nonfiction should also be considered nonliterature, a suggestion that is, well, nonsense.
>
> —Robert L. Root Jr. and Michael Steinberg, *The Fourth Genre*

PRACTICE 2.11

Using Classification

1. Work with a partner, and divide the following subjects into mutually exclusive categories: study-abroad programs, computers, films, gyms, relatives, and college classes.
2. Make a list of categories you would use when writing about college classes for the following purposes:
   a. A registration pamphlet
   b. A letter home
   c. An article on grade inflation
   d. A source guide written by students to give helpful advice to other students
   e. A humorous editorial for your school or community newspaper

CAUSES AND/OR EFFECTS Another way to explain and develop concepts is to explore the reasons why an event or a trend occurred or to discuss its aftereffects. Exploring causes means finding out why something happened; exploring effects means finding out—or sometimes speculating about—what the results will be. This excerpt from a historical article about the Great Depression focuses mostly on two causes of the Depression, the unequal distribution of wealth and speculation in the stock market.

> The Great Depression was the worst economic slump ever in U.S. history, and one which spread to virtually all of the industrialized world. The depression began in late 1929 and lasted for about a decade. Many factors played a role in bringing about the depression; however, the main cause for the Great Depression was the combination of the greatly unequal distribution of wealth throughout the 1920s, and the

> extensive stock market speculation that took place during the latter part of that same decade. The maldistribution of wealth in the 1920s existed on many levels. Money was distributed disparately between the rich and the middle-class, between industry and agriculture within the United States, and between the U. S. and Europe. This imbalance of wealth created an unstable economy. The excessive speculation in the late 1920s kept the stock market artificially high, but eventually led to large market crashes. These market crashes, combined with the maldistribution of wealth, caused the American economy to capsize.
>
> —Paul A. Gusmorino III, "Main Causes of the Great Depression"

PRACTICE 2.12

Using Cause and Effect

1. Choose one of these topics, and make a list of its possible causes.
   - The breakdown of the traditional nuclear family
   - The popularity of a specific musical style
   - The popularity of cell phones
2. Choose one of these topics, and make a list of its possible effects.
   - Cloning humans
   - Prohibiting alcohol on all public college campuses
   - Establishing an effective rapid-transit system for large cities

DEFINITION A basic definition puts a word or an idea into a recognizable category and then explains how it is like or different from all others in that category. For example, the writer of this editorial defines the term *microcredit* in the first paragraph by putting the term in the category of "a small loan" and showing how it is different from all other small loans by saying it goes specifically to poor women.

> These small loans, as little as $25, go to the poorest people, mostly women living on $1 a day or less. These loans could protect against terrorism by undermining the poverty that feeds social decay and destruction.
>
> —"Microprogress," from the *Boston Globe*

LINKING IDEAS CLEARLY WITH EFFECTIVE TRANSITIONS

Coherent paragraphs link ideas clearly, from one paragraph's main point to the next. Transitions are words that link ideas within paragraphs and that link paragraphs to one another. Transitional words and phrases such as *first of all, then, next, on the other hand, interestingly*, and *however* signal your intentions and keep readers moving smoothly from idea to idea. You can think of transitions as having three main functions—to show changes in time, in space, and in logic.

- Time transitions like *then, after*, and *meanwhile* are used when the piece is reporting a process or another series of linked events. They link elements in a timeline.
- Space transitions like *under, above, behind*, and *near* act as directions. Usually found in articles that describe places or objects, they show connections between the component parts. They help move readers around in a space the way a camera would control and move the audience's point of view in a film.
- Logical transitions like *on the other hand, however, therefore*, and *likewise* emphasize the logical connection between ideas. For example, when you are comparing opposing ideas, you would explain one theory, then indicate that you are moving on to an opposing point of view with the phrase *on the other hand*. In writing an extended definition, you might conclude your article with a sentence that begins with *therefore*.

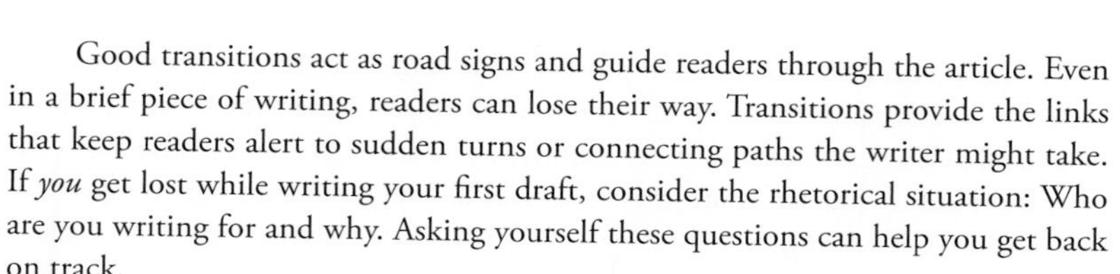

Good transitions act as road signs and guide readers through the article. Even in a brief piece of writing, readers can lose their way. Transitions provide the links that keep readers alert to sudden turns or connecting paths the writer might take. If *you* get lost while writing your first draft, consider the rhetorical situation: Who are you writing for and why. Asking yourself these questions can help you get back on track.

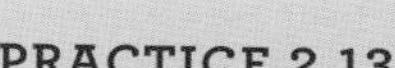

PRACTICE 2.13

Using Definition

In one or two sentences, write your own definition of one of the following words, putting it in its appropriate category and then showing how it is different from all others in that category.

- Techno music
- Cyberspace
- Terrorism
- Indie films

Asking Questions about the Rhetorical Situation

- What is the purpose of this writing? Is it going to *tell* a story or *report* on an event, *review* a book or *analyze* a poem, *argue* for building bicycle lanes in city streets or *lobby* for an internship?
- What development strategies will best support my points? Some development strategies are examples, stories, definitions, analysis of causes and effects, facts, details, and comparisons.
- Who is my targeted audience? You may be writing for a teacher or for a scholarship committee. If you are writing a news report, for example, it may be helpful to think of people reading it over morning coffee or on a bus or train on their way to work. Always think of your readers as intelligent and interesting people.

REVISING

> When I see a paragraph shrinking under my eyes like a strip of bacon on a skillet, I know I'm on the right track.
>
> —Peter DeVries

Revision consists of more than finding and fixing surface errors like typos or finding livelier synonyms for dull words. Changing words, checking spelling, and cleaning up grammatical and mechanical errors are all important end-stage writing activities, but they are not the essence of revision. Successful revision consists of truly rethinking your draft. You have to be willing to change your focus, reorder your thinking, lop off whole sections, and develop others.

You might need some time and distance between writing the first and second drafts to do this. Most writers depend on taking some kind of break between writing

and include a reader in the revision process. Your reader can be a teacher or a classmate who understands that your aim is to find the places where your writing is both on and off key, where you need more, and where you need less. You can also read your draft out loud to yourself. Both these activities allow you to gain new perspectives and look at your writing with fresh eyes, especially if you have just finished a marathon writing sessions. Ideally, leave a day or two for end-stage revising. Collaborating on a final draft—"peer review"—is covered in more depth in the next chapter.

Five Steps of Revision

- **Refocusing**
  Did your big idea hold up over the course of your writing? If not, a good way to start your revision is to rewrite that one-sentence statement. Answer the question "What is the main point (or thesis) of this paper now?"

- **Reordering**
  Does your organization pull your readers in and keep them reading? Sometimes moving the elements of a piece of writing to another place can change the meaning, pacing, and logic. Outlining what you have written can be extremely useful at this point.

- **Adding**
  Is your writing specific? Can you give an example? *Can you explain that in more detail? What is your evidence?* Do not let yourself get away with sloppy thinking, unexplained ideas, and unsupported generalizations.

- **Cutting**
  Do you need all these words? Despite what most beginning writers believe, extra words can cut back on clarity, losing the point. Cutting, can be a painful but necessary part of revising. "Murder your darlings," as the writer, Arthur Quiller-Couch advises.

- **Editing and Proofreading**
  Have you caught all the spelling and grammar errors? Nothing destroys a writer's credibility like a simple typo.

REVISING FOR STYLE

Enhancing style does not mean adding linguistic flourishes to your writing but rather improving its sound, rhythm, flow, originality, and impact. Style is not an add-on to a piece of writing—it is an integral part of it—the sum of all the choices you have made about words, sentence length, and paragraph structure. For most writers,

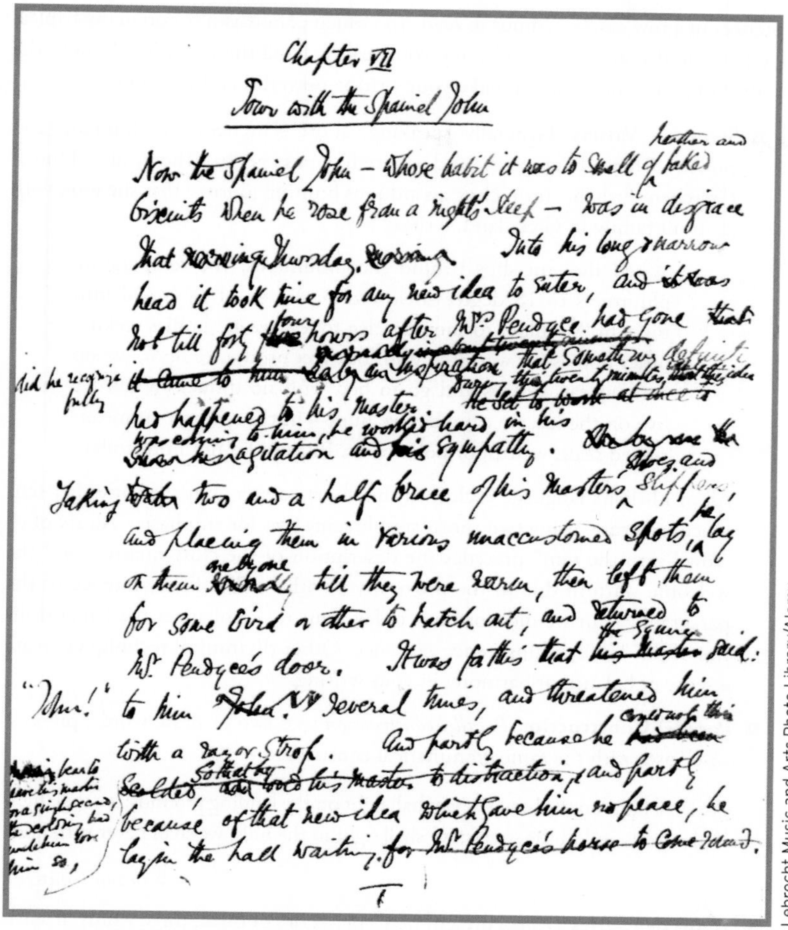

This manuscript page from "A Country House" shows John Galsworthy's revisions.

sentence crafting occurs during revision, not during the initial rush to commit ideas to paper. It makes sense to wait until your ideas are focused and fully developed before you work on style since many of the passages you might need to work on might not appear in the first draft. The more you pay attention to the details of good style, however, the more doing so will become second nature, and the more you will find yourself making deliberate choices even as you begin writing your first draft.

THE RHYTHM OF SENTENCES As you write, pay attention to the rhythms you can create with language, but, as with all creative techniques, be careful not to overdo it. Too many overly long sentences can create confusion, just as too many short

sentences in a row can be tedious to read. Too much parallelism or too many triplets sound silly and may distract or annoy your reader. Used thoughtfully, though, the rhythms of your sentences can make your writing powerful and memorable.

- **Sentence Variety** Generally speaking, short sentences are dramatic and punchy. They add emphasis and variety to a passage. In "The Endless Hunt," Gretchen Ehrlich, chronicling an arduous hunting journey that she took with an Inuit family in Greenland, writes,

  > When the sun slips behind the mountains, the temperature plummets to 18 degrees below zero. All six of us crowd into the tent. Shoulder to shoulder, leg to leg, we are bodies seeking other bodies for warmth. With our feet on the ice floor, we sip tea and eat cookies and go to bed with no dinner. When we live on the ice, we eat what we hunt—in the spring that means ringed seals, walrus, or polar bears. But we did not hunt today.

  All of Ehrlich's language is clear in this short passage, but she varies her sentence structure, using two short, simple sentences for emphasis. "All six of us crowd into the tent" precedes the description of the close quarters and the welcome warmth due to the proximity of others. The final sentence of the paragraph, "But we did not hunt today," quietly emphasizes the harsh realities of this family's subsistence existence. Other rhythmical techniques create a sense of balance or harmony in your writing.

- **Parallel Construction** *Parallel construction* uses two or more words, phrases, or clauses with the same grammatical construction:

  We shall fight on the beaches; we shall fight on the landing grounds; we shall fight in the fields and in the streets; we shall fight in the hills; we shall never surrender.

  — *Winston Churchill*

- **Items in a Series** *Triplets* present items in a series of three: three words in a list, three parallel phrases or clauses, or three sections in a paper:

  The outdoor play area contains picnic tables, chairs, and swings; indoors, two-story playrooms are packed with toys, blankets, and more swings.

THE SOUND OF WORDS When you speak words aloud, you can hear that some sounds are pleasing while others are harsh. Some letters and combinations of letters—like *s*, *sh*, *l*, *oo*, and *m*—make soothing sounds. Words like *smooth*, *shush*, *lull*, and *momma* use the sounds of those soothing letters to augment the meaning of the words. Conversely, some letters sound harsh, usually those that are called *plosives*. Plosives are made with a small explosion of air, as in the letters *k*, *p*, *t*, and *b*. (You can test to determine whether a letter is a true plosive by saying it aloud in front of a burning match. A well-articulated plosive can extinguish the match.) The word

cacophonous uses the *k* sound to create a harsh sound for a word that means "noisy, harsh, or disharmonious."

Playing with sound techniques is not only the purview of poets and creative writers. Good writers in all fields pay attention to the sound as well as the sense of language. They use *alliteration*, the repetition of consonant sounds at the beginning of a string of words, and *onomatopoeia*, words that "speak" their meanings, like *click*, *snap*, and *buzz*.

In a paragraph filled with alliteration and onomatopoeia, writer Philip Gourevitch describes Ralph Bass, the talent scout who first discovered James Brown, "the godfather of soul":

> So Ralph Bass knew the repertoire; he'd heard more gravel-voiced shouters, high-pitched keeners, hopped-up rockers, churchy belters, burlesque barkers, doo-wop crooners, and sweet, soft moaners—more lovers, leavers, losers, loners, lady-killers, lambasters, lounge lizards, lemme-show-you men, and lawdy-be boys—than any dozen jukeboxes could contain.

FIGURES OF SPEECH Poets often use figures of speech: fog creeps on little cat feet; love is like a red, red rose; a life choice is a road less traveled. But personification, similes, and metaphors do not belong exclusively to poets. Copywriters, journalists, corporate executives, scientists, and students also use figurative language to extend the literal meaning of their words.

Figures of speech such as personification, metaphor, and simile add nuance and depth to writing. When you personify a nonhuman object, you give it human qualities: *the wind shrieked*, for example. Metaphors and similes compare unlike things. Metaphors imply the comparison (*the wind was an angry ghost*) and similes state the comparison by using the words *like* or *as* (*the wind was like an angry ghost*).

In *The Good Doctor*, his *New Yorker* profile of Dr. Paul Farmer, an American doctor who has been treating AIDS patients in Haiti for twenty years, writer Tracy Kidder uses a metaphor to create a visual image of Farmer:

> Farmer is an inch or two over six feet and thin, unusually long-legged and long-armed, and he has an agile way of folding himself into a chair and arranging himself around a patient he is examining that made me think of a grasshopper.

This grasshopper metaphor enhances the visual image of an agile, long-limbed man. You can also be playful and use puns or other kinds of wordplay, when appropriate, to emphasize serious themes. One public service campaign for a homeless shelter shows a picture of a bedraggled man sleeping on a steam grate on a city sidewalk. The copy reads, "Imagine waking up and feeling this grate." Though the message is serious, the writer's play on the words *grate* and *great* makes the reader stop, think about, and perhaps pay more attention to the problem of homelessness. (See Chapter 13, Creating Visual Arguments, for more on using literary techniques in writing.)

A short step away from thinking about your writing process is thinking about when you first became aware of yourself as a literate person, someone who could read and write. The literacy narrative, a form of memoir (see Chapter 6 for more on the memoir), reveals these moments and relies on the elements of storytelling: scenes constructed with characters, conflict, and setting. Told in first person, the literacy narrative allows a glimpse into how a writer got started, the struggles of writing, or the process of the discovering the power of words. In *On Writing*, Stephen King—best-selling author of books such as *Misery*, *The Shining*, *It*, and *The Stand*, among many others—reflects on his beginnings as a writer.

On Writing[2]

Stephen King

Stephen King's writing memoir, On Writing: A Memoir of the Craft, *combines personal narrative with advice to writers. In the following excerpt, King tells how he made a sickly childhood year bearable by reading and eventually writing.*

THAT YEAR my brother David jumped ahead to the fourth grade and I was pulled out of school entirely. I had missed too much of the first grade, my mother and the school agreed; I could start it fresh in the fall of the year, if my health was good.

Most of that year I spent either in bed or housebound. I read my way through approximately six tons of comic books, progressed to Tom Swift and Dave Dawson (a heroic World War II pilot whose various planes were always "prop-clawing for altitude"), then moved on to Jack London's bloodcurdling animal tales. At some point I began to write my own stories. Imitation preceded creation; I would copy *Combat Casey* comics word for word in my Blue Horse tablet, sometimes adding my own descriptions where they seemed appropriate. "They were camped in a big dratty farmhouse room," I might write; it was another year or two before I discovered that *drat* and *draft* were different words. During that same period I remember believing that *details* were *dentals* and that a bitch was an extremely tall woman. A son of a bitch was apt to be a basketball player. When you're six, most of your Bingo balls are still floating around in the draw-tank.

"I read my way through six tons of comic books"

Eventually I showed one of these copycat hybrids to my mother, and she was charmed—I remember her slightly amazed smile, as if she was unable to believe a kid of hers could be so smart—practically a damned prodigy, for God's sake. I had never seen that look on her face before—not on my account, anyway—and I absolutely loved it.

She asked me if I had made the story up myself, and I was forced to admit that I had

[2]Reprinted with the permission of Scribner, an imprint of Simon & Schuster, Inc., from ON WRITING: A MEMOIR OF THE CRAFT by Stephen King.

copied most of it out of a funnybook. She seemed disappointed, and that drained away much of my pleasure. At last she handed back my tablet. "Write one of your own, Stevie," she said. "Those *Combat Casey* funnybooks are just junk—he's always knocking someone's teeth out. I bet you could do better. Write one of your own."

I remember an immense feeling of *possibility* at the idea, as if I had been ushered into a vast building filled with closed doors and had been given leave to open any I liked. There were more doors than one person could ever open in a lifetime, I thought (and still think).

"Four stories. A quarter apiece. That was the first buck I made in the business."

I eventually wrote a story about four magic animals who rode around in an old car, helping out little kids. Their leader was a large white bunny named Mr. Rabbit Trick. He got to drive the car. The story was four pages long, laboriously printed in pencil. No one in it, so far as I can remember, jumped from the roof of the Graymore Hotel. When I finished, I gave it to my mother, who sat down in the living room, put her pocketbook on the floor beside her, and read it all at once. I could tell she liked it—she laughed in all the right places—but I couldn't tell if that was because she liked me and wanted me to feel good or because it really *was* good.

"You didn't copy this one?" she asked when she had finished. I said no, I hadn't. She said it was good enough to be in a book. Nothing anyone has said to me since has made me feel any happier. I wrote four more stories about Mr. Rabbit Trick and his friends. She gave me a quarter apiece for them and sent them around to her four sisters, who pitied her a little, I think. *They* were all still married, after all; their men had stuck. It was true that Uncle Fred didn't have much sense of humor and was stubborn about keeping the top of his convertible up, it was also true that Uncle Oren drank quite a bit and had dark theories about how the Jews were running the world, but they were *there*. Ruth, on the other hand, had been left holding the baby when Don ran out. She wanted them to see that he was a talented baby, at least.

Four stories. A quarter apiece. That was the first buck I made in this business.

ANALYZING A LITERARY NARRATIVE

Write an analysis of Stephen King's *On Writing*. Include 1) a one sentence summary of the story, 2) an overview of your impression of the piece, 3) a description of King's style and voice, 4) a few examples from the text as illustrations.

CRITICAL READING QUESTIONS

1. Summarize the story King tells in a sentence or two.
2. What are the main development strategies King uses in this piece?
3. How would you describe King's voice in this piece? Give an example or two of lines you find particularly engaging.

PRACTICE 2.14

Identifying Rhythm, Sound, and Figurative Language

Read the following passages critically and identify their uses of figurative language, sound, and rhythm.

1. As pretty and varied as a bouquet of wildflowers, this trio of ceramic vases makes an elegant, eclectic statement of organic shapes and vibrant earth tones that are suitable for year-round display.
   —Catalog copy from Crate and Barrel Best Buys
2. Churchill once said that to encounter Franklin Roosevelt, with all his buoyant sparkle, his iridescent personality, and his inner élan, was like opening your first bottle of champagne. Roosevelt genuinely liked people, he enjoyed taking responsibility, and he adored being president.
   —Doris Kearns Goodwin, No Ordinary Time
3. The Maui surfer girls love one another's hair. It is awesome hair, long and bleached by the sun, and it falls over their shoulders straight, like water, or in

(*Continued*)

squiggles, like seaweed, or in waves. They are forever playing with it—yanking it up into ponytails, or twisting handfuls and securing them with chopsticks or pencils, or dividing it as carefully as you would divide a pile of coins, and then weaving it into tight yellow plaits.

— *Susan Orlean,* "The Maui Surfer Girls"

4. In the first paragraph, why does King mention his brother David? How does that mention help us understand Stephen King's character, and how does that understanding play into the bigger picture of the story?
5. King uses many images and figures of speech as he relates his story. Find a few lines that you think are particularly well written. Analyze his techniques (for example, exaggeration, metaphor, wordplay) and explain how you respond.
6. What is King's main point in this literacy narrative?
7. Why would someone be motivated to read about how Stephen King got started writing? Does he have an advantage that another writer of a literacy narrative or a memoir might not have?

WRITE YOUR OWN LITERACY NARRATIVE

Tell your reader about the process of your becoming a writer. Recount a pivotal moment in your reading or writing life—a moment of realization that came from frustration, accomplishment, or experimentation. Refer to Chapter 6 (Writing a Narrative: Memoirs) for more on how to create scenes, characters, conflict, and setting.

Collaboration, Peer Review, and Writing as a Public Act

Everyone needs an editor.

—Tim Foote

Most of your writing happens in private—just you and your empty sheet of paper or blank screen—but in the real world, the world of college classes and the workplace beyond, writing becomes a public act. You write for an audience: a professor or an editor or the people who sign on to your Twitter account or read your blogs. Authors of books and articles work with editors; proposal or report writers in community or workplace situations often write collaboratively, freely sharing ideas and criticism. All writers need a fresh pair of eyes to look at their writing in order to gain perspective and to find out how well they have communicated their ideas. It is always helpful to get feedback on your writing, especially from your peers who have tackled the same writing assignment and may have confronted the same writing problems.

WHAT'S TO COME

PEER REVIEW

Revision is the heart of the writing process and is an opportunity to look anew at what you have written. Of course, you are revising during the entire writing process, not just at the end. You revise as you plan and write, as you choose one idea or word rather than another. The most significant revision, however, usually occurs as you move from an early draft to a final one.

An x-ray of this painting, *Breezing Up*, by Winslow Homer reveals details of his earlier draft. In his revision, Homer eliminated an additional passenger near the mast and two extra boats that he had originally placed on the horizon.

Between drafts is a good time to have a trusted friend or someone from your college's writing center look over your writing with you. You can also read your draft out loud to yourself. Both these activities allow you to gain new perspective and to look at your writing with fresh eyes, especially if you have just finished a marathon writing session. Ideally, leave a day or two for end-stage revising.

Even if you have enough time between writing an early draft and a final draft to gain some perspective, editing your own writing can be hard. Your ideas may be clear to you, but are they clear to a reader? In the real-world of writing and publishing, writers have trusted colleagues and editors to give them "notes" or feedback on their writing before they tackle the final draft. The peer review process in college prepares you for these real-world writing situations. Many writing classes use the workshop method, having students read and critique each other's writing. As many writers have discovered, the peer review process can be extremely useful if the collaboration stays focused on

- Helping the writer strengthen the piece of writing
- Helping the peer reviewer strengthen his or her critical thinking

Your criticism should always be in the service of helping the writer improve. To make the peer review process work, and work well, you should understand the process and the roles of the writer and the peer reviewer.

THE PROCESS

Writing classes use peer review in different ways. Some use peer review groups of three or four students; others use peer review pairs. Some students e-mail drafts to peer reviewers; others bring hard copies to distribute in class. Some students write comments directly on the papers they are critiquing; some use separate peer review logs; and others just talk, letting the writer take notes. Regardless of the form, the peer review process allows each writer to have a set period of time in which to get specific feedback on a piece of writing.

THE WRITER

1. Bring in (or e-mail) enough copies so that each peer reviewer has a copy of your paper.
2. Read the piece aloud, or let someone else read it aloud. Reading or listening to your own writing is an extremely useful technique. You can pick up problems in logic, word choice, structure, grammar, and voice that you did not "hear" when you read your writing silently. Reading aloud also allows peer reviewers to hear the cadences of your writing while they read along.
3. Identify areas that you would like to receive feedback on. You can do this by jotting down questions before the session or by asking questions during the session.
4. Listen carefully to the feedback you get. Be open to new ideas about how to develop your paper or support your points.

5. Be selective in the advice you accept. Not all that you hear may be useful. Filter the advice through your intentions for that piece of writing. If the advice conflicts with what you want to do—or with what other readers have said—you can decide not to follow it.

THE PEER REVIEWER

Respond as a reader, not as a teacher. Some students feel uncomfortable in the role of peer reviewer, saying, "I am not a teacher." So do not respond as an expert in writing but as the intelligent reader you are. Tell the writer where the writing engaged you and where it lost you, where you were riveted by it and where your interest flagged. Point to sentences or images that worked well and those that seemed vague or confusing. This kind of reader response gives useful information to the writer.

Respond kindly and honestly. It should go without saying that criticism is meant to help, not to inflict pain on the writer. Caustic comments undercut the process, but so does being dishonest. If you find a piece of writing weak or undeveloped, say so. Conversely, if the writing is strong and effective, let the writer know.

Be as specific as possible. "I loved it" and "It was boring" are not useful comments. "I felt as though I could see the mountains you describe in the third paragraph" tells the writer why you loved the writing. "You make the same point in the first three paragraphs" tells the writer exactly why you were bored. The more specific you can be, the more useful the writer will find your comments, and the stronger your own critical thinking will become.

Focus on specific aspects of the writing. All the assignment chapters in this book include peer review logs that pose questions for your consideration. Copy these logs or download them from the Web site, and then use them to write responses to

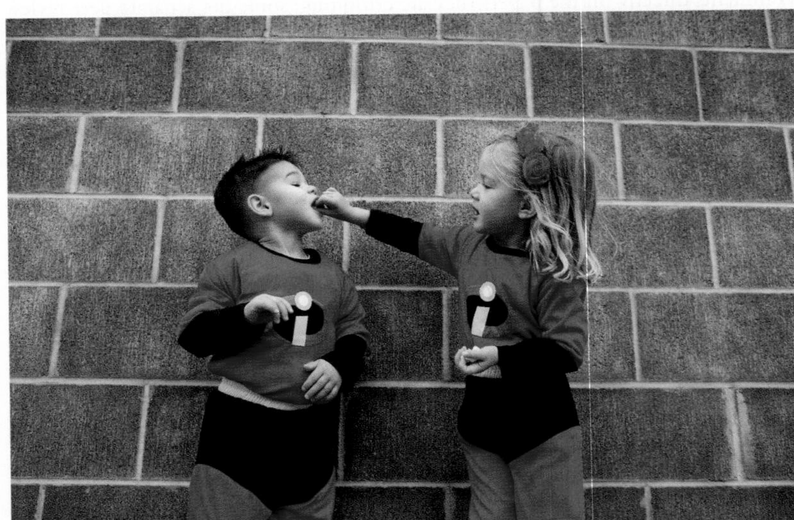

Solar Photographers

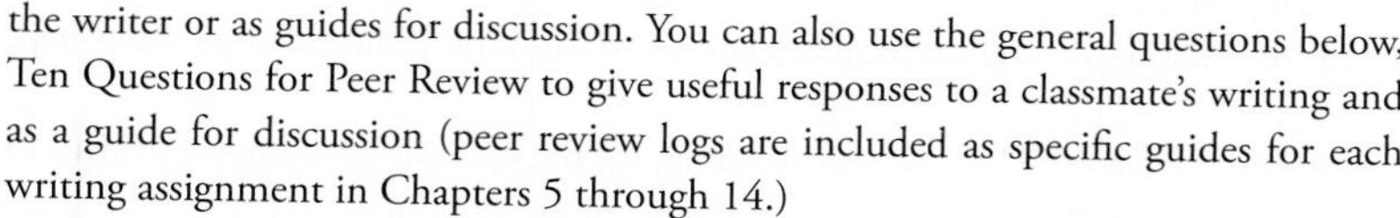

the writer or as guides for discussion. You can also use the general questions below, Ten Questions for Peer Review to give useful responses to a classmate's writing and as a guide for discussion (peer review logs are included as specific guides for each writing assignment in Chapters 5 through 14.)

Ten Questions for Peer Review

1. **Introduction:** What technique does the writer use to open the paper? Does it engage your interest? Could you suggest a better place for the paper to begin?
2. **Body:** Where does the body of the paper begin? Is the transition clear from the introduction to the body?
3. **Thesis or Big Idea:** What do you think is the paper's theme or thesis? Where is this theme/thesis stated explicitly? Where is it implied through images, language, or events?
4. **Title:** Does the title also direct the reader's attention to the theme? If the title is weak, can you suggest an alternative?
5. **Organization:** What structure holds up this piece of writing? Is the line of argument or the story line clear?
6. **Evidence:** Is there enough specific support for the argument or scenes that move the story forward? What else might the writer add or develop?
7. **Conclusion:** Does the conclusion provide a sense of completeness? Does it leave the reader thinking about the topic in new ways?
8. **Style:** Are all the sentences clear, concise, and economical? Is there clutter or redundancy that can be cut, or passive voice that should be active?
9. **Voice:** Are there places where the writer's voice is inappropriate for the subject or inconsistent? Does the voice get too formal or too colloquial?
10. **Grammar and Punctuation:** Are there any places where the grammar is nonstandard, or where the writer misspelled words, or punctuated incorrectly?

ONE STUDENT'S WRITING PROCESS: JUSTIN LIN

Justin Lin was assigned a memoir—a story about an important event in his life. The drafts below show how he developed his memoir from an initial freewriting exercise,

through peer reviewing, to the final draft. Note the significant changes and improvements he made as he received feedback and as his thinking about the topic deepened.

SAMPLE FREEWRITE In brainstorming for the memoir assignment, Justin Lin did a freewrite on the following topic: "Write about a moment you remember particularly vividly. Include weather, a gesture, dialogue, sound, a scent, and a color."

A cold aura loomed through the night. As it grew stronger, it engulfed me like a tidal wave. I voraciously devoured the air as my eyes shot wide-open. Their eyes moved left to right . . . right to left. I caught my breath in complete blackness and scanned the bunk above to collect my thoughts. Light footsteps from around the hammocks surfaced. I heard squeaky mice-like chatter get closer. The odor of sweat, vomit, and mud from the older boys soon filled my nostrils. Their eyes focused in on the target. Crack! In an instant, a barrage of socks filled with rocks crashed from above—Whack! Thump!

"Stop it," he shouted. As I listened to this beating, I slithered into my covers. I shut my eyes and held my breath. Gritting my teeth together, I waited for it to end. Sweat on my forehead formed when I thought to myself, "What if I'm next?" "Stop it! I'm sorry . . . !" Felix cried. The pounding stopped just like that; I could not make out the perpetrators—four, five, or six of them fled back to their bunks. In sheer flashes, all the damage was done. The deafening silence in this cold . . . cold summer night that entwined with puppy-whimpers from above, kept me awake. "He was just a little kid . . . he was just a little kid," I repeated quietly.

ANNOTATED FIRST DRAFT

THE PEER REVIEWER annotated the first draft following the direction provided by the peer review questions on page 49. For a completed peer review log, see pages 54 and 55.

"I Was Just a Little Kid"

JUSTIN LIN

The ninety-degree sun beat on his tan face. He had a scar across his right upper lip, most likely caused by a fight, that seemed to stretch more and more every time he barked at us. "You imbeciles, get down and give me push-ups," he commanded. Down-up "sir one sir," down-up "sir two sir," we screamed back the count in unison until the hundredth push-up

puts you in the middle of a scene

D

was completed. Sergeant Haines was not a very nice man—he just seemed bitter with his life. "Get up, dammit. Get up," he screamed. "Sir yes sir," we screamed back while falling into formation. Sergeant Haines began lecturing us about life while we were enduring the desert heat in the peak of summer. "What does he know about life," I mumbled quietly while trying to catch my breath from the push-ups. This was the eighth day out of this grueling ten-day ordeal.

conflict?

While he yapped on and on, I drifted off into a daydream and tried to remember how I got myself into this predicament. My right brow lifted and I grinned as I recalled how stupid I was to let my Dad persuade me to endure boot camp. He made this Devil Pups Military Program sound fun, and convincingly he told me that it was a chance to become a man. Ever since I was ten he would say, "Justin, you will amount to nothing if you don't grow up." Repeatedly saying this to me, I naturally began to believe him—I was scared of growing up, but in actuality I was more scared of not growing up.

IM

too much IM

✔ *conflict*

I jumped trains of thought to when he dropped me off. He was so proud. I do not believe I have ever seen my Dad stand as proud as he did on that day. I remembered his proud grin as he grabbed me to hug me. He whispered, "When you are done with this, you will be a man." Then he stepped into his Lexus and drove away. I saw the car whip a cloud of dust from the dirt roads. In moments he had stranded me at Camp Pendleton, imprisoned with malevolent juvenile delinquents and evil Drill Sergeants. I was thirteen years old, my dad's decision to send me to Devil Pups was just as wrong as my willingness to come.

end of setup? I'm not sure

"What the hell are you grinning for?" Sergeant Haines' beady eyes pierced mine. My pre-pubescent voice managed to squeal out, "Sir, nothing, sir." The older boys in my platoon snickered in the background, but I was too afraid to look. Sergeant Haines walked away, but I knew he was keeping his eye on me. I stood like a statue; my feet together making a forty-five degree V, my hands clenched together at pocket side, my head up with my eyes looking straight forward. We were drilled on staying in this form since the first day. My legs got tired the first couple days because each muscle had to be tensed up, but I got used to it. I could not even wipe the sweat running down to my eyebrows, but worse yet was a little dime-sized itch in the middle of my back. I could not scratch lest he would catch me and make the platoon do something horrible. I no

narrative detail

continues next page

longer could abstain from scratching. Just as I went to scratch, Sergeant Haines caught someone up the line sway back and stumble. The platoon was going to pay for making another mistake.

Surprisingly, Sergeant Haines did not scream at us, but we all knew he had just about had it with our crap. He told us to face right and march on. The four rows of ten turned in accord and began to march. He took us to the track. "Two-hundred meter sprints, up and back . . . until I get tired," Haines said as he signaled us to begin. "Until I get tired . . . until I . . . get tired," rang through my ears as I paced myself. There was no doubt we would keep running until we vomited. I knew I would wear out fast, and I did not want to be the first one to stop. The day got hotter reaching well past a hundred. Sweat drops from my face hit the pavement and evaporated as I ran. "Left . . . right . . . left . . . right," I thought as I sucked in air. I finished three lines and then my mouth dried up—I started getting dizzy—I stopped—I leaned over and threw up all my breakfast.

Sergeant Haines ordered me to keep on running. I could not move. He signaled me to come to him. I hunched over and slowly dragged my legs to him. I reached him and I barely could stand in correct form—feet by my side, and hands clenched at my pocketside. "You must be kidding me . . . you ran half ass like that and couldn't even finish four . . . Why?" he screamed at me. I was afraid of this man. I just wanted to crawl into a hole and never see his face again. I cleared my throat and said, "Sir, I'm just a little kid, Sir." He scoffed back at me and said, "Little baby, if you want to be a man in this world, you need to suck it up."

"Sir, Yes, Sir!" I yelled.

good detail

He spat on the pavement and ordered me to do a hundred push-ups. I saw his spit sizzle and fry on the hot pavement, and I knew the pavement would burn my hands. I bit my lip. I knelt down. Feeling my hand melt on the pavement, my eyes stung a little as they started to water. The heat was unbearable—down-up . . . "Sir one Sir"—down-up . . . "Sir two Sir." Each tear ran down the bridge of my nose and splattered on the pavement and hissed away. I was too weak to do this . . . couldn't he see! I struggled for the third push-up. I felt his boot nudge me on the right side just before he kicked me. I fell down. My back burned on the pavement, so I began to get up. I stopped as he neared me. I had cried so much that I could only see Sergeant Haines's silhouette along with the bright

beams of sun that outlined his figure. "You might as well stay down there," as he kicked me back down and walked away.

summary Cuts, bruises, and burns can only hurt for so long. They at least heal.

I cried a little longer, but everyone was done vomiting, and Sergeant Haines called us to form together and march to the classroom. As we prepared for the graduation of the Devil Pups Program, the older kids that sat by me were whispering to each other about what had happened this afternoon. Later, I found out all this running was caused by my bunkmate, Felix. Felix was just as young as I, but shorter in height. I knew the older kids were upset about this and I knew something horrible would happen to Felix.

The day was a blur because I was lightheaded from all the vomiting I had done from the running. I cried myself to sleep, and wished for the couple next days to come quickly.

good detail A cold aura loomed through the night. As it grew stronger, it engulfed me like a tidal wave. I voraciously devoured the air as my eyes shot wide-open. Their eyes moved left to right . . . right to left. I caught my breath in complete blackness and scanned the bunk above to collect my thoughts. *vivid* Light footsteps from around the hammocks surfaced. I heard squeaky mice-like chatter get closer. The odor of sweat, vomit, and mud from the older boys soon filled my nostrils. Their eyes focused in on the target. Crack! In an instant, a barrage of socks filled with rocks crashed from above—Whack! Thump!

"Stop it," he shouted. As I listened to this beating, I slithered into my covers. I shut my eyes and held my breath. Gritting my teeth together, I waited for it to end. Sweat on my forehead formed when I thought to myself, "What if I'm next?"

"Stop it! I'm sorry . . . !" Felix cried. The pounding stopped just like that; I could not make out the perpetrators—four, five, or six of them fled back to their bunks. In sheer flashes all the damage was done. The deafening silence in this cold . . . cold summer night was entwined with puppy-whimpers from above and kept me awake. "He was just a little kid . . . he was just a little kid," I repeated quietly.

PEER REVIEW LOG

As you work with a writing partner or in a peer editing group, you can use these questions to give useful responses to a classmate's memoir and as a guide for discussion.

Writer's Name: **Justin Lin**

Date: **February 8**

1. Bracket the introduction of the memoir. What technique does the writer use to open the story? Do you find it effective, or could you suggest a better place for the story to begin?

   The writer is putting us in the middle of a scene, but the scene is interrupted by lots of telling—he seemed to be bitter with his life. This slows down the action of the scene. But the description of the sergeant—what he looks like, etc.—it's easy to picture him.

2. Put a line under the last paragraph of the set-up. How effectively has the writer set up the story? What other information or sensory details might help you better understand the events that follow?

   Not sure I can do this—the whole thing seems like set-up. I think the focus of the story is the night-time beating and how this might have affected the writer, so everything that leads up to that scene seems like set-up, but it's hard to tell.

3. Box a section that presents the setting of the story. What details might make the setting stronger, more vivid, or more specific?

   The paragraph that starts "He spat on the pavement . . ." seems to give setting, but the whole description of the sergeant and what the "pups" were asked to do also seems to be setting for the violent scene at night. It's a place that's tough to be in. The spit sizzling seems exaggerated, almost like something you would see in a cartoon. Is that what you wanted? You might think about adding some more details of things you can see while you feel sick, how the yellow dust seemed sickly yellow, or what you stare at as you try not to think about your pain. You might be looking at the mountains way off in the distance or the shade trees that are really far away from the place you are standing.

4. Write a sentence that expresses the theme of the story as you understand it. What images, language, and events point to that theme? Does the title also direct the reader's attention to the theme? If the title is weak, can you suggest an alternative?

   The father says, "When you are done with this, you will be a man." This seems like part of the writer's theme, that he is just thirteen but looking for some kind of big change. He seems ready for a change. The title "I Was Just a Little Kid" shows me that some kind of change will take place, but I don't see it (the change) in the rough draft. Part of the theme seems to be the writer's definition of what makes a "man," what being a "man" will mean to him after this experience.

5. Put a check mark next to the first place you notice the conflict beginning to emerge. What is the conflict? What are the obstacles for the central character? What is at stake?

   I see two conflicts here: surviving the camp and the sergeant, and impressing dad. The writer seems to want to make his father proud of him, and he has to get through the camp in order to do that. The conflict becomes really clear when the writer says the father was wrong, and so was he. What is at

stake for the writer is his chance to become a man, at least in his father's eyes, and also staying physically strong throughout the ordeal. He is physically threatened, too, and part of what makes this story interesting is the question of whether he will hold up through the pain. Will he get really hurt—injured by the other "pups" or by the training somehow?

6. What is your impression of the main character(s)? Suggest places where the characters' actions and dialogue could be strengthened to develop them more fully.

   The main character is a mixture of frightened and willing. The writer says, "My right brow lifted" when he thinks back on how he got to the camp. It seems more like something somebody could see him doing, not something he could see. The main character could have some things he does when he's nervous, like cracking his knuckles or biting his tongue really hard when he wants to talk back but shouldn't.

7. Look at the narrative techniques the writer uses in the memoir. Identify places where the writer uses summary and places where the writer creates a scene through narrative detail. Identify places where the writer uses dialogue with a *D* and places where the writer uses internal monologue with *IM*. Which sections might be strengthened by *showing* through narration and dialogue rather than *telling* through summary and internal monologue?

   I like the part where he drifts into the IM of saying how he got to the camp in the first place, but it seems like too much at one time, and there might be more dialogue or description here. It seems like a lot of telling about the background, too much IM.

8. What kind of voice does the writer use to tell the story? Is it appropriate and consistent with the narrator's age and circumstance? How might the voice better reflect the narrator's character?

   The voice is good in the story. It seems like the right age, especially the things he notices in the night scene when he can't see anything. These things seem childlike—the way the main character is on the inside even though he seems tough on the outside. Some sentences seem more like the adult talking—"desert heat in the peak of summer"—this is not a thirteen-year-old talking, obviously. It's the more grown-up writer talking here. The voice is a good mixture of the two perspectives.

9. Draw a box around the conclusion. What technique does the writer use? Is the conclusion effective in leaving a last impression that fortifies the theme? Does the last paragraph add anything necessary to the story? Would the story be injured by cutting it?

   This is hard to do because the last paragraph seems less like a conclusion and more like the climax of the story. "He was just a little kid" is the conclusion somehow. It is the moment the main character sees how stupid it is to put these boys through all this just so they can be taught a lesson. He seems to realize something here, but there is too much packed into the image, and it doesn't seem to relate back to the theme of becoming a man in his father's eyes, which is the main conflict. The ending doesn't seem like an ending.

10. Comment briefly on the writing style. Write "vivid" next to a passage you think is particularly well written.

    I like the way the story is written. I was interested in finding out what happened to him, and it kept me reading. I don't see any major problems with the style.

FINAL DRAFT Using the peer reviewer's comments and his own sense of where he wanted his story to go, Lin wrote this final draft.

READING

When I Was Just a Little Kid

Justin Lin

I REMEMBERED HIS confident grin as he went to hug me. He whispered, "When you are done with this, you will be a man." Glancing down, I watched the summer sun hit his shiny leather shoes as he glided across the rocky path back to his Lexus. As he went to open the door, his new clean-cut hairstyle and facial features reflected off the window. Standing at the car door in his black suit, my dad turned to check on me one more time. In hindsight, there was nothing he could do to prepare me for the terror I would face in the last three days of Boot Camp. Then, he swiftly took his black coat off, placed his right leg into the car first and then maneuvered into the seat. He closed the door and drove away. I saw the Lexus whip a cloud of dust from the dirt roads. In an instant, he had stranded me at Camp Pendleton for the next ten days—imprisoned with juvenile delinquents and Drill Sergeants. I had once believed that I would be scared to grow up, but in actuality I was more scared of not growing up. I was thirteen years old, one of the youngest at the Devil Pups Military Program, and my dad's decision to send me here was just as wrong as my willingness to come.

"What the hell are you grinning for?" said Sergeant Haines, with his beady brown eyes piercing mine. I snapped out of my daydream to notice the scar across his right upper lip. My prepubescent voice managed to squeak out, "Sir, nothing, Sir." The older boys in my platoon snickered in the background, but I was told never to fidget. I stood like a statue. My feet were together making a forty-five degree angle, and my hands were clenched together at my side pocket. My head did not drop, and my eyes were focused straight ahead into space. We were drilled to stand in attention since the first day.

Sergeant Haines' six-foot frame towered over me, and the momentary shade he created disappeared as he walked away. I knew he was keeping his eye on me. He was a lanky Caucasian, and if he wanted to hurt somebody with his shiny black boots, he would. Having already been seven days into boot camp, I knew better than to be caught off-guard. Just as I thought this, a cadet two rows in front of me fell to the black pavement. The cadet was disoriented, and as he turned around to jump back into formation, I discovered it was my bunkmate, Felix. Felix was from South American descent. He was just as young as I, but shorter. He stood about five feet tall, where I was five feet, two inches. Like me, he had come to Devil Pups to be a man but was falling short of the mark. Although he was my bunkmate, there was no time for me to get to know him.

Surprisingly, Sergeant Haines did not scream at us, but I knew he was irritated. He told us to face right and march on. The four rows of ten turned in accord and began to march. He took us to the track. "Two-hundred meter sprints, up and back . . . until I get tired," Haines said as he signaled us to begin. "Until I get tired . . . until I . . . get tired," rang through my ears as I paced myself. There was no doubt we would keep running

until we vomited. The day got hotter, reaching well past a hundred degrees. As I ran, sweat drops from my face fell . . . skipped from my wet shirt to my dirty jeans and hit the track only to be evaporated. "Left . . . right . . . left . . . right," I thought as I gasped for air. Just as I turned the corner to finish the fourth line, my mouth dried up. I started getting dizzy—I stopped—I leaned over—I let the stomach acids leave my burning abdomen to pour onto the track.

From the side of the track, Sergeant Haines ordered me to keep running. I could not move. He signaled for me to come to him. I hunched over and slowly huffed-and-puffed my way towards him. When I reached him, I barely could stand in attention—feet by my side—hands clenched by my pocket-side.

"You must be kidding me . . . you ran half ass like that and couldn't even finish four . . . Why?" he screamed into my left ear. My heart raced a little faster.

"Cuts, bruises, and burns can only hurt for so long. At least they heal."

I cleared my throat and said, "Sir, I'm just a little kid, Sir."

He scoffed at me and replied, "Little baby, if you want to be a man in this world, you need to suck it up."

"Sir, yes, Sir!" I yelled.

He spat on the pavement and ordered me to do a hundred push-ups. Watching his spit sizzle and fry on the hot pavement, I knew the pavement would burn my hands. I bit my lip. I knelt down. I felt my hands melt on the pavement, and my eyes stung a little as they started to water. Down-up . . . "Sir, one, Sir," down-up . . . "Sir, two, Sir." Each tear ran down the bridge of my nose—splattered on the pavement and hissed away. I was too weak to do this . . . Couldn't he see! I struggled and shook for the third push-up. I felt his black boot nudge my right side just before he kicked me. I fell down. My back cooked on the pavement, so I began to get up. I stopped as he neared me. With my swollen eyes, I could only make out Sergeant Haines' silhouette against the bright sun. "You might as well stay down there," he said, and with that, he kicked me back down and walked away.

Cuts, bruises, and burns can only hurt for so long. At least they heal.

I cried a little longer, but everyone had finished vomiting, and Sergeant Haines called us to form together. We marched to the classroom so we could prepare for the graduation of the Devil Pups Program. While in class, the older kids who sat by me were whispering to each other. I listened closely as they talked about being upset with Felix for making us run. Intuitively, I knew something horrible would happen to Felix.

The rest of the day was a blur because I was lightheaded from all the vomiting I had done. I cried myself to sleep and wished for the next couple days to pass quickly.

An eerie sensation loomed through the night. As it grew stronger, it engulfed me like a tidal wave. In a panic I voraciously devoured the air as my eyes shot wide-open. My eyes flickered anxiously—left . . . right . . . right . . . left. I caught my breath in the blackness and scanned the bunk above to collect my thoughts. My ears perked up to hear light footsteps surface around the hammocks. The squeaky mice-like chatter got closer. The odor of sweat, vomit, and mud from the older boys soon filled my nostrils. I saw their eyes

narrow and focus in on their target. Crack! In an instant, a barrage of socks filled with rocks crashed from above. Whack! Thump!

"Stop it!" he pleaded, as the rocks pounded his flesh. As I listened to this beating, I slithered into my covers. I shut my eyes and held my breath. Gritting my teeth together, I asked God in a silent prayer to make it end quickly. With each swing, I felt my innocence slip away. I had never seen anything like this before. Sweat formed on my forehead when I thought to myself, "What if I'm next?"

"Stop it! I'm sorry . . . !" Felix cried. The pounding stopped just like that; I could not make out the perpetrators—four, five, or six of them fled back to their bunks. In an instant, all the damage was done. The deafening silence in this cold . . . cold summer night was entwined with puppy-whimpers from above that kept me awake. "He was just a little kid . . . he was just a little kid," I repeated quietly.

The sun's rays peeked through the little opening under the door. At any moment Sergeant Haines' boots would crunch on the gravel outside the door, and he would barge in screaming crude lines, flipping on the lights as he had done in the past mornings. I lay in bed for a moment and then I sat up. Indeed, it was a new day.

The door handle rattled a little and Sergeant Haines stomped in. This time I was ready for him. I stood in attention next to my already made bed. The sheets wrapped around the bed so tightly that even quarters could bounce off of them.

The last day was relatively simple. We marched for most of the day in preparation for the ceremony, "Left . . . right . . . left . . . right . . . skip step . . . halt . . . attention." We were prepared for the graduation. The American Flag, the Marine Corp Flag, and beside it the Devil Pups Flag, which the color guard held, danced and fluttered like butterflies in the wind. Before I knew it, I was seeing the same flags fly high during our graduation.

The day I had prayed for since I stepped into Camp Pendleton had come. I should have been filled with joy, but I wasn't. I should have felt as if I had conquered something, but I didn't. I should have become a real man, but I wasn't.

After the ceremony, my mom with her reassuring smiles and kisses came to retrieve what remained of the Justin she had left behind ten days earlier. Behind her, my dad stood in his three-piece suit and leather shoes. As if he were a military cadet, he stood at attention, feet together making a forty-five degree V, hands clenched together at pocket side, head up with eyes locked into space. He extended his hand to congratulate me and saw everything he had wanted to see—himself. In the car ride out of Camp Pendleton, my dad, like a curious child, asked me questions about Devil Pups. I answered concisely, trying not to reveal the trauma I had endured. He asked the one question that has stuck out these past seven years, "How does it feel to be a man?"

I thought about what I wanted to say: "Dad, I'm thirteen years old. I was just a little kid."

Awake from the fleeting daydream, I wet my chapped lips and gave him a fake half-smile. That day, I told him what he had wanted to hear. "Dad, it's just a great feeling." The Lexus got onto the on-ramp of the freeway and drove home.

QUESTIONS FOR DISCUSSION AND WRITING

1. What connections can you see between the freewrite and the final draft?
2. Did the peer reviewer give any advice that you disagree with? If so, what advice would you have given instead?
3. What specific advice that the peer reviewer gave did Lin successfully integrate into the final draft?
4. Compare the introductions to the first draft and the final draft. In the first draft Lin begins the story with a scene at the Devil Pups Military Program. In the final draft he begins earlier, in the car with his dad. What did Lin gain by changing the introductory scene? What did he lose? Which do you like better, and why?
5. The peer reviewer comments that, in the first draft, he doesn't see the writer's change from being a kid to understanding what it means to be a man. Does Lin make this change more apparent in the final draft? If so, how does he make it more apparent?
6. The peer reviewer comments that the ending does not seem conclusive enough. Compare the endings of the first and final drafts. Which do you think is more successful, and why?

WRITING PORTFOLIOS

Building a portfolio of your writing and your writing process creates a record of your progress as a writer. Electronic or paper, portfolios allow you to collect your writing in one place, reflect on your growth as a writer, and eventually select pieces that you might want to develop further or even send off for publication. In the Peer Review section, Justin Lin's freewrite, first draft, the peer reviewer's comments, his final draft, and eventually the professor's evaluation would provide good material to file in a portfolio. Together they provide an overview of his writing process and interesting material for him to reflect on and to evaluate.

Tips for Building a Writing Portfolio

1. File all your freewriting, research, notes, drafts, peer responses, and teacher evaluations for each piece of writing.
2. Label each stage of this process carefully.

(continued)

3. Write notes about your process as you proceed through each piece of writing. Note places that you might develop further or where you got stuck and need some advice.
4. At certain intervals (maybe mid-semester and towards the end of term), read through your portfolio.
5. Write a short reflection on how you see your development as a writer. What was your writing process? How would you assess your overall performance?

If you build an online portfolio, you can also upload photos, music, or videos to complement your writing.

A writing portfolio can be useful beyond your writing class as well. In the following section on Publishing, Andrew Waite's profile shows how important college writing can be. Andrew Waite's essay is a perfect example of a piece that should go into an ongoing portfolio of writing. You can use your portfolio to store pieces you may eventually use to apply for internships, jobs, or graduate school. Professional writers create portfolios of their published writing to submit to editors and often pick and choose the pieces most appropriate for the publication. However you use your portfolio, it is an important record of your work and your progress as a writer.

PUBLISHING

Writing matters in college. Whether you are writing an explication of an essay for your literature class, a poem for your creative writing class, a research paper for sociology, or a lab report for biology, you will be evaluated not just on your ideas but also on how well you express them. Your writing will be held to the same high standards in your community and in your workplace. In education, in business, and in the arts and sciences, employers' biggest complaint is the unclear writing produced by their new hires. You will be ahead of the game if you learn how to write your cover letters, grant applications, blogs, reports, memos, analyses, and evaluations clearly and compellingly.

One of the goals of this book is the publication of student writing. Internet technology has made it easier for you to get your writing published. In blogs and in Facebook or MySpace pages, you can, in effect, become the publisher of your own writing. For many, it has become almost second nature to post thoughts and feelings in some public space on the Web. College magazines, newspapers, and Web sites are

perfect places to publish your writing beyond your circle of friends. You can also find professional—and maybe paid—possibilities for publication.

Newspapers, magazines, and Web sites look for fresh voices on topics that you may be writing about for your writing class: your views on politics, popular culture, films, books; your stories about personal moments that others your age could relate to; or your stories about people who intrigue you.

On the *Writing in the Works* Web site, you can find helpful information about publishing your work. This section of the Web site contains specific suggestions about how and where to market your writing, whether it be your memoir, news story, film review, profile, or one of the other kinds of writing you will be doing. Check it out. Many students, like Andrew Waite, took the advice to heart and got their pieces in print.

READING

NEW YORK NURSE: FEBRUARY 2007

"Recovery Is Not Something You Get Over": SPAN Provides Lifelong Support for Nurses with Addictions[1]

by Andrew Waite

GINA HAS sparkling green eyes and white teeth that flash when she smiles. She puts down her coffee cup and pulls a buzzing cell phone from the pocket of her coat.

You'd never guess that she is recovering from addiction to drugs.

"No, I don't think I'm going tonight," Gina says into the phone. "But you still want to go rollerskating this weekend, right?" She closes the phone and puts it back into her pocket. She smiles as she sips her coffee, "See—I made friends there."

"There" is a support group sponsored by the NYSNA Statewide Peer Assistance for Nurses (SPAN) Program. The program helps nurses support one another as they recover from addiction. Gina is one of about 1,200 New York State nurses who have participated in SPAN since 2001.

EARLY PROBLEMS WITH ADDICTION

When Gina moved to New York from Connecticut in 1992, she was 22 years old and recovering from a heroin addiction that had

[1]Andrew Waite, "Recovery Is Not Something You Get Over," New York Nurse (February 2007). Reprinted with permission from the New York State Nurses Association.

begun in college. She started using marijuana at the age of 12 and continued experimenting with other drugs. She had been arrested twice for heroin use.

Gina tried to put her problems behind her by moving to Schenectady. She attended Narcotics Anonymous (NA) meetings and received outpatient treatment. She had a job in the field of substance abuse and worked at a clinic. She became a licensed practical nurse (LPN) in 1996 and an RN in 2001. She got a job in the intensive care unit at a local hospital.

It would have appeared that Gina had made it. She was married. She had a daughter and a great job. She had been "clean" for nine years.

But with her apparent success, Gina stopped attending NA. "I started to slack on recovery," she says, shaking her head. "I stopped going to meetings, stopped talking to my sponsor. My career became more important. I was forgetting that the only reason I was a nurse was because of my recovery."

THE DRUG DIVERSION TRAP

The pressure of the job became too much for Gina. She began diverting medications from the hospital. With careful planning and calculated manipulation, she was able to obtain quantities of morphine and hydrocodone.

According to Barbara Waite, one of five SPAN regional coordinators, many nurses fall into a trap of becoming addicted to the medications they are supposed to administer to others: "Stress and access makes nurses susceptible," she said. "Nurses take care of other people, but at a cost. They want to help others but often fail to take care of themselves."

Knowing she was in trouble, Gina did the only thing she thought she could do—run. She took a leave of absence and went back to Connecticut. But she could not outrun her addiction. She began seeing different physicians, complaining about fake ailments so they would prescribe medications for her. She needed more and more drugs just to feel normal.

One day she was at home with her six-year-old daughter. High on medication, she passed out on the living room floor. Her daughter called Gina's mother, who found her face down on the carpet.

Gina's husband convinced her to move back to Schenectady, but she still was not ready to quit using drugs. "I don't think I was ready because I hadn't had a jarring experience to bring me back to reality. I was unable to stop," Gina confesses.

FIRST VISIT TO SPAN GROUP

Back in Schenectady, Gina joined a SPAN support group. Linda English, a volunteer group facilitator, says, "The goal of these groups is to foster support, encourage sobriety, focus on recovery, and deal with licensure issues."

Currently, 38 states have similar peer support programs. Nurses meet, discuss their problems, and support one another. Entry into the program is completely voluntary, but participants are strongly encouraged to attend meetings. Some participants, who don't really want to be there, attend meetings grudgingly.

In the beginning, Gina was one such participant. She had a new job at a rehabilitation center and attended SPAN meetings, but used drugs in between. This pattern continued for three years. "I was making attempts, but I wasn't really stopping," Gina says.

Gina's employer caught her giving out medications while on restriction, and she was fired instantly. Before, Gina had been able to leave her job without actually getting in trouble. Not this time. This was her "jarring experience."

She went home in tears, dejected, confused, and lonely. Her husband was not sympathetic. He held her purse upside down, and pills poured out on the floor. Furious, Gina's husband gave her an ultimatum. It was either go to treatment or lose her daughter forever.

TIME TO GET SERIOUS

For the first time in her life, Gina called SPAN with serious intentions of ending her addiction. She went to a 28-day inpatient substance abuse program and applied to enter the New York State Professional Assistance Program (PAP). PAP is an alternative to discipline for licensed professionals. It does, however, require participants to surrender their licenses temporarily. Gina did this in March 2005. She cried all the way home.

"When you become a nurse, your profession becomes who you are," said Ellen Brickman, director of the SPAN program. "Nursing becomes a part of your identity, and a threat to your license is big."

At SPAN meetings, Gina began to see that she was not the only nurse with an addiction problem. This is the value of SPAN, Brickman said: "Talking to other people who have done similar things is very helpful. People benefit from hearing their story told in a slightly different way. To hear someone say, 'You won't believe what I did, but look at me now' can be very beneficial."

While her license was inactive, Gina followed protocols that included going to treatment, taking urine tests, and attending support meetings four or five times a week.

With a letter of recommendation from the SPAN regional coordinator and a lot of hard work, Gina's RN license was restored, but with some stipulations. She could not work in "high risk" situations without being monitored, she could have no access to narcotics, and she couldn't work nights. She got a nursing job at a physician's office, but still went to support meetings, talked to her sponsor, and called her mother daily for support.

Gina kept working hard. She began taking classes toward a BSN, attended the SPAN support group meetings, passed urine test after urine test, continued outpatient care, and returned to PAP for progress meetings. When she regained narcotics access, she took her current job on the cardiac floor of a local hospital.

NOT "JUST A NURSE" ANY MORE

Going through recovery has humanized nursing for Gina. "I'm more aware of patients; I'm not just caught up in the job. I realize that their needs are more important. I am not just a nurse. I am a person."

Gina will continue to go to SPAN meetings because she knows it will help her beat the odds. "They say only 3 percent of addicts recover," Gina says, "but those are just statistics. Everyone has the opportunity to live a good life."

After every meeting, Gina and her friends from the group talk about their progress, "We ride home from SPAN every week and say 'I can't believe we made it this far.'" But she knows her recovery continues: "Recovery is an ongoing event. Forget that—it's a process, not an event. It's not something you'll ever get over."

EDITOR'S NOTE Andrew Waite is the son of SPAN regional coordinator Barbara Waite. He is a student at Boston University.

"Writing for a public audience has made me aware of how careful you need to be."

Q&A with Andrew Waite

Writing, Marketing, and Publishing a Classroom Assignment

As an assignment for his writing class, Andrew Waite wrote a profile of "Gina," the pseudonym for a recovering drug addict who was also a nurse. Soon after the end of the semester, Waite's article was published in the magazine New York Nurse.

Q: How did you choose the topic of a nurse who was a recovering addict?

A: I chose the topic because the story of a recovering addict is always interesting, especially when the addict has a job or is in a position that is supposed to be ethically pure. The irony and struggle of the story were too rich to ignore.

Q: How did you get connected with your profile subject?

A: I was connected with "Gina" through my mother. She works with nurses who have addictions and knew "Gina" would be willing to talk about her life because she is in a good place now. My mom also said "Gina" has a bubbly personality and would be a good interviewee, and Mom was right.

Q: How difficult was it to interview someone about such a personal topic?

A: It was tough because you always have to find the line between too personal and acceptable, but "Gina" was really forthcoming. She was comfortable talking about everything because she has had to do it so often in the recovery process. Plus, "Gina" got so wrapped up in her own storytelling that she let details come out without my having to pry.

Q: What sort of research did you do before the interview? Did you do any research after the interview?

A: Research was definitely key. I read up on the history of the program on its Web site. The SPAN coordinators were good resources as well, telling me not only "Gina's" background but also some general info about SPAN. That way when I talked to the director and "Gina," the context really fit. After I wrote the story, I had SPAN coordinators read the story just to fact-check. They advised a few terminology changes.

Q: How did you go about publishing the profile?

A: I knew that the New York State Nurses Association has a monthly publication and that this story might work for them because it really shows the success of one of the union's programs. I e-mailed the editor saying this is what I have written, you may be interested in it, and let me know if you are. The document was attached to the e-mail. She e-mailed me back saying the story would be published after a bit of trimming.

Q: Has publishing your work given you insight into writing for a public audience? Have you gotten any feedback or reactions from readers?

A: Writing for a public audience has made me aware of how careful you need to be. Every detail matters because someone might scrutinize it and say it isn't quite correct. With writing solely for class, those missed details will probably not be read so critically. Overall, I received good feedback from readers.

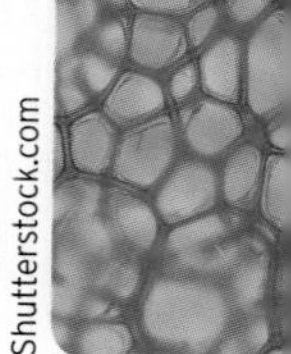

4 Reading, Thinking, and Writing Critically

When you start reading in a certain way, that's already the beginning of your writing.

—Tess Gallagher

Typically, our paths to literacy began with having picture books read to us, progressing to reading "chapter" books and comic books on our own. In these childhood books, words and images play off each other, each giving meaning and resonance to the other. Try thinking about *Where the Wild Things Are;* if this book was part of your childhood, images of Maurice Sendak's monsters probably leap to mind, maybe even before you remember Max shouting, "Let the wild rumpus start."

Even as children, the way we engaged with a text started with questions: Where will the story lead? Who is telling me about this? How does it make me feel? Why would I believe in wild things? Consciously, as well as subconsciously, the questions we ask open or close the gates to what we read.

As college students you are bombarded with words and images in books, articles, and Web sites. Sometimes a text simply speaks directly to you. Something about the way it is written or its something about its subject matter takes hold. Other times what we read seems foreign to us—even if it is written in our native tongue. It might have specialized language, or be written about a topic that requires some insider knowledge. We cannot seem to cut our way through the thicket of it. The message is wordy, convoluted, or illogical.

Knowing how messages take form and what effect they have on us as readers is what it means to read, think,

WHAT'S TO COME

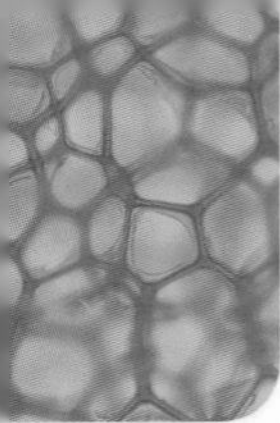

david pearson/Alamy

lvatore Dali museum illustrates the importance of looking at both the entire picture as well as the component pieces.

and write critically. When we read, think, and write critically, we do not necessarily criticize or find fault. Reading, thinking, and writing in college is an analytical processes whereby we develop a healthy skepticism about the messages we read in textbooks, trade books, advertising, classroom presentations, television news broadcasts, and YouTube videos. We start to understand the connection between the words in a message and the way that message appears: the design of the message and the visual images that accompany it.

Or so we should.

It all begins with the kinds of questions we ask. What's to come in this chapter is a method for reading and thinking—a method that offers questions to guide your inquiry—questions, because that is

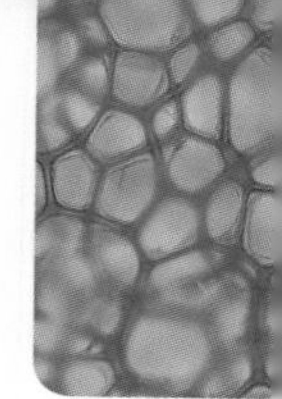

really where understanding a text lies. Without asking questions, you are a passive receiver, neither intercepting tricks nor helping yourself to the good stuff. You are on the outside, looking through a window.

Questions get you inside.

Ten Questions for Critical Thinking and Reading

These ten general questions provide an overview of critical thinking and reading skills. You can use these questions to begin thinking critically about any text you are reading.

1. What genre (type of text) are you reading? Is the piece a story, a review, an argument, or a factual article? Does it conform to the expectations and conventions of its genre or vary from them?

2. Who is the intended audience? How do you know?

3. What is the topic of the piece of writing? Is it something you know about, or is the information new to you?

4. How credible is the writer? Is the writer an expert, a scholar, or an authority? Is the writer exploring ideas or authoritatively presenting information?

5. What is the writer's overall point (thesis)? What kind of evidence does the writer use to support this point? Is the evidence taken from credible sources?

6. What are the main points of each paragraph or section? Do they further support the thesis or digress from it?

7. What is the writer's conclusion? Does the conclusion flow logically from the evidence?

8. What kind of language does the writer use? Is some of the language nuanced, having more than one meaning?

9. What kind of voice does the writer use? Can you locate any irony, sarcasm, anger, passion, or pomposity?

10. Do you agree or disagree with the writer's ideas? How do you respond to the overall thrust of the piece of writing?

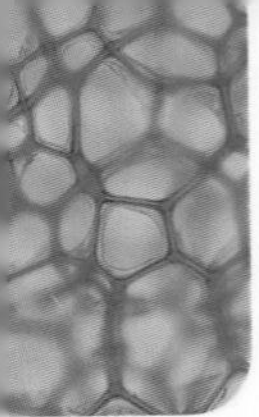

DEVELOPING A HEALTHY SKEPTICISM:
BELIEVING AND DOUBTING

Maybe you have heard of healthy skepticism before. It probably referred to holding off complete acceptance of something until after you had really thought it through. Sometimes a piece of writing might seem difficult because it is actually written without much regard for readers and their ease at understanding and following the logic. Many times, messages can be intentional traps or well-designed lures. The packaging of these messages is aimed directly at attracting us. Promotion and arguments can be disguised as information and even entertainment in order to gain entry through the gates. Too often we wholly accept writing that we do not completely understand.

On the other hand, you can miss out on a deep understanding of a text if you only doubt. Holding off acceptance until you have looked closely can also mean you

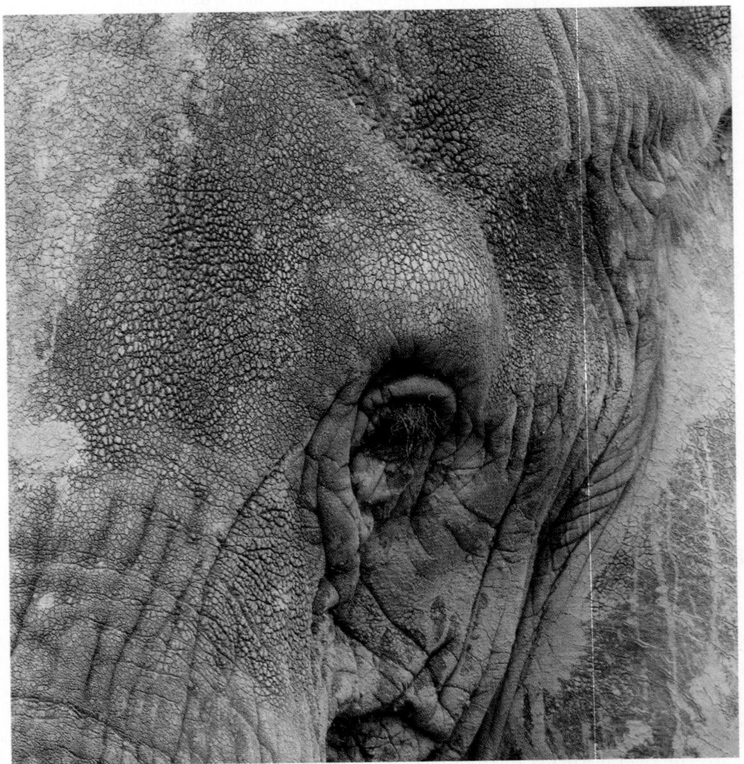

Roger Cicala

Spider's eye? Elephant's eye? Crag in a hillside? What evidence leads you to doubt or believe it is one of these?

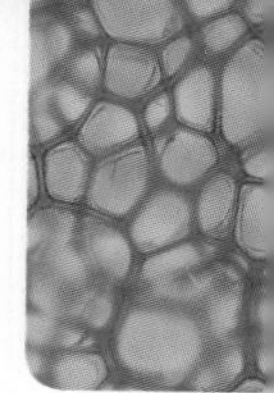

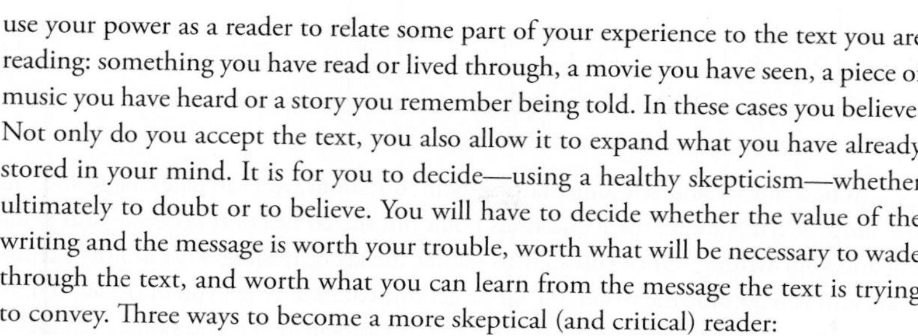

use your power as a reader to relate some part of your experience to the text you are reading: something you have read or lived through, a movie you have seen, a piece of music you have heard or a story you remember being told. In these cases you believe. Not only do you accept the text, you also allow it to expand what you have already stored in your mind. It is for you to decide—using a healthy skepticism—whether ultimately to doubt or to believe. You will have to decide whether the value of the writing and the message is worth your trouble, worth what will be necessary to wade through the text, and worth what you can learn from the message the text is trying to convey. Three ways to become a more skeptical (and critical) reader:

- Ask questions about the text
- Determine the bias of the sources
- Distinguish facts from opinions

ASK QUESTIONS ABOUT THE TEXT

Looking beneath the surface to analyze words and images helps you to decode subtle messages in all that you read and observe. Your critical thinking, reading, and observation skills make you an informed and educated person, one who can think independently and not be swayed by deceptive or false information. First, you have to actively engage with the text, whether it is a Facebook page, a blog, or an article in a scholarly journal. Then you have to begin to decode its meaning.

- Question the text's authority
- Challenge, or show a healthy skepticism about, the ideas presented
- Look for patterns of meaning
- Determine the context of the text
- Make connections between the text and other works or between the text's words and its images
- Read for explicit and implicit meanings—what is said, what is implied, and what is intentionally left unsaid

Use the Ten Questions for Critical Thinking and Reading at the beginning of this chapter to help you decode meaning, understand nuance, and uncover authors' intentions. Make those questions personal with the starting-point questions that follow. Together, these sets of questions will help you form a clear opinion about a text.

- Do I believe what I am reading?
- Do I have any doubts?
- Do I understand the point?
- Who is writing the message? What is the purpose behind the message?
- Is the message aimed at my doing something afterward? Is that "something" desirable to me?
- Is the message trying to convince me of something? Is that "something" I am open to?
- Do I find myself agreeing or disagreeing?

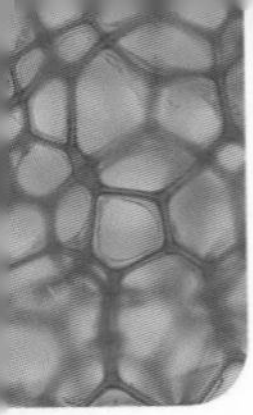

- Does the message surprise me or confuse me in any way?
- Is the writing—organization, word-choice, sentence structure, style—unusual or unexpected? Does it remind me of other writing I have read?
- How does the message make me feel?

When you ask yourself some starting-point questions, you can take charge and call the shots. What is more, these questions point out the connection between your reading and your writing. Once you start to master the art of reading with healthy skepticism, and you become the writer, the tables get turned: As a writer, you understand how to have the control over the reader *because* you can anticipate the questions. Imagine—no make that *expect*—a reader is asking the exact same things about your writing.

DETERMINE THE BIAS OF SOURCES

A great deal of your reading requires you to extract information from sources. But not all sources are credible or reliable; some are biased, expressing only one side of an issue. Some information is misleading, some is just plain wrong, and some writers have agendas and want to convince you to believe as they do.

How do you know whether sources are credible and provide a balanced view or whether they are trying to manipulate you to believe their perspective? Sometimes it is obvious. A writer who represents a national tire company is going to have a different slant on tire safety than a writer representing a consumer advocacy group. At other times bias is more difficult to detect. For example, political campaigns often produce videos that look and sound like news reports, although the issues are clearly slanted toward the political views of the candidate. In this and in all cases, it is important to be skeptical and consider the source.

You can go a long way toward determining whether a source is distorted by bias by researching the writer's background and the type of publication in which the writing appears.

PRACTICE 4.1

Detecting a Source's Bias

Read any two editorials from periscopepost.com. and answer the following questions:

1. What facts or details establish each writer's credibility? What research could you do to find out more?
2. What are each writer's biases? How do you know?
3. How fairly does each writer present his or her point of view?
4. What, if anything, detracts from the fairness of either piece?

Ask Questions about the Writer's Background and Publication Type

- Can you assess the writer's expertise by looking at the writer's degrees or affiliations? What is the writer's profession? What else has the writer published?
- Can you tell whether the writer has a vested interest in this topic? Does the writer work for an organization that has a vested interest in the topic?
- Who published this information? Does it appear in a well-known journal, magazine, Web site, or newspaper? In a book published by a mainstream publishing house or university press? Is it self-published on a Web site?

- When was this information published? Is it recent?
- Is the work a classic in its field? Have any significant knowledge, discoveries, and theories been added to the field since the work was published? (You can figure out the answer to these questions, in part, by reading other bibliographies in the same field and noting how often the source is cited and which other sources are most often cited.)
- What sources does this work cite? What is listed in its bibliography? Are these sources ones you have read about in other works?

Ask Questions about the Way the Material Is Written

- Does the writer disclose a particular bias?
- Does the writer fairly present other viewpoints or conflicting information?
- Does the writer ridicule other points of view or attack people who disagree with him or her?
- Is the writer's thinking illogical or careless? (See Chapter 12 for a more in-depth discussion of logical fallacies.)
- Does the writer furnish clear explanations and supporting evidence for his or her bias?

You can always use a writer's bias to understand one side of an issue as long as you understand where that writer is coming from—what assumptions and values the writer expresses.

DISTINGUISH FACT FROM OPINION

When someone begins a sentence with "it is a fact that," often what follows is an opinion, not a fact at all. "It is a fact that Dino's is the hottest club in town" is a fact only if you are talking about room temperature and have literally checked the temperature of every nightspot in the area.

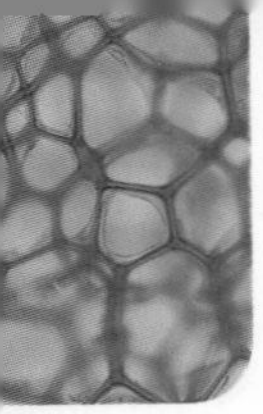

PRACTICE 4.2

Distinguishing Fact from Opinion

Decide which of the following sentences present facts (F), which present opinions (O), and which intermix facts and opinions (F & O). Choose two sentences that intermix facts and opinions, and rewrite them to make them completely factual.

1. The price to attend, a $10 donation, was not a problem for supporters.
2. More than two hundred college women attended sorority rush this year.
3. Jamnesty is a yearly event that raises money for an Amnesty International letter-writing campaign.
4. After last night's hockey game, which the team lost 0–6, senior captain Scott Gomes argued with head coach Don Webster.
5. "Gomes told Coach that he should tell the players to keep their heads up," said teammate Joe Friendly, who witnessed the exchange.
6. The argument dealt a serious blow to the team's ongoing struggle for unity and improved morale.

- *Facts* provide information that can be checked and definitively proved to be true not just once but repeatedly. That Saddam Hussein, the former leader of Iraq, was found hiding in a spider hole on December 14, 2003, is a fact. That the boiling point of water is 212 degrees Fahrenheit is a fact. That the planets revolve around the sun is a fact.
- *Opinions* are subjective. They present a person's perspective, and they can vary from person to person. That Saddam Hussein was the most evil despot in history is an opinion. That you should drink green tea made only with freshly boiled water is an opinion. That a person's astrological sign can control his or her personality and destiny on a day-to-day basis is an opinion as well. For example, if you wrote, "Saddam Hussein, the most evil despot in history, was found in a spider hole on December 14, 2003," you would be inserting your opinion into a fact.

Understanding the difference between fact and opinion allows you to see when opinion masquerades as fact and to hold writers accountable for clear and logical thinking. In your own writing, be careful not to blur the line between opinion and fact. Report writing (observation reports, lab reports, news reports, business reports) requires you to maintain as much objectivity as possible. You have to present facts—what you can verify through your own observations or through research—and present opinions only in quotations from experts, participants, or observers. Distinguishing fact from opinion is not as easy as it may seem, in part because writers often intermix the two, blurring the line between what is an indisputable fact and what is a subjective opinion.

READING ACTIVELY

Active reading exercises your mind and should also exercise your hand. When you read with a healthy skepticism, plan to underline, box, or star passages, and to write notes in the margins. If the book is not yours, take notes, or photocopy the section you need and mark up the copy. As you read, annotate the text. Look for key ideas, subordinate points, evidence that supports the points, and the writer's conclusion. Also be alert for loaded language, for what is unsaid as well as what is said.

Active reading, by definition, disallows mental passivity. You have to be aware of the questions you have, the feelings, ideas and connections the text provokes within you. Remember, you are in control of the text—the text does not control you. Question what you are reading. Do not accept what you read as gospel or dismiss it out of hand. Weigh it against your own opinions and knowledge. Allow yourself to be convinced by a well-reasoned argument, but make sure the argument is bolstered by clear and convincing evidence. The following activities help fine-tune your critical reading skills.

- Underlining key points
- Annotating and making marginal notes
- Outlining or clustering
- Paraphrasing and summarizing

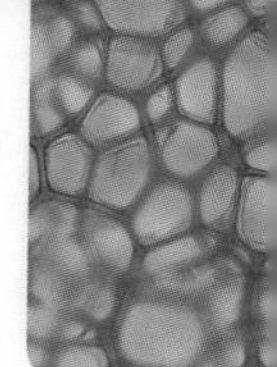

UNDERLINING KEY POINTS

Underlining key words and ideas as you read helps you concentrate on what you are reading and store information in your long-term memory. When you review the material, your underlining serves as a shortcut to key points. Be selective in what you underline. Weed out the essential from the nonessential; do not underline every word, only the words that convey important points.

While reading an explanatory essay, "How Bullets Tell a Tale" by Janet Rae-Dupree, one student underlined the following points. The underlining shows one way to highlight the essential information in these paragraphs.

> *Investigators have a tragic abundance of one kind of clue: "ballistic fingerprints," the scratches, dimples, bumps, and grooves that a gun leaves on a bullet and its shell casing. Like human fingerprinting, ballistics is all about matching: determining whether two rounds came from the same gun. It can be a powerful tool for crime-solving when investigators have a suspect's weapon and can compare a slug from the crime with one test-fired from the gun. Failing that, investigators can use it to link separate crimes, as in the Washington shootings. To make a match, an examiner places the rounds to be compared inside a special double microscope that displays images side by side or overlaps them. Larger markings, such as the ridges on a bullet left by rifling grooves in the barrel, can be enough to show that the samples came from the same gun model. Shell casings like the one that Washington investigators have found can also be revealing because they can record the position and shape of the firing pin and, on semiautomatic weapons, the extractor and ejector that expel spent rounds.*

Too much more underlining would make the strategy less useful since it would require rereading almost all the original text. You should be able to understand the essence of the two paragraphs by reading only the underlined words.

ANNOTATING AND MAKING MARGINAL NOTES

Annotations are the marks you make on a piece of writing: underlining, highlighting, bracketing, boxing, starring, numbering, drawing arrows between points, putting check marks in the margin. As you read, annotating aids your comprehension of the material and it saves you time when you review the material later. You can productively annotate most texts by creating your own set of lines, boxes, or stars. Here is one system of marks:

> * Star the overall point (thesis) of the piece.
>
> Underline the topic sentence (main point) of each paragraph.
>
> Next to each paragraph, summarize its main point in a phrase or two. | Summarize
>
> Box the evidence that supports each topic sentence.
>
> Put a wavy line under the conclusion.

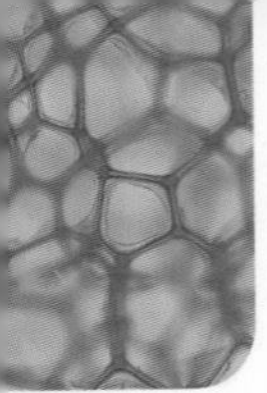

Some readers use colored pencils, marking different elements in different colors. You can annotate at any time in your reading and research, but annotating as you first read a text has the advantage of recording immediate impressions and keeping you alert and interactive. You cannot fall asleep—or at least nodding off is more difficult—when your mind is engaged and you are marking the text in a systematic way. It is also useful to go back to a text and look for different elements on a second or third reading. For example, the first time through you might underline unfamiliar words or put question marks next to confusing passages. The second time you might mark main and supporting points to highlight the writer's argument and organization.

As you annotate, also make notes in the margins, calling attention to and defining the points that the annotations mark. Interact with the text by writing questions, comments, and other responses. A "Huh?" in the margin will remind you to go back and reread a confusing passage. Have a conversation, even if it is one-sided, with the writer.

The reading that follows, "Hardscrabble Salvation," is annotated, so you can see how someone might have this kind of conversation with the text. In this piece, Joel Preston Smith offers homage to his mother. How you bring your readers into agreement that your mother is worthy of homage requires you to step outside your feelings about your most basic, and arguably most significant, relationship and yet be deeply embedded in those emotions at the same time. What is even more difficult is knowing how to cast the picture you might see in a mirror—the self you rarely see, but must portray for a reader. Joel Preston Smith has fashioned a hybrid homage/memoir/literacy narrative.

OUTLINING OR CLUSTERING

Once you have read and annotated a text, *outlining*, which you probably learned as a way to organize your thoughts before or during the writing process, can be used as a reading strategy for creating a map of the writer's thinking. An outline helps you understand the main points and notice any detours or dead ends in the writer's thinking. More importantly, an outline reveals the writer's principles of division, that is, how the writer breaks down the topic into categories.

An alternate way to understand a writer's thinking is to create a visual map: a *cluster* or a word web. Put the writer's main point in the middle of a page, circle it, and as you read, take notes that radiate out from this central idea. After you draw lines to show the relationships of the ideas to one another, you have created a visual map of the key ideas in a text. People who are visual thinkers often favor this strategy over outlining. (The technique of clustering is explained and illustrated in more detail in the box on Getting Unstuck, Getting Started, and Getting Refreshed in Chapter 2, pages 25–27.)

- Outlines of readings tend to be informal, quick sketches. Even if you do not produce an outline with Roman numerals and capital and lowercase letters, be sure to organize the outline or word web so that you can visualize the relationships among the ideas.
- Put bibliographic information (author, title, place of publication, publisher, date) at the top of your outline so that you will be able to find the original source.

ANATOMY OF A READING

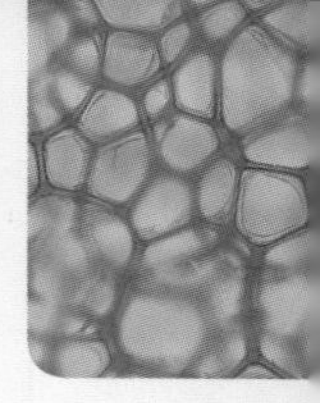

JOEL PRESTON SMITH Reprinted from *In Good Tilth* (May-June 2010), a bimonthly magazine of Oregon Tilth.

Hardscrabble Salvation[1]

Courtesy Joel Preston Smith

In 1974 my mother, my father, and I moved from a trailer park in Cleveland to a 97-acre farm in Liberty, West Virginia. I was 13, a city brat, an only child, and I thought I'd died and gone to hell. The world I left was coated in concrete, which led to shopping centers and movie theaters. The world to which I was banished was covered in corn, beans, potatoes, and squash, which led to blisters.

word choice reveals his point of view

typical story of moving to the country. Predictable change of heart coming by the end?

A wise child would have been grateful. He would have seen that so much land, so much freedom, is worth a little blood. He would have thanked his mother for this second birth, and his father for teaching him how to care for land.

What child would do that?

I was not that child. I fought against the land, against the work. I doubt that I passed up many opportunities to complain to my mother, and I'm sure all my grievances could be summed up as "You did this to me. You're working me to death. You're killing me."

sounds like a typical kid

My father, who was once a tree surgeon, died of a heart attack four months after we moved, age 40, sitting in his Chevy pickup in the parking lot of an auto-repair shop, waiting to fill out a job application. My mother's voice was hoarse when she told me. I'd woken to the sound of crying to find strangers from the funeral home sitting in our living room. She assured me that everything would be all right.

detail that shows scene of sadness

he says these two things, that her voice is hoarse and that she's trying to reassure at the same time she is suffering

It was not all right. With winter on our doorstep, we had no running water, no heat, no electricity, no money. She did what many people in small towns in West Virginia do—she found work at a plant, and drove two hours a day, round trip from the boonies to South Charleston, which bills itself as the "Chemical Capital of the World," to earn enough money to afford the privilege of owning and tending land.

detail that shows her work is gritty, dangerous, unappealing—implied

continues next page

[1]Joel Preston Smith, "Hardscrabble Salvation," from In Good Tilth - November-December 2010. Reprinted with permission.

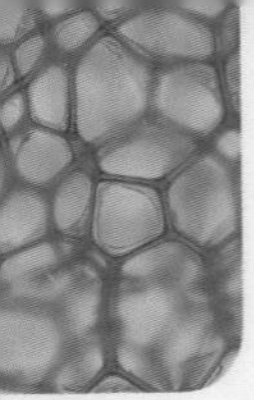

In the evenings she came home and worked with me on the hillsides, hobbling over stumps on her one strong leg, swinging an ax, helping me clear land. She'd contracted polio at age 2, and her left leg, from the thigh down, was mostly bone.

Courtesy Joel Preston Smith

She was relentless. She shamed me. Standing under 5 feet 2 inches, she weighed less than 100 pounds. She was a crippled widow, young and frail. Everything was against her. Yet every day she came home and worked me into the ground.

sad detail, shows her, physically

I don't remember her ever telling me "You have to do this." I learned my work ethic from watching her refuse to quit, refuse to succumb to poverty, refuse to allow grief to crush her and take her home and her land.

Now I measure all my work by whether it would live up to her standards. I learned from my mother that pride in one's work is a better reward than comfort. I learned tenacity. What courage I have is rooted in her, in my memories of how hard she worked to keep us clothed, sheltered, fed. There have been times in my life—divorce, two trips to Iraq, the bitter loss of people I have loved—when I have nearly given up, but each time I turn to these memories of my mother, and I keep going. When I was 23, still working on the farm, I stopped having normal dreams. My dreams were sightless and soundless, yet I saw stories. Words on paper, line after line after line . . . neatly typed. The stories were beautiful, and I would wake up with the last lines echoing, happy at first, then worried. Normal people—especially farm kids—shouldn't be dreaming in Courier 12-point type.

we wouldn't have believed this without seeing all the earlier detail

Twenty-five years have passed since then. I'm 48, a journalist, and my work as a writer and photographer has led me 2,500 miles away from my mother and our farm in Liberty. I write about agriculture for *In Good Tilth* and *Sound Consumer*, and about the environment for other publications. I wish I could say that the words that once came to me in dreams now just pour themselves effortlessly onto paper. They don't. Every story I write feels like five acres of corn, shot through with crabgrass, in the hot sun.

this is what he did with his hardship

stories hurt him—why write?

writes because that's what he dreams of—making his own dreams come true.

What I lack in talent, I try to make up for with tenacity. Each day I write, I try to find something that resembles the beautiful words I once dreamed. I would have given up long ago were it not for the memories of my mother's courage. When I feel impoverished—in spirit or intellect or ability—I call to mind an image of her propping herself up with a double-bladed ax on a hillside, her face smeared with dirt, beautiful, weary, but relentless. That image has sustained me. I hear myself saying, often, "You are not killing me. You are saving me."

Courtesy Joel Preston Smith

the writer's main point—to honor his mother

I was wondering how to write this story. I was worried about what I could possibly say that would honor my mother in so few words. I dreamed I was standing inside some kind of rock shelter. There was a cleft in the stone, and outside stood a forest bathed in light. The forest is real. I've seen it many times, hiking through our woods in Liberty, where the trees are as familiar to me as old friends. I felt as though the light and the warmth of the forest were an invitation. I was being welcomed.

The ending takes us back to the opening image—rural, natural—but his feelings about the land have changed.

- Begin the outline with the main point or thesis statement. If you cannot find a sentence in the text that presents the specific point, use your own words to summarize the main point.
- Link elements of the same importance (main points, supporting points) visually by aligning them in similar ways. Use numbers, bullet points, or indentations to show which ideas have similar weight.
- Be selective. Reduce a great deal of information to its essential points. You are creating an outline or a sketch, not an oil painting.

Sample Student Reading Outline

Source: "Hardscrabble Salvation" by Joel Preston Smith, http://www.utne.com/Great-Writing/Joel-Preston-Smith-Hardscrabble-Salvation.aspx (reprinted from *In Good Tilth*) November-December 2010.

Main Point: "I was worried about what I could possibly say that would honor my mother in so few words."

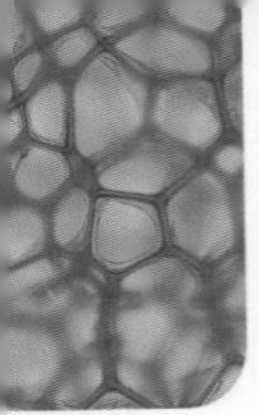

(His mother provided a role model for him that taught him how to survive and transcend hardship.)

-How he got to W. Virginia
  Resisted moving to the country
  Was angry, ungrateful, complaining
-Father dies and the circumstances change
  Watches his mother's relentless struggle
-Shift to now "I measure"
  Mentions dreams about words
  Recalls mother's struggles when he is struggling
-Pays homage to his mother
  He is a writer because of her
-In the forest, he is now "welcomed." (full circle)

PARAPHRASING

When you *paraphrase*, you put material that you have read into your own words. By paraphrasing passages as you read, you reinforce your understanding of the material.

- Look up unfamiliar words so that you have a thorough understanding of the writer's points.
- Put the main ideas in your own language *and your own sentence structure*, making sure not to simply substitute a few words in the sentence but to actually rewrite it without distorting the meaning or adding any details not in the original text.
- Put quotation marks around words or phrases you take from the original.
- Cite material you quote and material you paraphrase in your bibliography and in-text citations.

As you read new material, finding your own words to explain concepts helps you understand and "own" them. As you integrate quotations from print, electronic, or expert sources into your writing, you will often want to paraphrase them, saving direct quotations for especially articulate passages or original ideas.

Sample Student Paraphrase

Original: I fought against the land, against the work. I doubt that I passed up many opportunities to complain to my mother, and I'm sure all my grievances could be summed up as "You did this to me. You're working me to death. You're killing me."

Paraphrase: The author resented his mother and complained that she was responsible for working him "to death."

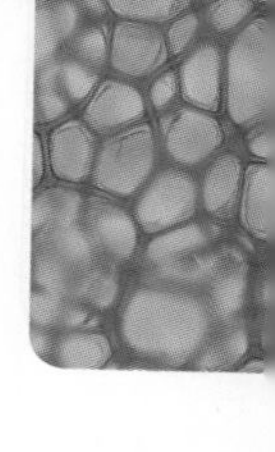

SUMMARIZING

Summarizing shows your understanding of a text. As you distill the main point in your own words, you might note the important highlights, but you will not include examples, anecdotes, digressions, or elaborations that enliven or illustrate the writing. Most summaries are significantly shorter than the originals, perhaps a third or a fourth of the original article's length.

To write a good summary, you have to distinguish between the essential points and the nonessential points. Underlining or highlighting the topic sentence of each paragraph is a good way to begin writing a summary.

Put any material taken directly from the original text in quotation marks. Maintain the integrity of the original text. Do not change the intended meaning, interpret the text, or add your own opinions to a summary. The following paragraph summarizes "Hardscrabble Salvation":

Sample Student Summary

> "Hardscrabble Salvation" tells the story of how the author watched his mother struggle to work the land and survive following her husband's death. The author reveals the inspiration his mother provided for his own struggles, later in life, especially those he encounters as a writer.

ANALYZING AND SYNTHESIZING

Analysis and synthesis, in general, can help you understand a piece of writing on a deeper level. When you analyze a text, you break it down into its component parts, which you can then examine more closely. Synthesis helps you connect the parts with other information to form generalizations or conclusions about the work.

ANALYSIS

Different kinds of materials require different criteria for analysis. You might analyze a memoir, for example, by looking at the narrative elements of character, setting, conflict, plot, and theme. On the other hand, you would analyze an editorial or argumentative essay by focusing on the individual points that support the argument and the kinds of evidence (facts, statistics, anecdotes, and examples) used to illustrate each point. You might analyze a photograph, a painting, or an ad in purely visual terms: How do the colors, shapes, or images create meaning?

The purpose of analysis is to gain a clearer understanding of the individual parts so that you better understand the composition and meaning of the whole. Often, analysis leads you to make connections and uncover assumptions you might not understand or see on a first reading or a first viewing.

One way to analyze text is to take a close look at the language the writer uses. As you decode meaning, understand nuance, and uncover authors' intentions, you learn to identify language and images that are full of truth and wisdom as well as

PRACTICE 4.3

Deciding on Principles of Division for Analysis

Decide on a principle you might use to divide each of the following topics for analysis. For example, to analyze a photograph, you might divide it into technical elements (composition), aesthetic elements (balance and harmony), and narrative elements (story and theme).

1. A cartoon
2. A novel
3. An advertisement
4. A textbook
5. A painting

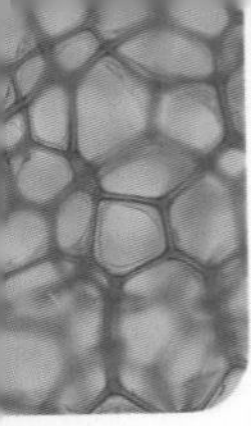

language and images that may be filled with half-truths and deception. As a reader, you can better understand a writer's meaning by detecting and interpreting irony and figurative language. Writers use irony and figures of speech such as metaphors, similes, personification, and hyperbole to create mood, tone, and nuance in order to add layers of meaning to their writing. Understanding how writers use these techniques will help you determine the writer's purpose, detect bias, and think critically about the subtexts of works you are reading.

PRACTICE 4.4

Irony

Try writing an ironic comment or two to suggest the absurdity of the following situations.

1. You discover that a course you need to graduate is offered only once every three years.
2. You find out that the entry-level job you applied for went to someone who has five years of experience in the field.
3. You read that health benefits were denied a family because it had too many seriously ill members.
4. Your dog gets a credit card offer in the mail.

INTERPRETING FIGURES OF SPEECH A *metaphor* is a figure of speech in which dissimilar things are compared to or substituted for one another. What is important in metaphorical language is not the comparison itself but rather the qualities that are implied in the comparison. As with irony, if you miss the implied meaning, you misread the writer's intention. Writers use metaphors to write with economy while enhancing meaning. If you understand the nuance suggested by figures of speech, you are better able to detect the writer's mood or bias.

> Metaphor (from "Hardscrabble Salvation"): *"I felt as though the light and the warmth of the forest were an invitation."*

Writers use various other types of figures of speech to imply meaning. A *simile* is an explicit comparison between two unlike things using *as* or *like*:

> Simile: *"Every story I write feels like five acres of corn, shot through with crabgrass, in the hot sun."*

Other common figures of speech are *personification,* which gives human qualities to nonhuman things: The mountains glowered in the distance, and *hyperbole,* which is intentional overstatement: It would take us *a lifetime* to climb the peak.

PRACTICE 4.5

Metaphor

Create a metaphor or simile for a person you see often: a bus driver, a cafeteria worker, a security guard, a dog walker, or a professor. Use the metaphor to reveal your bias toward this person.

Example: My boss scuttled across the floor, his antennae alert for any fun we might be having.

IRONY Writers often create or point out situations that are *ironic,* those in which there is conflict between what is said and what is meant, or between what one expects to happen and what actually happens. It would be ironic, for example, if a company that promoted itself as family-friendly cut its day-care and family-leave programs at the first budget crisis. An example of irony comes from an editorial in the *Chicago Tribune* about surgeons who take out the wrong organ or perform the wrong procedure on a patient. The writer's outrage is magnified by her discovery that the Joint Commission on Accreditation of Healthcare Organizations has decided that patients, not surgeons, are responsible for making sure the correct surgery is performed.

> As a result the commission is suggesting that the patient take matters into her own, uh, two hands. So carry a Magic Marker or a waterproof laundry pen with you to the hospital, not to fill out all those interminable haven't-I-answered-this-five-times-before printed forms, but so

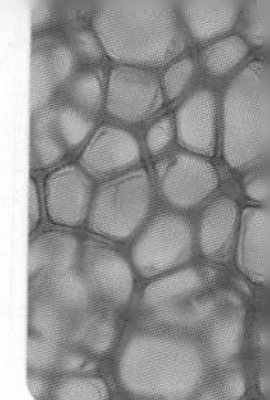

> you can draw a dotted line around the part requiring work and write in bold letters "CUT ALONG DOTTED LINE."
>
> —Dianne Donavan, "Hipbone's Connected to . . .," *Chicago Tribune*

Irony is a wink from the writer to the reader. The astute reader sees the wink and understands the writer's true intention. The danger comes when the irony—or the wink—misses the mark, and the reader winds up believing the opposite of the intended meaning. Certainly, this barb would hit the wrong target if the reader took seriously the writer's suggestion to write "cut along dotted line" on a body part before undergoing surgery. As a reader, you have to be alert to the cues that signal irony. Often, a writer employs irony to point out the absurdity or illogical nature of a situation or to express anger or outrage.

SYNTHESIS

Synthesis helps you pull together information from different sources and integrate previously learned information with new information. This combination of old and new material may lead to original insights into the work. For example, have you read other pieces that are similar to "Hardscrabble Salvation"—other memoirs or stories about the influence of mentors and parents? What elements of those stories remind you of the writing here?

Synthesis also occurs when you read many sources on the same topic, perhaps as research for an argumentative essay or editorial. As you read different views, you begin to notice patterns of thinking. By synthesizing the information you read, you build an understanding of the relationships among the ideas, deciding which you agree with, which you might challenge, which you might use to support your arguments, and which you will refute. Here are some questions to ask as you pull together ideas from different sources:

- Where are the points of similarity? What main points about the topic appear in all or most of the readings?
- Where are the points of dissimilarity? Where do the writers disagree about the topic?
- What kind of interpretations do different writers present? For example, is one writer exploring a topic from a psychological angle and another from a historical or literary point of view?
- What aspects of the topic do different writers focus on? Is one writer looking at causes and another at effects? Is the writer identifying a problem, proposing a solution, or both?

Understanding patterns and their organization, generalizing from given facts, relating knowledge from various sources, and predicting and drawing conclusions are all part of synthesizing information. In synthesizing, you connect different pieces of information to make the material more memorable and manageable and to prompt original thinking.

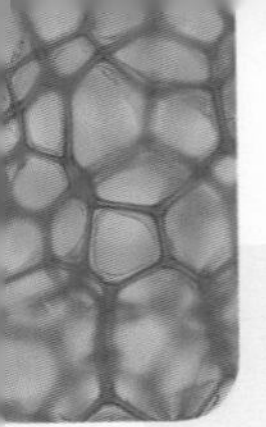

VISUAL LITERACY: ANALYZING IMAGES THAT COME WITH TEXT

PEOPLE MAIL their "secrets" anonymously on one side of a post card and the results are collected on postsecret.com. Some questions, below, will help you analyze the connection between image and text. Use the Post-Secret examples to practice analyzing how images connect to text by answering the following:

- What kind of image is it—a photograph painting, portrait, or computer-designed image?
- What tone or mood is created by the image? What elements in the image (line, color, shape, texture) create this mood?
- How does the image relate to the text? Is it a literal illustration or does it take the topic in a new direction?
- Does the image add information to the text?
- How do the text and image work together?

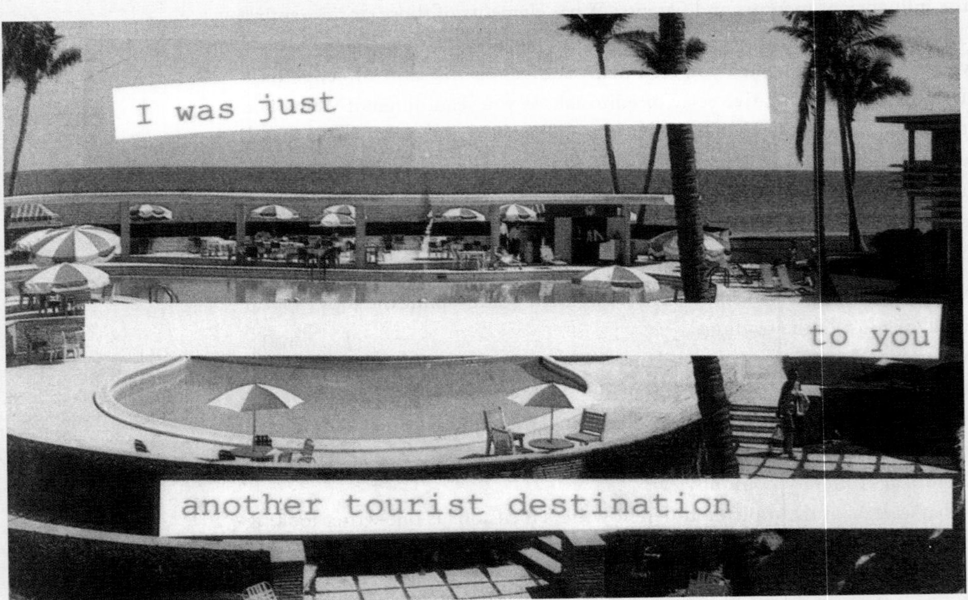

Harper Collins Publishers

People anonymously reveal their secrets through messages that are made up of words + pictures on the Post Secret Web site and books.

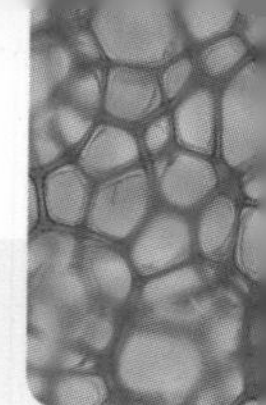

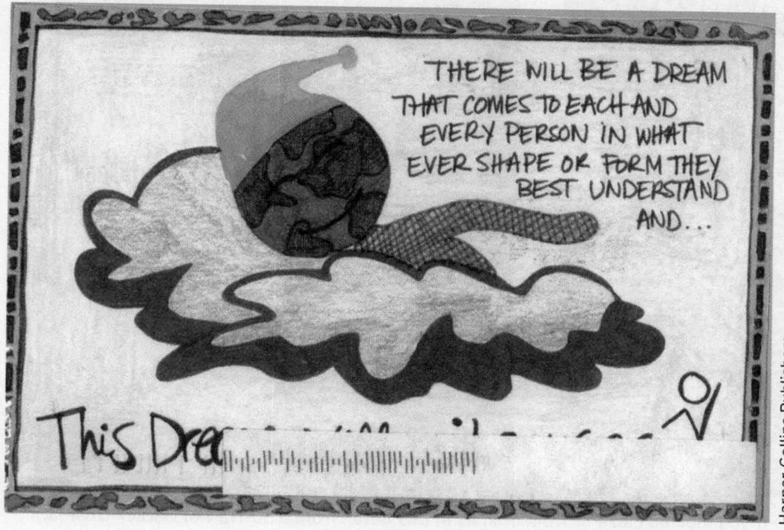

Harper Collins Publishers

PRACTICE 4.6

Analyzing Words and Images

1. Choose any short essay in Chapter 8 for analysis. Read it carefully, and answer the general questions on page 67 about analyzing readings.
2. Write a sentence that draws a conclusion about the essay's meaning.
3. Choose any image in this chapter. Look at it carefully, and answer the general questions about analyzing images on this page.
4. Write a sentence that draws a conclusion about the meaning of the image you chose to analyze.
5. Find your own image+text example from the Web or from print (advertising and children's books make great subjects for this) and write an analysis of how the images work with the text.

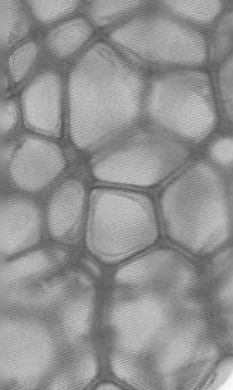

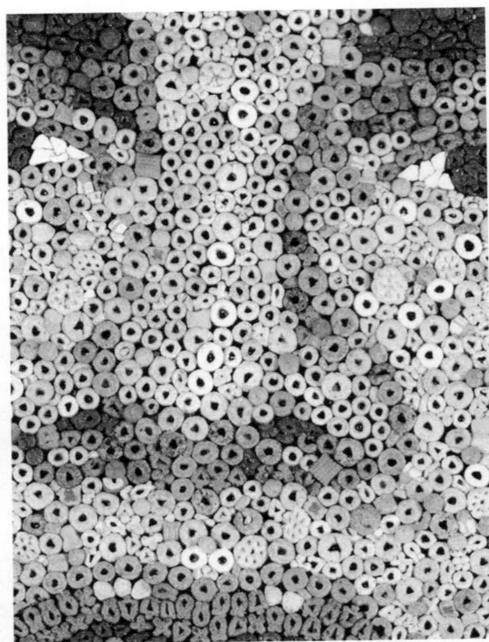

Ryan Alexiev

You can see things differently if you look up close or from afar, as in this detail from a portrait of Barack Obama, rendered in breakfast cereal.

A good test of your ability to synthesize material from different sources is writing a *synthesis sentence* that pulls together and summarizes the material in broad terms. Read two or more sources carefully. Underline, annotate, and make notes in the margins that help you understand the meanings. Then write a sentence combining this information. For example,

> In his new book of photojournalism, *Night of a Thousand Stars*, Smith puts a human face on the everyday struggles of Iraqis much the way he portrays his mother's battle to work the land after her husband's death in his piece "Hardscrabble Salvation."

UNDERSTANDING LOGICAL APPEALS

Writers want to keep you connected, even riveted, to their stories and ideas. They want to convince you that their writing is worth the time and energy you spend reading it. Appealing to their reader's logic and emotions and establishing themselves as trustworthy are ways writers have connected to their readers since ancient Greek thinkers identified these appeals. Classical thinking breaks logical appeals down into

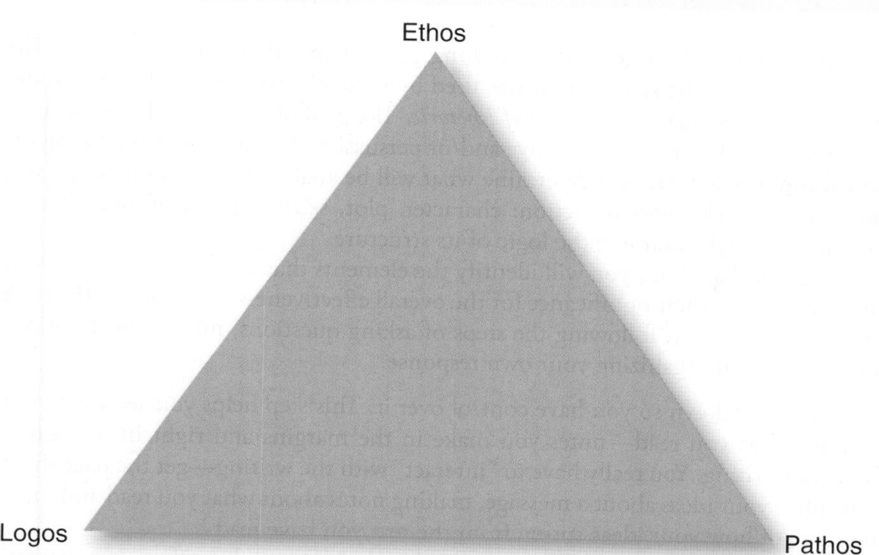

pathos, logos, and *ethos*. These might appear to be distant, ancient concepts, but you might be surprised by how thoroughly they address almost every writing situation you could find yourself in. Learning to identify these appeals in others' writing is yet another part of thinking and reading critically.

Briefly, *pathos* refers to how you connect to your reader's emotions. Joel Preston Smith, for example, had to walk that fine line between evoking his reader's emotions and being overly sentimental as he remembered his hard-working mother. His careful description of her, complete with the details of her polio, does indeed create emotion.

Other kinds of writing relay much more on *logos*, or appealing to the mind. The yearly State of the Union address needs to include some of this kind of logic, perhaps a few statistics that tells us the country is sound and safe. Yet, presidents often begin their assessments of the state of the union on an emotional note by honoring audience members who have overcome obstacles or demonstrated courage. Almost every state of the union address will include both an appeal to the head and to the heart.

The most abstract of these appeals is *ethos*, which is attached to the writer's trustworthiness. How qualified is the writer to state this opinion or tell this story? Most people have some area of expertise, a reputation, and credentials that make their statements credible. Their "wisdom" gives their statements that seal of approval. Think about how Joel Preston Smith creates *ethos* by including these details about himself.

> *I'm 48, a journalist, and my work as a writer and photographer has led me 2,500 miles away from my mother and our farm in Liberty. I write about agriculture for* In Good Tilth *and* Sound Consumer, *and about the environment for other publications.*

PRACTICE 4.7

Writing a Synthesis Sentence

Read the two reviews of the film *Fight Club* printed in Chapter 10. Choose one of these reviews to consider in relation to the other.

1. Read the reviews carefully, underlining and annotating their main points.
2. Write a sentence for each review that summarizes its main points.
3. Write a sentence that synthesizes the two reviews.
4. If you have seen this film, add a sentence that draws a conclusion about the film from your own perspective.

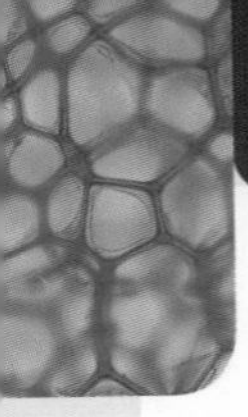

WRITING A RHETORICAL ANALYSIS

The word "rhetoric" does not mean anything goes, as in "That is just rhetoric." The word is used here in the sense that it was used by Aristotle, who wrote the first guidebook to effective persuasion, *The Art of Rhetoric.* The goal of a rhetorical analysis is to explore why a text is (or is not) effective and/or persuasive. As with any textual analysis, the key features of a genre will determine what will be analyzed. For a short story, you might review the elements of fiction: character, plot, setting, point of view. For an argument, you might examine the logic of its structure.

In a rhetorical analysis, you will identify the elements that will be the focus of your writing and analyze their significance for the overall effectiveness of the piece. The trick to writing an analysis is following the steps of asking questions, making observations about the text, and organizing your own response.

- Break the text down so you have control over it. This step helps you see what your thinking is as you read—notes you make in the margins and right in the text—*inside* the writing. You really have to "interact" with the writing—get the page dirty.
- Formulate your ideas about a message, making notes about what you read and making sense of how your ideas spring from the text you have read.
- Write an analysis that shows your command of the text and that offers your insights based on your response. It is important to remember the "your" in that last sentence: All readers bring their own experiences to a text, and yours has as much to offer as anyone's.

ASSIGNMENT Choose a text and write your own rhetorical analysis using the lists of questions in this chapter to guide you through reading, formulating ideas, and summarizing. Write an analytical thesis that explains a pattern you observed or a decision you made about the text.

A step-by-step guide follows, along with a sample of the notes and a rhetorical analysis by Elizabeth Ramsey-Vidales.

STEPS IN WRITING A RHETORICAL ANALYSIS

***Step One:* Consider the rhetorical situation, in particular the purpose, and audience of the text you are analyzing.**

- What genre is the piece?
- How is the writing going to be used in the world?

Step Two: **Think about the components of the genre in general.**

- Does the piece I am analyzing fit neatly into that genre or is it exceptional?
- Among others in its genre, what personality does this piece of writing have? Which words, phrases, or organizational structure make it fit in? What makes it stand out?

Step Three: **Make some judgments.**

- What is outstanding (good, bad, outrageous, noteworthy, unusual) about the piece of writing?
- What do I remember when I have finished reading?
- What is engaging? Boring? Fascinating?

Step Four: **Write your rhetorical analysis. Include:**

- An analytical thesis that gives an overview of a pattern you observe or a decision you have made about the text.
- Summary of the text.
- Examples that support your thesis.

Student Elizabeth Ramsey-Vidales went through these steps as she wrote her rhetorical analysis of "Hardscrabble Salvation."

Step One: Consider the rhetorical situation, in particular the purpose and audience of the text you are analyzing. What genre is the piece? How is the writing going to be used in the world?

> *The genre is literacy narrative. This is an essay of ideas about how or why someone writes. I do not know how it will be used, except to tell people that it is always hard to write—or do anything, and Joel Preston Smith finds inspiration in his mother. People might enjoy reading this, but it is not a very specific genre.*

Step Two: Think about the components of the genre in general? Does the piece you are analyzing fit neatly into that genre or is it exceptional?

> *It does tell me about how Joel Preston Smith started to write and how he keeps going, even though it is hard. He uses his mother's work with her hands, working the land, and compares his work to hers. If she would not give up, he will not.*

Among others in its genre, what personality does this piece of writing have? Does it sound like the others? Which words, phrases, or organizational structure make it fit in? Which devices make it stand out?

> *I could really see this piece of writing as a graduation speech, something that makes people motivated, inspired. It is a typical story of hardship, but I do not remember her ever telling her son "You have to do this." What makes it different from other overcoming-hardship stories is the lack of preaching or moralizing. I notice he uses a lot of repetition of sentence structures—like speech writers might. It sounds Biblical a little. I can hear Martin Luther King in the rhythm of the sentences. He uses direct quotation, descriptive details—very specific detail. He also leaves things implied. When he says "Chemical Capitol of the World," we get an impression without the writer having to explain. It fits into the pattern. This story could seem very pitiful, but the writer holds back and does not allow it to go there. He is not pitying; he is showing what she overcame, how brave his mother was.*

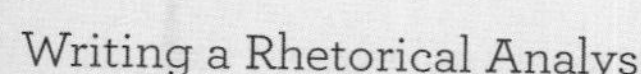

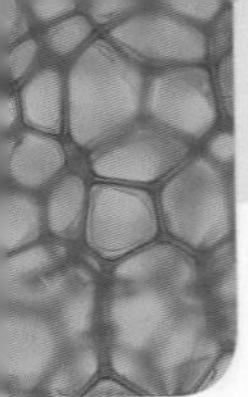

Step Three: Make some judgments: What is outstanding (good, bad, outrageous, noteworthy, unusual) about the piece of writing? A good question to ask is, what do I remember when I have finished reading? What is engaging? Boring? Fascinating?

> *I was interested in the story he told. I notice he never mentioned writing until very late in the piece. The story starts when he is 13 and they are poor. He tells about how hard his mother worked. He really does not talk about himself too much, except to say what he did not do—he did not appreciate things. And then about half-way through he states his thesis: "Now I measure all my work by whether it would live up to her standards."*

Step Four: Write your rhetorical analysis:

Craft an analytical thesis that identifies the pattern you observe or a decision you have made about the text.

THE ANALYTICAL THESIS

> *In "Hardscrabble Salvation," Joel Preston Smith tells the story of his mother's struggle to survive and work the land. His narrative uses the same style as a Southern Revival preacher might, expressing the complexity of suffering while offering inspiration.*

INCLUDE A SUMMARY OF THE TEXT See Ramsey-Vidales' rhetorical analysis of "Hardscrabble Salvation (page 89)."

CHOOSE EXAMPLES THAT SUPPORT YOUR THESIS You do not have to include every observation you have made in your annotation, outlining, and note making, but you do have to provide enough examples to prove the pattern you observed really does exist, or that the decision you have made about the text is logical.

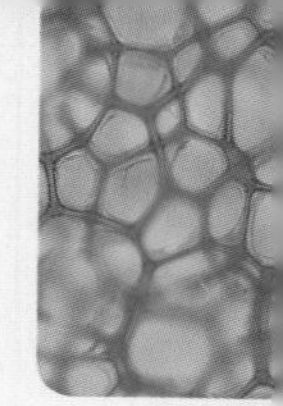

A Rhetorical Analysis of "Hardscrabble Salvation"

ELIZABETH RAMSEY-VIDALES

From the first few lines of his literacy narrative, you suspect the writer, Joel Preston Smith is going to fall in love with the countryside his parents have moved him to from his home in Cleveland with its "concrete, which led to shopping centers and movie theatres." It's not hard to imagine he might fall in love with the land that is covered in "corn, beans, tomatoes, and squash," even it if it does lead to "blisters."

discussion of first impression, where the writer intentionally begins

But what he reveals to his reader is not just another Hallmark movie about a 13-year-old brat who comes to appreciate nature. Instead, he focuses on his mother. She is the star of the story. And with just the sound of a preacher's cadences, but absolutely no preaching, he shows us his mother's struggle to survive, "a crippled widow, young and frail," and her determination to work the land. He uses a Southern Revival preacher's speaking style in his narrative about hardship and "salvation."

summary

Thesis: this is the main point: a pattern in the writing. It needs defending, but also fleshing out. In what ways is his narrative like a preacher's?

That very word, "Salvation" in the title, in fact, establishes the religious overtones in the narrative. In the first few sentences the writer mentions "hell," but it's only a "lite" version of hell he sees during his first four months of moving to Liberty, West Virginia. After his father dies suddenly, leaving his mother and him with "winter on our doorstep, we had no running water, no heat, no electricity, no money," his picture of hell changes. Joel Preston Smith immediately turns our attention to his mother, "a crippled widow, young and frail," as she struggles to work a factory job, driving two hours a day "to afford the privilege of owning and tending the land."

The first way it is like a kind of preaching: word choice. The writer uses preaching words

summary

Though the structure of the narrative takes on a "testimonial" feel of an inspirational revival story, the sentence structures remind us of the sound of a

continues next page

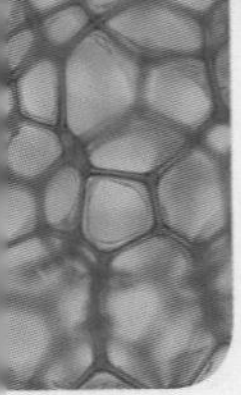

Southern preacher's rhythms and cadences, particularly in the repetition of sentence structures:

the structure of sentences

> A wise child would have been grateful. He would have seen that so much land, so much freedom, is worth a little blood. He would have thanked his mother for this second birth, and his father for teaching him how to care for land.
>
> I was not that child. I fought against the land, against the work.
>
> And another example a bit later in the piece:
>
> In the evenings she came home and worked with me on the hillsides, hobbling over stumps on her one strong leg, swinging an ax, helping me clear land. She'd contracted polio at age 2, and her left leg, from the thigh down, was mostly bone.
>
> She was relentless. She shamed me. Standing under 5 feet 2 inches, she weighed less than 100 pounds. She was a crippled widow, young and frail. Everything was against her. Yet every day she came home and worked me into the ground.

The author weaves powerful details of his personal story into the language and rhythms, avoiding almost all mention of abstraction. Instead he says simply that his mother worked at the "Chemical Capital of the World," allowing the reader to fill in the blanks of what that might have meant what that might have meant to her spirits and her already compromised health.

comment on how the writer uses specifics

When he says "normal kids, especially farm kids, shouldn't be dreaming in 12-point Courier type," we get another taste of how powerfully his specificity defines the characters of the story. And through this example, Joel Preston Smith shows has a way of hinting at religion without being religious, and likewise when he turns to his own writing, he has a way of shaking off self-importance. He makes a little joke.

a tie-in to the thesis

figurative language

His metaphor for farming—"Every story I write feels like five acres of corn, shot through with crabgrass, in the hot sun,"—might seem trite considering his mother's struggles, but Joel Preston Smith makes it seem honest and forthright and self-effacing. "What I lack in talent, I try to make up for with tenacity. . . .When I feel impoverished—in spirit or intellect or ability—I call to mind an image of her propping herself up with a double-bladed ax on a hillside, her face smeared with dirt, beautiful, weary, but relentless. That image has sustained me. I hear myself saying, often, "You are not killing me. You are saving me."

And when the story concludes with him finding the trees in woods of Liberty are as "familiar as friends," the readers find themselves where they expected they might end up—with the speaker finding a home in the country. Because Joel Preston Smith so expertly led the readers through his mother's struggle, the end transcends predictable and moves into salvation—through writing.

something mentioned at the opening that comes back into focus

PART II

Writing to Explore

Enrique's Journey © 2002 Los Angles Times. Photos by Don Barletti

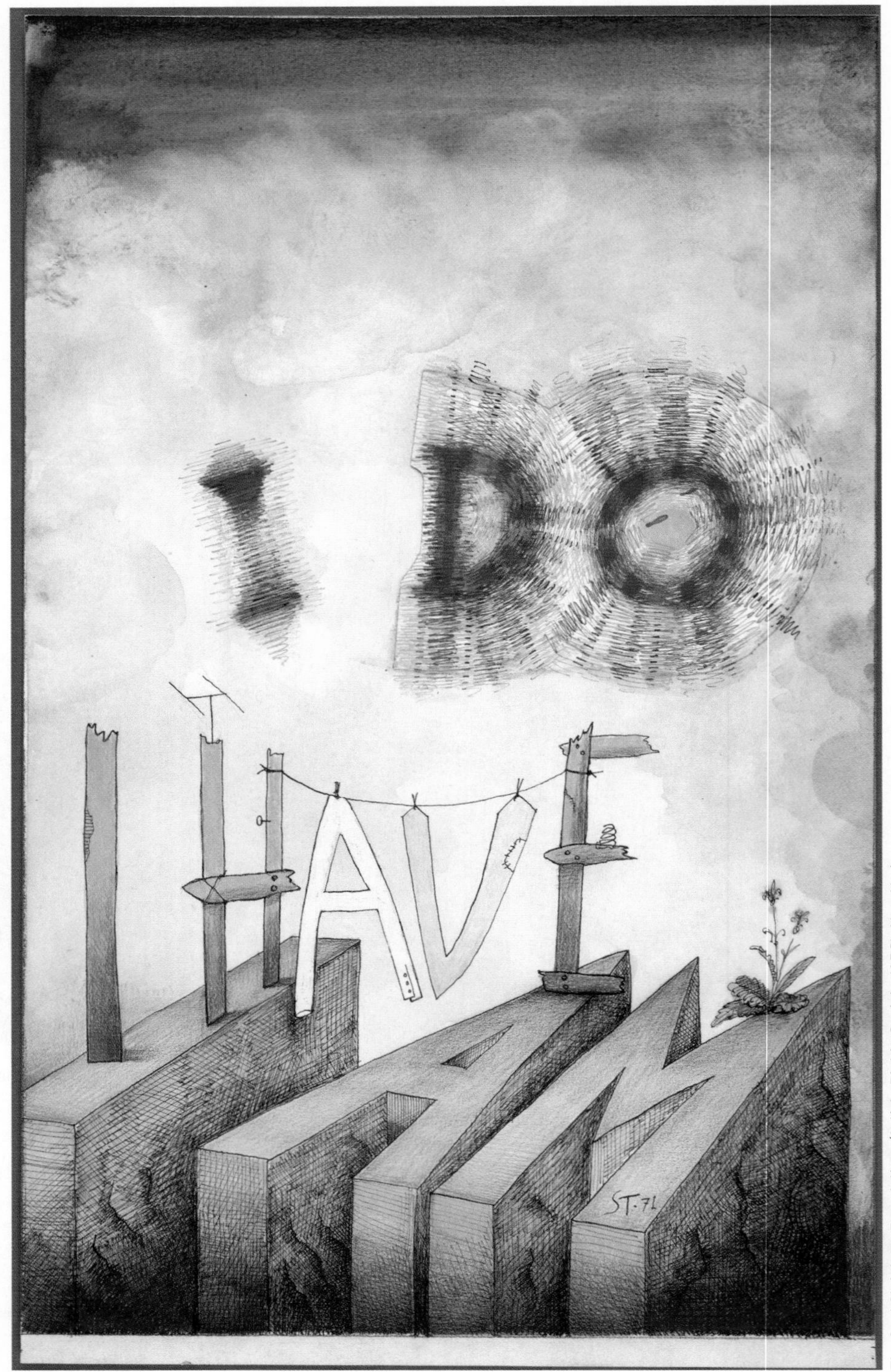
I DO
I HAVE
I AM
ST.71

Writing a Personal Statement

5

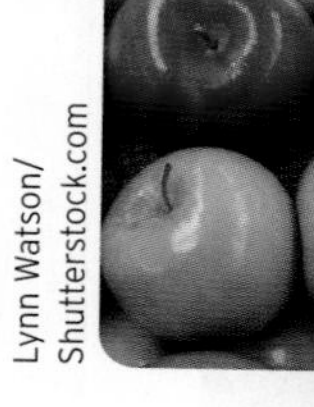

Lynn Watson/ Shutterstock.com

APPLICATION ESSAYS

No matter which question, we are asking what is really important to you, who you are, and how did you arrive where you are.

—Delsie Z. Phillips

When writing an application essay, you face what seems like a contradiction: writing in a formal voice while expressing your individuality. One student compared writing application essays to going to an interview and finding a one-way mirror. Her interviewers could see her, but she could not see them. Who were they? What mysterious elements made one application essay different from another? What made some of them winners?

Many students say they were never taught how to write application essays. They believe that some people have an intuitive sense of how to write outstanding essays and that other people do not. The truth is that you can learn to write application essays that will impress your readers. The keys are

1. understanding the reason for writing the essay—the rhetorical context
2. understanding the question that you are being asked, often called a *prompt*, so that you can focus your essay.

Your personal statements will stand out among the others in a positive way if you can engage your audience and become part of the "ones you do not forget."

WHAT'S TO COME

PROCESS PLAN

PROCESS PLAN

PREPARE

- Analyze the prompt carefully; what exactly are you being asked?
- Determine what you want your readers to know about you, and plan to answer the question while asserting your individuality

DRAFT

- Introduction
  - Catch attention in the opening: Create a scene, make a statement, offer an insight or opinion
  - Avoid overstatement and vague language
- Body: Support your thesis with examples that help reveal who you are
- Conclusion: Sum up your essay with a memorable image or insight

REVISE

- Include transitions to help guide the reader through your essay: Remind the reader of the main point by restating a phrase from a previous paragraph
- Have a friend read over your essay and check grammar, punctuation, and spelling
- Make sure the names of the organization, institution or people are correct

UNDERSTANDING THE WRITING PROJECT

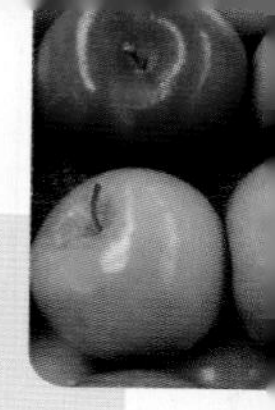

Thinkstock/Getty Images

THE PURPOSE of the application essay is to allow you to reveal something significant about yourself, something that makes you stand out among the crowd of other applicants. Also called "personal statements," these essays asking you to reveal some of your personality, beliefs, and goals are a standard part of college and scholarship applications. They are also often required when you are applying for jobs, internships, volunteer positions, or working with community service projects.

To write a stand-out personal statement, you need to understand your audience—what they might be looking for—and to define your connection to the audience and your reason for writing. Your ultimate goal is to have your brief statement be one the readers remember. Think of these personal essays as invitations to persuade your readers of your worth. According to the acting director of admissions at Haverford College,

> ". . . the essay is a way to put your personal adventure into words. It is a summing-up, maybe a catharsis. You need not expose all of your innermost thoughts, but you must share some part of yourself."—Delsie Z. Phillips, "The Question of the Essay"

Some questions that writers are asked in application essays follow:

- **Who speaks for our generation, and what are they saying? If you answer *no one,* why? What needs to be said?**—Scholarship application
- **Why would you like to be a Discovery Corps volunteer and how do you plan to inspire through science and nature?**—Volunteer internship application

Access an interactive eBook, and chapter-specific interactive learning tools, including flashcards, quizzes, videos and more in your English CourseMate via www.cengagebrain.com.

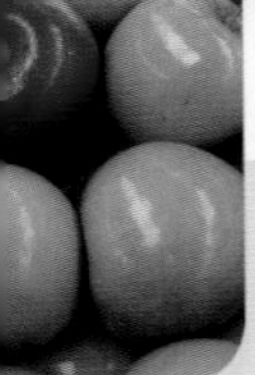

- **Discuss your interest in your major. Tell how your interest developed and describe a related work or volunteer/service experience.**—Transfer application
- **What personal characteristics do you possess that would make you a good health-care provider? Give some examples from your experiences that show your characteristics in practice.**—Job application

ASSIGNMENT Target an audience: Choose a job, a scholarship, or an internship, that you might be interested in getting. Write your own prompt like the ones above, or respond to a prompt from the audience you have targeted. Then write your essay response. Your personal statement should show that you understand your audience, their goals and philosophies. Present yourself as a stand-out applicant.

ANATOMY OF A PERSONAL STATEMENT

"THAT OTHER PART" is Nitya Venkataraman's essay from her graduate school application. Like many application essays, this personal statement is about how a person shapes his or her identity.

That Other Part

NITYA K. VENKATARAMAN

I wasn't White, Black, or Mexican. But to a six-year-old, what's an "Other"? White. Black. Mexican. Other.

opening catches attention

I stared blankly down at the page in front of me and tried to answer a question that would echo throughout the rest of my life every time I sought to define an identity for myself.

THE BIG IDEA = findi[ng] a racial identity

The year was 1985 and the California Achievement Test was the most grown-up undertaking that had collided with my six-year-old existence. And even though I promised my very Indian

personal voice

parents that my teacher said the test "didn't count," they had sailed to this country on the tide of education, and a test was a test was a test. I spent the week preceding the test doing math problems and taking spelling tests hosted by my mother around our kitchen table.

But what I'll never forget is the one question on the test that my mom never prepared me for.

I was giddy with excitement at the thought of answering multiple choice questions in a Scantron bubble format. With three newly sharpened No. 2 pencils, a gruff "good luck!" from my dad, a kiss from my mom, and my prettiest peach frock with puffed sleeves, I dismounted the bus and ran into my first-grade classroom, waiting for my first real test to commence.

specific detail

I remained optimistic as we were instructed to fill in basic information about ourselves, feeling slightly worried that the California Achievement people might mistake me for someone else—my name amounted to "Nitya K. Venkatar," in a test-taking land where after the eighth Scantron box, the letters in your last name were irrelevant.

narrative detail helps your reader follow

Sex: M or F? With little hesitation, I marked in the oval next to "F," giggling along with my classmates at the word *sex* printed on a test.

Birthday. That was easy: April 13, 1979.

So far, so good.

Ethnicity (Optional). I am: White. Black. Mexican. Other.

Our teacher told us that optional meant we didn't have to answer it. But part of my test preparation included the speech that I never skip questions (lest I lose points), and I assumed that if I thought and thought and thought hard enough, the right answer would come to me.

White? Black? Mexican? Other?

a distinct voice

I knew I wasn't White. White was Stephanie, my best friend next door, and Peaches-and-Cream Barbie. It was the Pledge of Allegiance, potato salad, and the Nina, Pinta, and Santa Maria. White was my dad's boss. And I knew I wasn't any of those things.

I knew I wasn't Black. Black was the little girl across the street with hair that could be braided once a week and clipped at the ends with colorful plastic barrettes. Black was Willis on

continues next page

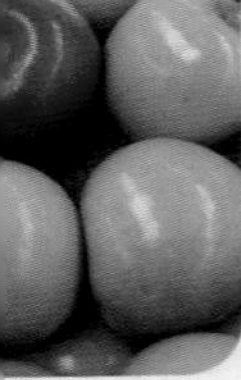

Different Strokes and the kind lady with shiny, dark skin at the grocery store who told me I was as "sweet as brown sugar." Black was Stevie Wonder. And I knew I wasn't any of those things.

public references and private details

I knew I wasn't Mexican. Mexican was enchiladas and tacos and adios. It was the "Uno Dos Tres Quatro Cinco Seis" song. Mexican was the man at the Farmer's Market in Berkeley who sold us fresh grapes every Saturday. And I knew I wasn't any of those things.

But Other. Who was Other?

I sighed, disheartened. After so much excitement, so much preparation, I was not going to be able to take the test. Ethnicity (Optional) didn't really apply to me. With a heavy heart, I collected my materials and tried to unobtrusively make my way to the front of the classroom to Mrs. Palmer's desk to tell her of this latest calamity.

dialogue

"Mrs. Palmer, I don't think I can take this test." I showed her the question and I'll never forget the look that washed over her face.

"You're 'Other,' Nitya," she whispered with a kind smile. "You're a little bit special on this test."

I grinned, at the thought of being special, and pushed away all thoughts of confusion and unhappiness, even though something about bubbling in Other didn't exactly sit right with me. What was Other?

revealing personal detail

Was Other the plates and plates of sweets I ate every Diwali? The classical dance classes I took every weekend at the temple? The Hindi lullaby my mother sang to me before I slept?

On the way home, I overheard a Chinese girl on the bus telling the person sitting next to her that she "got to be an Other" on the test. And that is when I realized: Other was Chinese New Year and Egyptian pyramids. It was falafel, origami, and Hindi lullabies. Other was the little piece of everyone that had been forgotten somewhere else.

reference to the larger issue > connecting her personal story to a larger issue

Years later, multiculturalism became politically correct. Having a specific ethnic identity was beyond OK—it was chic, trendy, encouraged, and evidenced in the Ethnicity (Optional) boxes, once reserved for White, Black, Mexican, Other.

Chinese New Year became Chinese-American. Falafel was Middle Eastern. Origami was Japanese-American. And Hindi lullabies? Well, they were Asian, Asian-American (Indian sub-continent included), and on special occasion, lucky enough to be considered Indian-American.

But what happened to Other? It was still there, lurking in the bottom right-hand corner of every Ethnicity (Optional) box, glaring at all the turn-coats who had left it for their own identities. And yet, Other remained, proud to claim those without identity as its own.

her conclusion about multiculturalism—her personal statement

As for me, I never really decided where I belonged. As much as I longed to bubble myself in as Asian-American, I always felt torn, like I was leaving Other behind. But Indian-American? Could I really be two things at once? Could I represent a culture of arranged marriages and another of sexual freedoms all at the same time? Was I Kulfi and apple pie? Bindis and blue jeans? Something in the picture didn't fit together.

As a newly defined Indian-American, I realized something that many hyphenated Americans recognize when their worlds collide: My identity lay not really in the Indian, and not really in the American, but more like that Other part.

a memorable closing

The hyphen in between.

"I always remind myself that real people are reading my essay, not robots. And in the middle of a mundane application process, it is a brief, shining opportunity to be creative and unique."

Q&A with Nitya K. Venkataraman

How One Student Envisioned her Audience to Tap into her Creativity

Q: What have you encountered as obstacles in writing essays for applications? What, for you, is the most difficult part of writing essays for applications?

A: The most difficult part of any application essay process, I think, is staying original and trying to say something old in a new way. We have a natural tendency to write what we think admissions committees want to hear, which sometimes makes essays generic and cookie cutter; as a result, we end up staying away from the stories and topics and anecdotes that make us unique and personal.

Q: How do you imagine your reader when you write essays for applications? Does your version of that reader shape your style?

A: It sounds kind of funny, but I envision my reader as a member of an admissions committee who is surrounded by stacks and stacks of application essays (sometimes I even imagine them looking a little bit bored!). For some reason, when I think about the volume of generic essays these committees probably consume, I am forced to be creative [and] punchy and take more chances with my writing, tone, and style.

Q: How do you balance personal writing with the formality of an application essay? Or do you?

A: Application essays should be personal. In a lot of cases, this is your one and only opportunity to speak to the selection panel, so you need to paint a picture of yourself to a group of people who have never met you before. I always remind myself that real people are reading my essay, not robots.

Nitya K. Venkataraman

Ken Andreyo/Carnegie Mellon

Q: Your essay has a definite narrative thread that makes the essay really engaging. You seem like a real person, an individual rather than a type. What do you think you included to make yourself more of an individual, to help your reader remember you?

A: I think it's all in the details. The details make it vivid and real and an experience that you share with your reader. I wrote about the standardized test because I knew it was an experience that anyone could relate to, but the ethnicity-optional box was a minute detail that changed my entire life. Without that small, poignant detail, I might have forgotten that I even took that test in 1985. The details are everything.

Q: Would you say you enjoy writing application essays?

A: I do. I think that writing application essays is a good time to do some personal soul-searching. It is not necessarily a good time to put it in an essay and send it off to an admissions board, but it's a good time to remember what your goals are and why you are pursuing them. And in the middle of a mundane application process, it is a brief, shining opportunity to be creative and unique.

PRACTICE 5.1

Writing a Prompt

Students transferring into your college are stuck responding to a standard, dull essay question: "Why do you want to transfer to this college?" As part of a student recruitment team, you have been asked to come up with a prompt that allows for more creativity and still asks the basic question of why the student is applying to your college. Write a prompt that captures a bit of the spirit of your school.

THE RHETORICAL SITUATION: THINKING ABOUT YOUR READERS AND YOUR PURPOSE

Why would your readers remember you?

Your application essay will be read by someone who has most likely not met you, someone who will be reading a stack of essays all written from the same starting-point prompt. Think about *that* reader, and what that reader might want to know about you, and you will begin to write an effective essay.

So, how do you make your personal essay stand out positively from the rest? Readers of application essays say that disorganized, unfocused, generic, and carelessly proofread essays go into the discard pile. First and foremost, consider your reasons for applying. Then organize your ideas into a clear structure. Make sure that your grammar is technically perfect.

Remember what you have to say is every bit as important as how you say it. The content of your essay should:

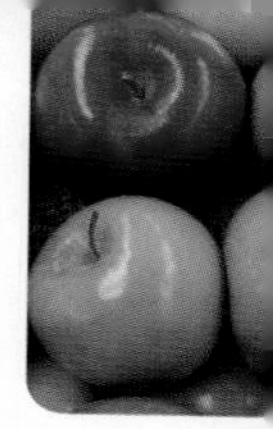

- provide useful information about you
- reveal a sense of your personality and style
- engage the interest of your readers, and even inspire them

Your readers want to know that you have given thought to *them.*

Make no mistake: Writing an application essay is entering a competition with a lot at stake. You will be judged by your writing. The people who read your application essay have no personal interest in your success.

RESEARCH PATHS: USING RESEARCH TO APPEAL TO YOUR AUDIENCE

You have a clearly defined audience for your application essay: the person or committee in charge of evaluating applications for the scholarship, study-abroad program, internship, college, or job to which you are applying. It makes good sense to do some research about the goals and missions of your audience. Each has a different orientation; even though it might be tempting to recycle the same essay for all applications, tailoring the application to the specific audience is a much better idea.

If, for example, a scholarship is named after a prestigious alumnus, you should learn about that person. Find out what qualities the person embodied, who endowed the scholarship, and what prompted that person or group to endow it. You might want to begin your application with an acknowledgement of the person's contribution or importance, showing that you did your homework. Any group or organization that funds a scholarship—whether a religious group or a corporate one—wants to know that you have considered its reasons for offering the scholarship and that your values are harmonious with its values.

Since an internship application usually asks for a personal statement or a statement of purpose, become informed about the company or organization to which you are applying. You do not need to show comprehensive knowledge of the company's net profits or overall business plan, but you should be able to write convincingly about how your skills and abilities are a good fit for the work and how your values mesh with the company's values.

If you are applying to study abroad, know something about both the program and the country. Do you need to speak a foreign language? Will you be taking classes with native students? Will you be living in a dorm or with a family? Do not make the mistake that one student did when he wrote an essay about how much he wanted to learn about the English parliamentary system for his application to study at the University of Dublin in Ireland.

If you are seeking a transfer or admission as a graduate student, know the programs and the identities of the eminent professors. Check out a Web site; read the publicity

PRACTICE 5.2

Research

1. Do some research to find a scholarship or internship that you might be interested in applying for and obtain application material. You can locate opportunities by doing a Web search, reading bulletin boards at your school, or talking to professors in your field of interest. Public and college libraries usually have books that list scholarships students can apply for.
2. After reading the application material, list the qualities that the scholarship or internship committee might be looking for in an ideal candidate.
3. In a brief paragraph, explain how your experience and education fit those expectations.

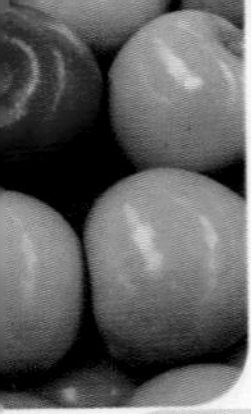

materials; and talk to people who have gone before you. Gather as much information as possible so that you can write from a firm base of knowledge about the school or program.

After attending an inspiring workshop with a writing professor, a student decided to apply for a fellowship to work with that professor. She began her application essay with a paragraph narrating her experience at the workshop. Too obvious? Maybe. But it was honest and heartfelt, and it worked: She got in.

All this advice boils down to one point: Know your audience. Making an effort to research your audience will help you write a focused and successful essay in a confident voice.

FINDING YOUR FOCUS IN THE APPLICATION QUESTION

Like an academic essay on a specific question or theme, the application essay has a built-in focal point: the question or, as many call it, the prompt. If you make the mistake of forging ahead without reading the requirements, you may write a 2,000-word essay when the prompt asks for 500 words, or you may not fully address the question. Read the question or prompt carefully. Pay attention to the rules or parameters of the application. The language of the prompt suggests ways to focus your essay. Most prompts fall into one of the following categories.

- Past experiences and achievements
- Future plans
- Values or personal philosophy
- General knowledge
- Ability to analyze ideas

Understand what each kind of question is trying to elicit.

PAST EXPERIENCES AND ACHIEVEMENTS

Questions about your past experiences and achievements usually sound like this question on the application to the University of California, Los Angeles:

- What do you consider to be your most important personal and professional accomplishments to date?

Other prompts might be worded like this one:

- Describe an experience that has helped change your perspective.
- Describe a challenge you have successfully met.

These kinds of prompts ask you to focus on something that reveals who you are by relating and interpreting an experience. Remember that the word *describe* asks you to provide concrete details and to be specific about your experience.

Even small events such as winning a race or a prize, an unexpected friendship, or a setback are all fine topics for this kind of essay. One student wrote a memorable and compelling application essay on the unlikely topic of shopping for prom shoes.

PRACTICE 5.3

Analyzing Prompts

1. Analyze each of these typical application prompts. What are they asking? What might you focus on in an answer?
   a. Describe a personal experience that has profoundly changed your perspective on an issue of regional, national, or international importance. In what way has this event impacted your previous perspective? How will it change your approach to this issue (or similar issues) in the future?
   —UCLA, undergraduate application
   b. Why do you want to intern at the Office of Exhibits Central, and what do you hope to learn?
   —Smithsonian Museum, internship application
   c. You have just completed your 300-page autobiography. Please submit page 217.
   —University of Pennsylvania, undergraduate school application
   d. Tell us about an opinion you have had to defend. How has this affected your belief system?
   —Cornell University, undergraduate application
2. Write the first fifty words of one of these essays.

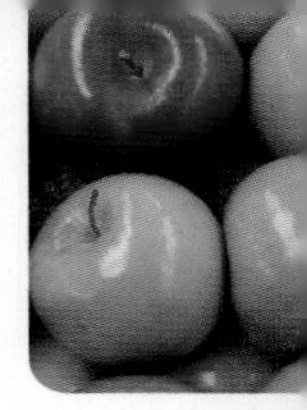

The important point is that you need to describe the event and then interpret it. Explain to your reader why the event was significant to you.

FUTURE PLANS

When an application asks about your plans, you can assume that the employer, college, or program wants to know whether your goals match the open position or the mission of the college or program. In a sense, readers want to know whether they should invest in your future by giving you a job, a scholarship, an internship, or an opportunity to study abroad. Your focus should be on convincing them that the fit is right. If you are applying for an internship in a political organization, for example, make sure you know and are in agreement with the organization's positions on major policies and candidates before you elaborate on the legislation you would sponsor in your future role as senator.

VALUES OR PERSONAL PHILOSOPHY

Questions about your values or philosophy can sound like this one from a scholarship application:

- If your education had no limits, you could stay as long as you wanted, and money were no object, what would you hope to get out of your time at college?

By asking you to strip away practical limitations, the question, in effect, is asking you to focus on and articulate your core philosophy about education. In your response, you should be honest as well as insightful about what you want from school.

GENERAL KNOWLEDGE

Sometimes transfer or internship applications allow you to demonstrate your expertise in a subject. Such questions are opportunities to reveal your passion for and understanding of a subject of special interest.

- Describe how a work of art, music, dance, theater, or literature has inspired you.

ABILITY TO ANALYZE IDEAS

Some questions ask you to analyze a quotation and relate it to your life.

- Pearl S. Buck once said, "You cannot make yourself feel something you do not feel, but you can make yourself do right in spite of your feelings." Tell us about an experience in which you felt that you did the right thing in spite of your feelings.

You will not be able to give a correct or incorrect answer to this analytical question, but you will have to be careful to stay on track and focus on having done the right thing when you did not feel like doing it. The important word in this question is *right*. You will want to take into consideration the moral issues suggested by the word as you form your answer. The prompt is not asking you to write about a decision that was "different" from other people's decisions or one that was "wrong." Reading the question carefully and analyzing its language and intent can help you come up with a focused and persuasive answer. Understanding what the question

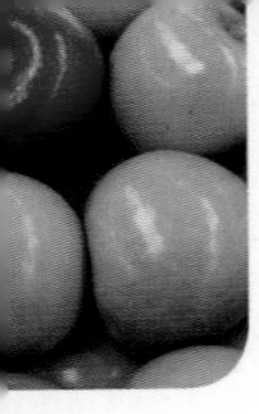

is asking can save you countless hours of frustration, not just in writing application essays but also in answering questions wherever you encounter them.

THE BIG IDEA: THE THESIS OF AN APPLICATION ESSAY

Your thesis in an application essay is an explicit statement of your idea or interpretation of your topic. Make sure it also answers the prompt. Often you will state your thesis at the beginning of the essay as either the first or last sentence of your introduction. However, if you are trying to build suspense or lead your reader to your main point by first presenting evidence, you might state your thesis later in the essay. Whereever you put it, make sure that you know, and that your reader knows, what your thesis, your big idea, is in this essay

In "Smoke," an application essay in the readings (page 120), Jessica Polanski addressed the question of why she wanted to enter the public health field. Her essay presented vivid accounts of people in her life who smoked and suffered from this habit. Her thesis, which she placed at the end of her essay, was

> I think I can make a difference: help inform and motivate people, and help them lead longer, and maybe happier lives. Receiving a School of Public Health scholarship will help me take my first step towards my goal.

By waiting to state her thesis until the end of her essay, Jessica allowed the narrative details and specific examples to build a convincing argument for her decision to work in public health. Some writers like to work in this model, building their case, then ending with a thesis. Others state their thesis in the opening section of the essay and then support it with specific examples and details. Whichever way you decide to structure your essay, be sure your thesis is **narrowly focused on a single belief, philosophy, decision, or conclusion.**

PRACTICE 5.4

Analyzing Thesis Statements

Read the following thesis statements from application essays.

And, over the years, there have been times when my future character was decided in a conflict between fear and morality.
—Application essay about a friend with Down syndrome

My life is based upon two very simple, sweeping philosophies: pragmatism in actions and idealism in thought.
—Personal identity essay

A typical teen's room? In some respects, yes, but in many ways, my room has become an extension of my personality, interests, and values.
—Essay on giving a tour of a room

Living behind the Orange Curtain, I feel that my sexuality has grounded me outside society.
—Personal identity essay by an Asian gay-rights activist

Thesis in an Application Essay

- Limit to a single conclusion, belief, philosophy, or judgment
- Reveal something personal about you or your background
- State either at the beginning or the end of the essay
- Use as the general focus; all the details add up to your thesis.

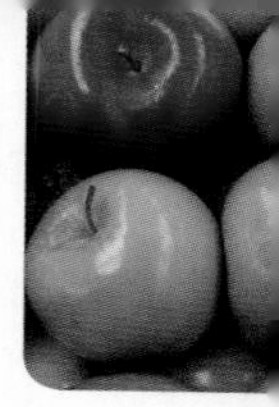

CHOOSING A DEVELOPMENT STRATEGY

Depending on the prompt and your topic, you can choose from a variety of approaches to develop your essay. Three basic approaches are narration, analysis, and argumentation. Each has strengths, and each can be appropriate for an entire essay or part of one.

NARRATION

Stories allow you to be personal, even confidential, as you engage the reader's attention. "Show" your story with vivid description, well-selected detail, and maybe even some dialogue or a scene to make it more engaging and memorable.

The following opening, from an application essay about living abroad, uses narrative to draw the reader into the scene.

> NARRATIVE DRAWS THE READER INTO THE SCENE ▶ "Je deteste des Americains" [I detest Americans], said the old Swiss woman sitting across from me. Her face contorted into a grimace of disgust as she and her friend continued to complain that Americans had no culture, that they never learned another language, and that their inferior customs were spreading throughout Europe like an infectious disease. Each hair on the back of my neck sprang to attention as I strained to hear the woman's inflammatory remarks. I gripped my bag of McDonald's harder with each insulting phrase.
>
> —"Essay 32, Harvard, International Experience: Living in Switzerland," *Barrons*

The opening dialogue creates immediate tension. The reader wants to know who the Swiss woman is and how the writer responded to her angry outburst. The writer offers some description—the woman's "grimace of disgust," the hair on the back of the writer's neck, and finally the ironic detail of the "bag of McDonald's" gripped in the writer's hand. The introduction has characters, setting, and conflict, all the ingredients of a good story.

ANALYSIS

Even if you have chosen to tell a story, it is important to analyze the events—that is, to break them down into their parts in order to explain or interpret them. Some prompts may explicitly call for analysis to be a major part of the essay. An application essay should not be creative writing that leaves the reader wondering what the meaning of it all is. Instead, you want to show that you have understood the experience and its impact on your life and that you can articulate its meaning.

One applicant wrote about a summer job "detasseling" corn—"removing the tassel from a corn stalk so that pollinization of the plant can occur and hybrid seed corn can grow." A variety of Midwesterners, many of them students, do this work

(*Continued*)

I have had a lifelong fascination with mathematics, a fascination that I perhaps owe to my mother, who has a degree in mathematics and who encouraged me to study it extensively.

—Essay on hobbies and interests

—All quotations from Amy Burnham, Daniel Kaufman, and Chris Dowhan, *Essays That Will Get You into College*

1. Which statements present the most interesting and original ideas?
2. Which, if any, are vague or unfocused?
3. Rewrite one thesis to make it more interesting or more specific.

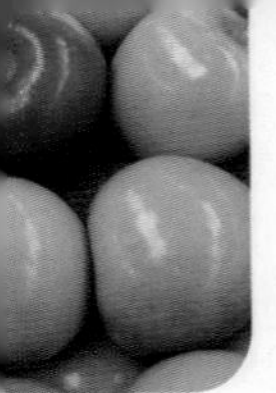

each summer. The writer's experiences with coworkers who were "different kinds of achievers" from the people she had previously known led her to analyze her own experience of working under difficult circumstances, sometimes from sunrise to sunset.

> ANALYSIS EXPLAINS AND INTERPRETS EXPERIENCE ▶ "While discovering the strengths of so many different kinds of people, I also discovered some of my own strengths. . . . I realized that I am able to depend on my own inner resources. This discovery of my own physical strength and my ability to endure came as a revelation to me."
>
> —Celia E. Rothenberg, from *One Hundred Successful College Application Essays*

You may also be asked how a work of art or literature has inspired you or how you expect this internship (or scholarship or study-abroad program) to affect your future.

ARGUMENTATION

In a sense, everything you write in an application essay is an argument in favor of your worth as a candidate. But mostly, an application essay is a demonstration of your personality, your ideas and experience, that you are a good fit for the program. What you choose to write about and how you express yourself—your voice and style as well as grammar and vocabulary—together persuade your reader that you are an interesting and intelligent person who stands out among your peers.

More specifically, some essay prompts require you to make an argument to support an opinion. In making this kind of argument, you claim a distinct position on an issue and present evidence that defends your position. For example, a prompt used by Cornell University was "Tell us about an opinion you have had to defend. How has this affected your belief system?" For this application essay, you would need to state your position as well as your reasons for holding that view in the same way that writers of editorials or opinion essays do. One student who was applying for a scholarship wrote about the controversial topic of federal funding for stem-cell research.

> ARGUMENT SHOWS REASONING ABILITY AND DEMONSTRATES IDEAS AND EXPERIENCE ▶ "The federal government should fund stem-cell research because the government can make funds equally available to all scientists. If the government does not take the responsibility for research on stem cells, some private research group certainly will, limiting the amount of information available to scientists. Also, more researchers working on developing cures could speed remedies for chronic and deadly illnesses like diabetes and Alzheimer's."
>
> —Chisom Aganabe, scholarship application

The student takes a clear stand on a controversial scientific topic: that the federal government should fund stem-cell research. She supports her argument with two main points: The federal government can make funds equally available to all researchers, and more scientists working on a problem can solve the problem more quickly. Another student might argue that stem-cell research is immoral or that there should be less government regulation of research. Whatever your opinion, make sure you state it clearly and support it with specific reasons that reveal your logic.

See the box Tips for Giving Your Application Essay the Personal Edge on page 111 for more help presenting yourself as an interesting, one-of-a-kind person while keeping your style and tone consistent with formal writing.

MAKING YOUR ESSAY STAND OUT

You want your reader to have a strong impression of your distinct personality—as someone who is interesting, confident, capable, and professional. Most likely you would not go to an interview dressed in jeans or in a costume. Likewise, your essay should be written in a style and tone that fits the formality of the situation.

Gavriel Jecan/Encyclopedia/CORBIS

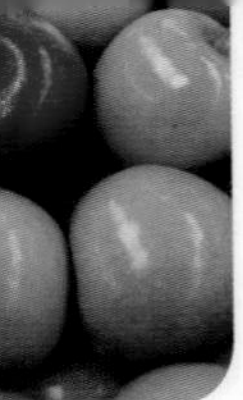

THE OPENING SENTENCE

Remember that your goal is to have your writing leap off the page and into the mind of a tired reader who has a mailbox full of files to read. That first sentence should create interest as this opener does.

OPENING SENTENCE ▶ *I know I shouldn't, but I always hesitate to tell people that when (and if) I go to college I'll be the first person in my immediate family to do so. Why do I hesitate?*

THE LAST SENTENCE

The conclusion in an application essay not only sums up your essay; it also provides a last glimpse of your personality. You want to convince your reader that you are the best candidate for whatever it is you are applying for—a job, an internship, a study-abroad program, or a scholarship. Your last sentence is your last moment with your reader. Do not fade out. Being memorable means using each and every word you have to create a distinct impression.

"I think I've finally found my own voice."

Bernard Schoenbaum/Cartoonbank.com

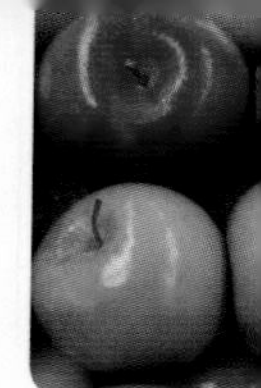

From an essay about being identified as dyslexic, the writer uses a quotation from Samuel Beckett as his last line:

LAST SENTENCE ▶ *I am the first to admit that I've had academic challenges. But I'm not going to let them stop me. As Samuel Beckett said, "Ever tried. Ever failed. No matter. Try again. Fail better."*

PERSONAL VOICE

Aim to sound as if you are talking to just one person—but in a formal setting, such as an interview. In other words, even though you are not familiar enough with your reader to use slang or inside jokes, you are not addressing a large lecture hall either. One mistake writers make is to "institutionalize" their application essays, making them sound more like policy statements than personal statements:

TOO IMPERSONAL ▶ *Utilizing coalitions built within family, friends, and acquaintances might be a way to succeed in the business world, but that is not what initiative is all about.*

PERSONAL TONE ▶ *Many people use their family connections to succeed in business, but I have a different sense of initiative.*

Tips for Giving Your Application Essay the Personal Edge

1. **Use the first person.**
   In a personal essay, the first person (*I*) is required, not optional.

2. **Be specific and concrete.**
   - *Too general:* Working on the farm helped me define "free time" in a new way.
   - *More specific*: That summer on the farm, I would wake up at four in the morning and eat lunch at 1. I would not finish with my chores until 3. I did not have a car, and I was too tired to walk the five miles into town. I often found myself lying under my favorite tree in the pasture, with only the cows for company. It was a new way to think of "free time."

3. **Write in the active voice.**
   Make the subjects of your sentences the doers of the action. In other words, avoid the passive voice.
   - *Passive:* "A scholarship was awarded to me."
   - *Active:* "I received a scholarship."

   The active voice is clearer and more appealing.

(continued)

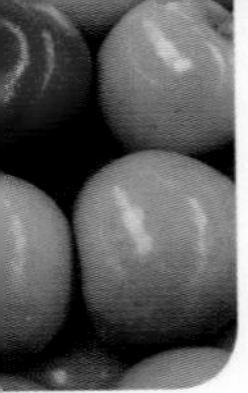

Tips for Giving Your Application Essay the Personal Edge (continued)

4. **Use your own vocabulary.**
   Do not replace simple words with long or obscure words that you have found in a thesaurus. Inflated language is inconsistent with a personal voice.
   - *Inflated Language:* My intransigent goal has consistently been to utilize my superlative business training for intromission to an appropriate salaried position.
   - *Appropriate Language:* I want to use my business training on the job.

5. **Use understatement rather than overstatement.**
   Modesty is more appealing than bragging. Avoid aggressive or pompous business-speak.
   - *Overstated:* I have a proven record as someone who succeeds in anything he tries to do.
   - *More Measured:* My friends sometimes make fun of my determination. Truthfully, since I am the only one in my family who has had the opportunity to go to college, I *am* determined to work hard and succeed.

6. **If possible, use few or no contractions.**
   (I've, there's, haven't, would've). Some readers do not find them appropriate in written works of importance.

7. **Avoid gimmicks.**
   Creative writing and an engaging personal voice cannot take the place of having something substantial to say and a good focus. Give careful thought to your topic, trying several before settling on one, and avoid high-risk gimmicks. The problem with taking risks is that sometimes they fail miserably, and even the ones that are not total failures can be jarring to some readers.

8. **Use humor carefully.**
   Your readers do not have your facial expressions to help them understand subtle jokes, so weigh the risk of using humor. Sarcasm, for example, is always risky because sarcasm can be easily misread and brings a negative tone to your writing.
   - *Sarcastic Tone:* Working hard for no money is the way I want to spend my professional life.

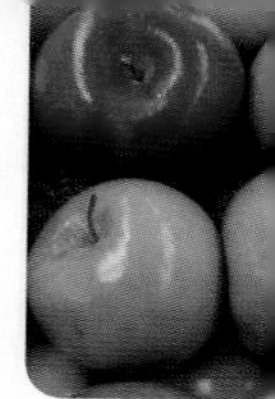

Starting an essay with the sarcastic statement is provocative, but it also sets up a negative tone. The first impression your reader has of you is as someone who is angry and sarcastic.

9. **Avoid application clichés.**
   Clichés are predictable expressions that have grown so familiar people no longer think of them as fresh or interesting.

   When readers hear clichés, they tune out. Application essay clichés are particularly deadly, though, because they do not allow you to stay in the crowd. Even if your message is similar to others, it does not have to sound like all the others. Use specific details to make your story individual:

   - *By my junior year in high school I had been thrown over saloon tables, stabbed to death in a knife fight, strangled in my own bed. I was not the scared, shy, slightly overweight fourteen-year-old who entered that theatre three years earlier. I had fallen in love with stage combat, had discovered a part of myself that was indeed a fighter. I was altogether different.*
   - *I have always hated winter and it does not help that freezing temperatures are the mortal enemy of my violin. But standing on that street, playing back-up for the cheerily Victorian-dressed Christmas carollers, I will never forget making eye-contact with one audience member during my single solo.*
   - *I was deathly afraid of butterflies the summer I turned seven. I awoke covered in sweat from nightmares about the winged creatures. I even tried not to leave the house for the entire month of July. And then my mother tricked me into going to the science center, to the place I feared most in the world, a long series of screened rooms called The Butterfly House. It was there I came face to face with my fear. It was right there and then, I am certain, that I became a scientist.*

10. **Reconsider experimental techniques.**
    Writers will often try to brighten stories by writing in unusual points of view. One writer told a story from his dead grandmother's point of view, a technique that overshadowed the real point of the writing. If you are going to write in verse, or limit yourself to words that begin with the letter "c," for example, you are going to draw a great deal of attention to your technique—more to the technique than the content. This is a risky gamble—one that is not worth the possible cost. Instead of spending your time thinking up clever packaging, think about developing yourself as a "brand." What makes you genuine, real, and valuable to the organization or school?

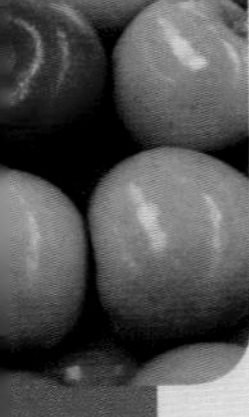

D I Y

DIY MEDIA AND DESIGN

THE RÉSUMÉ AND APPLICATION LETTER

IN THE WORLD of applications, the application essay is sometimes accompanied by a résumé or letter.

RÉSUMÉS

Résumés are usually your first introduction to organizations, and are almost always a component of applications. Put your best foot forward. A résumé is a personal statement, a summary, an informational report, and an argument for why you should be hired. You need to provide basic information about yourself in an easily scanned list. You may include a brief description of jobs that require additional detail, but if you are sending a print résumé, keep your résumé limited to one or two pages, maximum. Conciseness is your goal, but providing a full picture of your credentials is also essential. If you have the option of including an application letter (or e-mail), the letter can make connections and fill out some of the details not included in your résumé. In your résumé, arrange the following information into categories with titles:

- up-to-date contact information: name, address, phone, and e-mail
- education or training
- relevant job experience
- relevant volunteer positions
- relevant course work
- special skills (foreign languages, computer, or technical skills)
- awards, honors, publications, leadership positions, and details that show substantial commitment to something (track team—four years, for example)

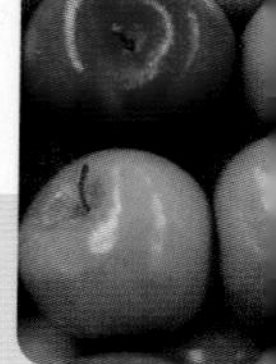

DIY

TRICIA GONZALES

tgonzalez@umass.edu

set up an email address with a professional-sounding name

56 Falstaff Lane
Northampton, MA 01065

EDUCATION

2010-present University of Massachusetts/Amherst-Elementary Education major/Math minor, 3.5 GPA

provide some detail, but only if it flatters you

2010—2006 Hadley High School, graduated with high honors

EXPERIENCE

2010-present Resident Assistant, Adams Hall—currently working as an advisor and resource to 28 undergraduates. Responsibilities include enforcing university housing policies, planning social functions, and peer counseling.

briefly list the responsibilities using fragments of sentences—make sure the fragments are parallel

2007–2009 Summers Swimming Instructor, Northampton YMCA—instructed children ages 3-12 in swimming skills and water safety.

list in descending order of chronology, from most recent

2008–2009 Server Amazing Bean Coffee, Amherst, MA—worked behind the counter, 25 hours per week during high school. Responsibilities included maintenance of kitchen equipment, clean-up, and management of cash tally and deposit at the end of the day.

RELATED EXPERIENCE

2008–2010 Volunteer Tri-City Shelter—worked as an after-school tutor for third through fifth grade students who were homeless. Each Tuesday, Sept-May.

time spent shows commitment, good detail

SPECIAL SKILLS

Spanish—Four years, high school. Two years college. Currently enrolled in Advanced Spanish Literature and Composition.

Computer skills—Photoshop, Final Cut.

AWARDS AND HONORS

Massachusetts Cross-Country Championships (6th place award), 2009
National Forensics League Debate State Finalist, 2010
Rotary Club Scholarship 2010

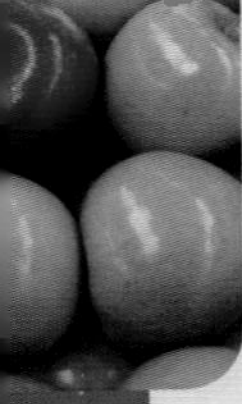

DIY

APPLICATION LETTERS

Knowing how to write a brief but revealing application essay is one step away from being able to write a good letter of application—a writing task that will most likely follow you around your whole life. Think carefully about the organization you are writing to: What sort of person is a good fit for it? What is the organization's central philosophy? Make sure you understand the job or post announcement. Get to know this by reading company Web sites and mission statements. The purpose of your letter is to garner the attention of the readers while outlining your particular qualifications. You should never reveal what you do not have or how you can catch up with skills on the job, for example. Focus instead on the details of your résumé. Sum up your experiences, emphasize highlights, and connect the dots that the "listing" of a résumé cannot. Be brief. Use proper business letter format. Application letters include:

- Your reason for writing (the job, internship, promotion)
- A specific connection to the organization in a thesis
- A demonstration of how your experiences connect directly to the job or organization
- An explanation of how unrelated experiences might relate
- An assertion of your qualities that is self-confident but not arrogant

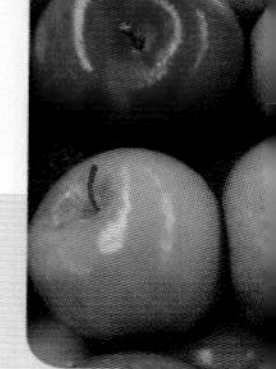

SAMPLE APPLICATION LETTER

890 Lisbon Street
Milton, MA, 02186
Jan. 19, 2011

return address—and date

use the title of the person, followed by a colon

Dear Professor Frederick:

I am writing to apply for the position of intern at Satellite Pictures. Roger Flynn suggested that I write to you.

State your reason for writing and how you heard about the job

I first became aware of Satellite Pictures when Roger Flynn approached the head of Milton High School's theatre and film department, Ian McDowell, last Fall, looking for student interns. Though I was very interested when Mr. McDowell recommended I look into the position, I could not work out the schedule, especially with the commute to Plymouth. I am hoping this summer you can find a spot for me with Principle Pictures.

Mr. McDowell identified me as a candidate because he has seen my work in my "Moving Image" film class at Milton High. I have experience shooting with Canon GL and GL2's, and editing films on Final Cut and Adobe Premiere Elements. I have produced several of my own documentaries for my class at Milton. I write screenplays, shoot, edit, and act in my films. My short Live Type music video was a selection at the Williston Northampton School film festival last May. I have produced films that were used as part of theatrical productions at the Lyric First Stage Program in Boston. At school, I use my film skills in community service: I have produced PSAs for the Tibet club, have shot dance video for our annual dance concert, and have produced humorous-yet-informative videos for my student government association. In addition to shooting and editing live action, I have made several stop-animation shorts.

putting experiences from the resume into context, showing connections. outlining qualifications for this particular job

moving into personal reasons, philosophy, ideals or beliefs.

My interest in Satellite Pictures comes partially from my interest in women's issues, gender equality, and civil rights. Though I am at the beginning stages of my studies, I am aware that women are in the minority in the filmmaking world—even as students in film classes. I am also aware that the voices and perspectives of women are, in general, not well represented in the world of film and are largely absent from documentaries. Even more important is that those voice are missing from feature films. I am drawn to the work of Satellite Pictures because of the many films Satellite has made that spotlight the stories of women. Perhaps, as a mixed-race woman who views this issue of under-representation from a couple of different angles, I feel the attraction to Satellite's work even more acutely.

a kind of argument

personally revealing, arguing from a personal perspective

clearly states reasons for wanting the post

I would love to discuss my work, and also for you to visit my Youtube address listed on my résumé, to see the range of my projects and get an idea of my skills. I look forward to hearing from you.

closes with a polite, general statement. Shows self-confidence.

Sincerely,
Yoshi Makishima

D I Y

READINGS

TWO STUDENT essays show how personal details can take even very typical experiences—like watching a sick relative or going through the college application process—and make them fresh, personal, and memorable. The third reading is a job application for "the best job in the world" with Tourism, Queensland in Australia.

Looking for Students Like Me![1]

Tess Langan
New York Times
November 5, 2010

Langan leads us through what might be familiar territory to anyone who has ever applied to college, but creates a distinct sense of mystery about what will happen next, in the style of a narrative-based essay.

IT WAS early in my junior year, before my college search had begun in earnest, that the letters started coming. It began as a trickle, but I was quickly inundated. One stands out in my mind: a letter informing me in a manner both presumptuous and peremptory that "at long last" my college search was over. Soon after, I received a letter from clairvoyant admissions officials at another college, asking me to gaze into the future with them and envision myself at their school. Having already learned of the end to my college search, I was confused to find myself frolicking on the greens of another university.

Despite the confidence of these courting colleges, I was still a directionless junior. So I started clocking in hour after hour with my small library of guidebooks, fretting over student-to-faculty ratios and weighing the advantages of large versus small schools. For days I would be besotted with a school. Then I would find out that it rains perpetually in the region where the school is located, or that it is a "beer and football" school, or that it got a pitiful two-and-a-half-star quality-of-life rating from Fiske. I did find my dream school, Antioch College, only to go online and discover that it was "in a period of transition"— that is, it had closed.

"Choosing the right college felt like trying to answer one of those dreaded multiple-choice questions that has two right answers."

Choosing the right college felt like trying to answer one of those dreaded multiple-choice questions that has two right answers. You march up to your teacher's desk to expose the flaw, and she tells you to pick the best answer. Sometimes I would simper like a child, intimidated by the gravity of the adult decisions I was being forced to make, and that would mold my future.

I began my college sojourn in earnest with a tour of Colgate. We were all handed Chipwiches, those spectacular amalgams of cookies and ice cream. That gave Colgate the

[1]Tess Langan, "Looking for Students Like Me!" from The New York Times, November 7, 2010. Reprinted with permission of PARS International.

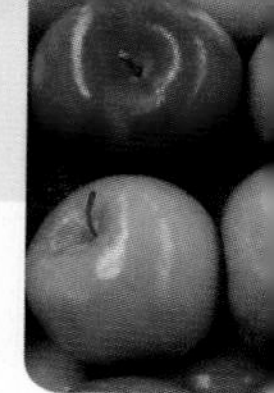

early lead until I took a tour at nearby Hamilton College. Not to be outdone, Hamilton was doling out coupons for the locally famous half-moon cookies and some pretty excellent stir-fry vegetables, courtesy of the cafeteria. Admitted applicants could look forward to a pair of Hamilton flip-flops if they visited campus before deposits were due. Colgate followed up by sending me an idyllic poster of the campus lake along with a handwritten note from the admissions director.

Now I was extremely conflicted; anyone who thinks teenagers cannot be bribed with food and flip-flops does not know teenagers. And the more time passed, the more muddled my mind became.

Even harder to ignore was a Princeton Review e-mail cajoling me to patronize their Web site by offering a personalized list of colleges "looking for students like you!" And there were simply so many colleges like Franklin & Marshall that e-mailed periodically to remind me that they "look forward to hearing from you!" Others, like Ursinus College, extended a special Priority Select application deadline, after their regular decision deadline. A painless application with no teacher recommendation, no essay and no fee, it was a hard offer to resist. But I did.

"Anyone who thinks teenagers cannot be bribed with food and flip-flops does not know teenagers."

The sheen of a college brochure is yet another distraction from the substance of a school. My glossy Vassar brochure boasted a student circus troupe called the Barefoot Monkeys. And though the ground might freeze over from November to April, the brochures of Northern colleges invariably depict eternal spring. The University of Vermont has an elaborate tunnel system that allows students to move from building to building without fear of frostbite. But you'd never guess it from the mail you get, filled with kids in shorts playing Frisbee in the sun.

Soon I had whittled down my options and applied to college. The letters I began to receive from colleges now were less fluffy and more portentous. Bleary-eyed and near-blind with anticipation, I would rip them open and scan frenetically for key words. Words like "regretfully," "welcome" and "congratulations" shouted at me like McDonald's signs on the side of the highway. Vassar and William & Mary "unfortunately" told me thanks but no thanks, while Colgate and the State University of New York at Geneseo declared it a "thrill and a privilege" to offer me admittance.

Now it was time to decide exactly where I would like to play Frisbee in the sun. I attended accepted students days at Geneseo and Colgate. Both involved guided tours, reception speeches, free prizes and current students who had "drunk the Kool-Aid," as my dad liked to joke, milling around wearing "Ask Me Anything" T-shirts and spouting canned lines about student life. ("There are going to be big drinkers everywhere, but there is no pressure to drink here.") My parents enjoyed the cocktail party Geneseo hosted at a historic inn, and Colgate wowed its teenage audience with an ice cream social—eating ice cream is, it seems, a tradition at Colgate—and the tantalizing promise of many more to come.

I really like my Colgate water bottle and my many nearly identical totes emblazoned with college logos. But rather than enlighten me, the presidents' addresses and the facts that ran together like slush and the

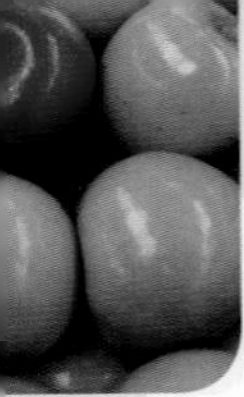

pamphlets and the complimentary ice cream all threatened to immobilize me. I was more confused than ever, but of one thing I was certain: the dogged marketing of the admissions process had left a bad taste in my mouth that no half-moon cookies or ice cream social could wash away.

After all my researching and hand-wringing, I turned down Geneseo and Colgate. And my rejections were not "unfortunate" or "regretful" but, rather, freeing.

When I found out about a gap-year program, Global Citizen Year, I did not need any prodding to apply or any encouragement to commit. I knew instinctively I would do anything to go.

I am spending my year in Senegal. College will have to wait.

Tess Langan graduated from Verona High School, in Verona, N.J., last June.

QUESTIONS FOR RHETORICAL ANALYSIS

1. **CONSIDERING THE RHETORICAL SITUATION:** What does Langan assume her readers already know about the subjects she mentions?
2. How does Langan manage to keep a reader's attention in spite of the fact that the story is typical and familiar to many?
3. Describe Langan's voice. If you were on an admissions committee, would this essay stand out?

QUESTIONS FOR WRITING AND DISCUSSION

1. How did you feel about the end? Were you surprised? Is it a flaw in the writing that she ends up in a different place than the reader expects?
2. What does Langan leave unstated in this piece? What is she implying?
3. Why does Langan include all the details—about the ice cream, and stir-fry vegetables, and the rest?

STYLE PRACTICE: IMITATION

Write one paragraph of a first-person experience you have had that others have shared. Use details to make the experience individual to you and yet familiar at the same time.

Smoke

Jessica Polanski

Jessica Polanski wrote this essay to apply for a scholarship to a school of public health. She relates her personal experiences directly to her purpose for the application essay and describes in precise detail so her readers will have a specific and detailed picture in their minds—a technique that makes her essay hard to forget.

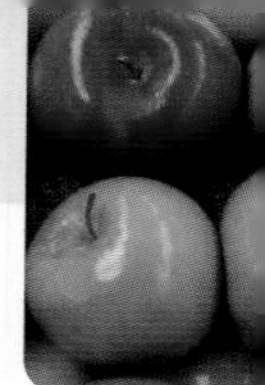

As LONG as I can remember, someone in my house was always smoking a cigarette. My mother would have one smoldering in an ashtray next to her as she read the newspaper while my father would be smoking in another room. He even smoked while he was changing clothes. He would be smoking as he rushed to get out of his overalls, coated with oil from the shift at Midas Mufflers and into his bartender clothes. I often wondered how he didn't catch fire.

It was what I was used to; the smell of cigarette smoke was for me the smell of home. Smoking was what my hard-working mother, father, and grandparents did to relax.

> "The smell of cigarette smoke was for me the smell of home."

Many people in my town in Pennsylvania are smokers. There were so many, in fact, that you routinely see the medical supply truck stop at three or for houses on the same block, delivering oxygen to elderly people, many of whom have emphysema – a preventable disease, one you only get from smoking. Everywhere you go you can see people with tubes leading from their noses, behind their ears, and over to portable oxygen tanks: in grocery stores, in cars, at Bingo, and at my family reunions.

The first of my relatives to die of cigarette-smoking-related ailments was my grandfather, who succumbed to heart failure at 67. His doctors had been urging him to quit smoking for years. I remember him when he was near the end of his life, lying almost motionless on the hospital bed they installed in his living room, the way he would get my grandmother to prop him up with pillows and folded-up blankets so he could smoke a cigarette. He was too weak to light up by himself.

My grandmother died of cancer about two years later. It was then I finalized my decision to work in a field that would help people fight addictive behaviors. I'm not naïve enough to think that my grandparents didn't know smoking was bad for them. Who doesn't know that? Still, though the message was out there, it didn't get through to them. The fact that friends of mine are already hooked on cigarettes, despite all the information that's out there about the dangers, also makes me determined to work in the field of Public Health Education and concentrate on smoking cessation programs. I think I can make a difference: help inform and motivate people, and help them lead longer, and maybe happier lives. Receiving a School of Public Health scholarship will help me take my first step toward my goal.

QUESTIONS FOR RHETORICAL ANALYSIS

1. **CONSIDERING THE RHETORICAL SITUATION:** how does Jessica speak to her readers? What makes her writing seem authentic and honest? What technique does Jessica use to get attention?
2. What do we learn about Jessica in this essay besides the fact that she grew up sharing a house with smokers, and that smoking is harmful and she is committed to raising awareness about the dangers? How do those additional details define her as a person, as worthy of a scholarship?
3. Describe the voice of this essay. Comment on Jessica's choice of language like "smoking cessation programs." Does this seem out of place? Is it helpful? How and why?

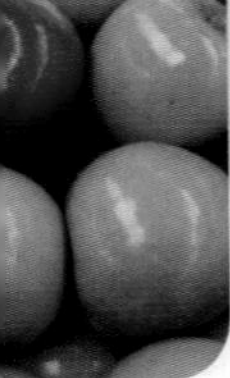

QUESTIONS FOR WRITING AND DISCUSSION

1. What are the risks of taking a stand that your reader might personally disagree with? For example, if you have a view point that is controversial, could this have an effect on your reader? Which topics might you consider too controversial to tackle?
2. Can we learn too much about a personal in an application essay? What sort of material would you avoid in your essay?

STYLE PRACTICE: IMITATION

In a paragraph, describe an experience you had that motivated you to do something. Do not explain why or how you were motivated, though. Allow the description to move your reader emotionally as well as logically towards seeing what inspired your choice.

In 500 Words or Less[2]

Anny Chih

Anny Chih applied for the "best job in the world" with Tourism, Queensland in Australia with this "500 words or less" essay.

A DANDELION. That's how my best friend in high school described me. At first I wondered if I should be insulted – it is a weed after all, and a pesky one at that! But after she explained why, I thought it was the best one-word description I could've been given.

"Have you ever tried to pull a dandelion out of the ground?" she asked. A dandelion is strong and stubborn. Once it's decided to grow somewhere, there's no stopping it. "No matter how high the altitude or how rough the climate, a dandelion will thrive in the environment it's given" she explained. And in the spring when a dandelion has decided to move on, "it can go anywhere the wind will blow." A dandelion is bright, strong, determined, carefree, and full of potential. "You're a dandelion" she said to me.

My roots are Taiwanese but I sprouted in the states during a trip my mom had taken to visit relatives. At the time, my parents and two older siblings, Angela and Andy, were living on a desert off the coast of Chile where my dad worked as a factory manager producing motorcycle parts. Being piggybacked up sand dunes was probably a lot of fun, but in 1988 we settled our roots in the lush West Coast city of Burnaby, BC Canada. Once Angela, Andy and I grew up though, my parents began travelling the world again and now spend a good portion of their time in Asia.

While planted in Burnaby to finish my degree in Marketing and Entrepreneurship from Simon Fraser University, I worked in a variety of customer service and administrative roles. My sunny outlook on life and exceptional organizational skills allowed me to flourish in both school and work where I eventually began taking on more

[2]Anny Chih, "The Best Job in the World: In 500 Words or Less," Posted by Anny Chih on annychih.com. Reprinted with permission.

managerial responsibilities at a medical clinic, while continuing my regular volunteer activities.

BC is the ideal place to grow a bright dandelion. We have hundreds of hiking trails rich with flora, stunning ocean views, and great easygoing people. But, by the time I graduated I was just itching to get out and explore the rest of the world. The wind blew me all the way to Vladivostok and across Russia on a solo adventure. Family and friends tried to convince me not to go, but being as stubborn as I am and determined to see the world, I went anyway. It was the best decision I've ever made, and one that taught me that the most important thing in life is just to live it.

David Koscheck/shutterstock.com

I hope that the next gust of wind will take me to Queensland, Australia with my sister Angela and brother-in-law Morten. They are the most down-to-earth, supportive and considerate people around. They also happen to know just the right angles to make any dandelion look like a pretty flower.

QUESTIONS FOR RHETORICAL ANALYSIS

Watch a video application for the same position: http://www.youtube.com/watch?v=m45nZbcEKRA&feature=related.

1. **CONSIDERING THE RHETORICAL SITUATION:** both the essay and the video have the same audience and purpose. How does the choice of medium—a video or an essay— affect each candidate's personal message?
2. What kinds of personal detail does each applicant include? What picture do those details paint about the applicant?
3. How would you describe the tone of the essay versus the tone of the video? Point to specific word choices the author uses to create that tone.
4. Identify the big idea in each candidate's application.
5. Describe the structure the writer chooses? Does the video use a similar structure?

QUESTIONS FOR WRITING AND DISCUSSION

1. What are the risks of including a video with your application? What are the benefits?
2. Which applicant would you give the job if you had to choose? Defend your views on which application is more successful and why?

STYLE PRACTICE: IMITATION

Write the first 100 words of an application for a job you would love to have. Include dialogue.

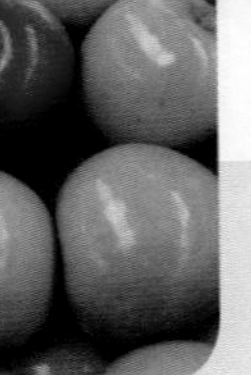

WRITING AND REVISION STRATEGIES

Three interactive sections here will help as you write, revise, and think about the design of your application.

- Writer's Notebook Suggestions
- Peer Editing Log
- Revision Checklist

WRITER'S NOTEBOOK SUGGESTIONS

These short exercises are intended to jump-start your thinking as you begin to write your application essay.

1. Write a letter of recommendation for yourself.
2. You have been asked to go back to your former high school and give a useful two-minute speech to the senior class. Write the speech.
3. Describe your single best asset in one paragraph. Do not brag, but sell yourself.
4. List all the things you wish to accomplish in the next five years.
5. Give one example of a time when you succeeded against the odds.
6. Write one paragraph explaining a disappointment and how it affected you.
7. Write about an experience that made you aware of a skill you have.
8. Write a paragraph about one goal you have. Be as specific as possible.
9. Link a personal experience with a career goal, in 300 words or fewer.
10. Create a visual image (a short video, a collage, a drawing) that communicates something about who you are.

PEER REVIEW LOG

As you work with a writing partner or in a peer review group, you can use these questions to give helpful responses to a classmate's application essay and as a guide for discussion.

Writer's Name: ______________________________

Date: ______________________________

1. Underline the essay's thesis. Make suggestions to strengthen it by rewording it or placing it elsewhere.
2. Put brackets around the introduction. Does the introduction announce the topic clearly?

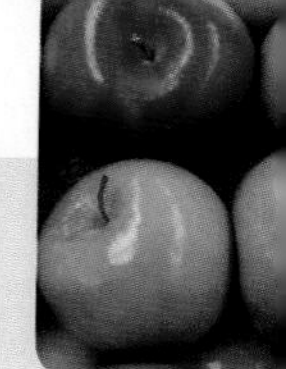

3. If there is a prompt, has the introduction addressed the prompt specifically?
4. What development strategies does the writer use? Can you suggest specific places where narrative detail or supporting evidence might strengthen the essay?
5. Put brackets around the conclusion. What impression does it leave? Suggest ways for the writer to strengthen the final impression.
6. Put wavy lines under any application clichés the writer has used; put check marks next to any language you find particularly fresh and appealing.

REVISION CHECKLIST

As you do your final revision, check to make sure that you

- Stated your thesis clearly and accurately
- Wrote an engaging and focused introduction
- Clearly answered the prompt, if there was one
- Organized the body of the paper in a logical pattern
- Used elements of narration, analysis, and argumentation where appropriate
- Wrote in a personal yet not informal voice
- Avoided using application essay clichés
- Concluded with the impression you wanted to leave with your reader
- Wrote a memorable essay that reflects some aspect of your values, interests, and personality

TEXACO
COLLEGE
COLLEGE
LUTHER
TEXACO

Writing A Narrative

Kate Burak

MEMOIRS

> If you speak with passion, many of us will listen. We need stories to live, all of us. We live story by story. Yours enlarges the circle.
>
> —Richard Rhodes

Stories wallpaper our daily lives. Think of how many times a day you hear stories—in the news, in songs, in advertisements—in all media, new and old. So much information comes to us in the form of narrative because people have always found stories irresistible and memorable. They entertain us and teach us. They give us a laugh. They make us cry. Good stories mark the memory. They leave footprints.

We watch movies and read fiction and nonfiction books because we like the feeling of getting lost in a story. Sometimes we do not care whether we remember details or whether the story has deep significance. But the best stories, the ones that leave marks, are well told and offer something beneath the surface action. These provide not just a record of what happened but also a reason for listening to the story and understanding why it matters.

Memoirs are true stories, nonfiction narratives. They engage readers the way fiction does, by taking them into scenes. Films use the same techniques, creating scenes that show more than they tell. Think of pictures, like the snapshots on these pages, as small scenes from a memory book. Memoirs are personal like these photos—and certainly they also record a time and place in someone's life.

WHAT'S TO COME

PROCESS PLAN

PROCESS PLAN

PREPARE

- Choose a true story with personal meaning, maybe about a transformational moment or series of events.
- Figure out the best structure: chronology, flashback, flashforward, another?
- Choose key scenes to render in detail. Do some research about when the story took place. What else was happening in the world?

DRAFT

- Introduction: Create scenes through detail and description. Introduce characters, create the conflict.
- Body: Develop the plot logically and incrementally. Bring the story to some high point of tension, the climax.
- Conclusion: Resolve the conflict subtly with an image or a line of dialogue that resonates and reinforces the theme.

REVISE

- Clarify your theme. What is the bigger picture? Seed in the theme.
- Add details or images that reinforce the theme.
- Be sure your title points your reader toward your theme.

UNDERSTANDING THE WRITING PROJECT

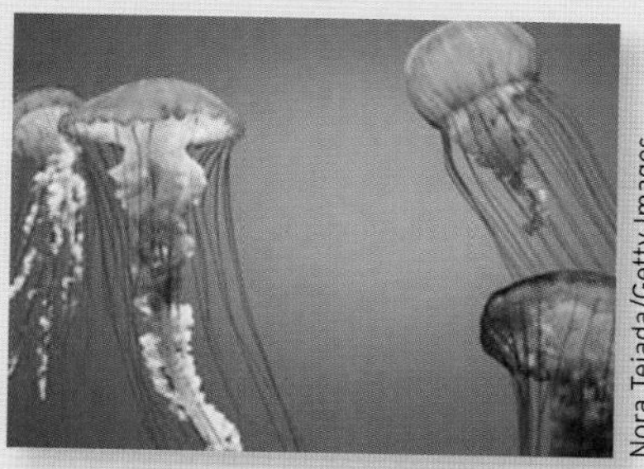
Nora Tejada/Getty Images

YOUR MEMOIR is not private writing. You are telling a story that has to have meaning for your readers as well as for yourself. People read to be entertained and informed, but with memoirs, people are interested in the fact that the story is true, that it really happened. Part of the appeal is the knowledge that the same thing could happen to them—or that maybe in some way, on some level, it already has. This thematic connection with the reader gives memoirs their universal appeal.

Because narratives are both engaging and personal, you can use them to persuade people when you write proposals, brochures, and letters for work or for community service. You have probably read many letters of appeal, for example, that begin with testimonials, true stories that relate personal or eyewitness accounts. Such stories often engage readers' emotions while also establishing the writer's credibility.

Narratives about you or about someone else reveal an insider's knowledge of time periods and cultural experiences. Narrative writing is not just for memoirs; it can add color, provide evidence, and persuade readers as you examine your values or cultural identity or compose an oral history or historical profile.

ASSIGNMENT Write a memoir, a true story about some part of your life. Your story can relate a single event or a series of closely linked events. Show a change of

Access an interactive eBook, and chapter-specific interactive learning tools, including flashcards, quizzes, videos and more in your English CourseMate via www.cengagebrain.com.

mind or heart, a discovery, a confirmation or contradiction of a belief, a disappointment, or a decision. Include the following narrative elements:

- scenes full of detail and imagery
- characters with motivation and depth
- incremental, logical development of the plot
- conflict and theme

Another possible way to tell your story is to use both words and images as you might see in a graphic novel. The DIY section of this chapter (page 150) will give you some pointers.

ANATOMY OF A MEMOIR

WRITER ANTONYA NELSON remembers the time she was fired from her waitressing job.

All Washed Up[1]

ANTONYA NELSON

My boss that summer prided himself on having kissed all the waitresses. According to others, he had made them all cry. I swore that he would neither kiss me nor make me cry.

announcement of conflict

This was a busy restaurant-bar in tourist-laden Telluride, Colorado. My job was to bus tables and wash dishes. I also played first base for the restaurant's softball team. At eighteen, I wasn't old enough to wait tables and serve drinks; at eighteen, I was still living in my parents' summer house, so my work felt casual. I had another job, at the local historical museum, where the crazy curator was constantly giving me pieces of the exhibits, like double-headed railroad spikes or articles of a prostitute's clothing. I would take the gifts home, then sneak them back the next day. At night, I worked at the restaurant.

setup

why mention? effect?

[1]Antonya Nelson, "All Washed Up," as appeared in The New Yorker, April 21 & 28, 2003, p. 152. Reprinted by permission of Frederick Hill Associates.

Like the waitresses, I divided my time between the public front and the private kitchen. Like the waitresses, I was a girl. But, unlike them, I didn't feel superior to the bartenders (front) or the cooks (kitchen), nor did I receive tips. I was not only the worst-paid but also the youngest staff member, which encouraged avuncular treatment from the men—the bartenders would send me shots of tequila, which I tossed down in between sending loads of steins through the Hobart. The waitresses liked to bestow advice—depilatory, pharmacological, chauvinistic. They thought I was pretty good at softball, and I didn't present a threat in the restaurant, stuck as I was elbow-deep in sludgy black water.

That busy kitchen combination of steam, grease, and tequila was heady and golden. The cooks fought with one another, dashed outside to get stoned, retreated to the walk-in to feed their munchies, and argued volubly about skiing or women or spices; about the bluegrass festival at the town park; about our boss, who was universally disliked but not universally understood. Some of these people intended to remain in the restaurant business. My status as temporary drudge made me stand out—that and a lack of humility. I was a college student; I had places to go when the summer ended.

theme

first plot point

On the night that I was fired, James Taylor was singing in the park. He'd seen fire and he'd seen rain.... My back was quacked from softball—a torqued swing had sent me into a cataclysmic spasm—and I couldn't haul the pony keg up from the basement. So I got one of the cooks to help, along with the drug-addled brother of my boss's silent partner; I recruited my own brother, two years younger, to haul the trays of beer steins to me from the front. I was still running the dishwasher. And I was still slamming shots. When the boss—nicknamed the Fireplug, two inches shorter than I, a dead cigar always between his lips—took me to task, I pointed out that I'd covered for myself rather than phoning in injured. Who cared if my brother wasn't on the payroll, or that No Man, the cook, had temporarily been away from his burners? But the Fireplug didn't see it that way.

I should have told him what I knew about the damage his vengeful staff had done behind his back. They'd contaminated pots of soup and tubs of dressing, thrown away dozens of plates and sets of cutlery, played bombs away with brandy snifters. They swindled and overcharged, sneaked in after hours to eat and steal, refused to wash their hands or scour the cutting surfaces, had sex in the walk-in. Flabbergasted and tongue-tied, attempting to say "I quit" before he said "You're fired," I didn't have the chance to rat on the others. I did, however, let him know that, as far as I was concerned, earning a college degree meant never having to work for someone like him again.

telling

continues next page

We'd been having this conversation at the sink. He turned to the busy kitchen and whistled it quiet. "Hey," he yelled. "How many of you went to college?" Everyone there raised a hand—even the dimwit brother of the silent partner. *showing: details*

"We're gonna miss you, First Base," my boss announced as he rocked forward and delivered a liver-lipped, ashtray-flavored kiss to my chin. Then he disappeared into the dining room. That's how he brought me to tears.

conclusion My own brother merely shrugged when I called to him from the back door. Already, he was rolling up his sleeves, eying my tequila nuggets. He'd been hired on the spot to replace me. Up the hill I stormed, back to our house, where my family sat around the kitchen table playing bridge and drinking gin, the front door closed against the "caterwauling" coming from the festival grounds—James Taylor's encore. My little sister was pleased to see me; she was terrible at bridge, and got ragged in only when no one else was available. A visiting cousin, between semesters at Baylor, was her partner. He's the one who started the pitying refrain that has become part of family lore: "Nobody gets fired washing dishes."

"I have an internalized rhythm that means something to me. It dictates how I write, how I pattern sentences, what vocabulary I choose, and so on."

Q&A with Antonya Nelson

Discovering Voice and Developing Style in Narrative Writing

Q: Your memoir, "All Washed Up" reads a lot like a short story. It is sometimes hard for writers to imagine using a "real" event and making it into something that reads like a piece of fiction. How do you take real life and make it into art?

A: Sometimes I like to pose the opposite question: how can you write about something that hasn't happened to you, that you know nothing or care nothing about, and turn that into fiction? That seems like the more challenging task, especially the not caring part. Ideally, finding fiction in one's factual life means locating a stance that will accommodate genuine feeling, on the one hand, without hurting genuine feelings, on the other hand.

Q: Readers might notice your techniques of using parallel sentences, repeating certain phrases, and listing. Are you conscious of these techniques as you write, or are they part of your internal writing mechanism?

A: I'm pretty sure this is a matter of what we loosely call voice. I have an internalized rhythm that means something to me. It dictates how I write, how I pattern sentences, what vocabulary I choose, and so on. I know what sounds good to me. I'm sure I learned it reading books, reading aloud, hearing the spoken word when it's at its most seductive, and I'm sure I've attempted, pretty unconsciously, to channel that which pleases my own ear. I sing aloud in the car too. Sometimes I just chat at the dog.

Antonya Nelson

Scott S. Warren/National Geographic Society/Corbis

Q: Much of the story happens "off-screen" and is revealed in the form of exposition. How do you decide when to let the camera roll and show the action in a scene rather than [using] a "voice-over"?

A: Again, this has to do with some sense of being both writer and reader simultaneously. I tell my students this all the time: imagine you are reading what you are writing. What do you want (need) to know (hear) next? I really do believe in the internalized sense of pattern and variation, of some monitor lodged behind the reader/writer's eyes or brain or heart that dictates when a line of dialogue needs to emerge, when a repeated background note needs striking, when a sentence containing only one word needs to fall. There.

Q: Your voice in "All Washed Up" captures the essence of being eighteen and full of yourself, which is essential to the theme of the story. When you were learning the craft of storytelling, how did you go about finding a voice for yourself as a writer?

A: I imitated people for a long time. I still might be doing that. But I read enough people that the combo plate is pretty varied. I love Flannery O'Connor's precise humor. I love Carson McCullers's swampy psychotic emotional terrain. I love the scalpel-like descriptors of John Updike. I want David Sedaris's irreverence. I wish I had plot under control like Pete Dexter or Larry Brown or Elmore Leonard. I long for the dreamy, unstated business Mavis Gallant goes about. In short, I think I'm still an apprentice writer whose voice, insofar as I could claim it, has the virtues of the mutt: mixed breeding.

THE RHETORICAL SITUATION:
PERSONAL STORIES FOR PUBLIC AUDIENCES

Although memoirs are true stories, memoirists borrow techniques from fiction to make their stories feel personal to a public audience. They create scenes full of narrative detail—scenes that leave footprints in their readers' memories. They explore

themes that connect to their readers' lives. Some inexplicable chemistry of the elements in a story gives it the power to get and keep readers' attention and to make an impression. Compare these two versions of the same story.

NARRATIVE A

Ironically, it was a beautiful day, and I felt quite relaxed as I rode the train from upper Manhattan, and we passed by the more run-down buildings. Suddenly we came upon a gruesome scene. A little boy had been hit by the train. A crowd of people stood around, as well as police and other rescue workers. Near me two men were playing a game of cards. This game of chance reminded me of the danger in the world: Life is a game of chance. As I thought about it, I noticed the men pay attention to the poor dead boy for just a second and then turn right back to their bridge game.

NARRATIVE B

One afternoon in late August, as the summer's sun streamed into the car and made little jumping shadows on the windows, I sat gazing out at the tenement-dwellers, who were themselves looking out of their windows from the gray crumbling buildings along the tracks of upper Manhattan.

As we crossed into the Bronx, the train unexpectedly slowed down for a few miles. Suddenly from out my window I saw a large crowd near the track, held back by two policemen. Then, on the other side from my window I saw a scene I would never be able to forget: a little boy almost severed in halves, lying at an incredible angle near the track. The ground was covered with blood, and the boy's eyes were opened wide, strained and disbelieving in his sudden oblivion. A policeman stood next to him, his arms folded, staring straight ahead at the windows of our train. In the orange glow of late afternoon the policemen, the crowd, [and] the corpse of the boy were for a brief moment immobile, motionless, a small tableau to violence and death in the city.

Behind me, in the next row of seats, there was a game of bridge. I heard one of the four men say as he looked at the sight, "God, that's horrible." Another said, in a whisper, "Terrible, terrible." There was a momentary silence, punctuated only by the clicking of the wheels on the track. Then, after the pause, I heard the first man say: "Two hearts."

—Willie Morris, *North Toward Home*

Narrative A provides information about an incident but does not invite you into its world. The writing does not create a sense of place, nor does it put you in the middle of a scene. Though explaining can be important in making a vague point

clear, when you write a narrative, you want to *show*, rather than tell, all you can. You want to roll the tape, run the movie.

On the other hand, in Narrative B writer Willie Morris uses description to invite you into a scene and create a mood. The opening takes you to a specific moment, place, and mood, a late August afternoon on a train moving through the tenements of the Bronx. From this setting the story can progress.

People inhabit this setting. The narrator introduces himself as a train-rider, an observer of the scene about to unfold. Through his eyes you can see the tenement-dwellers and the tableau of the boy, the policemen, and the crowd. Then the writer shifts his and your attention to the four card players on the train. Morris creates many characters for such a brief story, but each plays a part in building the scene.

If you think of narratives as movies rather than as still photos, you can see why something must happen in order for a story to develop. Even though the story is very short, Morris lets the tape roll to show a specific picture: an unforgettable scene of the tragic death of a small boy. Vivid pictures like this create the footprints.

Morris creates a setting and moves characters into it. Something happens there: a story filled with tension unfolds. By the end of the story, the meaning of this scene emerges. Memoir—like other exploratory writing—does not always have an explicit thesis. When we think of thesis for a work like a memoir, we talk about its *theme.* When you begin, you might have a theme in mind for your memoir. It should provide an insight into who you are, but at the same time reveal something universal to which your reader can relate. Even in a scene as brief as this one, you can see the elements of story: setting, character, conflict, and the way the theme is a cumulative result of the story that has been told, a part of the process of exploration.

CREATING A VIVID PICTURE: SHOWING AND TELLING

Storytelling invites your reader to enter a world that you create. A memoir should allow your reader to experience your story as it happens, as you, the narrator, may have experienced it in real life. Mark Twain advised writers, "Don't say the old lady screamed. Bring her on and let her scream." However, "show; don't tell" is one of those rules that may be easier to understand than to do. Writing your memoir is a prime time to practice this skill.

If you want to evoke a feeling, description and well chosen detail should lead your reader to that feeling. But, not every moment in a memoir needs to be created in such detail. Sometimes you might need to get from one time period to another with a quick explanation rather than a descriptive scene, and so you might summarize or use internal

PRACTICE 6.1

Six-Word Memoir

Write a true story in six words. Ernest Hemingway wrote: "For Sale: Baby shoes, never worn."

Here are some other examples from a collection of six-word memoirs ("Not Quite What I Was" from *Smith Magazine*, edited by Rachel Fershleiser and Larry Smith, Harper Perennial, 2008):

Bad brakes discovered at high speed. (Johan Baumeister)

Watching quietly from every door frame. (Nicole Resseguie)

I asked. They answered. I wrote. (Sebastian Junger)

Nobody cared, then they did. Why? (Chuck Klosterman)

Never really finished anything, except cake. (Carletta Perkins)

Student Diana Yin wrote:

Youngest of 14 kids; was skinny.

On page 142 you can see a six-word memoir accompanied by a photo that illustrates the story.

PRACTICE 6.2

Show and Tell: Read this scenario.

> Fifteen-year-old Angela is arguing with her mother. She wants to wear a tight purple tube top to school. Her mother has forbidden her to wear revealing clothing and will not let Angela out of the house until she changes.

Write a short scene using description and dialogue to show and using summary and internal monologue to tell. Choose one point of view to write from—Angela's, her mother's, her father's, her sibling's, or her best friend, who is waiting to walk with her to school.

monologue to clue your reader into what you are thinking. "Showing" can emphasize a moment while "telling" allows you to fast-forward over unimportant details.

SUMMARY: TELLS

Summary can give you a chance to advance the story to an episode or scene that you want to focus on. Summary will not offer pictures for your reader to remember, so you should keep it to a minimum, using it as a transitional device to connect moments and to help your story flow.

> Later that night I called each member of my mother's family. I assured them that the accident was minor. At that point, nobody could know what would happen one month later.

NARRATIVE DESCRIPTION: SHOWS

Narrative description puts you into a scene the way a camera would. Every detail you mention becomes significant to your reader. Detail slows down the movement of the story, focusing carefully on the moment. Use narrative description to emphasize dramatic and important moments.

> Sophie stood shivering on the porch. Her eyeliner was smeared, and her hair was slicked back by the rain. Her light jacket clung to her sharp, bony shoulders. As she started to speak, the thunder roared. I could see her mouth moving, but I could not make out the words.

INTERNAL MONOLOGUE: TELLS

Internal monologue is like the voice-over in a film. It is the script of what is going on in your head. Use it sparingly to add drama or to help clarify a scene. Remember that this type of explaining will not create pictures your reader can remember.

> I wondered why my father would be up so late. Did he know about the argument? I wished I had one of those dads who works all the time and never pays attention to what is going on in the house.

DIALOGUE: SHOWS

Use dialogue to reveal character, not to provide information. You can combine full dialogue with summary to advance the dialogue. Write conversations or parts of conversations rather than speeches.

> "Where is the car key?" I asked, opening the door.
> "In the ignition," she said.
> "You keep the key in the ignition?"
> "No, of course not," I said. "I would not keep the key in the ignition. It is stuck."

Kate Burak

For more on the snapshots in this chapter, see Visual Literacy: Snapshots, page 138.

RESEARCH PATHS: FINDING DETAILS THAT BRING YOUR STORY TO LIFE

Recalling the cultural and historical details of a time period can enrich the texture of a story. It can also help to create a sense of place—not just a physical place but also a place in time. Time markers can provide a larger context for your story and help deepen your theme, the central insight you embed in your story. One student, writing about a particularly disappointing moment for her that occurred in February 2002, used an image of American flags as a backdrop to her story. She described the flags as tattered from having been displayed all winter after the patriotic awakening brought on by the terrorist attacks of September 11, 2001. Though the narrative had little to do with patriotism, the image added historical context and depth to her story about expectations and being let down.

VISUAL LITERACY: SNAPSHOTS

THE ILLUSTRATIONS in this chapter are personal photos—the kind that people keep on their refrigerators and in little frames on their desks or nightstands. These images take people back to places and times they want to remember always. Choose one of these pictures, describe what you see, and give reasons why this photo might be important to its owner. Find a snapshot that is important to you, and write about the moment that it freezes. Write in the present tense.

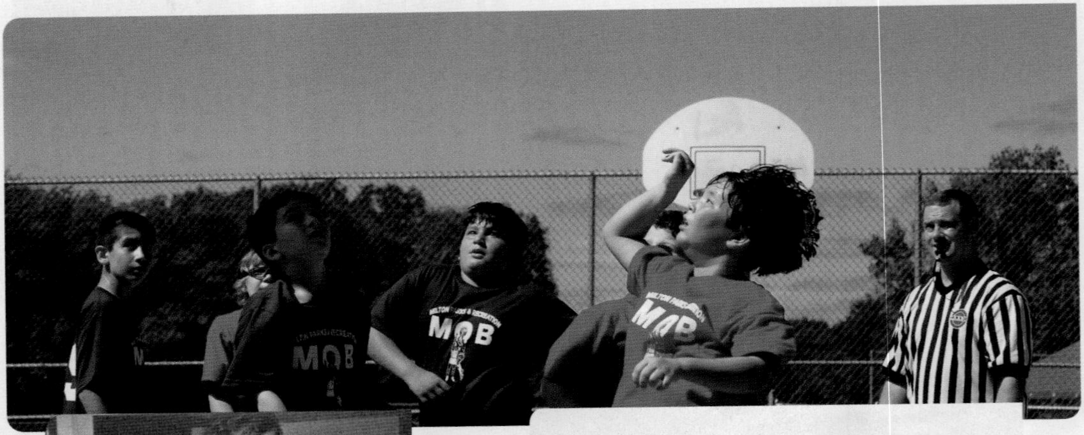

Elizabeth "Yoshi" Makishima

007 by Smith Magazine. Reprinted by permission of HarerCollins Publisher, photo Elliott David

©unshovelingthepast.blogspot.com/Sarah Ambrose

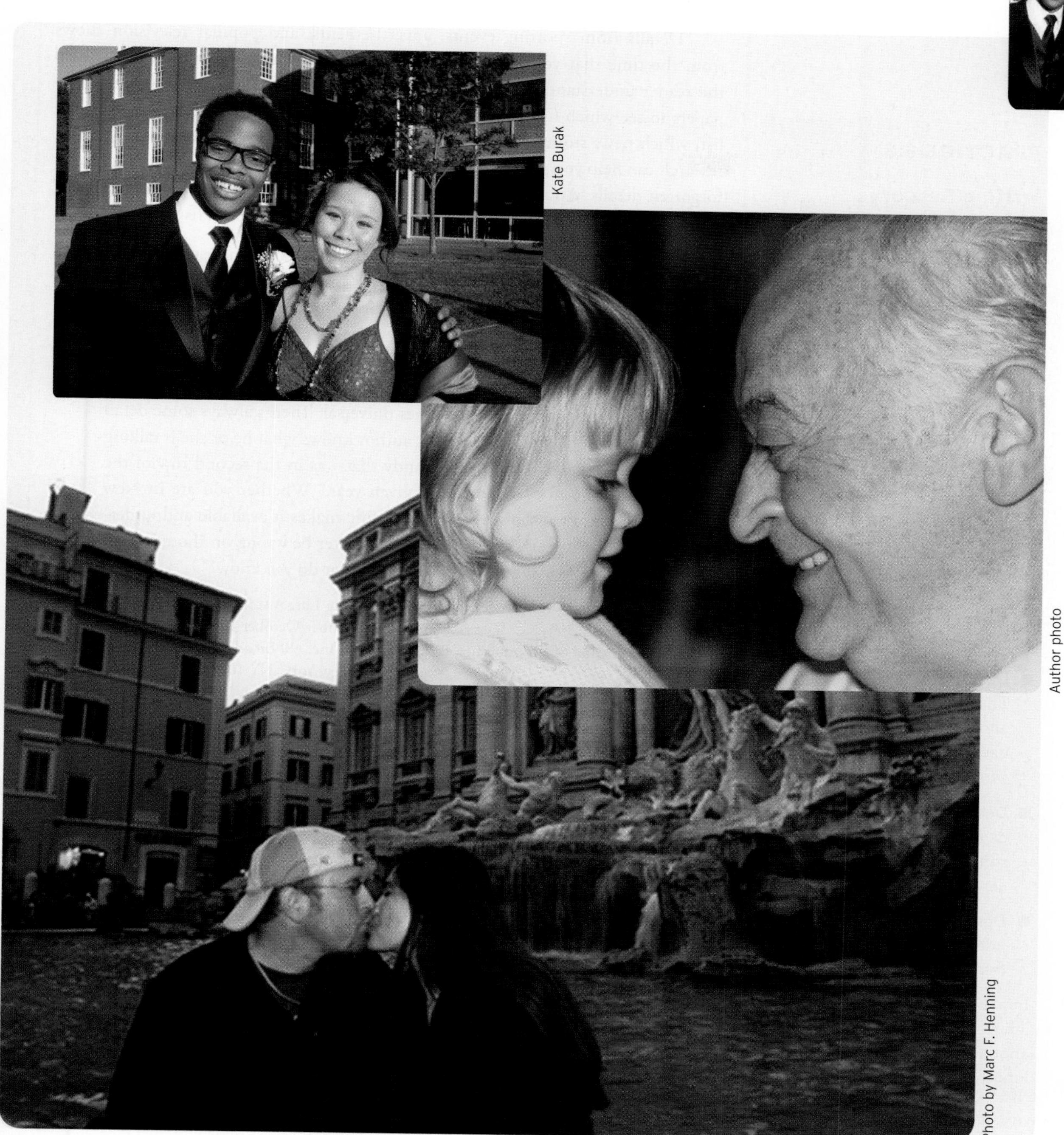

Kate Burak

Author photo

Photo by Marc F. Henning

Details from sporting events, advertisements, and popular television shows from the time that you are writing about can add irony or humor and can help the reader understand characters in your story. Consult old magazines and newspapers to see which films were being reviewed, which books were on the bestseller list, which news stories were in the headlines, and which songs were popular. This research can help you gather details for your story and jog your memory about long-forgotten details. An interviewer once asked Pete Hamill, author of the memoir *A Drinking Life*, how he captured the Brooklyn of his childhood. His response:

> You can get help with memory. You can look at old newspapers. You can listen to the music that was played. In my case, I got the *Billboard* lists for the different years I was writing about and made tapes. I went to oldies record shops like Colony Records on Broadway. I would be driving with the tape player on, and it would create whole rooms, you know? I think if you get the details right, if you get the thing very specific, it inadvertently becomes universal. There's always some detail that someone says, "Damn, the author knows what he or she is talking about. That was the kind of candy that was in the second row of the candy store in New York in a given year." Whether you are in New York or Tokyo, the sense of the specific makes it available and understandable. It feels true. You can't as a writer be wrong on those things. Otherwise, you'll get letters saying, "What do *you* know?"
>
> —Carolyn T. Hughes, "A Thinking Life: A Conversation With Pete Hamill," *Poets & Writers Magazine*, September/October 1999. Reprinted by permission of the publisher, Poets & Writers Inc., 90 Broad Street, Suite 2100, New York, NY 10004. www.pw.org.

Pay attention to all the details you can gather from a source published on the date of your memoir. If you can, get a local newspaper or check the headlines on a "This Day in History" Web site for the place where your story was set, and look at the weather for that day and the forecast for the next day. A brewing storm and an unusually warm February day can be authentic details and can possibly add thematic significance to your story.

Talk to your friends about what they remember about the time period. What were the trends? The gossip of the time? What music would have been playing on the radio?

PRACTICE 6.3

Writing Sensory Description

This exercise is based on the game "Taboo," in which certain words are banned. The object of the exercise is to write descriptions without using taboo words. Here are some practice examples using the five senses:

- Describe the feeling of getting into a hot car on a summer day. Do not use *hot, heat, burning, sun,* or *melt*.
- Describe the sounds of waking up in the morning. Do not use *clock, ring, buzz, shower,* or *birds*.
- Describe the smell of Thanksgiving (or choose another holiday). Do not use *turkey, good, delicious, warm,* or *sweet*.
- Describe the look of a rainy day. Do not use *gray, drops, rain, water, puddle,* or *clouds*.
- Describe the taste of orange juice. Do not use *sweet, sour, fresh,* or *acid*.

In pairs or groups, create challenges like the ones above for another group. Exchange challenges and write descriptions.

NARRATIVE ELEMENTS: SETTING, CONFLICT, CHARACTER, POINT OF VIEW

Every story happens in a specific place, is inhabited by characters who have to overcome some kind of obstacle, and is told from a particular vantage point. These essential elements of narrative are setting, conflict, character, and point of view.

SETTING

The setting is the time, place, and social or cultural context of a story. Most memoir writers establish the setting early in the piece to bring the reader more fully into the remembered place. In the excerpt from *North Towards Home* (page 134), Willie Morris sets the mood for his commuter train ride with a sense of late summer and the hypnotic shadows of the train. The larger elements of the city and the impersonal way people sometimes treat each other in cities also are essential in understanding the meaning of the story.

Consider the setting of a rundown horse stable. Stables in general might make you think of the daily chores of farm life or the privileges of the wealthy. But the following description of the horse stable at the Diamond D Ranch creates an "air of neglect."

> No one at Diamond D knew how to properly care for horses. Most of the animals were kept outside in three small, grassless corrals. The barn was on the verge of collapse; our every entry was accompanied by the fluttering sounds of startled rats. The "staff" consisted of a bunch of junior high and high school kids willing to work in exchange for riding privileges. And the main source of income, apart from the pony parties, was hacking—renting out the horses for ten dollars an hour to anyone willing to pay. Mrs. Daniels bought the horses at an auction whose main customer was the meat dealer for a dog-food company; Diamond D, more often than not, was merely a way station. The general air of neglect surrounding the stable was the result more of ignorance than of apathy. It's not as if we didn't care about the horses—we simply didn't know any better.
>
> —Lucy Greely, *Autobiography of a Face*

A story can also be set at a particular time. In the following example, a brutal winter becomes the setting for a story about finding shelter—in a literal and a figurative sense.

> Winter was like a dark and endless tunnel I entered when I left the house for school. The clouds pulled themselves down around me, reducing clear sky to a place just above my head. I could almost touch those gray clouds that blotted out the sun for weeks and weeks on end. The cold was sometimes so intense that my nostrils would freeze, sticking together, and the coldness could transform the snow. There were days when it did not melt, or adhere to anything, but lasted as a fine powder that squeaked under my boots. The prowling winds skulked through the maze of buildings of the housing project where I lived, waiting behind corners to attack, to shoot icy blasts up my nose, down my throat. And then there was inside.
>
> —Connie Porter, "GirlGirlGirl"

IBM brat broke back; twins, Mac.

–John Hockenberry

"IBM brat broke back; twins, Mac" is a six-word memoir from Larry Smith's *Not Quite What I Was Planning and Other Six-World Memoirs*.

CHARACTER

Creating character through dialogue

You are the narrator of your memoir, and in telling your story, you communicate how the experience affected you, how it mattered to you, and how it changed you. You introduce the other characters and show their actions and their personalities.

The people in your memoir are characters with needs, motivations, and choices. They can act and react, change or refuse to change. In Willie Morris's scene, the main characters are the card players who are as anonymous as the boy who is killed by the train. This anonymity helps express the theme of the story—namely, how impersonal tragedy can be. The true center of Morris's tale, though, is the speaker, the person who observes the action and understands the irony of the bridge player's comment, "Two hearts."

As a narrator, you need not explain your feelings or explain at length about the characters. Instead, you are a lens for the action. Your goal is to show, not tell. Rather than tell the reader what you are thinking through internal monologue or explain what a character is like, you reveal character through details or incidents. Rather than explaining, imagine how you would film such material. Keep asking, "What is my movie showing now?"

Not every character in your story has to be fully developed. Some minor characters will be in the story simply to move the plot along. The police officer with the big sunglasses that made him look like a bug, the one who gave you the speeding ticket on the fateful day when you also got caught running a red light, will appear only for a moment. Still, all characters require careful attention. They should be clearly drawn and have clear motivation. What they do develops logically from *who* they are.

Dialogue allows the reader to hear the characters' voices, letting the writer reveal characters effectively through their own words. The challenge of using dialogue in a memoir is trying to stay true to your memory while selecting just the right language to reveal character. The reader will not expect you to remember the exact words you uttered five or ten years ago or even a month ago, but the reader will expect you to recreate conversations as accurately as possible.

People have "signatures" in their speech—words, gestures, pauses, or subject matter that reveal who they are. Think about how people actually speak. One character might say "like" a lot or ramble from one subject to another. Another might pause often, be evasive, answer questions with few words, or repeat questions. Dialogue can highlight personality and emotion and can create drama.

Punctuating Dialogue

Here are a few tips on the technical aspects of writing dialogue:

- Begin a new paragraph with each new speaker.
- Put quotation marks around each speaker's words.

(continued)

PRACTICE 6.4

Description of Character

In the following passage author David Eggers describes a trick his mother often did.

> She used to do a trick where it looked like she would be pulling off her thumb, when in fact she was not. Do you know this trick? Part of one's right thumb is made to look like part of one's left hand and then is slid up and down the index finger of the left finger—attached, then detached. It's an unsettling trick, and more so when my mother used to do it, because she did it in a way where her hands shook, vibrated, her neck's veins protruding and taut, her face gripped with the strain plausibly attendant to pulling off one's finger. As children we watched with both glee and terror.
>
> —*David Eggers, A Heartbreaking Work of Staggering Genius*

Describe a character you know by writing a passage about one physical feature, gesture, or habit.

Punctuating Dialogue (continued)

- Place periods and commas inside the quotation marks.

"All right," I said, "I will walk with you."

- Place a question mark and an exclamation mark inside quotation marks if the quotation is itself a question or an exclamation. Place the question mark or exclamation mark outside the quotation marks if the sentence around the quotation poses the question or makes an exclamation.

"When can we start walking?" she asked.
"When did you say, "I would rather drive"?
"I want to go now!" she said.

- Use *said* or *says* for most attributions.

PRACTICE 6.5

Dialogue

1. To understand how dialogue reveals character, go to a public place—a café, a dining hall, a bus, a subway car, a lecture hall—and eavesdrop on a conversation. Write down as much of the conversation as you can in ten or fifteen minutes.
2. As soon as possible, rewrite the conversation, adding all the details about setting, appearance, gestures, and tone of voice that you can remember.
3. Read over this version of the conversation, and write a paragraph about what the speakers' language reveals about them. Focus less on content and more on who dominates the conversation, how colorful or dull their words are, how expressive or monotonous their voices are, and what their verbal idiosyncrasies are.
    a. What can you tell about each speaker's character from this dialogue?
    b. Which pieces of dialogue would you choose to reveal a specific personality?
    c. Which sections of dialogue would you eliminate?

CONFLICT

The struggle, search, or mystery that drives the story forward comes from internal or external conflict. Conflicts can originate from inside (such as when you begin to outgrow a friend) or from outside (as when your parents say that they are getting a divorce and that you must decide with whom you will live). Once introduced, conflict advances through scenes. The conflict gets more complicated as the main character encounters obstacles along the way. This development of conflict is the backbone of a narrative, and it must develop incrementally and logically.

A character requires motivation to grapple with a conflict and also needs to have a stake in the outcome. Think about telling a story about becoming so fed up with a frustrating boss that you quit your job. The story could center around your personal conflict: Should you quit the job and suffer the consequences of unemployment? What is your motivation to quit? You may have been harassed or felt intimidated. The stakes also need to be clear. If you quit, you have to change your lifestyle, live on less, or perhaps move home. Readers want to know why the conflict is important. The motivation and stakes create the tension and reveal the significance of the conflict.

POINT OF VIEW

Art students will tell you that the most difficult assignment—and they are almost always given this assignment in a beginning drawing class—is to draw a self-portrait. Drawing yourself is complicated not only because drawing and studying the shape and shadows of your own face are very difficult but also because objectifying yourself compounds the challenge. You are not used to looking at yourself from an emotional distance. Writing about yourself as a character is the same sort of challenge.

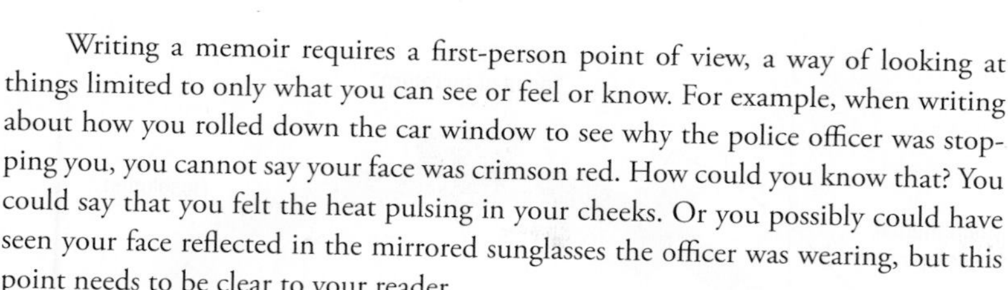

Writing a memoir requires a first-person point of view, a way of looking at things limited to only what you can see or feel or know. For example, when writing about how you rolled down the car window to see why the police officer was stopping you, you cannot say your face was crimson red. How could you know that? You could say that you felt the heat pulsing in your cheeks. Or you possibly could have seen your face reflected in the mirrored sunglasses the officer was wearing, but this point needs to be clear to your reader.

Your point of view might be limited to your knowledge and understanding at the time of the story: "I am looking at the officer for some signal that he is not mad. All I see is me, my red face, all guilty-looking, staring back at myself in his big, mirrored sunglasses."

You might also write in the first-person point of view that expresses an understanding of an event that has ripened with time:

> I looked at the police officer's face for some signal that he was not mad at me. I would not find out until later that the officer was my mom's high-school sweetheart and a really nice guy. At that moment all I saw was me, my red face, all guilty-looking, staring back at myself in his big, scary, mirrored sunglasses.

You cannot know what the officer is seeing (unless you see it, too) or thinking. "He thought I was a stupid kid" is expressed from a third-person point of view—*he*, not *I*, thought. You should use one point of view throughout a story unless you are experimenting with a special effect.

THE NARRATIVE ARC (PLOT): SET-UP, RISING ACTION, CLIMAX, RESOLUTION

All stories have to start somewhere and end somewhere else. As a writer, you have choices to make about where the story should begin and what the best structure would be to move the events to a satisfying conclusion. Whatever choices you make, the basic requirement of narrative order remains the same: that the story progresses incrementally, in steps.

A typical narrative structure has a beginning, a middle, and an end, making up a *narrative arc*. A narrative arc provides a visual map of a story, showing how writers typically build up tension to a climactic moment and then allow the tension to decrease to the story's resolution. A classical story arc looks like the arc on page 146.

Some writers emphasize different parts of the story and may make their readers wait to begin the climb. In the opening memoir in this chapter, "All Washed Up," Antonya Nelson spends the first half of the story on set-up. Her story arc might look more like the alternative story arc on page 146.

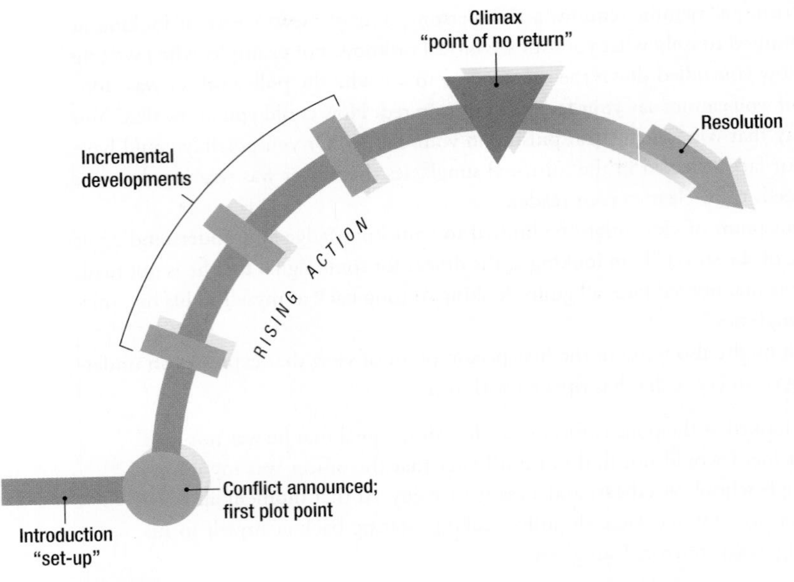

Conventional Story Arc

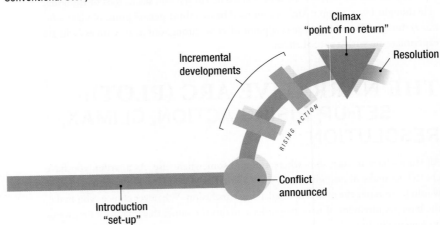

Climax
"point of no return"
Incremental
developments
Resolution
RISING ACTION
Conflict
announced
Introduction
"set-up"

Alternative Story Arc

You can structure your story in a number of ways. The most common is straight chronology, starting at the beginning and working your way through an event as it occurred. You can organize sections of your story by using flashbacks and flash-forwards. You might begin the story at the end as Bernard Cooper does in "Dream House," flashing forward and then moving back to the beginning. If you use this technique, be sure to provide clear transitions. Cooper tells us directly: "But none of this had happened yet." In effect, he restarts the story, using straight chronology this time.

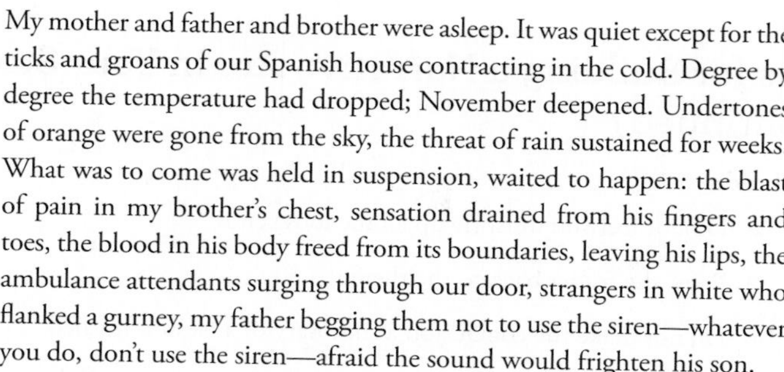

My mother and father and brother were asleep. It was quiet except for the ticks and groans of our Spanish house contracting in the cold. Degree by degree the temperature had dropped; November deepened. Undertones of orange were gone from the sky, the threat of rain sustained for weeks. What was to come was held in suspension, waited to happen: the blast of pain in my brother's chest, sensation drained from his fingers and toes, the blood in his body freed from its boundaries, leaving his lips, the ambulance attendants surging through our door, strangers in white who flanked a gurney, my father begging them not to use the siren—whatever you do, don't use the siren—afraid the sound would frighten his son.

But none of this had happened yet. It was just after dawn. A pale light filled the hall. I stood in the doorway and stared at my parents sprawled in sleep. Their limbs were flung at improbable angles. Their mouths were slack. Beneath closed lids, eyes followed the course of dreams whose theme I tried to guess. But their faces—sunken in a stack of pillows, released from the tension of fear and hope—were emptied of all expression.

—From Bernard Cooper, "Dream House," Harper's Magazine, July 1990.

Tips for Building a Narrative Arc in Your Story

Introduction and Setup

- Hook the readers by tempting them to read the story
- Set the readers on the path that leads to the conflict
- Build the narrative using one, two, or more paragraphs
- Give readers essential information or context for the story
- Announce or suggest the story's conflict.

Rising Action

- Create a series of events that heighten the conflict
- Make events occur incrementally, one step at a time
- Use one, two, or many events
- Do not include every step along the way, just essential ones

Climax

- Make the climax the moment of highest tension
- Be sure the climax brings the conflict into high relief
- Create the climax as the "point of no return," when things can never be the same

(continued)

Tips for Building a Narrative Arc in Your Story (continued)

Resolution

- Do not feel you must tie up all the loose ends
- Point the reader back to the theme
- Do not make the conclusion a summary of a "lesson learned"
- Reveal how you have—or in some cases have not—resolved the conflict

THE BIG IDEA: THEME

Unlike a traditional essay where the thesis is explicitly stated in the first paragraph and the rest of the paper emerges out of that thesis (see Chapter 2, The Writer's Process), exploratory writing such as the memoir often does not have an explicit thesis. Its theme often reveals itself to the writer at the end of the essay as a cumulative result of the story that has been told—a part of the process of exploration. Simply put, the theme is what your story is about: its point and its larger significance.

The theme you choose to reveal in your memoir depends on what actually happened, how it affected you, and what it helped you understand. Often stories about significant events in childhood, for example, have to do with coming of age or experiencing a rite of passage as you leave some part of your childhood behind. It does not matter what theme you reveal in your story, as long as you make a point that has meaning for you as well as for your readers. Readers want to take something away with them and gain a greater understanding about the world, about people, and about life experiences.

Finding out what a story means can be a challenge. Sometimes you need to write the story several times before you see the meaning. Often you will find clues in your language and the imagery you intuitively use. For example, one student drafted a story about her embarrassment while dancing on the stage in middle school. The other students were talking, laughing, and making fun of her. It was a pivotal moment for her, but she could not figure out what the story was really about on a thematic level. When she reread her own language about her "flesh-colored leotard" and her "naked feet," she realized that she was writing about being metaphorically stripped of her dignity. With that insight, she was able to deepen her story, add language that emphasized her sense of exposure, and find more universal themes about vulnerability and violation.

Thematically, a story about moving to a new place could be about how you reinvented or transformed yourself. The theme of a story about winning over a difficult stepparent could be about gaining control, being out of control, being rejected,

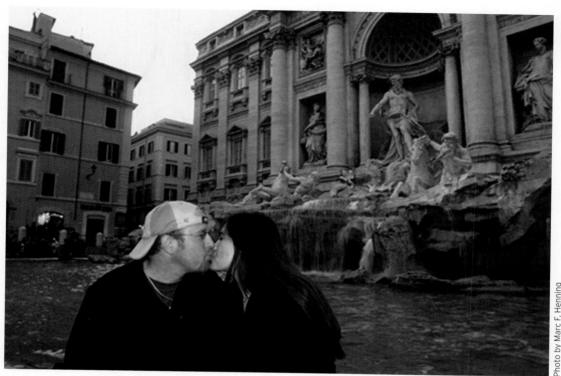

Photo by Marc F. Henning

For more on the snapshots in this chapter, see Visual Literacy: Snapshots, pages 138–139.

or being accepted. A story about meeting your Internet friend face to face could have the themes of trust and taking chances. The theme comes from your story, but it also reveals a more universal truth that you and your readers share, even though you have not had duplicate experiences.

Once you discover your theme, you will need to use it to revise your memoir. Make sure to seed it into your story. Refer to it from the beginning. Even a short scene like Willie Morris's experience on the commuter train on page 134 begins developing the theme in the first sentence. Morris is looking out at tenement-dwellers who in turn are looking back at him. The idea that people look at each other without really seeing each other—a theme that is hinted at in the first sentence—germinates and ripens throughout the story.

One caution: Do not confuse *theme* with *moral.* A moral reduces the entire meaning of your story to a boring and trite cliché, such as "you can't tell a book by its cover" or "easy come, easy go." Most memorable stories are about something deeper, more meaningful, and less clichéd. Surprising or unexpected twists, complex responses, and expectations turned upside down make for interesting and realistic themes.

D I Y

DIY MEDIA AND DESIGN

THE GRAPHIC MEMOIR

A GRAPHIC NOVEL is an excellent example of how to tell a story more by "showing" than "telling." Graphic novels use the conventions of comic book design. Each page is segmented into panels, often six or eight. The illustration can reveal many small details that you might not be able to capture in language. Although their images are static, graphic novels are similar in some ways to films. They can both "show" through images and dialogue and "tell" through voice-over narration. To create a graphic memoir out of a scene of your memoir, or to create a scene from scratch, you will have to consider how to show through illustration, tell through narration, and reveal internal monologue and dialogue through speech and thought bubbles. Tips for creating a graphic memoir follow:

- Limit narration to concepts not easily drawn or time segues.
- Let the images and dialogue tell most of the story.
- Remember that captions interrupt and slow down the action.
- Reveal character through the dialogue.
- Limit the speech and thought balloons to two or three in a panel.
- Show the characters in action in the panels.

Captions appear in boxes in the corners or on the top or bottom of the panel for narration. Usually captions indicate a change in setting or time—the fast-forward or backward kind of time-travel more easily accomplished in verbal narrative. Dialogue appears in speech balloons or thought balloons (a series of small balloons leading to the speech balloons).

As an example, look at how this excerpt from Marjane Satrapi's memoir of coming of age in Iran in the 1980s, the graphic novel *Persepolis,* defies the limits of "written" stories because it is able to "show" through illustrations. To further explore the difference between a narrative and a visual genre, take the graphic representation and translate it

Note how Satrapi reveals three things in her first drawing: The main character is a girl; she is one of many girls wearing veils; and she is in a segregated school. The illustrations also establish point of view; Sartrapi, for example, captures a child's perspective in her drawings. (This is the beginning page of the story.)

D I Y

into narrative prose. Using only words (no pictures), evoke the scene on page 153. Begin with the sentence, "I turned around to see them one last time," and end with the sentence, "It would have been better to just go."

Note how Satrapi ends with a powerful visual image. The last words of your memoir should be a distinct statement, a bit of poetry, an unforgettable image that lingers long after the reader has finished.

READINGS

WHAT IS it like to be a college student serving on a jury for a murder trial? A high school student who has conflicting emotions about a marginalized classmate? Or a fifth-grader locked out of his house with his sibs on the fifth snow day off from school? The memoirs in this section offer insights into these characters as the writers look back at defining moments that were sometimes funny and sometimes serious and sometimes both.

Duties of Adulthood[2]

David Tanklefsky

Student David Tanklefsky wrote this memoir about his first time serving on a jury. The trial was for murder.

"IS THERE anything, young man, which would prevent you from being impartial in this case?" I peered up at the bench; the big bulging eyes of the judge stared back at me. To my right, the lead prosecutor—with his pudgy face and baggy, weighty, wrinkled eyes—stared back at me; the bottom of his chin made a little fat frown. To my left, the public defender, a man of about 60, pursed his lips and, touching his hand to his face, adjusted his broad-rimmed glasses.

I thought through many of the possible irrational and quasi-incoherent answers to that question. Everyone knew that was a sure-fire way out of jury duty. "Just look at this guy, Your Honor," I'd say, pointing to the defendant who sat in the middle of the courtroom. "He's got guilty written all over his face! We oughta throw him into jail right now and let him rot!" I could have offered that the female prosecutor bore a striking resemblance to a girl whom I had just gone through a painful breakup with, and every time I looked at the prosecutor, I felt angry and duped and sheepish. That really would have been true. They looked a lot alike. I could have run out of the courtroom screaming, "I'm only 19 years old! I can't even drink a beer legally! How the hell can you possibly expect me to be up to the task of deciding whether or not this man (who, by the way, was accused of murdering someone) should go to jail for the rest of his life?"

"I looked over at the defendant, who looked back at me. ... Yeah, we are both in way over our heads here."

Instead I steadied myself, looked up at the judge in his black robes, and said, "No, Your Honor."

The lawyers briefly conferred at the bench. The defense attorney turned and cast me a sidelong glance before looking back at the judge and shrugging in a "He'll do" kind of way.

"Have a seat," the judge said. "You're juror number four." I looked over at the defendant, who looked back at me. We both exchanged

[2]Reprinted by permission of David Tankelfsky.

bewildered looks that said, "Yeah, we are both in way over our heads here."

I took my seat to the left of the judge's bench next to a kindly looking gentleman who appeared to be in his mid-60s. He looked at me—the shaggy-haired teenager who had just sat down next to him—and gave me the quizzical look that an elder gives to a youngster who is way on the other side of the generation gap.

I couldn't say I blamed him for his confusion. I wondered why I had been selected myself, especially when 75 people before me had been dismissed, including every other college student who had been called to the bench. Besides the fact that I was only 19, I was notoriously bad at coming to judgments on anything. Was David Ortiz worthy of winning this year's MVP? Should I call the newspaper company back about that summer internship? Does the car need an inspection? These were the problems of my everyday life that I couldn't answer, never mind trying to decide the guilt or innocence of an accused murderer.

"The more I tried to psychoanalyze, the more I realized I'd work myself into a senseless frenzy trying to figure out who he was as a human being."

When you're a teenager, you don't want to make judgments. You want to sit around and think about things forever. And maybe eat a pizza. However, painful as it is, when it comes to facing adulthood or staying oblivious forever, sometimes you don't have a choice.

The details of the case were fairly easy to ascertain. A stocky, middle-aged man had walked into a 7-11 convenience store with a towel over his face and stabbed the store clerk to death before grabbing a few hundred dollars from the cash register and running from the store. Darnell Wilcox had been arrested and accused of committing the crime.

During the first few days of the trial, the prosecution called nearly 20 witnesses to the stand. I tried to write down as much as I could about the testimony that each witness gave, but the flow of witnesses was so constant that I found myself writing extraneous notes about each just to remember what differentiated one from the other.

"Lieutenant Wilson has a big mole on his forehead," I wrote. "Captain Pierce looks like Teddy Roosevelt." Sometimes I drew little caricatures of particularly colorful witnesses.

While prosecution witnesses gave testimony, Wilcox sat quietly in a wooden chair. He looked comfortable in the courtroom, as if he'd been in that chair before. He remained attentive for most of the trial, sometimes turning to whisper something to his attorney or writing a few notes on a legal pad. Wilcox was a huge specimen of a man. He was built like a linebacker with broad shoulders and thick legs. He had worked for years lifting heavy appliances off delivery trucks.

I observed his demeanor carefully. He looked like a nice enough guy. What could he be thinking as he listened to testimony from police officers and from the wife of the man he had allegedly killed? Was this a man who was capable of it? Could he have murdered in an act of desperation? Could he have been on drugs? The more I tried to psychoanalyze Wilcox, the more I realized I'd work myself into a senseless frenzy trying to figure out who he was as a human being.

The jury has the same role in every trial: to look at the facts of the case and the evidence presented. Whether or not Wilcox was a nice guy was irrelevant. I began to develop callousness to the situation at hand.

As the days dragged on, I became accustomed to the routine of the trial. We heard testimony for three hours each morning with a short 15-minute break (for the judge to take a cat nap, as he cleverly quipped). At lunchtime there was a one-hour recess. This was the time that I got to know my fellow jurors. Gordon, the older gentleman who had eyeballed me with surprise on the first day, was a mathematics teacher who was on his summer break from a nearby college. Larry was a thirty-something who made "shitloads of money, dude" at a car dealership and was losing "literally a fuckload of money" by sitting in this "shitty courtroom every day listening to this shit." Susan was a blonde mother of four who constantly bit her nails, and Bill was an oddball music teacher who was always quietly humming to himself.

"If you find him guilty, ya'll will pay."

During the first days of the trial, we were allowed to leave the confines of the courtroom to grab lunch at one of the local restaurants. However, the judge quickly became concerned for our safety. At noon as we exited the courthouse for lunch, the defendant's six children sat on the courthouse steps and made casual remarks such as "You know my dad didn't do it" and borderline threats such as "If you find him guilty, y'all will pay." This situation marked the end of our restaurant lunches, and we spent the rest of the trial eating in a stuffy, unair-conditioned upstairs meeting room as the June heat sweltered all around us.

The only witness the defense called to the stand was Wilcox's wife, Molly. With all six Wilcox children looking on from the back of the courtroom, Molly quietly explained that her husband led a difficult life. He worked long hours and weekends to make enough money for his large family. He had never graduated from high school. He took in a number of neighborhood troublemakers and treated them like his own sons. "Sure, Darnell can use some bad language or smack the kids every once in a while or steal my cigarettes. He's not the best guy in the world, but deep down he's just a big teddy bear." Even Wilcox had to scoff a little at his wife's character analysis, and the judge quickly asked the jury to excuse that comment from Molly's testimony.

As Molly Wilcox stepped off the witness stand and marched to the back of the courtroom, she looked at Darnell and whispered the words "I love you." Wilcox, seeming to finally grasp the direness of his situation, grew teary-eyed and echoed back, "I love you" to his wife.

During closing statements, the prosecution told us that Wilcox was a monster who had killed a decent, hard-working man for no reason but to snatch a few hundred dollars out of a cash register. The chubby prosecutor did most of the talking. He worked himself into a sweat describing Wilcox's grisly act. For theatrical effect he picked up the knife that had been entered into evidence as the murder weapon and plunged it into an imaginary victim to show the raw horror of the crime.

The defense attorney, on the other hand, spoke at length about Wilcox's character. Wilcox, he said, was a "tough guy" but a good man who had a devoted family he was trying to support. He added his own theatrical touch by walking over to Wilcox and touching his

shoulders to show that they were buddies and that Wilcox was an average Joe.

Then deliberation began. We remained confined to the same stiflingly hot meeting room that had served as our lunch room for the final days of the trial. We spent the morning looking over the evidence. We watched the video of the stabbing repeatedly and then looked carefully at still photos that had been lifted from the surveillance footage.

As I watched the stabbing on video, a wave of nausea hit me and I excused myself to the bathroom. Gordon, the teacher, met me as I washed my face in the sink.

"If this is too much for you, we can deliberate without you," he said. "Hell, I don't like doing this neither, but people do it. People kill people."

"I'm fine."

"Yeah?" he said.

"I don't know."

I walked back to the meeting room. I re-wound the VCR and watched the tape of the crime again. This time I noticed a small white emblem on the jacket of the suspect. It seemed to match a jacket of Wilcox's that had been entered into evidence. A number of jurors crowded around to check my observation.

"They certainly do look the same," said Susan in a calming, motherly way.

"Fuck yeah, they do," said the car dealer.

After a few more grueling hours of discussing and looking over the evidence, things seemed to be pointing towards Wilcox's guilt.

"I'm not afraid to say it; he's guilty," said Susan.

The rest of the jurors slowly followed suit and agreed that the evidence overwhelmingly pointed to Wilcox as the murderer. I felt a second wave of nausea hit me, this one more pronounced than the first.

As we lined up to walk downstairs and deliver the guilty verdict, I felt time get hazy that way you hear happens to people who have delusions. The twelve of us stood, still relative strangers to the goings-on of each other's lives but bound by this excruciating process. Under state law, a guilty verdict for first-degree murder comes with an automatic sentence of life in prison. From here on out, every day that I took a walk to the store, went to a ball game, watched a movie, called a girl, Darnell Wilcox would be in a penitentiary due, in part, to my decision.

In the courtroom, the judge asked if we had reached a verdict.

"We have, Your Honor," replied the car dealer, who had been randomly selected as our foreman.

The judge rose. The chubby prosecutor and the prosecutor who looked like my ex-girlfriend rose. The defense attorney rose. Wilcox rose. Wilcox's wife rose. His six children, the eldest of whom I could now see looked to be my equal in age, rose.

"And how do you find the defendant on the charge of first-degree murder."

"Guilty," said the car dealer.

Before we were quickly shuffled out of the courtroom, I saw Wilcox collapse into his chair and put his hands over his head. The defense attorney put a fatherly hand on his back. Wilcox's wife and children wailed in disbelief.

A police escort walked us to our cars in a parking lot adjacent to the courthouse. We walked quickly and in a single-file line. A soft rain had started falling, and I zipped my raincoat. As we reached our cars, Gordon turned to me and shook my hand.

"Justice is served, but it ain't fun," he said chuckling. "Nice meeting you, son; ain't you a man now?"

I pulled my hood over my head and made it four steps to my car before throwing up in the rainwater.

QUESTIONS FOR RHETORICAL ANALYSIS

1. **CONSIDERING THE RHETORICAL SITUATION:** The general characteristics of three of the jurors are sketched in by their voices. Look at the dialogue written for Gordon, Susan, and Larry. What does their language reveal about their personalities?
2. Identify the lead, or the introduction, to this story. What technique does Tanklefsky use? Where does Tanklefsky break from the story and provide some setup or background information?
3. What is the conflict in this story? Where do you first become aware of it?
4. The main character of this story is the narrator. How does he present himself in the story? Cite some specific passages to support your interpretation.
5. Tanklefsky introduces you to the other characters in this story by providing "telling" details and by describing their actions. What do you know about the following characters? How does each reveal something about the narrator?
   a. Darnell Wilcox
   b. Darnell Wilcox's wife, Molly
   c. Gordon, the juror who is about sixty
   d. Larry
   e. Susan
6. The writer moves his story forward by presenting a number of connected scenes. What does he accomplish by using this structure? Are there any scenes you think could be eliminated? Why?
7. What stated and unstated themes does the writer embed in this story?
8. How effective are the last two lines of dialogue and the final image of the story? Do you find the conclusion satisfactory? Why or why not?

QUESTIONS FOR WRITING AND DISCUSSION

1. Even if you have never served on a jury, can you relate to Tanklefsky's story? Why or why not?
2. Tanklefsky tells readers that he was the juror who first noticed the detail that ultimately caused the jury to convict Wilcox. How does knowing this information affect your feelings about the writer? Would the story be better or worse if he had not told readers this information?

STYLE PRACTICE: IMITATION

In the opening paragraph, Tanklefsky describes the lead prosecutor and the public defender with a few details that make them memorable. Write a similar few lines of specific description about two of the characters in your memoir.

Unrolling a Twisted Impression[3]

Melissa Hochman

Melissa Hochman's memoir "Unrolling a Twisted Impression" was selected for a reading at her college. The memoir was also published in the writing program's online magazine. Read it and see why.

I HATED TERRY. He sat next to me in Creative Writing and plucked keys off the keyboard to serve as his own personal set of Scrabble pieces. He'd form various words from curses to body parts, SAT vocabulary to interjections. He'd make a ruckus by both stripping and then replacing the entire components of the keyboard as I struggled to write a story or a poem on the computer beside him. He took great pleasure in restarting my computer while I was on page four of an unsaved document (I could never grab his dirty fingers in time to stop him from pressing the button). He wore the same outfit every day: green flannel button-down with an Allman Brother's Peach album t-shirt underneath, faded blue jeans, brown oversized belt (oversized so that the leather after the buckle swung low to his knee) and brown combat boots. He carried a distinct odor with him that smelled of tuna fish and peanut butter and intensified from the tips of his shaggy hair to the soles of his clunky combat boots. When he wasn't destroying the computers, he was sleeping. When he wasn't sleeping, he was roaming the halls looking for trouble.

"I hated Terry…He took great pleasure in restarting my computer while I was on page four of an unsaved document."

When I first met him, I had attempted to talk to him, befriend him even. I brought up an Allman Brother's concert I had gone to over the summer and how I had seen him working at Auntie Anne's in the mall. He took one look and scoffed at me; he would have none of my company. I decided I didn't like him. For the rest of the four years, he kept to himself, drew cartoons, and created random objects from long pencil shavings. But the thing about Terry was that he was a genius, and everyone in the class knew it.

My intensive creative writing class consisted of 12 people and spanned my entire high school career. We shared our most intimate thoughts, our most private work and our most absurd ideas, as well as a passion for creating beauty from 26 letters. Although our small family all shared talent, we did not all share an appreciation for it.

While we all worked, Terry goofed off. While we all spent time and exerted will power for a contest piece, Terry slept. When we read our own pieces aloud and engaged in constructive criticism, Terry remained silent.

When he did write, which was only during times of mandatory in-class story development and workshops, it was flawless. He drafted screenplays I could envision on the feature screen. He crafted characters and defined not just what they did for a living, but

[3]Reprinted by permission of Melissa Hochman.

how their morning coffee order included two espresso shots, soy milk, and the plop, plop of three sugar cubes, which set off a series of waves whose waters rose and broke against the interior of a recycled cup—every detail, every grimace, and every conversation came full circle. When he tried, he made allusions of the rarest form, had impeccable word choice, and wrung sentences with syntax so right it made you want to call a publishing company and exclaim, "Yes it was I; I discovered him and I want half the profits." A film of jealously clung to my body like thick sea foam when he read his pieces aloud because I knew I was not as gifted as he was and that his potential far exceeded my own. I couldn't help but wish that I could capture dialogue as he did; understand and describe distinct movements as he did; set up a solitary scene with comedic, horrific, romantic and dramatic elements as he did.

"During the September of senior year, Terry decided to bring a BB gun to school."

However, outside of the creative writing classroom Terry was not viewed as brilliant. Consistently in the principal's office for various acts of vandalism, setting off the fire alarm and cursing at a teacher, Terry spent his weekends smoking marijuana alone outside of the 7-11.

During the September of senior year, Terry decided to bring a BB gun to school. He brought it to lunch, drew it from his backpack while he was outside, and pretended to fire the pellets at his surroundings. Though he never aimed it at another person, the administration dealt with the matter seriously. Considering Terry's record, they decided to search his locker. They found Shakespeare plays, textbooks that did not belong to him, and a poster of Sigmund Freud. Behind the poster of Freud was a half-filled Ziploc bag of marijuana and a separate bag containing three LSD tabs. Terry was expelled and placed in a juvenile detention facility 20 minutes away from the high school.

After the news surfaced, there was a shift in our creative writing class. I looked over at the keyboard that had all of its keys intact. I looked at the electric pencil sharpener that had all of its shards still entangled within its clear plastic base. Gone were the intermittent grunts, gone were the strumming sounds of five fingertips on the desk next to mine. In some strange way, I sincerely missed that smelly genius.

Three months after Terry left, my creative writing teacher carried two manila envelopes into the classroom. Her normally pale complexion was rosy and bright. She proudly laid the envelopes on the table and allowed everyone to take note of the return address: The Scholastic Art and Writing Awards. An award from Scholastic meant you had it. It meant a certificate; it meant an awards ceremony; it meant a cash prize, and it meant that someone besides your mother saw a spark in something you had written. My name was on one envelope, and Terry's name was on the other.

After the excitement settled, my teacher wondered what to do with Terry's envelope. She didn't want to send it to him at his new school, and she didn't trust his family to recognize the significance of the award. No one had Terry's phone number or had kept

in contact with him since he had left, but we couldn't allow it to just sit there. I assumed that Terry still worked at Auntie Anne's, so I volunteered to deliver the envelope.

As I walked up the mall staircase to the second floor, I could hear his familiar, raspy voice chanting, "Roll, twist, pat." As I hid out of sight behind a tall beam, I watched him continue to roll, twist, and pat pretzel dough for a few more minutes before someone came over to him and told him he could go on a break. Terry threw off his hat and apron and jumped over the side of the counter, heading for the staircase. I stepped to the side of the beam so that he could see me and he made his way over to where I stood. As he came closer he extended his arm and pointed at the envelope clutched in my hand.

"That my X-Mas gift?"

I handed him the envelope. After a moment, he lifted his long, shaggy hair to reveal a large forehead with a furrowed brow.

"No fuckin' way," he said, before opening the envelope. He took out a small gold key, a certificate with his name on it, and a copy of his science fiction short story.

"This was the only thing I typed up all year. It was a first fuckin' draft."

It was the first emotion I had ever seen him display: he was surprised, humbled, and in disbelief.

"Yeah, winning that's a pretty big deal," I told him, ignorantly assuming that he hadn't realized the significance of what he was holding.

"No shit," he said. "You win regionals and then you're eligible to go to nationals. You get to nationals and it means you get to go to D.C. for free. Get out of here for a little while." He ran his fingers over the raised seal on his certificate and traced the letters of his name.

"Well, uh, congratulations," I said. "Maybe I'll see you around."

He held up his hand and told me to wait a minute. He went back the Auntie Ann's and came out with a notebook that had doodles and holes on the front cover with loose paper sticking out of the sides. He rolled the notebook, making a twisting motion with his two palms before patting the notebook flat again.

"I've been workin' on some stuff, nothin' great. But I want you to take this back and have everyone look at it. You know, just a couple pieces, if you guys have time."

I was in shock. I couldn't believe that he still wrote, let alone had enough work to fill a notebook. I couldn't believe that he cared about the opinions of his fellow classmates, or that he hoped to improve. I couldn't believe that he was capable of saying so many words at once.

I nodded and walked away. As I placed the notebook in my bag, a card fell out. It was an Auntie Ann's frequent buyer card, with six pretzel punches already stamped through. According to the card, I had purchased six pretzels and was due for a free one.

I turned around and Terry said, "That's to make sure you come back."

QUESTIONS FOR RHETORICAL ANALYSIS

1. **CONSIDERING THE RHETORICAL SITUATION:** Hochman doesn't allow her reader to hear Terry's voice until the final scene of the story, until after she paints a portrait of a disaffected "genius." Reread the dialogue in the final scene. How does that dialogue reveal Terry's character? What does it reveal about the narrator?
2. Where does the writer first engage the reader and introduce the story's conflict?
3. This story has a long set-up before the story actually begins. Identify the place where the story is set in motion. Why do you think Hochman has such a long set-up? Is it effective?
4. The narrator seems to be on the sidelines of this story, but it is her character and her character arc that is of central interest. What change does she experience? Cite evidence from the story to support your answer.
5. In what way do pretzels and pretzel-making serve as metaphors in this story?
6. The final scene at the mall is rendered in great detail. Is it an effective conclusion to the story? Why or why not?

QUESTIONS FOR WRITING AND DISCUSSION

1. Terry is a recognizable character—a kind of disaffected student who has great intellectual promise. What other characters from literature or film have these qualities? Do you find Terry a sympathetic character? Why?
2. What motivates the narrator to reach out to Terry? Would you have done the same?

STYLE PRACTICE: IMITATION

Begin a paragraph with the sentence, "I hate (fill in the blank). Then, as Hochman does in the first paragraph, explain what is hateful, but also intriguing, about this person.

Let It Snow[4]

David Sedaris

David Sedaris has written humorously about his time as a Macy's elf in Santa Land Diaries *and about his life as an expatriate in France. He writes about his family and about growing up in Raleigh, North Carolina in his well-known books* Barrel Fever, Naked, *and* Me Talk Pretty One Day. *His short pieces appear in the* New Yorker, Esquire, *and other magazines and are often aired on National Public Radio. Sedaris often uses humor to critique social norms, to deflate pretensions and political correctness, and to reveal—with uncompromising honesty—messy and complicated human relationships, as he does in "Let It Snow."*

WINTERS WERE frustratingly mild in North Carolina, but the year I was in the fifth grade we got lucky. Snow fell, and, for the first time in years, it accumulated. School was cancelled, and two days later we got lucky again. There were eight inches on the ground, and, rather than melting, it froze. On the fifth day of our vacation, my mother had a little breakdown. Our presence had disrupted the secret life she led while we were at school, and when she could no longer take it she threw us out. It wasn't a gentle request but something closer to an eviction. "Get the hell out of my house," she said.

We reminded her that it was our house, too, and she opened the front door and shoved us into the carport. "And stay out!" she shouted.

My sisters and I went down the hill and sledded with other children from the neighborhood. A few hours later, we returned home, surprised to find that the door was locked. "Oh, come on," we said. I rang the bell, and when no one answered we went to the window and saw our mother in the kitchen, watching television. Normally she waited until five o'clock to have a drink, but for the past few days she'd been making an exception. Drinking didn't count if you followed a glass of wine with a cup of coffee, and so she had a goblet and a mug positioned before her on the countertop.

"Hey!" we yelled. "Open the door. It's us." We knocked on the pane and, without looking in our direction, she refilled her goblet and left the room.

"One us us should get hit by a car," I said. "That would teach the both of them."

"That bitch," my sister Lisa said. We pounded again and again, and when our mother failed to answer we went around back and threw snowballs at her bedroom window. "You are going to be in so much trouble when Dad gets home!" we shouted, and in response my mother pulled the drapes. Dusk approached, and as it grew colder it occurred to us that we could possibly die. It happened, surely. Selfish mothers wanted the house to themselves and their children were discovered years later, frozen like mastodons in blocks of ice.

My sister Gretchen suggested that we call our father, but none of us knew his number, and he probably wouldn't have done anything anyway. He'd gone to work specifically to escape our mother, and between the weather and her mood it could be hours, or even days, before he returned home.

"One of us should get hit by a car," I said. "That would teach the both of them." I pictured Gretchen, her life hanging by a thread as my parents paced the halls of Rex Hospital, wishing they had been more attentive. It was really the perfect solution. With her out of the way, the rest of us would be more valuable and have a bit more room to spread out. "Gretchen, go lie in the street."

"Make Amy do it," she said.

Amy, in turn, pushed it off on Tiffany, who was the youngest and had no concept of death. "It's like sleeping," we told her. "Only you get a canopy bed."

Poor Tiffany. She'd do just about anything in return for a little affection. All you had to do was call her Tiff, and whatever you wanted was yours: her allowance, her dinner, the contents of her Easter basket. Her eagerness to please was absolute and naked. When we asked her to lie in the middle of the street, her only question was "Where?"

We chose a quiet dip between two hills, a spot where drivers were almost required to skid out of control. She took her place, this six-year-old in a butter-colored coat, and we gathered on the curb to watch. The first car to come along belonged to a neighbor, a fellow-Yankee who had outfitted his tires with chains and stopped a few feet from our sister's body. "Is that a person?" he asked.

"Well, sort of," Lisa said. She explained that we'd been locked out of our house, and, while the man appeared to accept it as a reasonable explanation, I'm pretty sure he was the one who told on us. Another car passed, and then we saw our mother, this puffy figure awkwardly negotiating the crest of the hill. She did not own a pair of pants, and her legs were buried to the calf in snow. We wanted to send her home, to kick her out of nature just as she had kicked us out of the house, but it was hard to stay angry at someone that pitiful-looking.

"Are you wearing your *loafers*?" Lisa asked, and in response our mother raised a bare foot.

"I *was* wearing loafers," she said. "I mean, really, it was there a second ago."

This was how things went. One moment she was locking us out of our own house and the next we were rooting around in the snow, looking for her left shoe. "Oh, forget about it," she said. "It'll turn up in a few days." Gretchen fitted her cap over my mother's foot. Lisa secured it with her scarf, and, surrounding her tightly on all sides, we made our way home.

QUESTIONS FOR RHETORICAL ANALYSIS

1. **CONSIDERING THE RHETORICAL SITUATION:** One purpose of dialogue in narratives is to reveal character. Reread the dialogue Sedaris writes in this story. What is revealed about each character through his or her dialogue? What does Sedaris reveal about his mother when he writes, "Oh forget about it," she said. "It'll turn up in a few days."
2. Identify the place where the set-up ends and the narrative begins. What tone does Sedaris establish in the set-up?

3. On the surface, the story is about a mother who drinks and locks the children out of the house in the snow. How do you think Sedaris wants the reader to react to this story: seriously, humorously, or both? What evidence can you find in the story to support your view?
4. What image does Sedaris leave with you in his conclusion? What feelings does this image evoke?
5. What is at the heart of this story? What is Sedaris' theme?

QUESTIONS FOR WRITING AND DISCUSSION

1. The subject of this memoir, a snow day off from school, usually suggests a positive, if not lighthearted tale of most every child's winter dream: a serendipitous day of free play. How does Sedaris use this setting to help the reader see things in a different way?
2. Some have described Sedaris' stories as "darkly comic." Is that an apt description of this story? Explain.
3. Listen to the "Fresh Air" Public Radio interview with Sedaris at http://www.npr.org/templates/story/story.php?storyId=4247938 . What insights do you get from the interview that help you understand his writer's voice and themes in "Let it Snow"?

STYLE PRACTICE: IMITATION

David Sedaris is known for his darkly playful humor, which is beautifully illustrated in the conversation among the three oldest children as they pass down the task of lying in the street to Tiffany, the youngest. Using this dialogue as a model, write a few lines of dialogue for these same three children as they try to get Tiffany to do a different task to get Mom's attention, such as throwing a rock through the window or running naked through the snow.

WRITING AND REVISION STRATEGIES

Gathered here are three interactive sections for you to use as you write and revise your memoir.

- Writer's Notebook Suggestions
- Peer Review Log
- Revision Checklist

WRITER'S NOTEBOOK SUGGESTIONS

You can use these exercises to do some start-up thinking and writing for your memoir.

1. Write about a moment that you remember well. Include all of the following: weather, a gesture, dialogue, music, color, a smell. Do not exceed 250 words.
2. Using the writing you did for the first question (or some other memory), change the voice. Use one of the examples in the chapter as a model.
3. Take any paragraph of memory writing and change the verbs to the present tense.
4. Write two different openings for a story about your first day at school or your first day on a job. Choose from the following types of openings:
   a. Start in the middle of action.
   b. Start by describing a photograph of that day (real or imagined).
   c. Start by seeing your reflection in a mirror or window.
   d. Start at the end.
   e. Start with dialogue.
5. Choose a day from your life that you remember well, not necessarily because it was dramatic or important but because you can recall many of the details. Write a diary entry as if the day were yesterday.

6. Write a paragraph that combines internal monologue, dialogue, summary, and descriptive narrative.
7. Write about yourself in the third person.
8. Describe the weather on a day that was important to you.
9. Remember a phone call that was hard for you to make. Write the dialogue.
10. Describe someone who has left an impression on you by describing a place in which that person belongs. How does the place represent the person?
11. Use the letter-to-a-friend technique: Write a letter explaining an event to someone you know well.

PEER REVIEW LOG

As you work with a writing partner or in a peer review group, you can use these questions to give helpful responses to a classmate's memoir and to guide your discussion.

Writer's Name: ______________________________

Date: ______________________________

1. Bracket the introduction of the memoir. What technique does the writer use to open the story? Do you find it effective, or could you suggest a better place for the story to begin?
2. Put a line under the last paragraph of the setup. How effectively has the writer set up the story? What other information or sensory details might help you better understand the events that follow?
3. Box a section that presents the setting of the story. What details might make the setting stronger, more vivid, or more specific?

4. Write a sentence that expresses the theme of the story as you understand it. What images, language, and events point to that theme? Does the title also direct the reader's attention to the theme? If the title is weak, can you suggest an alternative?
5. Put a check mark next to the first place where you notice the conflict beginning to emerge. What is the conflict? What are the obstacles for the central character? What is at stake?
6. What is your impression of the main character(s)? Suggest places where the characters' actions and dialogue could be strengthened to develop the characters more fully.
7. Examine the narrative techniques that the writer uses in the memoir. Identify places where the writer uses summary and places where the writer creates a scene through narrative detail. Label places where the writer uses dialogue with *D* and places where the writer uses internal monologue with *IM*. Which sections might be strengthened by showing through narration and dialogue rather than by telling through summary and internal monologue?
8. What kind of voice does the writer use to tell the story? Is it appropriate for and consistent with the narrator's age and circumstance? How might the voice better reflect the narrator's character?
9. Bracket the conclusion. What technique does the writer use here? Is the conclusion effective in leaving a last impression that fortifies the theme? Does the last paragraph add anything necessary to the story? Would the story be injured if this paragraph were cut?
10. Comment briefly on the writing style. Write *V* where the writing could be strengthened by substituting active verbs for "to be" verbs and *T* where the writer could use a better transition. Put an asterisk (*) next to places where the writer uses interesting verbs and good transitions.

REVISION CHECKLIST

As you do your final revision for your memoir, check to make sure that you

- used an interesting, attention-getting opening
- set up the story
- created a setting that helps develop the mood of the story
- presented a clear conflict
- developed the conflict incrementally, in steps
- presented a climax
- described your characters
- made your main character's motivation clear
- explored a theme that has significance for you and your reader

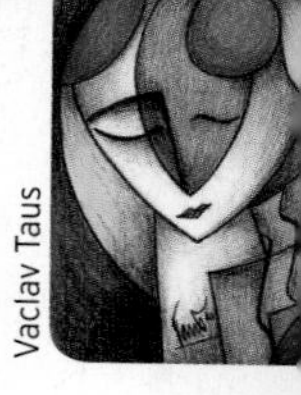

Writing About Others 7

PROFILES

An ordinary life examined closely reveals itself to be exquisite and complicated, somehow managing to be both heroic and plain.

—Susan Orlean

In painting a portrait, an artist sets out to create a likeness of a person, a recognizable image. The artist's aim, however, is only in small part to record the details of the subject: color of hair, slope of nose, or smile. The real art of portrait painting lies in the way the artist interprets and reveals the subject. In a good portrait, through some combination of light and shadow, expression, and detail, the essence of the subject emerges, not just the likeness but also the character of the subject.

A profile is a portrait in words. It provides an in-depth look at a person or sometimes a group of people from a specific perspective or angle. This angle makes the portrait very different from a general picture of a person, what might amount to a simple "driver's license" description: height, weight, and date of birth, for example. As we look at the more in-depth issues of character: the struggles, commitments, and decisions of others, we may even recognize ourselves. Along the way, we also learn about the professions, passions, and lifestyles of famous, infamous, and even ordinary people, and perhaps extend the boundaries of our own lives.

WHAT'S TO COME

Andy Warhol's interpretation of Marilyn Monroe

PROCESS PLAN

PREPARE

- Find a profile subject you can interview who represents a career, a trend, a movement in history, a philosophy or lifestyle.
- Become an expert: Research the subject's area, read similar profiles, read about the issues the subject represents.
- Write interview questions: Ask for stories, examples, experiences that will concretely illustrate the ideas your subject represents.

DRAFT

- Introduction: Hook your reader with a scene, anecdote, or statistic.
- Body: Develop the "big idea," the interpretive thesis of your profile. Organize the profile to explain this thesis.
- Include physical description, moments where the reader sees the subject in action, and comments from others who know the subject or the ideas represented.
- Conclusion: End with an image or a memorable quotation.

REVISE

- Remind your reader of your thesis at strategic points to stay focused.
- Cut references to the interview itself. For example, avoid saying, "Next I asked. . ." Focus on the subject not on yourself.
- Check for two types of transitions:
  1) those that connect paragraphs and
  2) those that remind us of the big idea

UNDERSTANDING THE WRITING PROJECT

Shanna Baker/Getty Images

PROFILES ARE word portraits. They are not biographies, filled with facts about when someone was born, where the person grew up, went to school, got married, had kids, and so on. Instead, profiles paint a picture of some piece of a person's life, leading to an interpretation of what is interesting or important about that person and that person's world.

Look at this biographical entry about a writer whose books you are likely to know, but you may not recognize from the facts about his life.

> He was born in Springfield, Massachusetts, on March 2, 1904, and graduated from Dartmouth College in 1925. At Oxford University, he studied towards a doctorate in literature. There he met Helen Palmer, the woman he eventually married. After returning to the United States, he worked for a humor magazine. Later, he joined the army during World War II and was sent to Hollywood, where he won several Oscars for his documentaries about Adolph Hitler, and one for a cartoon called *Gerald McBoing-Boing.*

These dryly listed facts do not give a clue about who this man really is. Instead of a portrait, which reveals some basic element of character, we get a snapshot—information without interpretation.

The following paragraph, which interprets this person's character, provides a perspective, and it helps reveal the writer, whom you will now most likely recognize.

> He used to doodle in school, strange little drawings. His high school art teacher told him never to plan a career in art. Likewise, his writing teacher at Dartmouth

Access an interactive eBook, and chapter-specific interactive learning tools, including flashcards, quizzes, videos and more in your English CourseMate via www.cengagebrain.com.

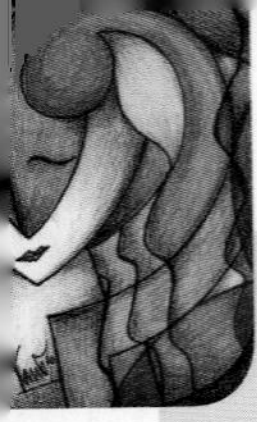

Library of Congress

College discouraged him from becoming a writer. Even his fraternity brothers voted him least likely to succeed. Being misunderstood, though, would not get in his way. This writer's first children's book was rejected 43 times. Then a friend agreed to publish it. The writer went on to win an Oscar for a cartoon, but even more importantly, he kept trying new things. At the encouragement of his publisher, he set out on a campaign against boring children's books, hoping to make learning to read more interesting than Dick and Jane had. And, in 1954, using a list of 220 words he thought a first grader could learn, he wrote an instantly successful book. It was called *The Cat in the Hat.*

—Adapted from *Outpost 10F, Poetry Guild,* and *Stories for a Teen's Heart*

The writer, of course, is Theodore Geisel, known all over the world as Dr. Seuss, author of *How the Grinch Stole Christmas, Green Eggs and Ham*, and forty-two other children's books. The second paragraph, rather than just listing biographical facts, creates a portrait of this unique artist, focusing on his quirky sensibilities, his "misunderstood" character, and his early conflicts.

At their best, profiles invite the reader into the subject's world. Malcolm Gladwell, author of many *New Yorker* profiles, says that profiles should be more sociological than psychological.

He claims no interest in a profile subject's childhood or even the intimate details of that person's life. What interests him is the subculture in which the subject belongs. He writes that "the individual is a means to examine another world—the world in which that person lives."

ASSIGNMENT Write a profile of a person or a group. Focus on some specific aspect that is noteworthy. You do not have to admire the people you write about, but you should find their accomplishments, lifestyles, or philosophies interesting and maybe even fascinating to explore. (Oral history is another avenue to explore for recording fascinating people's lives. See the DIY on page 192 for some pointers.) You also do not have to choose someone who is rich and famous. Sometimes the most interesting profiles are about ordinary people as in the following profile of Michael Cresta, a carpenter and a "Scrabble king."

ANATOMY OF A PROFILE

CYNTHIA ANDERSON journalist and fiction writer, explores the nuances of "fame" as she portrays this king of an off-beat domain.

Of Carpenters and Scrabble Kings[1]

CYNTHIA ANDERSON

introduction

LEXINGTON, MASS.—Michael Cresta is the reigning king of Scrabble, but you'll have to excuse him if he wears the crown a tad uneasily.

interpretive thesis: Unlikely King

nut graf

Unassuming by nature—a carpenter from Saugus, Mass., who bowls on Tuesday nights and plays Scrabble on Thursdays—Mr. Cresta is, well, horrified by the attention that has ensued

continues next page

[1]Cynthia Anderson, "Of Carpenters and Scrabble Kings," from Christian Science Monitor November 11, 2006. Reprinted with permission.

since that fateful game on Oct. 12 at the Lexington Scrabble Club during which he toppled three national records.

Hence, he is not returning the many calls from the media or answering the phone. That task has fallen to his wife, Dianna, who says, "Michael is just not that kind of guy." For that matter, Cresta didn't share the news with his own father, who found out almost a week after the fact. "Why didn't you tell me?" his dad asked, to which Cresta could only shrug.

quotes from secondary sources: wife and father

Diffidence notwithstanding, Cresta receives an imperial welcome when he shows up on a recent evening at the club in suburban Boston, his first appearance since the win. "There he is!" shouts someone as Cresta—a compact, curly-haired man in jeans and sneakers—materializes in the doorway of the group's church-basement headquarters.

thesis reinforced

scene

Cresta is late for the meeting, having been stuck at work waiting for a plumber who was supposed to help with a bathroom renovation. Nobody seems to mind. Instead, his club mates clap and cheer. Cresta reddens, looks at the floor. "It's really not that big of a deal," he tells the first person to approach and congratulate him. "But thank you very much."

revealing detail

quote from subject

According to the National Scrabble Association, Cresta set three records in that game. His individual total was 830 points, besting the previous North American high of 770. He and his partner, Wayne Yorra, together scored 1320, the most points ever achieved in a two-player game. Cresta also broke the record for points scored in a single turn, garnering 365 for the triple-triple QUIXOTRY. His other big play was FLATFISH, also a triple-triple, for 239.

researched facts and stats/ background

If on that night a month ago Cresta was HOTHOTHOT at the table, he is less so this evening. He sits across from Hilda Siegel, both of them focused on the letters in their trays. The 15-by-15 square board is filling with respectable combos like ZING, JOLLY, and QUIRE but nothing too remarkable. Cresta is a bit ahead.

Then Ms. Siegel "bingos," emptying her tray of seven tiles in a single play. With the 50-point boost from the bingo, she takes the lead. "Nice work," says Cresta, peering down at his own letters, mostly a mess of vowels.

Ten other games are in progress at nearby tables. An air of happy concentration fills the room. Other than the click of tiles being arranged and the hushed tally of numbers, quiet prevails. Every so often a pair of players rises from their chairs and hurries across the room to a laptop set up to settle challenged words. Chit-chat will come later, when people take a break for tea and cookies in the corner.

observed scene at scrabble club interwoven with exposition

With the clock ticking, Cresta leans closer to the board. The skin around his nails is white from the grouting he did at work. He refuses to use certain words—profanity and "phonies," made-up combos passed off as real. "Not ethical," he says. Finally he responds with OORIE, a low scorer that at least provides the chance to draw consonants. He rummages in the tile bag, extracts four pieces, grins.

revealing detail

Siegel eyes him. "Be kind," she says.

Cresta keeps smiling, but in the end she takes the game, 416 to 383.

exposition: history of the game/background

Scrabble was invented in 1931 by an out-of-work architect, Alfred Butts, who wanted to create a board game that combined skill and chance. To determine a letter's frequency (and inversely its "value"), Butts scrutinized the front page of *The New York Times.* He discovered that vowels appeared far more often than consonants, and the E was the most common letter. Least common (i.e. most valuable) were Q and Z. The game's big break came in the 1950s, after the president of Macy's discovered it while on vacation and ordered it for his store. Within a year, clerks couldn't keep the game in stock.

exposition: cresta's history with the game

Cresta himself started playing in 1973, when he was 10. He continued to play casually as an adult, only joining the club two years ago. Since then, he has worked to sharpen his skills. "When I first came here, I thought I was good," he says. "I soon found out I wasn't."

quote from subject

interesting details about Cresta's preparation/anecdote

While watching TV at night with Dianna, he often reads from the Scrabble dictionary. He's memorized many of the J, Q, X, and Z words, as well as most of the two-letter and a lot of the three-letter ones. Describing his tactics, Cresta lowers his voice. "Actually I'm a bad speller. English was my worst subject." Then he brightens. "I do have a good memory."

Which brings up the matter of the cassettes he listens to at work. He records them himself, 45 minutes to a side, reading aloud from the dictionary. Recent tapes include words that begin with "out" and "over." Each word is pronounced and then spelled. (Cresta avoids playing the tapes when a homeowner is around.)

Though intent on improving his game, Cresta seems less serious about competition. He and Mr. Yorra joke about a previous champion who wears a cap inscribed with his winning score, and—this cracks them up—drives a car with the score on his license plate. Cresta regards a club member hunched over a board across the room. "Look at that frown," he says. "Come on. This is supposed to be fun."

continues next page

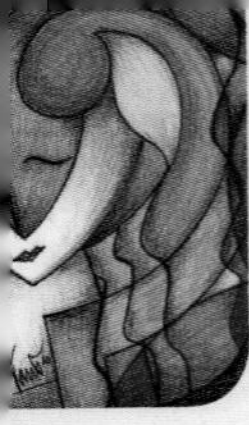

At the Lexington club, where some members have been playing seriously for decades, Cresta's position as a hobbyist and relative beginner is not news. "Michael's not one of our top players. In fact, he's near the bottom," says club statistician Mike Wolberg matter-of-factly. Indeed, of the club's 42 ranked players, Cresta is 35th, even after last month's record breaker. The win was statistically anomalous for him, besting his previous high score by more than 200 points. Nor was the game he played considered tactically brilliant.

conclusion: back to scene at Scrabble club

supports "uinlikely king" interpretation

"Technically, Cresta's strategy was unsound," wrote Stefan Fatsis in the online magazine *Slate*.

"[E]xchanging letters three times, as Cresta did, to enhance some combination of Q, U, I, and X (for the word QUIXOTRY) is unorthodox at best, suicidal at worst . . . In Scrabble, the player who waits for the miracle word usually loses."

quote from online source: reinforces the thesis

With all of this, Cresta concurs. "I come here to play and have a good time," he says. He pauses. "Also to learn." Recently he decided to learn the definitions of all the words he memorizes. "It'll help make me smarter," he says.

concludes with quote from subject: reveals his down-to-earth perspective.

QUIXOTRY, as it turns out, implies "visionary schemes," which perhaps relates to what Cresta really hopes could come of his Scrabble reign: "It might bring me some carpentry jobs."

Writing short is harder for a simple reason. Every piece of writing, every story, has to do some basic things: it needs a beginning, a middle, an end. It needs a plot or a structure, a story, exposition, and all the elements of any story—and all that takes up space. So in a short

"A good written scene should be like a film clip, with forward motion and an arc."

Q&A with Cynthia Anderson

The Interview Process and Writing "Scenelets"

Q: Since Cresta is unused to the glare of publicity, was it harder to interview him than some of the more public figures you have written about?
A: Everyday people are easier to write because they're generally more candid. Once you make them comfortable, they tend to talk openly. They're less rehearsed. That said, often they speak too candidly, tell you too much about their lives, and you have to make judgment calls when putting the story together to protect their privacy.

Q: How do you use scenes and exposition in your profiles? How important were scenes in this piece?
A: Watching Cresta actually play Scrabble was not critical, but in addition to providing scene, it offered an opportunity to insert observations about his character into the story.

In terms of process, though, it's crucial to dedicate part of your time with your subject to the interview itself, and part to observation of him or her actively doing something. Otherwise both aspects get watered down. I usually spend some time on the interview first so that my subject doesn't find the observation part awkward with me as a silent spectator.

Q. What were the challenges of writing about a process (the game) that does not provide much to look at—it is a little like watching paint dry?

A: Right, that's why I included a lot of sounds! Actually, the real challenge wasn't the absence of visual detail as much as it was the lack of action. Nothing moves a scene along like action. A good written scene should be like a film clip, with forward motion and an arc. You need strong verbs to move those characters around on the page, so the characters—your subject or subjects—have to be doing something.

Courtesy Cynthia Anderson

Cynthia Anderson

Including anecdotes that are anchored by "scene-let" (such as the one in which Cresta memorizes the Scrabble dictionary while watching TV at night with his wife) also helps enliven a story that's not inherently active. Make sure you get enough details when assembling an anecdote to give it a scenic context.

Q: You are a writing teacher as well as a writer, so what is the most important advice you give to students about writing profiles?

A: The interview and the writing itself should be an act of discovery. Prepare enough questions to give the interview shape (and be sure you know as much about your subject beforehand as you can), but then let yourself be surprised. Even though it's helpful to go in with a working nut graf, it's important to adjust it according to what you actually find. In Cresta's case, I had no idea he'd be a reluctant "king," but that wound up driving the whole story.

THE RHETORICAL SITUATION:
THE WRITER'S STANCE

Published profiles appear just about everywhere in community, workplace, and professional settings. Many community and special-interest groups produce specialty publications profiling members or groups of people who might be noteworthy to members. Newspapers also often profile ordinary people who have faced extraordinary circumstances. In college, you might compose oral histories or historical profiles that shed light on a social movement, discovery, medical breakthrough, or phenomenon. In all these cases, you will want to find a narrow angle or perspective and focus on a specific aspect of the person's life rather than write a comprehensive biography of an entire life.

As you explore your profile subject's life, you will undoubtedly learn about yourself—your own interests, values, and beliefs—and you will be able to help

Pam Berry

Portrait of a man with a cigar, Lubbock, Texas, by Pam Berry.

PRACTICE 7.1

Defining Style and Voice

1. Go out to a public place: a restaurant, park, or lobby, for example. Choose one person to observe for as long as ten minutes. Make note of the person's gestures, body language, clothing, and hairstyle. If you can catch a few words of dialogue, write them down.
2. Decide what impression that person made on you.
3. Without telling your reader what you think about the person, describe, in one paragraph, what you observed. Select and arrange details and choose words that will help shape your reader's impression.
4. When you return to the classroom, read your paragraphs out loud. Have classmates tell you what impression they get from your writing.

your readers discover something in your profile subject's life that reflects on their lives as well. To do this, you need to keep the spotlight on your subject. So, it is usually best to keep your subject in the foreground and yourself in the background unless there is a compelling reason for you to be in the story. In a profile of a businessman who dropped out of the corporate world to become a teacher, you might be tempted to write:

> "Why did you leave your successful career in business to become a teacher?" I asked him next. He told me he left to "follow a voice [he] heard every morning just as [he] was waking up."

But you can use the same material without reference to yourself and without inserting your questions:

> Monroe left his successful career in business to "follow a voice I heard every morning just as I was waking up," he says.

(See also the box on the Key Elements in Effective Profiles on page 183.)

CHOOSING A GOOD PROFILE SUBJECT

The media are starting to heed the old axiom that everybody has a story. The ordinary-person genre has become a professional crusade for one reporter. David Johnson, at the Lewiston, Idaho, *Morning Tribune*, selects a name randomly out of the phone book for his features about people not normally considered newsmakers. Johnson has been writing his column "Everyone Has a Story" for twenty years and has written more than one thousand pieces about ordinary people.

FINDING YOUR TOPIC

This following list of profile topics demonstrates the range of topics students have written about. Student writers discovered these topics at their colleges, in their neighborhoods, in their family's circle of acquaintances, and by word of mouth.

- An 89-year-old Russian immigrant who has lived through "World War II, Communism, Stalin, Brezhnev, Gorbachev, and the breakup of the Soviet Union"
- High school chess players who challenge the "chess nerd" stereotype as well as one another
- A local band that combines punk rock with Irish sentimentality
- A college woman who wears the college mascot suit and views college sports from this unique perspective
- A director of a summer arts camp for inner-city kids who believes that the arts teach essential cognitive skills

FINDING YOUR FOCUS

Finding the story in your subject's life that resonates and will have meaning for your reader is just as important as choosing a good profile topic. You can often locate this meaning in a point of tension or conflict. If you were writing a profile of a professional wrestler, for example, a point of conflict might be whether professional wrestling is above-board and how this particular wrestler deals with the perception of fakery in the sport. A profile about a student athlete might explore the tension between the demands of academic work and athletic training.

Five Questions to Help Focus Your Profile

1. Is your subject in some way related to a news story or a current trend or idea?
2. Is your subject in some way unusual, odd, or offbeat?
3. Can you link your subject to a noteworthy achievement, an innovation, a contribution, or a discovery?
4. If your subject is not unique, how does he or she fit in? Does your subject represent what is typical about a profession, interest, lifestyle, or conflict? Can your subject reveal something found in others with the same profession, interest, lifestyle, or conflict?
5. Why would readers be interested in this person? What is the payoff for readers?

PRACTICE 7.2

Finding a Good Profile Topic

1. List five possible profile topics. Think of people you know or people you have heard about who have had interesting experiences, do interesting work (perhaps in a field you might want to enter), have interesting unusual hobbies interests, or espouse interesting philosophies.
2. Choose one person from your list and freewrite for five minutes about that person. What are possible points of tension or conflict in the person's story? What would you want to find out about him or her? What questions would you ask?

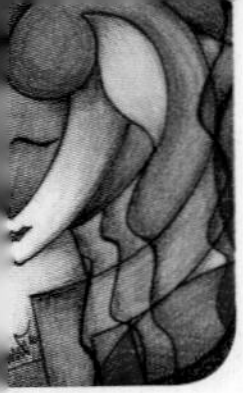

PRACTICE 7.3

Identifying the Nut Graf or Interpretive Thesis

Find three profiles published in newspapers, magazines, or Web sites. For each, identify and underline the nut graf. If you do not find a nut graf directly after the lead paragraph(s), see if it has been pulled out and used as a subhead after the title. For each nut graf you identify, comment on how well you think it presents the profile's focus. Explain your reasoning.

THE BIG IDEA: THE NUT GRAF OR INTEPRETIVE THESIS

A profile usually explicitly states its thesis directly after the lead, the introductory paragraph or paragraphs. This thesis is often embedded in a paragraph that journalists call the *nut graf. Nut* means the kernel of the idea; *graf* is journalistic shorthand for "paragraph." Some call this paragraph the "bridge," and another way to understand its function is to understand that it bridges the lead and the body of the paper.

When you write your profile, you might not find your focus until you have completed your research. Research often uncovers a new insight as you explore your subject, and may help you unearth a compelling, previously untold story. Peter Scanlan, in *The Quill*, a publication of the Society of Professional Journalists, gives this advice for finding or developing a profile focus: Look for conflicts, questions, obstacles, or "pivotal moments" in someone's story:

- When things have changed
- When things will never be the same
- When things have fallen apart
- When you do not know how things will turn out

The nut graf announces your focus—that is, your interpretation of your subject—and it stems from your exploration of your subject. If you are having trouble finding your own focus for a profile, sometimes it is helpful to use this template to help figure out your thesis:

(Name of your profile subject) is a ____________ who ____________.

For example, for the profile of Theodore Geisel (Dr. Seuss), you could fill in the blanks in a number of ways.

Theodore Geisel was *a writer and artist* who *changed the way children read forever.*

Theodore Geisel was *a visionary* who *never let fate govern him.*

A word of caution here: Remember that an interpretive thesis is never a factual statement about the person (Theodore Geisel was the author *of Green Eggs and Ham*) but rather stems from your interpretation of your profile subject, an interpretation that you then have to support through your research.

Next, figure out a logical pattern of development that stems from your nut graf. Select quotations, anecdotes, facts that support your interpretation.

Key Elements in Effective Profiles

- **Physical description:** Physical description should be brief and relevant. Give your reader a glimpse of some defining characteristics that reflect your interpretation but not a feature-by-feature portrait.
- **Quotations from the subject:** Quotations are the lifeblood of profiles. Quotations from your subject allow your reader to actually hear your subject's voice and to bring that person to life.
- **Quotations about the subject:** Quotations from others allow for multiple perspectives and allow you to draw a complex character, who, like all of us, has many layers.
- **Examples:** Your profile needs proof, examples that illustrate how or when your subject did something noteworthy or revealing of character.
- **Anecdotes:** Some of the best examples come in the form of anecdotes, or small stories. Your source can be your subject or people who know your subject well.
- **Factual information (background and context)**: Embedded in your profile should be factual information that deepens your reader's understanding of the subject. Explanatory, or expository, passages explain everything from background information on the subject's life to concepts needed to understand the world in which the subject lives.

For example, in "The Quietest Mogul," on page 191, the nut graf is the third paragraph, which begins with the interpretive thesis, "Le may be the quietest titan of the Boston food scene." Le's story flows from this point; it is one of how quiet determination and hard work brought him to the pinnacle of success in the extremely competitive restaurant business. The dominant impression of Le, that he is "the quietest titan," weaves its way through the entire profile.

PRACTICE 7.4

Identifying Profile Elements

1. Find a published profile you like (from a recent publication, Web site or from the readings in this chapter), and get a handful of highlighters. As you read the profile, use different colors to highlight all the following elements you can find:
   - Physical description
   - Quotations from the subject
   - Quotations about the subject
   - Examples
   - Anecdotes
   - Factual information
2. By looking at the color patterns, make an assessment of the kinds of elements the writer used. Which elements did the writer rely on most?

VISUAL LITERACY: ANALYZING PORTRAITS

EXAMINE THE TWO PORTRAITS OF ANDY WARHOL

1. Look at each portrait carefully. Pay attention to
   - the background (context)
   - the focal point of the portrait (where the artist directs your attention first)
   - the pose of the subject, his body language
   - the positioning of the subject in the frame—his size and presence
   - the colors and design of the clothing and the background images

Jamie Wyeth/Collection of Cheekwood Botanical Garden and Museum of Art

Portrait of Andy Warhol, by Jamie Wyeth (1976)

Portrait of Andy Warhol, by Hans Namuth (1981)

2. What impression do you get about the character in each painting or photograph?
3. Does the artist refer to other paintings or images in the style or design?
4. Does the author refer to other characters—from literature, popular culture, mythology, or stereotypes?

What specific details contribute to your interpretation?

- Write an interpretive thesis using the steps under The Big Idea, pages 182–183.
- Answer these questions for the other portraits in this chapter.

RESEARCH PATHS

How interesting your reader finds your story hinges on what you discover and uncover in your research. The more you learn, the stronger and more credible your voice becomes, and the more you will enliven and focus your writing. A well-researched profile includes

- Print and electronic sources, including social networking sites like Facebook as well as sources about the subject's field of interest
- Direct observation of the person in a place that has relevance for him or her
- Interviews with many people (multiple sources)

SOCIAL MEDIA

Social media sites are quickly becoming ways to get in touch with people whom you might not have met any other way. Facebook, LinkedIn, or other social networking sites provide good entry points for learning details about your subject's interests, getting some contact information, or finding out some basic information about your subject's biography. Message boards and forums as well as Twitter can lead you to people who might know about the field your subject represents, and lead you to possible outside interviews to help contextualize your subject. Be careful, though, to assess your source's credentials for acting as an "expert" whose comments have worth in your work. Make sure you verify your source's identity and claims. The rule of thumb for journalists is to make sure you can find a second source offering similar information. Statistics, documents, and other people can help verify claims.

PRACTICE 7.5

Search for Sources

Possible profile subjects include the following:

- A high school teacher who has just been named Math Teacher of the Year
- A college student who is a professional figure skater
- An inventor who is working on creating a nonpolluting combustion engine
- A marathon runner

Choose one of these subjects, or one from the "Finding Your Topic" on page 181, and do a search for print and electronic sources that you could read for background information. List at least three sources. Use correct bibliographical citation, as shown in Chapter 16.

ONLINE SEARCHES AND DATABASES

Other useful contextual information—facts and statistics—are available on databases. Through online searches, you can find the names and contact information for authors or members of groups. Often you will find links or lists of sources that lead you to people who might be willing to offer an expert opinion on your subject or topics.

DIRECT OBSERVATION

Novelist Eudora Welty said, "Stories don't happen nowhere." She was talking about the significance of setting in creating an impression. Characters in profiles, as in fiction, inhabit places, and the places they inhabit reveal something about who they are.

One student, writing a profile of a nutritionist, visited her office. The student begins her profile this way.

> Bright red Coca-Cola bottles intermix with Special K cereal boxes on the top of her food pyramid shelf. Tiny sugar cubes, used to illustrate how much sugar is in different sizes of soda, form geometric shapes from the size of a three-ounce piece of steak to an extra-large pancake. On the shelf below, [a] vitamin C–dense Tropicana orange juice box mingles with the fiber-rich Quaker Oats box, decked out in its reds, whites, and blues. Every flavored water drink out on the market from pineapple to strawberry line[s] the third shelf like a row of soldiers.
>
> —Yoonie Park, "Hold the Line in Body Fat"

The description of the office shelves brings the reader into the subject's nutrition-savvy world and leads to the writer's assessment that the subject "does not offer the quick fix; instead, she brings us a pinch of fun and enjoyment with eating healthfully." If you can shadow your profile subject for a day or an afternoon and observe him or her in daily life—teaching nutrition, racing dirt bikes, or painting a picture—you will find revealing details and establish a solid narrative base for your profile.

INTERVIEWS

Interviews are the mainstay of field research. Through interviewing sources, you gather firsthand information from experts as well as opinions, responses, and thoughts from anyone familiar with the subject. (For more information on Interviewing, see the box on Tips for Good Interviews and also page 497 in Chapter 15, Research.)

Charles Fishman, whose short article about Disney's laundry service you can read in Chapter 8, is an award-winning journalist who has also written articles and books about Tupperware, bomb-making factories, NASA, and Wal-Mart. We asked him about his reputation for gaining unusually good access to sources. His response follows:

> I have gotten into some amazing places. I talked my way into the nation's only bomb factory—the factory where the U.S. military makes every non-nuclear bomb dropped in Afghanistan and Iraq, a facility six times the size of Manhattan. I spent two weeks on the busiest maternity ward in the U.S., I actually attended the births of something like 40 babies. I not only got to write about the creation of the largest cruise ship in history—I spent four days in the shipyard where it was being constructed. I have stood at the top of the launch pad from which the space shuttles are launched.
>
> You don't get invited into any of these places. You have to ask.

Tips for Good Interviews

Although conducting an interview might seem as simple as having a conversation, planning ahead and being well prepared will help you get the best material possible.

- **Start Early.** Leave plenty of time for phone or e-mail tag.
- **Set Up the Interview.** Arrange to meet at a specific time and place, preferably in the subject's workplace or home.
- **Make a Contact List.** Compile a list of people who know your subject and the issues discussed in the profile. As you interview your subject and the secondary sources, ask for names of other people knowledgeable about the subject or the subject's field.
- **Do Your Homework.** Go into the interview informed. Enter your source's name—and the topic's name—into an Internet search engine and check out the results before you sit down to talk.
- **Prepare for the Interview.** Write at least ten questions. Make them open-ended, not ones that can be answered by *yes* or *no*. Ask "How do you think the Internet will be used in the future?" rather than "Do you think the Internet will only be used for shopping?"
- **Conduct the Interview.** If you find it hard to start, ask some general questions to warm up. "What are you doing when you are not working (or in school)?" often opens up an interesting path of inquiry.
- **Be a Careful Observer.** Pay attention to small details. A small detail of dress or an idiosyncratic gesture can bring your subject to life for your reader.
- **Transcribe Your Notes.** Add any details of physical appearance or setting that might be useful to remember later.
- **Read Your Notes Critically.** Annotate your notes as you read through them. Underline important information. Make stars next to or highlight good quotations.

Peter Doyle

Portrait of Shantay, a male performer.

MULTIPLE POINTS OF VIEW

If you just tell a story from your subject's perspective, you have not written a profile as much as an as-told-to story—a story told from only your subject's point of view as he or she tells it to you. Your reader gets only your subject's point of view. To develop a more balanced and more complex perspective (even a contradictory or negative one), provide your reader with multiple points of view about your subject. These secondary sources can be coworkers, relatives, neighbors, or competitors, to name a few.

If you are writing about the owner of the first Vietnamese noodle shop in town, for example, interviewing nearby restaurant owners might give you an interesting perspective on the business. Interviewing the owner's spouse, children, chef, and servers adds other, more personal layers to the story. Phoning the restaurant reviewer who gave the new restaurant four stars might tell you even more about the owner's abilities.

Portrait, Girl with Pearl Earring, by Jan Vermeer (1632-1675).

PRACTICE 7.6

Choosing Good Quotations

Below is a list of quotations gathered for a profile written about Damian DiPaola, the owner and chef (or as he prefers it, "cook") at an Italian restaurant. Journalist David Maloof gathered these quotations from interviews with DiPaola and from observing DiPaola in conversation with coworkers. Decide which quotations you would (a) quote fully, (b) quote partially, (c) paraphrase, or (d) omit. Explain why you made these decisions.

BEGINNINGS AND ENDINGS

How to start and how to end are often the trickiest parts of writing a profile. You want to capture your readers' attention from the very first line of your piece, and you want to end gracefully, giving a sense that your exploration of the subject is complete and satisfying.

BEGINNINGS

Of all the types of introductions (leads) available, three are the most common and most useful: the setting, the anecdote, and the generalization.

SETTING LEAD: The scene-setting lead can use description, detail, and direct quotations to bring the reader directly into a scene that introduces the profile subject in his or her milieu:

> At the Holiday Inn in Bismark, N.D. Heidi Heitkamp, the Democratic candidate for governor, charges to the podium, her trademark mane of red hair moussed into submission. Heitkamp, 45, is big, beautiful and lit up from the inside. The election results aren't all in, but she appears jubilant.
>
> —Judith Newman, "Running for Life" from SELF. Reprinted with permission.

ANECDOTAL LEAD: An anecdotal lead hooks the reader by telling a brief but complete story that gives the reader some insight into the person's character:

> China's Cultural Revolution was in full force in 1968, when Shen Tong was born. His grandparents had been among its first victims; when his grandfather openly criticized the village mayor, he and his wife became targets for the Red Guards.
>
> The day before they were to be paraded through their village in dunce caps, they hanged themselves from their bamboo bed frame.
>
> —Midge Raymond, "The Long Journey Home"

GENERALIZATION LEAD: A generalization lead begins with a broad, umbrella statement, then narrows down to the specific point, or person, of the profile:

> Tonight, an artist in Allston will eat tripe. On Newbury Street, a weary shopper will eat beef tendon. And in Harvard Square, students and parents and the odd out-of-towner will slurp their way through a selection of intensely flavored and very inexpensive noodle soups they'd probably never heard of just two years ago.
>
> These parallel dining adventures come courtesy of Duyen Le, the accidental noodlemonger from Vietnam whose Pho Pasteur restaurants have taken pho, the steaming soul food of northern Vietnam, from Formica tabletops in Chinatown and Dorchester to higher-rent neighborhoods where, not so long ago, the prevailing notion of ethnic food featured spaghetti carbonara.
>
> Le may be the quietest titan of the Boston food scene.
>
> —Kelly Horan, "The Quietest Mogul"

ENDINGS

The best kind of conclusion in a profile presents an image or a quotation that leaves a final impression on readers, reminding them of your focus.

Good quotations can be irreverent, eccentric, funny, witty, wry, angry, or emotional. What they should not be is boring, self-evident, or confusing. Quotations can reveal character; sum up a point; create an image; or provide irony, insight, or tension for the piece. Quotations should be articulate, clear, and accessible, unless what they are intended to reveal is a person's nervousness or perhaps evasiveness.

Often profile writers return to the introductory scene to create a sense of coming full circle. In Cynthia Anderson's "Of Carpenters and Kings" notice how she returns in the conclusion to the opening scene at the Scrabble club. She ends with a quotation from Michael Cresta, the reluctant "king" of Scrabble. His response to his fame, "It might bring me some carpentry jobs," reinforces Cresta's down-to-earth personality and reminds the reader of Anderson's opening paragraph where she asserts that he "wears the crown a tad uneasily."

(Continued)

- "I've been making cappuccinos since I was four years old in my Dad's café."
- "My mother had a knack for making the greatest dinners with the least ingredients. She used lots of vegetables and fish and pasta. My father would make the elaborate meals, such as lobster *fra diavlo* and rack of lamb."
- "A chef is someone who runs around with a clipboard and a pen and then goes out in the dining room and takes credit for everything."
- "I did have a house, but when I bought my [business] partner out I had to sell the house."
- "About a year ago, I weighed 205. I lost 35 pounds. I ate a lot of angel hair pasta with escarole in chicken broth."
- "We're not 'chefs' here. We prefer to be called 'cooks.' *Chef* is a French word. It means 'chief' or 'commander of the kitchen.'"

—David Maloof, "Notes for Pan Music,"• a profile published in the Hampshire Life Magazine section of the Daily Hampshire Gazette, June 27, 1997. Reprinted by permission of the author.

D I Y

DIY MEDIA AND DESIGN

ORAL HISTORY: A SPOKEN WORD PROJECT

TELLING ANOTHER'S STORY through the spoken word is the core of oral history projects. The most interesting subjects are people who have lived through an era or experience that has historical significance but, just as with written profiles, everyday people living ordinary lives have memories worth adding to the historical record.

You might want to think about parents, grandparents, or friends of the family who might have been in World War II, Vietnam, or Iraq. Or think of people who have been on the cutting edge of social or political movements.

One important caveat about oral history is that it must be an accurate account of your subject's story and not include rumor or hearsay. Since oral history depends on the spoken word and your subject's memory, it is important to record the story accurately, whether you take notes by hand or use audio or video recordings. When conducting interviews for an oral history:

- Be sure your subject understands that the conversation is not private but will become part of a historical record.
- At the beginning of each recording session, state the name of the interviewee, the place, and date of the session.
- Keep the tone conversational.
- Allow your subject to tell the story in his or her own time and manner.
- Do not try to fill in dead spaces in the interview. Silence allows your subject to recall events.
- End the interview after an hour, two at most.
- Have your subject sign a release form that simply includes the subject's name, your name, the date, and the subject's permission to use the interview for a school project.
- Transcribe your notes soon after the interview.
- Analyze the interview. What other information do you need? What new questions come to mind? Are all the facts and dates correct?

One nonprofit group, StoryCorps began recording and collecting interviews between parents and their children, siblings, or friends in 2003. Since then it has archived tens of thousands of interviews, which you can listen to on its Web site, StoryCorps.com.

READINGS

AUTHOR JACK FALLA profiles the college teacher who taught him how to write; student Thanos Matthai explores the world of a Muslim teen, and journalist J. R. Moehringer visits a Vermont farm to explore the former life of a Holocaust rescuer.

The Top Drill Instructor in Boot Camp 101[2]

Jack Falla

Jack Falla was a writer, teacher and sports journalist who spent many years on the staff of Sports Illustrated. *He wrote this profile of the teacher who really taught him how to write for* Campus Voice, *the alumni magazine of his* alma mater, *Boston University. This piece is slightly adapted, with the author's permission.*

THE BULLWHIP lay on the bookcase, coiled around its wooden handle like a snake around its rattle.

I was in the second-floor office of associate professor Gerald Powers at Boston University's College of Communication. A student carrying a sheaf of papers had slunk away from Powers's desk as I entered, "REWRITE" scrawled across the top paper in red pencil. The whip had struck again.

"Not my day to be popular," said Powers, rising from his chair to shake hands. He is a slight man, perhaps 5 feet 9, with close-cropped graying hair, and a reserved, somewhat bemused manner.

"At least you spared him the stamp," I said, nodding toward the open door. We could hear the retreating student's footsteps in the hall.

"Oh, I still have it," said Powers, smiling for the first time and opening his desk drawer to take out a rubber stamp that says REWRITE in block letters. "And I have the other one at home."

The other stamp is even more succinct; it simply reads BULLSHIT.

The stamps and Powers's willingness to use them on students' papers are two of the reasons he carries the reputation that inevitably falls upon one faculty member at every college in the world: toughest sumbitch on campus. Powers is one of those professors from whom hordes of students recoil at preregistration, choosing instead to slink over to the "twinkies" courses. Yet somehow the sumbitches manage to endure.

"Powers is one of those professors from whom hordes of students recoil at preregistration."

For 20 years, Powers has taught various writing courses within BU's Public Relations Department. And for 20 years he has ritualistically slain compromise in the first minute of the first class. His usual greeting:

> "Deadlines are immovable. Meet them if it kills you. The only excuse for failing to turn in a paper on time is a death in the family. In which case," he adds, "I prefer that the death be yours."

[2]Jack Falla, "The Top Drill Instructor in Boot Camp," adapted from Campus Voice, August/September 1984. Reprinted with permission.

Neal Boudette, a recent survivor of a Powers class, recalls another intimidating tactic: "One day Powers opened his briefcase in class and took out that whip. He said, 'This is a gift from former students. They thought it symbolized the way I work.' I said to myself, 'This man is a lunatic. He uses terror to teach.'"

"I try to set the tone early," says Powers, describing his First-Day-of-Class Grand-Entrance Fantasy. "I think I should enter the class ahead of a train of graduate assistants carrying my briefcase and books, backed up by an orchestra playing the march from Verdi's *Aida.*"

That would certainly get the class's attention, I agreed.

It is also a day-one ritual for Powers to tell his students that almost every assignment will have to be rewritten—twice. At which point some unfortunate will inevitably raise his hand and ask, "What if you do it right the first time?"

"Humor me," he will say.

"I think students take his classes as some kind of self-flagellation," says BU grad Denise Graveline. "They know Powers's reputation, and they want to see if they can meet the challenge."

Meeting the challenge takes a strong self-image on the students' part because Powers, like many professors of the hard-line persuasion, can be brutal in class.

For example, one student began an editorial with "In this modern world of ours today …"

Powers read it aloud. "Nice lead," he said, then commented, "if we don't count its being dull, pointless, and triply redundant."

Then there was the now-famous classroom argument between Powers and a student who tried playing hardball in defense of his use of the alleged word *irregardless.*

"Not a proper word," said Powers.

"It's in the dictionary," yelled the student, who then had the temerity and monumental bad judgment to charge to the front of the room and bang his *Webster's* down on the table.

"My dear boy," said Powers, picking up the dictionary and sliding into what he calls his full William F. Buckley, "let us read the definition. '*Irregardless:* illiterate use of the word *regardless.*'"

Powers's students routinely receive graded papers bearing so much red penciling that it looks as though Powers has bled on them.

"Nice typing. Horrible writing" is a frequent comment in the river of red. And to a student who once argued that good layout photos would help "carry his story," Powers replied, "Illustrating that story would be like perfuming a pig."

"Three or four weeks into each term, the school's advising center begins to resemble a refugee processing station."

"He demeaned us," says former Powers student Bob Hughes, "until most of us rose above ourselves in the effort to prove we were better than he gave us credit for being." No one escapes Powers's sarcasm. A graduate assistant once gave a lecture while Powers observed from the back of the room. The students were less than animated, prompting the grad assistant to say with forced good humor, "Professor Powers, is there something you can do to wake up the class?"

"Begging your pardon," replied Powers, "I wasn't the one who put them to sleep."

And to a student who was considering a freelance writing career, Powers advised, "An excellent idea, particularly if you had the

foresight to be born the daughter of a railway magnate."

Three or four weeks into each term, the school's advising center begins to resemble a refugee processing station with students in dazed or indignant retreat from Powers's thermonuclear teaching.

"Students would come in crying 'mental abuse' or 'I can't take it in there,'" says BU grad Maryellen Kennedy, who observed these semiannual crises during four years of working in the advising center. "A lot of people transfer to other courses, but all that does is add to the Powers mystique."

"Students genuinely fear him," adds Graveline.

But, like other sumbitches from the football field to the physics lab, Powers claims he doesn't care.

"I'm an elitist," he says, pointing out that his teaching methods derive from the classical private-school tradition as he experienced it at Boston Latin, St. Sebastian's, and Harvard.

"I actively detest . . . the brownnosers, grade grubbers, and B.S. artists."

"I divide students into four categories," he says. "First are those I actively detest. The brownnosers, grade grubbers, and B.S. artists. Then there are what I call the Rimless Ciphers. They're neuter. They occupy space. I'm neither for them nor against them. The largest group is made up of pleasant, nice people. I have great empathy for students in this group who try hard. Finally, there is a small group—the select and gifted few—the ones you never forget."

Powers may be harder on his protégés, however, than on any of his other students. I recall one of the chosen, a senior who had done well in two of Powers's courses and who was suddenly doing poorly after going through that most painful of undergraduate crises: Breaking Up with the Girlfriend. There were some of us who feared for the young man's emotional stability. Powers was not among us.

"Do you know what Robert Frost once said was all he knew about life?" Powers said to the student. "'It goes on.' When you come into this class, you leave your personal problems outside."

Yet Powers has a single overwhelmingly redeeming feature that he probably shares with a good many other campus SOBs. He will go to the mat for his students.

Kennedy describes a typical scene at the student advising center: "The reception room would be crowded with students waiting to see advisers, and suddenly Powers would burst in with a student in tow. Immediately, Powers's student would become the best kid with the most pressing problem in the entire university. Powers would have to get him into this course or out of that course, and it would have to be done that minute. Sometimes Powers would just bypass everyone and go charging into a dean's office."

"When alumni return to school, the one name you hear most often is Powers," says Graveline. "The message is usually 'If you can get through Powers's courses—and put up with him telling you to straighten your tie and shine the back of your shoes—you can probably survive the transition from campus to the world of work.'"

Powers readily admits that he is more concerned with his students' job search than with their paper chase. Each year he places dozens of students in high-paying internships with such

corporate giants as Ford, Alcoa, and General Electric. He sends these former waitresses and lifeguards away in May with the admonition "Screw up and you'll answer to your boss this summer and to me next fall."

But Powers's students—those who survive, that is—don't often screw up. And as much as they may curse his name as they're plowing through yet another endless rewrite, a large percentage will someday look back and realize that he was the one professor who made a difference in their lives.

I lifted the bullwhip off the bookcase and let it uncoil on the floor.

"So why do you keep teaching?" I asked.

"Same reason most of the other SOBs in this profession do it," he said, leaning back in his chair. "I do it for the money."

I put the bullwhip back on the shelf. We went to lunch. I bought.

QUESTIONS FOR RHETORICAL ANALYSIS

1. **CONSIDERING THE RHETORICAL SITUATION:** In this profile, Falla uses the first person in the very first scene: "I entered the second-floor office ..." and he uses the first person again in the final scene: "I lifted the bullwhip off the bookcase...." Why do you think Falla put himself in the story? In what way is it effective? In what way is it intrusive?
2. Where does the lead or introductory section of the story end and the body of the story begin? What do you learn about Powers in the introduction?
3. Identify the argumentative thesis in the nut graf. Cite at least two sentences in the body of the profile where this thesis is supported and expanded.
4. Give an example of each of the following elements from this profile:
   - Physical description
   - Quotations from the subject
   - Quotations about the subject
   - Examples
   - Anecdotes
   - Factual information
5. What does Falla imply about his ex-teacher in the last two sentences of this profile: "We went to lunch. I bought."?

QUESTIONS FOR WRITING AND DISCUSSION

1. Falla adds to the mythology of the enduring value of a "tough" teacher. Do you agree that "tough" teachers are the most effective ones? Explain your answer.
2. The bullwhip and the rubber stamps define Powers' teaching style. Think about a teacher who affected you in some way—positively or negatively. What symbols would you use to define that teacher? Why?

STYLE PRACTICE: IMITATION

Falla opens this profile with a simile, comparing Professor Powers' bullwhip to a snake. "The bullwhip lay on the bookcase, coiled around its wooden handle like a snake around its rattle." Create a simile using some symbolic object you might find in one of your professor's office.

A Fine Balance: The Life of a Muslim Teenager[3]

By Thanos Matthai

Thanos Matthai wrote this profile of his fellow student, Mohamed Ahmed, for his writing class. Matthai examines the tension between Mohamed's Islamic faith and his college culture.

MOHAMED AHMED arrives at the frat party with several of his friends. After putting his coat away, he talks to his friends for a little before going to the bar to get a drink.

"Can I get a Coke?" he asks the guy behind the bar. The bartender tells him that the Jack Daniels is running out, but that there's still some left for another rum and Coke.

"No, I only want Coke," says Mohamed. The bartender gives him a puzzled look, but obligingly pours him a Coke. Mohamed rejoins his friends, who are all embracing their plastic cups of Bud Light. He decides to go watch the "Beirut" game in the next room and passes several couples grinding to Sisqo's "Thong Song." The "Beirut" game becomes boring, and he goes back to find his friends completely drunk.

A month later Mohamed returns home during a break from college and its party life and catches up with all his high school friends. While hanging out at a friend's house, they all talk about the people whom they've met at college. Some of Mohamed's friends are in relationships while the rest have "hooked up" with people.

"Hey, Mohamed, how many girls have you hooked up with?" asks one friend chuckling.

Mohamed blushes a little and laughs quietly along with his friends.

"You know I'm not allowed to do that," he replies, stating what his friends already know.

Islam is the reason that Mohamed doesn't behave in the same manner as his friends. His parents emigrated from India in 1980; his is the only Muslim family in a wealthy suburban town outside of Boston of which only 196 out of 10,000 residents are not white. Always surrounded by people who held beliefs almost directly contrary to his own, Mohamed has had to make tough choices, sometimes forcing him to almost lead two separate lives.

"Mohammed has had to make tough choices, sometimes forcing him to almost lead two separate lives."

As a Muslim, Mohamed is forbidden from many things that his friends take for granted, such as drinking alcohol, having sex outside of marriage, and even eating pork. If Mohamed eats out with his friends, he usually has to order vegetarian dishes because the meat in most restaurants isn't *zabiha*: slaughtered in a manner that the Koran, the holy book of Islam, deems *halal*, or fit for a Muslim to eat. "The nearest *halal* restaurant to me is a 25-mile drive to either Boston or Providence," he says. When offered a Starburst candy, he declines it, saying that it is *haram,* or completely forbidden by the Koran, because it contains enzymes and emulsifiers that could have been obtained from pigs.

"Starting from middle school, I was raised to hang out only with Muslims because they

[3]Reprinted by permission of Thanos Matthai.

were good influences," says Mohamed. "I had no friends in school, but I did a lot of stuff with my cousins and people I knew from the mosque." Walking around his room at home, he points to the old history and biology books that he used to read in his free time. "I was a real geek," he says, laughing as he flips through *The World's Greatest Cities.*

Although initially quiet and not very social, Mohamed became heavily involved with school activities during his junior and senior years. "Mohamed's mother really pushed him to take part in things and to succeed," says his cousin Kareem Ahmed.

According to Mohamed, football and student council were the two activities that really changed him. "The football team wanted me to hang out with them and made me hang out with them," he says as he picks up a football and tosses it in the air. With a husky 6 foot 3 inch frame, dark complexion, thick eyebrows, and close-cropped black hair, he was a fierce-looking outside linebacker. "Their popularity and the fact I was vice president of the student council really helped me get to know people," he adds. Mohamed was also valedictorian and a member of many service-oriented groups like the National Honor Society and the Leo Club, which helped him meet more people.

"Many kids found him interesting because he was so naïve and different from them," says his friend Jim Dorsey. "As they spent more time with him, they began to like him and become friends."

Many people find Mohamed to be a welcome change from the average teenager. "He's so different from my other guy friends because he's not caught up with material things and not obsessed with beer," says Shannon Riley, one of Mohamed's closest friends. "He's more interested in other things like religion and politics."

"In the beginning of high school, no one had any idea what Islam was," says Mohamed. "Even though nothing bad happened to me after 9/11, I really made it a point to talk about Islam because all people knew about it was what they saw on television."

"Even though nothing bad happened to me after 9/11, I really made it a point to talk about Islam because all people knew about it was what they saw on television."

"Mohamed was much more aware of things outside America because he was a religious minority," says Jim. According to Jim, very few of Mohamed's friends were knowledgeable enough to be concerned about such things and discuss them, so they usually avoided discussions about politics and religion with him.

"I talked about Islam and politics so much that people got sick of it, but I felt I had to give them an accurate picture of what was going on," says Mohamed as he scrolls through the BBC Web site.

As Mohamed became more social and more involved in school activities, the differences between him and his friends became more apparent. "He had no idea about things that we thought were common knowledge," says Todd Shuman, a friend who also became Mohamed's roommate at college. Mohamed was not exposed to the same TV shows, jokes and experiences as his friends, and often found it hard to relate to them. *Sheltered, innocent, inexperienced* and *gullible* are some adjectives his friends use to describe him.

"It's almost as if things he couldn't do intrigued him, so he always asked questions about things like sex and being drunk," adds Todd.

More than reveal cultural differences, greater interaction with his friends forced Mohamed to walk a fine line. "He was always motivated to be in the public eye, but this kind of backfired because he became almost too social," says Kareem. Kareem has a good understanding of Muslim teenagers because he studied at a school in Pakistan for one and a half years. According to him, most first generation American Muslims are raised much more strictly than those living in predominantly Muslim countries like Pakistan or Egypt. "Parents are often scared that their kids are going to lose touch with their cultural roots, so they give them much less freedom," says Kareem. Many of his friends in Pakistan went to dance clubs, stayed out late, and socialized with girls.

"My dad didn't want me to hang out with anyone except Muslims because they could be a bad influence," says Mohamed. "I was raised to never be friends with girls or even to talk to them unless they were family," he adds.

While the Koran does not explicitly state that interaction with the opposite sex is wrong, it does state that men should not have impure thoughts about women other than their wives. At family functions, men and women are segregated and eat separately. Many traditional Muslims also encourage their children not to be friends with members of the opposite sex, says Kareem.

When asked about simply being friends with girls, Mohamed hesitantly replies that it's okay to be friends. "But I still kind of believe what I was raised to believe," he says. "I don't really know," he adds quickly, a pained expression on his face as he looks away.

Group projects for his classes were the initial excuses for staying out late. Then it was hanging out with the guys. "I kind of got used to people drinking at parties, so I went to them sometimes," he says. But according to his friends, at parties he would only stop by for five minutes to say hello to people.

Mohamed eventually told his mother that he spent time with girls. "She was ticked off at first, but then she became okay with it because she knew that I wouldn't do anything like date or have sex, which would violate Islamic principles," he says.

"Most first generation American Muslims are raised much more strictly than those living in predominantly Muslim countries like Pakistan or Egypt."

"I don't even know if my dad knows," he says with a faraway expression. "I didn't say anything to him because he's very traditional."

Then there was the one party that changed everything. "I stopped by this one party and Michelle, one of my best friends, was really drunk," says Mohamed as he remembers the evening. Michelle insisted that he have a sip from her cup, saying that it was only Sprite. Mohamed spit it out when he realized that the cup also had some alcohol (he would later find out it was vodka) in it.

"He got so angry that he started yelling at Michelle and pushed her over," says Shannon. "Michelle's boyfriend wanted to start a fight with Mohamed, but people broke it up."

"That really changed my outlook on things," says Mohamed. "That one of my best friends could do something like that

knowing full well that I couldn't drink alcohol." Michelle apologized repeatedly, but it took almost a year and a half for Mohamed to finally forgive her.

"When I look back at things now, I kind of regret a lot of things," says Mohamed as he looks around his dorm room. "I feel like in some ways it was a waste of time because I angered my parents for being out all the time and grew kind of distant from my cousins and other Muslim friends."

Sitting on his bed, he quietly contemplates his situation. "Sometimes I feel I've done wrong by even going to parties and stuff and it really depresses me," he says slowly and softly as he looks at a copy of the Koran on his desk.

Shannon, on the other hand, thinks otherwise. "Sometimes something bad needs to happen to shake you up so you realize how things really are," she says.

Mohamed will sometimes go to college parties with his friends because he wants to meet new people and because "the dorm gets boring when nobody is around." Instead of remaining on campus during the weekend, he often goes home; however, he knows that he can't keep returning home for the rest of his life.

"Sometimes I feel that there are two different voices or sides to me," he says. "One side is Islam and its principles and the other . . . well, I don't know what it is."

Mohamed reads a lot of Nietzsche, Aristotle and Plato in his college classes. "I like reading their books because their thoughts and ideas are so logical and make so much sense to me," he says while looking through Aristotle's *Nicomachean Ethics.*

He looks again at the copy of the Koran on his shelf. "But it's totally different from anything in Islam," he says with a sigh.

QUESTIONS FOR RHETORICAL ANALYSIS

1. **CONSIDERING THE RHETORICAL SITUATION:** The writer does not appear at all in this profile but stays in the background. What effect does this have on the reader? Look particularly at the scenes that the writer must have observed.
2. What impression do you have of Mohamed Ahmed in the opening scene at the frat party? What details contribute to your impression?
3. Identify the nut graf in this profile. What phrase in this paragraph encapsulates the writer's thesis? Where else can you find language or details that express the tension in this profile?
4. How does Matthai develop his profile? What elements—physical description, quotations from and about the subject, examples, anecdotes, factual information—does he weave into the portrait? Which are most memorable?
5. What research has Matthai done for this profile? Are there places where you think the profile needs more information?
6. The concluding scene is set in Mohamed's dorm room. What details in the conclusion reveal Mohamed's character and the quality of his life? In what ways has your impression of him changed or deepened from the opening scene?
7. How effective is the title of this profile in summing up its central points?

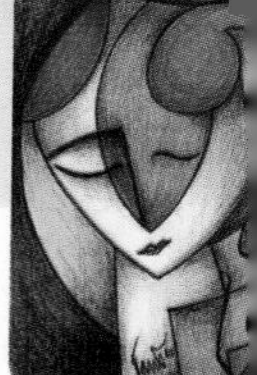

QUESTIONS FOR WRITING AND DISCUSSION

1. This profile is one of many stories told about cultural differences; this one is specifically about a Muslim teen. Does Mohamed Ahmed's story change your understanding of Islam? In what way?
2. Where do your values conflict with mainstream culture in your community?

STYLE PRACTICE: IMITATION

This profile concludes with a contrast between the secular books Mohamed reads and the Koran. The profile ends with this quotation:

> "I like reading their books because their thoughts and ideas are so logical and make so much sense to me," he says while looking through Aristotle's *Nicomachean Ethics.*
>
> He looks again at the copy of the Koran on his shelf. "But it's totally different from anything in Islam," he says with a sigh.

Choose a quotation from your subject that might end your profile and that would reveal your profile subject's conflict. Conclude the sentence with a gesture, like a sigh.

A Hidden and Solitary Soldier[4]

by J. R. Moehringer

Pulitzer-prize winner J. R. Moehringer was the Atlanta bureau chief of the Los Angeles Times. *In addition to his many profiles, he has published a memoir,* The Tender Bar, *and collaborated with Andre Agassi on his memoir* Open. *The following 'profile in courage' is about Marion Pritchard, a grandmother living quietly in Vermont who, while living in Holland during World War II, rescued people from the Holocaust, shot a Nazi policeman, and survived imprisonment. The profile was published in the* Los Angeles Times.

AS THE SUN dips behind the Vermont tree line, the family sits down to dinner and the talk goes in a thousand directions-books, politics, the Red Sox. Eventually the conversation turns to Grandma, and the Nazi she gunned down.

Grandma looks into her lap, shyly. The adults discuss the story in low voices while the children strain to hear from the far end of the table. "What are you talking about?" says Marion Pritchard's 12-year-old granddaughter, Molly.

Silence. "Grandma and the policeman," someone says.

"Oh," Molly says-not shocked, but bored. She's heard that story a million times.

It often happens this way. Pritchard's family doesn't get too excited about her daring past. They glide over the fact that she rescued scores of children from the Holocaust, survived seven months in a Nazi prison and killed one Nazi who got in her way. They take for granted that Grandma is a war hero—or else they can't

[4]J.R. Moehringer, "A Hidden and Solitary Soldier," from LA Times, January 20, 2002. Reprinted with permission.

quite believe it. The stories of extraordinary bravery don't fit with the aproned woman they see before them, who is frightened of squirrels and public speaking and who feels guilty when she swats a fly.

Strangers tend to be less casual about Pritchard's past. Psychologists study her, biographers woo her, governments fete her and invite her to speak. Visitors occasionally appear at her door, unannounced, to meet her, shake her hand, thank her.

Lately interest in Pritchard has grown even more avid. People want to be around her, now more than ever, because they know she's been here before: a nation under attack, a constant state of fear, a fanatic enemy bent on killing innocent civilians, especially Jews. The last time, Europe was ground zero, and Pritchard was one of those who ran into the fire.

But for a profile in courage, she keeps a fairly low profile. She lives at the end of a dirt road, in the middle of a sparse woods, on the outskirts of a town—Vershire, Vt.—that doesn't appear on many maps. She spends her days reading, teaching, seeing patients—she's been a psychoanalyst most of her working life—and listening to her beloved Verdi. You might hear "Chorus of the Hebrew Slaves" wafting from the open windows of her big white farmhouse when you turn off the dirt road.

As history does its ominous U-turn, she watches quietly from a safe distance. This isn't her fight. And yet, when hatred hits closer to home, she reverts instantly from recluse to rescuer. When anti-Semitism and homophobia flared in her corner of Vermont not long ago, Pritchard fought back with everything she had.

People want to know where this 81-year-old woman gets her grit. She eludes the question the way she once eluded her pursuers. "There's nothing you can tell somebody that's going to make them less fearful," she says in her faint Dutch accent. "I was scared stiff all the time during the war."

She prefers to let her life speak for itself. And its lessons are clear:

You can't always hide from hate.

Or from history.

And sometimes it's best not to try.

"The stories of extraordinary bravery don't fit with the aproned woman they see before them, who is frightened of squirrels and public speaking and who feels guilty when she swats a fly."

Standing in her garden, not much taller than her sweet peas and daylilies, Pritchard doesn't look like the intrepid rescuer who defied the Third Reich. Sitting in her book-lined living room, speaking in a thin voice that crackles like a fire, she gives no hint of the cunning rebel who risked her life for strangers.

She hides the hero somewhere inside.

When the memory of an injustice comes up, though, her blue eyes darken, her voice takes on a ragged quality, like a gypsy violin, and there she is, in plain sight, Marion van Binsbergen, the young girl who tried to save the world one child at a time. It happens when she remembers Hitler's shock troops devouring Europe in 1940, smashing into Amsterdam, where she was living with her younger brother and her parents. Overnight, the streets were filled with Nazis, "all 6 feet tall" and smug, she says.

She heard stories. Mass arrests. Night trains. Camps. She knew what was happening, but she didn't really know, until one day: She was 20 years old, riding her new bicycle near the school of social work where she was a graduate student, when she saw a truck double-parked outside a Jewish children's center. Some Nazi soldiers were rousting the children—all between 2 and 8 years old—and rushing them onto the truck. The children were sobbing. The soldiers were pitiless and efficient.

"It didn't take long," she says.

One soldier grabbed a little girl by her pigtails and hurled her onto the truck.

"I couldn't believe what I was seeing," Pritchard says. "Two women came from the other side of the street to try to stop them, and [the Nazis] threw them in with the kids."

She seems to be watching the 60-year-old scene play out in the middle of her living room, each detail as clear as the books and rugs and potbellied stove, and she becomes angry all over again. "That," she says, "was indeed the moment when I decided what was the most important thing to do."

Pritchard decided to rescue Jews—hide them, smuggle them, help them however she could. Though not Jewish herself, she made rescuing Jews her mission, for no reason other than that it was right.

People who make such decisions are the products of extraordinary parents, says Eva Fogelman, who has studied Holocaust rescuers, including Pritchard, for years. Most rescuers, Fogelman has found, were given an exquisite sense of justice as children, along with an unwavering self-confidence, "so they could withstand fears."

Pritchard remembers, for example, an ex-change between her mother and the Germans. "The Nazis were looking for able-bodied men," she says. "They came and made my brother get out of bed. He was 14 at the time. Fortunately, he was still small and skinny, and they told him he could go back to bed. Then they said to my mother, 'What are you doing with all that bunting?' My mother had all this red, white and blue material out on the kitchen table. My mother was a lady. She never swore. But she said, 'I'm making a Union Jack—to hang out the window when you sons of bitches get kicked out of here!' "

"She heard stories. Mass arrests. Night trains. Camps. She knew what was happening, but she didn't really want to know."

Pritchard coughs and covers her mouth. She looks away, and her eyes fill with tears. "It's funny," she says. "You can tell a tale a lot of times, and then suddenly, for some reason, it gets harder."

Pritchard estimates that she helped 150 Jews, nearly all of them children. She doesn't know the precise number. She didn't keep track, in case she was caught. "The less you knew, the better."

Nor does she know how many of the children she helped were able to survive the war. She would hide a child for a day, an hour, then pass the child along, into the night, into the woods, into history. She only knows that most of Holland's 140,000 Jews were killed, so it's likely that most of the children she met didn't make it. She gave them, at best, a few more days, or hours. Hers may have been the last kind face they saw.

Every rescue was different. She'd bring a child home, or simply to the next rescuer. She'd guide a child in the night to a safe house, or a clearing in the woods. She'd place a Jewish newborn with a non-Jewish couple. Occasionally, she'd walk a child in the light of day right past a group of Nazi soldiers.

In 1981, Pritchard was honored by Yad Vashem, Israel's official Holocaust authority, as one of the "Righteous Among the Nations." Her name was placed in the pantheon of Israel's national heroes, alongside Holocaust rescuers such as Oskar Schindler. She was recognized as one of the great moral exemplars of the century, from whom, the writer Cynthia Ozick wrote, "we can learn the full resonance of civilization."

And still she regrets not doing more. She's haunted by the children she couldn't save, the countless Anne Franks. She knew Anne Frank, in fact. And Anne's older sister, Margot. She met them once at a birthday party. Years later, a mutual friend met the Frank sisters at Bergen-Belsen, and saw them die.

"Every rescue was different."

Besides the children who passed briefly through Pritchard's hands, she hid one Jewish family for the duration of the war. She took Fred Polak and his three children—Lex, 7, Tom, 4, and Erica, an infant—to a farmhouse on the outskirts of the city and cared for them as though they were her own while their mother fought with the Dutch Resistance.

By day, Pritchard and the family kept to a routine, playing and walking in public, pretending to be non-Jews. At night, when the Nazis came around and demanded everyone's papers, Pritchard hid the family in a pit beneath the living room floor. Whenever Pritchard heard a motor coming up the road, she hurried the Polak family into the pit. "Regular people didn't have motors," she says. "Only Germans. So when you heard a motor, you knew."

Even when the Nazis weren't coming, she made the Polaks practice sliding away the coffee table, pulling up the floorboards, diving into the pit. Survival hinged on doing the drill faster and faster. "We got it down to 30 seconds," she says, still proud.

Pritchard was arrested during the war, but not for rescuing Jews. She was simply studying with friends who were part of the Dutch Resistance, and when the Nazis raided the apartment, everyone was taken, Pritchard included.

Memories of prison return to her, unbidden, at odd moments. In an elevator or a strange bathroom, if the door doesn't open right away, she feels trapped. Having a manicure, she recalls the way she filed her nails in prison, by rubbing them against her cell walls.

Every detail of prison remains vivid, but she doesn't share them. "I never have told, and I don't know whether I ever will tell, about the relatively minor torture I underwent."

She does describe, with a self-mocking smile, her sudden surge of religion. "It came naturally. 'Dear God, if you let me out of here, I'll be good forever after.'"

She was better than her word. When the Nazis set her free after seven months, she went back to rescuing Jews and took even greater risks, helping to pull off a daring kidnap in which she stormed a house and snatched a 2-year-old girl whom the Nazis were about to torture—their way of making her parents name members of the Dutch Resistance.

Then there was the Nazi she killed, a sadistic Dutch policeman she'd known all her life. He surprised her one night at the farmhouse, no sound of a motor to warn her, no time to hide the Polaks in the pit. Acting on a tip, the policeman crept up to the farmhouse on foot and burst in the door. "Somebody must've betrayed us," Pritchard says.

In that terrible moment, Pritchard says, there was no choice. Behind some books on a shelf was a gun given to her by a friend. She grabbed the gun and fired. "One shot," she says. "Dead as a doornail."

She doesn't remember pulling the trigger. She doesn't remember feeling anger or regret. "I remember the exhilaration when he was lying on the floor," she says. After covering the policeman with a sheet, she phoned a friend, Karel Poons. He arranged for the body to be smuggled to an undertaker, to be buried secretly with a recently deceased resident of the town. "Oh," she says, in the ragged violin voice, "Karel was wonderful."

> **"Pritchard gave Vermonters a stern history lesson, reminding them that Hitler began by persecuting everyone 'different.'"**

She thought of him often in 2000, when Vermont legislators voted to let gay couples "marry," plunging the state into a yearlong political crisis. Poons was gay, and it couldn't have mattered less to Pritchard. She loved him, trusted him with her life. So when the debate over gay rights in Vermont turned ugly, she took it personally.

But she kept quiet for the sake of her patients. "If someone comes to me who is an ardent Republican," she says, "I want them to be able to tell me anything."

Eventually, as she feared, the anti-gay rhetoric spawned something darker. Swastikas began to appear all around her, on lawns and mailboxes and the elementary school across the street from her office. She couldn't keep quiet any longer.

In a letter to the local newspaper, Pritchard gave Vermonters a stern history lesson, reminding them that Hitler began by persecuting everyone "different." Then she hammered signs into her front yard, supporting candidates friendly to gay rights.

One night her phone rang. A menacing voice told Pritchard to take down her signs "or you'll be sorry."

The signs stayed.

The voice called again.

The signs stayed.

Finally, someone crept up to Pritchard's farmhouse in the middle of the night, no sound of a motor to warn her, and stole the signs. It felt, she says, as if the past itself had crept out of the shadows. "I never thought," she says, "in Vermont of all places-"

Meeting Pritchard many years after the war, Erica Polak had trouble believing that this small, dignified grandmother was once all that stood between her and the camps. "She's such a tiny woman," Erica says by phone from her home in Holland. "She came from a very sophisticated family. And then, to go underground, to do such brave things? It's unbelievable."

Erica's mother never discussed the war. And with Pritchard, Erica feels the same reticence. Revealing means reliving.

"She lets go of a tiny piece at a time," Erica says, "and most things she doesn't let loose at all."

The honor from Yad Vashem seemed to loosen Pritchard a bit. She began to accept speaking invitations. Last fall she even helped teach a seminar at Clark University in Worcester, Mass., the only college in the nation to offer an advanced degree in Holocaust Studies. Despite cataracts and heavy traffic on the interstate, Pritchard sometimes drove herself to the school, four hours each way.

Deborah Dwork, who heads the center for Holocaust Studies at Clark and taught the seminar with Pritchard, says the students would fall perfectly silent whenever Pritchard spoke. One young woman confided to Dwork: "I never thought in my life I'd have the opportunity to be at the same table as a saint." Dwork feels the same way. "Just being with her makes me calmer," she says.

Each class began with Pritchard sharing a wartime memory. Then there would be a discussion of the week's assigned reading. The final hour of class was given over to the latest news. The students asked Pritchard for her take, and she gave it, unvarnished. One day she spoke about walking the razor's edge, about living each day in danger. She told the students that terrorism is yet another of life's perils, no more lethal than all the others. Evil didn't end with World War II, she said.

You can't always hide from hate. Or from history.

It was as close as she comes to giving advice. "The notion that someday everything in the world is going to be lovely, I haven't had that for a long, long time," Pritchard says. "I guess I hoped that right after World War II. But humans don't change, it seems."

In those heady days after the war, there were many reasons for optimism, but the main reason was U.S. Army Lt. Tony Pritchard, who did what the Nazis couldn't. He found Marion van Binsbergen.

He spotted her at a Paris rail station, where they were both bound for the refugee camps—he with the Army, she with the United Nations. They got into an argument immediately. She scolded him for complaining to a fellow soldier about all the "awful Dutch girls." He told her that he was simply remarking, "What an awful lot of Dutch girls."

She laughed, and so it began.

"It's summer, it's peace," she says. "After years of deprivation, of no food and no fun, suddenly you're on the French coast. We got American officer Army rations, which included liquor and wine. I'd never had hard liquor before."

They married in 1947, her wedding dress sewn by concentration camp survivors. A few months later, they came to the U.S., first to Cambridge, Mass., where they started their family, eventually to Vermont, in 1967. It was Tony who found the Vermont house, part of an old dairy farm, with 120 acres of white birches and sugar maples, set in the middle of raw wilderness.

Rebuilding the house was Tony's passion until he died 10 years ago. Now keeping the house is Pritchard's mission. It takes daily courage. Besides intruders in the shadows, she must contend with the brutal cold, the isolation, the temperamental septic tank and the steep staircase, down which she recently took a bad fall.

She deems it a small price to pay for staying connected to Tony, her fellow hero, who fought with Patton at the Battle of the Bulge and went with the first troops into the nightmare of Buchenwald. She and Tony could talk about anything, Pritchard says, which was vital, because they often couldn't talk to anyone else. At dinner parties and other social events, they were

discouraged from describing the horrors they witnessed. Too depressing, friends said. Move on.

Over time, their silence included their children. Pritchard's three sons—52-year-old Arnie and the 49-year-old twins, Ivor and Brian—didn't know much about their mother's past until 1981, when Israeli officials phoned to say that Pritchard would soon receive one of their nation's most sacred honors.

In Israel, Brian watched as his mother received the thanks of a nation. She was showered with praise, he says, and blinded by flashbulbs. Then the ceremony ended and everyone started for the doors-except for a group of sad-faced men and women. They moved closer to his mother, their hands extended, and he wondered who they could be.

Then he realized. They were survivors of the camps.

"That," he says, his voice unsteady, "was when I knew. . . ."

Once, at a school, Brian heard his mother reveal the thing she never reveals, the details of her time in prison. A boy in the audience asked politely and Pritchard wasn't able to deny him a straight answer. She told how the guards pressed a knife in her arm, demanding information. When she wouldn't talk, they pressed harder.

It was the first time Brian had heard the story, and it explained the scar on his mother's left forearm. It also made him wonder how many other stories and scars will remain hidden forever.

"It was the first time Brian had head the story . . . It made him wonder how many other stories and scars will remain hidden forever."

"We'll never know all there is to know," Arnie says. But he quickly adds: "I think I know enough."

What the brothers do know is always hard to reconcile with the woman their children call Grandma. "It challenges the imagination," says Ivor. "To put these two things next to each other-these extraordinary heroic things and the very ordinary experience of your mother, who's afraid of some things and doesn't like to do some things, and is shy and uncomfortable in front of people-it's incongruous."

And so, after dinner, it may be the incongruity that causes Pritchard's granddaughter to brush off the story of Grandma and the Nazi. Instead, Molly wants to hear the birds.

"Please, can we hear the birds?" she pleads.

Inside the cage are two birds made of luminous paper, and underneath is a key, which Pritchard now winds tight. When she releases it, the birds spin to face each other, and their beaks fly open. The room suddenly fills with bird song.

The children stare in awe. The adults tilt their heads and smile. The sound is beautiful but also haunting. Like voices from a vanished world. It's not possible to know what they are saying. But it's clear that they are somewhere other than this delicate hiding place above Pritchard's kitchen, and that they are happy and free.

QUESTIONS FOR RHETORICAL ANALYSIS

1. **CONSIDERING THE RHETORICAL SITUATION:** It is clear from the narrative portion of this profile that the writer visited and observed Marian Pritchard at her Vermont farm, yet his first-person voice is absent from this profile. What effect does this have on the reader?

2. Identify the portion of the profile that is the lead. In what ways do the dialogue and setting in the lead introduce Marian Pritchard to the reader?
3. What is the dominant impression of Pritchard that Moehringer creates in this profile? Support your answer with a few details from the profile.
4. Identify places in this profile where Moehringer used

   direct observation
   print or electronic sources
   interviews with the subject
   interviews with secondary sources

   What kind of research did he use most heavily? What do these multiple sources of research add to the profile?
5. Does the scene between Pritchard and her granddaughter provide an effective conclusion to the profile? Why?

QUESTIONS FOR WRITING AND DISCUSSION

1. Moehringer writes, "You can't always hide from hate. Or from history." In your experience, is this statement true? Explain.
2. Taking action against intolerance, as Pritchard did on a grand scale in Nazi Europe and on a smaller scale in rural Vermont, takes conviction and courage. Do you agree? What other stories—from your life or the life of others—could illustrate this statement?

STYLE PRACTICE: IMITATION

Find an instance where Moehringer uses metaphorical language, a balanced sentence, a telling detail, or a vivid description. Then, imitate that technique using your own material from your profile.

WRITING AND REVISION STRATEGIES

Gathered here are three interactive sections for you to use as you write and revise your profile.

- Writer's Notebook Suggestions
- Peer Review Log
- Revision Checklist

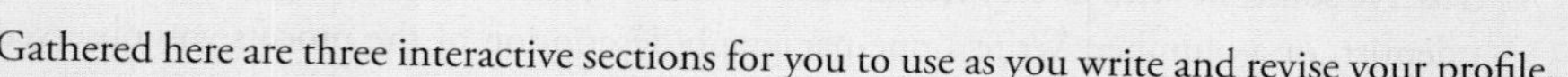

WRITER'S NOTEBOOK SUGGESTIONS

These short exercises are intended to jump-start your thinking as you begin to write your profile. They also might provide some useful topic suggestions.

1. Choose a person to describe, perhaps a classmate. Describe the subject's clothing in three sentences that also give your reader a strong impression of character. Here is an example.

   > He's clad in wrinkled khakis and a long-sleeved shirt adorned with a fine patina of fuzz, and his steel wool-colored hair hasn't recently encountered a comb. If Fay looks like hell, he feels even worse. While on the trip, he contracted filaria, a blood-borne infestation of tiny, threadlike worms that, if left untreated, can block the flow of lymph inside a victim's body and cause the extremities to swell to a grotesque size. . . . Fay grimaces and peers through Coke-bottle glasses—he's had trouble with his eyesight since childhood—into a forest of Brooks Brothers suits and elegant dresses.
   >
   > —Patrick J. Kiger, "Grand March of an American Misfit"

2. Listen in on a conversation—in a café, in a bookstore, or on public transportation. Take notes, and then write up a page of your overheard conversation. Use spoken and unspoken communication: include all gestures, facial expressions, pauses, and inflections (when voices rise or fall, become whispers, and so on).

3. Look through the business section of the phone book for interesting occupations. Make a list of businesses you want to know more about.

4. Write a brief portrait introducing your best friend. Focus on a single aspect of his or her life or a single character trait.

5. Watch a profile documentary film. Make notes about how many quotations from the subject you hear. What sources are quoted, and what do they have to say? How many anecdotes do you hear? How does the filmmaker move the story from one time period to another?

6. Attend a sporting event and observe one player during play, on the bench, and after the game. Record all gestures, signs of emotion, and actions. Afterwards, write a descriptive lead for a profile on the player.

7. Observe someone with a technical skill, such as a bread-baker, an interpreter for the deaf, a dentist, or a plumber. Write a one-paragraph description of the process you observed, making it easy to understand.

8. The following description is from a profile of Lieutenant Colonel Robert O. Sinclair, commander of the 13th Marine Expeditionary Unit of Camp Pendleton, California. Look at the way the writer uses the present tense to pull readers into the scene. Note how he uses repetitive sentence structure, verb choice, and sensory detail and emphasizes the details of the description with explanation.

    His pale-blue eyes are bloodshot from lack of sleep. His face is camouflaged with stripes and splotches of greasepaint—green, brown, and black to match his woodland-style utilities, fifty-six dollars a set, worn in the field without skivvies underneath, a personal wardrobe preference known as going commando. Atop his Kevlar helmet rides a pair of goggles sheathed in an old sock.

    —Mike Sager, "The Marine" Esquire 136, no. 6 (December 2001). Reprinted by permission of the author.

    Choose someone to describe. Write a one-paragraph description, imitating Sager's style. Use similar sentence structures, details, and combination of description with explanation.

9. Choose one of the paintings or photographs that create visual profiles in this chapter, and write a paragraph translating what you see into descriptive language.

PEER REVIEW LOG

As you work with a writing partner or in a peer editing group, you can use these questions to give helpful responses to a classmate's profile or as a guide for discussion.

Writer's Name: ______________________________

Date: ______________________________

1. Bracket the lead of this profile. What kind of lead is it? Could the profile start with a more interesting scene, anecdote, or generalization, perhaps one found later in the piece?
2. Underline the nut graf. Does the nut come too early or late in the profile? Judge this by asking whether the lead has set up the nut sufficiently. Does the focus seem like a natural extension of the opening? Does it seem artificially tacked on? Can the wording be more specific?
3. Is the nut graf a good overview of the story? Does it deliver everything it promises? Point out places where the writer refers to the idea in the nut, reinforcing and developing the thesis as the profile progresses. Locate any missed opportunities to remind the reader of the focus of the profile.
4. Look at the way the profile is organized. Make a quick outline of the profile's structure. What might strengthen the organization?
5. Circle major transitions between sections. Do the sections have good transitions? Do the narrative sections tie in with the factual, expository ones?
6. Does the story show and tell? Identify places where the writer uses description, anecdotes, examples, and facts. Does the profile need more of these elements to illustrate the generalizations made in the paragraphs?
7. What is the major impression you get of the profile subject? What details lead you to this impression? Could the writer insert more description, anecdotes, or character-in-action scenes to reveal character?
8. Annotate the sources the writer integrates into the profile by marking the places where the writer uses direct observation (DO), interviews from the subject and about the subject (I), and print or electronic sources (PS or ES). Could the profile use another source or two? Are there good quotations from reliable sources? Is the attribution clear?
9. Does the profile achieve a sense of balance? Does it have quotations from enough sources to create multiple perspectives of the subject? If the subject is being praised, are there enough illustrations, quotations, and evidence to support this praise?
10. Bracket the conclusion. Does the profile end with a memorable image? Is there a way to strengthen the conclusion?

REVISION CHECKLIST

As you do your final revision, check to make sure that you

- Wrote an engaging lead
- Announced your thesis in a clear nut graf or in the deck
- Created a major impression of your profile subject
- Used some or all of the typical profile elements to add color, interest, and depth:
  - Physical description
  - Quotations from the subject
  - Quotations about the subject
  - Examples
  - Anecdotes
  - Factual information
- Created a multifaceted portrait by using different perspectives from your sources
- Clearly attributed research from direct observation, interviews, and print and electronic sources
- Limited or eliminated the use of the first person (*I*)
- Provided clear transitions for your reader
- Concluded memorably, perhaps with a lingering image of your subject

PART III

Writing to Inform

TAO Images/SuperStock

Writing an Exposition

8

SHORT ARTICLES

Frontpage, 2009/Used under license from Shutterstock.com

I have made this letter longer than usual, only because I have not had the time to make it shorter.

—Blaise Pascal, Letters Provinciales (1657)

"In 300 words or fewer, tell me…"

How can I explain anything using so few words?

In just 269 words, Abraham Lincoln delivered a defining statement about freedom that most Americans can quote at least a small piece of: "Four score and seven years ago…" This enduring message, the beginning of the official end of slavery, was so concise that the photographer did not even have time to set up before Lincoln was walking away from the podium.

Tell me, in 300 words…

Short expository articles are the bread-and-butter of magazines and Web sites. They put a magnifying glass on a remote concept or idea, enlarging it enough for us to look carefully, but briefly, so our understanding of that subject expands. These short articles demand precision while providing fine detail on subjects we do not know much about. Short expository messages can also shape-shift. They can take the purely visual form of a photo essay, like the one in this chapter, or a more hybrid version featuring pictures and words, like the illustrated essay that appeared in a blog, featured in the DIY section of this chapter.

WHAT'S TO COME

Photo from the collection of photos that appeared on the Web site *Foreign Policy* accompanying "Oil, Oil Everywhere." For more photos, see pages 224–225.

Photo by John Moore/Getty Images

PROCESS PLAN

- Choose a general subject and start reading to become informed.
- Narrow your topic to a claim by asking "What"? And "So what?"
- Write your thesis statement, and ask yourself if your thesis holds up under this question: "What do you mean?"
- Collect "sticky stuff": interesting material that sticks in your reader's mind and defends your thesis.

DRAFT

- Introduction
  - Begin with your thesis (deductive organization) or lead the reader to it (inductive organization).
  - Write an introduction that hooks the reader with a scene or specific story.
- Body: Organize for logical flow.
- Conclusion: Write an ending that restates or makes a comment on the main subject.

REVISE

- Add good transitions.
- Check your obligation to your reader: Do you have enough proof to back up your thesis?
- Cut any extra words: Combine sentences and make sure all adjectives and adverbs are necessary.

UNDERSTANDING THE WRITING PROJECT

Thinkstock/Getty Images

SHORT WRITING is deceptively difficult. A short article is not just brief; it is also jam-packed with meaning. Your readers—in print or on the Web—expect to be surprised, to learn something new. This means you have to find a fresh, inviting topic and sources to help develop an understanding of your topic.

Your style also counts: You just do not have the luxury of extra words or repetition to make your points. Abraham Lincoln, in his under-300 word statement, was refocusing what was at the heart of the Civil War—that all men are created equal, according to the Constitution, and that "government by the people, for the people and of the people" should not perish. This was no small goal. Scholars marvel at the precision and power of his word choice, and that he did so much with so few words.

ASSIGNMENT Write a short article about something most people do not know about—a new discovery or trend, or a bit of insider's knowledge of a subject. Your article might focus on a place, a process, a person, a phenomenon, or a theory or discovery.

As you begin to think about subjects, consider your purpose. Imagine that your article puts a magnifying glass on a little-known piece of the world. The view you offer should be tightly focused and intensely detailed. Using multiple sources—print, online, and observation and interview when you can—helps you develop original articles. Compressing and combining the details from your research provides a brief, but still rich view of this small slice of life.

Access an interactive eBook, and chapter-specific interactive learning tools, including flashcards, quizzes, videos and more in your English CourseMate via www.cengagebrain.com.

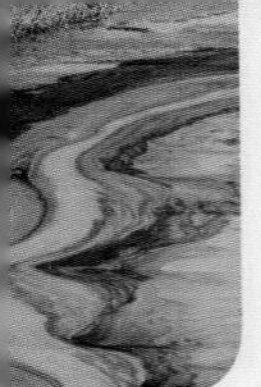

ANATOMY OF AN EXPOSITION

CHARLES FISHMAN wrote this short for the *Orlando Sentinel's* Sunday magazine. He implies as much as he "tells" in this short article about the inner workings of Disney World.

The Scoop on Disney's Dirty Laundry[1]

CHARLES FISHMAN

There are no illusions in Ed Fox's shop at Walt Disney World. There are no animatrons; no goofy, grinning characters; no artificial cheer. Ed Fox's shop is where Disney comes clean—the laundry.

opening attracts attention and announces the general subject.

There's not much magic to it, just a lot of work: 400 people on duty 365 days a year, two full shifts a day, with a little linen left over for a third shift.

lots of numbers show the scale of the work done at the laundry. Factual detail

Disney's dirty linen gets done in a nondescript, two-story building the size of a city block. Labeled, "Laundry and Dry Cleaning," it has a logo that looks at first like just a group of bubbles, but on reflection resolves itself into a soapy Mickey head.

description, shows.

Inside, the place looks truly un-Disneyesque—industrial, in fact. There is no air conditioning, no one wears a uniform, the staff contains a good measure of immigrants and many of the signs on the walls contain instructions in Spanish.

more showing, but also an implied idea—that the workers are immigrants. Not told, but implied through the detail.

The machines look vaguely familiar, except for their size. The clothes dryers are the size of dump trucks. The machine that irons and folds 915 queen-sized sheets an hour (one sheet folded every 4 seconds) looks like a printing press. The washers hold 900 pounds of laundry at a time; computers control the mix of detergents.

more researched details, specific

example of the "sticky stuff" from the interview on page 220

The laundry uses 400,000 cubic feet of natural gas a day and 350,000 gallons of water. It is one of the biggest facilities in the country. Every towel, napkin, bed sheet, table cloth, pillow case, bath mat—every piece of linen used in any Disney hotel or restaurant, every uniform or costume used in the Magic Kingdom or Epcot or Pleasure Island—they all come here.

comparing to others in its class, put this place into a context—also reveals the relevance of the topic.

catalogue that reveals the equality of all laundry.

Every sheet in every occupied room is changed every day; every employee gets a freshly dry-cleaned uniform. Designed, as Fox says, for the 1,500 hotel rooms and "one little

[1]Charles Fishman, "The Scoop on Disney's Dirty Laundry" from The Orlando Sentinal Sunday Magazine, February 4, 1990. Reprinted with permission.

Magic Kingdom" that existed when Disney first opened in 1971, "We're just bursting at the seams now."

quotation shows a variety of research

His people clean up after 6,100 hotel rooms and three big parks, plus a couple of smaller ones. When Disney planners talk of new facilities, all Fox sees is more linen and no more capacity.

The operation is full service. Drivers pick up dirty laundry and return clean laundry to 260 locations at Disney on 13 pick-up routes.

The facility is divided roughly in half—laundry on one side, dry-cleaning on the other.

During a holiday week, the facility did 818,000 pounds of laundry. Incoming laundry is dumped onto a conveyor belt, which takes it to a second floor sorting room. It returns to the first-floor washing area through stainless-steel chutes that dump dirty linens directly into washing machines. Eventually, closet-sized carts filled with pristine linens wait to be trucked out.

Dry cleaning is also sorted first, according to color and pattern and the kind of attention it needs. The dry-cleaning ranges from ball gowns and full-dress tuxedos to chefs' hats and emergency medical technician uniforms to Mickey Mouse costumes. Much of it makes its way through the laundry on hangers dangling from elaborate moving conveyors, about 25,000 pieces a day.

explanation of a process

thesis: all the details relate to this statement. It's the claim—the idea that accumulates after the details are laid out. Proving this is your "obligation to your reader."

All of Disney is at the mercy of the laundry. According to Fox, most hotels, restaurants and parks have no more than a four-day supply of their laundry. To forestall disaster, three maintenance men work full-time each shift.

Last summer, when a machine that provided heat to dry and iron sheets broke down, Fox says, "I just started calling every laundry guy I knew on the phone, and the first one who said yes got all my business." He ended up trucking Disney's sheets to Space Coast Hospital in Rockledge.

anecdote about a specific example—illustrates the point

Among the secrets revealed amid Disney's dirty laundry is that the linens you sleep on and towel off with in your suite at the new, luxe Grand Floridian may have last done duty in the most ordinary room at the Contemporary.

At Disney, all linens are created equal.

conclusion—this is what all the details add up to. Inductive reasoning.

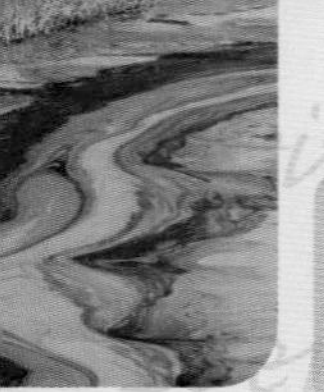

"My goal is to make sure a piece has 'sticky stuff,' the bits that people remember . . ."

Q&A with Charles Fishman

What Readers Want

Q: Since you also write books, you are a good person to ask: Is writing short pieces really more difficult than writing long ones?

A: Absolutely. Writing short is harder for a simple reason. Every piece of writing, every story, has to do some basic things: it needs a beginning, a middle, an end. It needs a point. It needs some explanatory, expository material. That's the basic bones of any story—and all that takes up space. So in a short space, it can be very hard to handle those basics and also get in color, fun, telling detail, a good anecdote (or two good anecdotes), humor, drama. My goal is always to make sure a piece has as much of that kind of material in it—what I think of as the "sticky stuff," the bits that people might remember, might tell a friend—as possible, while also fulfilling whatever obligations the piece must fulfill for readers.

Courtesy Charles Fishman

Charles Fishman

Q: Do you always know what the article is about when you begin your research, or are you sometimes surprised by what you find?

A: Both. You must know what the article is about in some way before you do it because you not only have to have a topic; you have to have a framework, a theory, so you can ask some questions that are interesting. But you also have to follow your curiosity and let the story, the people, the details surprise you (and correct you).

Q: Describe your writing process for the Disney laundry piece. Was the topic assigned? Did any parts of the research surprise you?

A: The writing here—for me, the writing for any story—begins with the reporting, and not everyone knows how to report a "scene story" like the Disney laundry in a way that will send them back to their keyboard with what they need to write a good story.

Here are my two hints: Ask lots of questions, and write down all the answers. We've all done laundry, we've all folded sheets. There's a machine folding sheets—one every four seconds. Well, that's the moment: A machine that can fold fifteen sheets a minute. Most of us can't fold a single sheet well in a minute. You have to ask every question—particularly dumb questions—and write the answers down. You won't use every single factoid, but you'll never be sorry you have twenty-seven instead of seven.

You learn a lot from bafflement. Don't nod and say "uh-huh" and pretend to understand if you don't. That's why you're there. Not to prove that you "knew it all along," but to be surprised for readers, to learn something new.

Look around. Listen. Smell. Notice what's clean and what's rusty. Notice how big things are (a clothes dryer the size of a dump truck). Notice it, and write it all down.

THE RHETORICAL SITUATION: WHY READERS WILL STAY WITH YOU

In the Q&A Charles Fishman mentions the writers "obligations" to the reader. Start understanding these obligations by asking why someone would want to read your article. What will a reader gain?

Most likely the answer to this question is that the reader wants information. True enough, but the short article is more than an encyclopedia entry, more than a listing of information. The reader also wants an *understanding* of the subject. So, your first obligation is to provide a thesis worthy of a reader's time—a thesis that moves beyond basic fact. You must interest the reader by writing in a style that engages.

And your second obligation is to deliver whatever you have promised in that thesis. You are also the trusted authority. Your research needs to be thorough, but also easily understood.

THE BIG IDEA IN SHORT ARTICLES: WRITING A THESIS

Short expository articles should surprise as much as they inform. Their point, or thesis, should be interesting and fresh. If you hold your topic selection to the criteria that the subject should explain some little-known phenomenon or place that is new to readers, you need to prove to your readers that the subject is worthy of their time.

In making your writing appeal to readers, the first steps are (1) to make sure your article has a thesis statement worthy of proof (2) to make sure you have enough detail to back up your thesis. This detail comes from research in print and online sources and from people you interview—practitioners and experts. The detail might be statistics, facts, or quotations that reveal opinions or recount experiences.

Your subject might be new or unfamiliar to your reader, but you should have command of it. You should understand it inside and out, so that your explanation is easy to understand. You need to examine the context for the subject—where it fits in with others, how it works, what its significance is. After you do that kind of thinking, you can form a theory that helps you explain the relevance of the subject. The theory does not have to be original, but it does need some defending. A good thesis is one that—only through a body of evidence—will seem reasonable and convincing to a reader. That all of Disney is at the mercy of the laundry might be considered factual, but it is also a way of looking at the facts—a theory that needs explanation.

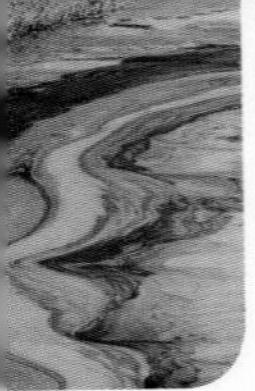

THE BIG IDEA in an explanatory article reveals **WHAT** and a **SO WHAT** in a single sentence.

The **WHAT** of the Disney article: One laundry serves all the needs of Disney in Orlando.

The **SO WHAT**: If that laundry stops, so do all the hotels, imaginary characters, food service, and basically everything.

The *thesis*, or the concise statement that sums up the **WHAT** and the **SO WHAT** is:

> All of Disney is at the mercy of the laundry.

This is a theory because, although it may be true, it is not a fact that is self-evident, such as saying the laundry is divided in half, laundry on one side, dry cleaning on the other. A thesis, instead, is big enough to bear the question: What do you mean?

In a short article, the thesis needs to be focused tightly enough to have that question answered in just a few pages.

WHAT SHOULD I WRITE ABOUT? WAYS OF LOOKING AT A SUBJECT

With any writing, the most difficult part is getting started. But the old maxim, "I will not know what I mean until I see what I say," can direct your writing process toward generating ideas. Several "systems" for looking at a topic can help you examine where your subject fits in the world—its context. Asking questions about the subject will help you see its significance and relevance to a reader, and will also help direct your research.

METHOD OF INQUIRY: QUESTIONS TO ASK ABOUT YOUR SUBJECT

1. Separate the subject into parts. What are its individual parts?
2. Put the subject into a category. How is your subject different from the others in the category?
3. Has your subject changed over time?
4. How can the subject be "measured" or "calculated"?
5. What is a metaphor for your subject?
6. Can you describe a process involved with your subject?
7. How can you look at your subject from different points of view—magnified, cut into cross sections, from far away, from an outsider's viewpoint?

PRACTICE 8.1

Finding and Testing Topics

1. Look at today's headlines to find topics that people might like to know more about. Make a list of possible subjects for short researched articles.
2. Think about current trends in health, beauty, fitness, and lifestyle that you might like to know more about. Make another list.
3. Reader-test your topics. Pitch the topics to a group of classmates. See which ones they would be most likely to read. Find out what they want to know.

PRACTICE 8.2

Using Methods of Inquiry Questions

Choose a topic you might write about and use questions about your subject to generate interesting ways to write about your topic.

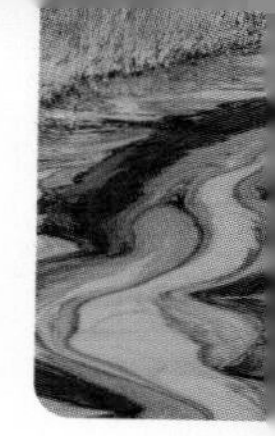

RESEARCH PATHS:
USE PRIMARY AND SECONDARY SOURCES

To begin your search for facts, and even as a part of your brainstorming, you will probably do a keyword search on the Internet. Of course you should take care in evaluating sources, and take good notes along the way. (For more on evaluating sources and taking good notes, see Chapter 15, Research.) Most importantly, do not limit yourself to one source. Using only a dictionary or an encyclopedia for the question about whether a tomato is a fruit or a vegetable, you might miss some interesting information. For example, the Supreme Court ruling in 1893 that declared tomatoes would be classified as fruits can be found on a Web site. On the other hand, you might find a Web site that offers information that contradicts authoritative sources and would thus not be a good source. With Web material, it is best to find at least two sources that agree on information.

When you use sources in your article, be sure to provide clear and accurate attribution. For a short article, you might integrate the source material and the attribution into the text of the article. For example, you might write, "The *Encyclopaedia Britannica* defines *tomato* as 'any fruit of the numerous cultivated varieties of *Lycopersicon esculentum*, a plant of the nightshade family (Solanaceae); also, the fruit of *L. pimpinelli folium*, the tiny currant tomato.'"

Remember to keep track of your sources as you find them. (Academic essays call for a complete citation of sources on a Works Cited page. This source from a Works Cited page uses *Modern Language Association (MLA)* style. For more on ways to keep track of your sources, see Chapter 15, Research. See chapter 16 for guidelines on citing and documenting your sources.)

> Jacob, Mark, and Stephen Benzkofer. "10 Things You Might Not Know about Tomatoes." *Chicago Tribune*. 20 Mar. 2011. Web. 18 July 2011.

If you can, talk to people with experience in or knowledge about the subject area. These primary sources can provide examples and illustrations that you will not get anywhere else.

PRACTICE 8.3

Finding Sources and Integrating Research

Choose one of the topics below, and list at least one Web site, one print source, and one expert whom you might consult to get information.

- Learning disabilities
- Ethnic food
- A historical event in your community
- Encryption
- The infield fly rule
- Postmodernism

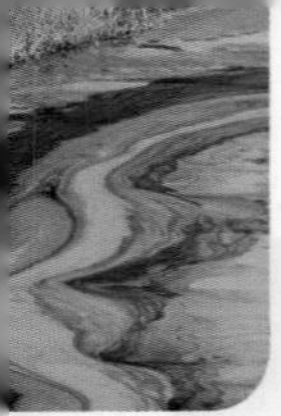

VISUAL LITERACY: FINDING A THESIS IN A PHOTO ESSAY

PHOTO ESSAYS are a visual method of developing a thesis. This photo essay from the Web site *Foreign Policy* accompanies Brian Fung's article about the BP oil spill in 2010. It begins: "A spill of epic proportion: The explosion of the BP-leased Deepwater Horizon drilling rig on April 20 that killed 11 workers has produced the largest oil spill ever in U.S. waters. The leak began 50 miles off the coast of Louisiana, caused by a burst pipe that BP then failed to shut down."

- Write a thesis for this essay that uses information from the photos and the above introduction to the article.
- Create your own photo essay (with five to seven photographs) that reveals a main point about a place, process, person, or phenomenon that might be new to your subject, or that might reveal an insider's view of a familiar subject. Write the thesis that would accompany your photo essay.

John Kepsimelis/U.S.Coast Guard via Bloomberg

Joe Raedle/Getty Images

John Moore/Getty Images
John Moore/Getty Images
John Moore/Getty Images
John Moore/Getty Images
John Moore/Getty Images

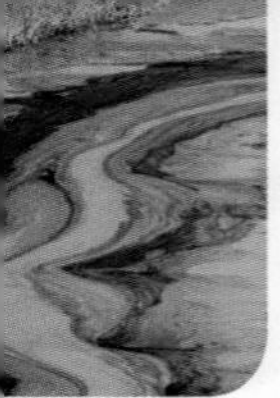

ORGANIZE YOUR THINKING:
STRUCTURE YOUR WRITING

INDUCTION OR DEDUCTION?

Once you have done your brainstorming and researched your topic for good details and accuracy, it is time to start organizing your points. A common way to organize your points is to include your thesis early in the article, shortly after introducing the general subject, and then to follow it with proof that it is a reasonable theory. This is *deductive* organization. Beginning with the thesis can be useful for grabbing the readers' attention. In the article about earwax on page 233, the author, Gunjan Sinha starts by promising readers they will understand why new research might be important:

> Well, it turns out earwax says a lot about a person.

If we continue to read, we will find out what the author means, that is, the reasons this theory is valid.

Charles Fishman, on the other hand, uses *inductive* organization in his article about Disney's laundry, laying out his collection of facts and then announcing what they add up to: his thesis or theory about how all of Disney is at the mercy of the laundry.

Mystery drives inductive reasoning, with the reader following along like a partner in detecting the point to the pattern.

INTRODUCTION

Keep in mind your obligations to your reader. The beginning of a short article should announce the general topic and provide something "sticky"—an unusual fact, a telling detail, or vivid description—to hook the reader. This "sticky" material, as Charles Fishman describes it, is something that stays with your reader—something your reader might mention to a friend, later. You promise your readers more of that, if they continue, and that is why they do.

BODY

The body contains the substance of your piece: the explanation, evidence, or support for your thesis or main claim.

CONCLUSION

Conclusions often restate the main subject, but in a short article, you do not have words to waste. So what might be a general statement of introduction, in "Disney's Dirty Laundry," becomes the conclusion: All linens are created equal. Other choices for conclusions are facts or quotations that comment on the material or put it in context.

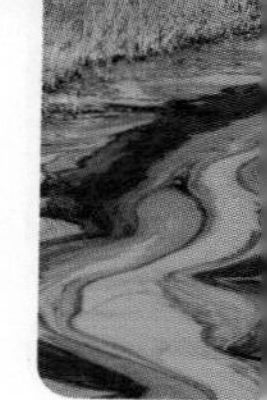

Show Don't Tell: "Sticky Stuff"

- Details of place or character that create "pictures": the soap suds in the shape of Mickey's ears, for example.
- Observations: "There is no air conditioning."
- Specific examples: full-dress tuxedos, emergency medical technician uniforms, instead of "costumes and uniforms."
- Anecdotes that provide illustration: "Last summer, when a machine that provided heat to dry and iron sheets broke down. . . ."
- Quotations from experts: "Designed, as Fox says, for the 1,500 hotel rooms and 'one little Magic Kingdom' that existed when Disney first opened in 1971, 'We're just bursting at the seams now.'"
- Insider information: "Most hotels, restaurants and parks have no more than a four-day supply of their laundry."

PRACTICE 8.4

Showing Detail

Select a topic you might want to write about and describe it in action. Use well-selected and specific detail to set your reader directly into the scene.

DIY MEDIA AND DESIGN

THE HYBRID ESSAY: WORDS AND PICTURES

READ AND VIEW "Vote for Independence for Southern Sudan" from the *Boston Globe* as an example of one hybrid short essay. Then create your own hybrid short essay, including words and pictures—photos, drawings, illustrations—that inform your readers about a single concept they would find new and interesting.

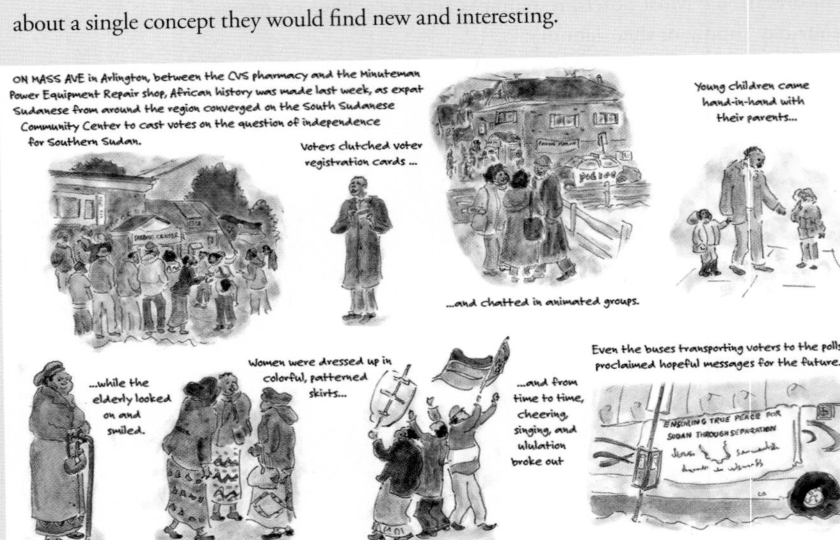

ON MASS AVE in Arlington, between the CVS pharmacy and the Minuteman Power Equipment Repair shop, African history was made last week, as expat Sudanese from around the region converged on the South Sudanese Community Center to cast votes on the question of independence for Southern Sudan.
Voters clutched voter registration cards ...
...and chatted in animated groups.
Young children came hand-in-hand with their parents...
...while the elderly looked on and smiled.
Women were dressed up in colorful, patterned skirts...
...and from time to time, cheering, singing, and ululation broke out
Even the buses transporting voters to the polls proclaimed hopeful messages for the future.
ENSURING TRUE PEACE FOR SUDAN THROUGH SEPARATION

All the while, looking on from across the street sat an unprepossessing colonial.
It is, according to the plaque in its front yard, the Butterfield-Whittemore House, one of "few surviving 'eyewitness buildings' of the first day of the American Revolution, when British troops marched past on their retreat from Lexington and Concord."

Two-hundred and thirty-six years later, the flags have changed ...

...but from the windows of the Butterfield-Whittemore House...
...the eyewitness view to history remains.

Sage Stossel/Boston Globe Magazine January 16, 2011

DIY

READINGS

SHORT ARTICLES help readers understand a topic they find useful, new, or related to something in current thinking or in the news. Sometimes called sidebars, they can appear alongside a longer article in print. On Web sites, a term that appears in hot type will often direct you to a short article that provides a detailed look at a subject. The five readings that follow demonstrate the range of topics you can find in short articles. They describe "how bullets tell a tale," define the term "reading at grade level," explain the significance of ear wax in genetic research, explain the importance of rice to the Ojibwa, and report on the history of the laboratory mouse.

How Bullets Tell a Tale[2]

Janet Rae-Dupree

The following selection originally appeared as a sidebar in an article about a sniper. The writer used the sidebar to explain how a number of shootings might be conclusively connected by looking at the impression guns can leave on bullets they fire. At the time the article and this companion sidebar were written, two snipers, who were later captured, were at large in the Washington, D.C., area.

INVESTIGATORS HAVE a tragic abundance of one kind of clue: "ballistic fingerprints," the scratches, dimples, bumps, and grooves that a gun leaves on a bullet and its shell casing. Like human fingerprinting, ballistics is all about matching: determining whether two rounds came from the same gun. It can be a powerful tool for crime-solving when investigators have a suspect's weapon and can compare a slug from the crime with one test-fired from the gun. Failing that, investigators can use it to link separate crimes, as in the Washington shootings.

To make a match, an examiner places the rounds to be compared inside a special double microscope that displays images side by side or overlaps them. Larger markings, such as the ridges on a bullet left by rifling grooves in the barrel, can be enough to show that the samples came from the same gun model. Shell casings like the one that Washington investigators have found can also be revealing because they can record the position and shape of the firing pin and, on semiautomatic weapons, the extractor and ejector that expel spent rounds.

Then comes a more painstaking task: matching two rounds to the same weapon, based on the smaller marks left by microscopic imperfections in the gun's mechanisms. Individual lines inside the rifling grooves are one clue. "It's not unlike the lines left by a knife when cutting hard cheese," says John Nixon, ballistics expert at Athena Research and Consulting in Indiana. Because the markings appear different depending on viewing angle and lighting, Nixon says, there are "an infinite number of permutations."

"It's not unlike the lines left by a knife when cutting hard cheese"

Fragments. All of this is often more difficult with rifles than with handguns.

[2] Janet Rae-Dupree, "How Bullets Tell a Tale," from US News & World Report, October 21, 2002. Reprinted with permission.

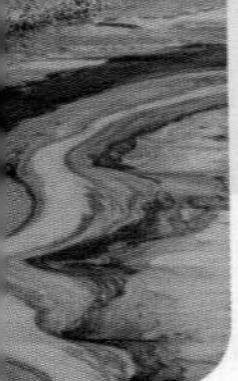

High-velocity rifle rounds usually break into fragments, marring identification lines.

Besides comparing bullets and shells one by one, ballistics investigators can consult a national database. About 235 police departments are equipped with $100,000 stations linked to the National Integrated Ballistics Information Network, which stores the markings on bullets and shell casings as electronic signatures. It includes only ballistics data from crimes, although gun control advocates want firearms makers to test-fire all new weapons and deposit the data in the national system along with the weapons' serial numbers. But the 1968 federal Gun Control Act blocked any national gun registry, and the National Rifle Association opposes changing the law. States, however, can require gun makers to provide test-fired samples from new weapons. So far, only two have done so: New York and Maryland.

QUESTIONS FOR RHETORICAL ANALYSIS

1. **CONSIDERING THE RHETORICAL SITUATION:** Would readers be interested in a story about bullets and guns if the story was not tied to current news?
2. What is the thesis of this article?
3. Reread the quotation by ballistics expert John Nixon. Why do you think the writer included this quotation?
4. How has the writer organized this sidebar? Can you suggest a different, or more effective, organization?
5. Although this short piece is explanatory in nature, its conclusion advocates for a particular position. What is this position? Is this an effective conclusion for the article? Why?

QUESTIONS FOR WRITING AND DISCUSSION

1. How much would readers connect this information to material they might have seen in crime dramas on television? Would that exposure increase or hinder their interest?
2. Research the Washington sniper story, and write a brief update on what happened or on where the case stands now.

STYLE PRACTICE: IMITATION

Write one paragraph description of a process.

Reading at Grade Level[3]

Katie Koch

Katie Koch wrote this short article for her college writing class. She writes, "The assignment was basic: Write a short article explaining a concept, trend, or place. It was very open-ended, so I went into it with an activist mindset. I wanted to use an explanation of a commonly misunderstood subject to allow readers to see an issue in a new light. I was taking a course on the politics of education at the

[3]Reprinted by permission of Katie Koch.

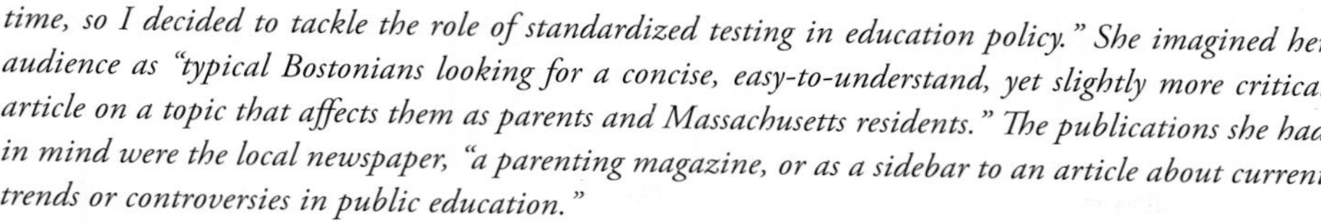

time, so I decided to tackle the role of standardized testing in education policy." She imagined her audience as "typical Bostonians looking for a concise, easy-to-understand, yet slightly more critical article on a topic that affects them as parents and Massachusetts residents." The publications she had in mind were the local newspaper, "a parenting magazine, or as a sidebar to an article about current trends or controversies in public education."

ANYONE WHO has taken a standardized test in school recognizes the phrase "reading at grade level." If you're old enough to have attended school in the good old days before national testing, perhaps the term entered your consciousness in the mid-1990s, when Bill Clinton took to the campaign trail with the conviction that "within five years, all of our children will be reading at grade level!" Chances are you've heard a doting mother brag that her nine-year-old daughter reads at a tenth-grade level. You've probably also heard of educational initiatives to promote literacy that sound a lot like this proposal from the Oregon Department of Education: "All 4–12 students will meet grade level." But what does "reading at grade level" actually mean?

> **"What does 'reading at grade level' actually mean?"**

"Reading at grade level" simply means that a child is scoring exactly "in the middle range of his or her peer group on a standardized test of reading skills," according to Gerald Bracey, author of *Put to the Test: An Educator's and Consumer's Guide to Standardized Testing*. However, the term has a much broader implication and meaning than that, and without context, this definition is almost meaningless.

A student earns the title of "reading at grade level"—or, for that matter, reading above or below grade level—according to how well he or she scores on a standardized test. You may have heard of some of the nationwide tests, such as the Terra Nova, the California Achievement Test or the National Assessment of Educational Progress, or the Massachusetts-wide test known as MCAS. Whether national or local, these tests contain almost strictly multiple-choice questions. Students can be assigned a "grade level" for any kind of standardized tests subject—say, math or science—but, for some reason, the phrase "reading at grade level," which refers to a score on a reading comprehension test, gets tossed around most often.

Most people know that the term "reading at grade level" is a byproduct of standardized tests, but very few understand how these scores, which are pretty meaningless on their own, translate into significant tools for determining whether or not a child can read up to standards. (If you're among the uninformed, don't be embarrassed. According to education policy analyst Christine Rossell, most teachers and administrators have no idea what their students' scores actually mean statistically.)

The way it works is as follows. Students are ranked by percentiles according to how well they score on a test (that is, the 1 percent with the highest scores will be in the 99th percentile; the 1 percent of test takers with the lowest scores will be in the 1st percentile). Then "grade levels" are spread out over this distribution of scores to mirror the student's

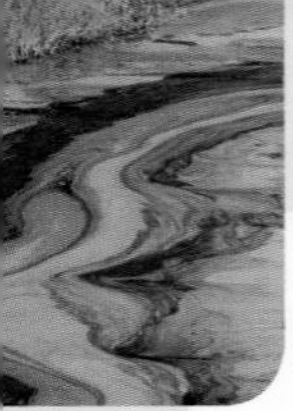

percentile ranking. A student in the middle—the 50th percentile—will be exactly at his or her "grade level."

For a better understanding, let's examine the cases of three hypothetical fifth-grade students—Sarah, Jane, and Johnny. Sarah comes home from school with a government-issued printout of her MCAS scores. Sarah's mother looks over the busy mish-mash of graphs and numbers and glosses over fancy terminology like "stanines" and "normal-curve equivalents"—after all, Sarah's mother hasn't taken statistics since high school—and sees that Sarah's grade level for reading is 5.2. Sarah is "reading at grade level," and so her mother is pleased, without ever knowing that what the 5.2 actually means is that Sarah scored exactly in the middle range of her peers.

Jane comes home from school and shows her parents her scores. They can't believe their eyes: according to the MCAS results, Jane is reading at a twelfth-grade level! Of course, Jane's parents always knew she was smart, but they never thought she could handle twelfth-grade work! As they busily map out a reading list spanning Homer's *The Odyssey* to Joyce's *Ulysses* for their child prodigy, Jane's parents fail to realize what her score actually means. Jane's projected "grade level" of 12.1 indicates that she scored as well on her test—a test of fifth-grade-level reading skills—as a twelfth grader would on that *exact same test*. Jane is doubtlessly one of the brightest children in her class (her score must be somewhere near the 99th percentile), but she couldn't even tell you Shakespeare's first name, let alone demonstrate from her MCAS the ability to read what high school seniors are reading.

Finally, let's hear the sad tale of Johnny. Johnny gets off the bus, enters his house and tosses his MCAS results on the kitchen table. His father picks them up when he arrives home from work and is disappointed to find that his firstborn son just can't read. Johnny is eleven years old, and according to his test scores, he's reading at a "grade level" of 1.5—a kid who's halfway through the first grade. Johnny's father remembers the rote simplicity of his first-grade reading class and imagines his son struggling to read even the easiest words. However, what Johnny's father doesn't know is that Johnny may be a perfectly decent reader for his age. All his scores indicate is that he is in the bottom 15 percent of his peers—not great, mind you, but not necessarily illiterate, or even close. Then there's also the possibility that Johnny just didn't put any effort into the test that day because, as an eleven-year-old boy, he wasn't aware that the results might label him for the rest of his public school career as a "bad reader."

"He wasn't aware that the results might label him for the rest of his public school career as a 'bad reader.'"

Despite its deceptively straightforward-sounding name, the "grade level" measurement is one of the most commonly misunderstood features of already-confusing standardized tests. A better understanding of what "reading at grade level" actually means may not shake up anyone's worldview, but it may have the effect of making the whole process of standardized testing seem a little less scary for parents who undoubtedly have enough to worry about these days.

WORKS CITED

Bracey, Gerald. *Put to the Test: An Educator's and Consumer's Guide to Standardized Testing.* Bloomington: Phi Delta Kappa International, 2002. Print.

Oregon. Dept. of Education. Office of Educational Improvement and Innovation. *Oregon's Literacy Initiative* 2.3 (2005). Web. 9 Nov. 2006.

Rossell, Christine. "Test Scores and Their Meaning." Lecture to Political Science 548. Boston University, Boston. 17 Sept. 2006. Lecture.

QUESTIONS FOR RHETORICAL ANALYSIS

1. **CONSIDERING THE RHETORICAL SITUATION:** What does the writer do to hook the reader? Does the introduction make you want to read on? Why, or why not?
2. How would you define Koch's voice in this article? Quote a few lines that support your judgment.
3. Who is Koch's intended audience for this article? How do you know?
4. What is Koch's thesis in this article? Is the article's organization deductive or inductive?
5. Identify the development strategies Koch uses in the body of this article. Which do you find most effective?
6. What transitions does Koch use to help her reader follow her explanation of "reading at grade level"?
7. Identify the conclusion. What is Koch's point in the conclusion?

QUESTIONS FOR WRITING AND DISCUSSION

1. Knowing what you now know about "reading at grade level," write a note to your parents explaining why your younger sibling should not be grounded for "reading below grade level."
2. How might the voice of this article differ if it were written for educators? For fifth-grade students? Write an introduction suitable for each of these audiences.

STYLE PRACTICE: IMITATION

Write a short definition for a term readers might not understand, like "reading at grade level."

Genetics: The Moistness of Your Earwax Is Controlled by a Single Gene—and That May Be More Important Than You Think[4]

Gunjan Sinha

No topic is really too small for a short article, especially if the article is reporting new developments in thinking about a subject, as is the case with this short article concerning a topic almost no one talks about—ear wax.

[4]Gunjan Sinha, "Listening to Earwax," from Popular Science, September 2002, p. 31. Reprinted with permission.

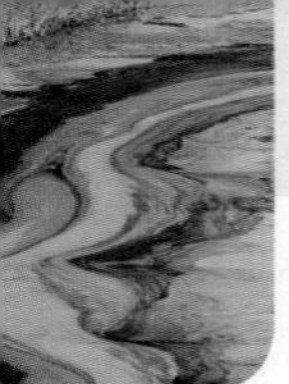

OK, IT'S a geneticist's job to hunt for all sorts of genes. But now that Japanese researchers, led by Norio Niikawa at the Nagasaki University School of Medicine, are zeroing in on the gene that makes earwax, the question is: Who cares?

Well, it turns out earwax says a lot about a person. It comes in two varieties: moist and gloppy, or dry and flaky. (The wet kind is more common in Americans, Europeans, and Africans; the dry type more frequently found in Asians and Native Americans; both types are also found in chimpanzees.) A few years ago, epidemiologist Nicholas Petrakis at the University of California San Francisco found evidence suggesting earwax contains hints of a woman's risk for contracting breast cancer. Ears and breasts both contain apocrine glands, and women with too much apocrine tissue—and moist earwax—have a tendency to form breast cysts. Finding the gene that orchestrates apocrine development might one day help doctors predict a woman's risk of developing the disease. In addition, people who have moist earwax tend to have more pungent body odor. Armpits also contain apocrine glands, which secrete oily chemicals that stink-producing bacteria feed on. So the earwax gene might also clue researchers into ways to better fight B.O.

QUESTIONS FOR RHETORICAL ANALYSIS

1. **CONSIDERING THE RHETORICAL SITUATION:** What is the effect of starting this article with "OK," and including "Well," as a transition?
2. What is the thesis of this article?
3. What does the author do to make the reader interested in a topic that might be considered distasteful?
4. How much technical, scientific detail does the writer use to explain her point?
5. How does the author organize this material?

QUESTIONS FOR WRITING AND DISCUSSION

1. What type of magazines or Web sites would be interested in a subject like this one?
2. How do you think the writer went about researching this topic?
3. How do you think you might find out about new developments in science?
4. Where would you go for news that the average person might not read?

STYLE PRACTICE: IMITATION

Write one paragraph explaining a scientific concept in a conversational tone.

Going with the Grain[5]

Lauren Wilcox

Lauren Wilcox shows her reader a place as well as a process they would otherwise not know anything about since the tradition of harvesting true wild rice is rarely practiced. Notice how she adds a human face to the centuries-old process.

[5]Lauren Wilcox, "Going with the Grain," from Smithsonian Magazine, September 2007. Reprinted with permission.

COME SEPTEMBER in northern Minnesota, on lakes on the Ojibwa lands, harvesters, two per canoe, pole through thick clusters of wild rice plants growing along the marshy shores. One stands in the stern like a gondolier; the other sits midship and uses a pair of carved cedar "knocking" sticks to sweep the tall grasses over the bow. The rice, still in its hull, falls into the boat with a soft patter.

Ricing is a picturesque tradition, but on the White Earth Indian Reservation, where unemployment approaches 50 percent, it spells survival. "It's not a pastime," says Andrea Hanks, a local Ojibwa. "It's work." Each autumn, several hundred Ojibwa harvest more than 50,000 pounds of wild rice, selling most of it to local mills. Unlike commercially grown wild rice—which is crossbred for hardiness, raised in paddies and harvested with combines—the Ojibwa's grows naturally, in muddy shallows. Called *manoomin* in Ojibwa, it is the mature seeds of several varieties of the grass species *Zizania aquatica.*

"It's not a pastime," says Andrea Hanks, a local Ojibwa. "It's work."

The White Earth Land Recovery Project, run by political activist and tribe member Winona LaDuke, was started 18 years ago to preserve the harvest and boost the tribe's share of the proceeds. It operates a mill on the reservation and markets Native Harvest wild rice to specialty stores around the country (and through nativeharvest.com). Ojibwa wild rice is one of only five U.S. products supported by the Slow Food Foundation for Biodiversity, an international organization based in Italy that aims to preserve traditional or artisan foods.

On a drizzly September morning, the Recovery Project's mill is a dusty, smoky hive of activity. Bringing the freshly harvested rice in still-dripping sacks, the ricers come by twos: fathers and sons, uncles and nephews, husbands and wives. Most are straight from the lakes, their cuffs still wet, inchworms clinging to their clothes, canoes lashed to their cars and pickups. Fresh-off-the-stalk rice is pale green and encased in a long, thin hull. In the old days, Native Americans toasted it over fires and stomped on it to remove the husks. The mill parches the covered seeds in great wood-fired ovens that can turn a total of 600 pounds at a time. "I can tell just from listening when it's done," says Pat Wichern, who has operated the parchers for ten years. "It starts sizzling, kind of singing in there."

After the rice has cooled, machines remove the hulls and sort the grains by size. The final product, cooked, tastes nothing like commercially grown wild rice: it is toothsome and nutty, with the exotic, earthy tang of fresh lake water. Some local residents say they can tell which lake a batch of rice came from just by the taste of it.

At this time of year, Wichern keeps the parcher stoked from sunup to sundown. Today, the mill is paying $1.25 a pound; in a few days, it will be $2, the highest in 20 years, to draw more ricers to the mill. Tribe member Donald Stevens has gathered seven bags in two days, for a total of 353 pounds. LaDuke hands him $441. He grins. "Not bad for the weekend, eh?" he says.

Many people on the reservation, says LaDuke, patch together a living off the land: trapping leeches for bait stores, ice fishing, berry picking, hunting and trapping, making maple syrup. And the men and women who bring rice to the mill do seem drawn by the prospect of cash in hand. Several wear boots

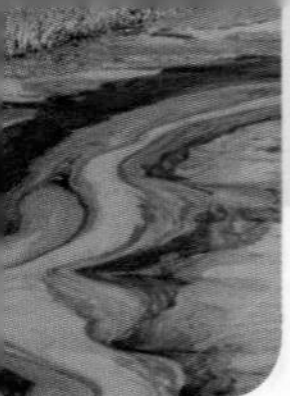

that gape at the seams. One man stops his car at the end of the road and staggers with his bags of rice almost a hundred yards on foot. His car, he says, is running out of gas.

Yet there's no denying the appeal of being out on the lakes during the "wild rice moon," a part of tribal life for some 600 years. Ricing is so central to the Ojibwa it's part of the tribe's founding myth—the creator told the tribe to seek out the place where food grows on the water. Tribesman George Chilton, 90, last went ricing five years ago. "I poled and knocked," he recalls. "Oh, it was hard work. But I sure wish I could get out there now."

QUESTIONS FOR RHETORICAL ANALYSIS

1. **CONSIDERING THE RHETORICAL SITUATION:** What effect does writing in the present tense have on this short article?
2. What do the details in the last paragraph add to this article about rice?
3. What is the writer's obligation to the reader in this short article? What does the writer need to explain?
4. Which of the brainstorming strategies, "Ways of Looking at a Subject," on page 222 can you see in this article?
5. What does the concluding quotation add to the article?

QUESTIONS FOR WRITING AND DISCUSSION

1. Think of a process or tradition that happens in the area of your hometown that might make an interesting short article.
2. Write a list of sources you might consult—literature, Web sites, and individuals you could interview for your article.

STYLE PRACTICE: IMITATION

Create a description of a scene that could begin a short article.

Mighty Mice[6]

Charles Fishman

Charles Fishman uses an entertaining voice to describe the use of lab mice in experimentation in this article from Fast Company, *a magazine that covers business news in a style that appeals to leisure readers.*

THERE IS NO CATEGORY of Nobel Prize called "best supporting researcher." But if there were, it would surely be awarded to the unassuming lab mouse. Last year, the distinguished British scientific journal *Nature* concluded that 17 Nobel Prizes have been awarded for research in which a lab mouse was indispensable.

Why are mice so nice for biological research? They are small and easy to care for—and, in 12 months, a pair of mice can produce the equivalent of a century's worth of human descendants.

[6]Charles Fishman, "Mighty Mice," from "Agenda Items," Fast Company, June 2001, p. 147. Reprinted with permission.

Plus, "mice basically have the same genes as humans," says Joyce Peterson of the Jackson Laboratory, the premier breeder of research mice. "Mice have the same systems as humans, all the same little organs, plus a couple more. They get the same diseases for the same reasons."

The lab mouse has a long history. Clarence Cook Little was an undergraduate at Harvard College when he started breeding mice in his dorm room as a way of testing his theory that some kinds of cancer might be hereditary. Little became president of the University of Maine, and then the University of Michigan. Ultimately, he returned to research, founding the Jackson Laboratory as a cancer-research center, using money from auto moguls he met while in Michigan, including Roscoe B. Jackson, head of Hudson Motorcar Co.

"In 12 months, a pair of mice can produce the equivalent of a century's worth of human descendants."

Since then, the mouse has helped discover penicillin. Vaccines for a range of ailments, from polio to rabies, were developed using mice. Much of what scientists and physicians know about the immune system comes from working with mice—including techniques that have made the transplants of kidneys and hearts routine.

And mice are big business. The journal *Science* has estimated the total market for research mice at more than $200 million a year, in excess of 20 million mice. Manipulation of mice genomics has become routine, and the mapping of the human genome is expected to lead to an explosion of demand for mice to test new drugs, new theories about disease, and new methods of treatment.

Cutting-edge research on Alzheimer's, AIDS, multiple sclerosis, almost all kinds of cancer—even heart disease—relies on mice. "The mouse is in the vanguard of research," says Robert Jacoby, a veterinarian and research scientist who heads Yale University's Animal Resources Center. "The mouse is at the fulcrum of understanding how genes actually operate in whole living systems."

QUESTIONS FOR RHETORICAL ANALYSIS

1. **CONSIDERING THE RHETORICAL SITUATION:** Comment on the style and voice in this short article. Does it sound like the kind of writing you would do for any particular class? Point out specific spots in the writing that you could use to defend your opinion.
2. Does the writer need the quotation in paragraph 2? Could the writer have stated this as a well-known fact? Why use the quotation?
3. Which details about the mice seem to be the most important? Which the least important? Why?

QUESTIONS FOR WRITING AND DISCUSSION

1. What do you think about referring to the lab mouse as someone's "invention"?
2. Select and research another widely used device or item, and write a short history about its invention.

STYLE PRACTICE: IMITATION

Define a technical, scientific, or medical term using a conversational style.

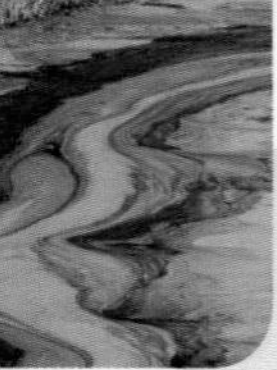

WRITING AND REVISION STRATEGIES

Gathered here are three interactive sections for you to use as you write and revise your short article.

- Writer's Notebook Suggestions
- Peer Review Log
- Revision Checklist

WRITER'S NOTEBOOK SUGGESTIONS

You can use these exercises to do some start-up thinking and writing for your short article.

1. Explain a process you are familiar with, or choose one of the following:
   - Preparing yeast dough for bread
   - Pumping gas at a self-service station
   - Making coffee
   - Changing a flat tire
   - Starting a campfire
2. Research the origin of the three-ring circus, and write a paragraph about it, using narrative.
3. In three concise sentences, explain the historical background of any issue currently in the news.
4. Explain an unusual way of making money that most people do not know about.
5. Compare bottled water with tap water in several paragraphs. Write for a general interest publication.
6. Report on a small but remarkable episode in your school's history.
7. Write several paragraphs about postage stamps—their design, their price, or some other aspect.
8. Write the beginning of a short article related to sports. Choose your topic, or use one of the following:
   - Explain the shape of a football.
   - Describe the different tennis court surfaces.
   - Report on the origin of synchronized swimming.
9. Explain the origin of Labor Day, Arbor Day, Kwanzaa, or some other holiday.

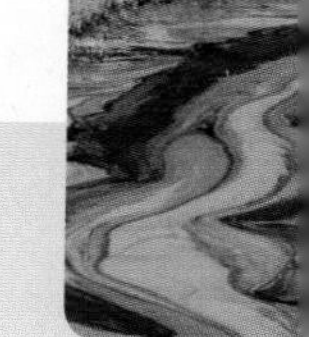

PEER REVIEW LOG

As you work with a writing partner or in a peer review group, you can use these questions to give useful responses to a classmate's short article and as a guide for discussion.

Writer's Name: ______________________________

Date: ______________________________

1. Identify the explanatory thesis (underline it). Does it reveal the focus clearly? Why? What might make it stronger?
2. Identify any development strategies the writer uses by making a note in the margin.
3. Who do you think is the audience for this article? In what ways are the strategies appropriate or inappropriate for this audience?
4. Do you understand the writer's explanation of the idea, process, event, person, or place? Put a question mark next to any point that you find confusing or that needs more explanation. What other information might you need?
5. List the main points of the article. Can you suggest other points the article might cover?
6. Does the writer have a sense of the purpose of the article—as a school assignment, an article, or a Web site? Identify any places that seem too formal or too informal for the purpose. Put a check mark next to any material that seems at odds with the formal or informal approach, and make a note.
7. How well does the author use transitions? Write *T* where the writer could use a transition or might change a transition. Write a brief note to the writer.
8. Does the article come to a satisfactory conclusion? How would you suggest that the writer improve the conclusion?

REVISION CHECKLIST

As you do your final revision, check to make sure that you

- Wrote an engaging opening sentence
- Stated your thesis clearly and accurately
- Explained your point with "sticky stuff," details, descriptions, quotations.
- Used clear transitions keyed to the development strategies you used
- Wrapped up your explanation in a clear concluding sentence or two
- Acknowledged your sources

US AIRWAYS

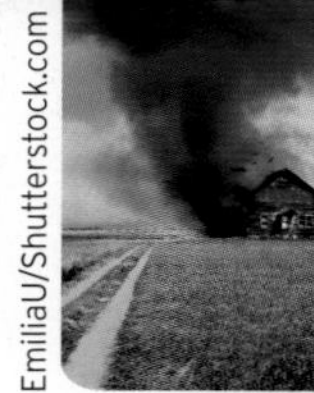
EmiliaU/Shutterstock.com

Writing a Report 9

NEWS FOR PRINT, WEB, AND SOCIAL MEDIA

Journalism is literature in a hurry.

—Matthew Arnold

The first reports of Flight 1549—when a jet bound for North Carolina lost all engine power three minutes after taking off from LaGuardia airport and then ditched safely—came on Twitter, with photos of the scene taken and transmitted via cell phones. The images showed an incredible sight: people standing on the wing of an airplane partially submerged in the Hudson, on a freezing cold January day, waiting for rescue. In more than one way those photos were historic—documenting the event, yes, but also demonstrating how the public has become part of the news media.

Really, anyone with a cell phone can contribute to the public record about big events that attract interest. So many people can have a voice in reporting, in fact, that the noise of it all can prove distracting and confusing. It can be difficult to find the truth amidst all the choices. But people do wade in and sort through it, gravitating to old media (traditional newspapers and broadcast stations) as well as sampling the new.

Their quest is to find very good *and* very current information. It may even be a basic human drive—the desire to become an "eyewitness" to the dramatic, the controversial, the mysterious, the odd. Perhaps we are hard-wired to want to know what is happening, when it is happening. Over time, technology has given us many more options to feed this need. We are, more than ever, tied to real-time updates. Understanding how to speak to an audience that wants information is not old-school at all; in fact, writers with the skills to research and report useful stories are more in demand than ever.

WHAT'S TO COME

Janis Krums

PROCESS PLAN

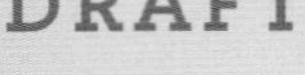

PREPARE

- Choose a current topic and test it for newsworthiness.
- Interview people involved with the story—eyewitnesses, experts.

DRAFT

- Introduction (or lead)
  - Write a summary of the main point answering Who? What? Where? When?
  - Incorporate the angle into the summary. How? Why?
- Body
  - Arrange quotations so that your story is a kind of conversation about the news—with one quotation logically following another.
  - Write sentences that set up each new topic in quotations and function as transitions.
- Conclusion: End with a quotation that offers the "human side" of the issue.

REVISE

- Cut back on all unnecessary words—no phrases like "there are" or "it is."
- Make sure paragraphs are brief: limited to one idea and/or one quotation each.
- Check the use of a consistent objective voice: third person, past tense, and none of your own opinions.

UNDERSTANDING THE WRITING PROJECT

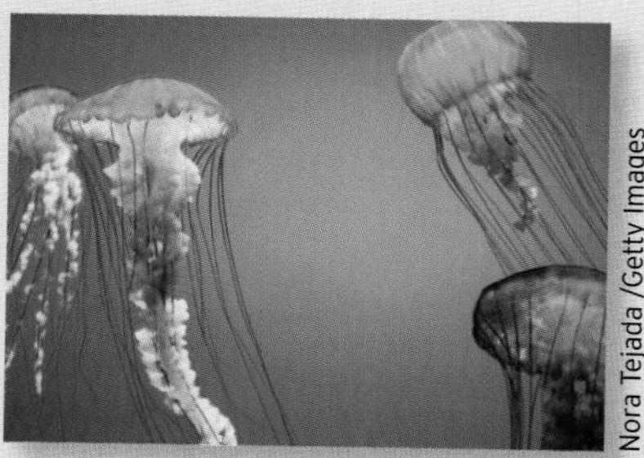
Nora Tejada /Getty Images

TODAY EVERY second of every day somebody is reporting news: on Facebook, Twitter, and blogs; on newspaper, radio, television, Web sites; and on broadcasts and narrowcasts going out over cable, the airwaves, and high-speed phone lines. The way we reach these stories is constantly changing, but what readers ask for in good news reports is not. They want writing that is fair, balanced, well-researched, reliable, and probably more than anything—concise.

The concise form of news writing, with a focus on abstracting the main point from a whole collection of information, will provide you with skills that serve you well in school. Often you are asked to provide a very brief overview of reading, write an annotated bibliography, or propose a complicated research project in a few paragraphs. In research papers this kind of overview is called an abstract. In summarizing literature, the summary is called the précis. This skill of summarizing is the cornerstone of all critical, analytical writing—and also at the heart of news reporting.

ASSIGNMENT Report on recent events or a trend that has significance for your community—school, town, group— and publish your story in a newspaper, newsletter, blog, or Web site. Write a story with a good headline that focuses and summarizes the news. Your report should include the following key features:

- *The Lead.* Leads should include what happened, who was involved, where, and when.
- *Details.* Details should follow the lead in order of importance.
- *Quotations from Sources.* Eyewitnesses, people involved, and experts should tell the story for you.

Access an interactive eBook, and chapter-specific interactive learning tools, including flashcards, quizzes, videos and more in your English CourseMate via www.cengagebrain.com.

ANATOMY OF A REPORT

KATHERINE DONNELLY was asked to write a news report about some trend she observed on her campus. As a soccer player at a Division One school, she, herself was part of the story. The challenge for her was to report the news without using her opinions. She uses primary sources—players diagnosed with concussions—as well as secondary sources to fill out the details of the story for her readers, and provides a balance of insights and opinions on the issue.

Concussions: A Hidden, but Potentially Deadly Sports Injury Gets a Closer Look[1]

KATHERINE DONNELLY

time element

angle: why or how the events happened

After Boston University researchers proposed, earlier this month, that a depression-inducing illness caused by frequent hits to the head in football games might be to blame for the death of a University of Pennsylvania student, coaches, trainers and students are speaking out against the danger athletes can cause themselves by keeping their concussions quiet.

lead paragraph—provides who, what, where, and when.

context: provides background details that help explain the angle

The autopsy of 21-year-old Owen Thomas revealed that the UPenn student was suffering from Chronic Traumatic Encephalopathy – a brain disorder that has affected a number of NFL players – before his suicide. The disease, which can cause paranoia, aggression and dementia, is typically associated with athletes who have had long careers and experienced multiple concussions. Thomas's diagnosis makes him the youngest and first collegiate athlete on record to have suffered through CTE.

This discovery has more recently triggered fears that repeated blows to the head during the physical sport could put young athletes in high school and college at risk. According to a recent story from ESPN.com, every year more than 50,000 high school football players, between 14 and 18 years old, suffer from concussions, especially dangerous at this age because brain tissue is still growing.

quotations from secondary sources—sources cited within the text

[1]Reprinted by permission of Katherine Donnelly.

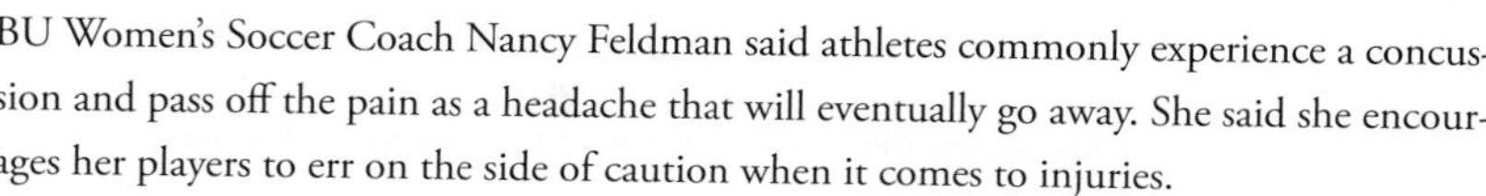

BU Women's Soccer Coach Nancy Feldman said athletes commonly experience a concussion and pass off the pain as a headache that will eventually go away. She said she encourages her players to err on the side of caution when it comes to injuries.

Thomas – who would have been one of his team's senior captains this season – hanged himself in his apartment off of UPenn's campus five months ago. His mother told ESPN in a Sept. 14 story that he had never been formally diagnosed with a concussion and that he had not shown any obvious indicators of depression in the time leading up to his death.

source cited accurately, in text

"You can't take chances with injuries to the brain," Feldman said. "[Athletes] must seek medical attention right away or it will only get worse."

BU Athletic Trainer Erica Shaya pointed out that athletic departments at BU and beyond have begun to address the issue of head trauma and its consequences more adamantly in recent seasons. She said BU requires athletes to sign a specific concussion waiver before their seasons that makes the reporting of concussion symptoms and corresponding seeking of medical attention mandatory. "Some leagues actually have kids taking pre-season brain scans now," Shaya said. "All concussions are serious and may result in complications including prolonged brain damage and death."

details that fill out the local angle: what this school does, specifically

Shaya added that athletes at BU must take and pass a computerized concussion test prior to the season in order to be eligible to play. The "Impact Test" organizes students' medical profiles, asks them questions about their health history and leads them through a series of neurophysiological tests, such as word discrimination, symbol and color matching, and design memory, to clear them for competition.

details about the concussion test—what does it ask?

Set up for the quotes that follow, a transitional device in news writing

Some students say the testing is patronizing and needless. Junior Michelle Kielty – a member of the women's soccer team – said student athletes should be able to determine for themselves if their condition is worthy of medical attention.

establishes the identity and credibility of the speaker

provides a different opinion, balance for the story

"To me, it's kind of a waste of time," she said. "I think we can judge for ourselves if we feel the injury is that bad."

gives a sense of how the community is responding, fills out the details, all sides of the story

continues next page

College of The Holy Cross senior and soccer player Jessica Pham said she supports the testing, but understands that some athletes have an "invincibility complex."

partial quotation

quotations respond to one another, showing all the sides, providing a kind of conversation about the topic. good source, who is a practitioner—has experienced the phenomenon, first-hand.

"I used to think the test was useless too," said Pham, who has experienced seven concussions as a collegiate athlete. "But after I kept getting headaches. I had to report it, and the test showed I had one."

Pham said she is now required to wear a protective headband known as a "Total 90" during practices and games to soften the blow another hit to the head might deal her. She said now that she has taken the steps to keep herself safe, she wants to help other students to understand that owning up to injury is not the end of the world.

"It's easy not to want to let your coaches down – your teammates down," she said. "You think you can overcome it."

provides some explanation of the denial, from a practitioner

"It just isn't worth it not to report it or at least get it checked out," Pham added. "What's missing one practice compared to a whole season? Or your life, for that matter."

powerful quote saved for the ending—memorable, emotional

"I had to go back and ask Jessica if she actually had 7 concussions because I couldn't believe that myself."

Q&A with Katherine Donnelly

A soccer player/writer uses her personal experience—and her teammates'—to help report news

Q: How did you become familiar with the topic, Katherine?

A: I became familiar with the topic being a student-athlete myself. Jessica was one of my teammates at Holy Cross. Coming in freshman year I didn't really understand why she wore the protective headband, I thought it was more for show than anything. After learning how many concussions she had experienced, however, I began to understand much better.

Joseph Lee

Writer/athlete Katherine Donnelly, in the white uniform.

Q: Where did you find sources? How much of your interview notes finally made it into the story? Did you need to go back to your sources for more information?

A: I knew Jessica's mom because she came to the games. One source coached Jessica since she was in middle school I believe, so she was a good resource. As for the concussion testing itself, I asked the trainers in the Athletic Training Room at BU who had more facts. I had to go back and ask Jessica if she actually had 7 concussions because I couldn't believe that myself!

Q: How did you feel about including the student source who said the efforts to detect concussions are too much—that athletes should be allowed to self-report?

A: I wanted to include Michelle because I think her opinion is the reason why concussions are becoming such a big issue now. Most cases they don't report it in fear of letting teammates and coaches down. It's a scary fact, but it's one that I'm sure most college athletes are guilty of.

Q: Did you have any experiences that helped you write the story?

A: When I was 12, I had a concussion in a game. I didn't tell my coach, but at the end of the game my parents could tell I was out of it. I had more headers in that game than in a whole season combined.

Q: How did you keep your personal opinions out of the story—or did you?

A: I tried not to make any biased opinions on the topic, but I did want to stress the fact that athletes don't report it—as Michelle's said—when they should. I wanted there to be both sides of the story told, but Jessica is a good friend of mine, and I think her courage is something very admirable and I wanted to make sure that came across. She actually had a concussion again this year, and she is done for good.

John Tlumacki/ South Boston/ January 29–This photo was taken at Gavin Middle School. The assignment desk asked me to go see whether there were any photos of Acia Johnson that we could use because the trial in her death was about to start. The principal said: "Let me get her teacher. You probably want to talk to her." As the teacher opened this case dedicated to Johnson's memory, she was hunched over. Then she turned around and just started crying. At that point, there are two things going through your mind: Are you the human, compassionate person who's going to go over and say, "I'm sorry. Is everything all right?" And then the journalist in me kicks into high gear and says, "That's a great picture." Sometimes one wins over the other.

John Tlumacki/Globe Staff/Getty Images

THE RHETORICAL SITUATION: THE VOICE OF OBJECTIVITY

Whether we are consciously aware of it or not, the conventions of news style are ingrained in our heads and in our culture. We know that no other writing quite sounds like news reporting. We know it when we hear it, and we lean on that knowledge when seeking sources for information that are current, concise, and, more importantly, credible. And even though some networks have a clearly specific viewpoint, you can hear in the *formal* reporting of news on television broadcasts that the tone still sounds the same. Readers want news reports that are accurate, balanced, thorough, and not driven by a desire to promote products or ideas.

Balance is a term journalists use to describe the content of a news story. A close relative of *objectivity*, and certainly an ingredient in the voice of objectivity, balance refers to the inclusion of many points of view. Quotes that reflect opposing opinions help news writers avoid one-sided writing. Showing your readers that you have reported the full spectrum of observations and points of view helps establish the voice of objectivity in your writing. Some specific "rules" of news voice and style:

1. Write in third person.
2. Use simple past tense.

Suzanne Kreiter/Globe Staff/Getty Images

Suzanne Kreiter/Chelsea/May 16
It was a Sunday, and some robbers had barricaded themselves in a home with people in it. The police surrounded the house, and then the people and the bad guys had come out, but the police and the SWAT team had no way of knowing whether there were still people in the house. There was an element of street theater about this. These people here, no one was really in danger. It was an inconvenience with a little bit of stress. I saw this little girl and her mother, and I would imagine at that age, you really don't know what's going on. I felt that her face was going to give readers an idea of what it would be like to wake up in Chelsea on a Sunday morning and have your neighborhood taken hostage.

3. Include careful citation of sources (names, titles of people, in-text citations of researched material).
4. Use phrases like "according to" and "as reported in" to help establish this voice of objectivity.
5. Never, ever include your opinion. Instead include the opinion of others.

Since the early days of newspapers, the voice of news writing has become an identifiable style with the information that readers find useful being reported and written in the same way: with a focus on what the readers want to know. In addition to following the cardinal rules just mentioned for establishing the objective voice, the credibility of your voice depends on addressing the readers' expectations that they will find verifiable information that is organized, succinct, and up-to-date. Accuracy is a high priority in news stories and one of the most significant draws for readers.

PRACTICE 9.1

Practicing Voice

Choose a fairy tale—*Cinderella, Hansel and Gretel, Little Red Riding Hood,* or *Snow White*—and rewrite it in the voice of news writing.

NEWSWORTHINESS

In choosing a topic for a news story, the first step is to figure out what makes a story newsworthy—of interest to readers of newspapers, newsletters, or Web sites. Ask yourself these questions as a first test for story ideas:

1. Is the story timely or about an issue that is currently "in the air?" A story about football is best reported leading up to or during football season, for example. Issues in the news such as concerns about the economy or up-and-coming elections can be timely.

Bill Greene/Globe Staff/Getty Images

Bill Greene/Hull/April 26
It was just a slow day. Oftentimes you're driving around trying to find something, and it can be very frustrating because sometimes you just don't. So I headed down to Hull. I was driving down the street, and I noticed two trees moving on the sidewalk. I stopped and I shot them. I introduced myself, and it turned out just to be two 14-year-old boys trying to cause a commotion. It became clear to me what the picture was going to be when they came upon an unsuspecting person.

PRACTICE 9.2

Looking for News Worth

Evaluate the following for newsworthiness. If worthy, identify the place the story would be posted or printed:

1. When the university opened this fall, authorities discovered cracks in the walls of a brand-new dormitory.
2. A restaurant in your town has lost its liquor license.
3. The town little league snack shack accidentally burned down.
4. Students at your school are complaining about the student center closing on Sundays at 3 o'clock.

2. How many people have a stake in the topic? Are many people involved? Does the issue have the potential to reach out to a big group?
3. Is the story interesting because it involves people from my community? Even a plane crash that is far away could be newsworthy if someone from your hometown is involved.
4. Is a celebrity involved? This does not just mean Hollywood stars, but your town's state champion wrestler or a well-loved teacher.
5. Is the story off-beat in some way? Report stories that many people would agree are worth reading about, like someone who sells her house to devote a year to community service in Africa. Not everyone does that. People would want to know why she did.

RESEARCH PATHS: CURRENT, ACCURATE, AND RELIABLE

Doing the reporting for news stories will be similar, in some ways, to the kind of research you probably have done for term papers, but it will be markedly different in other ways as it will require you to deal with primary sources as well as secondary ones. In developing the story, you will rely on the observations, knowledge,

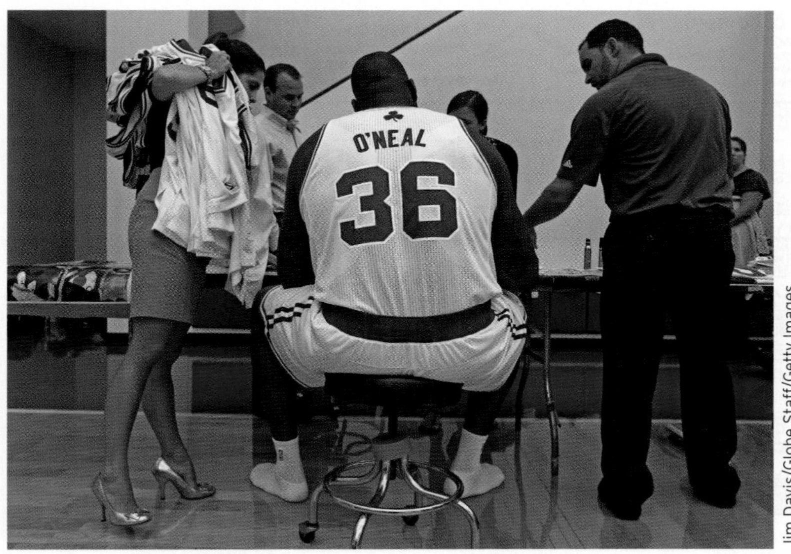

Jim Davis/Globe Staff/Getty Images

Jim Davis/Waltham/September 27
That was the media day the Celtics held at their training camp. They set aside three, four hours. It's a good thing for feature photos, because we don't need to capture the promotional stuff the team is doing or the TV stations are doing, we can just pick off what is going on there. We look for an offbeat moment. This particular picture is of Shaquille O'Neal, and, for some reason, he had taken off his sneakers. I think he was done with them for the day. He was just sitting there, signing jerseys.

and insights of experts, analysts, and eyewitnesses. Information from these sources is valuable in helping advance a reader's understanding not just of what happened, but of its significance and context. You may also be consulting academic, political, or legal documents, which can help ensure the veracity or accuracy of your report. This kind of direct, raw information is referred to as *primary source* material as it represents original research.

Take the following police report from Kent, Washington on page 252 as one example of a primary source. News writers often have to gather stories from reports—like this police report—that offer a raw form of information. When examining a primary source, you have to be your own detective. In this report, for example, a news writer would need to decide whom to interview to bring in the human perspective and how to create a summary of the events from the raw data.

Writers of news reports prefer to do their own research so they can be personally sure of its validity. Rarely do reporters rely solely on other stories, though occasionally looking at previous reports about the same issue can help reveal context. Knowing what was reported in the past can give you a sense of whether a recent event seems atypical or a continuation of a larger pattern of events or behaviors. These kinds of published accounts, called *secondary sources,* can be useful in helping you become expert on the topic you are writing about.

Just keep in mind that most of your reporting needs to be original reporting: You will talk to people. You will look for facts in the form of data from studies, books, and reports.

PRACTICE 9.3

Summary

Read the police report on page 252 and summarize what happened as part of your lead for a story you might write about this event.

MASTER CASE REPORT FORM

MASTER INCLUDES
- ☐ SUSPECT FORMS
- ☐ ADD'L PERSONS/VEH
- ☐ ADD'L PROPERTY REPORT
- ☐ EVIDENCE LOG
- ☐ VEHICLE FORM
- ☐ MISSING PERSONS

KENT WASHINGTON

City of Kent Police
220 4th Avenue South
Kent, Washington 98032
(253) 856-5800

MASTER CASE REPORT NUMBER: 03-5152
Cross-Ref 1 | Cross-Ref 2 | Cross-Ref 3 | Cross-Ref 4

CASE SUMMARY

☒ RCW ☐ KCC ☐ NO CRIME ☐

PRIMARY STATUTE	CRIME/INCIDENT TYPE	PRIMARY COUNTS	2ND	3RD
9A56040	THEFT 2	060070 / 1	1	1

ADDRESS	APT/SUIT	BUSINESS NAME	LOCATION IF NO ADDRESS	CITY
1810 MAPLE LN	M72	HOLLYGLEN CONDO		KENT

OCCURRENCE DATE/TIME	DATE/TIME	REPORTED DATE/TIME	HOW TKN
4/28/3 1100	4/28/3 1430	4/28/3 1510	D

RPT OFFICER ID#	LAST NAME, INITIALS	REVIEW BY ID#	LAST NAME, INITIALS	CASE STATUS
23970	SPOONER, AZ	92021	PAGANUCCI	C

PERSONS/BUSINESSES

INVOLVED	NAME (Last, First, Middle)	SEX	RACE	DOB (AGE)	OCCUPATION/EMPLOYER
RP/VM	☒ PERSON ☐ BUSINESS BALLANTINE, ROBERT	☒ M ☐ F	W	6-4-39	—

ADDRESS	APT/SUIT	CITY	STATE	ZIP	HOME PHONE	BUS PHONE
1810 MAPLE LN	M72	KENT	WA	980		—

IF PERSON WERE THEY (1P) INJURED? ☒ NO ☐ YES — INJURY RELATES TO: ☐ FEL CRIME ☐ MIS CRIME ☐ IND ACCID ☐ ACCIDENTAL ☐ OTHER ☐ UNKNOWN — EXT-INJ — TAKEN TO — BY — STATEMENT ☐ YES ☒ NO

INVOLVED	NAME (Last, First, Middle)	SEX	RACE	DOB (AGE)	OCCUPATION/EMPLOYER
	☐ PERSON ☐ BUSINESS	☐ M ☐ F			

ADDRESS	APT/SUIT	CITY	STATE	ZIP	HOME PHONE	BUS PHONE

IF PERSON WERE THEY (1P) INJURED? ☐ NO ☐ YES — INJURY RELATES TO: ☐ FEL CRIME ☐ MIS CRIME ☐ IND ACCID ☐ ACCIDENTAL ☐ OTHER ☐ UNKNOWN — EXT-INJ — TAKEN TO — BY — STATEMENT ☐ YES ☐ NO

PROPERTY

OWNER-LAST NAME, INITIALS	GENERAL DESCRIPTION	TYPE	CATEGORY	WACIC NO
☒ SAME PERSON AS ABOVE — SAME AS VM	SEGWAY			

RECORD ARTICLE CD	BRAND	MODEL	SERIAL NO	QTY	$VALUE	BY
				1	5000.00	

COLOR(S)	PREMISE/AREA/ROOM TAKEN FROM ADDITIONAL NOTES
BLK	2-WHEEL MOTORIZED VEH

OWNER-LAST NAME, INITIALS	GENERAL DESCRIPTION	TYPE	CATEGORY	WACIC NO

RECORD ARTICLE CD	BRAND	MODEL	SERIAL NO	QTY	$VALUE	BY

COLOR(S)	PREMISE/AREA/ROOM TAKEN FROM ADDITIONAL NOTES

OWNER LAST NAME, INITIALS	GENERAL DESCRIPTION	TYPE	CATEGORY	WACIC NO

RECORD ARTICLE CD	BRAND	MODEL	SERIAL NO	QTY	$VALUE	BY

COLOR(S)	PREMISE/AREA/ROOM TAKEN FROM ADDITIONAL NOTES

VEHICLE

INVOLVED	LICENSE	STATE	LIC-TYPE	YEAR	MAKE	MODEL	BODY	COLOR(S)	UNIQUE ID

VIN	R/O NAME ☐ PERSON ☐ BUSINESS	ADDRESS	APT/SUITE

CITY	STATE	ZIP	HOME PHONE	BUSINESS PHONE	DAMAGE TO VEHICLE

SUMMARY OF INCIDENT

RP/VM ROBERT BALLANTINE STATED THAT AT THE ABOVE DATE, TIME AND LOCATION HE HAD CHAINED UP HIS UNIQUE MOTORIZED TWO WHEELED WALKING MACHINE. BALLANTINE INDICATED THAT HE WAS THE ONLY ONE TO HAVE THE MACHINE IN SOUTH PUDGET SOUND.

THE MACHINE WAS PARKED AND CHAINED AROUND 1130 ON 4/28/3 WHEN BALLANTINE RETURNED TO THE MACHINES LOCATION, THE CHAIN HAD BEEN CUT OFF AND THE MACHINE WAS GONE.

THERE ARE NO SUSPECTS

C-CLOSED ☐ ADDITIONAL NARRATIVE

OFFICER ID	LAST NAME INITIALS	DATE/TIME	APPROVE ID	LAST NAME INITIALS	DP BY
23970	SPOONER, AZ	4/28/3 1600			

KPD1218 5/22/02 rev

Police report from Kent, Washington.

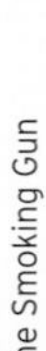

Tips on Sources for News

- **Interviews:** Take good notes and make sure you write down names and phone numbers. Steer the conversation into specifics whenever you can. Instead of asking yes or no questions, ask for stories, examples. Follow up on interesting answers asking for more details. (More on interview tips can be found in Chapter 15, Research.)
- **Observations:** While testimony from eyewitnesses is useful and interesting, you can also use your own direct observations. Does that politician sometimes park illegally in a handicapped spot? Did the fire burn the whole house? Were protesters chanting obscenities? Use your observation to help set the scene of news events, noting telling details like the "sea of green tee-shirts at the rally" or the icicles clinging to the building after a fire.
- **Documents:** Marketing studies and governmental statistical reports and surveys are widely available online, but you have to be aware of the source. Increasingly, public legal documents like deeds, lawsuits, licenses, and court records can also be found on the Web.

DEVELOPING THE BIG IDEA: THESIS OR ANGLE IN A NEWS STORY

One of the paradoxes of a news report—like other kinds of reports (see the selection on abstracts on page 258)—is that yes, it is a story, but no, it is not written chronologically—at least not from the very beginning. This organization may seem at odds with the way people tell stories to their friends: "I had to go the store for some milk, so I drove over the 7-Eleven and parked, and after I got my milk and got in line at the counter, I heard the crash outside." Instead, news stories flip right to the outcome: "Five people were seriously injured when a car being pursued by a police cruiser collided with passenger van pulling out of the parking lot of a convenience store on the outskirts of town last night." So, why would I read the rest? Some readers do not, but others are intrigued enough to want to find out all the details of the story.

The importance of the *news lead*—which is the journalistic term for the opening paragraphs of a news story—is to summarize the whole event (to answer *who, what, where, when*)—but also to provide an angle. As a reporter, you slice into a story and decide what is most significant in these events. And although it seems at odds with the goals of keeping your own opinion out of the news story and remaining

PRACTICE 9.4

Looking at Angle

Choose two stories in today's news. Read them carefully, and figure out their angles. See how many other angles you could approach the stories from. Generate at least three other angles for each story. Write a lead sentence for each of the new angles you created.

VISUAL LITERACY: EYEWITNESS ACCOUNTS

BRINGING YOUR READER INTO THE MOMENT WITH PHOTOGRAPHS THAT TELL STORIES

PHOTOGRAPHS—and film and video—make everyone an eyewitness to event. The best examples of photojournalism capture more than just the landscape of that moment, though. They also tell a story with characters and conflict. They make us all eyewitnesses. Read the captions that accompany these news photos and the other photos in this chapter to get the photographers' insights into what they were thinking.

Jonathan Wiggs/Globe Staff/Getty Images

Jonathan Wiggs/Fall River/March 30
We'd had several days of heavy rain in Massachusetts, causing a lot of flooding. Reports were coming in that there was heavy damage in Fall River. The damage was a little difficult for me to find, because streets were blocked off. But I eventually found where several streets had buckled. The neighborhood had just undergone extensive reconstruction of its sewer system and repaving of its streets, so the damage was a particularly cruel blow.

USING ANY KIND OF CAMERA, GO OUT AND TAKE PHOTOS THAT REVEAL STORIES. Once you have collected three photos, bring them into class. Ask yourself: Which story does my photograph tell? On a sheet of paper you will keep secret, write down the narrative you intended to convey in the photograph, like the captions with the photos. Ask classmates to write down the story they detect in the photograph. Compare the reactions to your intention, and discuss the elements of the photograph that led your viewers to your intention—or away from it.

Boston Globe via Getty Images

Pat Greenhouse/Boston, March 7
This is in the Cathedral of the Holy Cross, and Cardinal O'Malley was saying a memorial Mass for the victims of the Haitian earthquake. I just caught this woman at the right moment. When I look at it, just the way her hands are held, I get a sense that she's shielding her face from the horrors of everything that happened, but with the rosary in her hand, it's revealing hope at the same time. She was singing a song.

objective, the angle does provide a kind of interpretation—a way of understanding the news.

Think about this lead:

- This Fall, Boston University is stepping up precautions for athletes in regard to head injuries.

  In this lead, we do have the *who, what, where, when* questions answered, in keeping with traditional news form. But, we do not yet know why the university is stepping up precautions.

Consider how much this extra information shapes your understanding of the story:

> After Boston University researchers proposed, earlier this month, that a depression-inducing illness caused by frequent hits to the head in football games might be to blame for the death of a University of Pennsylvania student, coaches, trainers, and students are speaking out against the danger athletes can cause themselves by keeping their concussions quiet.

The angle of the news story, the *how* or *why*, helps the reader see the context and significance of the story. With this additional information, we can see that the angle of this story is the danger of athletes keeping quiet about their concussions. Other reporters might choose other angles from which to report this story. perhaps focusing on the depression caused by head injuries. The angle reveals its newsworthiness.

Summary + *How* or *Why* = News Angle

So, if the story's lead and angle tell you what happened why read on? Because the lead still has an element of mystery, still needs more explaining.

PRACTICE 9.5

Finding an Angle

Write down some possible angles that might come out of the facts of this story:

> You go to a book signing at your campus bookstore and the author, who is originally from your town, has written a book about his hunting expedition in Africa. Animal rights advocates are picketing outside. People have trouble getting past them and into the store. Inside the store, eight people are waiting to have books signed.

CLEAR AND CONCISE: TWO TYPES OF SUMMARIES

When you write summaries and abstracts, you condense many words into few. You state the main point, "the bottom line," in your own words, and leave out the details. To summarize an event, you would want to focus on the outcome and perhaps generalize about the causes and effect. In writing an abstract, which is a summary of a piece of report or analysis, you will state the overall conclusion.

THE NEWS LEAD

A news lead is a concise summary of an event, with a sense of how or why the event has significance. One way to think of this summary is as an overview. Writing a good summary is particularly relevant in writing for the Web and social media where readers, or viewers, are less inclined to kick back and spend a long time with information. "Quick and hot" is one way experts describe digital information.

WRITE A SUMMARY: THE NEWS LEAD To practice your skills at writing a summary lead, read the following Toland Foods press release. Translate the press release into the style of news and write a concise, straightforward news lead giving an overview of what happened and how Toland Food is reacting. Limit yourself to one to two sentences.

RELEASE DATE: 1 NOVEMBER 2011

Toland Foods Announce Rebate on Earth's Own Organic Broccoli

TOLAND FOOD DISTRIBUTORS ANNOUNCED today that they are extracting Earth's Own Organic Broccoli from markets, starting immediately. Consumers who had previously purchased Earth's Own Organic broccoli are welcome to a full refund from vendors.

Broccoli purchases between the dates of October 1 and October 28, 2011 qualify for the refund.

"We are responding in a proactive fashion to the possible connection between our fresh vegetable products and Listeria, and the 47 reported cases of illness in the tri-state area. We always advise consumers to wash their hands before preparing fresh vegetables, to make sure their food preparation areas are sanitized and to cook food thoroughly," said Frederick Grimes, Toland Food spokesperson.

According to FDA standards, a product can be labeled "organic" if it is produced without pesticides and abides by water conservation standards set by the governmental organization.

Toland Foods Announce Rebate on Earth's Own Organic Broccoli

continued

"Since organic fruits and vegetables are not chemically treated in the same way conventional produce is, the opportunity for bacteria to grow is naturally higher than it might be," said Grimes. "We stand by our food. It's 100% organic, according to FDA requirements."

THE ABSTRACT

An abstract, similarly, is a summary, but a summary of a research paper. Like news leads, abstracts can function as a freestanding source of information, independent of the context in which they might appear. You can read a news lead and know what happened. You can read an abstract and understand the main claim of a research paper. In the Readings section of this chapter, you will see examples of both an abstract and a news lead, which is part of a news release, to use as examples.

The following exercise on abstracts and the preceding one on the news lead will allow you to practice reading material and extracting a concise summary of its information.

WRITE A SUMMARY: THE ABSTRACT Read the following report and summarize the Institute of Medicine Committee's conclusions in a single sentence.

REPORT BRIEF • SEPTEMBER 2009

Local Government Actions to Prevent Childhood Obesity

IN THE UNITED STATES, 16.3 percent of children and adolescents between the ages of two and 19 are obese. This epidemic has exploded over just three decades. Among children two to five years old, obesity

prevalence increased from 5 percent to 12.4 percent; among children six to 11, it increased from 6.5 percent to 17 percent; and among adolescents 12 to 19 years old, it increased from 5 percent to 17.6 percent (see Figure 1). The prevalence of obesity is so high that it may reduce the life expectancy of today's generation of children and diminish the overall quality of their lives. Obese children and adolescents are more likely than their lower-weight counterparts to develop hypertension, high cholesterol, and type 2 diabetes when they are young, and they are more likely to be obese as adults.

In 2008, the Institute of Medicine (IOM) Committee on Childhood Obesity Prevention Actions for Local Governments was convened to identify promising ways to address this problem on what may well be the epidemic's frontlines. The good news is that there are numerous actions that show potential for use by local governments. Of course, parents and other adult caregivers play a fundamental role in teaching children about healthy behaviors, in modeling those behaviors, and in making decisions for children when needed. But those positive efforts can be undermined by local environments that are poorly suited to supporting healthy behaviors—and may even promote unhealthy behaviors. For example, many communities lack ready sources of healthy food choices, such as supermarkets and grocery stores. Or they may not provide safe places for children to walk or play. In such communities, even the most motivated child or adolescent may find it difficult to act in healthy ways.

Institute of Medicine, Report Brief of September 2009, "Local Government Actions to Prevent Childhood Obesity." Reprinted with permission.

THE BODY OF THE NEWS STORY:

THE DEVIL IN THE DETAILS

Though the rules of news writing are changing as media becomes more tailored to the desires of readers who sometimes prefer a more narrative approach, the tradition of telling stories without opinion is still valued by readers. No matter their leanings, readers will return to a source that offers original, fully detailed reporting that is fair and intelligent. But readers are after more than just facts or data when they choose

to read a news story. They are interested in the characters, conflicts, and themes in those stories. Readers ask news writers to be observant and accurate, as their stories unfold mysteries and uncover important truths.

This is why quotations are a key ingredient in writing for this genre: Quotations from people who understand the circumstances can help us understand the story. The quotations in a news story can even be thought of as a conversation about the topic—a kind of back and forth between knowledgeable people. Through eavesdropping on that conversation our understanding of the story grows deeper. Because the news writer has done a good job gathering, selecting, and compressing information, we learn what the "experts" know. And we learn it quickly.

USING PARAPHRASE AND QUOTATION

There are three ways to use material from interviews and other sources: full quotations, partial quotations, and paraphrases.

FULL QUOTATIONS

Full quotations are usually a full sentence or two, transcribed exactly as they were spoken.

EXAMPLE: "There is no evidence, at this point in time, that the accident was related to alcohol," said Ted Vargen, Wake County district attorney.

Use full quotations especially for well-phrased thoughts, memorable language, and when accuracy is crucial.

PARTIAL QUOTATIONS

Selected material from an interview appears in a partial quotation, along with the attribution—the name of the source of the quotation.

EXAMPLE: People became "hysterical, running out of the lab screaming," according to Marisol Boulanger, an eyewitness to the chemical spill in the chemistry lab on Tuesday.

Use a partial quotation to capture the power of a direct quotation even though the full sentence may be too long, ungrammatical, or confusing.

Both full and partial quotations are most useful when they are clear, provide insight into a character, or help vary the presentation of information in a paragraph.

PARAPHRASES

Restating a quotation in your own language can help clarify meaning and can be a good way to make information more concise, easier to understand, or more relevant.

EXAMPLE: Students were instructed in how to handle accidents in the lab, according to Boulanger.

Paraphrase long or wordy quotations or quotations in which the language is fuzzy or vague, grammatically incorrect, or confusing.

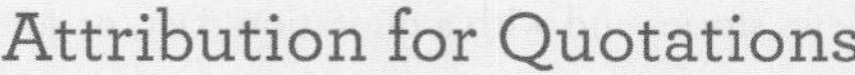

Attribution for Quotations

- Always give the name of the source of the quotation, citing the speaker's full name and title.

  EXAMPLE: "Pollution is causing asthma rates to soar," said Dr. Greg Spiro, head of pediatrics at Faith Hospital.

- Follow a full quotation with the simple verb *said*.
- If you quote the same speaker later, use just the person's last name in the attribution.

  EXAMPLE: Asthma is a major public health issue, according to Spiro.

- As a rule, do not start quotations with the attribution, as doing this tends to slow the story down. Instead, state the quotation and then cite the speaker's name.
- If you are using a quotation that you found in another source, you must also give attribution to the other source, citing the publication in which it first appeared and identifying the speaker.

  EXAMPLE: School board member Raisa Perez told the *Sun-Times* last Tuesday that more students would be left out of the free-lunch program if budget cuts continue.

- Use quotations from other printed sources sparingly and only if you absolutely must. If possible, replicate the quotation by calling the source directly or by substituting a similar source and quotation that you have collected.

PRACTICE 9.6

Class Press Conference

Use the following scenario to stage a press conference:

Your town is currently debating a new law that will outlaw text messaging while walking. The proposed penalty for text messaging while walking is $100 for the first offense, $250 for the second, and $500 for the third.

1. Five students from the class will answer questions. The interviewees should represent class members who have texted while walking, those who prefer not to text while walking, those who support the bill, and those who oppose it.
2. After the press conference, formulate a lead that summarizes student opinions of the bill.
3. Write a news story with quotations that reveal the various viewpoints on the issue.

ENDING THE NEWS STORY

The structure of the news story evolved because the technology has allowed news to be passed around at lightning fast speeds. For the same reasons, news stories do not have "conclusions" that summarize or tie up all the loose ends. As news was

updated, the tops of stories changed and the bottoms were chopped off, leaving the other stories on a page intact. Instead of changing the whole page, printers were able to change one paragraph of a late-developing story. Since stories were written in descending order of importance, what comes last should be the least important and the most expendable details. Traditionally, news writers have spent little time thinking about the ends of news stories for this reason. Stories seem to fade out rather than conclude. Nowadays, many news stories end with a quotation, fact, or statistic that shapes the impression of the story.

FINDING AN AUDIENCE: FLASH COMMUNICATIONS AND USING SOCIAL MEDIA

Though many people use social media simply for keeping up with friends, increasingly services like Twitter and Facebook are becoming important channels for sharing news and information with communities of users who share your interest. For example, if you are a health writer in Louisiana with a special interest in reporting the latest developments in diabetes research, you can quickly and easily connect to a global audience of "followers" or "friends" by tweeting your news or communicating it through a status update on your Facebook page. Your readers are not general-interest browsers, but insiders—possibly doctors, researchers, or patients and their families. They are following you because you are a source of information about a subject they care about.

The best social media writing is taut and concise. Twitter posts are limited to 140 characters, which tends to dictate what and how you communicate. Like Twitter, Facebook limits the number of characters permitted in its status updates, but Facebook allows a much more generous 410 characters. Still, brevity and conciseness rule. Think of an extended headline with more detail, but still highly concentrated.

Social media writing is essentially like writing headlines. It must inform and grab the reader. A useful thing to keep in mind is the dictum laid down by old-school newspaper editors. They say when writing a good headline, think about how you would draw the attention of people in a crowded bar if you had to shout out a single sentence. Keep in mind that key words, or specific detail, will draw readers in more than vagueness.

Which of these would be better to shout into the crowd?

- *Four arrested at protest*
- *Plainfield cops arrest four students at tuition-hike protest*

The second is clearly better. It is more concrete, highlighting key details that clearly reveal the content of the story while still being short and to-the-point.

Let's say you are tweeting or writing a Facebook update on a page for fans of the last Harry Potter movie. Which of these two is more informative?

- *Variety* says some characters get killed and Harry faces down Voldemort in "Harry Potter and the Deathly Hallows: Part 2."
- I have read that lives will be changed in the last installment of the Harry Potter movie.

The first sentence tells the reader much more and is more interesting and compelling.

Some Tips for Headline and Social Media Writing

- Avoid complex sentence structure.
- Use active verbs.
- Cut back on articles (the, a, an).
- Use concrete language.
- Be specific.
- Use key words that would show up in Internet searches.

Both Facebook and Twitter allow you to connect to a global community of users who care about you or share a specific interest. Most tweets notify registered followers about updates to personal, organizational, or corporate blogs or direct them to Web sites where there is content that may be of interest—news or feature articles or videos. Companies, organizations, and groups also create Facebook pages to keep interested individuals up-to-date on their doings. Hundreds of millions of individuals use Facebook to keep friends and acquaintances abreast of what they are doing.

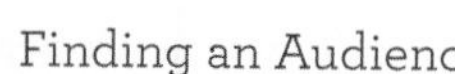

D I Y

DIY MEDIA AND DESIGN

WRITING FOR A BLOG: AN INSIDER'S VIEW

FIND A BLOG that covers an area you are particularly interested in and write a story for it, using Lee Feiner's advice (below) about understanding what your audience already knows and what you can offer that is fresh and engaging.

Strode chases open dream in qualifying draw[2]

Lee Feiner *Sports Illustrated*

Lee Feiner wrote for the Sports Illustrated *blog while he was a college intern. He says that a blog can present a different set of considerations than writing for print. He understood his readers would come to the subject with a deep understanding of the subject. "I knew I had a tennis-savvy audience reading my work." Feiner says he knew the piece, part of a "US Open Blog" feature of the SI Web, would need something extra to sell the story. "There isn't much that's going to make even the die-hard tennis fan read about a player ranked in the hundreds trying to win a qualifier. So with the producer I decided that the hook was Strode's not-so-common backup plan at one of the most prestigious law schools in the world." Here is Lee Feiner's lead for the* Sports Illustrated *blog.*

[2]Feiner, Lee. "Strode chases Open dream in qualifying draw." Open Source. 24 August 2010. Reprinted with permission.

Blake Strode has something most scholars would kill for: an acceptance letter to Harvard Law School.

He also has something most tennis players would kill for: an opportunity to make the main draw of the U.S. Open.

Starting today, Strode, a two-time SEC Scholar-Athlete of the Year who graduated from the University of Arkansas with a 3.98 GPA, will compete for a spot in the 128-player main draw alongside hopeful professionals ranked just outside the Top 100. His first-round opponent is Alex Bogdanovic of Great Britain.

For the first time, the USTA gave anyone 14 or older a chance to qualify for a Grand Slam that's become more "open" than ever before. The winners of 16 men's and women's sectional qualifying tournaments held around the country from April through June advanced to July's National Playoffs in Atlanta, where Strode navigated the draw to earn a place in this week's qualies at the Billie Jean King National Tennis Center.

READINGS

WRITERS OF news for journals, newletters, blogs and other sources use the same style and structure as newspapers for a reason: because readers trust objective reporting and also appreciate the idea that the events will be concisely summarized at the beginning. Readers also want to know how the events have an impact. In the following readings, you will get a sense of how a story may start out as a report for a specialized audience, but then can be transformed into news almost any reader would find useful.

Teach for America Impact Studied

This is a short news story from the Philanthropy Journal *on the study from the Urban Institute and Calder center, "Making a Difference?: The Effects of Teach for America in High School" It is followed by an abstract of the same study by three co-authors. Note how, as the rhetorical situation changes, and in turn the reader's expectations change, the voice does, too. The whole report can be found at the Web sites for the Urban Institute and the Calder Center: www.urban.org and www.CALDERcenter.org.*

TEACHERS FROM a nonprofit that deploys recent college graduates to teach in some of the neediest public schools in the U.S. are outperforming traditional teachers, a new study says.

High school students taught by Teach for America teachers perform better on end-of-course exams than those taught by traditional teachers, says an evaluation by the Urban Institute.

That finding holds true even when comparing Teach for America's teachers to more experienced educators, and even though the nonprofit's teachers are assigned to more academically-challenged classrooms.

And while gains are seen across all subject areas, math and science see particular benefits from the Teach for America program.

"Evidence shows that, in terms of test scores, TFA teachers are able to more than offset their lack of teaching experience, either due to their better academic preparation in particular subject areas or due to other unmeasured factors such as motivation," the report says. The 2009 report updates a 2007 report using a larger sample size and additional comparisons.

Making a Difference?: The Effects of Teach for America in High School[3]

Zeyu Xu, Jane Hannaway, Colin Taylor

CALDER Working Paper No. 17

The Urban Institute and CALDER

(Revised March 2009)

April 23, 2009

[3]From Xu, Zeyu, Jane Hannaway, and Colin Taylor. Making a Difference? The Effects of Teach for America in High School. The Urban Institute. 27 March 2008. Reprinted with permission.

ABSTRACT

Teach for America (TFA) selects and places graduates from the most competitive colleges as teachers in the lowest-performing schools in the country. This paper is the first study that examines TFA effects in high school. We use rich longitudinal data from North Carolina and estimate TFA effects through cross-subject student and school fixed effects models. We find that TFA teachers, on average, have a positive effect on high school student test scores relative to non-TFA teachers, including those who are certified in-field. Such effects exceed the impact of additional years of experience and are particularly strong in math and science.

1. Teach for America (TFA) recruits and selects graduates from some of the most selective colleges and universities across the country to teach in the nation's most challenging K–12 schools throughout the nation. TFA has grown significantly since its inception in 1990, when it received 2,500 applicants and selected and placed 500 teachers. In 2005, it received over 17,000 applicants and selected and placed a little over 2,000 new teachers, and the program anticipates expanding to over 4,000 placements in 2010. In total, the program has affected the lives of nearly 3 million students.

   The growth of the program alone suggests that TFA is helping to address the crucial need to staff the nation's schools, a particularly acute need in high poverty schools, but TFA is not without its critics. The criticisms tend to fall into two categories. The first is that most TFA teachers have not received traditional teacher training and therefore are not as prepared for the demands of the classroom as traditionally trained teachers. TFA corps members participate in an intensive five-week summer national institute and a two week local orientation/induction program prior to their first teaching assignment. The second criticism is that TFA requires only a two year teaching commitment, and the majority of corps members leave at the end of that commitment. The short tenure of TFA teachers is troubling because research shows that new teachers are generally less effective than more experienced teachers (Rivkin, Hanushek, and Kain, 2005; Rockoff, 2004).

2. In recent years, TFA corps members have also engaged in on-going professional development activities provided by TFA and whatever other supports school districts provide new teachers. The research reported here investigates the relative effectiveness (in terms of student tested achievement) of TFA teachers, and examines the validity of the criticisms of TFA. Specifically, we look at TFA teachers in secondary schools, and especially in math and science, where considerable program growth is planned over the next few years. To the best of our knowledge, this is the first study of TFA at the secondary school level. Using individual level student data linked to teacher data in North Carolina, we estimate the effects of having a TFA teacher compared to a traditional

"In total, the program has affected the lives of nearly 3 million students."

teacher on student performance. The North Carolina data we employ are uniquely suited for this type of analysis because it includes end of course (EOC) testing for students across multiple subjects. This allows us to employ statistical methods that attempt to account for the nonrandom nature of student assignments to classes/teachers, which have been shown to lead to biased estimates of the impact of teacher credentials (Clotfelter, Ladd, and Vigdor, 2007a; Goldhaber, 2007).

> "The findings show that TFA teachers are more effective, as measured by student exam performance, than traditional teachers."

The findings show that TFA teachers are more effective, as measured by student exam performance, than traditional teachers. Moreover, they suggest that the TFA effect, at least in the grades and subjects investigated, exceeds the impact of additional years of experience, implying that TFA teachers are more effective than experienced secondary school teachers. The positive TFA results are robust across subject areas, but are particularly strong for math and science classes.

QUESTIONS FOR RHETORICAL ANALYSIS

1. **CONSIDERING THE RHETORICAL SITUATION:** Why does someone read a report? Who reads them regularly?
2. Comparing the news story to the report does one source seem more factual than the other? Why or why not?
3. How do the details about the growth of the program (included in the report) shape your opinion about the issue? Do you think the news story should include the information? Why or why not?
4. Who is the audience for the study? Why might the identified audience think this is a well-written document?
5. What makes the news story seem objective?

QUESTIONS FOR DISCUSSION AND WRITING

1. Do you need to know something more about the program Teach for American to fully understand the significance of the news story?
2. How would more quotations from a larger variety of sources help develop your understanding of the news story?
3. If you were to develop a similar story about Teach for America participants at your college, what sort of questions would you ask? What information would help you develop this angle, that the program is successful?

STYLE PRACTICE: IMITATION

Write the lead for a news story that "translates" an article from an academic journal into a news story for your college paper.

Bearing the Burden[4]

Lauren McKown

thestatenews.com 9/23/10

Student loan debt, a perennially newsworthy issue, gets updated with the release of a government report—an opportunity to report the local angle of a national issue. In this case the reaction comes from the community at Michigan State University.

AS SOON as Ethan Davis was admitted to MSU, he set his sights on getting out. An economics freshman taking only core, required classes, Davis now is considered a sophomore credit-wise after loading up on Advanced Placement courses in high school. He's determined to graduate in three years.

It's not what he wants to do—it's what he has to do.

From Federal Stafford Loans to private loans to Parent Plus loans, Davis said he has plenty of borrowing options to pay for school. It's the precise reason he feels the pressure to leave East Lansing with a diploma and as little debt as possible.

"It's an incentive for me to get out of MSU as quick as I can," he said. "It's a bad thing because, for me, it's encouraging me to take only required classes and as many as I can, as soon as I can. And that's bad for my quality of learning and my health and well-being."

But Davis isn't the only one feeling the heat.

The State News/statenews.com

According to a 2010 report by the Department of Education, MSU students cumulatively owe about $433 million in government loan debt. That amount, which does not include private loans taken out by students, makes MSU the institution with the eighth highest total student debt nationally among not-for-profit universities.

MSU also has the second highest median student debt rate in the Big Ten Conference at $22,078 per student. Spartan debt is only trumped by students at private Northwestern University, according to the report's data.

All things aside, MSU students far exceed expectations in the area of loan defaults, according to student loan and financial aid experts. The national average for student loan defaults—or the inability to make continuous monthly payments on a loan—rose to 7 percent in 2010. MSU students have a 2010 average of 1.7 percent.

[4]Lauren McKown, "Bearing the Burden," from The State News, September 23, 2010. Reprinted with permission.

But to just glance over the statistics would be a mistake, said Rick Shipman, director of the Office of Financial Aid. Shipman said it's important for students to be knowledgeable about borrowing and the on-campus resources available before choosing how to pay for school.

"Of course students should be afraid of borrowing that much money, but they shouldn't be afraid of taking out the loans, getting the degree and a job and managing those payments (after graduation)," he said.

BREAKING DOWN THE NUMBERS

A simple math equation isn't enough to define the state of student debt at a university, Shipman said.

"When studies look at the average debt of a graduating senior, they look at all of the seniors who borrowed loans and divide the total dollars borrowed by the total numbers of students who borrowed," he said. "There are a small amount that take out private loans also, and you'll find that it really skews the results and makes the average higher."

Although having about $22,000 in debt upon graduation might seem outrageous, Melissa Hunt, vice president of client relations and education at Credit Union Student Choice, said the statistic isn't surprising.

Credit Union Student Choice is an organization that works with credit unions across the nation to help provide financial support services to students.

"I don't feel that that's extremely high," she said. "If you think about it, an average student is eligible for about $29,000 in federal loans already, so to be below that is definitely reasonable."

"An average student is eligible for about $29,000 in federal loans already."

Although MSU has one of the highest national student debt loads, James Monks, an associate professor of economics in the Robins School of Business at the University of Richmond in Virginia, said he's not surprised MSU students have low default rates on their loans.

"Generally, the better the school, the better the default rate," Monks said. "Students are able to go on and get good jobs and pay their loans."

MSU students are some of the best in the Big Ten Conference for avoiding loan default, Shipman said. Similarly-sized schools such as Pennsylvania State University, Ohio State University and Indiana University have default rates of 3.4 percent, 2.5 percent and 2.5 percent, respectively, he said.

"Students who default the most are students who do not complete their degrees," he said. "You don't have a lot of students at MSU that don't end up finishing a degree here or elsewhere."

Mark Kantrowitz, publisher of fastweb.com and finaid.org, said there are few reasons MSU's default rate could be lower.

Fastweb.com and finaid.org are Web sites devoted to helping students navigate financial processes associated with higher education.

"(It's) a better qualified college and therefore students are going to get better jobs after graduation," Kantrowitz said. "Schools also can manipulate their default rates by encouraging students that are struggling financially to defer payment or go into forbearance so they aren't included in the default statistics."

WORKING THE SYSTEM

Students have numerous options when it comes to managing loan debt post-graduation, Kantrowitz said, but most experts promote taking out federal loans first in all cases.

"They have fixed, lower interest rates," he said. "There is loan forgiveness on federal loans, but not private loans."

As part of a student loan reform package added on to the Health Care and Education Reconciliation Act of 2010, income-based loan repayment and loan forgiveness now are helpful options available for students, Shipman said.

"Most college students start out making less money than they are going to make over time," he said. "Knowing that their payments will always be reasonable based on their income level makes it less fearsome for them to borrow the needed amount. On top of that, if they are totally unemployed and have no income, they can file for forbearance and (the government) will let you wait to pay on your loans for up to 12 months at a time."

Monks said the policy is an important one, but warned that students should be cautious.

"It doesn't reduce the payment," he said. "It just stretches out the payment over a longer amount of time."

> **"Knowing that their payments will always be based on their income level makes it less fearsome for them to borrow the needed amount."**

Jane Glickman, a spokeswoman for the U.S. Department of Education, said most importantly, the department wants students to avoid default.

"Our goal is to make sure students don't go into default and have the opportunity to pursue teaching or whatever public service jobs they want after college that don't generate as much income," she said. "We don't want student debt to dictate what they go into, so this is a good option for them."

Hunt said it is vital that students in debt trouble communicate with their lenders.

"If you find yourself, as a student, in a situation where you might not be able to pay your loan payment, reach out to your lender," she said. "They do not want you to default. They want to assist you in staying in payment on this loan. Many, many lenders will work with you."

TAPPING INTO UNIVERSITY RESOURCES

As much as loans are financial strains, international relations and French junior Breanne Lewinski said they can provide students with important experiences, such as study abroad.

Traveling to Brussels this summer, Lewinski said many of her peers could not have made the trip without the help of federal loans.

"The experiences we got from visiting the different European Union institutions there were irreplaceable and the benefits those students got from the study abroad by taking out the loan were essential," she said. "Some of the programs are too expensive for students to handle without loans."

For those feeling the strains of financial stress, Olin Health Center can schedule student appointments with a financial awareness counselor who visits campus weekly, said Dennis Martell, health education coordinator for Olin Health Center.

"It's available for students to help them reduce mental, physical and academic difficulties," Martell said. "MSU students ranked money as the second highest rated thing that they're stressing about in a survey we did last year."

Davis said regardless of his options, the pressure is on. He said officials need to avoid making assumptions about the financial

situations of students when doling out grants and financial aid.

"There are classes that I really want to take and if they're not counting, I can't take them," he said. "I'm definitely missing out on part of the experience."

Shipman said students should take advantage of entrance and exit counseling available at the Office of Financial Aid for loan debt.

"You have the opportunity to come and meet with someone in our office individually or in a group setting," he said. "You can even do a Web version that tells you about the terms and conditions that are available as a borrower to avoid default."

Hunt worked with the Office of Financial Aid on many prior occasions and said students should take advantage of the resources the office has to offer.

"I would go to a school and they would do one great thing and another school would do another great thing," she said. "But at MSU they do a lot of great things. I am blown away at how phenomenal the financial aid office is. They're in a totally different class."

QUESTIONS FOR RHETORICAL ANALYSIS

1. **CONSIDERING THE RHETORICAL SITUATION:** What will readers need to understand about college loans an Advanced Placement classes in order to understand the opening of this news story?
2. What's the angle in this story?
3. How does the information about studying abroad help develop this story?
4. How does the writer make the facts from the study particularly focused on MSU? What issues does MSU, for example, reveal about the student loan picture?
5. This is the story of an ongoing trend. What makes it news?

QUESTIONS FOR DISCUSSION AND WRITING

1. What do you think about leading this story with a specific person's experience? Will it interest readers or put them off? Why?
2. The topic might make students feel stressed, but readers might find some uplifting material in this story. Where? Is this useful information?
3. Do you agree that one of the effects of student loan debt is trying to stick to the required classes and perhaps not making the most of your college years?

STYLE PRACTICE: IMITATION

Write the lead for the same type of article, but about your school. Start off with a student example, the way this one does.

WRITING AND REVISION STRATEGIES

Gathered here are three interactive sections for you to use as you write and revise your news story.

- Writer's Notebook Suggestions
- Peer Review Log
- Revision Checklist

WRITER'S NOTEBOOK SUGGESTIONS

You can use these exercises to do some start-up thinking and writing for your news story.

1. Read today's offering on a newspaper site. Make a list of newsworthy topics that are covered in the hard-news stories, not in the features or commentaries.

2. Brainstorm a list of topics at your school that you would like to know more about.

3. If your city or town has two competing newspapers, read the same story in both papers or read the same story in your local paper and in one of the national papers like the *New York Times, Washington Post, San Francisco Chronicle*, or *Chicago Tribune*, all of which you can find online. Compare the coverage of the stories, looking at the headlines, the leads, the angles, and the writing. Analyze any differences that you find, and note instances of bias or lack of objectivity, if any.

4. Using the topic of today's lead story on a news site, interview two friends and find out their opinions on the topic. Write a three- to four-paragraph news story on local reaction to this event, integrating at least two quotations from your friends.

5. Write a short news story about a trend you have observed, and explore its implications, effects, and/or causes by talking to people directly affected by it. (A weather pattern, poor turnout at elections, and parking problems are some examples.)
   - Report about the trend in the lead.
   - Get reactions to it and quotations about it from people.
   - Investigate to determine whether this trend occurs in other places.

6. Write a lead paragraph for the following story. Set it in the present time, and write it for tomorrow's paper.

   In Verona, Italy, the teenage children of two feuding families fall in love. Juliet Capulet and Romeo Montague, with the help of the local friar, Friar Lawrence, escape from their homes and plan to meet at a remote family tomb and then marry secretly. Juliet arrives first. She takes a powerful sleeping potion as she waits for her lover. When Romeo shows up, he mistakenly believes that Juliet has committed suicide, takes out his knife, and kills himself. When Juliet wakes up, she sees her dead lover and, tragically, kills herself with the same knife.

7. Write a letter home or to a faraway friend about your life this week, using news story form and structure. Make sure that your lead summarizes the news, that you have a clear angle, and that you organize your information in order of importance. Do not make anything up.

8. Write an "anniversary" story. Follow up on a story that was happening a year ago. Report any new developments or ongoing issues.

PEER REVIEW LOG

As you work with a writing partner or in a peer editing group, you can use these questions to give useful responses to a classmate's news story or as a guide for discussion.

Writer's Name: ______________________________

Date: ______________________________

1. Underline the lead. Put check marks by the *who, what, where, when,* and (if included) *how.* What is missing, if anything? What is the angle?

2. Is the topic of the story newsworthy? Is it interesting to readers? Why would readers find the topic useful?

3. Is the story objective and free of the writer's personal viewpoint? Does the writer seem to be advertising, promoting, or lecturing in the news story? Label any spots that seem biased or promotional with *OBJ?* (for *objectivity*).

4. Number the sources (1, 2, 3). Do the sources reflect different perspectives on the topic? Could the writer use an opposing or a different view?

5. Are quotations attributed to sources? Note any problems with quotations by writing question marks in the margin. Look for quotations that are too long or too confusing. If you can suggest that the writer paraphrase or use a partial quotation, make a note in the margin.

6. Does the story sound like something you might hear on the evening news? Is the style formal? Circle any words or phrases that jump out as being inconsistent with the voice of news reporting.

7. Does the body of the story reveal enough about the background of the story? Do you have questions about why or how the event happened?

8. Are paragraphs arranged to show order of importance? Draw arrows if you think some paragraphs might be rearranged.

REVISION CHECKLIST

As you do your final revision, check to make sure that you

- Chose a newsworthy, timely topic
- Wrote a concise lead including *who, what, where, when,* and perhaps *how* or *why*
- Included a clear angle
- Provided background information to give a full picture
- Used correctly attributed quotations from several sources
- Organized the story by order of importance
- Balanced your reporting to show several sides of an issue and to remain objective
- Consulted good sources

PART IV

Writing to Analyze

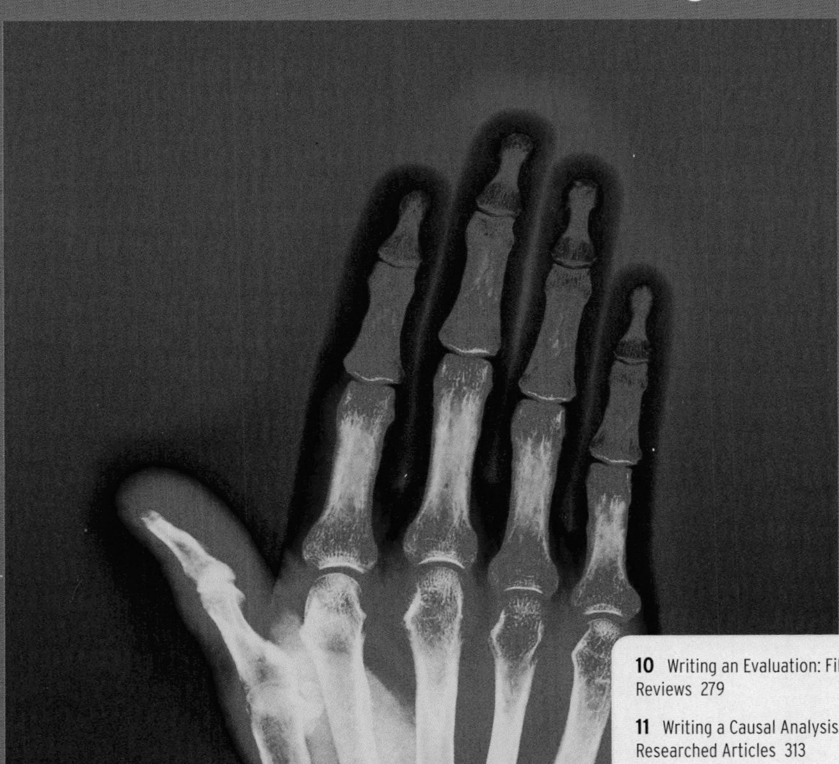

Image Source/Aurora Photos

akva/Shutterstock.com

10 Writing an Evaluation

FILM REVIEWS

I learn more from critics who honestly criticize my pictures than from those who are devout.

—Ingmar Bergman

When filmmaker James Cameron's *Avatar* was released in December, 2009, reviews differed. In *Rolling Stone*, Peter Travis wrote a rave:

> It extends the possibilities of what movies can do. Cameron's talent may just be as big as his dreams.

On the Salon.com Web site, critic Stepahnie Zacharek panned the film:

> It *is* a very expensive-looking, very flashy entertainment, albeit one that groans under the weight of clumsy storytelling in the second half and features some of the most godawful dialogue this side of "Attack of the Clones."

Film critic of the *Boston Globe,* Ty Burr gave the film a mixed review:

> James Cameron's gamble, in other words, has paid off in ways both problematic and successful beyond measure. (You can read Burr's full review on page 282.)

Part of the fun of reading film reviews is seeing how different writers admire and criticize different aspects of a film.

WHAT'S TO COME

20th Century Fox/Everett Collection

PROCESS PLAN

PREPARE

- Take notes as you watch the film. Pay attention to the story, acting, visual impact, and sound effects.
- Find out about the making of the film, the director, the stars—really any interesting context or background information.

DRAFT

- Introduction: Include background and contextual information about the film. Present thesis: evaluation of the film. Give a brief summary of the film.
- Body: Analyze the most significant criteria—the story, characters, direction, music, editing, cinematography, acting, costumes, special effects—that support your thesis: What are the film's strengths and weaknesses?
- Conclusion: Do not stop at a summary. A review requires an evaluation. Answer the question: Is it worthwhile to see this film?

REVISE

- Check to make sure evaluation is clear.
- Find more evidence to strengthen points.
- Be sure to acknowledge both the strong and weak points of the film.

UNDERSTANDING THE WRITING PROJECT

Shanna Baker/Getty Images

A FILM REVIEW cannot be a plot summary alone. You should reveal just enough of the plot to give your audience a context for your evaluation, and you should try to avoid "spoilers," those details that will ruin any surprises the film has in store for your reader. But whether you are analyzing a film, a work of literature, or an article for a psychology class, the basic review form is the same: evaluation supported by evidence.

Evaluations are determined by analyzing the key features of a work. Films tell stories as much through images as through words. In your film review, in addition to evaluating the characters, plot, conflict, and theme of the film, you will want to evaluate the visual elements that are specific to film: the cinematography, editing, acting, production design, music, and special effects.

ASSIGNMENT Write a film review of a movie in current release or on video. Choose a work that has some artistic merit and aims to provide more than light, mindless entertainment. For your film review:

- Look for a movie in current release or on DVD or go to the YouTube Screening Room <*www.**youtube**.com/**screeningroom***> to find a short, lesser known film to review.
- Choose the specific publication in which you would publish this review: a newspaper, a magazine, or an online site. Keep this audience in mind as you write the review.
- Research your topic by reading reviews in your chosen publication and finding out what you can about the context and any sources of the film you are reviewing.

Access an interactive eBook, and chapter-specific interactive learning tools, including flashcards, quizzes, videos and more in your English CourseMate via www.cengagebrain.com.

When you write your review, avoid the temptation to go through a laundry list of these film elements; rather, choose the ones that are important to the film. For a film made with such innovative technology like *Avatar*, for example, you would probably emphasize the computer-generated graphics and 3-D effects, while for a serious drama like *The Hurt Locker*, you would likely focus on the writing and the acting.

ANATOMY OF A FILM REVIEW

TY BURR has written three books about films and contributes film criticism to *Entertainment Weekly*. He currently works as a film critic at the *Boston Globe*.

Avatar[1]

TY BURR

Here is a glass of Kool-Aid - would you like to drink it? It's made up of equal parts expectation and hype: the long-awaited return, after 12 years, of a gifted filmmaker to the epic narrative form that's his true strength; the breakthrough technology to make visionary fantasy worlds seem more vivid than our humdrum reality. The glass holds the promise that our entertainment industry always makes and almost never keeps - the promise of the Brand New Thing, the pop artifact that changes *everything*.

provides the reader with a context for looking at the film—background

addresses the reader one-on-one. As in a conversation with a smart friend

Here is a movie called "Avatar." If you drink the Kool-Aid (it's for sale on every channel and in every magazine), the film may indeed look like the Brand New Thing. If you don't, "Avatar" may instead appear to be a long, tactile, visually revelatory, dramatically simple-minded 3-D science-fiction adventure made up of live-action sequences and photo-realistic digital images. (Instead of "computer animation," by the way, journalists

thesis statement

[1]Ty Burr, "Avatar," from The Boston Globe, December 17, 2009. Reprinted with permission of PARS International.

Photos 12/Alamy

have been instructed by studio publicists to use the phrase "the Next Generation of Special Effects." Mmm, mixed berry!)

thesis continues to second paragraph Opinion + Why

James Cameron's gamble, in other words, has paid off in ways both problematic and successful beyond measure. The 60 percent of "Avatar" that comes from the computer - either in wholly invented images or by wrapping human bodies in imaginary digitized forms - is bewitchingly, tantalizingly realistic. The film creates a planet called Pandora, a race of tall, blue cat-people called the Na'Vi, and gives them both a dazzlingly colorful rainforest reality - part Rousseau, part George Lucas on inhalants.

The roughly 40 percent of the film that is live action - those scenes involving human colonizers from Earth amid their predatory mining and military hardware - is, oddly, less convincing. "Avatar" focuses on a scientific team that has cloned Na'Vi bodies for human hosts to patch into as they (the humans) lie in high-tech tanning beds back at the base. With these biotech sock-puppets, head wonk Dr. Grace Augustine (Sigourney Weaver, juicily riffing on both Ellen Ripley *and* Dian Fossey) hopes to "win the hearts and minds" of the indigenous population. If she doesn't, the corporate suits and military men (represented, respectively, by Giovanni Ribisi and Stephen Lang, both of whom would twirl their mustaches if they had them) will happily force the issue.

premise

What Grace isn't expecting is that her newest team member, a paraplegic ex-Marine named Jake Sully (Australian actor Sam Worthington), will go native once he has found his avatar legs. In his long new blue body, Jake enthusiastically joins the Na'Vi as a sort

continues next page

of junior probationary member, quickly acquiring their jungle skills, the ability to tame and ride the local Pandoran horses and pterodactyls, and the respect and love of Neytiri, played by a fierce, inventive Zoe Saldana underneath all the pixels. From the way the local flying-jellyfish tree spirits alight on Jake in flocks, it's clear that our hero is the Chosen.

summary

When the earthlings come back with their bulldozers and cannons, and Jake has to choose sides. Hmmm, which will it be? The Na'Vi with their interconnected biosphere, their massive Tree of Souls, their literal genetic bond with the flora and fauna that surrounds them? Or the snarling humans addicted to hardware, despoilage, extinction, and big, snorting machines? Yes, "Avatar" is the latest high-tech entertainment to lecture us that technology is wrong. Human civilization, too. The movie's cultural politics are childishly two-dimensional, at times insulting (especially if you know anyone in the armed forces). Squint at "Avatar" the wrong way and it starts to look like a training film for jihad - not, I'm guessing, what Cameron had in mind.

conflict of the film

comment on theme

negative comment abou the oversimplification th reviewer sees

comment on how successfully the film reveals theme. Imbedded comment in the word choice.

In terms of plot, then, this is "Dances With Wolves." Seriously: It's *the same movie*, re-imagined as a speculative-anthropological freak-out. Because Cameron is a visionary and a perfectionist, though, it's possible to get lost in his created world, and this is where "Avatar" thoroughly lives up to its hype. I could go on about the depth of field in the rapturous 3-D landscapes, how cleanly each individual leaf and insect is realized, how fully visualized the critters, but words start to fail. "Avatar" is an entertainment to be not just seen but absorbed on a molecular level; it's as close to a full-body experience as we'll get until they invent the holo-suits. Cameron aims for sheer wonderment, and he delivers.

plot comment, first a comparison

comment on getting lost in the plot—in a good way

good element: the "look of the animation

(A side note: At the film's initial screening for Boston-area press, the 3-D visuals were noticeably off, causing image-doubling that made for a poor viewing experience. A hastily scheduled rescreening, overseen by a Fox technician flown in from the West Coast, resulted in a vastly improved "Avatar," although reflective surfaces in the live-action scenes are still hard for the eye to resolve. A projector setting was at issue, apparently, and you'd better hope the kid who sells you popcorn knows which button to push at your local theater, because the Fox guy has since gone home.)

What is clear is that Cameron remains a natural-born filmmaker, even when he gets obsessed by world-building at the expense of plot and dialogue. You feel you can almost reach in and touch Pandora, not because of the 3-D but because the director has imagined

plot and dialogue a bit off

the planet's dangers and beauties well beyond the borders of the screen. Other elements show the King of the World starting to repeat himself: The clomping exoskeleton from "Aliens" gets a redo here, as does that film's butch Latina Marine, now played (very engagingly) by Michelle Rodriguez. Worthington is solid and bland as both the human and Na'Vi Jakes, but since the hero is in effect *our* avatar, that vagueness makes a kind of sense. (It's up to Weaver, Saldana, and Rodriguez to provide the gumption - but Cameron has always loved powerful women.)

comment on special effects and characters

The director has said he has been carrying this story around since he was a teenager dreaming it up in his bedroom, and that makes sense, too. At night the jungles of Pandora bioluminesce like black-light posters, and there are times you may feel you've landed on the Disco Planet. The character Neytiri is a classic teenboy daydream - the wild woman conquered - and what's the whole avatar business but a way to imagine oneself out of a small, impotent body and into something stronger, truer, *realer*.

themes, what the story tells us

At the same time, "Avatar" is merely the latest white man's romance, and it hits every stop in the playbook: The broken hero who finds renewal by leaving his decadent people, who joins a tribe of noble savages and becomes purified, who leads his new children to victory (because they can't lead themselves) and becomes a legend in the doing. Tarzan has been here, and Herman Melville, and so has Kevin Costner. As a cultural cliché, it reflects profound disgust with the society of men and a yearning for authenticity - for a connection deeper than anything our fallen modern world can provide.

more on theme and premise—negative

Is Cameron aware of the traps of this fantasy? More than it might seem. "Avatar" is, after all, a movie where the hero dreams himself into a strong blue body and wakes, crestfallen, to find himself back in his own skin. The movie knows that Jake Sully is like Pinocchio, a human marionette aching to be a real alien, and at times it takes the measure of the distance between the two. Not for nothing is the standard Na'Vi greeting "I see you." Not for nothing is the scene in which Neytiri finally says those words to the human Jake the most emotionally powerful moment in the film.

reference to a specific scene that shows a strength

I think Cameron loves the fantasy more, though - enough to sail close to the edge of the ridiculous in the final moments of "Avatar." Enough to spend 15 years and hundreds of millions of dollars building a beautiful someplace that doesn't exist and into which we can blissfully, forgetfully project ourselves. Here's your Kool-Aid, he says. Drink deep.

ends with the beginning metaphor

"All reviews require nuance; a mixed review forces it."

Q&A with Ty Burr

A Film Critic Talks about the Reviewer's Responsibilities to His Readers

Q: You go out on a limb in this review suggesting that fans—especially Cameron's faithful—might have drunk "the Kool-aid." Did you think of it as a risky way to open this review?

A: Not particularly—I wanted to address the hype—which was ferocious in the weeks leading up to the film's opening—right off the bat. I'm never very concerned about alienating "the faithful" or not. My duty is to both the average *Globe* reader (whoever that may be) and my own response to any given film.

Courtesy Ty Burr

Ty Burr

Q: It is a mixed review—with the film being both "problematic and successful,"—in your opinion. Is it easier or more difficult to write a review that is mixed?

A: It's much easier to write an unqualified rave or a pan than a mixed review: You have to sort out your own, sometimes inchoate, response and assign positive and negative values to storytelling, camerawork, acting, etc etc. The flip side is that with a rave or a pan, it's easier to give into cheerleading or a beat-down, respectively. All reviews require nuance; a mixed review forces it.

Q: Were there any challenges reviewing this film (are partially animated films a different set of problems for you as a reviewer)?

A: The challenge is more with the pop-culture event trappings surrounding a movie this big—can you cut through the media noise to get a bead on the film itself? With *Avatar*, the challenge was taking stock of the technological breakthrough and adequately conveying it to the reader. You have to get more into the nuts and bolts than with a standard animated or live-action film.

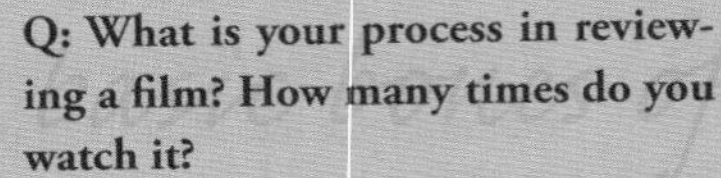

Q: What is your process in reviewing a film? How many times do you watch it?

A: It varies. Major studio films are screened for us in a commercial movie theater. Art house films, foreign language films, and documentaries we will often but not always watch at home on DVD screeners, though if the film's visuals are an issue, the publicists will generally try to get us into a theater. We generally see a film once, though if we first see it at a film festival and many months have passed, we'll watch it again. In the case of *Avatar*, I did see it twice and was glad to do so, since technical projection issues made the first screening a bust.

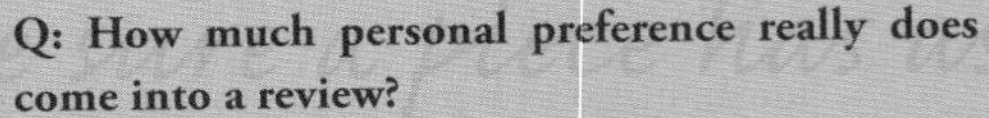

Q: How much personal preference really does come into a review?

A: Lots. At bottom, all reviews are subjective—are about **my** response to the movie. What a critic brings to the table is context: relevant information about the director, actors, the film industry, the subject and themes of the movie, and so on and so forth, depending on how much the movie itself demands details of this nature. I traffic in contextualized subjectivity, in other words, and unlike some other critics I try to be up front about that—that it is my opinion and that your own opinion may or may not vary.

THE RHETORICAL SITUATION: CONSIDERING VOICE AND AUDIENCE

Knowing your audience will help you find your voice. If you are writing for a general interest magazine or newspaper, you have to assume that readers may not know or care about film terminology. They want to read a clear review that is specific and well written; they do not expect a comprehensive analysis of film technique. Here is an example of a review of *The Departed* in *Newsweek*.

> Martin Scorsese's profanely funny, savagely entertaining *The Departed* is both a return to the underworld turf he's explored in such classics as *Mean Streets* and *GoodFellas* and a departure. What's new is that he's hitched his swirling, white-hot style to the speeding wagon of narrative. For all his brilliance, storytelling has never been his forte or his first concern. Here he has the devilishly convoluted plot of the terrific 2002 Hong Kong cop thriller *Infernal Affairs* to work from, and it's a rich gift.
>
> —David Ansen

Readers of online publications like Salon.com and others may be more knowledgeable about film, but these online critics also aim to engage and entertain their readers, perhaps with a livelier voice than in a mainstream publication.

> Oscar, Schmoscar—who needs one anyhow? Martin Scorsese made this one to please his fans and not the members of the Academy who continue to invite him to the dance only to make him leave the event without the night's most sought after party favor. With *The Departed*, Martin Scorsese returns full-force to the vulgar, sickeningly violent world portrayed in his critically acclaimed mob dramas. Thank you Mr. Scorsese. It's been a long wait but *The Depa*rted made it worthwhile.
>
> —Rebecca Murray from an online review at About.com

Readers of film magazines such as *Premiere*, *Cineaste*, and *Film Quarterly* probably do want the technique analyzed. These film journals are often written in a serious, academic voice, similar to the voice you would use for a literature or cinema studies class. Here is one more excerpt from a review of *The Departed* from *Cineaste*, one of the premiere film journals.

> Although Scorsese is well known as a film buff and has always quoted other films, *The Departed* is unusually packed full of such references. It is

PRACTICE 10.1

Collaborative Activity

While half the group watches the opening scene of a movie, the other half turns away from the screen and listens to the audio only. Then all class members do the following:

1. Describe the main characters
2. State the conflict
3. Describe the setting (if you can)
4. Describe the tone of the film—suspenseful, amusing, etc.

Compare impressions of each group. Did the viewers get a different impression of the film than the audio-only group did?

PRACTICE 10.2

Voice and Audience

1. For each of the three reviews of *The Departed*, describe the voice and explain what decisions the writer made about sentence length, sentence structure, word choice, and grammar that helped to create that voice.
2. Write the first few lines of the movie review you are writing for this assignment, or choose another movie you know well. Rewrite these lines for
   a. a scholarly film journal like *Cineaste*
   b. an online move review site
   c. a general circulation magazine like *Newsweek*

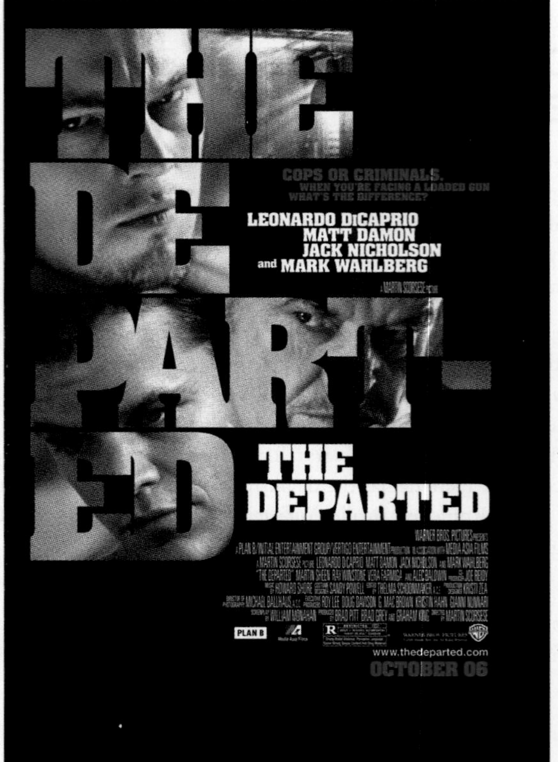

WARNER BROS./THE KOBAL COLLECTION/ART RESOURCE

as though the film represents a personal encyclopedia of cinema that races a path from John Ford to John Woo and the Hong Kong esthetic. Not only does Scorsese faithfully recreate scenes from *Infernal Affairs*; he also parodies, in the port-theater scene, the theater sequences in his own *Taxi Driver* and his remake of *Cape Fear*, making himself part of the geneaology. And he uses these allusions—which are precisely placed within the film—to deepen our understanding of the film's characters and situations.

—Rahul Hamid in *Cineaste*

Finding the right voice for a review can be tricky. Though it is fun to be irreverent—to skewer a bad film with wit and irony—you also have to be careful not to go overboard and sound silly or mean-spirited. Similarly, it is often easiest to write in a serious, even reverent voice about a film you love, but if your voice is overly earnest, your reader may find the review dull or believe that your ability to see the film's flaws has been compromised.

RESEARCH PATHS: FIND OUT ABOUT THE MAKING OF THE FILM

Film reviewers may seem to have a cushy job, watching movies and eating popcorn all day, but watching the movie is a small part of the process. Taking notes, researching the film, and putting it in context for a reader require strong research, analytic, and organizational skills.

You can find information about a film's director, writer, actors, and original source in a number of places.

- The movie's Web site is built by the promotion department and so has bias, but offers good information about the cast and production.
- Internet Movie Database at <http://www. imdb.com> catalogues a great deal of information about current movies, including biographies of filmmakers and casts, movie trivia, information about the locations, and relevant anecdotes about making the movies.
- Film encyclopedias and general histories are more scholarly sources. One of the best is David Cook's *History of Narrative Film,* which includes a detailed glossery of film terms. Another excellent resource is Gerald Mast and Bruce Kawin's *A Short History of the Movies..*

Use context and background information sparingly in your review, however. You do not want or need to sound as though you know every single detail about the film. The review is about your evaluation of the movie, not your comprehensive knowledge of it. Sometimes it is more important to have the information to add to your own understanding of the movie than to include it in the review itself.

Yet if you discover something important or interesting about the making or distribution of a film, by all means include it if it works with the points you wish to make. For example, on the Internet Movie Data Base you can find this interesting fact about the 2009 Oscar-winning film, *Slumdog Millionaire.* "Director Danny Boyle placed the money to be paid to the 3 lead child actors in a trust that is to be released to them upon their completion of grade school at 16 years of age. The production company has set up for an auto-rikshaw driver to take the kids to school every day until they are 16 years old." Knowing this fact might mollify some readers who felt that the film exploited some of the child actors.

Background information, often interesting in and of itself, adds even more value to a review if it leads the reader to your main point. Any background and contextual information you use should be done not in isolation but in service to your evaluation of the film.

PRACTICE 10.3

Exploring a Web Site

Go to the Internet Movie Database at <http://www.imdb.com>. Spend some time exploring this site. Write a list of the kind of information you can find at the site that would provide a reviewer with background and context information for the film you are reviewing.

THE BIG IDEA: WRITING THE EVALUATIVE THESIS

Talking about a film with friends can be half the fun of seeing one. If you have friends who like to talk about film, you probably have noticed in your discussions with fellow film viewers, people can arrive at different interpretations of what the message behind the story might have been. Your friends might disagree with your idea of the meaning, or theme in a film. What the film told you, your interpretation—about life, society, relationships, human nature, for examples—might be very different from theirs. So, you have to explain your reasons for the message you extracted from the story. You have to list evidence in things the characters said or did, in the logic of the plot, perhaps even in the premise of the story. As you talk about the main ideas the filmmakers wanted to get across, most likely, you are also expressing whether you liked the film.

In conversations like this, you following the steps of writing a review. You are discussing the meaning behind the story—the theme—and the execution of the message or theme. Maybe the message, in your opinion was fresh and original and earth-shattering, but the execution was flat. Or maybe the message was trite. Maybe you have heard it a thousand times, but something about the storytelling seemed original. Perhaps both the meaning and the execution were brilliant. Because the themes are really at the heart of films, you cannot evaluate one without knowing how you would express the theme in a concise statement. Your film review needs to include this statement along with an overview of your opinion of the film: Overall, was it good, bad, or mixed.

PRACTICE 10.4

Identifying Thesis Statements

Read two film reviews (from newspapers, magazines, or Web sites) of a film you have recently seen. Identify and copy the reviewer's thesis from each review.

1. How are the reviewers' theses different?
2. How are they similar?
3. Write a thesis for a review you might write for this film.

ANALYSIS OF THEME + YOUR EVALUATION OF EXECUTION = EVALUATIVE THESIS

In his review of *Fight Club*, printed in full in the Readings Section later in this chapter, Roger Ebert embeds his opinion in key phrases no one would mistake for flattery. He uses "cheerfully fascist" and "celebration of violence," along with the statement that the "heroes write themselves a license to drink, smoke, screw and beat one another up." You can see Ebert has made his decision that the theme of *Fight Club* is "macho porn" where "eroticism between the sexes is replaced by all-guy locker room fights." Ebert also mentions the execution of the film in his evaluative thesis, noting it is "well made and has a great first act."

> *Fight Club* is the most frankly and cheerfully fascist big star movie since *Death Wish*, a celebration of violence in which the heroes write themselves a license to drink, smoke, screw and beat one another up.
>
> Sometimes, for variety, they beat up themselves. It's macho porn—the sex movie Hollywood has been moving toward for years, in which eroticism between the sexes is replaced by all-guy locker room fights. Women, who have had a lifetime of practice at dealing with little-boy posturing, will instinctively see through it; men may get off on the testosterone rush. The fact that it is very well made and has a great first act certainly clouds the issue.

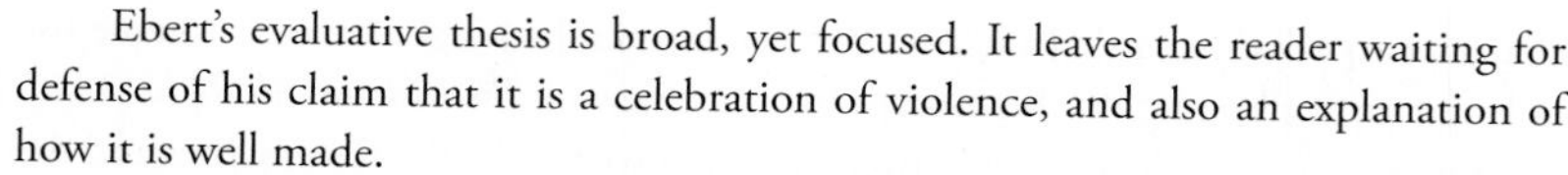

Ebert's evaluative thesis is broad, yet focused. It leaves the reader waiting for defense of his claim that it is a celebration of violence, and also an explanation of how it is well made.

Janet Maslin's review of the same film, also in the Readings section, reveals the type of contrast in opinion you might experience in your conversations with other film watchers—and with other film reviewers. Her interpretation of *Fight Club* is that it is the story of rebellion against "middle-class notions of masculinity." In asserting her perspective on the film, overall, she both describes and evaluates the execution, calling it "visionary and disturbing." She notes the "lightning-fast visual sophistication," in describing the execution of the film. Notice how that phrase also becomes a kind of positive evaluation. This kind of embedded opinion is hallmark of evaluation.

> Of the two current films in which buttoned-down businessmen rebel against middle-class notions of masculinity, David Fincher's savage *Fight Club* is by far the more visionary and disturbing. Where *American Beauty* hinges on the subversive allure of a rose-covered blond cheerleader, Mr. Fincher has something a good deal tougher in mind. The director of *Seven* and *The Game* for the first time finds subject matter audacious enough to suit his lightning-fast visual sophistication, and puts that style to stunningly effective use.

PRACTICE 10.5

Identifying Film Elements

1. On television, videotape, or DVD, watch a film with the sound turned off for five minutes. As you watch, take notes on the visual elements of the film. Pay attention to the acting, cinematography, editing, production design, and any special effects. Think about the *Mise en scene* as it is defined in the Visual Literacy exercise on page 294. List all you can tell about about character, conflict, and theme.
2. Listen to another five minutes of the same film with the picture hidden. As you listen, take notes on the aural aspects of the film—the dialogue, soundtrack, and sound effects. Note what kind of mood the sound elements create.

HOW TO VIEW WITH A CRITICAL EYE: THE ELEMENTS OF FILM

Your thesis stems from your evaluation of the strengths and weaknesses of the film. On its way to revealing the theme, your review should address how well or how poorly the film developed the plot, created characters, introduced special effects, or used music to set the mood. How original or fresh are the insights?

STORY ELEMENTS: CHARACTER AND PLOT

Script writers put characters in a variety of situations that reveal the film's major themes. You can begin to analyze a film by looking carefully at the characters, plot, and theme.

CHARACTERS The characters can be divided into major characters and minor or supporting characters. The main character will go through some sort of change or character development, often called a *character arc*. This change should grow out of clear motivation to be believable and should happen in increments, not all-at-once. A film that has character, rather than plot, at its center is said to be *character-driven*.

A screenwriter creates a character on the page, in large part, through what the character says, and the actor creates this character, in part, through the way the dialogue is delivered. Good dialogue is original, believable, and idiosyncratic. Well-drawn

characters speak differently from one another and can be judged by their unique use of language or phrasing. In this excerpt from a review of *The Kids are All Right*, A. O. Scott makes a careful distinction between the lines written by the screenwriter and the way they are delivered by the actors, Annette Bening and Julianne Moore.

> The screenwriters' ear for the way therapeutic catchphrases and hazy insights recalled from college reading lists filter into everyday conversation is as unerring as Ms. Moore's offbeat comic timing or Ms. Bening's tactical use of silence.
>
> —A. O. Scott in the *New York Times*

ACTING AND CHARACTER Actors get credit for portraying the basic role and delivering dialogue with imagination. Although actors speak the lines, screenwriters write them, so be careful in a review to separate the acting (the way the lines are delivered) and the writing (the lines themselves). Humphrey Bogart may have delivered one of the classic film lines in *Casablanca*, "Of all the gin joints in all the towns in all the world, she walks into mine," but the screenwriters, the Epstein brothers, penned it. Actors add nuance through facial expression, vocal techniques, gesture, and movement. When you consider the acting, think about the actor's believability. Focus on the way that an actor brings the character to life.

PLOT The plot is the story line—what happens to the characters in the film. The plot usually revolves around a conflict—a clash of ideas or forces, or internal tension of some kind. A good screenplay should not be boring or have puzzling plot twists or meaningless scenes.

As you analyze a film, you might hold the screenwriter responsible for a problematic story line or the director for cutting between scenes too quickly and not allowing enough onscreen time to develop parts of the story. In the following excerpt about *Shrek 4*, the reviewer criticizes the plot for being derivative and inappropriate for the intended audience.

> But the plot cuts closer to dystopian sci-fi than buoyant family cartoon, and Shrek is dragging around some awfully heavy psychological baggage for an ogre. "I didn't know what I had until it was gone," he mewls to Donkey, his existential crisis nicked whole from *It's a Wonderful Life*.
>
> —Amy Biancolli in *The Houston Chronicle*

VISUAL ELEMENTS: CINEMATOGRAPHY, EDITING, PRODUCTION DESIGN, AND SPECIAL EFFECTS

Films are visual stories, so understanding the visual elements is critical for effective analysis. Our emotional and intellectual reactions to a scene can be influenced by the arrangement of the visual image, so as you analyze the storytelling elements of a film also make note of the way the shot is framed—how the characters, furniture, or

other props are arranged within the margins of the shot. Also note costume, lighting, color, setting. In short, notice all the visual detail, even if you think it might be unimportant. Think about what the director's intention is in the shot and what it can tell you about the tone of the film. What do you know about the character, plot, and conflict from looking at the still shot from the film?

CINEMATOGRAPHY The cinematography is the way a movie is filmed: the shots, camera angles, and lighting. Camera angle and lighting can be used to create particular effects; for example, a camera might be pointed down on a dimly lit character to show the character's fright or confusion. But when analyzing the cinematography, you do not necessarily have to know a great deal about the technical aspects of filming. You can evaluate the results. Consider whether the movie is full of "talking heads" (still, close-up shots of people conversing) or of unrelenting, dizzying motion. In his review of *Slumdog Millionaire*, Stephen Rea shows how the cinematic style creates the *setting* and *tone*.

> *Slumdog Millionaire* careens with hyperkinetic energy—but the whooshing cameras and crazy jump-cuts, the flashbacks and flash-forwards, the thumping rhythms of the soundtrack, aren't mere show. They're in service of the narrative, and reflective of its setting: a country teeming with crowds, a noisy, mad, knockabout place, awash in color and contradiction.
>
> —Stephen Rea, *The Philadelphia Inquirer*

EDITING Film editing is the art of juxtaposing the individual camera shots into a coherent final product. Editing creates the sequences of images and the transitions from one scene to the next that tell and advance the story. Editors may splice shots together to create a jumpy mood or to show what is happening simultaneously in two places. Alternately, they may use a lengthy shot to create a naturalistic feel as the camera follows a character through a day's events.

Good editing allows the pace of the film to reflect the dramatic movement of the story. You might note in your review whether quick cuts from scene to scene create an artful effect, create tension, or call unnecessary attention to the editing techniques. *Memento,* a film that uses an unusual narrative structure, relied heavily on the skill of the editor. Critics, like Lisa Nesselson, credited the editor's skill in piecing together this story.

> Terrific idea and ingenious execution may wear thin or grow irritating for viewers unaccustomed to paying close attention. But anybody who dug the trippy triptych structure of *Pulp Fiction* should be able to keep up with the temporal shifts as narrative moves back, forward and sometimes sideways with the alacrity of a crab scuttling across the widescreen. Dody Dorn's editing is top-notch as pic—scripted, acted and lensed with precision—smoothly toggles back and forth between sequences in B&W and in color.
>
> —Lisa Nesselson in *Variety*

VISUAL LITERACY: *MISE EN SCENE*

MISE EN SCENE All shots in a well-crafted film are carefully planned because any good director knows the visual details of costume, lighting, blocking or placement of actors, and set design all contribute layers of meaning to the script. In fact, even without dialogue or music, the audience gets information about character, conflict, and theme. Film experts call this *mise en scene,* which means "to put in the scene." Examine the film stills from *Lost in Translation, Moulin Rouge,* and *Juno* to analyze the director's intentions in selecting and arranging the elements in the scene.

Focus Films/Zuma Press

Bill Murray in *Lost in Translation*

20TH CENTURY FOX/THE KOBAL COLLECTION/ADLER, SUE/Picture Desk

Nicole Kidman and Ewan McGregor from *Moulin Rouge*

FOX SEARCHLIGHT/THE KOBAL COLLECTION/GREGORY, DOANE/ ART RESOURCE

Ellen Page (center) from *Juno*

FILM 4/CELADOR FILMS/PATHE INTERNATIONAL/THE KOBAL COLLECTION/ART RESOURCE

Scene from Slumdog Millionaire

PRODUCTION DESIGN Production design includes the sets, costumes, locations, and props. For example, lavish period films may be filled with furniture, knick-knacks, and clothing that have to be thoroughly researched in order to give an authentic "feel" to the sets. Sometimes the physical world of the film is so elaborately imagined and created that it is worth a reviewer's commentary as in David Ansen's in-depth analysis of the production design of *Star Wars, Episode I.*

> The genuine magic in *Episode I* is all in its design. Conceptual artist Doug Chiang and production designer Gavin Bocquet give us breathtaking vistas, fabulous imaginary cities that range from the Florentine splendor of Queen Amidala's domain to the teeming metropolis of Coruscan. The vaultlike Galactic Senate, whose box seats float through the air, is a triumph of baroque futurism. The sunset-drenched, open-air Jedi council chambers (shades of *Blade Runner*) glow like a remembered childhood picture book. (The art nouveau, glass-bubble undersea city, however, looks like a floating Lamps Plus showroom to me.) The massive, tree-crunching tanks of the droid armies have a brutal beauty; there's visual wit in the insectlike robot soldiers who do the Trade Federation's dirty work. Indeed, there's often so much to take in you wish Lucas would hold his shots longer, and let us feast on the details.
>
> —David Ansen in *Newsweek*

SPECIAL EFFECTS The special effects are the animation, digital design elements, or stunts in the film. All effects, whether they are high-tech or low-tech,

should be meaningful within the world of the film. When innovative animation or computer-generated images enhance films, they are well worth mentioning in a review as David Edelstein does in his review of *Avatar.*

> The problem until now with CGI (Computer Generated Imagery) is that it didn't make the final perceptual leap. It was impressive rather than immersive. But Cameron moves the boundary posts. Beyond his motion-capture gizmos, he has an old-fashioned command of composition: strong foregrounds and layers of texture and movement reaching back into the frame and down to the teeniest pixel. On the moon Pandora, he creates a living ecosystem—and You (and Your 3-D Glasses) Are There.
>
> —David Edelstein in *New York Magazine*

SOUND ELEMENTS: THE SOUNDTRACK

The soundtrack is the musical score of the film (not the popular songs that often accompany film sequences such as love scenes). It should enhance the mood of the film and place the viewer within the world of the story on an aural level. If the music is inappropriate or distracting, it can achieve the opposite of its intentions and catapult the viewer out of that world. Anthony Lane talks about how the classical music in *The Royal Tenenbaums* introduces the film's "oddity."

> Slowly, however, the communal oddity of the new picture began to hit home. For some reason, I caught it first in the soundtrack, notably in the sharp sprinkling of Ravel that Anderson throws over his chosen people—a pizzicato passage from the String Quartet which tightens our sense of the Tenenbaums as unpredictable toys, either running down or whizzing out of control.
>
> —Anthony Lane in the *New Yorker*

THE REVIEW: PLOT SUMMARY PLUS EVALUATION

PLOT SUMMARY Somewhere in your review, usually near the beginning, you should include a brief overview of the film's plot. A plot summary, like a summary on a book jacket or on the first page of your phone bill, hits the highlights but leaves out the details. A summary should be both specific and concise.

Think of your reader when you write your plot summary. A reader turns to a review to find out what the movie is about and whether to spend time and money to see it. Most readers do not want to know every detail of the story and every twist of the plot. Be careful not to spoil any surprises.

PRACTICE 10.6

Writing Summaries

Choose a movie you know well—one you are reviewing for this assignment or have seen many times—and write a one- or two-sentence summary. Provide a reasonable overview of the film's story.

Brief and specific plot summaries often appear on film review Web sites, and might serve as good models. For example, here is the plot summary for the Oscar-winning war film, *The Hurt Locker*, from the Rotten Tomatoes Web site:

> Iraq. Forced to play a dangerous game of cat-and-mouse in the chaos of war, an elite Army bomb squad unit must come together in a city where everyone is a potential enemy and every object could be a deadly bomb.

This summary is about the cult comedy *Superbad*, also from Rottentomatoes.com.

> *Superbad* revolves around two co-dependent high school seniors (Hill and Cera) who set out to score alcohol for a party, believing that girls will then hook up with them and they will be ready for college. But as the night grows more chaotic, overcoming their separation anxiety becomes a greater challenge than getting the girls.

EVALUATION: THE RAVE, THE PAN, AND THE MIXED REVIEW

Combining your knowledge of these film elements with your personal taste in film, you can write with authority and select specific evidence to support your opinions. "I loved the movie" does not give your reader much information, nor does "It was the worst movie I ever saw." But if you can write "The acting was strong but the pace far too slow," you will have been specific and will have identified two elements that support your opinion: acting and pace.

As you choose the specific elements that support your overall evaluation, you will want to credit the right people for their roles in putting together this film. Film is a highly collaborative medium. If you stay to watch the credits roll at the end of a film, you know that hundreds of people contribute to its creation. Following are brief descriptions of the roles of some of the main players.

THE PLAYERS

Producer The producer pitches the project to potential funders, arranges the financing, monitors the budget, and advises on locations.

Director The film's director interprets the script, oversees the shooting and the actors, and determines the film's style.

Writer(s) One or more writers create the screenplay—that is, they create an original plot and characters, or they adapt already created ones.

Actors Actors translate the characters from the screenplay onto the screen. When the movie is being filmed, actors typically follow the director's instructions. Afterwards, they help promote the finished movie.

Cinematographer Also known as director of photography, a cinematographer makes decisions about lighting, camera angles, and camera movement, creating the visual style of the film.

Editor A film editor cuts the footage that has been shot to make a finished product. The editor's work is responsible for creating mood through the juxtaposition of shots and for establishing the pace of the film.

DIY MEDIA AND DESIGN

A SCENE IN A SCREENPLAY

WHEN YOU WRITE a film script, you begin to understand much more clearly the art of visual storytelling. The screenwriter writes the story that is then interpreted by the director, the cinematographer, the actors, and others. The screenwriter is limited to writing what can be seen and heard on the screen: description and dialogue. In a way, writing a screenplay is a perfect example of how to "show" rather than "tell."

You can find the exact format for writing a screenplay in a number of online sources such as <http://www.screenwriting.info/> or you can download a free screenwriting program like celtx. But, the most important elements of writing a screenplay are visualizing the scene, describing it in clear, direct sentences, and writing realistic dialogue for your characters. Every scene in a screenplay should

- have a clear beginning, middle, and end
- reveal a central tension between characters or within a character
- come to a climax or peak moment
- reveal some kind of change that the character experiences

This brief scene from Tom McCarthy's *The Visitor*, about a burned-out college professor, provides a good model of how a character can be defined through description and dialogue.

INT. CONNECTICUT COLLEGE, WALTER'S OFFICE—LATER

Walter is staring out the window in his simple but very lived-in office. Classical music plays softly in the background. A knock at the door.

DIY

WALTER

Come in.

A STUDENT opens the door and enters.

STUDENT

Hi.

He sits down and sets a paper on the desk.

STUDENT (CONT'D)

Sorry it's late

WALTER

Why is it late?

STUDENT

I had some personal things to deal with.

Walter hands back the paper.

WALTER

I'm sorry. I can't accept it now.

STUDENT

But…

WALTER

I'm sorry.

Walter goes back to work. The Student sits stunned for a moment and then gets up and picks up his paper. He opens the door and then stops.

STUDENT

You know you still haven't given us a syllabus.

WALTER (Lying)

I know.

The Student shakes his head and leaves without another word.

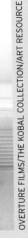

OVERTURE FILMS/THE KOBAL COLLECTION/ART RESOURCE

D I Y

READINGS

JANET MASLIN, reviewing for the *New York Times*, and Roger Ebert, reviewing for the *Chicago Sun-Times*, take radically different views of the 1999 film *Fight Club*, a film that some call a modern classic. Student Ryan Conrath writes a rave review of Martin Scorsese's *The Departed.*

Such a Very Long Way from Duvets to Danger[2]

Janet Maslin

Janet Maslin began her career in 1972 at Rolling Stone, *writing about rock and roll. She had brief stints at the* Boston Phoenix *and* Newsweek *and began reviewing films for the* New York Times *in 1977. She was chief film critic for the* Times *from 1993 until she resigned in 1999.*

OF THE two current films in which buttoned-down businessmen rebel against middle-class notions of masculinity, David Fincher's savage *Fight Club* is by far the more visionary and disturbing. Where *American Beauty* hinges on the subversive allure of a rose-covered blond cheerleader, Mr. Fincher has something a good deal tougher in mind. The director of *Seven* and *The Game* for the first time finds subject matter audacious enough to suit his lightning-fast visual sophistication, and puts that style to stunningly effective use. Lurid sensationalism and computer gamesmanship left this filmmaker's earlier work looking hollow and manipulative. But the sardonic, testosterone-fueled science fiction of *Fight Club* touches a raw nerve.

In a film as strange and single-mindedly conceived as *Fight Club*, Mr. Fincher's angry, diffidently witty ideas about contemporary manhood unfold. As based on a novel by Chuck Palahniuk (and deftly written by Jim Uhls), it builds a huge, phantasmagorical structure around the search for lost masculine authority, and attempts to psychoanalyze an entire society in the process. Complete with an even bigger narrative whammy than the one that ends *The Sixth Sense*, this film twists and turns in ways that only add up fully on the way out of the theater and might just require another viewing. Mr. Fincher uses his huge arsenal of tricks to bury little hints at what this story is really about.

"This film twists and turns in ways that only add up fully on the way out of the theater and might just require another viewing"

Fight Club has two central figures, the milquetoast narrator played by Edward Norton and his charismatic, raging crony played by Brad Pitt. The narrator has been driven to the edge of his sanity by a dull white-collar job, an empty fondness for material things ("I'd flip through catalogues and wonder what kind of dining set defined me as a person") and the utter absence of anything to make him feel alive. Tormented by insomnia,

[2]From Janet Maslin, "Such a Very Long Way from Duvets to Danger," New York Times, October 15, 1999. Reprinted by permission of PARS International.

he finds his only relief in going to meetings of twelve-step support groups, where he can at least cry. The film hurtles along so smoothly that its meaningfully bizarre touches, like Meat Loaf Aday as a testicular cancer patient with very large breasts, aren't jarring at all.

The narrator finds a fellow twelve-step addict in Marla, played with witchy sensuality by Helena Bonham Carter and described by the script as "the little scratch on the roof of your mouth that would heal if only you could stop tonguing it—but you can't." As that suggests, Marla's grunge recklessness makes a big impression on the film's narrator, and can mostly be blamed for setting the story in motion. Soon after meeting her he is on an airplane, craving any sensation but antiseptic boredom, and he meets Mr. Pitt's Tyler Durden in the next seat. Surveying the bourgeois wimp he nicknames Ikea Boy, Tyler asks all the hard questions. Like: "Why do guys like you and I know what a duvet is?"

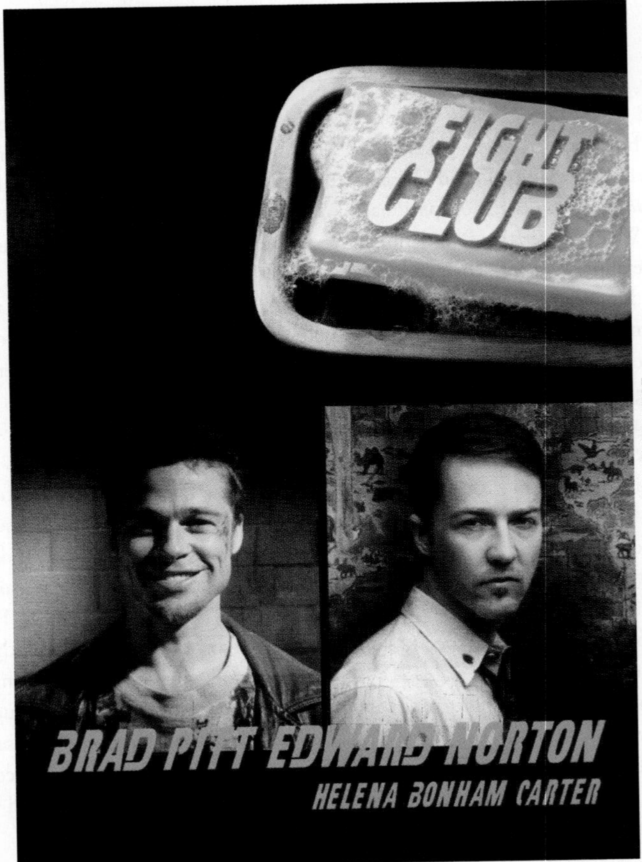

20TH CENTURY FOX/THE KOBAL COLLECTION/ART RESOURCE

Poster for *Fight Club* (1999)

Mr. Norton, drawn into Tyler's spell, soon forsakes his tidy ways and moves into the abandoned wreck that is ground central for Tyler. Then Tyler teaches his new roommate to fight in a nearby parking lot. The tacitly homoerotic bouts between these two men become addictive (as does sex with Marla), and their fight group expands into a secret society, all of which the film presents with the curious matter-of-factness of a dream. Somehow nobody gets hurt badly, but the fights leave frustrated, otherwise emasculated men with secret badges of not-quite-honor.

Fight Club watches this form of escapism morph into something much more dangerous. Tyler somehow builds a bridge from the anti-materialist rhetoric of the 1960s ("It's only after we've lost everything that we're free to do anything") into the kind of paramilitary dream project that Ayn Rand might have admired. The group's rigorous training and subversive agenda are as deeply disturbing to Mr. Norton's mild-mannered character as Tyler's original wild streak was thrilling. But even when acts of terrorism are in the offing, he can't seem to tear himself away.

"Even when acts of terrorism are in the offing, he can't seem to tear himself away."

Like Kevin Smith's *Dogma*, *Fight Club* sounds offensive from afar. If watched sufficiently mindlessly, it might be mistaken for a dangerous endorsement of totalitarian tactics and super-violent nihilism in an all-out assault on society. But this is a much less gruesome film than *Seven* and a notably more serious one. It means to explore the lure of violence in an even more dangerously regimented, dehumanized culture. That's a hard thing to illustrate this powerfully without, so to speak, stepping on a few toes.

In an expertly shot and edited film spiked with clever computer-generated surprises, Mr. Fincher also benefits, of course, from marquee appeal. The teamwork of Mr. Norton and Mr. Pitt is as provocative and complex as it's meant to be. Mr. Norton, an ingenious actor, is once again trickier than he looks. Mr. Pitt struts through the film with rekindled brio and a visceral sense of purpose. He's right at home in a movie that warns against worshiping false idols.

Fight Club is rated R (under seventeen requires accompanying parent or adult guardian). It includes bloody fights, grisly touches, sexual situations and nudity, profanity and assorted intentional gross-out shocks, including the rendering of human fat into soap.

QUESTIONS FOR RHETORICAL ANALYSIS

1. **CONSIDERING THE RHETORICAL SITUATION:** Define Maslin's voice in this review. Choose a few specific lines from the review, and explain how they helped you form your opinion of her voice.
2. What contextual and background information does Maslin include in her review? What would you like more of? Less? Why?
3. What does Maslin think are director David Fincher's intentions in this film? Does she think he fulfilled them? Cite a line from the review to support your answer.
4. How much of the plot does Maslin reveal? Where? Do you think she gives away too much? Just enough? Why?

5. What film elements does Maslin discuss to support her thesis that *Fight Club* "touches a raw nerve"? Do you think she makes a convincing argument? Why?
6. Maslin asserts that *Fight Club* "sounds offensive from afar." What argument does she put forth to explain the importance of the violence it portrays? Do you agree or disagree? Explain your answer.
7. Does Maslin end the review effectively? Why?

QUESTIONS FOR WRITING AND DISCUSSION

1. How explicit do you think filmmakers should be in depicting violence on the screen? When is violence appropriate, and when is it gratuitous? If you have seen *Fight Club*, comment on the violence in this film.
2. Maslin names a number of films that explore contemporary manhood. Some films, she says, are built around "the search for lost masculine authority." What do you think defines masculinity in contemporary society?

STYLE PRACTICE: IMITATION

In her final paragraph, Maslin gives the film's rating and then enumerates the reasons why it earned this rating in a list. Write a similar sentence (rating + reasons in a list) about the film you are reviewing.

Fight Club[3]

Roger Ebert

Roger Ebert is arguably the best-known film critic in the country. On his long-running television show Siskel and Ebert at the Movies *(then* Ebert and Roeper*), he popularized the "thumbs-up, thumbs down" motif. He is the film critic for the* Chicago Sun-Times, *has won a Pulitzer Prize for film commentary, and has published fifteen books on film.*

FIGHT CLUB is the most frankly and cheerfully fascist big-star movie since *Death Wish*, a celebration of violence in which the heroes write themselves a license to drink, smoke, screw and beat one another up.

Michel Bourquard/PACHA/Corbis Entertainment/CORBIS

Roger Ebert

Sometimes, for variety, they beat up themselves. It's macho porn—the sex movie Hollywood has been moving toward for years, in which eroticism between the sexes is replaced by all-guy locker-room fights. Women, who have had a lifetime of practice at dealing with little-boy posturing, will instinctively see through it; men may get off on the testosterone rush. The fact that it is very well made and has a great first act certainly clouds the issue.

[3]From Roger Ebert, Fight Club movie review, from the Roger Ebert column by Roger Ebert, copyright (c) 1999 The Ebert Company, distributed. by Universal Press Syndicate.

Edward Norton stars as a depressed urban loner filled up to here with angst. He describes his world in dialogue of sardonic social satire. His life and job are driving him crazy. As a means of dealing with his pain, he seeks out twelve-step meetings, where he can hug those less fortunate than himself and find catharsis in their suffering. It is not without irony that the first meeting he attends is for post-surgical victims of testicular cancer, since the whole movie is about guys afraid of losing their *cojones*.

These early scenes have a nice sly tone; they're narrated by the Norton character in the kind of voice Nathanael West used in *Miss Lonelyhearts*. He's known only as the Narrator, for reasons later made clear. The meetings are working as a sedative, and his life is marginally manageable when tragedy strikes: He begins to notice Marla (Helena Bonham Carter) at meetings. She's a "tourist" like himself—someone not addicted to anything but meetings. She spoils it for him. He knows he's a faker, but wants to believe everyone else's pain is real.

"A secret society of men who meet in order to find freedom and self-realization through beating one another into pulp."

On an airplane, he has another key encounter, with Tyler Durden (Brad Pitt), a man whose manner cuts through the fog. He seems able to see right into the Narrator's soul, and shortly after, when the Narrator's high-rise apartment turns into a fireball, he turns to Tyler for shelter. He gets more than that. He gets in on the ground floor of Fight Club, a secret society of men who meet in order to find freedom and self-realization through beating one another into pulp.

It's at about this point that the movie stops being smart and savage and witty, and turns to some of the most brutal, unremitting, nonstop violence ever filmed. Although sensible people know that if you hit someone with an ungloved hand hard enough, you're going to end up with broken bones, the guys in *Fight Club* have fists of steel, and hammer one another while the sound effects guys beat the hell out of Naugahyde sofas with Ping-Pong paddles. Later, the movie takes still another turn. A lot of recent films seem unsatisfied unless they can add final scenes that redefine the reality of everything that has gone before; call it the Keyser Soze syndrome.

What is all this about? According to Durden, it is about freeing yourself from the shackles of modern life, which imprisons and emasculates men. By being willing to give and receive pain and risk death, Fight Club members find freedom. Movies like *Crash* must play like cartoons for Durden. He's a shadowy, charismatic figure, able to inspire a legion of men in big cities to descend into the secret cellars of a Fight Club and beat one another up.

Only gradually are the final outlines of his master plan revealed. Is Tyler Durden in fact a leader of men with a useful philosophy? "It's only after we've lost everything that we're free to do anything," he says, sounding like a man who tripped over the Nietzsche display on his way to the coffee bar in Borders. In my opinion, he has no useful truths. He's a bully—Werner Erhard plus S & M, a leather club operator without the decor. None of the Fight Club members grows stronger or freer because of their membership; they're reduced to pathetic cultists. Issue them black shirts and sign them up as skinheads. Whether Durden represents hidden aspects of the male psyche is a question the movie uses as a loophole—but is not able to escape through, because *Fight Club* is not about its ending but about its action.

Of course, *Fight Club* itself does not advocate Durden's philosophy. It is a warning against it, I guess; one critic I like says it makes "a telling point about the bestial nature of man and what can happen when the numbing effects of day-to-day drudgery cause people to go a little crazy." I think it's the numbing effects of movies like this that cause people to go a little crazy. Although sophisticates will be able to rationalize the movie as an argument against the behavior it shows, my guess is that audiences will like the behavior but not the argument. Certainly they'll buy tickets because they can see Pitt and Norton pounding on each other; a lot more people will leave this movie and get in fights than will leave it discussing Tyler Durden's moral philosophy. The images in movies like this argue for themselves, and it takes a lot of narration (or Narration) to argue against them.

Lord knows the actors work hard enough. Norton and Pitt go through almost as much physical suffering in this movie as Demi Moore endured in *G. I. Jane*, and Helena Bonham Carter creates a feisty chain-smoking hellcat who is probably so angry because none of the guys thinks having sex with her is as much fun as a broken nose. When you see good actors in a project like this, you wonder if they signed up as an alternative to canyoneering.

The movie was directed by David Fincher and written by Jim Uhls, who adapted the novel by Chuck Palahniuk. In many ways, it's like Fincher's movie *The Game* (1997), with the violence cranked up for teenage boys of all ages. That film was also about a testing process in which a man drowning in capitalism (Michael Douglas) has the rug of his life pulled out from under him and has to learn to fight for survival. I admired *The Game* much more than *Fight Club* because it was really about its theme, while the message in *Fight Club* is like bleeding scraps of Socially Redeeming Content thrown to the howling mob.

"A man drowning in capitalism has the rug of his life pulled out from under him and has to learn to fight for survival."

Fincher is a good director (his work includes *Alien 3*, one of the best-looking bad movies I have ever seen, and *Seven*, the grisly and intelligent thriller). With *Fight Club* he seems to be setting himself some kind of a test—how far over the top can he go? The movie is visceral and hard-edged, with levels of irony and commentary above and below the action. If it had all continued in the vein explored in the first act, it might have become a great film. But the second act is pandering and the third is trickery, and whatever Fincher thinks the message is, that's not what most audience members will get. *Fight Club* is a thrill ride masquerading as philosophy—the kind of ride where some people puke and others can't wait to get on again.

QUESTIONS FOR RHETORICAL ANALYSIS

1. **CONSIDERING THE RHETORICAL SITUATION:** Define Ebert's voice in this review. Choose a few specific lines from the review, and explain how they help you form your opinion of his voice.
2. What is Ebert's opinion of *Fight Club*? Where do you first know this opinion?
3. Identify the positive and negative qualities Ebert writes about in his review.
4. How much of the plot does Ebert reveal? Where? Do you think he gives away too much? Just enough? Why?

5. Where in the review does Ebert give contextual and background information? Compare the amount and placement of this information with Maslin's review above.
6. What are the points on which Ebert disagrees with Maslin? Who do you think makes a more convincing case?

QUESTIONS FOR WRITING AND DISCUSSION

1. Ebert asserts that people will like *Fight Club* because of the violent behavior it shows and will ignore the film's argument against this behavior. He writes that "a lot more people will leave this movie and get in fights than will leave it discussing Tyler Durden's moral philosophy. The images in movies like this argue for themselves." Do you agree or disagree with Ebert?
2. Do you think violent movies promote violent behavior?

STYLE PRACTICE: IMITATION

In the last line of Ebert's review, he creates a metaphor, comparing the film to a "thrill ride," and then he extends the metaphor explaining that "some people puke and others can't wait to get on again." Create a metaphor that sums up your evaluation of the film you are reviewing, and like Ebert did, extend the metaphor in a phrase or two.

Scorsese Back at Film School, *The Departed*[4]

Ryan Conrath

Student writer Ryan Conrath brings his experienced film-watcher perspective to this review. He focuses on The Departed *as a film in which we find equal parts violence and poetry.*

WHILE MOST Hollywood directors are thinking about the box-office receipts and cramming extra special effects into a movie, Martin Scorsese is one of the only American directors alive who stays true to his artistic mission of making movies that are as poetic as they are violent. And he manages to package it all in a ferociously entertaining blockbuster film. *The Departed*, Scorsese's latest criminal epic, has cemented the filmmaker's role as perhaps the greatest Hollywood philosopher-bard of our time.

William Monahan (*Kingdom of Heaven*, *Blood Meridian*) adapted *The Departed* from Siu Fai Mak's 2002 script *Infernal Affairs*. The Hong Kong action film is still highly celebrated, even to a vexing level, considering that Monahan's script is considerably more thoughtful and layered.

William Costigan (Leonardo DiCaprio) and Colin Sullivan (Matt Damon) are two men who would perhaps have never met. But their lives become indelibly tied up with a notorious Boston crime boss Frank Costello (Jack Nicholson). Costigan's father had been somehow involved with the mob a long time ago, and as a result is still well known by the mafia. Sullivan, in his turn, was "adopted" by Costello at a young age. Both men end up becoming cops for the

city of Boston. But both also, in some way, end up working for Costello. Costigan is working for Costello, undercover as a mole for the Boston Police Department (BPD), and Sullivan is working for the BPD undercover for Costello.

If this makes your head spin, it's probably okay. In fact, things get considerably more complicated than that. While it might be interesting and even important to watch *The Departed* while still trying to keep track of who's who and what's what, it might, on the other hand, detract from some of the more subtle messages at work here. In fact, the lure of keeping track of characters and actions within this maze of events is part of Scorsese's layering of theme.

From the very beginning, William Costigan is made aware that he is not meant to be a cop—he's not meant ". . . to pretend to be a cop," according to Captain Queenan (Martin Sheen). For Queenan, all cops are cops because they like to pretend. The real cops are the ones without identities . . . the ones undercover. In some ways, this idea ends up being one of the truths of the film. Costigan, the man who is truly a cop, is the one pretending not to be, and the true rat is the one pretending to be a cop. Confused? Remember, that's the point—and the question this film submits: what counts—appearance or action?

"The real cops are the ones without identities . . . the ones undercover."

This question of reality and fiction is one of Scorsese's main themes in the film. In a session with Dr. Madden (Vera Farmiga), a police shrink, the always skeptical Costigan insists that cops only feel bad about using their weapons because they saw a cop react the same way on TV. "No one is more full of shit than cops," he asserts, ". . . except the ones on TV."

In one of the great sequences of the movie, Costigan chases Sullivan through Chinatown. Both are trying to find each other out for their respective roles as "rats." This scene marks the first moment in the film when the two get close to finding out about one another. The really interesting thing is that Scorsese presents Chinatown as a massive movie set. The two run out of the movie theatre into the heart of the district. The lighting, the steam, the neon lights, the sounds, the reflections off the puddles: all the details are stylized and overplayed. Scorsese seems to be reminding the audience that the battle arena here is that of the cinema, and perhaps the only place a battle over identity in our modern day can take place.

The fact that this movie deals with deep commentary about the dizzying effect of television on culture and the difficulty people have in defining themselves as individuals does not get in the way of its being a very entertaining suspense movie. Great acting from Jack Nicholson confounds as much as it enhances the epic quality of the movie. Leonardo DiCaprio, in perhaps his most defining role thus far, has figured out how to play the complex role of a character who is in some way aware of his state as a character. And not long after turning 30, Farmiga does an incredible job as Dr. Madden, who is also the love interest of both the main characters. Considering her shockingly measured role as a drug-addicted single mother in the 2004 *Down to the Bone*, it's no surprise she was cast in this important role. You'd be hard pressed to find a film this year with so many rewarding performances as *The Departed* has.

Then again, not many Hollywood movies these days even try to tackle such complex issues while giving audiences a good night at the movies. Ultimately, what makes *The Departed* one of the most exciting films of the new century is that it reminds us that art is not dead in Hollywood.

QUESTIONS FOR RHETORICAL ANALYSIS

1. **CONSIDERING THE RHETORICAL SITUATION:** Define Conrath's voice in this review. Does he attain the kind of conversational voice that Pauline Kael admired? Give specific examples to support your answer.
2. Which element does Conrath choose as the main focus for his film review?
3. What background information does the reviewer explain about the director, actors, and screenwriter?
4. What is Conrath's main point or thesis?
5. Conrath admits the plot might "make your head spin." How successful is he in providing a plot summary of *The Departed*?
6. How does Conrath use the look of the movie to make a point in his review?
7. How much time does Conrath spend on the acting? Why?
8. How does Conrath conclude this review?

QUESTIONS FOR WRITING AND DISCUSSION

1. Do you agree that a film can be violent and poetic at the same time?
2. If Conrath is correct, and Scorsese is making a point about identity, would you argue with the thesis that the search for identity is absent from daily life? Can you think of other films that question identity?

STYLE PRACTICE: IMITATION

In the third paragraph, Conrath summarizes the very complicated plot of *The Departed*. Choose a movie you have seen that has a similarly complicated plot, and summarize it in a paragraph.

WRITING AND REVISION STRATEGIES

Gathered here are three interactive sections for you to use as you write and revise your film review and as you apply what you have learned to writing in other classes.

- Writer's Notebook Suggestions
- Peer Review Log
- Revision Checklist

WRITER'S **NOTEBOOK** SUGGESTIONS

These short exercises are intended to jump-start your thinking as you begin to write your film review.

1. Write an e-mail message to a friend telling him or her about the most recent movie you have seen. Write the message in your own conversational voice.
2. You have just been hired to write blurbs for the backs of the boxes of new video releases. You are limited to one paragraph per film. Write blurbs for two movies you have seen recently, one you liked and one you did not. Remember that you have been hired to sell the films, not review them.
3. Decide on a movie, perhaps one that you have seen recently, perhaps the one you intend to review. Write its name in the middle of a blank sheet of paper and circle it. Create a cluster of words and phrases that express your varied responses to the film. (You may want to reread the section on clustering in Chapter 2 before you do this exercise.)
4. Make a list of the most clichéd movie review phrases you can find in ads or reviews in your local newspaper.
5. On a piece of paper, write the words *cinematography*, *soundtrack*, and *special effects*. Under each heading, write a list of excellent examples of that element from movies you have seen.
6. On a piece of paper, write the words *acting*, *production design*, and *screenplay*. Under each heading, write a list of terrible examples of that element from movies you have seen.
7. Write an advertisement for your favorite movie. It can be an ad for a newspaper, a radio spot, a poster, or a Web site.
8. Write a trailer for a movie you have seen recently. Include descriptions of the visual elements in your script.
9. Find a short film on YouTube or another Internet site and write a review.

PEER **REVIEW** LOG

As you work with a writing partner or in a peer review group, you can use these questions to give helpful responses to a classmate's film review or as a guide for discussion.

Writer's Name: ____________________

Date: ____________________

1. Bracket the introduction. Does it grab your attention? Why? Suggest one way to strengthen the introduction.

2. Can you tell by the end of the introduction what the reviewer's opinion of the film is? State it in a sentence.
3. Underline all the sentences that provide background or contextual information. Is the information interesting? Could any be cut? What other information would you like?
4. Underline the thesis when it is first stated. Also underline any places in which the thesis is restated in the review. Does the writer prove this thesis? Can you suggest a way to state the thesis more clearly?
5. Identify the paragraphs that give the plot summary. Does any information give away surprises or twists? Is there too much detail, and could some of it be cut? Do you need more information to make sense of the film's story?
6. Identify the film elements that the writer uses to prove the thesis. Does the writer use visual elements like cinematography, acting, and production design? Has the writer clearly tied the film elements to the thesis? If not, how might this be done?
7. Do any of the points need more support? Where could the writer use a quotation or a specific example from the film to pin down an idea?
8. Mark any places where the voice sounds lively and engaging. Mark places where it could be improved.
9. Is the conclusion satisfying? Make a suggestion to strengthen the ending.

REVISION CHECKLIST

As you do your final revision, check to make sure that you

- Wrote an introduction that brings your reader quickly into the film
- Stated your opinion of the film in a clear thesis statement
- Provided background or contextual information
- Wrote a plot summary that contains only essential information and at the same time does not give away any surprises or plot twists
- Selected the criteria that best support your opinion of the film
- Included some discussion of the visual aspects of the film
- Provided specific evidence to support your opinion of the film
- Wrote in a professional and lively voice
- Avoided using clichéd language
- Wrote for the specific audience you have selected
- Included a clear bottom-line evaluation of the film
- Concluded strongly, perhaps refocusing on your thesis

Hipster Tr

11 Writing A Causal Analysis

LONG RESEARCHED ARTICLES

ildogesto/Shutterstock.com

It is a capital mistake to theorize before one has data.

—Sir Arthur Conan Doyle

Why do people bowl alone? It all started with a question, based on an observation from a Harvard researcher named Robert Putnam about the decline of bowling leagues—down 40 percent between 1980 and 1993. Putnam's research, which revealed that people are now less likely to bowl in leagues—or to attend PTA meetings or even go on picnics—led him to argue that people are less connected to their communities and families. During the second half of the twentieth century, he concluded, people were more likely to watch *Friends* on television than make friends.

Putnam's book, *Bowling Alone: The Collapse and Revival of American Community*, became a bestseller as thousands of readers were drawn to his speculation about what happened in the United States to compromise community involvement. His inquiry started with a hunch—about what makes people join fewer bowling leagues—and speculation about how American society has changed over time. All sorts of fields—from sociology through marketing—follow the same method of analysis, looking at how small details can lead to an understanding of a bigger picture.

Looking closely at a trend can help you understand changes in the way we view culture, society, and technology.

Celeste Pille (www.celeste-doodleordie.blogspot.com)

WHAT'S TO COME

PROCESS PLAN

PROCESS PLAN

PREPARE

- Look for new patterns or trends, or fresh developments in familiar patterns.
- Ask a question: Is the pattern or trend significant?
- Talk to people who are involved in the trend: practitioners/experts

DRAFT

- Introduction: Show the trend in action. Write a scene or tell a story that hooks the readers' interest in the first paragraph.
- Body
  - State the trend clearly and either place it within a larger context or announce the significance of the pattern.
  - Use statistics, testimonials, or surveys to prove the trend exists.
  - Anticipate your reader's questions.
- Conclusion: Use a memorable quotation or image that reinforces the thesis.

REVISE

- Include reminders of your thesis, restated.
- Check source citations, in text and/or in end notes.
- Make sure your points have logical transitions.

UNDERSTANDING THE WRITING PROJECT

Thinkstock/Getty Images

IF YOU have ever participated in a survey—online, on the phone, even in a short response card that came with a product warranty—you have participated in causal analysis, as part of a data group. You have provided information about who you are and most likely what caused you to behave in a certain way: to purchase a product, to view a movie, or to vote for or against something.

Organizations might be interested in your personal information for different reasons: some for purely academic reasons, and some for reasons that are completely self-promotional. Regardless of the intentions, the research all begins with an observation—a theory. As you begin to observe and form theories, you have to ask yourself the question: Is the pattern or trend significant enough to be noteworthy? The best way to answer this question is to look at what might be the causes and/or effects. The word "might" is significant here. Though we can prove a trend exists—with measurements like statistics—our understanding of causes is always speculative. In other words, you have to create a well-reasoned analysis defending your conclusions about what the causes and/or effects of the trend are.

ASSIGNMENT Identify a pattern or trend—some new development in behavior you have observed—living "off the energy grid," for example. Or you might identify a new twist in a established phenomenon such as marriage among teens. You might be able to come up with a theory if you find the marriage rate is rising or falling among that age group. Write a trend analysis that includes multiple sources and speculation about the causes and/or effects of the pattern or trend.

Access an interactive eBook, and chapter-specific interactive learning tools, including flashcards, quizzes, videos and more in your English CourseMate via www.cengagebrain.com.

ANATOMY OF AN ANALYIS

VIVIAN HO was a senior journalism major when she was asked to write a story about a trend she observed in her own life for *Writing in the Works*. A seasoned news and features writer, she was the editor of her college newspaper and had several internships, including a co-op at the *Boston Globe*.

The New Trend in College Admissions: Using Social Media[1]

VIVIAN HO

Amanda Brasil-Leigh, a high school senior from Brazil, officially submitted her application to Tufts University on Oct. 29.

James Garcia Alver, a high school senior from Tampa, Fla., sent in his Common Application supplement to Tufts several months ahead of time, on Aug. 18.

example, illustration, or anecdote that hooks in the reader with specificity, helping to demonstrate the trend

Both applicants decided this information – information that used to be privy only to family, friends, and the admissions officers on the other side of the process –should be available to anyone with internet access. Brasil-Leigh and Alver both took to Twitter with their news, sharing what used to be fairly private information with thousands of strangers, possible future classmates, and possible future competitors. This might not seem surprising, considering how much information is shared on social media. But then the Tufts Office of Undergraduate Admissions tweeted back.

"It's hard to believe they actually take time to connect with you individually that way," said Elisabeth Watanabe, another applicant to Tufts University. "I'm not interested in having admissions people know all about my life, but I think it's interesting that other applicants do. You have to ask if it gives them an edge."

quotation from a practitioner, someone involved with the pattern, speculating about the effects of involvement with social media in the application process.

analytical thesis: announces the trend or pattern and asks a question about the significance—causes and/or effects. A two-part thesis.

In the age of social media, college and universities throughout the country have been changing the way they recruit and communicate with prospective students. Like most questions that revolve around the brave new world of social media: does it help, hurt, or just make more clutter?

proof that the trend exists.

To see the trend in action, look at a poll of four-year accredited universities, which states that of the more than 400 randomly polled, 59 percent of admissions offices use Twitter, and 87 percent uses some other form of social networking site, such as Facebook,

[1] Vivian Ho, "The New Trend in College Admissions: Using Social Media."

to recruit applicants, according to a study conducted by the University of Massachusetts-Dartmouth Center for Marketing Research.

in-text citation of source

The study, published in May 2010, revealed these new trends in the admissions process involving the use of social media. Center for Marketing Research Director Nora Ganim Barnes, who conducted the study, said she decided to include Twitter because use of the popular social networking site among admissions offices has skyrocketed this year. About 55 percent of admissions officers polled said they felt they were very familiar with Twitter. And many of them are using it to reach out to potential recruits. "You know the old saying, 'Fish where the fish are'?" she said. "This is where the fish are."

cause for the use of social networking. Quotation that makes the statistics fresh, personal, and authetnic

Admissions Twitters can run the gamut from formal and official to casual and fun. The @TuftsAdmissions Twitter account, run by Assistant Director of Admissions Dan Grayson, allows applicants to get a personal glimpse into his day-to-day life recruiting for the university. Information he shares via Twitter ranges from purely professional to trivial: Grayson's 631 followers can read about his recent recruitment trip to Asia, his lunch at a Baltimore tortilleria, or a Friday night admissions staff dodge ball game.

specific example helps to show the trend in practice

"Daniel Grayson would tweet, 'Oh we had brownies today and here's a picture of them, and oh we accepted 15 students today,' " said Tufts freshman Mayabea Schechner of Milburn, N.J. "I felt very much like I knew that it was real people reading my application. It put a face on the application process, when otherwise, you felt like there was a major 'they' that was reading it, not actual people."

quotation from an expert: a first-hand observation

Josh Lubben, senior admissions counselor at the University of Maryland Baltimore County, said he thinks the admissions Twitter, which he runs, is a healthy mix of casual and formal. @UMBCadmissions tweets new posts from the school's blogs, reminders of deadlines, and retweets of the school's other Twitter accounts.

"We want it to be honest," he said. "We want it to be coming from admissions staff. While I don't see my own individual personality come through, I see myself as an admissions official come across in the Twitter."

UMBC uses its admissions Twitter as "part of an overall marketing strategy," Lubben said.

"Social media is a way to get information out to students," he said. "We didn't start it for the reason to bring in more students, but it's just an opportunity for us to get in touch with them, and for them to get in touch with us and making information accessible."

causes

continues next page

Despite the new outreach through social media and the opportunity for applicants to use technology to better their chances at acceptance, some applicants will still choose to learn about their schools through more traditional methods.

effect—in general

Jessie Geoffray, a senior at Santa Monica High School in California, relied on the Fiske Guide to Colleges to choose which colleges were right for her, deciding to lug around a more than 700-page book rather than look to university-sponsored Twitters and blogs.

"All schools say the same sort of things that can't be true for every single school – they're diverse, they're academically-driven," Geoffray said. "The Fiske Guide is basically the same objective person's perspective on every school."

quote that shows the effects of social media are limited.

Meredith Principe, director of college counseling at the Massachusetts-based college counseling service, Campus Bound, said she thinks colleges will still have to rely on older marketing strategies for some time because parents are involved in the selection, and there are still some of gaps in technological knowledge within student and parent demographic groups.

effects, limited due to demographics

"Parents are still, to some extent, the bottom line audience – they're the ones that usually foot the bill," she said. "Until that generation moves on and the parents of applicants are more tech savvy, then colleges will have to find some way to appeal to the parents."

The potential for problems with such an informal outreach tool is a concern for some schools. Without a set policy on what can and cannot be said, the school can easily be misrepresented. Less than 20 percent of schools have a social media policy in place, said Barnes.

potential negative effects

"If the admissions office is allowing student interns to run their Twitters, run their blogs, and they don't have a social media policy about what you can say, that means you can actually give student intern free reign with these tools," she said. "The risk obviously for the school is that someone does or says something inappropriate or makes it too casual."

potential negative effects

While Tufts has guidelines and suggestions when it comes to social media use, the school has no set policy or restrictions, said spokeswoman Kim Thurler. UMBC also does not have a set policy, Lubbens said.

The new tool is a success according to some students who respond enthusiastically to an admissions process that brings them closer to the school through daily updates, regardless of how trivial the information might be. Tufts freshman Abby Setterholm of St. Paul, Minn., says she was won over by the school's presence on social media. "I got to know the school almost as if you would get to know a person," she said. "I picked Tufts as much as Tufts picked me."

effects—quotation from a practitioner.

"Ask yourself before you start, who does this topic involve? Who will it affect? Who won't it affect?"

Q&A with Vivian Ho

How I Find Topics and Sources

Q: How did you find this topic? Which questions do you ask yourself to get going?

A: The article was originally focused on Tufts University adding an optional video supplement to their admissions process, and the Class of 2014 being the first class to participate in that. I had already interviewed one student and was all set to pursue that topic when I made contact with Abby Setterholm, a freshman who had submitted a video and was accepted. I asked her to bring a couple freshmen friends with her for the interview because I wanted to talk to members of the Class of 2014 who had submitted videos and also members who chose to apply in the traditional way. I ended up speaking to her and her friends for almost an hour. While we did talk about the video supplement, I also learned that their application process was enormously different from what my application process was just three years earlier.

Robin Berghaus

Vivian Ho Robin Berghaus

Q: So, you changed focus—because you caught onto a string of something new, that you found interesting?

A: Yes. That's how I sort of judge whether or not I should be pursuing a topic for an article. I couldn't stop talking about it to my friends. And when people reacted pretty much the same way as I did, I knew there was a story there.

Q: What is your research process like? How did you come up with the sources to help you develop the ideas?

A: Ask yourself before you start, who does this topic involve? Who will it affect? Who won't it affect? Don't feel squeamish about asking sources if they know anybody else that would be good to talk to.

Q: How do you go about developing the cause/effect part of a trend article?

A: A rule I established as an editor at the *Daily Free Press* was that every trend story needs to have numbers to make it legitimate. While I know now that that is not a hard-and-fast rule, you need to be able to somehow prove that more people—or fewer—are behaving in a certain way, in comparison to the past.

THE RHETORICAL SITUATION: THE ETHOS OF SPECULATING WITH AUTHORITY

The first task in your analysis is proving the pattern or trend exists, so your reader can follow you to your next step, explaining why. You can prove the trend exists by using a measurement or testimonial, showing a statistical rise or fall, reporting the results of a survey, or reporting a series of observations by experts. Provided your sources are good (more on evaluating sources in Chapter 15) and current, the bulk of your job in writing an analysis of causes and effects is speculation about why the phenomenon has happened and/or what are its effects. Your speculation is tied to a collection of evidence that backs up your explanation, a kind of argument. In order to make this argument convincing to your reader, you need to establish your credibility, your reliability, and your authority—your ethos.

A convincing writer is trustworthy, anticipates the readers' questions, uses logic and evidence, and demonstrates no personal bias. Some ways to establish your credibility, or ethos, listed below, can help you demonstrate that you are a good, reliable source for information. Consider the points in the box on Tips for Establishing Your Ethos as you think about how to invite your readers into your speculation about causes and effects of a trend.

Tips For Establising Your Ethos

SHOW THAT YOU UNDERSTAND YOUR AUDIENCE

1. What do they already know about the topic? Do not talk down to them.
2. Why do readers not know—is the topic new? Highly technical? Do not confuse them.
3. Is it a topic some might find controversial? Do not offend your readers.

SHOW THAT YOU ARE AN AUTHORITY

1. Use precise measurable data like statistics, results of polls, and surveys.
2. Interview people who can talk about direct observation and personal experiences, anecdotes (practitioners).

3. Consult secondary sources for anecdotes, illustrations, and examples.
4. Quote experts on the topic (authors of books and articles, experts in the field) who can make generalizations.

WRITE IN AN OBJECTIVE VOICE

1. Avoid first person.
2. Do not directly state your opinion. Allow your sources to introduce opinion.
3. Use attribution well: "According to expert sources. . . "

CHOOSING A GOOD TOPIC

How do you find an engaging topic your reader will want to spend some time with? Two types of patterns make good topics: New patterns or trends, and new developments in familiar patterns and trends.

New patterns can develop along with changes in technology or medicine, laws, or political movements. Looking at the way "generation text" relies on digital communications is a good example of a pattern that is new and the result of technology. Some patterns in behavior that have been around for thousands of years can still make good subject matter, too. For example, people throughout time and in many cultures have gambled. You can start with gambling as a topic for your initial thinking, and describe some instances you have observed. For example:

1. Aunt Mary buys lottery tickets and plays poker on Tuesday nights.
2. Your state is voting on whether to legalize casino gambling.
3. You have a 13-year-old cousin who really loves online poker.
4. You read about a celebrity athlete who was convicted of gambling on dog-fighting.

Use the questions in the box below for testing the worth of developing these observations into an analysis.

PRACTICE 11.1

Testing Topics

Using the questions for testing topics, evaluate the following observations. Can you detect a possible trend worth investigating?

1. You have observed women wearing black lipstick.
2. The newspaper in your town has decided to publish only three days a week.
3. An elderly neighbor was swindled by a company who took her downpayment and never delivered her new windows.
4. Your college has stopped selling bottled water.
5. Your college turned off all wireless internet connections in classroom buildings.

Questions For Testing Your Topic

- Is this one isolated case, or can you find other examples?
- Does the topic have larger implications for society, commerce, education, health, or politics?
- Are there noteworthy increases or decreases in its occurrence?
- Are significant causes driving this change?
- Are there significant effects of this change?

THE BIG IDEA: THE ANALYTICAL THESIS

The analytical thesis—one sentence or several sentences—clearly defines the trend or phenomenon and presents the **THEORY** about it. The analytical thesis signals to your readers **WHAT THEY WILL UNDERSTAND** by reading your analysis

> In Japan, the number of female visitors to shogun castles, samurai battle re-enactments and history bookstores has recently increased. Observers attribute this to the rise of the "history girls"—a new urban subculture that some believe signals a kind of empowerment for female Japanese hobbyists.
>
> —"For Japanese Women, The Past Is the Latest Fad" (later in chapter)

If readers continue, the analytical thesis promises, they will understand the interpretation of what the trend might reveal: a signal that Japanese women feel empowerment. Clearly the theory that "empowerment for women," is an interpretation, one that will require some explanation. Every analytical thesis should offer your readers a theory that requires explanation.

The theory in causal analyses focuses on the **CAUSES** and/or **EFFECTS**. The trend involving "history girls" might have developed, the writer tells us, because of the underlying cultural conditions that have resulted in women feeling more powerful.

Another writer, whose topic is technology and distractions to students, focuses on the effects of technology on the attention spans of students:

> Students have always faced distractions and time-wasters. But computers and cellphones, and the constant stream of stimuli they

offer pose a profound new challenge to focusing and learning. Researchers say the lure of these technologies, while it affects adults, too, is particularly powerful for young people. The risk, they say, is that developing brains can become more easily habituated than adult brains to constantly switching tasks—and less able to sustain attention. "Growing Up Digital, Wired for Distraction" (later in chapter).

Remember that since your causal analysis includes a theory—speculation and not a fact—what follows will be a kind of argument, defending this theory, citing examples, illustrations, and making a case for why the theory is reasonable.

PRACTICE 11.2

Conducting a survey

Create a list of survey questions about transportation students at your college prefer to use. Depending on the location of your school, your questions could include public transportation (if available), carpooling, or walking. Include some questions about time spent traveling and cost. Make sure to get responses from a cross-section of people, and to ask twenty to thirty people for responses. Write a summary of your findings, focusing on two questions:

What was the most common response?

Which response was the most surprising?

RESEARCH PATHS: ORGANIZING YOUR INVESTIGATION OF CAUSES AND EFFECTS

To prove that a trend exists and to be able to speculate about its causes, you will be collecting materials online, in the library, and in interviews.

Keeping Track of Your Research

For each source you examine, make note of the following information:

- Author
- Article or chapter title
- Full journal name or book title
- Date and place of publication
- Page number(s)
- For Web sites, full URL and date

BOOKS

You might not think of books as the first place to begin research, but almost always, one source can lead you to another, and books can be a good way to get to high-quality information as well as additional sources. In current publications,

> **PRACTICE 11.3**
>
> **Causes or Effects?**
>
> Decide whether you would start exploring the causes or effects of the following trends (or both) and explain why.
>
> Increase in ROTC students
>
> Increase in students studying foreign languages
>
> Increase in students taking a "gap" year between high school and college
>
> Decrease in sports teams at high schools
>
> Decrease in numbers of children getting vaccinations
>
> Decrease in number of medical students becoming dermatologists

you can get a good understanding of what is new about a topic, even with a quick search of Amazon.com or your library's catalog. (On Amazon.com, you can even read a few pages and browse through the tables of contents for some books.) Often books, as well as articles, will include bibliographies that come in handy in finding more sources. Once you know of an author who has written about your subject, you can do an Internet search to see if more articles are available online or in the library. You can even e-mail the author and ask for an interview. Through e-mail or in person.

SOCIAL MEDIA

In your search for practitioners and experts you might want to take to Twitter, Facebook, and other message boards related to your subject matter. Often you can leave questions on message boards (like College Confidential Discussions, Absolute Write) and get answers from people with experiences with your topic. You might even privately e-mail some of the respondents for information they might not want made public. You can send out messages on Twitter that you are looking for information by using the # in front of key words. People who share the special interest could connect with you through that key-wording system. You could also put out a call to your friends via Facebook that you are looking for people who can share their experiences with your subject.

INTERNET SEARCH ENGINES AND DIRECTORIES

You will find some current information by using directories and search engines on the World Wide Web, so these sources are good choices for researching current trends. However, not all Web material is equally useful or accurate, so carefully evaluate Web sources. The U.S. government's official Web site at <www.usa.gov> is a portal that leads you to census data, studies, and other sources of statistical information that can be useful in writing about trends. Any state's department of public health can offer reliable information as well. In general, the most reliable, unbiased sources of statistical information are .gov and .edu sites

INTERNET DATABASES

Databases that are available on a subscription basis provide excellent material not usually available on the free Web. Databases like LexisNexis, Proquest, and InfoTrac, for some examples, may be available to you because your library has paid a fee. You gain entry by logging on through your library or by using a password.

INTERVIEWS

Ask yourself who is involved? Who are the stakeholders? Who is affected? Who is an expert on the topic? Interviewing is an important part of making your trend research original. Through interviews, you gather quotations that give your statistics human faces, real-life stories. The quotations you gather can provide your analysis with a much more engaging style. Two types of sources that can help give your writing authority:

1. **Consulting Experts** Experts are people who work in relevant fields and have a deep knowledge of the subject of your trend analysis. Doctors, researchers, and authors of books make good sources and can provide excellent primary source material, making your paper more original than if you relied only on published sources.
2. **Consulting Practitioners** Practitioners are people who have experienced or observed the trend or who personify it and are also experts. They help make the trend relevant and give it a human side. For some tips on interviewing, refer to page 497 in Chapter 15, Research.

Checklist for Authority, Currency, Bias

- ✓ Is the identity of the author of the book, article or Web site clear?
- ✓ Is the formality of the writing and graphics you find within the source suitable to the subject matter?
- ✓ Does the source include any references to other sources? A bibliography or Works Cited list?
- ✓ Can you find grammatical or factual mistakes?
- ✓ Does the material or Web site list a date of posting/publication?
- ✓ Is the source trying to sell a product or service or promote a particular point of view?
- ✓ Does the source link to or refer to other sources that espouse a distinct point of view?

VISUAL LITERACY: INFOGRAPHICS—DATA MADE VISUAL THROUGH GRAPHICS

Analyze the connection between the message and the information in "The Most Dangerous Species in the Boston Harbor."

How does the image draw the reader into the information?

How would you create a metaphorical image that illustrates some factual data—the number of teens who smoke, for example, or the number of songs downloaded from iTunes per day?

THE MOST DANGEROUS SPECIES IN BOSTON HARBOR

Aluminum foil and tin cans
Origin: Trash cans, litter, boaters' debris
Behavior: Once ingested by other harbor dwellers, the metal causes lacerations to internal organs. Smaller creatures can become trapped inside the metal and starve to death
Lifespan: 200-500 years

Food wrappers
Origin: Trash cans, careless picnickers
Behavior: They keep the food airtight without leaking grease because they are made from Mylar and plastic, often coated with a chemical that is carcinogenic—bad for humans and fellow harbor inhabitants
Lifespan: 25 years, average

Based on THE MOST DANGEROUS SPECIES IN THE MEDITERRANEAN
Agencia Catalana de l'Aigue
Generalutat de Catalunya
Departament de Medi Ambienti Habitge

Plastic bags
Origin: Beaches and trash containers
Behavior: They look a lot like jellyfish, and are eaten by other creatures.
Lifespan: Though they have only been around for 50 years, they will have a 500-1000 year lifespan, potentially, and are made of a polymer that never biodegrades. However, the bags break down and becomes brittle, scattering into all corners of the harbor and ocean.

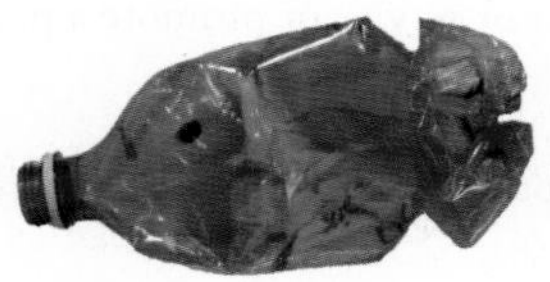

Plastic beverage bottles
Origin: Trash containers, boats.
Behavior: poisons and traps sea life
Lifespan: Average 350-400 years

Paper Bags
Origin: Beaches, boats
Behavior: Kraft bags degrade quickly, but cause digestive problems in hungry sea life.
Lifespan: 4 weeks

Cigarette butts
Origin: Toilets, city streets, careless motorists
Behavior: Their toxic blend of soluble chemicals can leach into water within 60 minutes of contact.
Lifespan: Filters—made of cellulose acetate— take three years to break down

Kate Burak

A JOURNALIST'S TIPS FOR SHOWING THE HUMAN SIDE OF DATA

To help your writing move beyond becoming a listing of data, consider ways journalists write feature articles that include statistical analysis (see also the poster on caffeine that brings in facts for interest):

1. **Find people who have experiences with the trend or pattern**. Interview them for realistic details.
2. **When you interview sources who have experiences with the trend, ask questions that lead to "stories."** ("When was the first time?" or "What did you see?")
3. **Begin with a "hook"**—a piece of someone's story, either in the form of a scene or an anecdote.
5. **Show the trend in action**. Include a demonstration of what the reader might see if he or she could observe a piece of the picture.
6. **Think of the writing as a conversation**. When you—through a source or statistic—make a point, allow a source (expert or practitioner or statistic) to provide a response: a comment or counter point—as if your sources were responding to each other.
7. **Do not forget to describe**. When you can, include a detail that shows what the trend looks like, feels like, how much something costs, or how it sounds.
8. **Save a good detail—an image or interesting quotation—for the end**. It is the reader's last impression.

PRACTICE 11.4

Showing Comparisons

Create your own poster like "The Most Dangerous Species in Boston Harbor" on page 326 or the "Caffeine Poster" on page 328 comparing similar products or practices. Include interesting "factoids" about the topic.

USING LOGIC TO ANALYZE CAUSE AND EFFECT:

AVOID JUMPING TO CONCLUSIONS

People can make errors when looking for reasons. Two common logical fallacies, as the following discussion describes, demonstrate how faulty reasoning makes for bad logic in causal analyses.

THE POST HOC FALLACY

Walking under a ladder causes bad luck; so does letting a black cat cross your path, breaking a mirror, and spilling salt. Dropping a glass means that company is coming. Finding a four-leaf clover brings good luck. These superstitions are all based on the

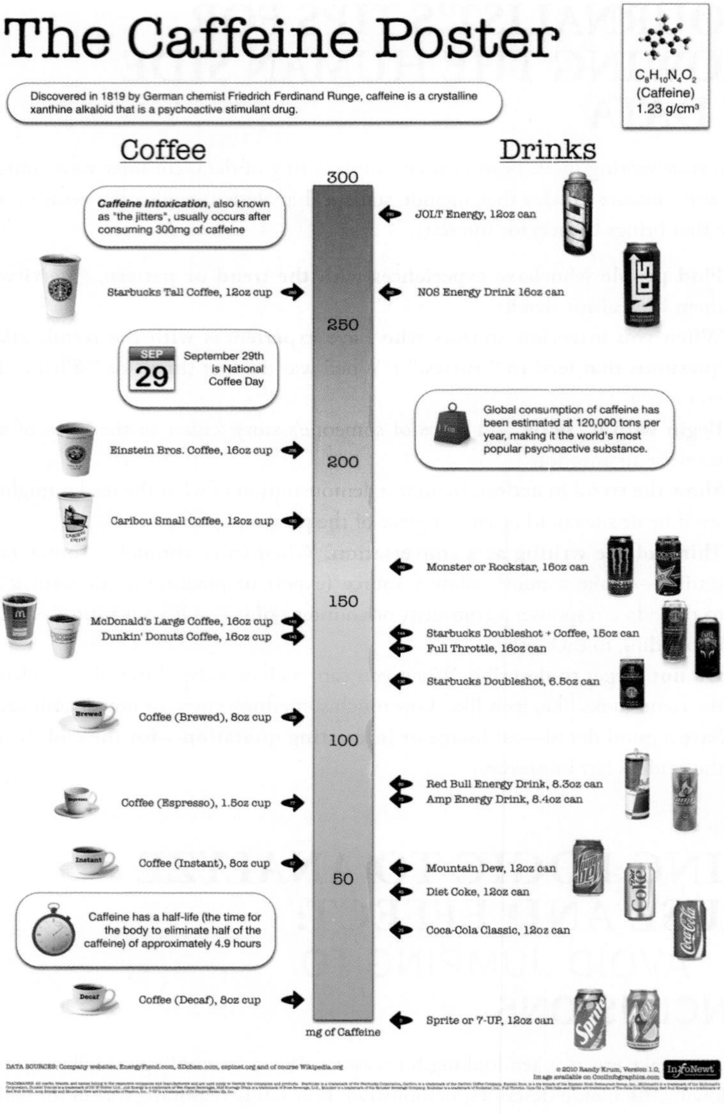

The Caffeine Poster

$C_8H_{10}N_4O_2$
(Caffeine)
1.23 g/cm³

Discovered in 1819 by German chemist Friedrich Ferdinand Runge, caffeine is a crystalline xanthine alkaloid that is a psychoactive stimulant drug.

Coffee

Drinks

300

250

200

150

100

50

mg of Caffeine

Caffeine Intoxication, also known as "the jitters", usually occurs after consuming 300mg of caffeine

Starbucks Tall Coffee, 12oz cup

SEP 29 September 29th is National Coffee Day

Einstein Bros. Coffee, 16oz cup

Caribou Small Coffee, 12oz cup

McDonald's Large Coffee, 16oz cup

Dunkin' Donuts Coffee, 16oz cup

Coffee (Brewed), 8oz cup

Coffee (Espresso), 1.5oz cup

Coffee (Instant), 8oz cup

Caffeine has a half-life (the time for the body to eliminate half of the caffeine) of approximately 4.9 hours

Coffee (Decaf), 8oz cup

JOLT Energy, 12oz can

NOS Energy Drink 16oz can

Global consumption of caffeine has been estimated at 120,000 tons per year, making it the world's most popular psychoactive substance.

Monster or Rockstar, 16oz can

Starbucks Doubleshot + Coffee, 15oz can

Full Throttle, 16oz can

Starbucks Doubleshot, 6.5oz can

Red Bull Energy Drink, 8.3oz can

Amp Energy Drink, 8.4oz can

Mountain Dew, 12oz can

Diet Coke, 12oz can

Coca-Cola Classic, 12oz can

Sprite or 7-UP, 12oz can

DATA SOURCES: Company websites, EnergyFiend.com, 3Dchem.com, cspinet.org and of course Wikipedia.org

© 2010 Randy Krum, Version 1.0. Image available on CoolInfographics.com

InfoNewt

Courtesy of Randy Krum/www.coolinfographics.com

faulty assumption that because two events happen sequentially, the first has caused the second.

You can see how the superstitions may have arisen: People walk under ladders at a building site and perhaps occasionally bricks fall on their heads, or company seems

to arrive just when you have dropped the crystal wine glasses. One coincidence leads to a generalization, but in fact the occurrence of one event does not necessarily mean the second will follow.

Statisticians phrase it this way: Correlation does not prove causation. Logicians use the Latin phrase *post hoc, ergo propter hoc*, meaning "after this, therefore because of this," to describe this error in reasoning. When you write about causes and effects, be careful to avoid this fallacy.

ASSIGNING SINGULAR CAUSE

If you have determined a cause-and-effect relationship between two events, do not assume that any one cause is the only cause. Sometimes a cause can be one of many; and other causes may be hidden or more significant.

For example, if you are looking at the growing problem of obesity among children, you might assume that the cause is the decrease in physical activity among children. You know that one reason for weight gain is burning fewer calories, so inactivity could certainly be a cause of obesity.

However, there are enough skinny couch potatoes around to make you look for other causes as well. A slow or malfunctioning metabolism might cause weight gain; calorie-laden fast-food can cause weight gain; and genetics may play a part. The causes of obesity are multiple and complex.

READING STATISTICS WITH A CRITICAL EYE

Statistics can be used or misused, depending on how ethical a writer is. Statistics might be distorted to understate or overstate a trend. For example, you might read that 50 percent of the police officers in a small town in Ohio were killed on the job last year. That rate is up 100 percent from the year before. The implication is that this is a dangerous town with a steeply climbing crime rate. The fact of the matter is that the town had two officers, and one was killed while helping a motorist change a tire. While it is true and unfortunate that one of the two officers was killed last year, it is misleading to say that 50 percent of the force was killed on the job last year.

Statistics, even those that are factual, are not always accurate without a clear context. You must be careful not to use every statistic you find without evaluating it and its source. You must also be careful to use statistics responsibly.

Here is an example of a statistic that needs a full explanation:

> The United States Fire Administration (USFA) announced today that 441 firefighters died while on-duty in the United States in 2001. This total, which is more than four and one-half times the average annual number of firefighter deaths for the last decade, includes 343 firefighters lost at the World Trade Center on September 11.

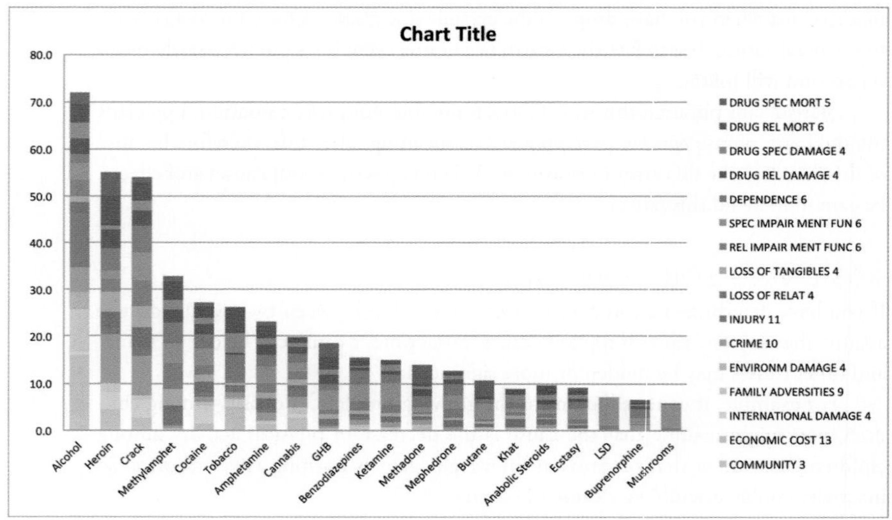

What surprises you about the conclusion you might reach after reading the data presented this way?

> The loss represents the worst total since the USFA began tracking firefighter fatalities in 1977. USFA is a part of the Federal Emergency Management Agency. "2001 was a tragic year for America's fire service," R. David Paulson, United States Fire Administrator, said. "In addition to the many local heroes who died serving their communities nationwide, the eyes of the world turned to New York City on September 11."
>
> —United States Fire Administration, Press Release

Numbers can also underplay a trend. It does not seem noteworthy to report that twenty students from the University of Cincinnati will spend spring break building houses with Habitat for Humanity. But if you find out that 600 students from all over Ohio are building houses for the poor, as compared with 200 last year, the numbers start to build a full and reliable picture of a trend.

Numbers can be translated to obscure information or to be more useful to readers. You can say that in 1999 there were 47,895 accounting majors at colleges nationwide. This seems like a lot of prospective accountants. Still, there were 13,325 fewer accounting majors in 1999 than there were in 1995. In context, this statistic can be even more accessible to readers. (See also the chart on consumer spending, Where Does the Money Go?)

PRACTICE 11.5

Evaluating a Chart

Examine the chart on this page; MOST DANGEROUS DRUGS.

Comment on the information, including the source. Research the claims made in the chart. Then write an evaluation of the chart commenting on:

Readability: Do you understand the points?

Design: Is the design distracting or engaging?

Credibility: Does the message include enough evidence?

Some industry specialists say interest in accounting careers has waned on campuses even though demand remains relatively strong. According to a 2001 study commissioned by the American Institute of Certified Public Accountants, the number of college students choosing an accounting major dropped more than 21 percent from a high of 61,220 in the 1994–95 school year to 47,895 for 1998–99, the most recent year for which figures are available.

—Barbara Claire Kasselmann, "More Than Debits, Credits"

PRACTICE 11.6

Making Claims Based on Data

Use the infographic on consumer spending to formulate some ideas about how people spend money. Make three claims based on the information in the graphic.

Then, list ways you could develop the causes and/or effect of the trends.

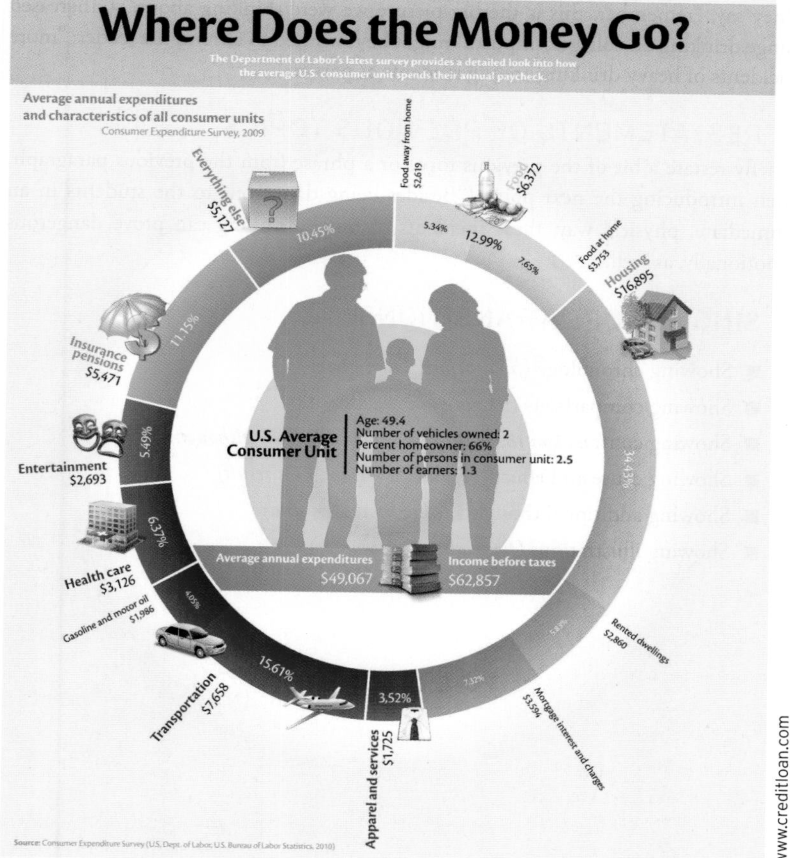

www.creditloan.com

REVISION:
MAKING YOUR LOGIC AIRTIGHT

Reasearch articles that explore the causes and effects of trends are complicated pieces of writing, and asking a reader to follow you through a collection of statistics, quotations, and explanations requires you to be a gentle guide. Transitions, which convince your reader that your analysis is logical and clearly guided in a particular direction, can be divided into three types:

1. BIG IDEA REMINDERS

You restate your thesis, reminding readers that you have a main point about a pattern. These reminders are like signposts and help you—and your reader—refocus. They say, "remember, this is the big picture we were thinking about." ("Increased binge drinking on college campuses" might be reworded to remind the reader: "more incidents of heavy drinking among students at parties."

2. RESTATEMENTS OF PREVIOUS TOPICS

Briefly restate a bit of the previous topic or a phrase from the previous paragraph, then introducing the next point ("Besides being dangerous to the students in an immediate, physical way, these incidents of binge drinking can prove dangerous emotionally, as well. . . .")

3. SINGLE WORD TRANSITIONS

- Showing chronology (*first, before, later, after*)
- Showing comparisons (*likewise, in this case*)
- Showing contrast (*on the other hand, however, but, although*)
- Showing cause and effect (*because, therefore, as a result*)
- Showing additional thoughts (*also, moreover, and*)
- Showing illustrations (*for example, so you see*)

DIY MEDIA AND DESIGN

INFOGRAPHICS

LIKE TREND STORIES, infographics give readers researched information about data, but the format relies on visual design to make its case. You can find several examples of infographics in this chapter, including one on the Social Media Effect on the following page. The idea of "visualizing data" is not a new one—charts and graphs are used in countless ways to condense a big message into an image, with words and numbers to guide the way. Not limited by media, infographics can include interactive Web sites and videos.

Conduct a survey (about health, fitness, consumer behavior, or lifestyle). Ask questions to a diverse sample of twenty to thirty people, minimally. Design your own infographic or video that makes your collected data visual.

Read more: http://www.pamorama.net/2010/03/03/35-great-social-media-infographics/#ixzz1BWqr4uta

D I Y

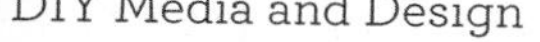

DIY

THE SOCIAL MEDIA EFFECT

CONTENT CREATED

STORY/CONTENT **HITS** DIGG'S FRONT PAGE

TWEET ABOUT STORY/CONTENT TO THEIR FOLLOWERS

Did you see...

TWEET USER **POSTS** STORY ON THEIR FACEBOOK STATUS

MAJOR BLOG SEES STORY ON DIGG'S FRONT PAGE, **LINK** TO POST ABOUT IT

Blog Blog Blog Blog

2.3 Million
UNIQUE VISITORS

34.7 Million
UNIQUE VISITORS

156Million
UNIQUE VISITORS

DIGG USER **SUBMITS** STORY TO REDDIT, MAKES FRONT PAGE

2 Million
UNIQUE VISITORS

SEVERAL FOLLOWERS **RETWEET** TO THEIR FOLLOWERS

DIFFERENT FRIENDS **SHARE** IT WITH THEIR FRIENDS

SMALLER BLOGS SEE STORY ON LARGER BLOGS, THEY **POST** ABOUT IT

STORY GETS **RETWEETED** ALL OVER TWITTER

STUMBLE UPON USERS **VOTE** UP STORY FROM THEIR STUMBLE TOOLBAR, MAKES FRONT PAGE OF STUMBLEUPON.COM

12.4 Million
UNIQUE VISITORS

GOOGLE SEARCH ENGINE RESULT FOR STORY/TOPIC

1. **YOUR SITE** (DUE TO ALL THE INBOUND LINKS)
2. **MAJOR BLOG #1** (W/LINK TO YOUR SITE)
3. **DIGG STORY** (LINKING TO YOUR SITE)
4. **BLOG #2** (W/LINK TO YOUR SITE)
5. **TWEET** (LINKING TO YOUR SITE)

AND SO ON...

IF CONTENT IS **GREAT**, CAN END UP FEATURED ON SITES LIKE:

AOL OR YAHOO!

49.3 Million
UNIQUE VISITORS

150 Million
UNIQUE VISITORS

INFO GRAPHIC WORLD

* Figures are From Compete.com as of 10/12/2011

READINGS

THE READINGS in this chapter analyze observable trends among young people—patterns that are shaped by a complex collection of causes. By looking at the variety of subjects here you can see how trends can be detected in a number of areas—technology, psychology, biology, and popular culture—and how these trends relate to matters of history, politics, and gender.

Race Remixed Black? White? Asian? More Young Americans Choose All of the Above[2]

Susan Saulny

This article explores a trend that was confirmed by the most recent census—a revised form that allowed respondents to check off more than one box in answer to the question about race. The form itself was historic, and the results quantified a trend that may have been in hiding for many years.

New York Times
January 29, 2011

COLLEGE PARK, Md.—In another time or place, the game of "What Are You?" that was played one night last fall at the University of Maryland might have been mean, or menacing: Laura Wood's peers were picking apart her every feature in an effort to guess her race.

"How many mixtures do you have?" one young man asked above the chatter of about 50 students. With her tan skin and curly brown hair, Ms. Wood's ancestry could have spanned the globe.

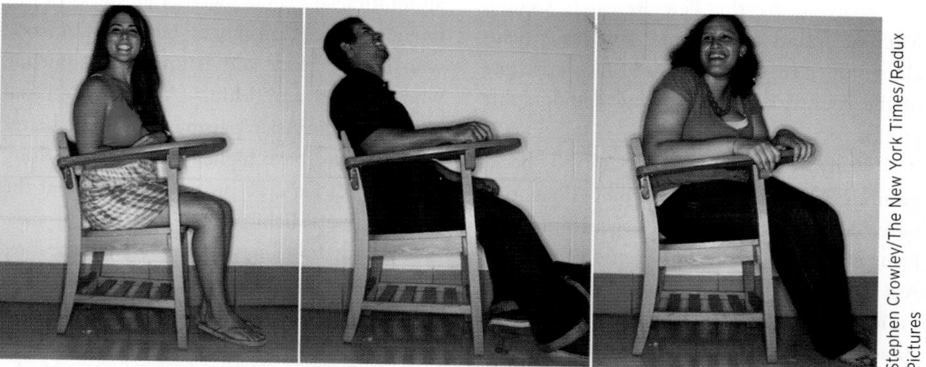

Stephen Crowley/The New York Times/Redux Pictures

Stephen Crowley/The *New York Times*. From left: Shannon Palmer, Japanese/Irish; Vasco Mateus, Portuguese/African-American/Haitian; Laura Wood, black/white.

[2]Susan Saulny, "Race Remixed," from New York Times, January 29, 2011. Reprinted by permission of PARS International.

"I'm mixed with two things," she said politely.

"Are you mulatto?" asked Paul Skym, another student, using a word once tinged with shame that is enjoying a comeback in some young circles. When Ms. Wood confirmed that she is indeed black and white, Mr. Skym, who is Asian and white, boasted, "Now that's what I'm talking about!" in affirmation of their mutual mixed lineage.

Then the group of friends—formally, the Multiracial and Biracial Student Association—erupted into laughter and cheers, a routine show of their mixed-race pride. The crop of students moving through college right now includes the largest group of mixed-race people ever to come of age in the United States, and they are only the vanguard: the country is in the midst of a demographic shift driven by immigration and intermarriage.

One in seven new marriages is between spouses of different races or ethnicities, according to data from 2008 and 2009 that was analyzed by the Pew Research Center. Multiracial and multiethnic Americans (usually grouped together as "mixed race") are one of the country's fastest-growing demographic groups.

Many young adults of mixed backgrounds are rejecting the color lines that have defined Americans for generations in favor of a much more fluid sense of identity. Ask Michelle López-Mullins, a 20-year-old junior and the president of the Multiracial and Biracial Student Association, how she marks her race on forms like the census, and she says, "It depends on the day, and it depends on the options."

"The crop of students moving through college right now includes the largest group of mixed-race people"

They are also using the strength in their growing numbers to affirm roots that were once portrayed as tragic or pitiable.

"I think it's really important to acknowledge who you are and everything that makes you that," said Ms. Wood, the 19-year-old vice president of the group.

"If someone tries to call me black I say, 'yes—and white.' People have the right not to acknowledge everything, but don't do it because society tells you that you can't."

No one knows quite how the growth of the multiracial population will change the country. Optimists say the blending of the races is a step toward transcending race, to a place where America is free of bigotry, prejudice and programs like affirmative action.

Pessimists say that a more powerful multiracial movement will lead to more stratification and come at the expense of the number and influence of other minority groups, particularly African-Americans.

And some sociologists say that grouping all multiracial people together glosses over differences in circumstances between someone who is, say, black and Latino, and someone who is Asian and white. (Among interracial couples, white-Asian pairings tend to be better educated and have higher incomes, according to Reynolds Farley, a professor emeritus at the University of Michigan.)

Along those lines, it is telling that the rates of intermarriage are lowest between blacks and whites, indicative of the enduring economic and social distance between them.

Prof. Rainier Spencer, director of the Afro-American Studies Program at the University of Nevada, Las Vegas, and the

author of "Reproducing Race: The Paradox of Generation Mix," says he believes that there is too much "emotional investment" in the notion of multiracialism as a panacea for the nation's age-old divisions. "The mixed-race identity is not a transcendence of race, it's a new tribe," he said. "A new Balkanization of race."

But for many of the University of Maryland students, that is not the point. They are asserting their freedom to identify as they choose.

"All society is trying to tear you apart and make you pick a side," Ms. Wood said. "I want us to have a say."

THE WAY WE WERE

Americans mostly think of themselves in singular racial terms. Witness President Obama's answer to the race question on the 2010 census: Although his mother was white and his father was black, Mr. Obama checked only one box, black, even though he could have checked both races.

"Some proportion of the country's population has been mixed-race since the first white settlers had children with Native Americans. What has changed is how mixed-race Americans are defined and counted."

Some proportion of the country's population has been mixed-race since the first white settlers had children with Native Americans. What has changed is how mixed-race Americans are defined and counted.

Long ago, the nation saw itself in more hues than black and white: the 1890 census included categories for racial mixtures such as quadroon (one-fourth black) and octoroon (one-eighth black). With the exception of one survey from 1850 to 1920, the census included a mulatto category, which was for people who had any perceptible trace of African blood.

But by the 1930 census, terms for mixed-race people had all disappeared, replaced by the so-called one-drop rule, an antebellum convention that held that anyone with a trace of African ancestry was only black. (Similarly, people who were "white and Indian" were generally to be counted as Indian.)

It was the census enumerator who decided.

By the 1970s, Americans were expected to designate themselves as members of one officially recognized racial group: black, white, American Indian, Japanese, Chinese, Filipino, Hawaiian, Korean or "other," an option used frequently by people of Hispanic origin. (The census recognizes Hispanic as an ethnicity, not a race.)

Starting with the 2000 census, Americans were allowed to mark one or more races.

The multiracial option came after years of complaints and lobbying, mostly by the white mothers of biracial children who objected to their children being allowed to check only one race. In 2000, seven million people—about 2.4 percent of the population—reported being more than one race.

According to estimates from the Census Bureau, the mixed-race population has grown by roughly 35 percent since 2000.

And many researchers think the census and other surveys undercount the mixed population.

MOVING FORWARD

The faces of mixed-race America are not just on college campuses. They are in politics, business

and sports. And the ethnically ambiguous are especially ubiquitous in movies, television shows and advertising. There are news, social networking and dating Web sites focusing on the mixed-race audience, and even consumer products like shampoo. There are mixed-race film festivals and conferences. And student groups like the one at Maryland, offering peer support and activism, are more common.

Such a club would not have existed a generation ago—when the question at the center of the "What Are You?" game would have been a provocation rather than an icebreaker.

"It's kind of a taking-back in a way, taking the reins," Ms. López-Mullins said. "We don't always have to let it get us down," she added, referring to the question multiracial people have heard for generations.

"The No. 1 reason why we exist is to give people who feel like they don't want to choose a side, that don't want to label themselves based on other people's interpretations of who they are, to give them a place, that safe space," she said. Ms. López-Mullins is Chinese and Peruvian on one side, and white and American Indian on the other.

That safe space did not exist amid the neo-Classical style buildings of the campus when Warren Kelley enrolled in 1974. Though his mother is Japanese and his father is African-American, he had basically one choice when it came to his racial identity. "I was black and proud to be black," Dr. Kelley said. "There was no notion that I might be multiracial. Or that the public discourse on college campuses recognized the multiracial community."

"Though his mother is Japanese and his father is African-American, he had basically one choice when it came to his racial identity. "I was black and proud to be black," Dr. Kelley said. "There was no notion that I might be multiracial."

Almost 40 years later, Dr. Kelley is the assistant vice president for student affairs at the university and faculty adviser to the multiracial club, and he is often in awe of the change on this campus.

When the multiracial group was founded in 2002, Dr. Kelley said, "There was an instant audience."

They did not just want to hold parties. The group sponsored an annual weeklong program of discussions intended to raise awareness of multiracial identities—called Mixed Madness—and conceived a new class on the experience of mixed-race Asian-Americans that was made part of the curriculum last year.

"Even if someone had formed a mixed-race group in the '70s, would I have joined?" Dr. Kelley said. "I don't know. My multiracial identity wasn't prominent at the time. I don't think I even conceptualized the idea."

By the 2000 census, Dr. Kelley's notion of his racial identity had evolved to include his mother's Asian heritage; he modified his race officially on the form. After a lifetime of checking black, he checked Asian and black.

(Dr. Kelley's mother was born in Kyoto. She met her future husband, a black soldier from Alabama, while he was serving in the Pacific during World War II.)

Checking both races was not an easy choice, Dr. Kelley said, "as a black man, with all that means in terms of pride in that heritage as well as reasons to give back and be part of progress forward."

"As I moved into adulthood and got a professional job, I started to respect my parents more and see the amount of my mom's culture that's reflected in me," he said. "Society itself also moved."

FINDING CAMARADERIE

In fall 2009, a question tugged at Sabrina Garcia, then a freshman at Maryland, a public university with 26,500 undergraduates: "Where will I fit in?" recalled Ms. Garcia, who is Palestinian and Salvadoran.

"I considered the Latina student union, but I'm only half," she said. "I didn't want to feel like I was hiding any part of me. I went to an M.B.S.A. meeting and it was really great. I really feel like part of a group that understands."

The group holds weekly meetings, in addition to hosting movie nights, dinners, parties and, occasionally, posts broadcasts on YouTube.

Not all of its 100 or so members consider themselves mixed race, and the club welcomes everyone.

At a meeting in the fall, David Banda, who is Hispanic, and Julicia Coleman, who is black, came just to unwind among supportive listeners. They discussed the frustrations of being an interracial couple, even today, especially back in their hometown, Upper Marlboro, Md.

"When we go back home, let's say for a weekend or to the mall, they see us walking and I get this look, you know, sort of giving me the idea: 'Why are you with her? You're not black, so she should be with a black person.' Or comments," Mr. Banda, 20, said at a meeting of the group. "Even some of my friends tell me, 'Why don't you date a Hispanic girl?'"

Mr. Banda and Ms. Coleman are thinking about having children someday. "One of the main reasons I joined is to see the struggles mixed people go through," he said, "so we can be prepared when that time comes."

And despite the growth of the mixed-race population, there are struggles.

Ian Winchester, a junior who is part Ghanaian, part Scottish-Norwegian, said he felt lucky and torn being biracial. His Scottish grandfather was keen on dressing him in kilts as a boy. The other side of the family would put him in a dashiki. "I do feel empowered being biracial," he said. "The ability to question your identity—identity in general—is really a gift."

But, he continued, "I don't even like to identify myself as a race anymore. My family has been pulling me in two directions about what I am. I just want to be a person."

"Despite the growth of the mixed-race population, there are struggles."

Similarly, Ms. López-Mullins sees herself largely in nonracial terms.

"I hadn't even learned the word 'Hispanic' until I came home from school one day and asked my dad what I should refer to him as, to express what I am," she said. "Growing up with my parents, I never thought we were different from any other family."

But it was not long before Ms. López-Mullins came to detest what was the most common question put to her in grade school, even from friends. "What are you?" they asked, and "Where are you from?" They were fascinated by her father, a Latino with Asian roots, and her mother with the long blond hair, who was mostly European in ancestry, although mixed with some Cherokee and Shawnee.

"I was always having to explain where my parents are from because just saying 'I'm from

Takoma Park, Maryland,' was not enough," she said. "Saying 'I'm an American' wasn't enough."

"Now when people ask what I am, I say, 'How much time do you have?'" she said. "Race will not automatically tell you my story."

What box does she check on forms like the census? "Hispanic, white, Asian American, Native American," she said. "I'm pretty much checking everything."

At one meeting of the Multiracial and Biracial Student Association, Ms. Wood shared a story about surprises and coming to terms with them. "Until I was 8 years old, I thought I was white," she told the group. "My mother and aunt sat me down and said the guy I'd been calling Dad was not my father. I started crying. And she said, 'Your real father is black.'"

Ms. Wood's mother, Catherine Bandele, who is white, and her biological father split up before she was born. Facing economic troubles and resistance from her family about raising a mixed-race child, Ms. Bandele gave her daughter up for adoption to a couple who had requested a biracial baby. But after two weeks, she changed her mind. "I had to fight to get her back, but I got her," Ms. Bandele said. "And we're so proud of Laura."

Eventually Ms. Wood's closest relatives softened, embracing her.

But more distant relatives never came around. "They can't see past the color of my skin and accept me even though I share DNA with them," she said. "It hurts a lot because I don't even know my father's side of the family."

Ms. Wood has searched the Internet for her father, to no avail.

"Being in M.B.S.A., it really helps with that," she said. "Finding a group of people who can accept you for who you are and being able to accept yourself, to just be able to look in the mirror and say, 'I'm O.K. just the way I am!' — honestly, I feel that it's a blessing."

"It took a long time," she said.

Now Ms. Wood is one of the group's foremost advocates.

Over dinner with Ms. López-Mullins one night, she wondered: "What if Obama had checked white? There would have been an uproar because he's the first 'black president,' even though he's mixed. I would like to have a conversation with him about why he did that."

Absent that opportunity, Ms. Wood took her concerns about what Mr. Obama checked to a meeting of the campus chapter of the N.A.A.C.P. last year. Vicky Key, a past president of the Multiracial and Biracial Student Association, who is Greek and black, joined her. The question for discussion was whether Mr. Obama is the first black president or the first multiracial president.

Ms. Key, a senior, remembered someone answering the question without much discussion: "One-drop rule, he's black."

"But we were like, 'Wait!'" she said. "That's offensive to us. We sat there and tried to advocate, but they said, 'No, he's black and that's it.' Then someone said, 'Stop taking away our black president.' I didn't understand where they were coming from, and they didn't understand me."

Whether Mr. Obama is considered black or multiracial, there is a wider debate among mixed-race people about what the long-term goals of their advocacy should be, both on campus and off.

"I don't want a color-blind society at all," Ms. Wood said. "I just want both my races to be acknowledged."

Ms. López-Mullins countered, "I want mine not to matter."

QUESTIONS FOR RHETORICAL ANALYSIS

1. **CONSIDERING THE RHETORICAL SITUATION:** Will some readers find the subject of this article controversial? Does it seem the writer has an opinion about how the readers will view the topic?
2. How does the writer prove the trend exists?
3. Where is the analytical thesis?
4. What are some causes of the trend? What are some effects? Which does the writer spend most time developing?

QUESTIONS FOR WRITING AND DISCUSSION

1. Project into the future and speculate about the meaning of race. Write from the point of view of someone in 2035, defining "race" as it might be defined then.
2. Do you think the piece includes enough sources? Why or Why not?
3. When are other times people are asked to label themselves or "choose a side"?
4. What do you think the purpose of quantifying race even in terms of "mixed race"—serves? How can such information be used and where?

STYLE PRACTICE: IMITATION

Write the opening of a trend story that starts with a conversation, like this article.

Chasing the Blues Away: Use of Antidepressants among Teens[3]

Meredith Jeffries

Student Meredith Jeffries explores the growing trend of prescribing antidepressents to adolescents.

THOUGH THE trend is difficult to follow because physicians are prescribing non-FDA approved antidepressants, the trend of using the drugs to help teens with emotional problems seems to be on the rise. The student–author uses many anecdotes to fill out a story that needs development: without the personal stories, our understanding of what causes teens and their parents to turn to mood-altering drugs would be vague. Our understanding of the drugs' effects on individuals is also clearer due to the writer's inclusion of personal stories.

Stephen Peterson's report card reveals he is nearly a straight A student. The fifteen-year-old high school freshman attends poetry club meetings every week. "I'm unathletic," he admits, self-consciously. He's just finished his shift bussing tables at the coffee shop where he works eight hours a week, and he slouches into his over-sized parka, his mop of dark hair obscuring his face. He's polite about answering questions but doesn't volunteer much. He is modest about his achievements: an award for a self-portrait he produced in his freshman art class goes

[3]Reprinted by permission of Meredith Jeffries.

unmentioned. His skill as a classical pianist also doesn't come up, though he has been accepted at a summer camp for gifted musicians. He also doesn't mention that after three years of battling depression, he's on Prozac. He also takes over-the-counter Melatonin to sleep at night.

"After we got home from the pharmacy with his prescription, Stephen told me he couldn't believe he was 'the kid on Prozac,'" his mother, Geena, says. "I didn't know what to do. I don't want my kid on Prozac, but everywhere we go for help, they keep saying we should try the drugs, that it's time to try them."

Stephen Peterson has joined the growing legion of children and teens who have been prescribed drugs to combat depression. It is difficult to account for exactly how many children and teens will be affected each year by depression. According to the National Institute of Mental Health "Fact Sheet for Physicians," up to 2.5 percent of children and up to 8.3 percent of adolescents in the U.S. suffer from depression ("Depression in Children and Adolescents"). The NIMH reports that depression is occurring earlier in life than it did in the past. "Is life more stressful?" asks Geena Peterson. "In my mother's day, boys would be drafted into the army the moment they got out of high school. Wasn't that more stressful? I think we just recognize depression more than we did before," she says.

"Up to 8.3 percent of adolescents in the U.S. suffer from depression."

Accounting for exactly how many of these depressed teens are being prescribed antidepressants is difficult, and since the FDA approved Prozac for use in children in 2003, much controversy has surrounded the drug. Further clouding the issue of the number of children on antidepressants is the practice of prescribing non-approved antidepressants "off label," or for purposes not included in the FDA screening. Many parents say they know at least one child or teen who takes a prescribed medication for depression. "When I started to tell people I was thinking about medication for Stephen's depression, friends came out of the woodwork with stories," Geena Peterson says. "Lots of kids are on antidepressants."

Dr. Peter Wilde, a pediatrician who practices in a Boston suburb, sees parents in his practice who come in asking for medication. "I first ask, 'What does your child do—come home grouchy and then go to his room without saying hello? I remind them that some of that is being a teenager.' " Dr. Wilde speculates that the growing trend of prescribing antidepressants for teens is tied with the overall trend in using them for adults. The Centers for Disease Control listed antidepressants as the "most frequently prescribed therapeutic class of drug" in 2005 ("Therapeutic Drug Use"). "Parents see the commercials and the ads on TV," says Wilde. "Most of the time they really want to help their kids suffering," he says, "and I have seen antidepressants work for some kids who really do need them."

Geena Peterson says Stephen was one of those kids. "We went through all the steps—the weekly meetings with his counselor, the vitamins, exercise, and even therapy with special lights. Then he started having trouble sleeping," Geena Peterson says. After about a month of [his] not sleeping and [having] terrible, violent dreams when he did sleep, Stephen's mother "caved in," as she puts it, to the pressure to use antidepressants. "Everywhere we went for help, we were told to try the drugs," she says. "I really resisted."

To explain how parents even started to consider drugs to treat their children's emotional problems, some people point at managed care and the push to make healthcare more efficient and cost effective. Others note the shortage of

child psychiatrists as one of the causes for prescribing drugs frequently. Still others say the aggressive marketing and lobbying of drug companies are factors contributing to the frequent use of antidepressants in children as young as 7.

Advocates claim that antidepressants have begun to supplant—rather than complement—the role of mental health counseling in treating young patients. Using national databases that tracked outpatient visits to hospitals and physician offices between 1995 and 2002, researchers from the Stanford University School of Medicine found a decreasing use of psychotherapy and increasing use of medication. Patients between the ages of 7 and 17 who were diagnosed with depression illustrated this trend. Between 1995 and 2002, their use of psychotherapy dropped from 83 percent of visits to 68 percent. Meanwhile, use of medication rose from 47 percent to 52 percent ("Antidepressants Potentially Misused in Treating Adolescents").

Prescribing medications and forgoing therapy [have] proven to be shortsighted, in the view of Dr. Mark Perrin, the author of *Psychiatric Medications for Children* and president of the New Jersey affiliate of the National Alliance on Mental Illness. "Because of the pressure from the pharmaceutical industry and the (shortage) of properly trained child psychiatrists, I think we're developing a very external approach to these childhood problems," says Perrin in an e-mail interview. "The approach is very superficial in dealing only with the external manifestations—we're not dealing with the internal causes."

"Stephen spent fifteen minutes with the psychiatrist before she prescribed," Geena says. "And he's really a high-functioning kid. On her intake form, the doctor noted, depression—moderate, impairment—mild." Geena says she was hoping the psychiatrist would have spent more time with Stephen getting to know him and the specifics of his depression. "She filled out an inventory form that asked questions like when was he potty trained, and then she wrote a prescription. I really wasn't any more confident I was doing the right thing even as I walked out of the pharmacy with our son's Prozac," she says.

Her husband, Mark, agreed with her reluctance to put their son on antidepressants. Mark Peterson thinks that, because of the ease of their availability, antidepressants are a convenient way—for the parents and the kids—to deal with the trials of adolescence. The availability of these drugs is a recent phenomenon, so the long-term effects are hard to predict. Mark asks what parents did with depressed kids in the past: "Wouldn't every character in a John Hughes movie be medicated? Wouldn't the whole Breakfast Club be on Prozac?"

"Wouldn't every character in a John Hughes movie be medicated? Wouldn't the whole Breakfast Club be on Prozac?"

Mark Peterson says the popularity of the drugs might even be chalked up to helping manage parenthood. "Who doesn't want a less moody teenager?"

Geena Peterson says her extended family was critical of her decision to turn to drugs. "My sister said, 'You just want to keep him a super-achiever,' " she said. Geena Peterson wonders herself whether part of [the] popularity of antidepressant use has as a goal keeping children highly competitive. "No parents want to see their children fall behind in any way," she says.

Stephen Peterson says he is very busy with all of his activities and that he often spends three hours or more on homework. Some nights, the honors student is still doing homework at 11:30.

"I know it's easy to see that over-working a fifteen-year-old might depress that child,

but how do you do it any differently?" Geena Peterson understands her sister's suspicion that some of what led to Stephen's medication was a desire to keep him "propped up" so he could continue to be an extremely successful person. "He's the one who wants to be busy," she says. Geena says that Stephen becomes even more depressed during school vacations when he has more free time. Those relaxation periods were always the times Stephen would fall into sadness, Geena says. "I guess in a way he's a workaholic. But would that be any different if we stopped treating his depression? I don't think so. It's who he is."

Loreen Lin, a close friend of Geena's, agrees with the speculation that the culture in which they are raising their children makes using antidepressants seem necessary, but she says that wasn't a factor for her. Her son, Jared, who attended a highly competitive private school in Boston, fell into depression during his junior year of high school. "He was off the charts on all the standardized tests, and then, boom, he stopped doing anything." Lin says Jared stopped attending school. "It was like he was completely detached, no longer really functioning." Lin dismisses the idea that she was trying to maintain a super-achiever's lifestyle by relying on a prescription. "I understand that might be true for some people, but for me it was a question of seeing my kid in pain—in real pain. Plus, we have a family history of major depressive episodes. The factors were there."

Their psychiatrist recommended Welbutrin, one of the non-approved antidepressants. According to Lin, the antidepressant "really did help." Jared repeated his junior year at a "very structured prep school" as a boarding student, living about 90 minutes away from his parents' home. He is now in his first year at Stanford University. After two years, he decided not to take the drug anymore, Lin says, and "he's doing fine."

One of the Peterson family's worries is that Prozac is a long-term treatment for Stephen. "I want to stop the medication at some point," says Stephen. "That's the other side of this—When?" "Everybody tells me that this is a problem in the chemistry of my brain, that I don't make enough serotonin. But if that's true, will that ever go away? Now that I'm getting extra serotonin, how will I live without it?"

The class of drugs that Prozac belongs in is known as Selective Serotonin Reuptake Inhibitors (SSRI's), [which] have been around only since 1987. Serotonin is believed to help regulate mood. Psychiatrists prescribe these serotonin-related drugs for a range of reasons, including to help patients suffering from obsessive compulsive disorders, eating disorders, and suicidal inclinations.

Melissa Bluestone, whose daughter is in Stephen's class, was not reluctant to try drug therapy with her child, even though parents are warned about the risks of increased potential for self harm among adolescents taking antidepressants. Raised the child of two physicians, Bluestone believes in using prescription drugs to address medical problems. "I do see depression as a very real medical problem," she says.

After Bluestone's daughter, Jayne, struggled with depression during her transition to a new high school, daily crying, and loss of appetite and ever-decreasing interest in her favorite activities—classic symptoms of depression—Bluestone agreed to try Prozac to help her fourteen-year-old. The effects, Bluestone says, were immediate. "It was as if we were watching a different person inside Jayne's body," Bluestone said. Though doctors say the full effects of the drug won't be evident until the child has been taking it for three weeks, Bluestone saw Jayne

change behavior in ten days. "It was subtle at first. She was brighter, happier, and we were glad to see the dark cloud start to lift," Bluestone says, "but then strange things started to happen."

Bluestone explains that Jayne's personality shifted. "She became more uninhibited—nothing too out there—but, for example, it was thirty nine degrees outside and she was walking around school without her shoes on. I said, 'Jayne, where are your shoes?' And she said, 'I just didn't feel like wearing any.'" Jayne also developed muscle spasms and experienced agitation. Bluestone says Jayne compared the feeling with having drunk a lot of caffeine, except it took a really long time for the feeling to wear off. When it did wear off, Bluestone says, Jayne "completely crashed." She would be chatting and chatting and then she would be asleep on the couch.

"What worried me was that Jayne saw positive side-effects," says Bluestone.

"I got really fast in Math and Spanish. I could never come up with the answers that fast before," says Jayne. "It was like I was more smart."

"Parents are warned about the risks of increased potential for self harm among adolescents taking antidepressants."

Jayne says she was able to stand up in front of a crowd and speak more comfortably. "It was as if my personality had changed, and I liked it, that I could have an easier time in school, and with people," Jayne says. "But the change didn't come from inside. It came from the outside, from the pills."

Jayne's mother adds her discomfort with the fact that Jayne began valuing the drug for the unexpected benefits. "I don't want Jayne to see Prozac as a performance-enhancing drug," Bluestone says. She admits, as a mother, she had to consider, also, whether she was "sending Jayne this message that the answer to the emotional rough spots in life might be found in a pill bottle."

Jayne does consider the possibility that the placebo effect kicked in a bit, that she may have believed the drug was having the effects when perhaps it was not. "But then I started twitching. My leg would jerk. I couldn't sit still."

The cautions that came with Jayne's prescription for Fluoxetine (Prozac) capsules say: "If you are experienc[ing] anxiety, agitation, . . . impulsive feelings, severe restlessness . . . contact your doctor as soon as possible." When Bluestone reported Jayne's agitation and other symptoms, their psychiatrist told them to discontinue the drug immediately. Parents of children who are prescribed Prozac are cautioned to monitor them carefully for changes in behavior—especially deepening depression. "We stopped the drug quickly," says Melissa Bluestone. "I shiver when I think of what might have happened had we doubled Jayne's dose as we were supposed to the following week."

"I can only imagine that twitchy feeling magnified," says Jayne.

After Prozac was approved for use in children and adolescents in 2003, the suicide rate rose among ten- [to] twenty-four-year-olds by 8 percent in 2004, the largest single year rise in fifteen years, according to the Centers for Disease Control and Prevention's (CDC) Morbidity and Mortality Weekly Report. Significantly, the spike followed a decline in the suicide rate of 28 percent ("CDC Report Shows Largest One-Year Increase in Suicide Rates in fifteen Years"). Many studies conducted since then have been unable to connect the prescribed antidepressants to what appeared to be a trend in suicide among teens. Some are suspicious about the lack of attention to the dangers in the U.S., pointing to the U.K., where much more is published about

the downside of antidepressants for children. Drug companies in the U.S. do promote the off-label use of psychiatric drugs in children and do not often reveal negative outcomes of studies. In 2004, the New York State Attorney General's Office filed a lawsuit against GlaxoSmithKline, complaining that the pharmaceutical company withheld four studies on the use of Paxil, an antidepressant, because of negative results (Harris).

As much as the drugs are prescribed by medical practitioners, the use of antidepressants has vocal detractors who emphasize what they see as the lack of a balanced view on the controversy. "We've seen that the effectiveness of antidepressants has been way overstated," said Daniel Buccino, a founder and director of the Baltimore Psychotherapy Institute who is on the clinical faculty of the Johns Hopkins University School of Medicine. "Some of the suicidal side effects, as well as agitation and withdrawal effects, have been underreported."

Stephen Peterson's mother and father continue to question his taking antidepressants. "All medication has risks," Geena Peterson says, "but when you're talking about something that you can't measure—you can't do a blood test and find out if your depression is any better—you are really just dealing with your instincts." Geena is currently looking for a good Cognitive Behavior Therapist to augment Stephen's drug therapy—a therapist who will keep Stephen talking about his feelings and strategizing coping mechanisms when he starts to get depressed. "I hope at some point his inner strength will take over," she says. "I don't want to think we've just gotten a lifetime prescription for antidepressants."

WORKS CITED

"Antidepressants Potentially Misused in Treating Adolescents, Stanford Study Finds." 16 Nov. 2005. *Science Daily.* Web. 20 March 2008.

Bluestone, Jayne. Personal interview. 20 March 2008.

Bluestone, Melissa. Personal interview. 20 March 2008.

Buccino, Daniel. Message to the author. 20 March 2008. E-mail.

"CDC Report Shows Largest One-Year Increase in Youth Suicide Rate in Fifteen Years." Press Release. 6 Sept. 2007. Web. April 8, 2008.

Harris, Gardiner. "Spitzer Sues a Drug Maker, Saying It Hid Negative Data." *New York Times* 3 June 2004. Web. 8 April 2008.

Kapalka, George. Message to the author. 21 March 2008. E-mail.

Lin, Loreen. Personal interview. 22 March 2008.

National Center for Health Statistics Fast Stats A to Z. "Therapeutic Drug Use." Web. 8 April 2008.

National Institute for Mental Health. "Depression in Children and Adolescents: A Fact Sheet for Physicians." Web. 8 April 2008.

Perrin, Mark. Message to the author. 19 March 2008. E-mail.

Peterson, Geena. Personal interview. 20 March 2008.

Peterson, Mark. Personal interview. 20 March 2008.

Peterson, Stephen. Personal interview. 20 March 2008.

Wilde, Peter. Personal interview. 22 March 2008.

QUESTIONS FOR RHETORICAL ANALYSIS

1. **CONSIDERING THE RHETORICAL SITUATION:** How does the writer convince the reader that the prescribing of antidepressants for teens is a trend? Does the writer prove that the trend affects enough people to make the reader think the article is worthwhile?
2. How does the writer establish herself as a reliable source for information?
3. What are the causes of the trend?
4. What are the effects?
5. How do the first-person accounts fill out your understanding of the trend? What do the secondary sources add to the piece?
6. Comment on the ending of the research article. Has the author reached a conclusion about whether the trend is positive or negative?

QUESTIONS FOR WRITING AND DISCUSSION

1. Which ads for prescription drugs to treat depression have you seen in magazines and newspapers and online? Which television commercials for those drugs can you remember seeing? What is your impression of drug therapy as a treatment for depression in general? Have the ads influenced your opinion?
2. Does the author's writing about this topic—using prescribed antidepressants for teens battling depression—serve the public?

STYLE PRACTICE: IMITATION

Write the opening for a story about a pattern you have observed at your college. Use one person as the focus for the opening so we can observe the trend in practice and hear some quotations that will make the ideas specific and personal.

For Japanese Women, the Past Is the Latest Fad[4]

Anthony Kuhn

This piece was written to be delivered via "spoken word," as a segment of cultural news broadcast on a radio show. See if you can detect any stylistic choices the writer might have made to tailor the piece for "listeners" as opposed to "readers."

NPR April 13, 2010

IN JAPAN, the number of female visitors to shogun castles, samurai battle re-enactments and history bookstores has recently increased. Observers attribute this to the rise of the "history girls"—a new urban subculture that some believe signals a kind of empowerment for female Japanese hobbyists.

One of the more public faces of the history girls, or reki-jo, is a fashion model named Anne. She's the daughter of actor Ken Watanabe, and she goes by one name. She's carved out a niche for herself writing and speaking about history and history buffs.

Reki-jo all have their favorite historical periods and characters. Speaking in a Tokyo cafe, Anne says hers is the Shinsengumi, the elite swordsmen of Japan's last shogun, or military ruler.

"The Shinsengumi is popular among Japanese girls because its members are all young, in their teens to early 30s," Anne says. "They changed Japan. The interesting part of their era is that we can see some photos of them, so we can imagine them better and feel closer to them. This history gives courage to young people today."

"The reki-jo idolize these historical figures like rock stars."

In TV dramas, the Shinsengumi are all played by popular, young male actors.

The reki-jo idolize these historical figures like rock stars.

PART OF THE NERDY COMIC BOOK SUBCULTURE

Ryo Watanabe (no relation to Anne) is one of the media and marketing entrepreneurs who has helped build the reki-jo phenomenon. He created music, a Web site, TV shows and a bar where they can congregate. Watanabe says that history girls populate both virtual and actual worlds.

"The virtual ones just play games and follow individual characters," Watanabe says. "The real ones start with games, but they also do research, read books and visit historical sites. These are the real history girls."

Anthropologists who study such things say that the reki-jo are actually a kind of otaku, a nerdy sort of fan of Japanese comic books and video games.

Otaku nerds build identities for their favorite characters—choosing, for example, kimonos, hairstyles and weapon—and give their characters attributes: three points for strength and four for charisma.

Patrick Galbraith, a doctoral student at the University of Tokyo and author of The Otaku Encyclopedia, says that the history girls signal the rise of the female otaku. And what do male otaku do?

"They're really kind of focusing on what types of women they're interested in, and they create this kind of fantasy discourse about the female, and they consume these fetishized fantasy images," Galbraith says. "And women also have been doing this for a very long time, but it's always been below the surface."

A WAY TO CONNECT

People in Japan increasingly define themselves through the media they consume rather than work, family or school ties. Of course, this is true elsewhere, but Galbraith says the 1990s decline of Japanese corporate culture has pushed the country's hobby culture into the mainstream.

"And so now we are seeing more and more people who are making connections through consumption, through shared media, through shared patterns of social existence," Galbraith says. "And maybe reki-jo is one example of that, because really they are, I think, people who share an interest, but almost nothing else."

On a Wednesday night, the reki-jo head down to Ryo Watanabe's bar to talk about warlords, sieges and assassins. In her metal-studded leather attire, Miyuki Miyamoto is

dressed more for a mosh pit than a history seminar. And she's proud of it.

"I like to be called a reki-jo," Miyamoto says. "Ten years ago, I had a negative image as a serious, isolated girl who likes history but has few friends. Now I feel more recognized as one of a group."

Observers say that even in the 19th-century Edo era, Japanese grouped around pop culture experiences as a way of coping with the anonymity and solitude of urban life. Their point: The otaku culture's roots run deep in Japan, and perhaps there's a little otaku in all of us.

QUESTIONS FOR RHETORICAL ANALYSIS

1. **CONSIDERING THE RHETORICAL SITUATION:** Who would be drawn to reading about this topic?
2. This piece was written first, for broadcast on the radio. Can you tell by reading it? How would a listener have different needs than a reader?
3. How will the reader respond to the use of "nerdy"? Is it a risk the writer is taking?

QUESTIONS FOR WRITING AND DISCUSSION

1. The author states that people in Japan often define themselves by the media they consume rather than work. Is this true in most cultures? Why or why not?
2. In some ways, this article is a kind of response to the "bowling alone" syndrome, with people bonding into communities around shared media. Miyamoto even says she is more comfortable, socially, now that she is part of a group. Can you see other evidence that people are interested in forming communities, connecting with other people?

STYLE PRACTICE: IMITATION

Introduce readers to a trend you have observed at your school. Start by describing a "practitioner" in action.

Growing Up Digital, Wired for Distraction[5]

Matt Richtel

From the title you can detect the author's conclusion about the effects of growing up exposed to digital technology, but read carefully to see whether this "distraction" is necessarily a negative outcome of this exposure.

November 21, 2010

REDWOOD CITY, Calif.—On the eve of a pivotal academic year in Vishal Singh's life, he faces a stark choice on his bedroom desk: book or computer?

By all rights, Vishal, a bright 17-year-old, should already have finished the book, Kurt Vonnegut's "Cat's Cradle," his summer reading

[5]From MATT RICHTEL, "Growing Up Digital, Wired for Distraction," from The New York Times. Reprinted by permission of PARS International.

assignment. But he has managed 43 pages in two months.

He typically favors Facebook, YouTube and making digital videos. That is the case this August afternoon. Bypassing Vonnegut, he clicks over to YouTube, meaning that tomorrow he will enter his senior year of high school hoping to see an improvement in his grades, but without having completed his only summer homework.

On YouTube, "you can get a whole story in six minutes," he explains. "A book takes so long. I prefer the immediate gratification."

Students have always faced distractions and time-wasters. But computers and cellphones, and the constant stream of stimuli they offer, pose a profound new challenge to focusing and learning.

Researchers say the lure of these technologies, while it affects adults too, is particularly powerful for young people. The risk, they say, is that developing brains can become more easily habituated than adult brains to constantly switching tasks—and less able to sustain attention.

"The worry is we're raising a generation of kids in front of screens whose brains are going to be wired differently."

"Their brains are rewarded not for staying on task but for jumping to the next thing," said Michael Rich, an associate professor at Harvard Medical School and executive director of the Center on Media and Child Health in Boston. And the effects could linger: "The worry is we're raising a generation of kids in front of screens whose brains are going to be wired differently."

But even as some parents and educators express unease about students' digital diets, they are intensifying efforts to use technology in the classroom, seeing it as a way to connect with students and give them essential skills. Across the country, schools are equipping themselves with computers, Internet access and mobile devices so they can teach on the students' technological territory.

It is a tension on vivid display at Vishal's school, Woodside High School, on a sprawling campus set against the forested hills of Silicon Valley. Here, as elsewhere, it is not uncommon for students to send hundreds of text messages a day or spend hours playing video games, and virtually everyone is on Facebook.

The principal, David Reilly, 37, a former musician who says he sympathizes when young people feel disenfranchised, is determined to engage these 21st-century students. He has asked teachers to build Web sites to communicate with students, introduced popular classes on using digital tools to record music, secured funding for iPads to teach Mandarin and obtained $3 million in grants for a multimedia center.

He pushed first period back an hour, to 9 a.m., because students were showing up bleary-eyed, at least in part because they were up late on their computers. Unchecked use of digital devices, he says, can create a culture in which students are addicted to the virtual world and lost in it.

"I am trying to take back their attention from their BlackBerrys and video games," he says. "To a degree, I'm using technology to do it."

The same tension surfaces in Vishal, whose ability to be distracted by computers is rivaled by his proficiency with them. At the beginning of his junior year, he discovered a passion for filmmaking and made a name for himself among friends and teachers with his storytelling in videos made with digital cameras and editing software.

He acts as his family's tech-support expert, helping his father, Satendra, a lab manager, retrieve lost documents on the computer,

and his mother, Indra, a security manager at the San Francisco airport, build her own Web site.

But he also plays video games 10 hours a week. He regularly sends Facebook status updates at 2 a.m., even on school nights, and has such a reputation for distributing links to videos that his best friend calls him a "YouTube bully."

Several teachers call Vishal one of their brightest students, and they wonder why things are not adding up. Last semester, his grade point average was 2.3 after a D-plus in English and an F in Algebra II. He got an A in film critique.

"He's a kid caught between two worlds," said Mr. Reilly—one that is virtual and one with real-life demands.

Vishal, like his mother, says he lacks the self-control to favor schoolwork over the computer. She sat him down a few weeks before school started and told him that, while she respected his passion for film and his technical skills, he had to use them productively.

"This is the year," she says she told him. "This is your senior year and you can't afford not to focus."

It was not always this way. As a child, Vishal had a tendency to procrastinate, but nothing like this. Something changed him.

GROWING UP WITH GADGETS

When he was 3, Vishal moved with his parents and older brother to their current home, a three-bedroom house in the working-class section of Redwood City, a suburb in Silicon Valley that is more diverse than some of its elite neighbors.

Thin and quiet with a shy smile, Vishal passed the admissions test for a prestigious public elementary and middle school. Until sixth grade, he focused on homework, regularly going to the house of a good friend to study with him.

But Vishal and his family say two things changed around the seventh grade: his mother went back to work, and he got a computer. He became increasingly engrossed in games and surfing the Internet, finding an easy outlet for what he describes as an inclination to procrastinate.

"I realized there were choices," Vishal recalls. "Homework wasn't the only option."

"As a child, Vishal had a tendency to procrastinate, but nothing like this. Something changed him."

Several recent studies show that young people tend to use home computers for entertainment, not learning, and that this can hurt school performance, particularly in low-income families. Jacob L. Vigdor, an economics professor at Duke University who led some of the research, said that when adults were not supervising computer use, children "are left to their own devices, and the impetus isn't to do homework but play around."

Research also shows that students often juggle homework and entertainment. The Kaiser Family Foundation found earlier this year that half of students from 8 to 18 are using the Internet, watching TV or using some other form of media either "most" (31 percent) or "some" (25 percent) of the time that they are doing homework.

At Woodside, as elsewhere, students' use of technology is not uniform. Mr. Reilly, the principal, says their choices tend to reflect their personalities. Social butterflies tend to be heavy texters and Facebook users. Students who are

less social might escape into games, while drifters or those prone to procrastination, like Vishal, might surf the Web or watch videos.

The technology has created on campuses a new set of social types—not the thespian and the jock but the texter and gamer, Facebook addict and YouTube potato.

"The technology amplifies whoever you are," Mr. Reilly says.

For some, the amplification is intense. Allison Miller, 14, sends and receives 27,000 texts in a month, her fingers clicking at a blistering pace as she carries on as many as seven text conversations at a time. She texts between classes, at the moment soccer practice ends, while being driven to and from school and, often, while studying.

Most of the exchanges are little more than quick greetings, but they can get more in-depth, like "if someone tells you about a drama going on with someone," Allison said. "I can text one person while talking on the phone to someone else."

"She blames multitasking for the three B's on her recent progress report."

But this proficiency comes at a cost: she blames multitasking for the three B's on her recent progress report.

"I'll be reading a book for homework and I'll get a text message and pause my reading and put down the book, pick up the phone to reply to the text message, and then 20 minutes later realize, 'Oh, I forgot to do my homework.' "

Some shyer students do not socialize through technology—they recede into it. Ramon Ochoa-Lopez, 14, an introvert, plays six hours of video games on weekdays and more on weekends, leaving homework to be done in the bathroom before school.

Escaping into games can also salve teenagers' age-old desire for some control in their chaotic lives. "It's a way for me to separate myself," Ramon says. "If there's an argument between my mom and one of my brothers, I'll just go to my room and start playing video games and escape."

With powerful new cellphones, the interactive experience can go everywhere. Between classes at Woodside or at lunch, when use of personal devices is permitted, students gather in clusters, sometimes chatting face to face, sometimes half-involved in a conversation while texting someone across the teeming quad. Others sit alone, watching a video, listening to music or updating Facebook.

Students say that their parents, worried about the distractions, try to police computer time, but that monitoring the use of cellphones is difficult. Parents may also want to be able to call their children at any time, so taking the phone away is not always an option.

Other parents wholly embrace computer use, even when it has no obvious educational benefit.

"If you're not on top of technology, you're not going to be on top of the world," said John McMullen, 56, a retired criminal investigator whose son, Sean, is one of five friends in the group Vishal joins for lunch each day.

Sean's favorite medium is video games; he plays for four hours after school and twice that on weekends. He was playing more but found his habit pulling his grade point average below 3.2, the point at which he felt comfortable. He says he sometimes wishes that his parents would force him to quit playing and study, because he finds it hard to quit when given the choice. Still, he says, video games are not responsible for his lack of focus, asserting that in another era he would have been distracted by TV or something else.

"Video games don't make the hole; they fill it," says Sean, sitting at a picnic table in

the quad, where he is surrounded by a multimillion-dollar view: on the nearby hills are the evergreens that tower above the affluent neighborhoods populated by Internet tycoons. Sean, a senior, concedes that video games take a physical toll: "I haven't done exercise since my sophomore year. But that doesn't seem like a big deal. I still look the same."

Sam Crocker, Vishal's closest friend, who has straight A's but lower SAT scores than he would like, blames the Internet's distractions for his inability to finish either of his two summer reading books.

"I know I can read a book, but then I'm up and checking Facebook," he says, adding: "Facebook is amazing because it feels like you're doing something and you're not doing anything. It's the absence of doing something, but you feel gratified anyway."

He concludes: "My attention span is getting worse."

"Downtime is to the brain what sleep is to the body," said Dr. Rich of Harvard Medical School. "But kids are in a constant mode of stimulation."

THE LURE OF DISTRACTION

Some neuroscientists have been studying people like Sam and Vishal. They have begun to understand what happens to the brains of young people who are constantly online and in touch.

In an experiment at the German Sport University in Cologne in 2007, boys from 12 to 14 spent an hour each night playing video games after they finished homework.

On alternate nights, the boys spent an hour watching an exciting movie, like "Harry Potter" or "Star Trek," rather than playing video games. That allowed the researchers to compare the effect of video games and TV.

The researchers looked at how the use of these media affected the boys' brainwave patterns while sleeping and their ability to remember their homework in the subsequent days. They found that playing video games led to markedly lower sleep quality than watching TV, and also led to a "significant decline" in the boys' ability to remember vocabulary words. The findings were published in the journal Pediatrics.

Markus Dworak, a researcher who led the study and is now a neuroscientist at Harvard, said it was not clear whether the boys' learning suffered because sleep was disrupted or, as he speculates, also because the intensity of the game experience overrode the brain's recording of the vocabulary.

"When you look at vocabulary and look at huge stimulus after that, your brain has to decide which information to store," he said. "Your brain might favor the emotionally stimulating information over the vocabulary."

At the University of California, San Francisco, scientists have found that when rats have a new experience, like exploring an unfamiliar area, their brains show new patterns of activity. But only when the rats take a break from their exploration do they process those patterns in a way that seems to create a persistent memory.

In that vein, recent imaging studies of people have found that major cross sections of the brain become surprisingly active during downtime. These brain studies suggest to researchers that periods of rest are critical in allowing the brain to synthesize information, make connections between ideas and even develop the sense of self.

Researchers say these studies have particular implications for young people, whose brains have more trouble focusing and setting priorities.

"Downtime is to the brain what sleep is to the body," said Dr. Rich of Harvard Medical School. "But kids are in a constant mode of stimulation."

"The headline is: bring back boredom," added Dr. Rich, who last month gave a speech to the American Academy of Pediatrics entitled, "Finding Huck Finn: Reclaiming Childhood from the River of Electronic Screens."

Dr. Rich said in an interview that he was not suggesting young people should toss out their devices, but rather that they embrace a more balanced approach to what he said were powerful tools necessary to compete and succeed in modern life.

The heavy use of devices also worries Daniel Anderson, a professor of psychology at the University of Massachusetts at Amherst, who is known for research showing that children are not as harmed by TV viewing as some researchers have suggested.

Multitasking using ubiquitous, interactive and highly stimulating computers and phones, Professor Anderson says, appears to have a more powerful effect than TV.

Like Dr. Rich, he says he believes that young, developing brains are becoming habituated to distraction and to switching tasks, not to focus.

"If you've grown up processing multiple media, that's exactly the mode you're going to fall into when put in that environment—you develop a need for that stimulation," he said.

Vishal can attest to that.

"I'm doing Facebook, YouTube, having a conversation or two with a friend, listening to music at the same time. I'm doing a million things at once, like a lot of people my age," he says. "Sometimes I'll say: I need to stop this and do my schoolwork, but I can't."

"If it weren't for the Internet, I'd focus more on school and be doing better academically," he says. But thanks to the Internet, he says, he has discovered and pursued his passion: filmmaking. Without the Internet, "I also wouldn't know what I want to do with my life."

CLICKING TOWARD A FUTURE

The woman sits in a cemetery at dusk, sobbing. Behind her, silhouetted and translucent, a man kneels, then fades away, a ghost.

This captivating image appears on Vishal's computer screen. On this Thursday afternoon in late September, he is engrossed in scenes he shot the previous weekend for a music video he is making with his cousin.

The video is based on a song performed by the band Guns N' Roses about a woman whose boyfriend dies. He wants it to be part of the package of work he submits to colleges that emphasize film study, along with a documentary he is making about home-schooled students.

Now comes the editing. Vishal taught himself to use sophisticated editing software in part by watching tutorials on YouTube. He does not leave his chair for more than two hours, sipping Pepsi, his face often inches from the screen, as he perfects the clip from the cemetery. The image of the crying woman was shot separately from the image of the kneeling man, and he is trying to fuse them.

"I'm spending two hours to get a few seconds just right," he says.

He occasionally sends a text message or checks Facebook, but he is focused in a way he rarely is when doing homework. He says the chief difference is that filmmaking feels applicable to his chosen future, and he hopes colleges, like the University of Southern California or the California Institute of the Arts in Los Angeles, will be so impressed by

his portfolio that they will overlook his school performance.

"This is going to compensate for the grades," he says. On this day, his homework includes a worksheet for Latin, some reading for English class and an economics essay, but they can wait.

interactivity. As he edits, the windows on the screen come alive; every few seconds, he clicks the mouse to make tiny changes to the lighting and flow of the images, and the software gives him constant feedback.

"I click and something happens," he says, explaining that, by comparison, reading a book or doing homework is less exciting. "I guess it goes back to the immediate gratification thing."

The $2,000 computer Vishal is using is state of the art and only a week old. It represents a concession by his parents. They allowed him to buy it, despite their continuing concerns about his technology habits, because they wanted to support his filmmaking dream. "If we put roadblocks in his way, he's just going to get depressed," his mother says. Besides, she adds, "he's been making an effort to do his homework."

"This is going to compensate for the grades," he says.

At this point in the semester, it seems she is right. The first schoolwide progress reports come out in late September, and Vishal has mostly A's and B's. He says he has been able to make headway by applying himself, but also by cutting back his workload. Unlike last year, he is not taking advanced placement classes, and he has chosen to retake Algebra II not in the classroom but in an online class that lets him work at his own pace.

His shift to easier classes might not please college admissions officers, according to Woodside's college adviser, Zorina Matavulj. She says they want seniors to intensify their efforts. As it is, she says, even if Vishal improves his performance significantly, someone with his grades faces long odds in applying to the kinds of colleges he aspires to.

Still, Vishal's passion for film reinforces for Mr. Reilly, the principal, that the way to reach these students is on their own terms.

HANDS-ON TECHNOLOGY

Big Macintosh monitors sit on every desk, and a man with hip glasses and an easygoing style stands at the front of the class. He is Geoff Diesel, 40, a favorite teacher here at Woodside who has taught English and film. Now he teaches one of Mr. Reilly's new classes, audio production. He has a rapt audience of more than 20 students as he shows a video of the band Nirvana mixing their music, then holds up a music keyboard.

"Who knows how to use Pro Tools? We've got it. It's the program used by the best music studios in the world," he says.

In the back of the room, Mr. Reilly watches, thrilled. He introduced the audio course last year and enough students signed up to fill four classes. (He could barely pull together one class when he introduced Mandarin, even though he had secured iPads to help teach the language.)

"Some of these students are our most at-risk kids," he says. He means that they are more likely to tune out school, skip class or not do their homework, and that they may not get healthful meals at home. They may also do their most enthusiastic writing not for class but in text messages and on Facebook. "They're here, they're in class, they're listening."

Despite Woodside High's affluent setting, about 40 percent of its 1,800 students come

from low-income families and receive a reduced-cost or free lunch. The school is 56 percent Latino, 38 percent white and 5 percent African-American, and it sends 93 percent of its students to four-year or community colleges.

Mr. Reilly says that the audio class provides solid vocational training and can get students interested in other subjects.

"Today mixing music, tomorrow sound waves and physics," he says. And he thinks the key is that they love not just the music but getting their hands on the technology. "We're meeting them on their turf."

It does not mean he sees technology as a panacea. "I'll always take one great teacher in a cave over a dozen Smart Boards," he says, referring to the high-tech teaching displays used in many schools.

"His advanced classes have one-third as many students as they had a decade ago."

Teachers at Woodside commonly blame technology for students' struggles to concentrate, but they are divided over whether embracing computers is the right solution.

"It's a catastrophe," said Alan Eaton, a charismatic Latin teacher. He says that technology has led to a "balkanization of their focus and duration of stamina," and that schools make the problem worse when they adopt the technology.

"When rock 'n' roll came about, we didn't start using it in classrooms like we're doing with technology," he says. He personally feels the sting, since his advanced classes have one-third as many students as they had a decade ago.

Vishal remains a Latin student, one whom Mr. Eaton describes as particularly bright. But the teacher wonders if technology might be the reason Vishal seems to lose interest in academics the minute he leaves class.

Mr. Diesel, by contrast, does not think technology is behind the problems of Vishal and his schoolmates—in fact, he thinks it is the key to connecting with them, and an essential tool. "It's in their DNA to look at screens," he asserts. And he offers another analogy to explain his approach: "Frankenstein is in the room and I don't want him to tear me apart. If I'm not using technology, I lose them completely."

Mr. Diesel had Vishal as a student in cinema class and describes him as a "breath of fresh air" with a gift for filmmaking. Mr. Diesel says he wonders if Vishal is a bit like Woody Allen, talented but not interested in being part of the system.

But Mr. Diesel adds: "If Vishal's going to be an independent filmmaker, he's got to read Vonnegut. If you're going to write scripts, you've got to read."

BACK TO READING ALOUD

Vishal sits near the back of English IV. Marcia Blondel, a veteran teacher, asks the students to open the book they are studying, "The Things They Carried," which is about the Vietnam War.

"Who wants to read starting in the middle of page 137?" she asks. One student begins to read aloud, and the rest follow along.

To Ms. Blondel, the exercise in group reading represents a regression in American education and an indictment of technology. The reason she has to do it, she says, is that students now lack the attention span to read the assignments on their own.

"How can you have a discussion in class?" she complains, arguing that she has seen a considerable change in recent years. In some classes she can count on little more than one-third

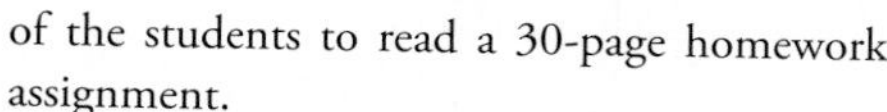

of the students to read a 30-page homework assignment.

She adds: "You can't become a good writer by watching YouTube, texting and e-mailing a bunch of abbreviations."

As the group-reading effort winds down, she says gently: "I hope this will motivate you to read on your own."

It is a reminder of the choices that have followed the students through the semester: computer or homework? Immediate gratification or investing in the future?

Mr. Reilly hopes that the two can meet—that computers can be combined with education to better engage students and can give them technical skills without compromising deep analytical thought.

But in Vishal's case, computers and schoolwork seem more and more to be mutually exclusive. Ms. Blondel says that Vishal, after a decent start to the school year, has fallen into bad habits. In October, he turned in weeks late, for example, a short essay based on the first few chapters of "The Things They Carried." His grade at that point, she says, tracks around a D.

For his part, Vishal says he is investing himself more in his filmmaking, accelerating work with his cousin on their music video project. But he is also using Facebook late at night and surfing for videos on YouTube. The evidence of the shift comes in a string of Facebook updates.

Saturday, 11:55 p.m.: "Editing, editing, editing"

Sunday, 3:55 p.m.: "8+ hours of shooting, 8+ hours of editing. All for just a three-minute scene. Mind = Dead."

Sunday, 11:00 p.m.: "Fun day, finally got to spend a day relaxing . . . now about that homework . . ."

QUESTIONS FOR RHETORICAL ANALYSIS

1. **CONSIDERING THE RHETORICAL SITUATION:** As a reader, what do you think of having the writer show you this whole issue through the lens of just one person, for instance, Vishal?
2. Is the writer objective, or has he made a decision about how technology is affecting young people?
3. Does the writer seem sympathetic toward Vishal?
4. How does the writer incorporate sources who have never met Vishal?

QUESTIONS FOR WRITING AND DISCUSSION

1. Do you think this article fairly reveals the typical student who is engaged in the digital world?
2. Does the article provide you with a full picture of Vishal or do you sense some things are missing? Does the author seem to withhold some details? Why or why not?
3. Does location have something to do with the kind of involvement this school has with technology, or does region not matter?

STYLE PRACTICE: IMITATION

Find a person who represents a trend (as Vishal does) and write a scene where the person is described in the process of doing something that shows the trend in action.

WRITING AND REVISION STRATEGIES

Gathered here are three interactive sections for you to use as you write and revise your trend research article.

- Writer's Notebook Suggestions
- Peer Review Log
- Revision Checklist

WRITER'S NOTEBOOK SUGGESTIONS

You can use these exercises to do some startup thinking and writing for your trend research article.

1. Go to a shopping center and choose a store. Interview sales staff about some new development in the store: a new product or style. Write one paragraph about your findings, incorporating quotations and statistics you have gathered.

2. Observe a high-traffic area for an hour, noting patterns in behavior. Choose one of the following behaviors, or identify your own.

   - The way people interact with ATMs
   - The way people behave on public transportation
   - The way people cross a busy intersection

   Write a generalization about behavior within the context. What can you say, in general, about people who ride the bus? Or about the way people behave when using an ATM?

3. Research the nutritional data from a fast-food restaurant. Write a paragraph for an average reader that clearly explains how much fat, sugar, and salt are in the most popular items. Use analogies to help make the facts clear.

4. Survey a group of college students. Ask how many hours they spend watching television or films on their computers. Ask how many of those hours are spent watching programming with others and how many are spent watching alone. Make a chart or graph to show your findings.

5. Do a survey in your writing class. How much time do students spend writing the average paper, how many drafts, etc. Find out whether each student's practice has changed since high school. Speculate why.

6. Describe a person who illustrates a trend.

7. Find out what are the most popular foods at your college dining hall, cafeteria, or coffee shop. Try one, and then describe the taste and texture. Interview people who have eaten the food (or cooked or served it), and collect quotations. Write a description of the food, incorporating the quotations.

8. Identify a trend at your school or in your community. The following are some examples:

   - Have you found that more (or fewer) of your friends are interested in food-service careers?
   - Do you find more interracial or cross-religion dating than there was previously?
   - Are there more smokers on your campus these days?

   Do at least three person-on-the-street interviews, finding out what people think are the causes and/or effects of the trend.

   Be sure to get names, approximate or accurate ages, occupations, and places of residence for all the people you interview. Try to get a mix of gender, age, and ethnicity, if possible. After you complete your interviews, write a page on your findings, integrating the quotations as you discuss possible causes and effects of the trend. Be sure to attribute quotations accurately and completely. For example: "Rebecca Wong, an eighteen-year-old freshman at Central College, says, 'Dating a guy on my floor would be like dating my brother.'"

PEER REVIEW LOG

As you work with a writing partner or in a peer review group, you can use these questions to give useful responses to a classmate's trend research piece or as a guide for discussion.

Writer's Name: ____

Date: ____

1. Underline the introduction. Did the introduction get your attention? Why? What might make it stronger?
2. Put two lines under the thesis. Does the topic seem noteworthy or interesting to you?
3. Put a star next to the area where the writer provides proof that the trend exists.
4. Note causes in the margins. Note effects in the margins.
5. Number the sources you find.
6. Put a wavy line under transitions, and identify any areas that need transitions with a *T.*
7. Does the writer explain the causes and/or effects well? Do you see the logic in the argument?
8. Can you think of anything else that the writer might add? More quotations from practitioners or experts? More facts or statistics?
9. Is all research well cited within the text? Do you wonder about the source of any facts or statistics? Note any place where the research needs a source or an attribution.
10. Bracket the conclusion. Does the writer end strongly?

REVISION CHECKLIST

As you do your final revision, check to make sure that you

- Wrote an engaging introduction
- Stated your thesis clearly and accurately
- Provided proof that the trend exists
- Provided an explanation of causes and/or effects
- Cited sources accurately and fully
- Used good transitions to show new aspects of your analysis
- Included a good ending that leaves the reader with a lasting impression

PART V

Writing to Argue

Luba Lukova

Ankush Trakru "Lord Q"

12 Writing An Argument

EDITORIALS, COMMENTARIES, AND BLOGS

An effective editorial has two ingredients... a position and a passion.

—Richard Aregood

In fall 2003, the Recording Industry Association of America (RIAA) brought lawsuits against 261 people, including a 12-year-old, for what some people called sharing music on the Internet and others called piracy. Since that time, illegal downloading of music has become a hot-button issue on college campuses, among recording artists, in the mainstream media and alternative press, and on thousands of blogs.

All over the country people reacted strongly to the initial lawsuits, some by writing letters to the editors of newspapers. Newspapers ran editorials on the issue of file sharing, and soon bloggers entered the debate.

File sharing and the RIAA's lawsuits prompted a national conversation about ethics, intellectual property rights, living in a digital age, corporate greed, and parental guidance.

When you take your argument to a public forum, you become a voice in the public debate of an issue. If you choose an issue worth arguing, you will no doubt find many avenues to explore and an audience ready to listen, to applaud, or to counter your claims.

WHAT'S TO COME

PROCESS PLAN

PROCESS PLAN

PREPARE

- Read newspapers and blogs to detect current issues, controversies, and public debates, and focus on an issue.
- Define the interest groups. Who has something to lose or gain in regard to the issue?
- Research the history of the issue, its origin, recent developments.
- Decide on a position and identify how you will enter the debate—how to promote your view through publication on blogs, letters to the editor, etc.

DRAFT

- Introduction
  - Find an illustration, statistic, or story that hooks your readers' interest.
  - State the issue and your position in a clear thesis.
- Body
  - Provide reasons to back up your position.
  - Include a refutation that addresses a reasonable aspect of the opponents' argument.
- Conclusion: End with a restatement of the position.

REVISE

- Check your word choice and tone, making sure your writing appears to be reasonable and authoritative.
- Consider whether your argument has a logical flow, using transitions.

UNDERSTANDING THE WRITING PROJECT

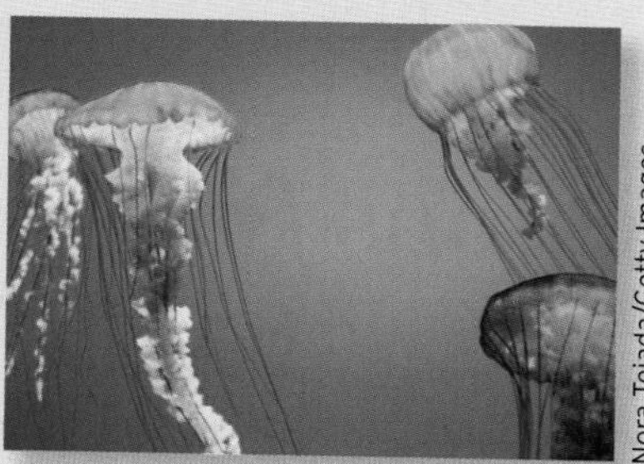
Nora Tejada/Getty Images

AN ARGUMENT is not a fight—at least not in the rhetorical realm, where your purpose is to use language well and persuasively. Convincing someone of your position on a controversial topic is an art form, and it requires strategy and solid information.

In college, you will be called on often to illustrate your understanding of history, government, or social issues by taking a side on an issue. You might be asked to write about welfare reform for a political science class or the impact of genetically modified food on public health for your biology class. When you write your opinion piece, you will need to demonstrate that you understand the issue fully—including all sides, not just the position you are defending. Your argument should include an informed perspective, moving beyond personal preference and into a logical argument based on research—one that relies on facts, illustrations, statistics.

ASSIGNMENT Choose an issue that is current and debatable, one that could be argued from different perspectives. The topic could be relevant at your school, in your town, or even globally. Define your position on the issue, and then find a good opportunity to add to the debate. You can consider writing a letter to the editor of a newspaper, writing a column for a magazine, or a blog for a Web site.

Access an interactive eBook, and chapter-specific interactive learning tools, including flashcards, quizzes, videos and more in your English CourseMate via www.cengagebrain.com.

ANATOMY OF AN ARGUMENT

STEPHEN BUDIANSKY has written 14 books on subjects as diverse as military history, espionage, and science. He blogs at liberalcurmudgeon.com.

Math Lessons for Locavores[1]

STEPHEN BUDIANSKY

the author uses "math" as the organizing structure for his argument

introduction

establishes his credibility

IT'S 42 steps from my back door to the garden that keeps my family supplied nine months of the year with a modest cornucopia of lettuce, beets, spinach, beans, tomatoes, basil, corn, squash, brussels sprouts, the occasional celeriac and, once when I was feeling particularly energetic, a couple of small but undeniable artichokes. You'll get no argument from me about the pleasures and advantages to the palate and the spirit of eating what's local, fresh and in season.

claim

But the local food movement now threatens to devolve into another one of those self-indulgent—and self-defeating—do-gooder dogmas. Arbitrary rules, without any real scientific basis, are repeated as gospel by "locavores," celebrity chefs and mainstream environmental organizations. Words like "sustainability" and "food-miles" are thrown around without any clear understanding of the larger picture of energy and land use.

argumentative thesis: answers "why" or "how."

The result has been all kinds of absurdities. For instance, it is sinful in New York City to buy a tomato grown in a California field because of the energy spent to truck it across the country; it is virtuous to buy one grown in a lavishly heated greenhouse in, say, the Hudson Valley.

refutation of opponents' argument.

reason #1

The statistics brandished by local-food advocates to support such doctrinaire assertions are always selective, usually misleading and often bogus. This is particularly the case with respect to the energy costs of transporting food. One popular and oft-repeated statistic is that it takes 36 (sometimes it's 97) calories of fossil fuel energy to bring one calorie of

[1]Stephen Budiansky, "Math Lessons for Locavores," from The New York Times, August 19, 2010. Reprinted by permission of the author.

iceberg lettuce from California to the East Coast. That's an apples and oranges (or maybe apples and rocks) comparison to begin with, because you can't eat petroleum or burn iceberg lettuce.

It is also an almost complete misrepresentation of reality, as those numbers reflect the entire energy cost of producing lettuce from seed to dinner table, not just transportation. Studies have shown that whether it's grown in California or Maine, or whether it's organic or conventional, about 5,000 calories of energy go into one pound of lettuce. Given how efficient trains and tractor-trailers are, shipping a head of lettuce across the country actually adds next to nothing to the total energy bill.

reason #2

evidence from a study

It takes about a tablespoon of diesel fuel to move one pound of freight 3,000 miles by rail; that works out to about 100 calories of energy. If it goes by truck, it's about 300 calories, still a negligible amount in the overall picture. (For those checking the calculations at home, these are "large calories," or kilocalories, the units used for food value.) Overall, transportation accounts for about 14 percent of the total energy consumed by the American food system.

factual evidence

Other favorite targets of sustainability advocates include the fertilizers and chemicals used in modern farming. But their share of the food system's energy use is even lower, about 8 percent.

factual evidence

The real energy hog, it turns out, is not industrial agriculture at all, but you and me. Home preparation and storage account for 32 percent of all energy use in our food system, the largest component by far.

presentation of writer's argument reason #1

presentation of argument with Reasons

A single 10-mile round trip by car to the grocery store or the farmers' market will easily eat up about 14,000 calories of fossil fuel energy. Just running your refrigerator for a week consumes 9,000 calories of energy. That assumes it's one of the latest high-efficiency models; otherwise, you can double that figure. Cooking and running dishwashers, freezers and second or third refrigerators (more than 25 percent of American households have more than one) all add major hits. Indeed, households make up for 22 percent of all the energy expenditures in the United States.

factual Evidence

continues next page

Agriculture, on the other hand, accounts for just 2 percent of our nation's energy usage; that energy is mainly devoted to running farm machinery and manufacturing fertilizer. In return for that quite modest energy investment, we have fed hundreds of millions of people, liberated tens of millions from backbreaking manual labor and spared hundreds of millions of acres for nature preserves, forests and parks that otherwise would have come under the plow.

writer's argument reason #2

Don't forget the astonishing fact that the total land area of American farms remains almost unchanged from a century ago, at a little under a billion acres, even though those farms now feed three times as many Americans and export more than 10 times as much as they did in 1910.

The best way to make the most of these truly precious resources of land, favorable climates and human labor is to grow lettuce, oranges, wheat, peppers, bananas, whatever, in the places where they grow best and with the most efficient technologies — and then pay the relatively tiny energy cost to get them to market, as we do with every other commodity in the economy. Sometimes that means growing vegetables in your backyard. Sometimes that means buying vegetables grown in California or Costa Rica.

conclusion

examples

Eating locally grown produce is a fine thing in many ways. But it is not an end in itself, nor is it a virtue in itself. The relative pittance of our energy budget that we spend on modern farming is one of the wisest energy investments we can make, when we honestly look at what it returns to our land, our economy, our environment and our well-being.

restates his acknowledgement of opposition's views. Provides ethos.

answer to the question "Why?" or "How?"

"I'm optimistic that the Web and blogs will help the public debate stay ahead of the idiocy."

Q&A with Stephen Budiansky

On Being Reasonable

Q: You have written fourteen books about history, science, and the environment. What sparks you to write? What, for example, was the impetus for giving this math lesson to locavores?

A: H. L. Mencken observed in his diary, "My one purpose in writing I have explained over and over again: it is simply to provide a kind of katharsis for my own thoughts. They worry me until they are set forth in words." That's exactly why I wrote my op-ed on local food: these were ideas that had been eating at me for some time.

Q: Do you add anything extra when you are arguing a stand you know others will examine closely and possibly even disagree with?

A: Absolutely: I always try—especially in an opinion piece—to anticipate objections and address them and acknowledge them. And this isn't just some rhetorical trick of trying to strike a tone of sounding "reasonable": it always greatly strengthens your argument, I think, to acknowledge as much as you can the validity of other viewpoints and to say in effect, "yes, but still . . ." rather than implying that there can be no possible other way of looking at things. You're never going to get people to reverse their opinions about fundamental beliefs. But you can, I think, push people to be a little less doctrinaire and absolute in their opinions, to see the grey areas in things that seemed black and white, and see things a bit more from others' perspectives.

Courtesy Stephen Budiansky

Stephen Budiansky

Q: Do you think you have to embrace a stand 100% to write about it? For example, clearly you see the virtue in the local food movement, and yet you argue against it—you even give ammunition to opponents.

A. You have to have a strong conviction to write with conviction. But that doesn't mean being doctrinaire or ideological or intolerant. I tried to make a very specific point in this piece: namely that many of the supposedly scientific claims advanced by the local food movement are based more on emotion and wishful thinking and belief than on reality. I certainly feel very strongly about the misuse of science, whether it's by environmentalists or ad men or quacks or anyone else. But that's quite different from saying: eating local food is complete nonsense, or environmentalists are the devil incarnate.

Q: What role do you think blogging about current issues plays in shaping public debate?

A: It is amazing the connections one can forge that would have been impossible or at least very difficult in the pre-Internet era.

THE RHETORICAL SITUATION: APPEALING TO YOUR AUDIENCE

As a writer of an argument, you first have to consider your audience. A good strategy is to assume that your audience is the unconvinced and that your job is to overcome your readers' resistance and persuade them to shift their perspectives or accept new ways of thinking. You cannot do this by making your readers angry or by insulting them. ("Only an idiot would vote for that candidate.") You can, however, argue effectively by appealing to your readers' minds or hearts.

The original Greek terms for argumentative appeals are *logos, pathos*, and *ethos*. Most arguments—whether in debates or in opinion pieces in newspapers, on radio, and on blogs—use these appeals either alone or in some combination.

USE LOGICAL APPEALS TO MAKE A REASONABLE CASE

When you present a logical argument (*logos*), you appeal to the reader's intellect and sense of reason. Using logic, you create a path of evidence for your reader that inevitably leads to your conclusion. To get your reader to follow you from point to point, your argument must be clear and supported by objective evidence: facts and statistics.

For example, an editorial titled "An Obesity Epidemic" asserts that "Overweight children . . . are the victims of an epidemic of childhood obesity in the United States." The writer provides evidence to support this assertion by citing statistics such as "The percentage of overweight young people has increased from 4 percent in 1963 to 15 percent in 1999" ("An Obesity Epidemic," *Boston Globe*, 27 May 2003).

Make sure that your evidence is relevant to your argument and that it directly supports the claim you are making. If the writer of the editorial on the obesity epidemic cited evidence from Sweden or Japan, then that evidence would not be relevant to the claim of an obesity epidemic in the United States. Be sure that your evidence is also accurate. Double-check your sources to make sure that the fact of an increase of overweight children from 4 to 15 percent is from a reputable, impartial source and not from one that was funded by a weight-loss company, for example.

By making a reasoned argument and using relevant and accurate facts and statistics to support your points, you make a logical appeal to convince your readers that your views are valid.

USE EMOTIONAL APPEALS TO CREATE EMPATHY

Because using emotion (*pathos*) to sway opinion has often been done manipulatively, the appeal to emotion has garnered a bad reputation. Sunlit children running through fields of flowers do not make a compelling argument to vote for Candidate X. However, if you use emotion appropriately, especially in combination with a logical

Food with a Face
Food with a Future
Mon. April 20, 6:30pm
in The Mountainview Room, 3rd floor
Keene State College Student Center
Keene State College students Amanda Abramson and Martin Hansen
discuss food choice and the sustainability of the food system.
With a short film edited by KSC film major Erik Breakell.
Part of the Keene Is Reading program inspired by
Michael Pollan's The Omnivore's Dilemma.

All arguments appeal to an audience. An emotional appeal for the "humanity" of locally grown food is made through the "Food with a Face" poster.

appeal, you can speak to readers' hearts as well as their minds, evoking anger at injustice, sadness at tragedy, or outrage at inequity.

Using emotion to support your points involves marshalling subjective evidence, such as opinions, anecdotes, and personal observations. An emotional appeal appears in "Make Chris Take His 'Meds,'" an editorial that supports legislation requiring California courts to take a person's mental illness into consideration before sentencing. To vividly illustrate the plight of mentally ill homeless people, the editorial tells the story of one man.

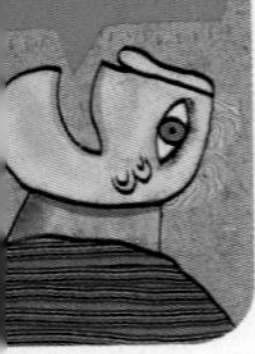

> Meet 22-year-old Chris Hagar, who is now locked up in the Sacramento Mental Health Treatment Center. Since age 15 Hagar has cycled in and out of six jails and mental hospitals, tormented by paranoid schizophrenia. He'd steal food from mom-and-pop grocery stores and promptly get arrested. He'd assault his parents and others. He'd break into a car to escape shadowy stalkers.
>
> —Alex Raskin and Bob Sipchen, "Make Chris Take His 'Meds'"

Even these few details of Chris's life evoke anger at the injustices he has had to face and sadness at the tragedy of his life.

The emotional appeal helps your reader connect with you and connects you with your reader. Emotion can be a way to find common ground and to say that you and your reader share a set of beliefs. In "Make Chris Take His 'Meds,'" the writer assumes the readers will be moved by Chris's story. The common ground is sympathy for a person who suffers from mental illness. In a way, the writer is complimenting the readers, saying, in effect, "We are all caring people who would want to help alleviate suffering in the world."

PRACTICE 12.1

Identifying Logical, Emotional, and Ethical Appeals

Read the following passages. For each, identify what type or types of appeal the writer is making—logical, emotional, ethical, or a combination of two or more of these.

1. A homeless Orlando couple with too little money to maintain a bank account must pay a fee and forfeit 3 percent of their meager earnings simply to cash a paycheck.
   —*Orlando Sentinel* editorial
2. As a professor at a liberal arts college, I must take a stand and refuse to take any more responsibility for student failure. If students plagiarize, it is not because my assignment was not creative enough.
   —Laura Tropp, Letter to the editor
3. An average of 78 percent of the convicted felons in that program stay clean and sober for one year or longer. Re-arrest rates for those participants after release is almost two-thirds lower than for non-participants.
   —Jim Gogek and Ed Gogek, "Drug War Solution between Legalization, Incarceration"

USE ETHICAL APPEALS TO CREATE A TRUSTWORTHY TONE

Although the word *ethics* suggests a moral code of behavior, the term *ethical appeal* (*ethos*) actually refers to the writer's credibility. To be swayed by your arguments, a reader has to trust you and know that the evidence you cite is accurate, valid, and reliable. If logic resides in the head and emotion in the heart, then perhaps *ethos* sits in your gut—your instincts about the worth of a person's character. You gain credibility in an argument, in part, through your authority and impartiality.

You do not have to be an expert yourself to establish authority in an argument. You can use authoritative sources to help support your positions. For example, your argument will be strong if you cite the surgeon general's warning about the effects of smoking rather than quote an actor who plays a doctor on a television show. Similarly, the Centers for Disease Control and Prevention is a better source for information about the latest flu epidemic than your runny-nosed roommate. You create your credibility, in good part, by clear and accurate attribution of your sources. Tell your reader who your sources are and why they are especially suited to speak to a particular subject.

Another powerful way to establish your authority and your credentials is to establish your expertise. Mark Edmundson, who wrote an editorial titled "How Teachers Can Stop Cheaters," is identified as "professor of English at the University of Virginia." The reader knows that he writes from experience. But, if Edmundson were to write about global warming, he would either have to establish himself as an expert in this field as well or rely on the expertise of environmental scientists to gain credibility.

Eat Local
Good for You
Good for Your Community

Indiana University-Purdue University Indianapolis

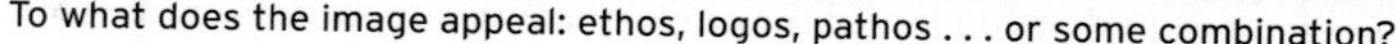

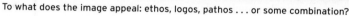

To what does the image appeal: ethos, logos, pathos . . . or some combination?

Being impartial is another aspect of the ethical appeal. If you want your reader to trust you and even to like you, you also have to demonstrate a lack of self-interest in the outcome of the argument. In classical argumentation, this position is called *disinterested goodwill.* If you or one of your sources has a vested interest in promoting a particular cause or course of action, your reader might question your credibility.

Let us say that you read an op-ed piece that argues in favor of more extensive use of nuclear power to address issues of energy supply and global warming. If you find out that the author works for the public relations department of your local nuclear power plant, you have to consider the argument in light of the plant's stakes in the outcome. Similarly, when pharmaceutical companies use television ads to plug the latest cure for arthritis, depression, or high blood pressure, you know that their interest in public health is affected by their interest in making money. Having a stake in the outcome undermines the *ethos* of the argument.

On the other hand, you can enhance the ethos of your argument by speaking from an altruistic position. An altruistic person believes in the moral obligation to help others and to do good work. The ethical writer has the public interest in mind and argues from a position of what will do the most good in the world. Instead of speaking on behalf of a group, you gain credibility when you speak from the outside as an impartial but authoritative commentator. Unlike the nuclear power plant or pharmaceutical company spokespeople, scientists or medical doctors might be better suited to speak to the issues of energy and health, especially if they have public welfare in the forefront of their concerns.

See Ten Tips on Avoiding Pitfalls in Logic to help you detect flaws in the logic of your own arguments—and in your opposition's.

PRACTICE 12.2

Identifying Fallacies

Identify the fallacies in these statements.

1. America—Love It or Leave It!
2. My dog was killed by a speeding car. We have to lower the speed limit in residential neighborhoods.
3. Women cannot be allowed to go to war because they are too feminine.
4. Of course, being wealthy, he would not know much about welfare reform.
5. You are either part of the problem or part of the solution.
6. Whenever I wear my lucky hat, I ace a test.
7. The company may have misrepresented its annual profits to the stockholders, but the real problem is that most companies underpay their accounting departments.
8. If we legalize medical marijuana, we will create a nation of drug addicts.
9. Our memories look more like impressionistic paintings than like TiVos.

Ten Tips on Avoiding Pitfalls in Logic: Fallacies

The strength of your argument can be undercut by faulty logic. Logical errors, commonly known as *fallacies*, destroy your credibility and weaken your argument considerably. If you can detect logical pitfalls in the work of people whose views differ from yours, you can begin to deflate an opposing argument. You can sharpen your skills in logic by searching out fallacies in your own and other's thinking.

BANDWAGON APPEAL

If everyone else jumped off a bridge, would you? This rhetorical question, usually attributed to a parent whose child is about to make a serious mistake in judgment, is a classic example of the bandwagon appeal.

A bandwagon was a wagon big enough to hold a band and often traveled through small towns promoting a political agenda or candidate. So jumping on the bandwagon meant that you joined the crowd that was supporting a cause or a candidate. The bandwagon appeal falsely suggests that an action is a good one because it is popular or endorsed by a popular person.

All good parents in this town support the school-budget override.

This assertion suggests that if you want to be counted among the good parents of the town, you would vote for the override. (You might also rightly ask how someone can measure who is a good parent and who is not.)

POST HOC FALLACY

Post hoc is short for the Latin term *post hoc, ergo propter hoc*, which means "after this; therefore, because of this." Just because a result happened after an event does not mean that the event *caused* the result.

Because a snack-cake company advertises aggressively during Saturday morning cartoon shows, obesity rates have risen among children.

Perhaps the obesity rate among children has risen at the same time that the advertising campaign has aired, but you cannot truly assert that the campaign *caused* the increase.

AD HOMINEM FALLACY

Ad hominem, Latin for "to the man," means an attack that targets a person rather than that person's views or arguments, a fallacy much in vogue during political campaigns. *Ad hominem* attacks ignore or sidestep the issue at hand.

Professor X dresses like a clown. How could anyone take his economics theories seriously?

Criticizing Professor X's appearance does not build an argument that convinces your reader that his theories on economics are flawed.

HASTY GENERALIZATION

A hasty generalization is a conclusion formed from only one or two examples. Avoid falling into this trap when looking for evidence to support your position. Remember that one case does not prove a point.

Airbags are not worth the risk because my friend was seriously injured when an airbag opened.

You could cite this example to illustrate the cautions that come with airbags should be taken seriously but not to argue the risks of airbags outweigh the benefits. When you also consider how many lives airbags have saved and note that injuries are much less frequent and less fatal with airbags, you avoid making this hasty generalization.

THE EITHER-OR FALLACY

The either-or fallacy oversimplifies a complex issue. It uses language that polarizes discussion into two extreme and mutually exclusive positions, leaving no room for nuances, other options, complexities, or the existence of common ground.

The school budget crisis can be solved either by reducing the teen center's hours of operation or by raising users' fees by $100.

This statement suggests that the budget crisis has only two possible solutions. Many ways exist to cut costs and raise money other than these two specific suggestions.

THE RED HERRING

A red herring used to be dragged across a fox's trail to put hunting dogs off the scent. Similarly, the red herring fallacy diverts a reader from the path of an argument, usually by going off in a new direction.

Since rowdy fans turned over cars and created a public nuisance after the soccer game, it is time to examine the importance of sports in our culture.

Instead of keeping attention on the acts of rowdy fans, this statement diverts the argument to the cultural importance of sports, a totally different path of inquiry.

SLIPPERY SLOPE

The slippery slope fallacy assumes that once you take one step, then a series of disastrous events will inevitably follow. The conclusion is usually that the only way to avoid a catastrophe is to not take that first step. This fallacy ignores other factors that might affect the outcome.

If we lower the drinking age to 18, eventually 10-year-olds will be able to drink.

This argument assumes that once you lower the drinking age to 18, then you might lower it to 17, then 16, and finally all the way down the slope to the absurdity of 10. The argument also ignores the developmental, psychological, and societal constraints that would apply the brakes well before the enactment of any legislation allowing children to consume alcohol.

(continued)

(Continued)

10. Senator Wu's youthfulness makes her unable to be trusted with the serious work of the Appropriations Committee.

PRACTICE 12.3

Researching Other Fallacies

Select one of the following common fallacies, research its meaning, find or create examples, and present your findings to the class.

- Fourth term
- Ad populum
- Begging the question
- Poisoning the well

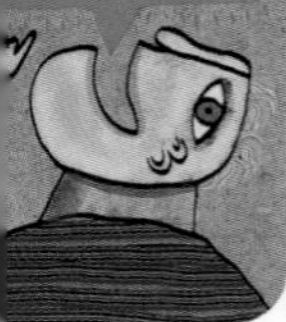

Ten Tips on Avoiding Pitfalls in Logic: Fallacies (continued)

NON SEQUITUR

The English translation of the Latin term *non sequitur* is "it does not follow," which gives you a clear idea of this fallacy. The conclusion does not follow from the premise of the argument.

If 18- year-olds can fight in wars, they should also be able to drink legally.

No logical relationship exists between fighting and drinking, so the conclusion that 18-years-olds should be able to drink legally does not follow from the fact that they can fight in wars.

APPLES AND ORANGES

When you compare two things that have no real basis for comparison, you can be accused of comparing apples to oranges.

Instead of recycling, we should just consume less.

Consuming fewer manufactured products has no real connection to the question of how we should deal with garbage, but rather that we should create less garbage. The cost—in terms of dollars and resources—of recycling compared to the cost of other methods of disposing of garbage is a more appropriate comparison.

CIRCULAR ARGUMENT

Like walking in a circle, a circular argument brings you back to the place you began—the end of the argument restates the beginning.

Pornography should be banned because it is obscene.

This statement is circular, saying that pornography is pornographic.

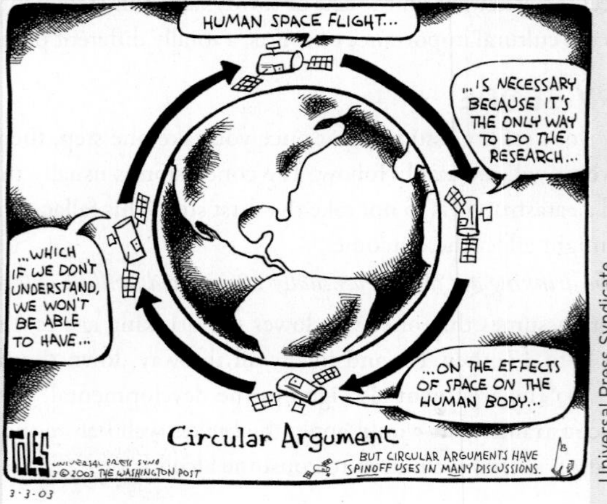

Universal Press Syndicate

VISUAL LITERACY: SEEING ARGUMENTS

THE FIRST POLITICAL CARTOON in America depicts the colonies as a snake divided into eight separate parts. Benjamin Franklin used the image to make the comment that without unity, the eight colonies would have no power in negotiating with the Iroquois. Franklin realized that the image would resonate with colonists, who were familiar with the belief that if sections of a snake were aligned, the snake would come back to life. The image became an important icon in the Revolution. Franklin's cartoon was an early American attempt at the art of editorial cartooning, in which a picture—with or without some text or dialogue—really does speak a thousand words of commentary. The political cartoon uses line drawings and a cartoon format to make a serious statement, usually ironic, always full of opinion. The popularity of the art form relies on the appeal of humor and the instant accessibility of a well-designed image.

- Look over the political cartoons in this chapter to see how editorial cartoonists express their opinions on contemporary issues.
- Choose an issue currently in debate and express a viewpoint by designing your own editorial cartoon.

CORBIS

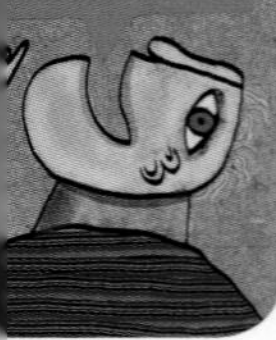

TAKING AN ARGUABLE POSITION

Arguable means that good points supported by solid evidence can be made on more than one side of the issue. You could not write much of an opinion piece, for example, asserting that ethnic or gender discrimination is illegal. Who could argue with that? However, if you wrote a piece that argued that ethnic or gender discrimination exists in college admissions policies, you would certainly have an arguable position.

Fact, Not Arguable: Ethnic and gender discrimination is illegal.
Arguable: Ethnic and gender discrimination exists in college admissions policies.

One way to find a specific focus for your argument is to break a topic down into its component parts. Social, political, economic, scientific, and cultural issues tend to be sprawling and multifaceted. People can spend years studying them. Find the aspect of the topic that affects you and people in your community. Stay local, and be specific. For example, assume that you have decided to write about global warming, a huge topic that interests you. As you read for background, you discover that people have focused on a number of specific solutions to global warming, including regulating automobile emissions, preserving green space, adding more-efficient mass transportation, and making buildings more energy efficient. Any one of these topics will narrow your focus. If your college or community is about to begin construction on a new

PRACTICE 12.4

Brainstorming for a Topic

1. List local or global issues about which you have opinions, preferably strong ones. Look at the editorial topics in your college, community, or city newspaper for ideas. Try to generate at least ten possible topics.
2. Choose one of the issues you listed, and make it the focal point for a freewrite. Write the topic on the top of a page; then write down as many different positions on this issue as you can imagine. Do not worry about logic, clarity, or grammar at this point. Just get your ideas down on paper. Write nonstop for ten minutes.
3. Alternatively, choose one issue that you listed, and make it the focal point of a clustering activity. Write the issue in the center of a page, circle it, and see how many points of view you can generate radiating out from this topic. (See Chapter 2 for more information on freewriting and clustering.)

©5/8/07 HARTFORD COURANT
BURGER
"NO PLASTIC BAGS, PLEASE. I DON'T WANT TO CONTRIBUTE TO GLOBAL WARMING!"

www.politicalcartoons.com

What arguments do these political cartoons on this page and the next make about global warming?

Eric Allie/www.politicalcartoons.com

building, you can further narrow your topic to that specific and local issue: persuading the builder to use solar panels or photovoltaic cells in the building, for example.

Too General, Not Arguable: Global Warming
Arguable: Regulating Automobile Emissions, One Solution to Global Warming

You will sometimes be writing a commentary on a topic for which you already have a "position and a passion," but when you write an opinion piece, you are writing about more than your personal preferences. To write knowledgeably about a public issue, you will need to be able to approach the topic in numerous ways: by examining history, reporting on current developments, citing anecdotes from a particular place or instance, noting a technological development, pointing to a change in trends, or looking through the lens of a certain discipline, such as sociology or psychology.

Personal Opinion, Not Arguable: Children should play more contact sports.
Arguable: The school day should be lengthened to allow all students one hour of physical education each day.

PRACTICE 12.5

Narrowing Topics

Choose one of these topics, and break it down into three or four narrower topics, as in the example on global warming. See if you can also find a local angle as you narrow the topic.

- Drug testing for athletes
- Airport security
- Film censorship
- Internet fraud
- New technologies

THE BIG IDEA: CLAIM AND ARGUMENTATIVE THESIS

Arguments begin with an informed opinion, usually a strong one, about an issue. Further developing that opinion and thinking about your reasons lead you to your *claim*, a general assertion of your position, stated or implied. Stephen Budiansky

in "Math Lessons for Locavores" at the beginning of this chapter explicitly states his claim when he finds fault with the local food movement. He says that ". . . the local food movement now threatens to devolve into a self-indulgent—and self-defeating—do-gooder dogma." This is the beginning of his argument, but his ideas become more sharply focused before he sets up his proof. He focuses as he articulates his *argumentative thesis* that "Words like 'sustainability' and 'food miles' are thrown around without any clear understanding of the larger picture of energy and land use." The argumentative thesis here gives specificity to the claim and gets us ready for examples.

Once you decide on your claim, the next step is to ask yourself "why?" or "how?" to develop an argumentative thesis that will provide a good blueprint for organizing your writing.

CLAIM + WHY or HOW = ARGUMENTATIVE THESIS

Let's say you are interested in gender differences in learning. After doing some research, you form a claim that says something like, "Separating boys and girls in school is bad for both genders." This is an arguable claim, with good reasons to support it, and you can imagine a counterargument, that separating girls and

PRACTICE 12.6

Crafting an Argumentative Thesis

Assume that your state legislature is considering a bill to make driving tests mandatory every time people renew their driver's licenses. According to the bill, mandatory road testing will reduce the number of accidents caused by young, inexperienced drivers and by older drivers whose eyesight and reaction time have diminished.

1. Make a list of four or five arguments on this topic, considering pro, con, and some positions in between.
2. Put the arguments in order of strength, saving the best argument for last.
3. Choose the position that you think is most compelling, and write a claim that promotes that position.
4. Edit your claim so that it is written as economically and clearly as possible.

Clay Bennett c 2002 The Christian Science Monitor

Christo Komarnitski/www.politicalcartoons.com

What arguments do the two political cartoons make about immigration?

boys in school has advantages for both genders. To help focus your argument, you want to think about "why?" This is where you have to make a decision about your angle. Why is it bad? You could probably think of many reasons, but let's focus on the limitations and say something like, "The current trend in separating boys and girls in school limits their futures." Then, you have to do the hard work of getting the facts, statistics, and expert opinion to support your thesis.

Other Examples:

TOPIC: Inequity in college acceptances
CLAIM: Many college applicants who were rejected were more qualified than those accepted.
Ask "why?"
ARGUMENTATIVE THESIS: Students from wealthy families and legacy students took the places that students with higher GPAs should have rightfully had.

TOPIC: Undue pressures to get high grades in college
CLAIM: The emphasis on high grades has had a negative effect on today's college students.
Ask "how?"
ARGUMENTATIVE THESIS: The emphasis on getting the highest GPA in college has prevented students from taking challenging and difficult classes.

RESEARCH PATHS: SUPPORTING ARGUMENTS WITH EVIDENCE

To argue persuasively, you have to be knowledgeable about the topic that you have chosen and its background. Inform yourself by reading back issues of newspapers, magazines, and journals in libraries or online. You can also talk to expert sources—people who know your topic well. As you research, keep your audience clearly in mind. Think of your audience as made up of intelligent people whose views differ from yours, and consider their arguments respectfully and thoughtfully. Use research to figure out what it means to have a different perspective on an issue about which you have strong beliefs. If you can understand other people's positions, you will be better able to argue ethically, logically, and passionately to change their minds.

- Many big-city newspapers publish indexes that organize previously printed articles by topic. Most college libraries keep at least the *New York Times Index* in their reference section and often have microfiche copies of editions going back many years. Check your college or local library to see what indexes are readily available to you.
- Many colleges and universities subscribe to the powerful online database LexisNexis and provide it as a resource for their students. The news section of this database catalogs thousands of periodicals from twenty or more years ago and from all over the country and retrieves information using keywords, writers' names, or article titles. The reference section gives biographical information, information from polls and surveys, quotations, and facts from the *World Almanac*.
- In addition to researching your chosen issue in newspapers and periodicals, you will often want to go to other sources for deeper information. For example, if you are writing about a scientific breakthrough like cloning, a social issue like homelessness, or an economic issue like Social Security, you will need to read journals, books, textbooks, and public documents. (For more information about consulting sources, see Research, Chapter 15.)
- Another research path takes you to experts. Take advantage of your college or university community. Professors spend their lives becoming experts in their fields, and most are more than willing to pass on their knowledge and their sources of information to students. For background information on current issues in science, psychology, politics, economics, medicine, law, or a variety of other topics, you can consult your teachers. If you know other professionals or practitioners in a field related to your issue, they can also be useful sources.

HOW MUCH BACKGROUND INFO[illegible]HOULD YOU INCLUDE?

You have to decide how much background information y[illegible] needs in order to understand your position on an issue. If your issue is curre[illegible] well covered in the news, sometimes all you need is a brief reminder. However, if the issue is complicated or not well known—for example, some little-known aspect of foreign policy or local politics—you need to provide enough background and context for the reader to understand the issue. Your research should help you find relevant background information, but do not try to include the complete history of the issue or a comprehensive overview. Define the out-of-the-ordinary terms, and summarize the important points for your reader. In a summary, you have to find the most concise way to put the issue in context.

TYPES OF EVIDENCE

As you read, collect supporting evidence—facts, statistics, public opinion polls, anecdotes, and experts—for all sides of the issue. What will convince your reader best are thoughtful, well-supported arguments. The stronger your support, the stronger your argument. Whether you search at the library, on your computer, or consult with experts, good research is key to developing your argument. The more variety of support you use, the more you demonstrate the truth behind your position. To set forth a convincing argument, amass a great deal of evidence, enough to convince your most skeptical critic.

So that you can later review and document your sources, take careful notes or make photocopies of all that you read and consult. Supporting material for your arguments can come in a variety of forms:

- *Facts* state objective reality. That you have blue eyes or brown eyes is a fact. That you are attractive is an opinion based on a fact. Your factual supporting evidence should be accurate and unadulterated by opinion.
- *Statistics* are numerical data that often seem to have the weight of irrefutable analysis behind them. Statistics can be slippery, however, and can be skewed or misinterpreted to fit the desired outcome, so you have to be careful to choose reputable sources.
- *Examples* and *anecdotes* illustrate your point. An example provides a single case, and an anecdote tells a story. You have to be careful not to generalize from a case or story, however, and commit the hasty generalization fallacy discussed earlier. Relevant examples and anecdotes often provide vivid support for an argumentative point.
- *Testimonials*, stories of experts or witnesses, provide excellent support for arguments as long as the source is well positioned to speak to the issue.

Every print source you use needs clear attribution. Make sure to note author, title, place of publication, publisher, date, and page number for all

PRACTICE 12.7

Providing Background Information

Assume that you are writing an opinion piece about changing your college's entrance requirements. You might be advocating making entrance requirements more stringent or less stringent, or you might have a new idea about attaining gender or ethnic equity. Assume that your reader has no knowledge of the current admission standards.

1. Write as brief a paragraph as you can to provide the background information your reader will need in order to understand the issue.
2. Choose two editorials from your local paper, and identify the background information presented in them. Note how much information is provided and where it appears in the editorial.

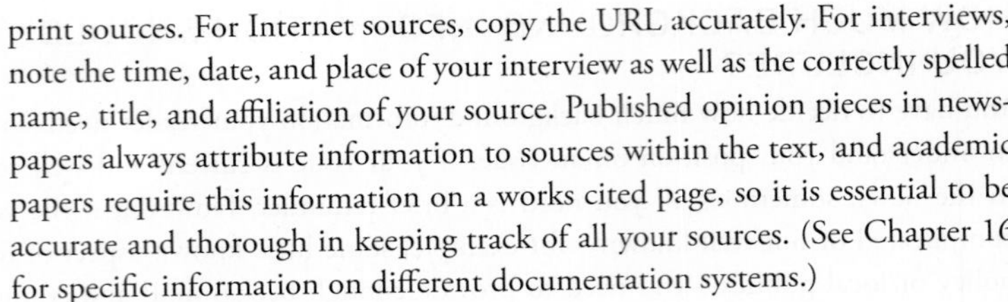
print sources. For Internet sources, copy the URL accurately. For interviews, note the time, date, and place of your interview as well as the correctly spelled name, title, and affiliation of your source. Published opinion pieces in newspapers always attribute information to sources within the text, and academic papers require this information on a works cited page, so it is essential to be accurate and thorough in keeping track of all your sources. (See Chapter 16 for specific information on different documentation systems.)

EVALUATING EVIDENCE

If you want to argue persuasively, your evidence has to be watertight. Evidence has to pass the tests of being reliable, timely, accurate, and relevant. Some questions you can ask to test your evidence:

1. **Reliability** Does the evidence come from a person who is an authority in the field?
   - What are his or her credentials?
   - Is this person cited in other sources?

   Does the evidence come from a reliable study?
   - Who funded the study?
   - Was the study sponsored by a government, university, or commercial source?
2. **Timeliness** Is the information up-to-date?
   - Has it been published in the last few years?
   - Have there been more recent studies that make this one outdated?
3. **Accuracy** Is the information correct?
   - Have you found a second source to corroborate the facts and figures, especially for information found on the Web?
   - Have you double-checked your transcription of this information?
4. **Relevance** Does the information support your point?
   - Does the evidence specifically address the point you are making?

   Have you tied this evidence clearly to the point?

ACKNOWLEDGING OPPOSING VIEWS AND REFUTING THEM

To make a convincing argument, you have to acknowledge opposing views and refute them, even if only briefly. Sometimes a single sentence that might begin "Granted" or "Still" states the opposition's strongest argument with a brief refutation to disprove that argument.

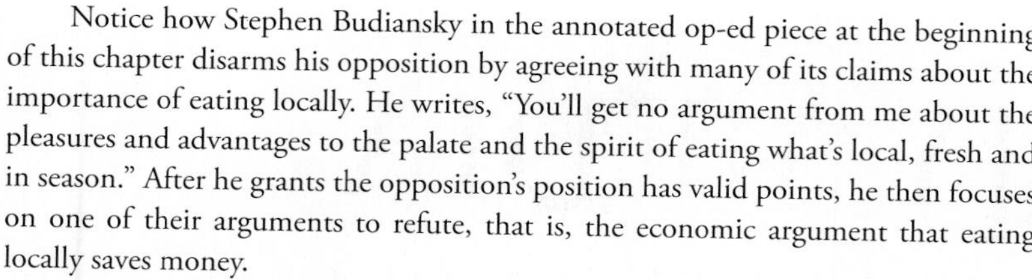

Notice how Stephen Budiansky in the annotated op-ed piece at the beginning of this chapter disarms his opposition by agreeing with many of its claims about the importance of eating locally. He writes, "You'll get no argument from me about the pleasures and advantages to the palate and the spirit of eating what's local, fresh and in season." After he grants the opposition's position has valid points, he then focuses on one of their arguments to refute, that is, the economic argument that eating locally saves money.

When you acknowledge and then dispense with your opposition's possible arguments, you enhance your credibility and build strength for your own position. Always support your counterarguments with solid research. In this way, you show that you understand and have thoughtfully considered the opposing views.

The Seven Habits of Highly Effective Arguments box also provides some insiders' tips on writing good arguments.

Seven Habits of Highly Effective Arguments

An argument should arouse curiosity, strong feelings, or both in your reader.

1. Hook your reader right away. Use a specific, personal story, or a quotation from someone you interviewed. A particularly surprising piece of data can attract attention.
2. Get to your point quickly—announce your topic clearly in the opening few sentences.
3. Keep your voice informal and engaging. Just because you are writing an argument, you do not have to sound stuffy or formal. Avoid jargon or wordiness: Instead of saying, "The accusation of censorship was erroneously reported in media sources." Say, "The news reports got the censorship charge wrong."
4. Make sure your research is current and accurate. Use factual material from unbiased sources (for example, major newspapers, .gov sites.)
5. Save your strongest argument for your conclusion. Leave your reader thinking about the most compelling reason to support your position.
6. Keep each paragraph to one main point. An additional or contrasting point should always begin another paragraph.
7. Leave your readers thinking about the implications of your argument. If the readers agree, what should they think or do, support or defeat?

PRACTICE 12.8

Acknowledging Opposing Views

Choose one of the following opinion statements and anticipate counterarguments by creating a list of opposing views. After you have generated a list of four or five con arguments, arrange them so that the strongest argument is first.

- Academic cheating can be stopped by having students endorse an honor code.
- Pulling vending machines out of schools will not make kids eat less junk food.
- Internet file sharing is no different from taping music from the radio or from a friend's CD.
- Drivers over 70 years old should have to take a driving test every two years.
- Drivers under age 21 should have to take a driving test every two years.

D I Y

DIY MEDIA AND DESIGN

CREATE A FACEBOOK PAGE TO BRING ATTENTION TO AN ISSUE

SOCIAL MEDIA CAN be powerful tools for organizing social or political action. Facebook has become the go-to medium for people who want to bring attention to a cause or an issue, often by organizing events that support those causes.

Create a Facebook page to encourage conversation around an issue you support. Post links to videos and blogs that support your viewpoint.

Social media allow you to reach many people quickly, but you also have to consider how to make a brief and persuasive argument through a combination of well chosen words and images. Post photographs and links to news and video clips that help support your position.

Facebook suggests four ways to create effective pages:

1. Be personal and educational: Keep your voice conversational by using the first person and talking directly to your readers.
2. Create content worth sharing.
3. Join the conversation: Poll your supporters and comment on the posts.
4. Use social plugins, such as the Like button, recommendations, and activity feeds, to increase the relevance of your page.

Craig Ruttle/Alamy

More than 450,000 Facebook users joined the Occupy Wallstreet Pages in the first two months of its creation.

D I Y

READINGS

THE FIRST TWO READINGS, a column and a response to that column from an online magazine, debate the influence of gangsta rap on our culture and abroad. The next set of readings comes from a discussion board on the online *New York Times*. The writers, a professor, a student, and a journalist, respond to the question of why today's students spend less time studying than did their predecessors. Finally, a journalist and an academic researcher present their argument debunking the popular notion that boys and girls learn differently.

Gangsta, In French[2]

David Brooks

New York Times *columnist David Brooks wrote this piece soon after riots erupted in the housing projects outside of Paris in 2005. Minority youth were protesting discrimination in jobs and a lack of opportunity in France.*

AFTER 9/11, everyone knew there was going to be a debate about the future of Islam. We just didn't know the debate would be between Osama bin Laden and Tupac Shakur.

Yet those seem to be the lifestyle alternatives that are really on offer for poor young Muslim men in places like France, Britain and maybe even the world beyond. A few highly alienated and fanatical young men commit themselves to the radical Islam of bin Laden. But most find their self-respect by embracing the poses and worldview of American hip-hop and gangsta rap.

One of the striking things about the scenes from France is how thoroughly the rioters have assimilated hip-hop and rap culture. It's not only that they use the same hand gestures as American rappers, wear the same clothes and necklaces, play the same video games, and sit with the same sorts of car stereos at full blast. It's that they seem to have adopted the same poses of exaggerated manhood, the same attitudes about women, money and the police. They seem to have replicated the same sort of gang culture, the same romantic visions of gunslinging drug dealers.

> "One of the striking things about the riot scenes from France is how thoroughly the rioters have assimilated hip-hop and rap culture."

In a globalized age it's perhaps inevitable that the culture of resistance gets globalized, too. What we are seeing is what Mark Lilla of the University of Chicago calls a universal culture of the wretched of the earth. The images, modes and attitudes of hip-hop and gangsta rap are so powerful [that] they are having a hegemonic effect across the globe.

American ghetto life, at least as portrayed in rap videos, now defines for the young, poor and disaffected what it means to be oppressed. Gangsta resistance is the most compelling model for how to rebel against that oppression. If you want to stand up and fight The Man, the Notorious B.I.G. shows the way.

[2]David Brooks, "Gangsta, in French" from The New York Times, November 10, 2005. Reprinted by permission of PARS International.

This is a reminder that for all the talk about American cultural hegemony, American countercultural hegemony has always been more powerful. America's rebellious countercultural heroes exert more influence around the world than the clean establishment images from Disney and McDonald's. This is our final insult to the anti-Americans; we define how to be anti-American, and the foreigners who attack us are reduced to borrowing our own clichés.

When rap first came to France, American rappers dominated the scene, but now the suburban immigrant neighborhoods have produced their own stars in their own language. French rap lyrics today are like the American gangsta lyrics of about five or 10 years ago, when it was more common to fantasize about cop killings and gang rape.

Most of the lyrics can't be reprinted in this newspaper, but you can get a sense of them from, say, a snippet from a song from Bitter Ministry: "Another woman takes her beating. / This time she's called Brigitte. / She's the wife of a cop." Or this from Mr. R's celebrated album *PolitiKment IncorreKt*: "France is a bitch. . . . [deleted] [O]ur playground is the street with the most guns!"

The French gangsta pose is familiar. It is built around the image of the strong, violent hypermacho male, who loudly asserts his dominance and demands respect. The gangsta is a brave, countercultural criminal. He has nothing but rage for the institutions of society: the state and the schools. He shows his own cruel strength by dominating women. It is perhaps no accident that until the riots, the biggest story coming out of these neighborhoods was the rise of astonishing and horrific gang rapes.

In other words, what we are seeing in France will be familiar to anyone who watched gangsta culture rise in this country. You take a population of young men who are oppressed by racism and who face limited opportunities, and you present them with a culture that encourages them to become exactly the sort of people the bigots think they are—and you call this proud self-assertion and empowerment. You take men who are already suspected by the police because of their color, and you romanticize and encourage criminality so they will be really despised and mistreated. You tell them to defy oppression by embracing self-destruction.

"Gangsta resistance is the most compelling model for how to rebel against that oppression."

In America, at least, gangsta rap is sort of a game. The gangsta fan ends up in college or law school. But in France, the barriers to ascent are higher. The prejudice is more impermeable, and the labor markets are more rigid. There really is no escape.

QUESTIONS FOR RHETORICAL ANALYSIS

1. **CONSIDERING THE RHETORICAL SITUATION:** What kinds of appeals does Brooks use in this piece? Identify a place where he appeals to logic, where he appeals to emotion, and where he establishes his authority.
2. Why do you think Brooks opens his editorial with a reference to 9/11? How effective do you find the opening paragraph?

3. What is Brooks's argumentative thesis? Where does he first state it?
4. Where does Brooks provide background information? Is it sufficient for you to understand his argument?
5. What connections does Brooks make between the French rioters and hip-hop culture in America?
6. Identify any fallacies in logic that Brooks commits in his argument.
7. Where does Brooks acknowledge the opposition?
8. Do you find Brooks a credible source to write about gangsta rap? Why, or why not?

QUESTIONS FOR WRITING AND DISCUSSION

1. Brooks uses the term *hegemony* in his argument. Define the word, and agree or disagree with his statement that American countercultural hegemony is more powerful than American cultural hegemony.
2. Do you agree with Brooks that "In America, at least, gangsta rap is sort of a game"? Explain your answer.
3. Write an e-mail to David Brooks at the *New York Times* responding to his argument.

STYLE PRACTICE: IMITATION

Write a short paragraph describing or defining a piece of popular culture (indie films, hip-hop, social media) and, like Brooks, use a formal voice with no colloquial expressions.

David Brooks, Playa Hater: The *New York Times* Columnist Grapples with "Gangsta Rap"[3]

Jody Rosen

The same day Brooks's "Gangsta, in French" ran in the newspaper, the online magazine Slate *posted this response from its music critic, Jody Rosen.*

DAVID BROOKS, the *New York Times* columnist and author who brought us Bobos, Patio Man, and other armchair sociological formulations, is at it again. In today's column, Brooks takes his shtick overseas and into the realm of pop music with a denunciation of "French gangsta rap." Citing the prevalence of hip-hop culture among "the rioters"—"poor young Muslim men" from Parisian *banlieues* and other French slums—Brooks goes on to spin a theory of global gangsta rap hegemony.

> It's not only that [the rioters] use the same hand gestures as American rappers, wear the same clothes and necklaces, play the same video games, and sit with the same sorts of car stereos at full blast. It's that they seem to have

[3]Jody Rosen, "David Brooks, Playa Hater," from Slate, posted November 10, 2005. Reprinted by permission of PARS International.

adopted the same poses of exaggerated manhood, the same attitudes about women, money and the police. They seem to have replicated the same sort of gang culture, the same romantic visions of gunslinging drug dealers. . . . The images, modes and attitudes of hip-hop and gangsta rap are so powerful [that] they are having a hegemonic effect across the globe.

The result, Brooks says, is a battle for the hearts and minds of Muslim youth "between Osama bin Laden and Tupac Shakur."

That anachronistic reference to Shakur isn't the only thing in the piece that gives off a musty stench. Brooks's entire rant is shopworn: He tut-tuts French rappers for having "nothing but rage for the institutions of society," infers a link between rap and "horrific gang rapes," and declares, in a breathtakingly doofy attempt to kick a little lingo, "If you want to stand up and fight The Man, the Notorious B.I.G. shows the way."

"Brooks's entire rant is shopworn."

If you feel like you've read this before, it's because you have. Way back in the late 1980s and early '90s, when Bill Bennett was at war with Ice-T and Time Warner—and Bill Clinton was triangulating his way through his first presidential campaign by dissing Sister Souljah—the op-ed pages were full of anti-rap fulminations. But Brooks is undismayed. It's tempting to imagine that Brooks actually wrote this article back in early '90s, when he was a lowly book reviewer for the *Wall Street Journal*. Picture Brooks, in the heady weeks after the Los Angeles riots, frustrated that he couldn't shoehorn his gangsta-rap riff into a piece on Andrew Morton's Princess Diana biography. It's been sitting in a desk drawer ever since, just waiting for some inner-city unrest to come along. *Et voilà*.

To be fair, Brooks is tromping into territory that has befuddled even hardened music critics. For at least a dozen years, the French hip-hop scene has been the world's most vibrant outside of the United States, yet it has been almost completely ignored by the American music press. And while rock critics have championed British grime, Brazilian baile funk, and other foreign hip-hop offshoots, they've completely missed the boat on IAM, Suprême NTM, Arsenik, TTC, Saïan Supa Crew, and dozens of other French MCs, who, in addition to voicing the disaffection of the French underclass, happen to be masters of the form—rappers of amazing skill, style, and wit.

On a certain level, it's hard to blame Anglophone critics. Your junior-high *être et avoir* won't get you very far with the torrents of slang that fill French rap. Even most French-speakers find it hard to follow along. Many MCs deliver whole songs in *Verlan*, the ingenious, dizzying slang in which words are reversed or recombined, turning *arabe* (arab) into *rabza*, *bourré* (drunk) into *rébou*, *bête* (stupid) into *teubé*, and so on. (*Verlan* is itself an example of the form: *Verlan* = *l'envers*, "the reverse.") It's not surprising that France, the nation that enshrines conversational grandiloquence as a civic virtue right up there with *fraternité*, would take to the most blabbermouthed genre in music history. France's *chanson* tradition is famous for emphasizing lyrics—the complete works of George Brassens and Charles Trenet are for sale in the poetry section of bookstores, right alongside Baudelaire and Rimbaud—and rappers are widely viewed as heirs to the *chansonniers*. The French Ministry of Culture, stodgy arbiters of all that is Truly French, has already

given one of its top music prizes to Marseilles firebrands IAM, largely because of the poetic skills of its lead rapper, Akhenaton.

It's safe to assume that David Brooks hasn't spent a whole lot of quality iPod time with the new Disiz La Peste album. Which is fine. But it might have made sense to do at least a *little* listening to French rap—or least some more thorough Web-trawling—before writing a treatise on hand gestures, hegemony, and "gangsta resistance." When Brooks starts citing lyrics, things get dodgy quickly. Midway through Brooks' piece we find the following paragraphs:

When rap first came to France, American rappers dominated the scene, but now the suburban immigrant neighborhoods have produced their own stars in their own language. French rap lyrics today are like the American gangsta lyrics of about five or 10 years ago, when it was more common to fantasize about cop killings and gang rape.

"Rappers are widely viewed as heirs to the *chansonniers*."

Most of the lyrics can't be reprinted in this newspaper, but you can get a sense of them from, say, a snippet from a song from Bitter Ministry: "Another woman takes her beating. / This time she's called Brigitte. / She's the wife of a cop." Or this from Mr. R's celebrated album *PolitiKment IncorreKt*: "France is a bitch. . . . [deleted] [O]ur playground is the street with the most guns!"

Problem: Brooks's first example of "French rap lyrics today" is, well, 13 years old. The song in question, "Brigitte (Femme de Flic)" appeared on the 1992 album *Pourquoi Tant de Haine*, by the long-defunct duo Ministère A.M.E.R. (The group's rappers, Passi and Stormy Bugsy, have gone on to successful solo careers.) Moreover, Brooks's research seems to consist of reading two articles in conservative-identified American periodicals. I suspect that Brooks's source is Theodore Dalrymple's article, "The Barbarians at the Gates of Paris," which appeared in the Autumn 2002 edition of the *City Journal*. Dalrymple provides the exact translation that Brooks cites as "Bitter Minstry's . . . best-known lyric"—though the lyric is not so well-known that (based on a Google search) anyone else appears to have ever translated it into English.

Now, there's nothing wrong with Brooks' using Dalrymple's translation, or even relying on his ideas. But isn't Brooks implying some broader knowledge of the topic at hand? Look again at his citation: "Most of the lyrics can't be reprinted in this newspaper, but you can get a sense of them from, say, a snippet from a song from Bitter Ministry." That "say" suggests that Brooks has any number of examples at his fingertips. The truth is, it's probably one of only two French rap lyrics he's ever heard—or, rather, read. The other he cites is the invective of "Mr. R," who, needless to say, the French know as Monsieur R. And lo and behold, a quick Google search turns up "France's Homegrown Gangstas," from the Sept. 28, 2005, issue of the *Weekly Standard* (where Brooks is an editor), which features the exact same English translation of lyrics from Monsieur R's "Fransse."

The crime here isn't just laziness. It's tackiness and gall. Did Brooks bother to notice that the rappers whose songs he cites in his piece about "the future of Islam" aren't Muslim at all, but two black Frenchmen and one black Belgian? There's a word for this kind of stuff. "Mr. R," I suspect, would call it *teubé*.

QUESTIONS FOR RHETORICAL ANALYSIS

1. **CONSIDERING THE RHETORICAL SITUATION:** Identify the appeals to logic and emotion in Rosen's response. Where does he establish his authority?
2. Look over the introduction. What does Rosen do to set up his counterargument to Brooks's thesis? How effective is this introduction?
3. What is Rosen's thesis? Where does he state it for the first time?
4. Identify paragraphs where Rosen acknowledges Brooks's position. How accurately does he present Brooks's argument?
5. What are Rosen's main points in his refutation of Brooks's thesis? How convincing do you find Rosen's points?
6. Look at some of the language that Rosen uses to dismiss Brooks's argument. Can you find any *ad hominem* attacks?
7. In the conclusion to this argument, Rosen uses the Verlan slang he discusses earlier in the piece. How effective is this conclusion?

QUESTIONS FOR WRITING AND DISCUSSION

1. After reading both Brooks's op-ed piece and Rosen's response, which writer do you think argues more effectively? Which writer is more credible?
2. Discuss your own response to gangsta rap.
3. Imagine that you are having dinner with David Brooks and Jody Rosen. The three of you are discussing the contemporary music scene. Write a page of dialogue. Try to capture the convictions and the language of each writer as they are reflected in their pieces above.

STYLE PRACTICE: IMITATION

Write a response to any argument in this chapter (or one you find elsewhere) using the same informal voice and tone as Rosen. Use many references to popular culture, directly address your reader, and use colloquial language to enhance your voice.

Room for Debate: Too Much Free Time on Campus?

Philip Babcock, "Falling Standards in Universities"
Raphael Pope-Sussman, "We Are Not Lazy"
Anya Kamenetz, "With a Job on the Side"

At the beginning of the college year, the New York Times *posted a discussion board question stemming from a recently published report by two University of California economists. The report found that today's students spend 10 fewer hours a week studying than they did 40 years ago. Another report by the Delta Cost Project found that colleges are spending more of their budgets on student services and a "declining share of their budgets on instruction." The following three readings are by a professor, a student, and a journalist who responded to the question, "What are students doing with their time?"*

FALLING STANDARDS IN UNIVERSITIES[4]

Updated August 23, 2010, 11:50 AM

Philip Babcock is an assistant professor of economics at University of California, Santa Barbara. He and Mindy Marks, an economist at the University of California, Riverside, recently issued a report *on the decline in studying time among college students.*

My co-author, Mindy Marks, and I found a whopping 10-hour decline in time spent studying outside of class for full time students at four-year universities between 1961 and the 2000s. We think it's because standards or requirements have fallen at universities.

Though we can't measure student learning in college, we do know that universities set standards for academic effort. We know that students don't come close to meeting these requirements, and that the shortfall has quadrupled over time.

> "Universities are marketing themselves as havens for fun and recreation, and students are taking them at their word."

Universities are marketing themselves as havens for fun and recreation, and students are taking them at their word.

Why did post-secondary institutions allow this to occur? It's hard to know for certain. One theory is that increased market pressures have empowered students, causing colleges to cater more to students' desires for leisure. Students do appear to prefer leisure and easier classes. A given instructor in a given course tends to receive lower ratings from students during terms when he or she grades less generously or requires more.

The *Delta Study* finding that spending for non-academic and recreation facilities has been increasing relative to spending on academic instruction also seems consistent with this explanation. Recreation facilities are a great way to advertise a lifestyle. One college even sent out Frisbees and chocolate chip cookies in its recruitment package. The message couldn't be clearer: Come to our college. It's a vacation spa. It's Club Med.

Some have argued that the decrease in study time has to do with advances in education technology. It's true that the Internet and word processors have made it easier for today's students to write papers and search for references. But because the largest portion of the study time decline happened between 1961 and 1981, before these advances could have been a factor, and because declines also occurred in majors that don't rely on writing papers or searching the library, we doubt this explains much of the story.

Others have argued that students are studying less because they are spending more time on work or internships. But the study time decline is clearly visible both for students who work for pay while in school and for those who don't. And while we don't have data on internships and other unpaid work-related activities in the early data sets, the later data show that students don't spend enough time on these activities to explain a 10-hour decline in studying.

Rather, students appear to have shifted time away from their studies toward leisure. If universities are marketing themselves as havens for fun and recreation, the time-use data show that students are taking them at their word.

[4]Philip Babcock, "Falling Standards in Universities," from New York Times Room for Debate, October 11, 2010.

WE ARE NOT LAZY[5]

Updated August 23, 2010, 11:53 AM

Raphael Pope-Sussman is a senior at Columbia University and the editorial page editor of the Columbia Daily Spectator.

The university student today may spend less of his time studying than students decades ago, but I see no evidence that he's lazier. On my campus, I've seen all manner of students: the hard-driving pre-med, cramming for his final in organic chemistry; the student-athlete, waking for practice at 6, going to class, then studying or returning to the gym; and the Platonic ideal of the scholar, the philosophy major, discussing Foucault in the corner of the library, late into the night.

None of these student types strike me as remotely lazy. Like my other classmates, they fill their days with their studies, but they also have jobs, hold internships, participate in student clubs, or work for campus publications.

My peers are pre-professional: they just want to be able to find decent jobs after graduation.

I've spent much of my time at college at the student newspaper, where unpaid editors often put in 50-hour weeks. Sometimes, after a late night at the paper, an editor will sleep in, maybe missing a class or two. Sometimes he'll skip his course reading or throw a paper together at the last moment.

As a student, that editor may be studying less. But he's not working less. Many editors at the paper hope to pursue careers in journalism. They aren't lazy; they're just pre-professional.

A lot of students today are pre-professional. The most common undergraduate major at four-year colleges isn't philosophy or English or astrophysics—*it's business.* The increasing focus on internships (often unpaid) is another symptom of this trend.

Perhaps all this pre-professionalism is a bad thing. If you believe a liberal arts education is intrinsically valuable, you might think it's a pity that students are increasingly focused on life after college. But that has less to do with the modern university—or the modern student—than it has to do with modern America.

"My peers aren't lazy; they're just pre-professional."

Every year this country pumps out *more and more college graduates* for fewer and fewer good jobs. Today, you go to college to learn, but you also go because you need a diploma for almost every stable career.

You can mourn the disappearance of an ivy-covered Arcadia where America's youth once went to discover Big Ideas. But don't blame the modern college student because he's spending less time with his schoolbooks.

He's not lazy. He's not incurious. He just wants to find a decent job after graduation.

WITH A JOB ON THE SIDE[6]

Updated August 23, 2010, 11:55 AM

Anya Kamenetz, a staff writer at Fast Company *magazine, is the author of "DIY U: Edupunks, Edupreneurs and the Coming Transformation of Higher Education."*

When I researched the history of higher education for *DIY U*, I was amused to discover that panic about declining rigor in

[5]Raphael Pope-Sussman, "We Are Not Lazy," from New York Times Room for Debate, October 11, 2010. Reprinted by permission of the author.

[6]Anya Kamanetz, "With a Job on the Side," from New York Times Room for Debate, October 11, 2010. Reprinted by permission of the author.

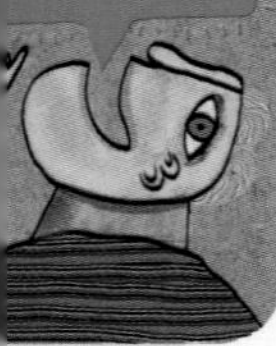

American universities has been a trope for centuries. When colonial colleges, the ancestors of the Ivy League and our fine liberal arts institutions, were founded in New England, history books say that academic standards were almost nonexistent; when the agricultural and mechanical schools opened in the Midwest, standards were lowered; when the G.I. Bill admitted two million vets, standards were lowered yet again.

Today we hear: "*Aggregate time spent studying by full-time college students* declined from about 24 hours per week in 1961 to about 14 hours per week in 2004." Are college students truly getting "lazier"?

Students have less time now because they have to work to pay for school.

Well, one thing is for sure: they have less time, because they have to work to pay for school. The percentage of full-time, traditional-age college students who have a job *increased from 34 percent in 1970 to 47 percent in 2008*, and the hours they worked went up too.

In addition, the demographics of college students have shifted significantly since the 1960s. There are more independent working adults and single mothers sitting in college classrooms than ever before. Three-fourths of all students are "nontraditional" in some way. Older students and part-time students overwhelmingly have jobs while in school.

"Professors feel pressure to grade students easier and to assign less homework when the students have so many outside responsibilities."

The Delta Project, which has done the most careful research on cost allocation in our college system, has found that students are staggering under the weight of "a continuous shift to ever-higher student tuition, which is the one constant across all of post-secondary education."

I've heard from professors—many of them overworked, part-time adjuncts themselves—that they feel pressure to grade students easier and to assign less homework when the students have so many outside responsibilities. This is no doubt detrimental to learning. It's yet another reason that it's so important we work to make college truly affordable and accessible to all.

QUESTIONS FOR RHETORICAL ANALYSIS

1. **CONSIDERING THE RHETORICAL SITUATION:** What is the main appeal (logic, emotion, or authority) that each writer uses in these three short essays? Give an example to support your answer.
2. Identify the sentence in each argument that presents the writer's thesis.
3. What kind of evidence (studies, facts, statistics, anecdotes, expert opinion) does each author use to support the argument's thesis?
4. What is the main appeal of each essay? Is it to logic or emotion or to the writer's authority? Find a sentence or two in each essay to support your answer.
5. Which of these three arguments is strongest, most logical and convincing? Explain your reasoning.
6. Three distinct voices emerge from these essays. Identify a few words, phrases, or assertions in each that help shape the voice of the professor, the student, and the journalist.

QUESTIONS FOR WRITING AND DISCUSSION

1. Kamenetz in "With a Job on the Side" asserts that today's students have more pressure placed on them to build their résumés and help out with spiraling tuition costs. Do you agree? Why or why not?
2. Pope-Sussman claims that today's students might be working less at academics but working more at extracurricular activities. Is that true in your experience? What are students doing with their spare time?
3. Have we really lost ". . . an ivy-covered Arcadia where America's youth once went to discover Big Ideas"?
4. What is the purpose of a college education?

STYLE PRACTICE: IMITATION

In his first paragraph, Pope-Sussman uses a common rhetorical strategy of list-making to create vivid pictures in his readers' minds about different "manners of students" and to support his idea that students may study less but work hard. Write a sentence modeled on his that lists different kinds of professors on your campus. Support the idea that professors work hard or that they too have more leisure time these days.

The Difference Myth[7]

Caryl Rivers and Rosalind C. Barnett

Journalist Caryl Rivers and senior scientist Rosalind Barnett have collaborated on numerous op-ed pieces, articles, and books about gender issues, including the book, Same Difference: How Gender Myths Are Hurting Our Relationships, Our Children and Our Jobs.

WOMEN ARE the chatty sex, using three times as many words each day as men. They are society's great communicators. The verbal parts of their brains are larger than men's, and they are hard-wired for empathy, but they lack a natural ability to reach the top levels of math and science.

Men, on the other hand, have brains that are good at understanding systems, and they are adept at acquiring and using power. They are hard-wired to excel at math and science, but lag behind women in reading ability. They talk less and are not naturally inclined toward caring for others.

"They are simply coating old-fashioned stereotypes with a veneer of scientific credibility."

Sound familiar? In the past decade, such claims have coalesced into an almost unshakable conventional wisdom: Boys and girls are different because their brains are different. This idea has driven bestsellers, parenting articles, and even—increasingly—American education.

[7]From Caryl Rivers and Rosalind Chait Barnett, "The Difference Myth," The Boston Globe, October 28, 2007. Reprinted with permission.

The problem is [that] a hard look at the real data behind these claims suggests they are simply untrue. Some of them are baseless, using the language of science to cloak an absence of serious research; others are built on tenuous studies, with methodological flaws and narrow margins of significance. More and more, they are simply coating old-fashioned stereotypes with a veneer of scientific credibility.

Scientists have turned up some intriguing findings of anatomical differences between the sexes. But we know very little about their real-world effect on how boys and girls behave—meaning that any conclusions based on these findings are premature.

Nonetheless, more policy makers, employers, parents, and teachers appear to be buying into the notion of great gender differences in cognitive abilities. The education world has seen a strong push for single-sex classrooms, with the Bush administration clearing the way for more public schools to segregate students by gender.

"There are now more than 360 gender segregated classrooms in the United States."

There are now more than 360 such classrooms in the United States, with more in the offing. And brain-difference theories are making their way into business, medicine, psychotherapy, and parenting. As they do, we risk letting an avalanche of dubious science overwhelm decades of legitimate findings—and, more importantly, we risk limiting the futures of a whole generation of boys and girls.

The idea that men and women are cognitively different has deep historical roots. Victorian-era scientists generally accepted as fact that the larger brains of men made them intellectually superior; women's smaller brains made them closer to children than to mature adults. Medical wisdom held that women's brains and ovaries could not develop at the same time, making education dangerous to motherhood.

The 20th century saw those ideas debunked. We now know, for instance, that brain size is proportional to body size and doesn't determine intelligence. A 7-foot man is not smarter than a woman who is 5-foot-2. By the 1970s, the women's movement was applying social pressure behind that science, breaking down the barriers that had kept women out of the top medical and law schools, the Supreme Court, the military, the astronaut corps.

But then, in the 1990s, the tide appeared to turn back. New neurological findings, provocative but inconclusive, began to surface. Female "essentialism," a strain of feminist thought, argued that women were more naturally caring than men in how they made moral decisions. Spurred also by a broader social anxiety about women's new roles, a cornucopia of books began tumbling from publishing houses and selling briskly. By now they include titles such as *Why Men Don't Listen and Women Can't Read Maps* (Barbara and Allan Pease), *Boys and Girls Learn Differently!* (Michael Gurian), *Why Gender Matters* (Leonard Sax), and the granddaddy of them all, *Men Are from Mars and Women Are from Venus* by John Gray. Though written by a family therapist whose Ph.D. came from a now-shuttered diploma mill, *Men Are from Mars* for a time outsold the Bible.

The broadest claim of the advocates of difference—and the most widely repeated—is the idea that boys and girls are innately different in math and science ability. One key piece

of evidence is that boys tend to dominate the upper reaches of SAT math scores: In the top 1 percent of scorers on the SAT math test, for instance, boys widely outnumber girls. And that performance gap seems to be echoed in math and science careers: There are very few top women professors in those fields.

The quest to explain those facts, however, has fallen back on some very thin neurological explanations. Best-selling author Gurian argues, in his books and his lectures, that boys have brains naturally wired for understanding systems, due to high testosterone, low serotonin, low oxytocin, and a smaller "corpus callosum," a bundle of nerve fibers that aids language by connecting the brain's two hemispheres. He's echoed by Sax, another best-selling author. In *Why Gender Matters*, Sax writes, "Girls and boys behave differently because their brains are wired differently."

"Their scientific-sounding lingo turns out to be not especially rigorous."

But their scientific-sounding lingo turns out to be not especially rigorous. A study published in the *American Journal of Psychiatry* in 2002 found there were no gender differences in the size of the corpus callosum, and recent studies using MRI images agree. Sax's argument that "boys have a brain-based advantage when it comes to learning math" is based on a very small study in which 19 participants looked either at faces or at a small white circle, while the blood flow in their brains was measured by an MRI. The data from the study, however, found so much variation among individuals that it would be meaningless to draw bigger conclusions about boys or girls as a group.

The SAT scores themselves are misleading as well. Though boys outnumber girls among top scorers, they also outnumber girls among the lowest scorers. The average score is nearly identical. And major new research finds that the gap at the top end is narrowing each year.

It's also not clear what very high SAT scores mean in practical terms. An exhaustive 2006 review of major studies, funded by the National Academy of Sciences, indicates no relationship between scoring in the upper tier of ability and eventual success in math or science careers.

In 2000, psychologist Diane Halpern of Claremont McKenna College reviewed a range of studies of cognitive abilities in areas in which you might expect to find sex differences, such as problem solving, computation, and spatial and verbal abilities. She found that differences were so slight as to be inconsequential. Cognitively, there is far more variation within each gender than there is between boys and girls.

Looking for explanations for the apparent boy-girl divide in math and science performance, some experts and numerous newspaper and magazine articles have seized on the idea that boys are biologically programmed to focus on objects, predisposing them to math and understanding systems, while girls are programmed to focus on people. This idea was based on a study of day-old babies done by British psychologist Simon Baron-Cohen in 2003. Baron-Cohen surveyed 100 babies and found that the boys looked at mobiles longer and the girls looked at faces longer.

His study, however, has since been attacked as unreliable by Elizabeth Spelke, a Harvard psychology professor. In an article

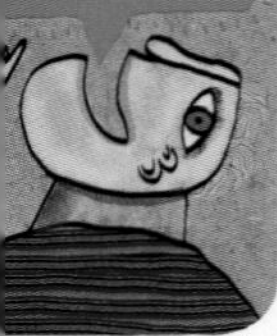

in *American Psychologist*, she pointed out that the experiment lacked critical controls against experimenter bias. Female and male infants were propped up in a parent's lap and shown, side by side, an active person or an inanimate object. Since newborns can't hold their heads up independently, their visual preferences could easily have been determined by the way their parents held them.

In fact, there's a vast scientific literature showing that male and female infants respond equally to people and objects.

If girls get the short end of the stick in the math and science wars, boys also get their share of knocks from the new biological determinism. Males are increasingly seen as inherently deficient in verbal abilities. In *The New Republic*, education author Richard Whitmire writes of a "verbally drenched curriculum" that is "leaving boys in the dust." One suggested solution is boys-only classrooms in which boys would be taught in boot-camp fashion, with diminished emphasis on verbal abilities. Gurian writes approvingly of the '50s-style classrooms "that kept a lot of boys in line."

"Male and female infants respond equally to people and objects."

Do most boys lack verbal skills? In a word, no. In 2005, the University of Wisconsin's Janet Hyde synthesized data from 165 studies on verbal ability and gender and found a slight female superiority—a difference measurable in statistics, but so small as to be useless in distinguishing real-world boys and girls.

But the idea that boys are less verbal has gained wide currency. In the 2006 bestseller *The Female Brain*, author Louann Brizendine argues that girls and women are the talkative sex, while males remain naturally strong and silent. A woman uses 20,000 words per day, while a man uses only 7,000, she asserts.

Brizendine is an academic neuropsychiatrist, and her statistic has been repeated in publications around the world. But it appears to be completely bogus. Brizendine's footnotes cite pop psychology writer Allan Pease—but Mark Liberman, a professor of linguistics and computer science at the University of Pennsylvania, has traced her citations in his popular blog Language Log, and says that Pease's work offers no source for the numbers.

In fact there is better, newer science that suggests those figures are wrong. The most recent study of word use found men and women in a statistical dead heat, with women clocking in at 16,215 words per day and men at 15,699. When that study was published earlier this year in *Science*, its coauthor, James Pennebaker of the University of Texas, Austin, made a specific point of debunking Brizendine's claims.

The lack of hard findings on the real-world difference between boys' and girls' brains hasn't slowed down the impulse to change education.

South Carolina, for instance, aims to have sex-segregated classrooms available in public schools for all children in five years, and gender difference theories are starting to drive curriculum. Teachers are allowing girls to evaluate cosmetics for science projects and assigning action novels for boys to read.

Gurian has exploited his ideas with great success as an educational consultant, claiming to have trained 30,000 teachers in 1,500 schools. Sax runs a lobbying group for more single-sex public schools. When we gave a speech at a national teachers meeting, one

private-school teacher in the audience stood up to say that his headmaster was revamping the entire curriculum based on Sax's theories of gender difference.

Of course, it would be naive and even harmful to pretend there are no differences between boys and girls. Boys, for example, are more vulnerable to autism and dyslexia—and teachers and parents need to be alert to that fact. But there's a mountain of evidence to show that gender is the wrong lens through which to view education policies and practice. Some kids learn best visually, others verbally; some do best in "boot-camp" type settings, while others thrive in informal classrooms with lots of freedom. But science and aptitude surveys tell us that gender isn't a helpful way to sort students into those groups.

> "There's a mountain of evidence to show that gender is the wrong lens through which to view education policies and practice."

As science becomes more central to our public and political conversations, it's perhaps not surprising that neurological factoids are being used to "prove" ideas on both sides of a debate. But science shouldn't be enlisted as an excuse for believing what we want to believe. Rather, it should be seen as part of a long series of steps that can lead to fresh understandings of the world.

What we can hope is that eventually, good science drives out bad, and that facts, by their sheer heft, ultimately crush the factoids. But we have to pay attention to make sure this happens. Otherwise, we will end up trusting our kids' futures to ideas and programs that—ironically—rely on science to shore up some of society's most unscientific prejudices.

QUESTIONS FOR RHETORICAL ANALYSIS

1. **CONSIDERING THE RHETORICAL SITUATION:** Where in this argument do Rivers and Barnett appeal to logic, to emotion, and establish their authority? Give examples to support your answers.
2. Rivers and Barnett begin their argument by presenting the gender myths they plan to debunk. How effective do you find this opening gambit? Why?
3. Identify the authors' main thesis. What is their central argument?
4. What evidence do Rivers and Barnett use to support their thesis? Where do they appeal to logic and to emotion? How do they establish their authority?
5. What counterarguments do they acknowledge? How well do they refute them?
6. What do the authors identify as the implications of their argument?
7. In the conclusion the authors compare "facts" to "factoids." What is this distinction? Have they presented the facts needed to support their argument?

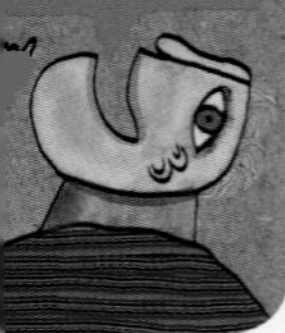

QUESTIONS FOR WRITING AND DISCUSSION

1. Which gender stereotypes exist in your culture? Which ones bother you the most?
2. What is your position on same-sex classrooms? Do you think education should move toward single-sex public schools?
3. Rivers and Barnett claim that both girls and boys are shortchanged by a belief in "biological determinism." Define *biological determinism*, and respond to this claim with evidence from your own experience.

STYLE PRACTICE: IMITATION

Write a two-paragraph opening, like the one from this reading, where you rely on stereotypes to help make your point. Be sure to make clear to your reader, through your tongue-in-cheek tone and style, that you are aware these are stereotypes.

WRITING AND REVISION STRATEGIES

Gathered here are three interactive sections for you to use as you write and revise your opinion piece.

- Writer's Notebook Suggestions
- Peer Review Log
- Revision Checklist

WRITER'S NOTEBOOK SUGGESTIONS

Many writers informally jot down their ideas and refine their thinking in notebooks that they keep handy. This compilation of suggestions for writing and thinking can be used to generate ideas at any point as you write your opinion piece.

1. Write an e-mail message to convince a friend to transfer to your college. Think about what would best convince him or her to make such a big change.
2. Cut out political cartoons that attract your attention, and paste them into your notebook. Write a claim for each cartoon.
3. Make a list of issues that appear on the editorial page of a local newspaper during the course of a week. Put a star next to the ones that you find interesting.
4. List policies at your college that you think should change. Choose one, and write a letter to the college president arguing against the policy or for a revised policy. Remember to consider the president's point of view.
5. Write an e-mail message to the student government president in which you take a stand on a campus controversy.
6. Read an editorial in today's local or school newspaper. Write the lead and thesis of a letter or column in response to the editorial, expanding on the writer's argument or disagreeing with the editorial.
7. You have been hired as a speechwriter for a candidate running for the student senate. The candidate has been asked to deliver a ten-minute speech on a proposed five-percent tuition hike. Outline a draft of this speech for your candidate, taking a stand for or against the hike.
8. The president of your college or university has asked you to serve as student consultant for a speech that proposes a five-percent tuition hike. Write an outline for the president's speech, aiming to convince students of the importance of raising tuition.
9. Draw a political cartoon that presents your opinion on an issue about which you feel strongly.

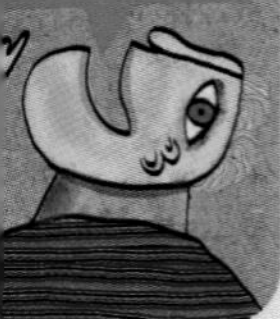

PEER **REVIEW** LOG

As you work with a writing partner or in a peer editing group, you can use these questions to give useful responses to a classmate's opinion piece and as a guide for discussion.

Writer's Name: ________________________________

Date: ________________________________

1. Identify the introduction. Did it get your attention? Why? What might make it stronger?
2. Underline the argumentative thesis in the paper that you are reading. Is the writer's opinion clear? Could you suggest better wording?
3. Do you understand the issue the writer is discussing? What other information might you need?
4. Put a star next to the main points of the writer's argument. Do they support the claim? Can you suggest other points the writer might consider?
5. How effectively does the writer appeal to the reader's heart or mind? Are there places that could use facts, statistics, opinions, anecdotes, or testimonials?
6. Can you identify any problems with logic? How could the writer solve those problems?
7. Does the writer effectively acknowledge opposing views? Are those opposing views refuted well?
8. Does the piece end strongly? Is there a call to action? What might make the conclusion more effective?
9. Comment on the writer's voice. Is it appropriate for this kind of opinion piece? Are there places where the writing gets bogged down? Can you suggest some places to insert stronger verbs or livelier language?

REVISION CHECKLIST

As you do your final revision, check to make sure that you

- Wrote an engaging lead
- Stated your argumentative thesis clearly and accurately
- Provided necessary background information
- Acknowledged and refuted counterarguments, if necessary
- Made clear points that supported your argument
- Used facts, statistics, examples, anecdotes, or testimonials to support your arguments
- Appealed to your reader's intellect and emotions
- Did not commit any fallacies in logic
- Wrote with clarity and conviction
- Concluded strongly, perhaps with a call to action

THERE'S NO BETTER FRIEND. ADOPT A DOG.
For more information about pet adoption visit www.spca.org.sg or call us at 62875355 ext 24.

SPCA-Singapore

13

Creating A Visual Argument

PUBLIC SERVICE MESSAGES

Yuliyan Velchev/ Shutterstock.com

A writer should write with his eyes, and a painter paint with his ears.

—Gertrude Stein

It is a familiar image: The room, dim, except for the television, broadcasting a sad movie. The shot even teeters on the brink of cliché, maybe, but then you look closer and see the dog is offering a tissue.

(*Insert the sound of a little chuckle.*)

Ah, that's my best friend! My dog.

Things happen when pictures tell us a story. Even more things happen when the story is a little about us—a situation we can put ourselves into, remember, recreate. The creators of this public service message have made the lonely-movie-night scenario fresh, given it a new twist, and in the process, have posed a visual argument: Why not adopt a pet?

Creators of public service messages may also give us reasons, charm us, warm our hearts. Sometimes they use images that make us cry, or make us angry, or puzzle us. Sometimes they give us something to read; other times, people who create visual arguments trust their pictures to say it all. This is what they know; they have a few seconds to get us interested, and maybe a few more to make their case.

They know a visual argument is an instant argument.

WHAT'S TO COME

PROCESS PLAN

PREPARE

- Choose an issue you care about, one that you want to support.
- Find an advocacy group that works on this issue.
  - Research past campaigns
  - Develop a fresh concept to help your argument

DRAFT

- Introduction: Create a headline that generates interest, attracts readers, and announces the topic of your argument.
- Body: Create copy that intrigues and concisely explains. Create visuals that complement the copy.
- Conclusion: End with a call to action: donate money, volunteer, change behavior.

REVISE

- Look for ways to strengthen the message either in words or with images.
  - Check to make sure you have appealed to your target audience's minds and/or hearts.
  - Be sure that you have established your authority or credibility through well researched information.

UNDERSTANDING THE WRITING PROJECT

Shanna Baker/Getty Images

WRITERS IN the information age cannot ignore the significance of the visual components of a message. In most advertisements, public service messages (PSMs) included, visuals work in conjunction with words. Building a visual argument gives you hands-on experience researching accurate and useful information, creating images to support that information, and having the words and images work in concert.

Images can work on many levels, calling on associations we all share to make sense of them. It is important to understand what motivates your audience in order to choose a medium that will persuade that audience. Professionals who create public service messages are aware of not only the general reluctance of people to listen to "what is good for them" but also of the specific obstacles that lie between a message and a particular audience. Thinking about the means of delivering your message dovetails with thinking about your audience.

ASSIGNMENT Find a nonprofit group or organization in your community that offers information or services that could benefit the public. This organization will be your client. Develop a portfolio of three public service messages and one pitch letter introducing your work to this new client. Your aim is to serve your community by raising awareness of an issue, initiating a new behavior or attitude, or changing a behavior or attitude. Choose from the following types of public service messages:

- Print advertisements for magazines, newspapers, posters, or billboards
- Storyboards and scripts for television commercials or for posting on YouTube
- Alternative media such as messages on shopping bags, installations in public spaces, bus or train wraps, or guerrilla theatre

Later in this chapter, the DIY will lead you to an example of a public service message in the form of a YouTube video.

Access an interactive eBook, and chapter-specific interactive learning tools, including flashcards, quizzes, videos and more in your English CourseMate via www.cengagebrain.com.

ANATOMY OF A PUBLIC SERVICE MESSAGE

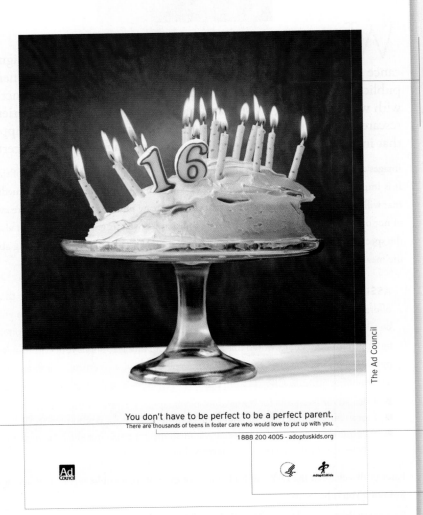

attract attention: familiar image—with a twist. creates a question (Why does the cake look lopsided?)

16

The Ad Council

headline focuses tightly on one thing the audience might be thinking about the argument, their obstacle, excuse, reason not to listen

You don't have to be perfect to be a perfect parent.

There are thousands of teens in foster care who would love to put up with you.

copy provides reasons why—thousands are waiting

1 888 200 4005 · adoptuskids.org

call to action: here's what to to—find out more at this place

Ad Council

"The 'aha' moment often occurs after you've left the project for some time and then come back to see your work in a new light."

Q&A with Tom Fauls

Getting to the "Aha" Moment

Tom Fauls has been a copywriter and creative director at major ad agencies.

Q: How is writing ads for public service different from writing ads for commercial use?

A: Public service ads are typically developed on a pro-bono basis. That is, the ad agency and copywriter/art director team receive no compensation. Their motivation may be (a) altruism and/or (b) the chance of getting an excellent and possibly award-winning sample that can attract new business or, in the case of the copywriter and art director, peer recognition and better jobs.

Q: Is it true that copywriters have more leeway to be creative and take risks when they write public service advertising?

A: Yes. Because they aren't paying agency fees, risk-averse clients have very little leverage and therefore [have] a harder time saying no when edgy, controversial, or confrontational work is presented. Moreover, the subjects of public service ads are often inherently emotional, dealing with disease, hunger, death, addiction, etc.—topics that most award competitions reward with recognition.

Courtesy Tom Fauls

Tom Fauls

Q: How do copywriters come up with concepts for a public service campaign?

A: Experienced copywriters and art directors all develop their own unique techniques for idea generation over time. But the general process involves the same steps detailed in James Webb Young's famous and short book, *A Technique for Producing Ideas.* Once you've gathered and absorbed the necessary research and background material, including competitive ads (for similar causes), you create a manageable way to quickly show your themes. This could be in any form that works for you but often involves (1) pages of rough sketches showing your ideas and metaphors and (2) pages of words and phrases beginning with key relevant themes expressed in one or two words. From there, you recognize that all ideas consist of new combinations of existing ingredients, and you begin to look for relationships between and among them. Webb notes that the "aha" moment often occurs after you've left the project for some time and then come back to see your work in a new light. Strive for original ideas that stem from connection to the core truth in your subject.

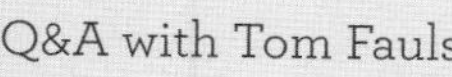

Q: What is the best advice you have gotten about writing public service ads? What is the best advice you can give?

A: The best advice is to keep focused on four things: (1) the client's objective; (2) how the target audience—not you or your friends—is likely to react to your message; (3) smart, original ideas that are relevant to the subject; and (4) powerful emotional motivators—as opposed to rational/logical motivators—associated with the cause. Finally, the hardest thing for inexperienced creative teams is to spend some time developing purely word-driven ideas when it seems much easier to generate visual ideas. If you don't spend an equal amount of time approaching the problem from both words and visuals, chances are you'll completely miss some of the best possibilities.

PRACTICE 13.1

Evaluate a Public Service Message

Collect examples of public service advertisements from magazines and online and grade them using the following scorecard. Award the PSM one point for every box checked.

Public Service Message Scorecard

- ☐ The ad attracted my attention.
- ☐ The ad kept me interested; I did not stop looking at it because I was offended, confused, or bored.
- ☐ The ad provided information that was new to me.
- ☐ I believed the ad.
- ☐ I would read the ad again.
- ☐ I would read more information about the topic.

THE RHETORICAL SITUATION: HOW IMAGES AND WORDS WORK TOGETHER TO TARGET YOUR AUDIENCE

While getting to work or school in the morning, you see or hear competing requests for your attention, time, and money. You are exposed to media messages constantly. Messages that try to change your mind—that make an argument—have an even tougher time breaking through all that noise. That is why your understanding of audience and purpose is critically important in designing your public service message. You want to change somebody's mind—to stop or start a person doing something. You have to think about exactly what that is and how best to get into your viewers' minds or hearts.

UNDERSTANDING YOUR AUDIENCE

In writing the message in your PSM, think about talking to one person and at the same time talking to a crowd. Each public service message is a personal appeal that just happens to be broadcast to thousands. Your target audience—that special group you want to listen to you—should be well defined in your mind. For example, if you are interested in helping the Red Cross with blood donations, you can choose from a variety of target audiences:

- First-time donors who might hesitate due to fear
- Businesses that might sponsor blood drives at their offices during work hours

- College-age donors who are healthy and have time to donate
- People between the ages of 30 and 50 who are busy but are motivated to help
- People between the ages of 30 and 50 who find lots of excuses not to help
- Retired people who have time and are interested in civic involvement

The writers and designers working on public service messages have a clear sense of *who* their intended audience is before they start to think about *how* to deliver the message. The group that you are working for, your client, may have ideas about whom it wants to target. Your client might have a number of different audiences in mind and create different campaigns to target these different audiences, but you will need to know, for example, whether you are pitching the material to children, teenagers, men between the ages of 18 and 24, affluent middle-aged businesswomen, or senior citizens. In marketing, breaking down a group into a profile of age, neighborhood, income, education, and gender is called *demographics*. Your client will probably be able to give you a good overview of the demographics it is targeting with its message.

CHOOSING YOUR MEDIUM

Where you decide to place your PSMs—in which publications, in what neighborhoods, on which modes of public transportation, on which Web sites, or at which television or radio stations—depends on *whom* you are aiming to persuade.

To assess how you will talk to an identified group, first think about where your target group is most likely to go for information so that you can place your message where its members will encounter it. In your community, which publications do women frequently read? What places would attract the attention of retired people? Would college students visit the same places? A poster in a coffee shop near a college would likely be seen by college students. A poster in a women's fitness center would be seen by women. But what about ads in the sports and business pages of the newspaper? Would these be good places to address a specific or a general group? Who would be exposed to a poster at the public library? A billboard on the interstate? How do you create a YouTube video that gets thousands of hits?

Thinking about how or when your audience will meet your argument will help you choose the best form for its function. Before you write and design your PSM, think about what form will best deliver your message. Although a few lines of copy that explain a headline are useful to a magazine reader, a driver speeding by a billboard at 60 miles per hour will never be able to read 2,500 words of copy. (See the box on Tips for Choosing the Best Medium for Your Message.) In general, talk directly to the audience you imagine. Sometimes

(Continued)

- ☐ I would act on the information.
- ☐ After reading, I remembered the message.
- ☐ I would tell my friends and family about the message.

_____ Total PSM score

Compare your totals with those of your classmates. Collect and examine the ads with the highest scores and the lowest scores, and decide which factors the best have in common and which factors the weakest have in common.

PRACTICE 13.2

Finding Your Target PSM Audience

1. Generate a list of possible target groups, like the one about blood donors on pages 412–413, for public service advertisements designed to solicit donations to the Every Child Is a Reader program, which gives new books to children in low-income school districts.
2. Decide where you would place the PSMs to reach each target group on your list.

PSMs need to be serious and somber. At other times PSMs attract the attention of a resistant audience by using humor. Use short sentences or phrases, and do not waste words. Most good copy is informal, brief, and to the point. It can also be playful and clever.

Tips for Choosing the Best Medium for Your Message

The following basic guidelines for some of the major ways to deliver PSMs should help you think about the best medium for your message. Your call to action, for example, will vary depending on the medium you use.

- **Print:** Print public service messages appear in magazines and newspapers and in the form of posters, flyers, and billboards. The way the ad looks is as important as what it says. But your call to action can be more specific in a magazine PSM than on a poster or billboard.
- **Web Pages:** Web sites can include hot type—so your reader can immediately link to the advocacy group's Web page for more information.
- **YouTube and Television:** YouTube and television offer all the benefits of the medium: pictures, sound, and text. Entice your audience to view your work through Facebook or Twitter. Open your video by being immediately engaging through the use of an arresting image, language, or music.
- **Alternative Media:** Outside-the-box thinking has created public service campaigns that do not use mainstream media to convey messages. Buses and trains are being wrapped with messages. Video is being projected onto buildings on busy city streets, and messages are being sprayed on streets. Think about using alternative media to catch the attention of an audience overly saturated with traditional advertising.

Image Courtesy of The Advertising Archives

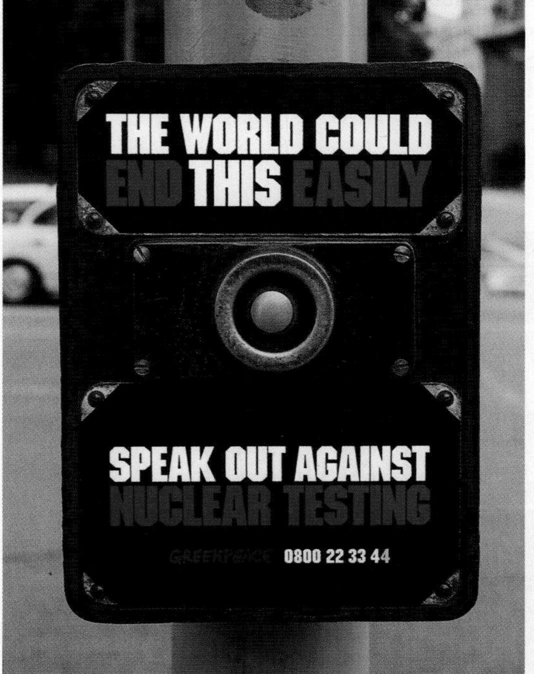

Image Courtesy of The Advertising Archives

Some Public Service Messages appear in unconventional places—as installations that draw attention to the novelty, first, and then the message.

PRACTICE 13.3

Using Alternative Media

You have been hired by Parents for Bike Safety, a group that is working to promote the use of bicycle helmets by school-age children. You have these statistics to work with: "Nearly 98 percent of bicyclists killed were not wearing a helmet at the time of injury. Helmet use is estimated to prevent 75 percent of cycling deaths." Write a memo to Parents for Bike Safety that lists three ways you might use alternative media to launch a bike-helmet safety campaign.

PRACTICE 13.4

How Text and Image Work Together

1. Analyze the image in the one of these public service messages.
2. What does the image tell you?
3. How does the text appeal to the audience—emotionally, intellectually, or both?
4. Using the same concept and the same text, create another image for the campaign.

WORDS + IMAGES IN VISUAL ARGUMENTS

The medium you choose will help you decide how visual and verbal elements work together in your argument. In creating an argument—any argument—your visual elements can be equal to the verbal elements. They can also be more important. In the split seconds it takes your retina to record a picture, you have already started to decipher the meaning and to respond both intellectually and emotionally. You see a photograph of sunglasses with one smashed lens, for example, and you think of something fragile that has broken. You may think about bad fortune or bad choices, accidents, damage, or loss. If that is what the sunglasses look like, what about the eye? The face? Pictures really can be worth thousands of words. When that image is partnered with a headline that states "Friends Don't Let Friends Drive Drunk," the image tells a terrible story and leaves a lasting impression.

Images can be photographs and illustrations, but they can also be just words. The typeface—its size and shape—becomes the image. Even the absence of a photo or an illustration delivers a powerful message. The "Buckle Up" billboard, which uses only type, exemplifies architect Mies van der Rohe's design principal that "less is more." The message is more powerful without a picture because it lets the viewer imagine his or her own child in the car, and makes a clear argument for the importance of buckling your child into a car seat. When the type is the only image, the choices about which text type and size, and how the text is arranged in the space, is crucial.

PRACTICE 13.5

Typography in Visual Arguments

Typography alone can sometimes make a powerful or witty statement. The poster on page 417 employs the shorthand of text messaging to draw people into an exhibition about the history of the English language. Write a text message to the creators of this poster and let them know whether or not you think it is effective.

A SUDDEN STOP AND YOUR UNBUCKLED TODDLER BECOMES A 35 LB. MISSILE.
BUCKLE UP.
Kansas Clicks
A public service message from the Kansas Department of Transportation

Kansas Department of Transportation Safety & Technology

VISUAL LITERACY: TEXT AS IMAGE

THE WORLD OF TYPOGRAPHY divides itself into two camps—*serif* typefaces and *sans serif* ("without serif") typefaces. Classical typefaces have serifs (those little lines at the feet of the letter), and modern typefaces do not have those serifs. Most typefaces come in different sizes (also called *font sizes*). But new typefaces are created every day, providing more options for using typefaces and font size to enhance the meaning of words. Which type—bold or script, chunky or delicate, might be the most effective?

Angry **ANGRY**

Terry Harris/Alamy

This exhibition poster uses text-messaging shorthand to suggest that language is constantly evolving.

Designers know the power of typography, and how words can shift personality through the choice of typeface. Even without pictures and illustrations, messages can have enormous impact and eye-catching appeal. But this was new thinking in 1962, when a group of graphic designers began to explore the possibilities in text. Ivan Chermayeff, Tom Geismar, and Robert Brownjohn limited themselves to one typeface and one size to create a small booklet titled *watching words move*. Their booklet caused a stir in the graphic design community and inspired designers to think about how the letters themselves could portray the meaning of a word. As simple as the concept seems, the result was revolutionary. Chermayeff and Geismar concluded that "the designer, using only the simplest means, can make certain words more evocative, and expressive of feelings, thoughts, and suggestions. In other words, words can have personality, and they don't need special typefaces or funny hats to do so."

addding
subtrcting
multimultiplying
div id ing

1. On an 8 1/2-inch × 11-inch page, use layout (placement of elements on the page), typeface, type size, and color to express the meaning of one of the following words:

   Timid
   Demagogue
   Contagious
   Existential
   Committed
   Fascist
   Deception

   Heed Chermayeff's and Geismar's admonition about using novelty typefaces—letters made of bamboo or letters that seem to be dripping blood, for example—and avoid them. Also, resist the temptation to include any illustration other than the letters themselves to convey meaning.
2. On a second page, use typeface, type size, layout, and color to express the opposite of what the word means.

You are more
It's hard to
likely to crash your
do two things at
car while talking
the same time.
on a cell phone.

Besides working with just the type, a designer can use layout (placement on the page) and color to add meaning to words, as in this ad based on a British public service advertisement called "Mobile Madness."

RESEARCH PATHS:
FINDING YOUR ARGUMENT STRATEGY THROUGH THE MISSION STATEMENT

Your first step in understanding how to relay a message is to interview the group for which you are designing your PSM. Understanding its mission will help you create a public service message.

YOUR "CLIENT" OR ADVOCACY GROUP

Start your research by contacting your "client" with a phone call or e-mail. Most Web sites include a contact section that offers a phone number. Contacting the group or agency that specializes in your topic could be a good way to get current information and insider sources. Explain that you are working on a project to raise awareness for a particular issue. People might be more inclined to answer your questions if they know what you want to accomplish.

The group will most likely be able to offer you the most current and relevant information you can use to become familiar with issues and previous campaigns. For example, this mission statement from Big Brothers Big Sisters of the Tri-State (West Virginia, Ohio, and Kentucky) clarifies the organization's goal.

> The mission of Big Brothers Big Sisters of the Tri-State, a nonprofit agency, is designed to provide guidance and companionship to youth from single parent homes through the provision of an adult Big Brother Big Sister volunteer. This is done through recruiting, screening, counseling, and supervision by a professional staff. The concept of our program is based on the premise that a child, in order to grow into responsible adulthood, needs a positive relationship with a mature adult figure. Where this influence is lacking, the child is handicapped in reaching his or her potential. Our clients are children needing friendship, affection, advice, and guidance. They may be emotionally deprived, in trouble at school, or just a lonely, unhappy child in need of a meaningful relationship. If the problems of the child are so severe that they require professional help exclusively, Big Brothers Big Sisters service will not be a consideration.

The mission statement informs you that Big Brothers Big Sisters' goal is to help children reach their full potential by giving them an adult mentor who will commit to a "meaningful" relationship. Knowing this information can help you design a public service message that fits them.

SEARCHES AND SOURCES

Once you understand your client's mission, look for material that will help you understand the issues your client needs addressing. You need to include up-to-date and quality

information, facts, and statistics from authoritative sources. Web searches are good starting places, but be sure to carefully evaluate your online sources. Some organizations with special interests might post misleading or inaccurate numbers. Look for information that comes from unbiased sources such as universities and government agencies.

A few good Web sources are the U.S. Census Bureau, state departments of public health sites, and the U.S. Government's Official Web Portal at www.firstgov.org. By using official statistical sources like these, you can create an argument that has authority.

Print sources help you to get information and double-check facts and statistics you find on electronic sources. Getting information from two sources helps to verify the information, and going to the original source is the best way to get reliable information.

THE BIG IDEA: THE CONCEPT BEHIND THE MESSAGE

A public service message begins with the big idea, the concept behind the message. Just like the claim in a written argument, the underlying concept in a PSM begins the process of figuring out your position. Remember that to become an arguable thesis, or the specific point of your message, a big idea needs to be refined and focused.

As soon as you identify an issue you want to work on, you begin to think about ways to bring your visual argument to your audience in a fresh way, a way that captures attention and brings results. Over the years, endless messages have been targeted at teens trying to persuade them not to drink. In the 1990s a now-famous public service campaign was built around a new concept. Channeling the strong bond teens have with their friends, and recognizing that teens will probably always experiment with alcohol, the PSM shifted the topic to drinking while driving and the concept to using peer group affiliation to argue against driving while drinking. The specific message, of course, is "Friends don't let friends drive drunk."

> Topic: Preventing teens from driving while drinking
>
> Concept: Using teen's peer group affiliation (positive peer pressure)
>
> Specific Point (tagline): "Friends don't let friends drive drunk."

Whole campaigns have been built around a single concept. The MADD campaign in the readings later in this chapter offers another example of a series of PSMs built around a single concept.

> Topic: Preventing teens from riding with drunk friends
>
> Concept: Recreate a specific teen's accident through typography and imagery and install in high school corridors
>
> Specific Point (tagline): "(Name of teen): One more reason not to ride with a drunk driver."

THE PERSUASION PATH

Visual arguments allow the viewer to make snap decisions about whether to engage in the message or turn away. Readers of verbal messages make the same decision, but once an argument takes a visual form and might include the layer of multimedia, the importance of the appeal factor increases exponentially. Your goal is to attract attention and keep it until you are finished making your point. These instantaneous steps viewers go through as they absorb your argument can be broken up into four parts. Think of this process as the *persuasion path*.

The Persuasion Path:

1. **Attract Attention and Generate Interest**
   —Use both the design and the verbal elements in your argument
2. **Appeal to Hearts and Minds**
   —Target your audience with your argument: Choose logos, pathos, or ethos
3. **Provide Reasons**
   —Make believers out of your viewers by giving them specifics
4. **Call Your Reader/Viewer to Action**
   —Do not be afraid to say exactly what you want your viewer to do

ATTRACT ATTENTION AND GENERATE INTEREST: HEADLINES AND VISUALS

A headline, like all titles, gives readers an entry point into a public service message. The headline can be at the top or bottom, or some place in the middle. Its job is to break through all the other conversations and to get attention by creating a sense of intrigue or mystery. Sometimes you will find yourself walking the thin line between intrigue and confusion. Keep in mind that you want your viewer to be curious, but not confused.

Much headline writing involves you speaking directly to the viewer—as a friend, an expert, an authority, or a colleague—one to one. A good headline establishes the role you are playing in language that is memorable—often quotable. Think of all the catchy slogans and zingers from advertising that go "viral" with people repurposing them as punch lines or using them as insider jokes. Those headlines illustrate the way well-crafted phrases or sentences, which are ever-so-brief, make their way through the noise. Most of the time the reason the headline achieves this kind of cultural currency is because the writer understands how important poetry is in making something so short speak volumes.

POETRY AND ADVERTISING COPY

Why do we remember so many advertising slogans through the years? Advertising copywriters often use poetic techniques to create language that stays in our minds—often pleasingly but sometimes also annoyingly. A few poetic techniques copywriters use effectively are metaphors, similes, alliteration, onomatopoeia, rhymes, hyperbole, repetition, rhythm, and parallel constructions.

Metaphors and Similes: Metaphors and similes compare unlike things.
A sudden stop and your unbuckled toddler becomes a 35 lb. missile.
Make your children superheroes. Teach them how to dial 911.

Alliteration: Alliteration is the repetition of a beginning sound.
Hopeless, hungry, hidden

Onomatopoeia: Onomatopoeia is the re-creation of sounds through words.
Every time the cash register goes ka-ching, we will donate part of the sales to helping keep the parks clean.

Rhymes: Rhymes are words with the same end sound.
Imagination and inspiration in education: Art in the schools.

Hyperbole: Hyperbole is exaggeration.
You can become a superhero by taking 20 minutes to become a blood donor.

Repetition, Rhythm, and Parallel Construction: Copywriters also use repeated words or phrases and song-like rhythms created by patterns of syllables.
Freedom. Appreciate it. Cherish it. Protect it.

PRACTICE 13.6

Using Humor

Use any humorous technique to create an ad that does one of the following:

- Encourages athletes to wear mouth guards to protect their teeth
- Asks people to conserve electricity by turning off lights in empty rooms
- Raises awareness about the importance of not driving when sleepy
- Encourages people to stop fertilizing their lawns to prevent groundwater pollution
- Motivates college students to vote

APPEAL TO HEARTS AND MINDS (*PATHOS, LOGOS, ETHOS*)

All arguments speak to hearts and minds, emotions and logic. In the world of classical appeals, these are called *pathos*, *logos*, and *ethos*. Many times you will find the appeals blended in ads.

USING PATHOS Appealing directly to the audience's emotions—pathos—in order to attract attention, is probably the most commonly used strategy in creating the images and text in public service advertisements. You can leverage emotional motivators such as guilt, fear, outrage, joy, and pride. You can inspire your audience or make it laugh. Sometimes humor can break down barriers between the message and the audience.

Irony is one of the most commonly used forms of humor in advertising. When you use irony, you rely on parallel logic—two-track thinking that leads to a surprising or counterintuitive outcome. Jokes work in a similar way: You set up a word or a situation, then deliver the opposite of what the audience expects, that is, the opposite of the literal meaning. Playing with your audience's expectations and assumptions can be a good way to get people interested in your message. One television ad for a fuel assistance program showed a mother dressing her daughter in snow pants, mittens, and a ski hat right before tucking her into bed for the night. The ad played on the assumption that the child was going out to play in the snow, not going to an icy bed in an unheated house. In a more humorous context, jokes often twist assumptions in the same way.

Image Courtesy of The Advertising Archives

Does this image appeal to the heart or mind or both?

Double entendre, like irony, plays with the meaning of words. When you use double entendre, your words have a second level of meaning, and the message resides in the double play of meaning. Double entendres may not be laugh-out-loud humor, but as with irony, your assumptions shift. An ad for a homeless shelter uses a

Susie.

A nice name doesn't make something less deadly.

Smoke 'Low tar', 'Lights' or 'Mild' cigarettes and despite their smooth taste, you are likely to inhale just as much tar and nicotine as from regular cigarettes.

For all the facts visit www.lowtarexposed.org **Low tar cigarettes. Death repackaged.**

CANCER RESEARCH UK

NHS THIS ADVERTISEMENT IS FUNDED BY THE DEPARTMENT OF HEALTH.

Image Courtesy of The Advertising Archives

How much does this PSM rely on the text to appeal to the viewer's logic?

play on the homonyms *grate* and *great*. The image is of a homeless man sleeping on a run-off grate, with the headline "Imagine waking up in the morning and feeling this grate." The fact that everybody understands the cliché of "feeling this great" after waking up is essential to the point. What kind of appeal does this ad make? Certainly, it rallies guilt in the audience, a put-yourself-in-somebody-else's-shoes kind of appeal.

Sometimes humor works well, and at other times it crosses the line and offends the audience. If you decide to use humor, keep in mind that offensive humor can turn off your audience, resulting not just in an ineffective ad but also in a counterproductive one.

USING LOGOS Another strategy is to use logic—logos. Advertisers who choose logic to attract attention often rely on statistics to make their points. Information is the focus of PSMs that use an intellectual appeal to get attention. Ads may have headlines that begin "two out of three" or sometimes use an analogy as does the Susie Shark magazine advertisement on page 424. Notice how your attention is attracted by the cavernous shark's mouth and the cute name "Susie." The headline promises "a nice name doesn't make something less deadly." You have to read the copy to see that a shark named Susie is being compared to a cigarette named "low tar." This analogy speaks to your common sense, your intellect.

The text, known as *copy*, needs to be spare, concise, and evocative because people resist reading the messages in ads. Your job as a copywriter who is writing a public service advertisement is to compress a great deal of information into a few words to deliver your message.

In their quest to get people to read or listen to their message, advertisers realize the audience has a natural reluctance to pay attention and perhaps may even be skeptical about the information. In the headline and in the text, writers try to draw in audiences by appealing to their emotions and their intellects.

USING ETHOS In creating public service messages your argument has extra weight with viewers because the sponsors—usually nonprofit groups—typically do not profit in a commercial sense. The groups whose argument you are positing, are looking to improve some aspect of society rather than sell a product. This fact helps your ethos, or a good reputation as a spokesperson. A PSM that encourages people to wear sunscreen to protect them from skin cancer will have more authority if "The American Academy of Dermatologists" is named as the sponsoring group in the PSM. The inclusion of this expert group gives the message as sense of trustworthiness and reliability. The group has nothing to gain from promoting the behavior. The real aim of the ad is not self-interest.

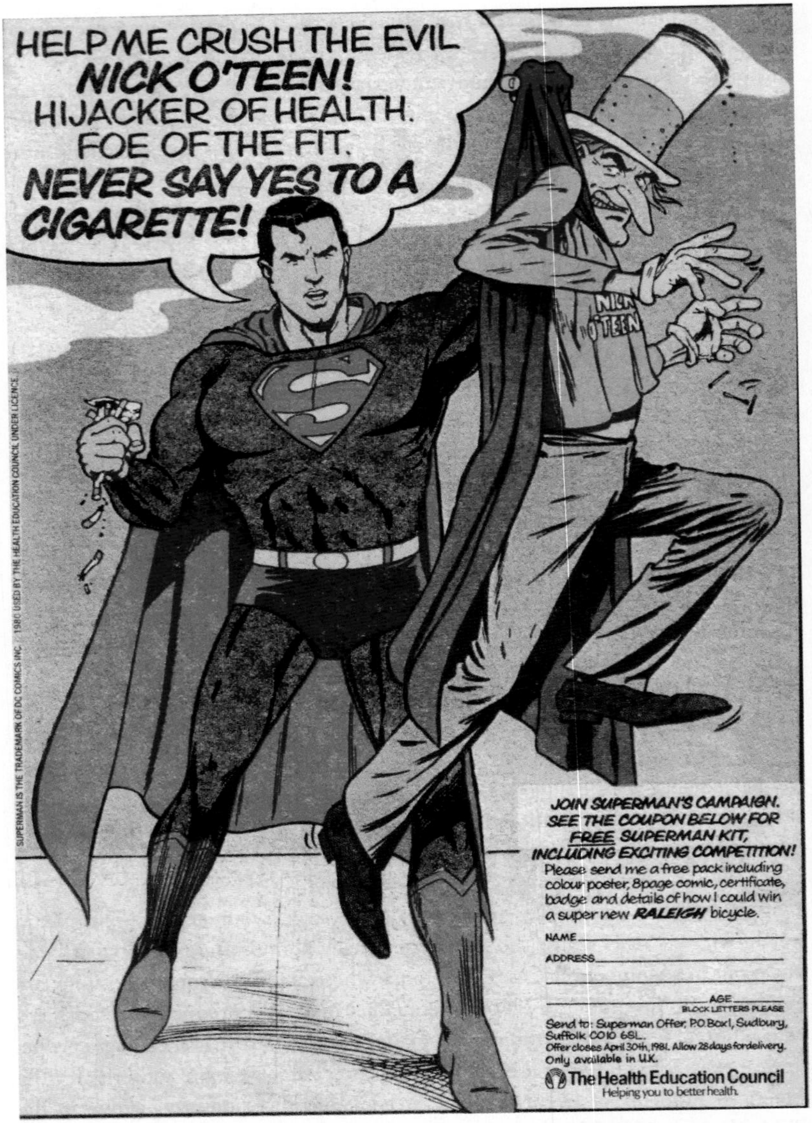

HELP ME CRUSH THE EVIL
NICK O'TEEN!
HIJACKER OF HEALTH.
FOE OF THE FIT.
NEVER SAY YES TO A CIGARETTE!

NICK O'TEEN

JOIN SUPERMAN'S CAMPAIGN. SEE THE COUPON BELOW FOR FREE SUPERMAN KIT, INCLUDING EXCITING COMPETITION!

Please send me a free pack including colour poster, 8page comic, certificate, badge and details of how I could win a super new **RALEIGH** bicycle.

NAME ____________________

ADDRESS ____________________

____

____________________ AGE ________

BLOCK LETTERS PLEASE

Send to: Superman Offer, P.O.Box1, Sudbury, Suffolk CO10 6SL.
Offer closes April 30th, 1981. Allow 28days fordelivery.
Only available in U.K.

The Health Education Council
Helping you to better health.

Image Courtesy of the Advertising Archives

Using a superhero to appeal to children, the Health Education Council launched this anti-smoking campaign in the early 1980s. Over 800,000 children sent in the form to request more information.

PROVIDE REASONS IN YOUR ARGUMENT

A visual argument can be mostly nonverbal—a message that happens in the brain, somewhere between the imagery and the viewer. Even a great image needs a few words that move beyond the showing and into the telling: A phase, clause, sentence or two that explains the why or the how.

> How could somebody like me be a foster parent?
>
> Because "you do not have to be perfect to be a perfect parent."
>
> Is hunger really a problem in America?
>
> Yes, "12 million children are fighting hunger."

CALL YOUR READER TO ACTION

The goal of a PSM is the "call to action." This is the final step in the persuasion path. If you have made your argument and persuaded your reader, it is now time to give your reader a clear course of action. Calls to action can take many forms, from asking people to get more information to asking them to do something or to stop doing something. Some calls to action ask people to donate money; some ask them to donate their time as a volunteer or as a mentor. Some calls ask for very specific actions: use a seatbelt, vote, do not drink and drive.

PRESENTING YOUR WORK: THE PITCH LETTER

Your public service message might be useful to the group or organization whose message you are promoting, so send a letter with a copy of the PSM. The letter, sometimes called a *pitch letter,* piques interest in your concept.

Choose any public service message in this chapter, and write a pitch letter to its sponsoring organization (see the box on Tips for Writing Pitch Letters). Assume that you have already created the public service message and that you are persuading the organization to use the message in its new campaign.

Tips for Writing Pitch Letters

- Write to a specific person, usually the public relations director of the organization. Do the research to find the contact person, the correct spelling of the person's name, and the person's title.
- Keep your letter brief. One single-spaced page is ideal.
- Make sure that your spelling, punctuation, and grammar are correct.
- Focus on what you can offer the organization. ("We have a fresh idea for making music piracy a thing of the past.")
- Remember that your reader is the expert in the organization. Do not tell the people in the organization things they already know, such as statistics that were generated by their organization. (Do not tell Mothers Against Drunk Driving, for example, that "drunk driving has serious consequences.")
- Use fresh, lively language and not bland, formal institutional phrasing. (*Bland:* "A group of students at our university has decided to devote time to helping to combat the enormous problem of music piracy on college campuses across this country." *Fresh:* "We want to help you help us not to steal music.")
- Be specific when you present your concept. ("Showing students where they can download free music legally will end music piracy.")
- Explain how your idea draws on your research and will bring the message to a new audience or to a traditional audience in a new way.
- Be clear about what you want the person to do if he or she likes your idea. ("Feel free to use our campaign. We consider it our contribution to helping combat drunk driving/music piracy.")

192 Freeman Street
Yardley, PA 19834

October 23, 2009

Hannah Blake, Director
MTV Think
1515 Broadway
New York, NY 10010

Dear Ms. Blake:

After spending four years at college, I have not met a single person who has been tested for HIV. I have heard many excuses from students about why they have not gotten tested, and I would like to show them the importance of testing. For a class project, three students and I created two public-service messages that we would like you to consider for your HIV testing campaign.

The current public service announcements for *Think,* MTV's HIV testing campaign, do a great job using humor to attract young people's attention. Our campaign has a serious tone that will complement your humorous approach and target the same young crowd.

Our print public service advertisement could appear in pop-culture magazines for the 18- to 24-year-old group, such as *Seventeen*, *Rolling Stone*, and *Maxim*. Our print advertisement features photos of four college students. Above each student is a speech bubble that reads, "I haven't been tested, but it's no big deal." The copy underneath the photos provides the shocking statistic that one out of every four people who are living with HIV has not had the infection diagnosed yet. The tag line of the ad reads, "That's a big deal."

We also created a radio spot that follows the same concept. Instead of photos, voices overlap saying, "I haven't been tested, but it's no big deal." After a beat of silence, an announcer reads the statistic and concludes with the tag line "That's a big deal." We conceive of this radio ad airing on national radio stations that play contemporary music, like New York's Z100.

Our goal is to encourage more young people to get tested for HIV.

Thank you for taking the time to look over these advertisements. If you would like to learn more about our campaign, you are welcome to contact us at the above address. We would be honored if you wished to use these materials to augment your current campaign.

Sincerely,
Monica Derevjanik

D I Y

DIY MEDIA AND DESIGN

YOUTUBE ADVOCACY VIDEO

A VIDEO VISUAL argument can use all the advantages of multimedia to engage the audience—sound, moving images, color, and action. This student-produced video won Third Place in a nationwide college PSA contest. The sponsoring organization, Screening for Mental Health (SMH), raises awareness abut signs of depression during their National Depression Screening Day. This Video was selected to be screened at high schools and colleges throughout the US. Look for other PSA contests online, and consider entering your video.

You can create your own video and post it on YouTube. Besides video images, you might use photography, typography, or animation to make your point. To get the full benefit of video, include music, sound effects, or voice-over.

Choose a process you can illustrate through a visual metaphor, like the one here using hands to illustrate symptoms of depression. Try to get your point across in a concrete way and raise awareness about an issue.

DIY

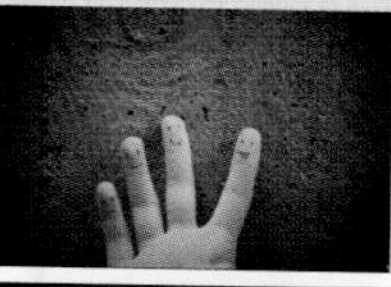

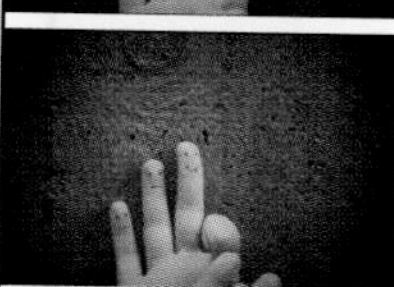

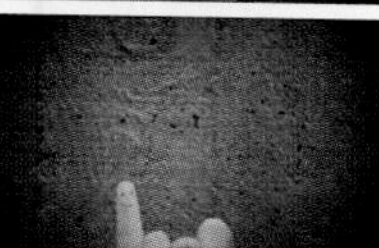

www.collegeresponse.org

SMH Screening for Mental Health

College Response National Depression Screening Day PSA

By Olga Khvan, Rachel Dushey, Kerry Aszklar, and Ephatha Park, Boston University

(Music starts -- a sad, slow tune. A shot of four fingers with faces on them wiggling, going down one by one until only the pinky is left.)

Voice Over: One out of four young adults will experience a depressive episode by their mid-twenties.

(Zoom in on remaining finger, fade out, zoom in on a girl's face. Hands with the symptoms written on them start moving in, pulling her hair and poking her face.)

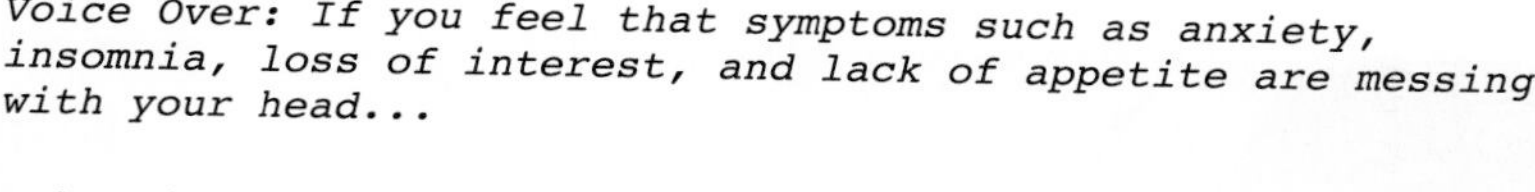

Voice Over: If you feel that symptoms such as anxiety, insomnia, loss of interest, and lack of appetite are messing with your head...

(The girl shakes loose of the fingers.)

Voice Over:...then break free.

(Music changes to a more upbeat tune. Fade out on girl's face, fade in on her now smiling face against a new setting -- a bridge overlooking the river. Two of her friends appear and embrace her.)

Voice Over: Take an anonymous depression screening...

(The website is typed out letter by letter on a blank screen and the logo appears.)

Voice Over: ...at www.collegeresponse.org.

Screening for Mental Health, Inc.

READINGS

ALL THE "readings" in this section showcase elements of contemporary public service campaigns. The first selection shows three installations created for Mothers Against Drunk Driving (MADD). The second pairs two posters from an anti-fur campaign. The final selection, shows a poster to raise awareness among teens about relationship abuse.

MADD High School Posters

Mothers Against Drunk Driving

These three photos show MADD's campaign to prevent teens from driving and drinking. The photos show actual installations in high school corridors with the accompanying informational text that was posted next to each installation.

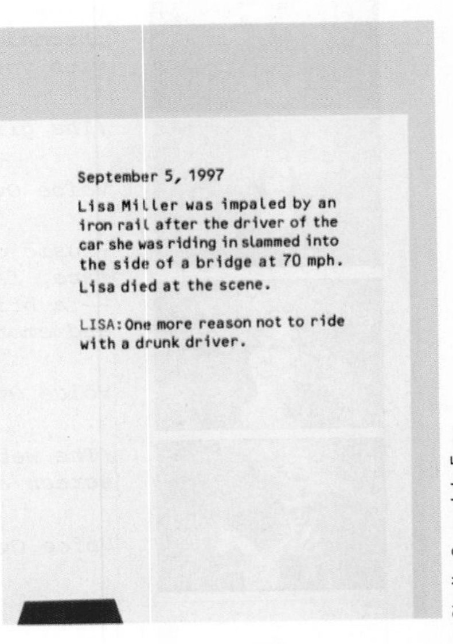

September 5, 1997
Lisa Miller was impaled by an iron rail after the driver of the car she was riding in slammed into the side of a bridge at 70 mph. Lisa died at the scene.
LISA: One more reason not to ride with a drunk driver.

Clarity Coverdale Fury

October 17, 2001

Jeff Wilson's body was crushed. The driver of the car Jeff was riding in drove into a ditch. The car flipped and Jeff's body was thrown underneath the vehicle. Jeff died at the scene.

JEFF: One more reason not to ride with a drunk driver.

MADD

Clarity Coverdale Fury

May 28, 2004

Amy Roberts was hooked up to a life support machine as a result of the injuries she sustained after the driver of the car she was in hit a parked truck. Amy died four days later.

AMY: One more reason not to ride with a drunk driver.

Clarity Coverdale Fury

QUESTIONS FOR RHETORICAL ANALYSIS

1. **CONSIDERING THE RHETORICAL SITUATION:** How does the material in the ad appeal to the target audience?
2. What effect does the installation have on the content of the ad? What are the potential risks of making this message large and public?
3. The appeal in the ad is frequently made to teens. Does this ad refresh the message? Why or why not?

QUESTIONS FOR WRITING AND DISCUSSION

1. What are the obstacles between the target audience and the message "Don't drink and drive"?
2. Are installations an effective method of raising awareness? Why or why not?

STYLE PRACTICE: IMITATION

You have been hired to do another in this series of PSMs, to install in your old high school corridor. Create a rough draft of how you would place this message in the corridor and what the copy would say.

Ink, Not Mink

Motley Crue's Tommy Lee and NBA legend Dennis Rodman are only two of a slew of celebrities who speak out against animal cruelty in PETA's anti-fur campaign.

Image Courtesy of The Advertising Archives

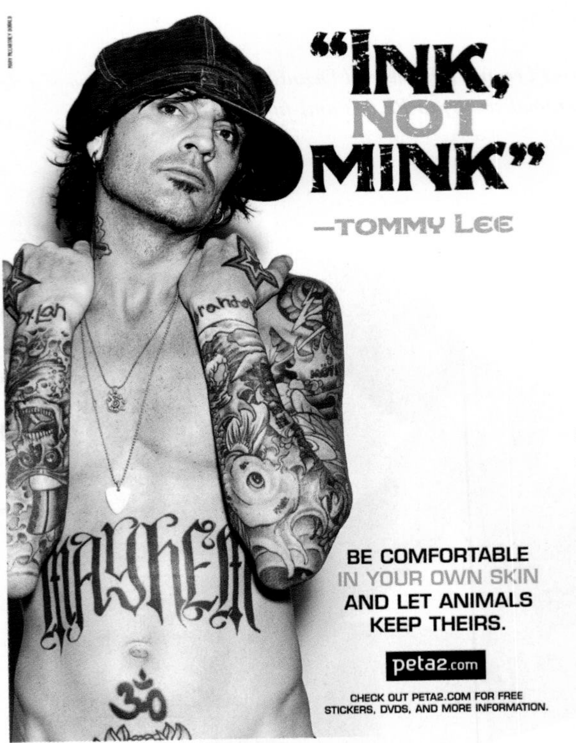

Image Courtesy of The Advertising Archives

QUESTIONS FOR RHETORICAL ANALYSIS

1. **CONSIDERING THE RHETORICAL SITUATION:** These two posters are examples of celebrity PSMs. What audience do they court? What audience might they alienate? What words or images support your answer?
2. What is the concept behind this campaign? Is it effective?
3. To what does this campaign appeal: *logos, pathos, ethos* or a combination?

QUESTIONS FOR WRITING AND DISCUSSION

1. Do you think having celebrities speak out about social issues is an effective persuasive technique? Why or why not?
2. What other approach might you take to persuade an audience not to wear fur?

STYLE PRACTICE: IMITATION

Create a rough draft of a poster for the "Ink, Not Mink" campaign targeting your parents' generation.

Talk About Your Boyfriend Trouble PSM

Seth Nichols, Emily Chang, and James O'Neill

This PSM that raises awareness about relationship abuse relies on the combination of typefaces to convey the message of its ad.

HE's **MY BOY**friend.

(I fell.)

I am high maintenance. I ASKED

for too MUCH **again**

He told me not to BUT I went anyway

(And I knew he was waiting for me to CALL)

I tripped: I am *so* clumsy.

Besides, he just lost it for a second

HE LOVES ME, *really*.

(That's what it means to be A girlfriend)

He didn't mean it!!!!!!!!!

It only happened once. *HE SAID*

HE LOVES ME.

It only happened

Once (or twice)

Love should never physically hurt.

Visit TalkAboutYourBoyfriendTrouble@yahoo.com if you want some anonymous advice on what to do next.

Kate Burak

QUESTIONS FOR RHETORICAL ANALYSIS

1. **CONSIDERING THE RHETORICAL SITUATION:** How do these writers attempt to break down the obstacles or barriers between their message and their audience?
2. How does the variety of typefaces work in this ad?
3. Who is the audience for the ad?
4. What is the purpose of the ad? What is the call to action?
5. Where would you place this ad?

QUESTIONS FOR WRITING AND DISCUSSION

1. This ad addresses an audience that might be reluctant to listen. What other audiences might not want to listen? Which other messages would be difficult to deliver? How have these messages been packaged in the past? For example, what kind of anti-smoking ads do you recall seeing?
2. In an ad directed at women, do you lose the interest of men? Do men need to hear this message as well? Which men?

STYLE PRACTICE: IMITATION

Using the same technique of using "excuses" in different typefaces, create a PSM for a seatbelt campaign, a skin cancer screening campaign, or a campaign to end drunk driving.

WRITING AND REVISION STRATEGIES

Gathered here are three interactive sections for you to use as you write and revise your public service message.

- Writer's Notebook Suggestions
- Peer Review Log
- Revision Checklist

WRITER'S NOTEBOOK SUGGESTIONS

Use these exercises to do some start-up thinking and writing for your public service message. Writers and designers say they often get the creative process started by looking at other advertisements, by looking at magazines, photography, and art books, and even by reading poetry. Inspiration can come in many ways. Short exercises like the ones that follow can help get your creative process going.

1. Design a public service advertisement that will appear on the side of a bus. The topic is raising awareness about the dangers of high blood pressure. Research the topic, and define the target audience. Alert and encourage your audience.
2. Use any news story as the basis for an ad: Use the real-life testimony about the event or some aspect of it as a cautionary tale or as an example of a behavior or policy that works well.
3. Read the editorial section of a newspaper and develop a PSM (print or television) based on the premise of one editorial or column. Raise awareness or call your audience to a more specific action.
4. Design a storyboard for a television PSM. Your goal is to raise awareness about eating disorders among teens. Your audience is parents.
5. Choose a nonprofit group in your community, and design a calendar for it. The group can either sell the calendar to make money or give it away. The calendar should have a different appeal every month to remind people of the group's activities or mission.
6. Design a new logo for a group in your community.
7. Use an existing image for a cause, and rewrite the headline and copy. Use the original call to action.

PEER **REVIEW** LOG

As you work with a writing partner or in a peer review group, you can use these questions to give helpful responses to a classmate's public service message or as a guide for discussion.

Writer's Name: ____________________

Date: ____________________

1. Where did your eyes go first? Second? Last? Note spots with the numbers 1, 2, 3, and so on.
2. To whom does the ad seem to address? Tell the writer to whom the ad would appeal. Tell the writer to whom the ad would not appeal. Who would stop reading or not be attracted at all?
3. Did you stop anywhere because you were confused?
4. Does the ad remind you of any other ads you have seen?
5. Does the design draw you in?
6. Is the language clear?
7. Did you have to start reading from the beginning to understand the point?
8. How did the ad make you feel? Did your feelings change as you progressed through the ad?
9. If you saw this ad again, would you stop to look at it or read it?
10. Tell the writer what you think the audience is called to do, and comment on this goal.
11. Is the call to action realistic?
12. Read over the pitch letter and look for
    a. Any spots that might insult the reader
    b. Any spots that assume the reader is not well informed
    c. Any places where the letter can be condensed

REVISION CHECKLIST

As you do the final revision of your public service message, check to make sure that you

- Used language appropriate to your target audience
- Created a headline that attracts attention
- Provided compelling reasons in the body of the message
- Included a clear call to action

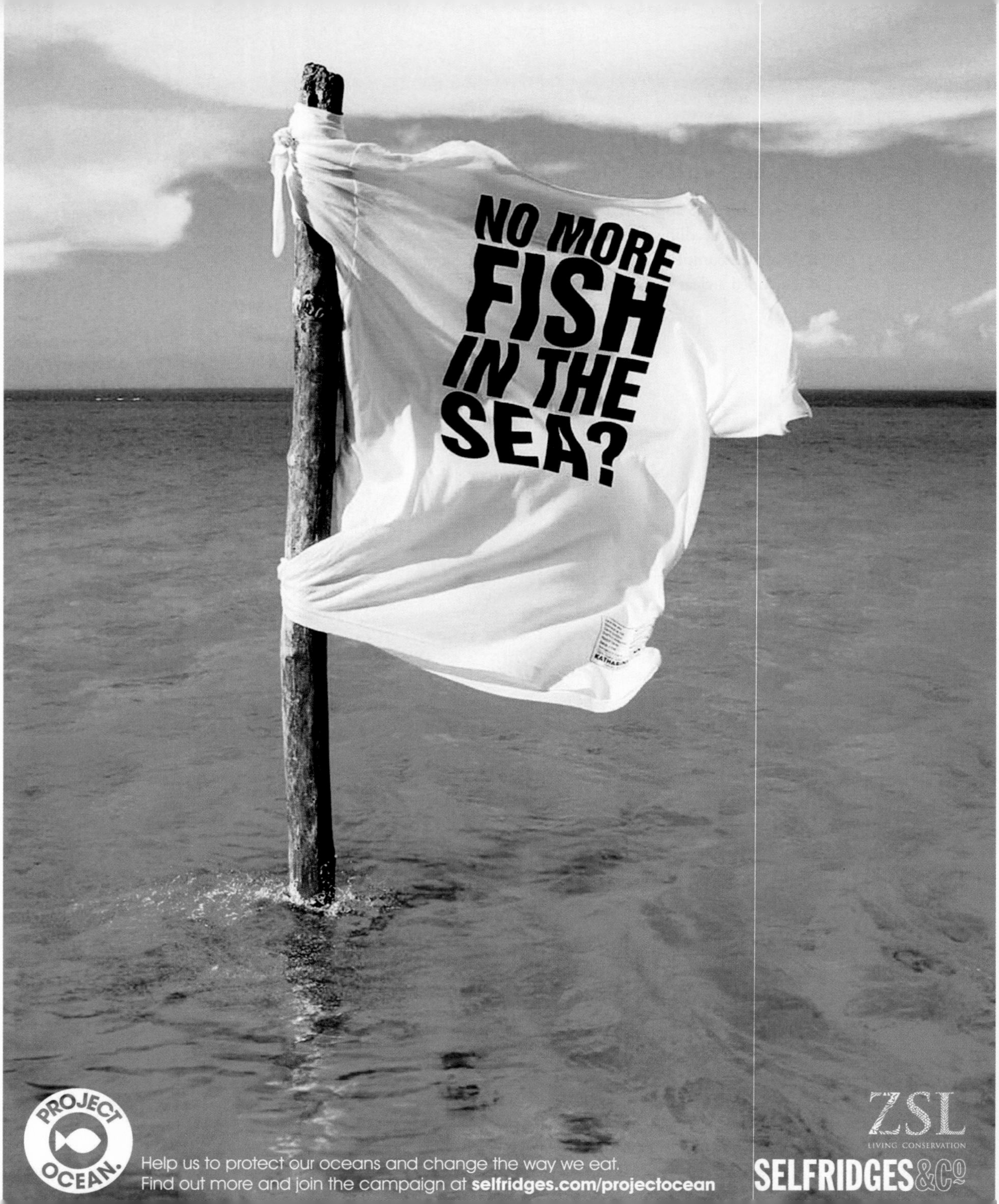

NO MORE FISH IN THE SEA?

Help us to protect our oceans and change the way we eat.
Find out more and join the campaign at **selfridges.com/projectocean**

ZSL
LIVING CONSERVATION

SELFRIDGES&Co

14

alterfalter/shutterstock.com

Writing for Your Community

PROPOSALS

When you sit down to write, you must have one clear goal in your mind. What is the ONE thing you want your reader [or] funder to remember?

—Garland Waller

A community group in a small town has taken on a project called Teddy Bears on Patrol. The group will provide teddy bears to the local police department. Police officers, in turn, will give the bears to upset or traumatized children who may have been involved in traffic accidents or domestic violence.

A high school student in a suburban community has helped found the Teen Action Board. The group's goal is to address the issue of sexual assault among high school students. With other teens around her state, she has created the See It and Stop It campaign. The campaign's primary focus is using teen peer groups to help recognize and stop behavior that can escalate to date rape.

A young woman who grew up in foster homes has spearheaded a campaign to create the Bridges to Independence program to provide transitional housing for 18-year-olds who are no longer eligible to live in foster homes. These young adults will be able to stay in this safe environment while being mentored in seeking jobs, filling out college applications, and learning independent living skills.

All of these projects began when individuals or groups identified problems: children traumatized by violence, the alarming incidence of teen date

WHAT'S TO COME

rape, the high rate of homelessness among 18-year-olds no longer in the foster-care network. The solutions to these problems are all being addressed through specific actions: comforting children with teddy bears, creating a public awareness campaign, and creating transitional housing for 18-year-olds who are former foster children.

Community service proposals offer plans to solve these kinds of problems. This chapter focuses on proposals concerning public issues. You will have the opportunity to think about problems in the public arena that you believe need to be fixed and to work on finding real solutions to those problems. Doing research will help you discover which solutions have been tried in the past and which are feasible in the present.

PROCESS PLAN

PREPARE

- Select a local or global problem to help solve.
- Figure out what background/contextual information needs to be researched.
- Come up with a solution, one that is truly feasible, targeted to a specific audience,
- Brainstorm a list of reasons that would persuade a targeted audience.

DRAFT

- Introduction: Clearly and briefly summarize the problem.
- Body:
  - Amass facts, statistics, anecdotes that show the scope and seriousness of the problem.
  - Provide a specific and feasible solution.
- Conclusion: Present the benefits of the solution.

REVISE

- Make sure the proposal has visual as well as verbal impact.
- Check that your evidence is solid and supports your proposal well.

PROCESS PLAN

UNDERSTANDING THE WRITING PROJECT

Thinkstock/Getty Images

MOST PROPOSALS identify a problem, suggest a feasible solution, and present the benefits of the solution. The purpose of any proposal is to persuade readers to take some action: to donate time or money or to create a program, plan, or public service campaign. Proposals come in many forms: formal grant proposals, letters to agencies or funders, editorials or articles that propose solutions to problems, and public petitions that lobby for change. Many college courses also require you to use the basic proposal form—problem, solution, benefits—in papers as well as in proposals for research projects and theses. Whatever the form, a proposal has to provide readers with compelling and logical reasons that prove the benefit of taking the suggested action.

ASSIGNMENT Suggest a fresh way to help solve a local, community, or global public problem. Your proposal might take the form of a grant proposal, a letter requesting funding or other support for a program, an editorial or article that proposes a solution to a specific problem, or an Internet petition that lobbies for a specific change. Organize your proposal into three sections:

- Problem
- Solution
- Benefits

Proposals are often written by teams such as groups of citizens or staff members. You can make this a group project and experience the kind of debate and compromise that goes into the process of effecting social change.

PowerPoint presentations often accompany proposals as they are brought to a public audience. You can read some tips on creating effective presentations in the DIY on page 460 of this chapter.

Access an interactive eBook, and chapter-specific interactive learning tools, including flashcards, quizzes, videos and more in your English CourseMate via www.cengagebrain.com.

Proposal for *The Silent Screams: Court-Ordered Abuse of Children*[1]

GARLAND WALLER

Garland Waller is an award-winning producer, writer, and director of nationally syndicated and local television programs and films. Her first independent documentary, *Small Justice: Little Justice in America's Family Courts*, has received national attention and was named Best Social Documentary at the New York International Film and Video Festival and the Key West Indie Film Festival. Waller wrote this proposal to fund a follow-up documentary. She sent it to a number of potential funders, including some national foundations dedicated to promoting peace and justice.

Dear Sir/Madam:

I am requesting support to conduct research, write and produce a one-hour documentary that explores an issue of national importance.

clear, specific statement of proposal's purpose

It is a little known secret that men who sexually abuse their children are MORE likely to get custody of their kids than non-abusive men. In fact, men with histories of sexual abuse are more likely to ask for custody. But the problem lies in the family courts. In my *proposed documentary, The Silent Screams: Court-Ordered Abuse of Children,* I intend to show how the family courts in America systematically send children in contested custody cases to live with a physically or sexually abusing parent. The goal of this film is to expose what in any other country we would call human rights violations.

draws reader in with attention-getting and shocking fact

identifies problem

proposes solution

explains benefits

I explored this general topic in my award-winning one-hour independent documentary, *Small Justice: Little Justice in America's Family Courts*. In this film, the focus was on mothers

establishes her credibility

[1]Reprinted by permission of Garland Waller.

who were victims of domestic violence and their courtroom trials. This documentary won the Best Social Documentary Award at the New York International Independent Film and Video Festival and was selected by the Key West Indie Film Fest as a winner. *Small Justice* was also shown at the NOW National Conference in 2002 and in 2003. The Museum of Fine Arts in Boston and the Boston Film and Video Foundation have screened *Small Justice* to shocked audiences. In addition, it has been used in numerous court cases across the country. Most recently, *Small Justice* as well as Antwone Fisher, received the Award for Media Excellence from the internationally respected Family Violence and Sexual Assault Institute.

elaborates on solution to identified problem

In the proposed follow-up documentary *The Silent Screams: Court-Ordered Abuse of Children* the focus is on the impact of family court decisions on the children who have spent months, years, or entire childhoods with abusers. Many of these children have come of age and are now free to talk. In fact, three interviews have already been shot. The following problems and issues will be addressed in this proposed project:

supporting Research

- Judges are awarding custody of children to men who physically and sexually abuse those children. New research from the Department of Justice, from the Wellesley College Centers for Research on Women, and Justice for Children supports this. What people are now realizing is that if a man beats his wife, sexually abuses his child, and then asks for custody, he has more than a reasonable chance of being granted custody. According to the American Judges Foundation on Domestic Violence and the Courtroom, batterers have been able to convince judges and legal authorities that they deserve shared custody in approximately 70% of challenged child custody cases. This statistic is more troubling because numerous studies show that batterers are twice as likely to seek custody.
- Children are suffering in record numbers. The National Organization of Women (NOW), the National Institute of Justice at the Department of Justice, Justice for Children, United for Justice, the Battered Mothers Testimony Project of the Wellesley Centers for Research on Women, the Massachusetts Children's Council and the Leadership Council are just a few of the advocacy groups that are researching the issue or going to court on behalf of child victims.

cites sources

appeal to emotion

supporting statistic—appeal to logic

acknowledges and refutes opposition

The question must be raised in the public forum, "Why are judges giving abusers custody?" One answer is the widespread use of the theory of "Parental Alienation Syndrome" (PAS) in court cases. PAS is defined as a syndrome in which a child is indoctrinated by one parent to unjustifiably insult the other, estranged parent. PAS is being used in courts by fathers with

continues next page

histories of domestic violence and/or child abuse. Dr. Richard Gardner coined the term and did "research," which experts now know is purely anecdotal. ALL the books on PAS are self-published. Yet this theory, taught in legal education seminars around the country, influences the outcome in thousands of custody cases. Because of the widespread use of PAS in custody cases, the courts often turn children over to abusers. It is important to note here that Professor Waller got the last recorded interview with Dr. Gardner before his suicide.

BUDGET ESTIMATE

The estimated overall budget for this one-hour documentary project is $175,000. This money will be spent over a two-year period when research and production will take place. Professor Waller has already begun shooting this project, but she can go no farther until there are additional funds.

establishes the feasibility of the proposal.

Research and development has already begun. Initial photography has begun. Interviews have been shot with three women who grew up in homes where, because a judge ignored their pleas to be protected from their fathers, they were raped and assaulted from childhood until they left home. The interview with Dr. Richard Gardner, his last before he committed suicide, is complete as are three interviews with women who were sexually abused and beaten by their fathers. Interviews are in line for a 14-year-old girl whose father, a felon, is seeking full custody. Despite substantial forensic evidence of sexual abuse, the judge has agreed to unsupervised visitation.

IN CONCLUSION

Recently the public became aware that members of the Catholic Church hierarchy had protected pedophile priests and ignored the words and needs of children. What people do not know yet is that judges, guardians *ad litem*, [and] even some social service agencies whose mandate is to protect children are not providing the protection that is expected from the justice system. This documentary will be the voice for children who have been silenced by the courts. It will focus public awareness on the failure of the judicial system to protect the children who have endured years of torture and abuse because of a flawed legal system.

connects to a current issue

restates problem

restates solution

restates benefits

"The more you read, the better writer you will be, and the better treatment or documentary you will write."

Q&A with Garland Waller

The Role of Research in Proposal Writing

Q: How much proposal writing do you actually do as an independent filmmaker?

A: A producer's life is writing and rewriting. You are either writing grants to foundations to try to get money or to broadcasters to try to get money. Your goal is to get your show made and seen by some particular audience. I would say that 75 percent of my day is writing and 25 percent is on the phone, talking about ideas, trying to sell an idea, getting someone excited and committed to an idea.

Q: You wrote this proposal to get funding for a follow-up film to your first documentary *Small Justice*. Both films have David-and-Goliath aspects to them, an independent filmmaker taking on a huge adversary, the American judicial system. How do you locate funders willing to take on these kinds of projects?

Garland Waller

Photo by Peter Smith

A: The trick is to make funders understand why your program is important. If you can't do that through your writing, you will never get a dime because the chance of a face-to-face to beg for money is pretty slim.

Q: You have obviously done a great deal of research on the topic of custody battles in family courts both for your first film and this one. How much research do you need to do before you propose a project?

A: I do an enormous amount of research before I get anywhere near a camera. I find out who the key people are that I should interview, what they will say and why, and who will say just the opposite. I think about where I will shoot them, how much access I will have to them, what makes their story different from any other story on the planet. I make sure I have spoken to experts who agree and disagree with my primary experts, and I read books and journals, both old and new, so that I can know the scope of the issue.

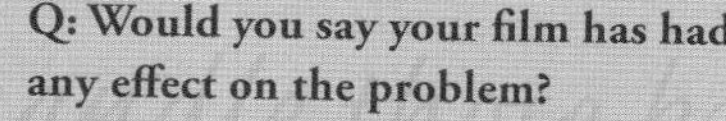

Q: Would you say your film has had any effect on the problem?

A: I am so lucky to know that *Small Justice* has been used in courtrooms as evidence and has also been used to raise money for women who have been jailed for protecting their children from abusers.

Q: Your proposal will be read by students who will be writing their own proposals to help solve problems in their communities. What proposal writing advice can you give them?

A:When you sit down to write, you must have one clear goal in your mind. What is the one thing you want your reader/funder to remember? It is important to keep to your topic, build on the reason for it, and make the writing as seamless as possible. Also, you must use your knowledge of the world around you. The more you read, the better writer you will be, and the better treatment or documentary you will write.

THE RHETORICAL SITUATION: DIFFERENT MEDIA (OLD AND NEW), DIFFERENT AUDIENCES

A written proposal to an individual or organization, like Garland Waller's proposal for funding her documentary film, takes into consideration the organization's mission and philosophy and so can have a very clear and narrow focus.

An Internet proposal, like the skateboard park proposal in the readings, targets a broad audience, one that is diverse and hard to define. The proposal has to cast a big net. Persuading any audience requires some strategic thinking.

IDENTIFYING YOUR AUDIENCE

Who has the authority to grant what you are seeking? This is the person or persons to whom you address your proposal. If you propose a change that requires support from the college community, figure out who is the person in charge. For example, for a student volunteer program to mentor local schoolchildren, collect used books for a literacy program, or help feed the homeless people in your area, you should be able to find the person in the college administration who is responsible for that area, perhaps a dean or director.

The community group working on the "Teddy Bears on Patrol" proposal might decide to target community leaders to sponsor a fundraiser or local toy stores to donate teddy bears. Proposals to help solve global social problems, like slavery in Sudan, can be directed to one of a number of nonprofit organizations already engaged in that area. In this case, the students addressed Christian Solidarity International, an organization working specifically in Sudan. You can often find the names of heads of organizations in a telephone directory or through a Web search or by making a simple phone call.

Familiarize yourself with the group that will read your proposal. Knowing the assumptions, philosophy, and history of your audience helps you understand possible obstacles. Why would audience members resist your proposal? Why would they embrace it?

Persuading someone to say yes to a proposal also requires some understanding of an organization's work. The mission of an organization or agency is the top priority of its administrators, so you need to show how your proposal fits with that mission. Most organizations and foundations have mission statements that you can study on their Web sites or in their promotional materials. Before you write your proposal, make sure you have thoroughly researched the organization's mission and philosophy.

GOING PUBLIC WITH YOUR PROPOSAL

Your proposal does not have to wait to find an audience. You can find a large audience for your ideas on the Internet—on a Web site or on a blog. Your proposal site—either blog or fully developed site—can include multimedia materials that help develop your argument. Viewers can see streaming video, link to sites that

PRACTICE 14.1

Choosing a Worthy Proposal Topic

Assume that your college has just received a donation from a wealthy alumnus to fund a community service project. The college president has created the President's Service Commission to decide which project should be funded. The commission has asked student groups, including yours, to come up with ideas for worthy projects. All the groups will present their ideas to the commission.

1. Create a list of at least five projects that would benefit your college or local community.
2. Choose the one project you think is most important, and prepare a brief position statement that
   - States the problem the funding will solve
   - Proposes how the money will be used
   - Predicts the benefits to the group and the community
3. Present your proposal to the President's Service Commission. You have only

support your cause, sign petitions, see design plans and blueprints, and even leave comments. The easiest way to post your proposal is on a blog dedicated to that topic, and you can even bring traffic to your blog by tweeting about it or starting a Facebook page and organizing an event that supports your proposal.

(*Continued*)

five minutes for your presentation. Keep in mind that the audience includes all of the other groups advocating for their projects to be funded.

IDENTIFYING A PROBLEM

Unfortunately, it is not all that difficult to identify a worthwhile issue for your proposal. Think about global problems like pollution, hunger, human rights violations, and underfunded medical research, or consider local problems like homelessness, lack of college scholarships for underprivileged students, and the need for bicycle lanes in your community. Find a problem that matters to you.

The problems you choose to work on are up to you. They can be local to your college campus, perhaps student safety after dark. They can involve your town or city, such as groundwater pollution caused by lawn fertilizer or rock salt deicer. Or the problems might be global, like hunger or disease in Third World countries. Whatever problem you choose to help solve, you will engage in a valuable process—one that helps create change in some aspect of community life, whether local or global.

Tackling a huge problem can be overwhelming, however. How can you find solutions to world hunger or war or hurricane relief when scientists and politicians around the world have failed? One way to create a manageable topic is to keep it narrow or local. Keep your goals realistic and feasible. For example, human rights violations are a vast global problem but one that you might be interested in helping to solve. To define the problem more narrowly, select a particular aspect of it or perhaps even a particular case.

One student group wanted to help eradicate human rights violations. The students began searching the Web using the keywords *human rights violations*. They discovered countries in which people are still enslaved. As they continued their search, they found the Christian Solidarity International (CSI) organization, which is actively working to end slavery in Sudan. They decided to narrow their focus to creating a public awareness and fundraising campaign in their communities. Helping CSI end slavery in Sudan became the focus of their community service proposal.

PRACTICE 14.2

Identifying Your Audience

Solve these research problems:

1. You want to write a proposal to post nutritional information in the student union or cafeteria. Find the name and e-mail address of the person in charge.
2. You want to send a letter supporting a proposal to create a food pantry in your hometown. Find the name and e-mail address of your local representative in the state legislature.
3. You want to locate a local environmental group. Find the names of the environmental groups active in your area. Get contact information for one group.
4. You are interested in finding out more about national service, and you know that AmeriCorps has a number of programs. Find the name and local contact information for at least one AmeriCorps program.

THE BIG IDEA: FROM CONCEPT TO PLAN

Just as the message drives a visual argument (Chapter 13) and an argumentative thesis (claim) drives an editorial, commentary, or blog (Chapter 12), the underlying concept of your proposal is the big idea that drives it. What is new or fresh in your thinking about the problem you are trying to solve? Many proposals have been built around the concept of empowering individuals to speak out against abuse or potential threats when they observe it. No matter whether the specific issue is domestic violence or terrorism, the underlying concept is that every person should

take responsibility for ensuring public safety. Once you move from presenting your ideas to your funding organization to posting your ideas for the public, you have shifted your audience and slightly changed your goals. Going public with your proposal means that you are speaking to a more varied group. Now, your readers might have different matters at stake, and your goal is not just funding but also gaining support for your cause—not necessarily a different aim but perhaps a different emphasis. Your proposal to build a skate park in a town will be met by neighbors whose concerns primarily are noise, parking, and crowds. Your Web posting can address these concerns by linking to similar projects in nearby towns, perhaps. Or you can show actual footage of an operating skate park so that residents can get a firsthand view of one. Whatever elements you choose, keep the audience in the forefront of your planning. Posting your proposal on the Internet allows you to link to a variety of media that will help enliven and support your proposal.

(*Continued*)

5. You are proposing that a local elementary school set up an e-mail pen pal program that pairs American students with kids from Europe, Asia, and Africa. Find out whether such a program already exists. Provide the names of existing programs and contact information.
6. Explain how you found the answers to each of these problems: whether by looking in a print source, online, or by asking a knowledgeable person.

Tips for Using Multimedia in Your Proposal

Use the medium to its fullest advantage. Posting to the Web means that you have the potential to include photography and video if you have access to film footage or slide shows. Adding video can be as simple as linking to a YouTube video you shoot or linking to a site with its own film clip. Blog-hosting sites also allow you to post video right on your blog. But remember that any material you include should fit in with your tone and be high-quality and credible. You will lose support if any of your claims are discredited or if the images and language in supporting Web links are inappropriate.

- Carefully check all videos and links to make sure the contents are consistent with the tone of your proposal.
- Make sure the multimedia material is of high-quality, both in its content and technology.
- As with all source material, be careful to attribute the source and check it for credibility and reliability.
- Avoid choosing material that includes offensive language or jokes. Your funders (and the community of viewers for your Web proposal) might not share your sense of irony.
- Be sure the material fits the assumptions of your funders. Avoid overtly partisan material. Even religious material may distract from your message (unless your funders are a political or religious group).

VISUAL LITERACY: USING IMAGES IN PROPOSALS

RARELY DO PROPOSALS COME without imagery: photographs, charts, graphs or art. For each of the images here, identify a problem the image might illustrate. Think outside the box (metaphorically or humorously). The image does not have to be a literal illustration of the issue.

Enigma/Alamy

Bill Heinsohn/Alamy

Vibe Images/Alamy

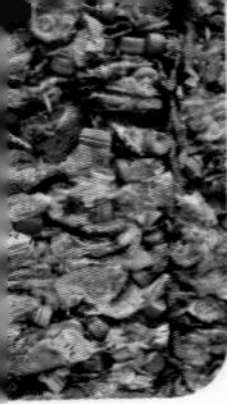

The specific plan emerges from this concept. In Garland Waller's proposal to fund her documentary film, her overall concept was to help stop abusive fathers from gaining custody of their children in divorce cases. Her specific plan, which she presented to funders, was to produce a documentary film on this topic. Often, if you ask yourself how you can translate your concept into a specific action, you can come up with your plan.

CONCEPT + HOW? = PLAN

> **PRACTICE 14.3**
>
> **Identifying a Problem for Your Proposal**
>
> Writing a proposal about a public issue allows you to suggest ways to make life better for yourself and others at your school, in your community, or in society at large. Often proposals originate in anger at injustice, unfairness, or lack of understanding. It is useful to begin thinking about proposing changes in public policy by determining what things anger you enough to want to devote time and energy to finding a solution.
>
> 1. Make a list of five things in your personal life that make you angry.
> 2. Make a list of five things about college life that make you angry.
> 3. Make a list of five things in society that make you angry.
> 4. Look over your fifteen items, and put a star next to those you think you could change.
> 5. Choose the item that most interests you.
> 6. Write that item on the top of a piece of paper and brainstorm ways that you could effect that change.

RESEARCH PATHS: TROUBLESHOOTING YOUR TOPIC AND USING EVIDENCE

AVOIDING PITFALLS OF PAST PROPOSALS

It is a good idea to do some research on past efforts to solve the identified problem before you propose your approach. Sometimes it is useful to interview a person in the organization, especially in the publicity department, to find out what the organization has accomplished and to see how it has targeted specific issues or particular populations. Become an expert on the group or individual who will read your proposal, and present yourself as someone who is not just knowledgeable, reasonable, and logical but also useful to the organization. Look for places where your plan might run into problems. One student group proposed a seemingly simple solution to feeding the local homeless population: pack up leftover food from student dining halls and bring it to homeless shelters. However, they discovered a serious impediment to this plan when interviewing the head of food services. He told them that the college was legally responsible for the quality of the food and that anyone who got sick after eating it could sue for damages. If the group had submitted its proposal before thoroughly researching the plan, the proposal would have been turned down immediately. Instead, the students altered their proposal to include a release form to be signed by the shelter absolving the college of legal responsibility, thus showing that their plan was fully developed down to the last detail. This kind of care in researching helps prepare you to face any hesitations your audience might have about accepting your proposal.

USING EVIDENCE TO APPEAL TO YOUR AUDIENCE

Evidence can help you appeal to your readers' logic and emotions and establish your own credibility. The original Greek terms for argumentative appeals are *logos, pathos*, and *ethos*.

Logos: Appeal to the reader's intellect and sense of reason by creating a path of evidence for your reader that inevitably leads to your conclusion. To get your reader to follow you from point to point, your argument must be clear and supported by objective evidence: facts and statistics.

Pathos: The emotional appeal helps your reader connect with you and connects you with your reader. Emotion can be a way to find common ground

and to say that you and your reader share a set of beliefs. Using emotion to support your points involves marshaling subjective evidence, such as opinions, anecdotes, and personal observations.

Ethos: To be swayed by your argument, a reader has to trust you and know that the evidence you cite is accurate, valid, and reliable. You create your credibility, in good part, by clear and accurate attribution of your sources. Tell your reader who your sources are and why they are especially suited to speak to a particular subject.

LOGOS—EVIDENCE THAT PROVIDES CONTEXT: FACTS, STATISTICS, AND STUDIES

Facts, statistics, and studies show the seriousness and scope of your problem. Facts, statistics, and studies make the abstractions of your ideas concrete and give context to the issues. In their research about the problem of slavery in Sudan, for example, the students found statistics from Amnesty International and the United Nations on the number of civilians who have suffered as a result of the civil war in Sudan.

> Civilians are the ones who suffer the most. Amnesty International estimates that more than two million people have died so far in the south alone. According to the United Nations, 700,000 are considered to be under a threat of death and 4.5 million have been driven away from their homes.
>
> —Dana Benjamin, Joanna Mayhew, Alexandra Mayer-Hohdahl, and Peter Myers, "Proposal to Help End Slavery in Sudan"

These numbers, from highly reputable sources, show the scope of the problem and the context in which the enslavement of civilians occurs.

In an article about "Bridges to Independence," the writer lists studies that prove "homelessness and foster care intersect at that alarming point in social research where the problem is clearly documented."

> A 1988 study of homeless persons in Lexington, Kentucky, determined that 16 percent had been in foster care, more than four times the rate for the general population. A federally funded study by Westat, Inc., in the late 1980s found that 25 percent of the emancipated youth had experienced at least one night of homelessness. A 1997 study of Wisconsin discharged foster youth indicated that 12 percent reported at least one experience of street or shelter homelessness.
>
> —Susan Kellam, "Give 'Em Shelter"

In a proposal for a child-care center at Northwestern University, writers use statistics to reveal the costs of private babysitting to help put the benefits of providing quality child care at the university into context. These statistics help make the abstract idea that child care is expensive more concrete.

> The combined impact of market forces and government regulation brings the total costs (with taxes) of hiring a full-time babysitter to $25,000, at a minimum. Those listed with employment agencies have salary expectations of $350–$500 per week, often with room and board expected as well. The pressure to provide health insurance adds further to the total cost of employment.
>
> —"Proposal for On-Campus Child Care at Northwestern University"

Facts, statistics, and studies go a long way toward making the issues understandable and putting the problem in a context. But how do you go about finding them?

First, consider who knows about the statistics. Who would know how many civilians have died in Sudan, the number of homeless people who have been in foster care, or how much it costs to provide day care for children? Chances are good that some international agency, government group, or university has researched many of the topics you will write about.

ETHOS—EVIDENCE THAT MAKES YOU CREDIBLE: CITING RELIABLE SOURCES

Digging up statistics relies in part on your intuition and common sense. It makes sense that Amnesty International would know about global human rights violations, that social scientists would study homeless populations, and that a university would have considered the costs of day care centers. You can try Internet searches for organizations with expertise on the issues you are writing about, or you can enter the name of the issue into a search engine and see which groups or agencies have studied the problem. As always, make sure your sources are reputable and credible.

Finding evidence from unbiased and expert sources is one important way to create your credibility. Sometimes it is hard to sift through all the information on a topic, especially on the hundreds of Internet sites, but it is important that you investigate the source of your information. Are the statistics about global warming that you are using to support your recycling program from a government agency, from a major research university, or from the research arm of a corporation? Who is funding the research? Answering these five questions will help you find reliable and unbiased sources for your proposal.

FIVE QUESTIONS FOR DETERMINING THE CREDIBILITY OF YOUR SOURCES

1. What are the author's credentials and affiliations?
2. What is the author's reputation? Has the author's work been cited in many sources?
3. Is the author known as an authority in this field?
4. Has the research been published in quality publications, especially scholarly journals?
5. When was the research done? Is it up-do-date?

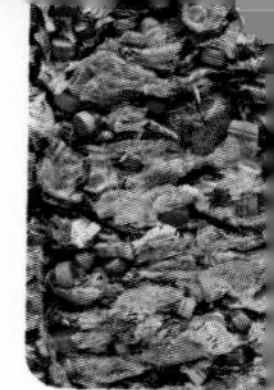

PATHOS—EVIDENCE THAT PRESENTS A HUMAN FACE: ANECDOTES, QUOTATIONS, AND VISUALS

Your research will help you find facts, statistics, and studies that provide logical support for your reasons. But the most persuasive reasons often combine logical and emotional appeals. Anecdotes, quotations, and visuals can provide the human face of an issue and bring home your point more compellingly. The "Bridges to Independence" article focuses on one young woman's story.

> A terrified young woman in Los Angeles walks into a lit office building because she has nowhere else to go. She's a decent kid and knows what it is like to be out there, having spent the better part of her 18 years bouncing between temporary homes. Later, after 18 months in transitional housing to dust herself off, and acquire the skills necessary to live independently, she emerges with a part-time job, her own apartment and a twenty-yard dash toward a nursing diploma.
>
> —Susan Kellam, "Give 'Em Shelter"

The proposal to fund the environmental education program for low-income youth includes a number of quotations from kids who have been on such trips. One elementary school student wrote this after a trip:

> I like how you took time out to ride with us people, and thank you for not giving up on me. And I like how you said, "Keep on going, Edric."
>
> —Rachel Kleinman, "Trips for Kids Proposal"

A number of proposals include photographs that illustrate the issue. Turn to the "CSI Proposal" in the Readings section of this chapter to see a picture of the children this group has rescued. Focusing on an individual example, telling a story, or giving a voice or face to a problem helps persuade a reader already hooked by facts and statistics. Logic and emotion combine to create a powerful case for any proposal. It is well worth the work to research your proposal issues as thoroughly as possible.

FORMULATING A CLEAR AND FEASIBLE SOLUTION

As in Teddy Bears on Patrol, and Bridges to Independence, a community service project often begins with a specific problem. Once you identify a problem, you can come up with a feasible solution. To persuade readers to accept your proposal, be positive and optimistic. You are not lodging a complaint but instead are presenting a plan of action. In an editorial or other opinion piece, you identify a problem and write an argument to change people's minds or behaviors.

PRACTICE 14.4

Generating Research Ideas

Choose one of the following proposals.

- Creating an antiviolence campaign on your campus
- Raising money for a local homeless shelter
- Advocating for 24-hour public transportation
- Lobbying against using live animals in science classrooms
- Creating a public awareness campaign about juvenile diabetes

Make a list of the kinds of research that would help you show the seriousness and scope of the problem. What facts, statistics, studies, anecdotes, quotations, and/or visuals would you want to find? First review this example.

Example: Creating a hotline for troubled teens

- Data on how many hotlines exist in nearby areas
- Anecdote about how a hotline has helped a specific teen
- Quotation from a counselor
- Quotation from a teen who was helped

(*Continued*)

- Studies about the usefulness of hotlines
- Expert opinion from psychologist about effectiveness of hotlines
- Costs of operating a hotline

PRACTICE 14.5

Creating Feasible Solutions

Create a feasible plan to help solve one of the following problems. List some resources you might need to accomplish that plan.

- Commuter students on your campus do not feel that they are part of campus life.
- The arts budget has been cut in elementary schools in your community.
- Summer residents of a beach community abandon their pets at the end of the tourist season.
- Over the past year, on your college campus or in your town, three people have been robbed while waiting for a bus.
- The local food pantry will run out of money next month.

Tips For Selling Your Solution

- Describe your vision in clear and specific language.
- Be positive and optimistic.
- Show your readers exactly how your plan solves the identified problem.
- Be brief. You are selling the concept, not describing every single detail of the plan.
- Write concisely but with impact.

Formulating a preliminary plan on how to solve the problem helps you focus your thinking and research. You may refine or even change your approach as you gather information. But generating ideas early in the process and putting them into clear language help you see their possibilities as well as their limitations. Once you have a plan in mind, test its feasibility by asking these questions:

- Does this plan actually solve the identified problem?
- Can this plan be accomplished with the resources I have or can get?
- Can this plan be accomplished within the time that I have?
- Has this plan been tried before?

But proposal writers go one step farther; they present a clear and feasible solution, a plan that is doable.

No simple blueprint exists for coming up with a creative solution, though it is always useful to begin by researching the issue. Read about the issue. Find out what has been done in the past. Talk to other people about the problem and past solutions. Freewrite to discover what you think about the issue. In other words, coming up with a possible solution starts with analyzing the problem.

Let us say you read a newspaper article about the lack of interest in environmental issues, especially among low-income city youth. Being an environmental activist, you decide that you want to ensure that today's young people become educated and involved. You think the first step could be to involve urban kids in outdoor adventures. One plan is to provide city youth with outdoor experiences, taking them on biking, hiking, and camping trips. What resources would you need to implement this plan? You might come up with this list:

- Volunteers from your campus outdoor club
- Support from parents and teachers
- Donations of bikes and camping equipment from local businesses

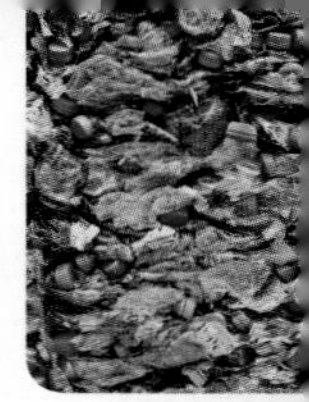

PROVIDING REASONS

Why should your reader accept your proposal? You have to provide compelling reasons, and you have to think about the possible downsides so as to counter possible objections. Generate as many reasons as you can, more than you will be able to use, to make sure you have considered all possibilities. Weed out the weak reasons, and select the ones that will be most persuasive.

One way to generate reasons is to analyze the problem. Break the problem down into its parts, and consider the different aspects. Working on the environmental education proposal, for example, you might think about what would compel parents, teachers, local businesses, and volunteers to support outdoor adventures for low-income city kids. Your list might be similar to this one:

1. Provides lessons in personal responsibility, achievement, and environmental awareness.
2. Helps kids develop practical skills and have fun.
3. Keeps low-income city kids away from gangs, drugs, and violence.
4. Provides guidance from supportive adults.
5. Helps kids get individualized attention.
6. Boosts self-esteem while kids learn about their role in protecting the environment.

—Rachel Kleinman, "Trips for Kids Proposal"

PRACTICE 14.6

Providing Reasons

1. Reread the six reasons for supporting outdoor adventures, and put them in order from strongest to weakest. Give reasons for your decisions.
2. Think of the different audiences: parents, teachers, local businesses, volunteer group leaders. Which of the reasons would you use to persuade each of these audiences? Explain your decisions.
3. What objections might someone have to any of these reasons?
4. What other reasons can you think of to support this proposal? Try to come up with at least three more reasons.

EXPLAINING THE BENEFITS

End by emphasizing the ways that the proposal will benefit your readers and the general public. What is in it for them? Be persuasive and specific as you present the benefits. Also, be specific about what you want the readers to do.

- If you want readers to fund a project, make sure you have clearly presented the budget and estimated the amount of money you need.
- If you want your readers to take action—support legislation or organize a charity bike ride, for example—explain exactly what steps you wish them to take.
- If you want readers to use your publicity campaign, explain your materials, the concept, and the audience that you are targeting.

You might even want to create prototype materials to accompany your proposal. All these possible approaches have a common goal: to convince readers of the benefits of accepting your proposal. However you decide to end your proposal, make sure your readers know how the community would benefit from the plan. If you want readers to do something, be clear, specific, and persuasive in your call to action. The conclusion gives you a final chance to motivate readers.

PROCESS PLAN

DIY MEDIA AND DESIGN

POWERPOINT PROPOSAL

CREATE A SHORT, 4-5 slide, PowerPoint presentation to present in class and perhaps even post on the Internet. Use the proposal you have written for the content, and be sure to cover the problem, solution, and benefits in your presentation. When you are designing PowerPoint Presentations, consider that your audience is listening and viewing. Display part of the text on slides, and deliver a talk to accompany the slides, but provide enough information that the slides might appear without the spoken text.

POWERPOINT DOs AND DON'Ts

1. Include powerful images that work in conjunction with your spoken text. A graph, for example, can speak a thousand words, while the narration points out a single conclusion.
2. Include charts that break down concepts visually (maps, pie charts, bar graphs can visually express statistics.).
3. Choose a style, vocabulary, and tone that illustrates the idea that you are "one person speaking to another person."
4. Use bulleted lists instead of blocks of text. The text on the slides is made up of titles or headlines and the main points are similar to an outline.
5. Remember the "one concept/one slide" rule.
6. Slide text, since the audience is reading while you explain further, does not need to be full sentences.

7. The text should be easily understood, brief, and concise. Slides should not be too detailed and should include illustrations the audience can read.
8. Organize your presentation so that it presents a kind of story with a beginning, middle, and end.
9. For a proposal, the structure is beginning (state the problem), middle (explain your solution), end (state the benefits).
10. Use a "take away" or handout for details like cost breakdowns.

Screen Shot: Proposal for a Skate Spot sponsored by the Superior Skatepark Coalition
The opening screen shot from the Superior Skatepark blog is included here. To see the complete PowerPoint proposal for a skate spot sponsored by the Superior Skatepark Coalition, go to the Readings section of this chapter. The PowerPoint proposal is posted on a blog that provides information and updates on fundraising efforts, skating events, and links to news stories.

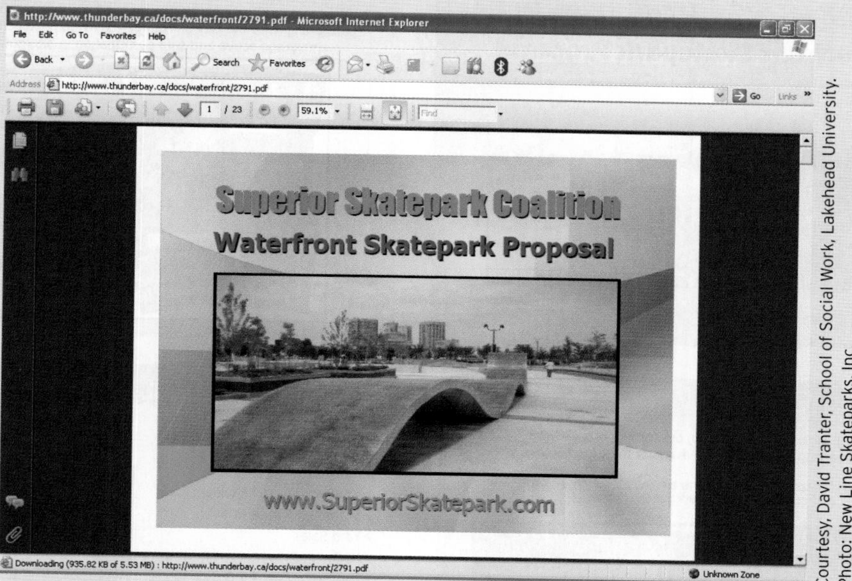

Courtesy, David Tranter, School of Social Work, Lakehead University.
Photo: New Line Skateparks, Inc.

READINGS

THE READINGS show the variety of forms proposals can take—a community group's Internet proposal to build a skatepark, an editorial that proposes a campaign to speak out against domestic violence, and a student-written proposal to help end slavery in Sudan.

Waterfront Skatepark Proposal

Superior Skatepark Coalition

THE FOLLOWING proposal is for a skatepark that would be part of a waterfront development plan. The proposal is a series of PowerPoint slides that include the elements of a good proposal. The Superior Skatepark Coalition has to sell the community on an activity that is growing in popularity but has some critics. Note how the group addresses the concerns of many constituencies within the community and makes a case for supporting the skatepark cause.

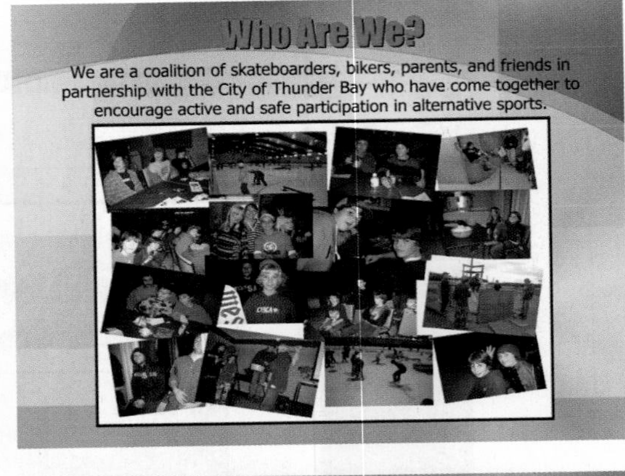

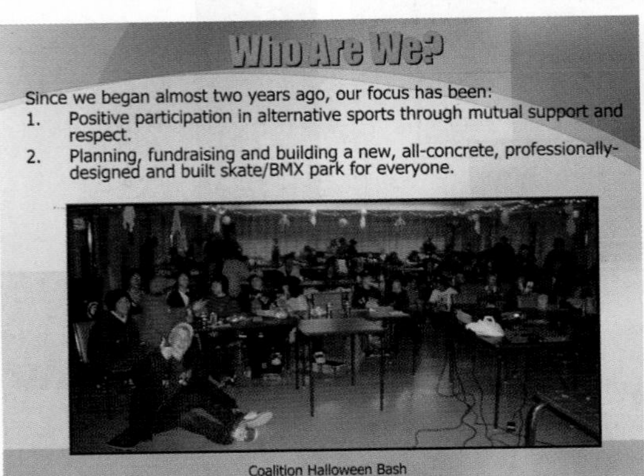

Coalition Halloween Bash

Our Activities:

- Biweekly planning meetings
- Skatepark design sessions
- Proposal writing
- Meeting with stakeholders
- Skateboarding Days
- Yard Sales
- BBQs
- Fun Skateboarding Competitions
- Skateboarding video nights
- Halloween Party
- T-shirt sales
- Video games competitions
- Skatepark clean-ups
- Road trips to visit other parks (Fort Frances, Kenora, Winnipeg, Dryden, Superior, Duluth, Terrace Bay)

Park Design Meeting

Why We Need a New Park

1. Our current parks don't support the demand.
2. Our current parks don't support the skill level of our skateboarders and BMXers
3. Our current parks are on the fringes of our community.
4. Our current parks don't capitalize on what a modern skatepark can do for a community.
5. Our current parks aren't appealing enough to draw skateboarders away from skating the streets.
6. Our current parks aren't as safe as modern ones.
7. We can learn from the experience of other cities.

Winnipeg Forks

The Old

Old Design: Linear flow, asphalt, small, placed on unwanted property, bleak, unwelcoming, single use (designed only for skateboarders).

West Thunder Skatepark

The New

New Design: Plaza style, larger, multiple use, blends with setting, thematic, open flow, smooth concrete, central, space for spectators, welcoming, a gathering place, landscaped, clean and bright.

Kettering, Ohio

The New

The new "plaza" design parks are among the centrepieces of modern public spaces where everyone is welcome. Below is the new Winnipeg Forks Skatepark:

Winnipeg Forks Skatepark

Why a Park is Good for the Whole Community

1. **Skateboarding is the fastest growing sport in North America.**

- Skateboarding has become more popular than basketball, baseball and even hockey in North America.
- There are over 1000 active skateboarders in Thunder Bay.
- Skateboarding clothing and shoes top all clothing sales.
- Skateboarding videos games are among the bestsellers of all time.
- Skateboarding is no longer a fad, it is the single fastest growing athletic activity on the continent and shows no sign of slowing down.

Burnaby, BC

Why a Park is Good for the Whole Community

2. **Skateboarding is also the most popular activity among kids who aren't in mainstream sports.**

- Not only has skateboarding surpassed mainstream sports, it is also the sport of choice for non-mainstream athletes.
- Youth who might not otherwise play organized sports (or exercise at all) get involved in skateboarding.
- Skateboarding breaks down barriers between sports and encourages youth of all ages, abilities and backgrounds to participate on their own terms.

Winnipeg Forks

Courtesy, David Tranter, School of Social Work, Lakehead University. Photo: New Line Skateparks, Inc.

Why a Park is Good for the Whole Community

3. Skateboarding is inexpensive, non-competitive and teaches skills for life.

- Skateboarding requires inexpensive equipment and emphasizes personal creativity and development, rather than "beating the other team".
- Skateboarding also requires extraordinary dedication and tenacity.
- Youth learn to compete against themselves instead of others, and focus on building personal skills rather than winning at all costs.

Why a Park is Good for the Whole Community

4. Skateboarding is not dangerous when done properly.

- Contrary to its reputation as being an "extreme sport", the rate of injury is well below other mainstream sports.
- When injuries do occur in skateboarding, it's usually a result of skateboarding at a poorly designed park or on private property.
- Skateboarding injuries are especially rare in well-designed, supervised skateparks.

Vancouver Skateplaza

Why a Park is Good for the Whole Community

5. If the city doesn't have a skatepark, then it will become a skatepark.

- The growth in popularity of skating has led to a growth in skating everywhere including on private property.
- The only way to draw skaters away from turning Thunder Bay's private and business property into skate spots is to give them a better alternative.

Winnipeg Forks

Why a Park is Good for the Whole Community

6. It's not just a skatepark, it's an accessible, supervised and safe outdoor youth centre for all.

- Unlike our current small skateparks that are exclusively for skaters and built on the fringes of the community, today's new skateparks are open and welcoming recreation centres for all youth and are easily accessible and situated in highly visible locations.
- They are built to rigorous safety standards and are usually supervised by a staff of volunteers.
- Thunder Bay's youth deserve a safe and accessible place to be.

Squamish, BC

Why a Park is Good for the Whole Community

7. Today's skateparks support urban renewal.

- The new skateparks are professionally designed to be aesthetically pleasing and complimentary to the surrounding landscape.
- They quickly become the centrepiece of a recreation area and draw skaters as well as many spectators.
- A new park will revitalize an underused part of Thunder Bay's community.

Winnipeg Forks

Why a Park is Good for the Whole Community

8. Today's destination skateparks create tourism.

- Skateboarding is a multi-million dollar industry and skateboarders are a dedicated group.
- They travel hundreds of kilometres just to skate a park.
- Thunder Bay's skateboarders regularly travel four hours to Superior, Wisconsin just to skateboard the park there.
- More parents are planning their family vacations around visiting popular skateparks.
- Also, families who are considering moving to a new city are increasingly investigating the availability of skateparks in the area.
- If you build it, they will come. If you don't, they won't!

Courtesy, David Tranter, School of Social Work, Lakehead University. Photo: New Line Skateparks, Inc.

Why a Park is Good for the Whole Community

9. The park planning and organization process teaches kids to be leaders in their community.

- The skatepark planning, designing and building process helps to teach Thunder Bay's youth the skills associated with project management, budgeting, fundraising, dealing with municipal government, grant proposal writing, public presentations, and working together to make our community stronger.

Why a Park is Good for the Whole Community

10. Invest in our youth to keep our youth in the community.

- Youth out-migration is at a critical level in Thunder Bay.
- If we want to keep our youth here, we need to show them that we are willing to invest in them and provide them with facilities that will make our city attractive to them.

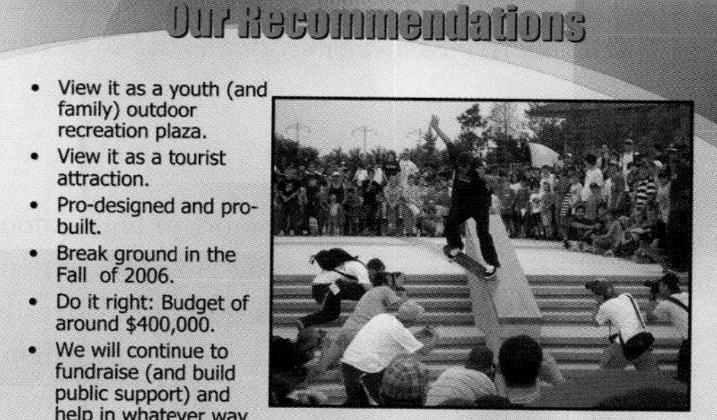

Our Recommendations
View it as a youth (and family) outdoor recreation plaza.
View it as a tourist attraction.
Pro-designed and pro-built.
Break ground in the Fall of 2006.
Do it right: Budget of around $400,000.
We will continue to fundraise (and build public support) and help in whatever way we can!

Winnipeg Skatepark

Opening Day (10,000 people showed up!)

Courtesy, David Tranter, School of Social Work, Lakehead University. Photo: New Line Skateparks, Inc.

QUESTIONS FOR RHETORICAL ANALYSIS

1. **CONSIDERING THE RHETORICAL SITUATION:** Who is the audience for this proposal? How do you know?
2. What sort of image does the proposing group seem to have? Who is in the group?
3. How does the group address the criticisms of both the sport and the skate park? Does the plan adequately address all counterarguments?
4. What kind of research has the group done? What does the information about sales of clothing and computer games add to the argument?
5. Who, aside from the skaters, would benefit from the proposed park? In what way does this information augment the proposal?
6. Does the plan's lack of financial details detract from the proposal? Why or why not?

QUESTIONS FOR WRITING AND DISCUSSION

1. What events could the group plan that might show civic leaders that this is a good and worthwhile proposal for them to consider?
2. In what other ways, besides a PowerPoint presentation, could the group present this proposal?
3. Would you support this proposal for a skatepark? Why or why not?

STYLE PRACTICE: IMITATION

Using three of the PowerPoint slides as models, design three slides for a proposal to create a dog park in your town or a community garden at your college.

Stopping Teen Dating Violence[2]

Jessica Hollander

This editorial was written by a Massachusetts student who was the victim of date rape. The editorial's publication in the Boston Globe *launched See It and Stop It, a campaign against sexual assault and domestic violence.*

EVERYONE WOULD like to believe that sexual assault or domestic violence happens only to someone else, somewhere else. We think of the perpetrator or even the victim as a faceless person one reads about in the papers.

Unfortunately, statistics show otherwise. One in five female high school students in Massachusetts reports being physically and/or sexually abused by a dating partner. Think of five teenagers you care about. Your daughter. Your little sister. Your best friend. Chances are they'll be affected by dating violence. It can be physical, emotional, or sexual. It starts with power and control. It starts early in our lives. And it happens everywhere.

"I sacrificed my own personal safety in the pursuit of what I thought was 'romance.' That night I sacrificed much more."

When I was a sophomore in high school, I learned this the hard way. An old boyfriend and close friend, one whom I not only trusted but believed I loved, snuck over to my parents' house in the middle of the night. Like many young girls do too often, I sacrificed my own personal safety in the pursuit of what I thought was "romance." That night I sacrificed much more.

When other students hear my story, they are surprised because I am not how they pictured a "typical" survivor. I lived in an affluent neighborhood, attended one of the best public school systems in the country, in a city that not only promotes but demands social awareness.

[2]Jessica Hollander (student), "Stopping Teen Dating Violence," Boston Globe, October 3, 2003. Reprinted with permission.

I have a wonderful, caring, and intimate family and friends.

Because I was so convinced that I was immune to these dangers, so certain that this individual would never consider hurting me, I ignored the warning signs, my very own intuition telling me something was wrong. I learned the hard way to follow your instincts and speak up, whether it's for your own safety or the safety of a friend. My friends and his friends ignored the signs too.

Teens need to be given more tangible tools, phrases, and words in our own language that we can use. And we need to have the confidence to know that if something in a relationship looks or feels wrong, it probably is.

The Teen Action Campaign is the long overdue vehicle to provide such tools to teens. For the past two years, I have been working with other teens from across the state to create the "See it and Stop it" campaign. We chose to launch in October for Domestic Violence Awareness month.

Because friends are such a major influence in teens' lives, the focus on bystanders is one of the main strengths of the campaign. Seeitandstopit.org asks teens to recognize the warning signs, be it jealousy, possessiveness, etc., in their friends' relationships and prevent them from escalating into a hazardous situation. The actions can be small, but can have a powerful impact.

We must all accept responsibility for the overwhelming presence of sexual assault and domestic violence in today's world. This is not just a woman's issue. Men of all ages must encourage each other not to be a man that women fear, but instead be a man that women can trust.

Those of us who helped create the "See it and Stop it" campaign are convinced that our generation has the power to speak up and change attitudes about gender violence before it becomes entrenched. But it takes resources and the support of everyone in our lives: parents, educators, faith-based leaders, philanthropists and government.

We had the help of the best experts and research in the country and the *pro bono* support of Hill Holliday Advertising, which took our ideas and made them into TV, radio, outdoor, [and] print ads; posters for schools and our website. We were supported by local philanthropists and corporations who shared our belief that we can end relationship violence as we know it. As we launch in Massachusetts, we've learned our campaign will be picked up nationally, by the Ad Council and Family Violence Prevention Fund.

"This is not just a woman's issue."

After my assault, my friends and I became vigilant in our daily activities to prevent such tragedy from occurring again. Simple things, like checking in with one another at parties, staying in groups, calling one another, and saying something out loud when something didn't feel right, became automatic.

Such precautions and social awareness can make the world a safer place for all of us. Check out our campaign so [that] the next time you see it, you'll know it. You just might speak up and do something to stop it.

QUESTIONS FOR RHETORICAL ANALYSIS

1. **CONSIDERING THE RHETORICAL SITUATION:** Who is the intended audience for this proposal? Where does the writer directly address her audience? Is this an effective technique?
2. What is the concept behind this campaign? Where specifically does Hollander state this concept?
3. In a sentence, define the problem Hollander identifies.
4. What is the solution to this problem?
5. Identify places where Hollander uses personal anecdotes, facts, or statistics to appeal to her readers' emotions and intellect.
6. What benefits will come from this proposal? Where does the writer mention these benefits?

QUESTIONS FOR WRITING AND DISCUSSION

1. Hollander writers that domestic violence ". . . is not just a woman's issue. Men of all ages must encourage each other not to be a man that women fear, but instead be a man that women can trust." Discuss your reactions to this statement.
2. Do you think that teens can be empowered to speak up against abusive behavior? What would stand in the way? What would pave the way?

STYLE PRACTICE: IMITATION

Hollander uses a personal anecdote at the beginning of her editorial to establish her credibility and to tell her story. Write a short personal anecdote that you might include in a proposal to stop bullying in school, to prevent teens from texting while driving, or some other issue in which you have a personal stake.

Proposal to Help End Slavery in Sudan[3]

Dana Benjamin,
Joanna Mayhew,
Alexandra Mayer-Hohdahl,
and Peter Myers

THIS STUDENT group proposed a media campaign to increase public awareness of the plight of enslaved people in Sudan. The students created this poster as an illustration of the public awareness campaign they describe in the proposal.

[3]Reprinted by permission of Dana Benjamin, Joanna Mayhew, Alexandra Mayer-Hohadahl, and Peter Myers.

DANA BENJAMIN, JOANNA MAYHEW
ALEXANDRA MAYER-HOHDAHL AND PETER MYERS
BOSTON UNIVERSITY

May 7, 2005

Christian Solidarity International
870 Hampshire Road, Suite 7
Westlake Village, CA 91361

Dear Sir or Madam:

While researching nonprofit organizations, we came across Christian Solidarity International, and your case immediately sparked our interest. We feel that our campaign will raise awareness for the problem of slavery in Sudan.

In the following proposal, we have put together a public-service campaign for both print and television.

Sincerely yours,

Dana, Joanna, Alexandra, and Peter

Cengage Learning

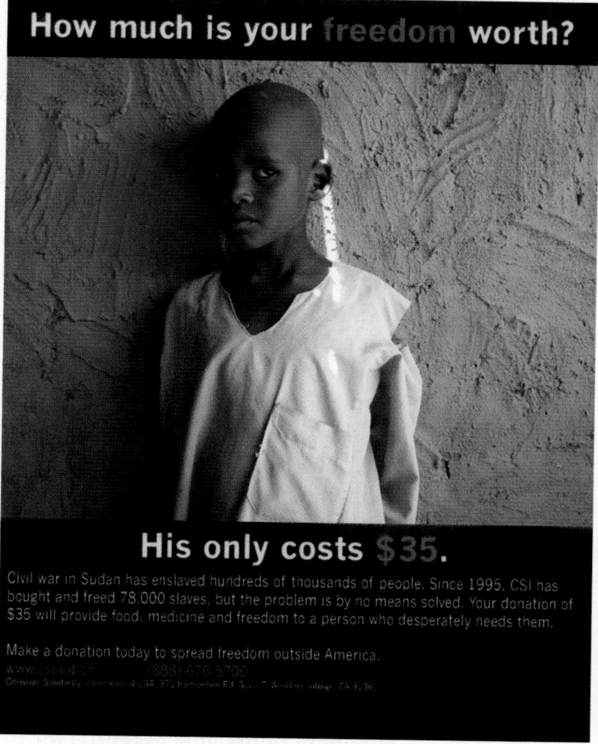

How much is your freedom worth?
His only costs $35.
Civil war in Sudan has enslaved hundreds of thousands of people. Since 1995, CSI has bought and freed 78,000 slaves, but the problem is by no means solved. Your donation of $35 will provide food, medicine and freedom to a person who desperately needs them.
Make a donation today to spread freedom outside America.
(888) 676-5700

Kate Burak Picture Contact BV/Alamy

This poster accompanied the students' proposal for Christian Solidarity International.

Proposal: A Public-Service Campaign for Christian Solidarity International to Raise Awareness of the Problem of Slavery in Sudan

1. Problem

The United Nations Universal Declaration of Human Rights states, "No one shall be held in slavery." However, slavery is still an everyday threat for a number of people around the world. Sudan, Africa's largest country, cannot provide complete protection for its inhabitants. A war-torn nation for decades, Sudan has become a scene of ethnic and religious discrimination.

The mainly black and Christian south regularly faces the Islamic north in bloody battles. Civilians are the ones who suffer the most. Amnesty International estimates that more than two million people have died so far in the south alone. According to the United Nations, 700,000 are considered to be under a threat of death, and 4.5 million have been driven away from their homes.

In addition to these overwhelming statistics, a new trend in warfare has appeared in the north's strategy. Soldiers, equipped with the most modern arms supplied by the northern government, regularly raid villages in the south. They are not only looking for loot: they are also searching for slaves.

Tens of thousands of children and women are abducted, forced to walk several days to the north, and then sold into bondage under conditions that go against all human rights. These slaves are mistreated physically and psychologically. Severe beatings, rape, female genital mutilation, death threats, torture, and forced conversion to Islam are the norm. The stories and testimonies they bring back, along with the bruises and scars, are proof enough.

5 Unfortunately, the international community has turned a blind eye to what is happening in Sudan. Their intervention is needed to stop the northern regime, based in Khartoum, from leading a so-called Jihad against the south. A sanction against companies doing business with or in Sudan had been considered by the United States, but this sanction has been forgotten in the midst of the antiterrorist work it is now involved in. In September 2001, the United Nations Security Council lifted its sanctions. Sudan is now to become part of the "civilized" world, even though such barbaric actions are still taking place.

Slavery and the actions of the Sudanese government remain a crucial violation of human rights. It is essential for the international community to react to this violation and apply pressure on the Khartoum regime to make sure it stops its inhuman warfare strategies. In addition, it is important to lend our support to nonprofit and nongovernmental organizations that fight slavery, CSI being one of the only ones to do so in Sudan.

2. Context

It is impossible to determine exactly how many people have been enslaved since the beginning of the civil war in Sudan. Yet the slave trade has been documented over and over again by journalists—from *Newsweek, Time, ZDF, and 3-SAT,* to name but a few—especially over the last years, when the organizations involved in Sudan have brought them into the country.

Today, CSI is one of the few nongovernmental organizations that remain in Sudan. A similar American organization, Christian Freedom International, was recently forced to discontinue its practice of buying back the slaves' freedom because of international pressure and criticism. Indeed, it has been said that organizations such as CSI only end up helping the slave traders to make more money. Still, CSI continues its work and is thinking of expanding its program.

Actions at a more global international level include the proposed Sudan Peace Act, which would stop companies that do business with Sudan from receiving any U.S. capital. However, this treaty now faces an uncertain future, as the United States is looking for allies among Islamic states to strengthen its fight against terrorism.

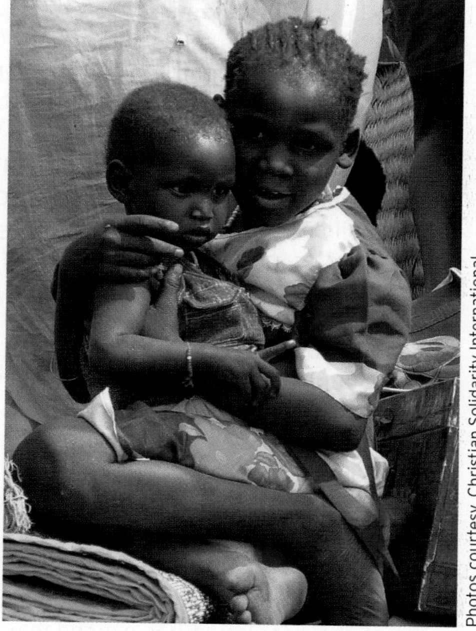

Photos courtesy, Christian Solidarity International

3. Research

10 Since 1995, over 78,000 black Sudanese slaves have been liberated through the CSI-sponsored "Underground Railroad." In this slave-redemption program, CSI pays networks of Arab retrievers a fixed rate of 50,000 Sudanese pounds—currently the purchase price of two goats or $35—for every slave freed and returned. Once returned, CSI provides food, medical aid, and education to the former slaves (www.csi-int.ch).

According to CSI, over 200,000 Sudanese are believed to currently be in bondage. Slavery is clearly defined in international law as a "crime against humanity." The U.S. State Department, several U.N. Special Rapporteurs, and many human rights organizations have implicated the government of Sudan in the revival of black slavery in Sudan. CSI's ultimate goal is nothing less than the abolition of slavery in Sudan.

Recently, CSI joined forces with the American Anti-Slavery Group and the National Black Leadership Roundtable to begin a project for documenting liberated and missing Sudanese slaves. The new documentation project aims to enable governments, human rights organizations, and the general public to better understand the extent of Sudan's revived slave trade. Sound documentation of this scourge of Sudanese slavery is essential for its complete abolition and the reunion of slaves with their families.

The documentation project is underway, and according to CSI, preliminary analysis of interviews with over 1,200 liberated slaves reveals that more than 70 percent of females over the age of twelve were raped while in bondage and over 15 percent

of boy slaves older than six years were sexually abused by their captors or members of their masters' households. Over 80 percent reported they had witnessed the execution of at least one slave by their mujahadeen captors or by their domestic masters. The same percentage said that they were forced to convert to Islam.

This documentation important, is also very new campaign propos- in a significant increase This support can then be tation program and other at aiding CSI [to] reach its ery in Sudan.

"70 percent of females were raped while in bondage and over 15 percent of boy slaves were sexually abused by their captors"

process, while extremely costly. We believe that our als will effectively result in monetary support. directed to the documen- areas, but it will be aimed ultimate goal: to end slav-

15 The opponents to CSI have only one complaint: by buying back slaves in Sudan, CSI is funding slave traders to buy more ammunition to perform further raids and thus increase the slave trade. However, this argument is easily refuted. CSI argues that all available research suggests that the number of slave raids has decreased since CSI began its slave-redemption program in 1995.

4. Solution and Analysis

Our campaign is targeted at the middle-aged American workforce. Usually, this segment of the population has expendable income to give to charity. Though the ads that we will be presenting may not seem target-based, their placement has been strategically planned for the middle-aged American businessperson.

To reach this target group effectively, we plan on putting our public-service announcement in *Newsweek*, the *New York Times Magazine, Time,* and the Sunday editions of various newspapers. In addition to publications, these advertisements will be placed on subways and buses.

Although appealing to both intellect and logic, our campaign focuses predominantly on an emotional appeal, using testimonials and pictures of Sudanese slaves. The more personal and truthful the ads are, the more likely the audience is to identify with the cause and invariably contribute to freeing the very people they see.

Our campaign consists of both print ads and television commercials. In the latter, the use of testimonials will bring people closer to the cause CSI is advocating. In both formats, we use emotion-evoking pictures and the slogan "How much is your freedom worth?" These common aspects of the ads help create an image of the organization and a sense of urgency for the cause. The dark backgrounds of both ads aid in creating the serious mood that accompanies CSI's cause. If we were to use twenty different slogans with catchy words and bright colors, the message would not be communicated nearly as urgently or effectively.

We also predict that our ads will create publicity for CSI, resulting in discussion 20
around the business community. Once CSI has established itself, we plan to integrate a cause marketing campaign, which would consist of a letter of appeal sent to large companies and their employees. Cause marketing links a nonprofit organization and a large company, forming a symbiotic relationship that results in publicity for both. There is a lot of potential for the bright future of CSI, and with our campaign, we feel that this potential will be reached and surpassed.

QUESTIONS FOR RHETORICAL ANALYSIS

1. **CONSIDERING THE RHETORICAL SITUATION:** To whom is this proposal addressed? What language or ideas in the proposal are tailored to this audience?
2. What are the visual design elements of this proposal in terms of the use of white space, headings, and typeface? How effective are they?
3. What techniques do the writers use in the introduction (the problem section) to focus readers' attention on the problem?
4. By the end of the introduction, is the problem clearly defined? Summarize the problem as you understand it.
5. What kind of research have the writers done? Where do they appeal to emotion and where to logic?
6. What solution do the writers propose? How feasible is this solution?
7. What benefits do the writers hope will emerge from this proposal? Can you suggest other benefits that might accrue?

QUESTIONS FOR WRITING AND DISCUSSION

1. How persuasive do you find this proposal? If you were in a position to work on this campaign, would you? Why?
2. How persuasive is the poster? To what does it appeal?
3. How do human rights issues like this one in Africa affect people in other parts of the world?

STYLE PRACTICE: IMITATION

Write a brief pitch letter, similar to the one written for this proposal, but address it to a local media outlet requesting that it support this issue by broadcasting or publishing your campaign.

WRITING AND REVISION STRATEGIES

Gathered here are three interactive sections for you to use as you write and revise your proposal:

- Writer's Notebook Suggestions
- Peer Review Log
- Revision Checklist

WRITER'S NOTEBOOK SUGGESTIONS

You can use these exercises to do some start-up thinking and writing for your proposal.

1. Write a one-page proposal aimed at the U.S. Postal Service recommending a commemorative stamp design. Choose a person or event you think worthy of a stamp, and make an argument for it.
2. You want to organize a fundraising barbecue to support a homeless shelter if your local chapter of the Salvation Army will sponsor it. Write a brief letter to the Salvation Army proposing this idea.
3. Talking with friends, you realize that each of you knows someone battling smoking or who has a smoking-related disease. You are irate that cigarette company advertisements target young people and poor people. Write a short letter to the American Cancer Society proposing that it pitch its next efforts to keep junior high kids from smoking.
4. Choose an editorial in today's paper. Write a letter to the editor proposing a solution to the problem discussed in the editorial.
5. Write a letter to your boss or former boss proposing improvements in the workplace. Consider your audience carefully.
6. You learn that your college is trying to recruit students from abroad to help create a more international student body. You decide to write and shoot a short promotional video to help recruitment efforts. Write a one-page proposal pitching your ideas to your college president and asking for funding for your project.
7. Write an e-mail message to a former professor proposing a feasible change to the course syllabus.
8. Valentine's Day is approaching. Write a proposal to your sweetheart.

PEER REVIEW LOG

As you work with a writing partner or in a peer review group, you can use these questions to give helpful responses to a classmate's proposal or as a guide for discussion.

Writer's Name: ____________________

Date: ____________________

1. Who is the specific audience for this proposal? What do you know about this audience? Can you make any suggestions on how the writer can more effectively tailor the proposal to this audience?
2. Bracket the introductory section. Does the introduction hook the reader? Can you suggest ways to strengthen this section?
3. Underline the problem statement. Can this statement be clarified? Does it need more support?
4. Underline the solution presented in the body of the paper. Is the solution feasible? What might make it more appealing or more doable?
5. Point out places where the writer has considered possible objections to the proposal. Can you suggest other points the writer might consider?
6. Mark places where research appeals to logic (facts, statistics, studies, graphics) and to emotion (anecdotes, quotations, visuals). Are the sources credible? Does the proposal need more or different kinds of support?
7. Bracket the conclusion. Underline sentences that explain the benefits of the proposal. Are these benefits clearly stated? Can you suggest other possible benefits?
8. Look at the overall design of the proposal. Could the writer use white space, headings, or different typefaces to help organize the proposal and make it more visually appealing?
9. Put a wavy line under writing that could be more concise, clear, positive, or specific. Can you make suggestions to strengthen the writing?
10. Does the proposal persuade you? If not, what else might the writer do to win you over?

REVISION CHECKLIST

As you do your final revision for your proposal, check to make sure that you

- Chose a specific audience for your proposal and tailored your writing to that audience
- Wrote an introduction that engages your reader
- Stated the problem clearly in the introduction
- Provided some background or contextual information
- Included research that shows the scope and seriousness of the problem
- Attributed your research clearly to credible sources
- Presented a clear solution to the problem
- Provided the necessary details to show the feasibility of your solution
- Explained the benefits of your solution to your audience
- Designed the proposal visually so that it is clear and easy to read
- Wrote with language that is concise, clear, positive, and specific

PART VI

Research and Documentation

Tony Law/Redux Pictures

“On the Internet, nobody knows you’re a dog.”

Research

15

Nejron Photo/
Shutterstock.com

Research is formalized curiosity. It is poking and prying with a purpose.

—Zora Neale Hurston

You are a student at the University of Nebraska at Lincoln. At lunch one day, your friends observe that, based on conversations they have had with other students, crime on campus seems to be rising.

Since you have a trend article due soon, you decide to look into the question of whether the crime rate at the university is rising, and you wonder how this shift may or may not compare with the crime rate at other four-year colleges in Lincoln and what all of this says about student safety on campus. You do a quick Internet search and you find crime rates for Lincoln, but your subject is so specific that you have trouble finding information on the topic of crime at colleges in Lincoln. Data must be compiled somewhere, you think.

Since you are walking by the library, you get the idea that you could ask a librarian for some advice. Why not? So you say, "I want some really quick, but reliable information." The librarian says, "It's simple. Just add an extra word to your search."

So you go to a computer and type in "campus crime statistics," and you include the word "database." You also ask yourself, "Why didn't I think of that?"

Just a second later, you have a source: The United States Department of Education collection of data on crime at colleges. High-quality source number one.

Your research has begun.

WHAT'S TO COME

UNDERSTANDING RESEARCH

More people than ever are incorporating research into their everyday lives, using the Internet for comparison shopping and finding out about medical conditions, and consulting experts through e-mail. The Internet makes it possible to research quickly and well, as long as you know the variety of tools available online.

Still, some inquiries need other approaches. Complex questions like "What were the effects of the Industrial Revolution on women?" might be best answered in a book or in a specialized database available at the library. Research for some projects may even take the form of interviewing experts or hunting through archives and public documents like birth and death records in the county courthouse.

Formulating a valid research question is the first step. Locating high-quality sources is the next. But the ocean of sources available to you through the Internet—including libraries, databases, journals, video, and audio files can be overwhelming. A huge array of research tools—books, Web sites, directories of experts, and public documents, to name just a few—is available through your Internet connection and at your school or public library. There are so many tools, in fact, choosing the right ones can be a researcher's most baffling problem. How do you find the best books among the stacks at the library? Why use a book if you have an Internet connection? Dealing with the vast array of sources may lead researchers into winding paths that consume lots of time and sometimes yield very few quality results.

Since you want your work to be as efficient as possible, making your research path as methodical as it is creative is key. A good method involves:

- refining a question
- knowing where to find sources
- knowing how to evaluate good sources quickly.

In this chapter, you will learn to research more efficiently and effectively, following a research path that ends in high-quality information.

No single tool can do every research task. A good researcher knows how to use a variety of search tools—including talking to experts, like librarians. As you will see in this chapter, the best research uses a combination of approaches. You will also learn some ways to make your writing more creative through research.

BRAINSTORMING: RESEARCHING TO DISCOVER TOPICS

Many people in creative professions—such as designers, architects, and film producers—use research to jump-start new projects and get ideas flowing. Some people in technical and scientific fields say that even before they have a topic firmly

fixed, they first brainstorm by doing a quick electronic keyword search. Many professionals report browsing "bricks and mortar" bookstores or even electronic bookstores like Amazon.com for inspiration.

Researchers who use this browsing method say they:

- look for unusual twists on familiar subjects by reading through titles and leafing through books, noting chapter titles and authors
- look at current journals that reflect recent topics and trends in specific fields of study

Browsing through journals and magazines at the library or bookstore might even be easier and more useful than surfing the Internet with keywords. Current professional and scholarly journals and other periodicals reflect the most up-to-date thinking, and it may be easier to evaluate the credibility of sources in the library than online. Later in this chapter you will see how important evaluating credibility is and why the publications you find in bookstores and libraries, which have been reviewed and selected, might be more reliable than Internet sources.

WIKIPEDIA

Wikipedia, a "collaborative" Web site that lets users contribute and edit material anonymously, is often criticized as being an unreliable source for facts. If you use Wikipedia to discover topics, remember most teachers forbid citations that refer to Wikipedia. Yet, it is a good place to go to get an initial overview of a topic.

VIRTUAL LIBRARY: THE ONLINE SUBJECT CATALOG

You can browse the "virtual shelves" at the library by beginning with a hunt through the online subject catalog. Libraries own a great variety of encyclopedias, guides, dictionaries, bibliographies, and other general reference works that can give you an overview of a subject you might not know much about. You can find these sources in the library catalog or with the help of librarians.

Online encyclopedias, such as *Britannica Online,* provide broad background information. For example, the following entry shows the result of a keyword search for "carbon dating" to research the way archeologists use carbon dating on digs.

> **Carbon-14 Dating and Other Cosmogenic Methods, from *Dating***
> The occurrence of natural radioactive carbon in the atmosphere provides a unique opportunity to date organic materials as old as 50,000 years. Unlike most isotopic dating methods, the conventional . . .
>
> **Radiocarbon Dating**
> Scientists in the fields of geology, climatology, anthropology, and archaeology can answer many questions about the past through a technique called radiocarbon, or carbon-14, dating. One key to understanding how and why something happened is to pinpoint when it happened. (See also Anthropology. . . .)

PRACTICE 15.1

Brainstorming through Research

Before you assign yourself a type of writing project (editorial, review, profile, short essay, trend analysis), identify a subject area you want to know more about.

Are you interested in green technologies or the history of the circus? Do you want to know more about a process or about the origins of something?

1. Divide a sheet of paper into six sections. Give each section a general subject (circuses, solar energy, the sport of lacrosse, for examples).
2. Write five questions in each section (Where was the first recorded circus? Where does the name "lacrosse"come from?).
3. Next, do a quick Internet search to answer your question. If you end up using Wikipedia, also visit the footnoted links.

Boston University Libraries

Telnet to Catalog

Web Catalog

Search
Author
Title or Journal Title
Word
Author / Title
Subject Headings
Call Numbers
ISBN, OCLC
Gov. Doc. Numbers

Reserve Services
By Course Number
By Professor's Name

Help and Renewal
Library Information
Borrowing Record
Book Renewal
Library Purchase Request

BU Library Web Sites
Boston University Libraries ▾ Go

Boston Library Consortium
BLC GatewayII Virtual Catalog II

Boston University
Page designed by the Web Catalog Committee.
http://library.bu.edu/

Mugar Memorial Library, Boston University

Library subject online catalog

Carbon
Without the element carbon, life as we know it would not exist. Carbon provides the framework for all tissues of plants and animals. These tissues are built of elements grouped around chains or rings made of carbon atoms. Carbon also provides common fuels—coal, coke, oil, gasoline, and natural. . . .

You can also search the *Britannica Elementary Encyclopedia* for articles about carbon dating.

Carbon Dating
Introduction to this technique. Contains information on its accuracy, applicability, and related theory.

Archaeology and Ancient History: Archaeology
British Broadcasting Corporation
Resource on various aspects of this study of the material remains of the past human activities. Includes illustrated articles on marine and virtual

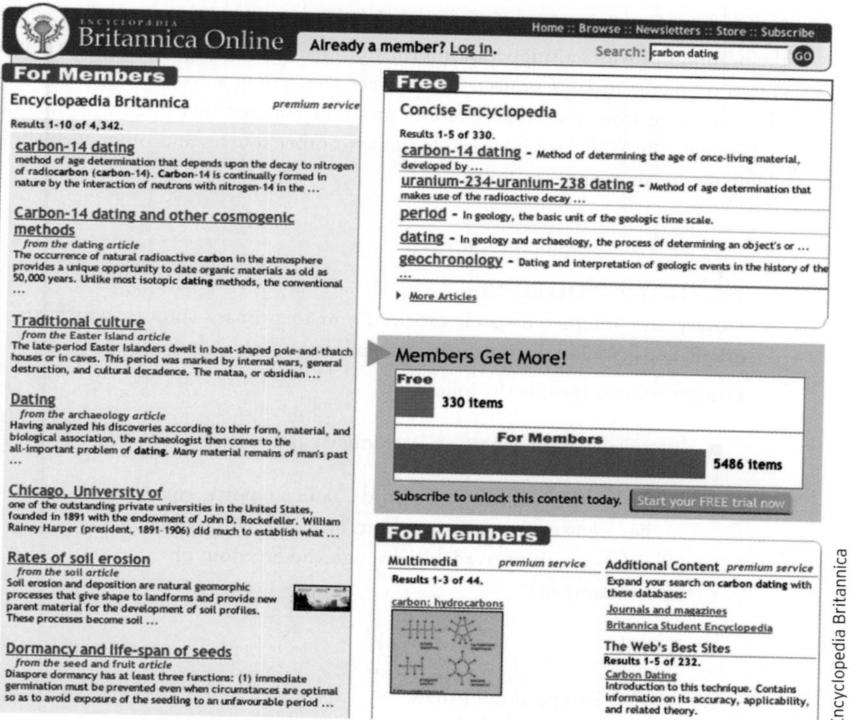

Encyclopedia Britannica

Online search for "carbon dating" from the *Encyclopeaedia Britannica*

archaeology, carbon dating, and the Piltdown man. Also contains reports on the British sites, and game.

Learning from the Fossil Record
University of California, Berkeley
Educational reference on paleontology, for students. Includes classroom activities and projects on plate tectonics, dinosaurs, carbon dating, fossils, and climate change. Provides access to related educational resources.

Prehistory
Teacher Net
Collection of resources on evolution, agriculture, tools, weapons, art, the major civilizations, and archaeology of this period of ancient history. Facilitates access to picture galleries, guided tours, interactive maps, timelines, and online books. Includes sections on dinosaurs and carbon dating techniques.

You can see the usefulness of this site for beginning your research path. Each of the headings provides a snippet of information that you can explore in more depth if it is pertinent to your project. If you were researching a coastal dig, for example, "Learning from the Fossil Record" promises material that deals with marine archeology. The Web site also provides links to other sources and other Web sites, giving you many avenues to follow.

Primary Sources

Library and Internet research can lead you to primary sources, which are original or firsthand documents that detail data.

Primary sources include the following:

- Interviews (with experts, practitioners, and witnesses)
- Public documents (like tax records, police reports, government studies, census data, minutes from meetings with public officials—anything available through the Freedom of Information Act)
- E-mail
- Diaries, letters, and journals
- Manuscripts, music, films, speeches, and works of art
- Experiments and observations
- Surveys and polls
- Autobiographies
- Journals

Using or consulting primary sources will tend to make your writing more credible and original, and less derivative. Sometimes, however, primary sources may be unavailable or not appropriate for your assignment.

SECONDARY SOURCES

In the course of your research, you may also want to read what other people have thought or figured out about a topic. Secondary sources analyze and interpret original sources.

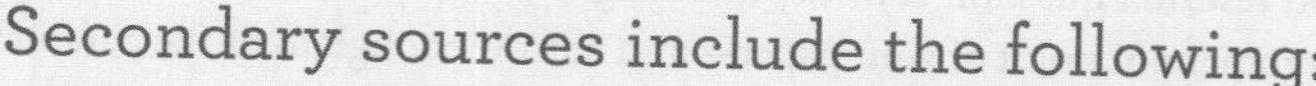

Secondary sources include the following:

- Analytical books
- Commentaries in magazines and journals
- Newspaper articles
- News broadcasts
- Reviews
- Online discussions, bulletin boards, and listservs
- Biographies

Remember always to give credit to the writer responsible for the research and ideas. See Chapter 16 on how to cite and attribute sources.

NARROWING YOUR TOPIC AND FORMULATING A SPECIFIC RESEARCH QUESTION

For each type of writing assignment you research, you will have to do some preliminary reading to help you narrow your topic. Assume you choose to look at new trends in the social life of college students. You do some preliminary reading in current newspapers and magazines to see what trends are in the news.

Once you have narrowed your topic, you can formulate a *research question*. Having a specific research question helps make your research efficient. It also allows you to enter into research with an open mind, genuinely seeking answers to a question you find interesting. A good research question might be "Why is crime rising at college campuses?" Another is "Are colleges required to report crimes in a different way than they did in years past?" If you begin to research without a question, you might spend a lot of time going in too many different directions. Even with a question in mind, you might start with one idea, begin reading and researching, and find that it is not interesting to you. You can always go back to your preliminary brainstorming and narrow your search to another branch of the topic and another question.

PRACTICE 15.2

Narrowing a Search Question

Using your questions from Practice 15.1, decide on a genre of writing. For example, you may have asked how solar panels are manufactured. You may have found yourself wondering about the cost of installing solar heaters.Why is it so expensive? How could the government help make it more affordable? This is a good question to investigate, especially if you are interested in writing an editorial.

1. Make a list of writing projects that correspond with the questions you started researching.
2. Once you have identified your writing project, write a one-sentence summary—a "pitch" or abstract—in which you tell your teacher/publisher/blog reader what the question in your piece is.

A good research question is in-depth enough to help you formulate a thesis—the main argument or point of your paper—and narrow enough to fit the parameters of your assignment. Your thesis probably will not be fully refined until you do your research and see where you want to go with an idea. Though following a single research question helps lead you to information, you should always be flexible in your researching. If you bump into another interesting trail of information, follow it. A solid thesis might occur to you after you follow different research paths and try several times to formulate a research question.

Your library may have a number of good ways to help you begin your reading and formulate your research question. Most libraries have research tools ranging from online catalogs to special databases available through computer terminals at the library or through "proxy" or home computer connections. Your library may pay fees to link to these databases. Most will provide citations for articles. You can track the articles down on microfilm or microfiche or even in back copies of journals at the library. Others provide full text of sources. (See the box on Databases for place to go to help you hone your research question.)

Databases

Some common databases are Ebscohost, CQ Researcher, and Twayne Series. Others include the following:

WORLDCAT

WorldCat lists and describes books and holdings from libraries in forty-five countries. The database includes journals, musical scores, video recordings, maps, magazines, newspapers, computer programs, manuscripts, sound recordings, visual materials, and Web sites.

INFOTRAC

InfoTrac is a searchable online library containing full-length articles, abstracts, and bibliographic citations from scholarly and popular periodicals, including a broad range of journals, magazines, encyclopedias, and newsletters.

LEXISNEXIS

LexisNexis provides legal, news, public record, and business information, including tax and regulatory publications in online, print, or CD-ROM formats. The database is searchable by field of interest like news, business, medicine, and law.

READERS' GUIDE FULL TEXT

Readers' Guide Full Text, produced by the H. W. Wilson Company, offers index listings—with full citations—and abstracts of the most popular general-interest periodicals published in the United States and Canada. You can get the full text for articles written after 1994. Some libraries also have Readers' Guide Full Text available in bound book and CD-ROM formats.

ISI WEB OF SCIENCE

The ISI Web of Science links to the Science Citation Index Expanded, Social Sciences Citation Index, and Arts and Humanities Citation Index. It provides access to multidisciplinary information from research journals, including full-text articles.

PROQUEST

Proquest provides the full text of current periodicals and newspapers and is updated daily, dating back to 1986. You can also link to e-journals and get information about dissertations. "Back files of record" pages from Proquest Historical Newspaper Collection show the pages exactly as they appeared to the original readers.

CREATING A WORKING BIBLIOGRAPHY

Keep track of all your sources, even if you are not certain you will use them in your writing. Careful record keeping will ensure that citations and quotations are accurate. Noting the title, author, publisher, date of publication, volume and page numbers, and Web page addresses while you are researching will make it unnecessary to retrace your steps after you decide which sources to include.

One useful way to create your working bibliography is to write all the information for each source on a separate index card. Using the correct documentation style when you write the information (see Chapter 16) will make it easy to type the *works cited* page when you have completed your paper: simply alphabetize the cards and copy the information. You might also want to make notes about the usefulness of the source or about what information it covers right on the card. Then, when you review your sources, you will know which source to consult for which information.

Another timesaving strategy researchers use is to give each source a code letter. If you put the letter on each note card you make from the source, you will not have

PRACTICE 15.3

Research Treasure Hunt

Find information that will help answer the following research questions. Make note of your research path: which books, experts, periodicals, and/or Web sites you consulted. Make note of where you started and how many sources it took to get to the answer.

1. For a profile on a local rap artist: What are the roots of rap?
2. For a short article on domestic terrorism: Can you really make a nuclear bomb at home?
3. For a news report: Find the number of registered independent voters in your state.
4. For a report on globalism and commerce: Get information about commercial trademarks found on Mount Everest.
5. For a technical report: Explain the migration of butterflies.
6. For a film review: How many films has Steven Soderbergh made?
7. For a trend article: How many McDonald's restaurants are in China?

to write all the bibliographic information on each card, but you will still keep your material organized efficiently.

A card might look like this:

A

Kauffman

Kauffman, Stanley. Regarding Film. Baltimore: Johns Hopkins University Press, 2001.

Compilation of his reviews from The New Republic, 1993–2000.

Cengage Learning

(*Continued*)

8. For a trend article about compulsive gambling: Why can you gamble on Indian reservations?
9. For an explanation of a trend: Are teens smoking more now than they were ten years ago?
10. For an editorial on schoolyard bullies: Find an expert to interview.
11. For a proposal: Get statistics on the number of dogs euthanized in your state last year.
12. For a proposal involving conserving fossil fuels: What was the top-selling car in the United States last year, and what kind of gas mileage does it get?

READING WITH FOCUS: TAKING USEFUL NOTES AND AVOIDING PLAGIARISM

Accuracy is essential when taking notes—and so is focus. As you read through your sources, look for ideas that support or refute your thesis. If you encounter ideas you have not considered, do not ignore them; read them and allow them to refine or qualify your original thinking. On the other hand, do not feel that you need to write down every fact, every example, or every quotation you find. Keep focused on your topic, and skip sections in your sources that are tangential or irrelevant to your concerns.

The most useful note cards tell you three things at a glance:

1. They tell you the source from which you got the information by including the code letter of the source or the last name of the author.
2. They tell you the page number(s) for a written source, the URL of an electronic source, or the date and time when an interview was conducted.
3. They tell you the general topic of the information on the card.

Try to create topic headings that are consistent. For example, do not write *film reviews* on one card and *movie criticism* on another.

The information you write on a card should be one of the following

- a summary
- a paraphrase of the material
- a direct quotation

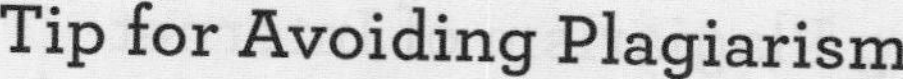

Tip for Avoiding Plagiarism

Take the time to put quotation marks around every phrase or sentence as you take it from a source so that you will not have to rely on your memory to determine which words are yours and which come from the source.

Using more than three words from a source without quotation marks or attribution is considered *plagiarism*. Passing off a source's original thinking as your own is also considered plagiarism. When you are working on a long-term project, even if you have the best of intentions, you will not remember whose words you are copying by the time you write the first draft. Most unintentional plagiarism can be avoided by being careful and accurate at this point in the research project.

SAMPLE NOTECARD

A note card might look like this:

Kauffman Themes A

Review of Eyes Wide Shut, August 16, 1999

—"Every married person has within himself or herself a secret cosmos of sexual imaginings, longings, fantasies, and perhaps extramarital actions."

—Original story written in 1926 by Arthur Schnitzler

p. 145

Cengage Learning

Key each note card to a main topic in your outline as this one does with "Themes."

Taking notes on cards is a good way to organize your material, but many people use photocopies to keep track of their sources. They print out copies of citations and full-text articles, and even e-mail themselves notes and copies. Whichever method you use, make sure to keep track of the origin of the ideas. Tracking down a source again to get the publication date or correct spelling of the author's name can waste a lot of your time. Making a quick notation of the full source as you read will save you time later.

Tips for Avoiding Plagiarism of Internet Sources

Plagiarism is defined as "the use of a source without giving credit to the author."

Online plagiarism includes cutting and pasting sections, paragraphs, and even phrases from online sources *without* using quotation marks or other indications that the material was written by someone else.

Plagiarism also includes taking ideas from sources without noting the original source of the ideas.

Even if you rephrase an idea or put it into your own words, always cite the source.

You can find more on how to attribute Internet sources in Chapter 16, "Documentation."

THE RHETORICAL SITUATION: EVALUATING YOUR SOURCES

Libraries all over the world share so much information that finding the few sources that are just right for your inquiry may be a daunting task. One online search for "the space program in the 1960s" returned 58,260 results or "hits." A library search was equally comprehensive, linking to sources covering rocket science and planet exploration, among others. Knowing how to evaluate your sources will save you time and will help you eliminate irrelevant information and focus on the information most useful to your research project.

A NOTE ABOUT WIKIS, BLOGS, AND MESSAGE BOARDS

Blogs can offer some of the best writing on the Web—insightful, well-researched, and current, and tools like wikis, blogs, and message boards can be useful in getting yourself educated about a subject. You can use blogs to link to studies, background news stories, and other commentary. Wikipedia also lists links and footnotes some sources you might not otherwise think of using. Message and bulletin boards can give you ideas that you might not get anywhere else. Still, you must be careful when using wikis, blogs, and message boards as sources of factual material. Remember, also, most teachers forbid citations that refer to Wikipedia.

Evaluating sources involves critical thinking and a system or set of criteria for judging their usefulness. Whatever you read, evaluate it in terms of its authorship, scholarship, bias, and currency. These criteria can help you decide what is useful and reliable; they can also help you narrow and refine your search by helping you select material. Remember that Web material, for the most part, is unevaluated. Evaluate sources by answering questions based on authorship, scholarship, bias, and currency.

CRITERIA FOR EVALUATING SOURCES

Authorship: *Who wrote the article and why?*

Scholarship: *Is the information credible and reliable?*

Bias: *What is the purpose of the work?*

Currency: *When was the work published or posted? Is it up-to-date?*

AUTHORITY

Finding out about the person who researched and wrote the information is key in evaluating books, articles, and Web material. What are the author's credentials? For example, has the author shown up in bibliographic lists you have found at the ends of articles or in textbooks or other books? Has the author written other books on the subject? Is the author connected with a school or organization? Connections to advocacy groups—groups that take positions on issues—can shape an author's point of view and make it closer to opinion than fact.

- Is there a clear statement of whose site it is and who is responsible for the content? Have you heard of the organization before? Are the articles signed? Is there a print version?
- Does the homepage include a phone number or postal address that indicates the company is legitimate?
- Can you find a link to information about the identity of the company, such as "About Us"?
- Is the formality of the writing or graphics appropriate to the subject matter?
- Is the material being provided as a public service?

SCHOLARSHIP

Quoting from works with good research makes your writing credible. Does the writing refer to other sources? Does it offer depth, or is it an overview? Are claims explained and documented? Does the work include a list of sources, links, or a bibliography that leads to other information? Is it well-written and free of typographical, spelling, grammatical, or other mistakes that bring its accuracy into question? Remember that what looks like a fact on a Web page might not be.

- Does the site include sources to document claims?
- Does any material that seems like a claim have a citation so you can check the source directly? Does the site link to sources?
- If the site includes excerpts from other published sources, are the sources complete? Have they been altered or shortened?
- Can you find errors in grammar or spelling that indicate there also may be incorrect information?
- Does the site include a bibliography?

PRACTICE 15.4

Detecting Bias

1. Take a look at the following book titles. Can you detect the author's bias from the title alone?

   a. *I am American (and So Can You!)* by Stephen Colbert
   b. *Fast Food Nation: The Dark Side of the All-American Meal* by Eric Schlosser
   c. *Nickel and Dimed* by Barbara Ehrenreich

2. Visit the library or a bookstore or go to <http://www.amazon.com>, and look at the tables of contents and excerpts from these books. Does getting more information further reveal the writers' biases?

3. Visit the following Web sites to see if you can discover a political bias from looking at the titles of pages and articles.

   a. The Drudge Report at <http://www.drudgereport.com>
   b. The *New Republic* online at <http://www.nr.com.>

BIAS

What is the purpose of the work: to argue, to report, to sell, to entertain? Who is the audience? Is the audience a specialized group with shared values? Is the audience general? How do the author's credentials imply a possible point of view in the writing? Is bias apparent? A source with a clear bias can be useful when you want a strong position on an issue rather than a balanced view. A researcher must understand the bias of a source in order to use the source well. In general, sources with the least amount of bias offer more reliable factual information than do biased sources. Quoting facts from sources that argue for a special point of view can make you seem like a spokesperson for the viewpoint rather than an objective writer.

Some Web sites conceal their purpose. Some might seem to be offering information but instead make sales pitches or arguments. Others lure you in with the promise of one thing and then switch to another topic or to a specific view of a topic. Expect promotional sites to present one side. Noncommercial sites might also be posted by advocacy agencies, so be aware of the purpose of the site. Is the purpose of the site to sell or promote a product or service?

- Is the information aimed at promotion of a specific point of view?
- Does the site link to other sites that espouse a distinct point of view?

CURRENCY

When was the book published, and by whom? Has the material been updated? Asking these questions is particularly important with sources that report new information—scientific publications, for example. Your research is fundamental to making your writing credible. Quoting outdated sources may show your reader that you do not understand the subject you are writing about.

Check posting dates and most recent updates when researching on the Web. It is especially important to do this with news sites, the best of which are updated frequently, sometimes hourly.

- Do the links work?
- Are the links current?

QUICK EVALUATION FOR WEB SITES

Use the type of domain in the domain name to help you evaluate Web sources and their likely usefulness.

.com business or marketing site, news site

.gov government site

.edu educational site

.mil military site

.org noncommercial site

Answering the questions on authorship, scholarship, bias, and currency can help you understand whether you want to use the source in your writing, though they don't necessarily eliminate a source. At times you may want to show an extreme viewpoint, when making a counterargument in an editorial, for example. You may want a historical perspective that you can get only from information that is clearly out of date to show the context of a social movement, for example, or thinking that has now changed. For example, the following book, published in 1953, might be useful to a researcher looking at women and society, even though the thinking about women and sexual behavior has changed since the book's publication date. Starting with an outdated notion that was considered state-of-the-art thinking in 1953 might make a really interesting—and creative—opening for an argument. Likewise, citing a well-accepted theory about women and behavior that has not changed since the 1950s might also make a thought-provoking opening.

> *Author:* Kinsey, Alfred C. (Alfred Charles), 1894–1956
> *Title: Sexual Behavior in the Human Female*, by the Staff of the Institute for Sex Research, Indiana University: Alfred C. Kinsey [and others]

THE SEARCH: SECONDARY SOURCES

The best researchers use multiple avenues of investigation. They consult a range of already published sources (secondary sources) and conduct surveys, polls, and interviews (primary sources).

USING BOOKS

Books are edited, reviewed, and selected by librarians for inclusion on the shelves. Most material on the Web, on the other hand, has not been screened. Anyone can post anything, so Web material ranges from worthless to exceptionally valuable. Sometimes the Web can be the place to find facts fast or to do general reading. At other times, books are the right place to go for research. For example, if you are researching the life of a slave in Georgia in 1860, books would probably offer more depth than Web pages.

HOW TO FIND BOOKS ON YOUR SUBJECT All libraries have catalogs, which today are mostly online catalogs rather than drawers of cards.

Catalog entries list author, title, publisher, and call number. Other information that might be helpful in assessing the source are number of pages, the presence of a bibliography and index, and a list of subjects related to the material in the publication.

PRACTICE 15.5

Reading a Catalog Entry

Compare the following entry with the previous one on page 492. How are these sources different? How are they alike?

Author: Menzigian, Margaret H.

Title: A study of the leisure time activities, television viewing habits, and the expressed interests of a selected population of fifth grade children in connection with their studying of natural science by television, by Margaret H. Menzigian [and] Ellen Marion Shepherd

Imprint: 1960

Location: Mugar

Call No.: EdM 1960 me

Status: Available

Descript: v, 65 p., 66 folded insert, 67–72 p. illus. 30 cm

Note: Thesis (M. A.)—Boston University, 1960

Alt author: Shepherd, Ellen Marion, joint author

PRACTICE 15.6

Evaluating a Catalog Entry

Evaluate this source based on the information from a library catalog.

1. Describe the bias you can detect from the catalog entry.
2. Would you eliminate this book as a source for information about bias in media? Why?

Author: Goldberg, Bernard, 1945–

Title: Bias: a CBS insider exposes how the media distorts the news/Bernard Goldberg

Imprint: Washington, DC: Regnery Pub.; Lanham, MD: Distributed to the trade by National Book Network, c2001.

Location: Mugar

Call No.: PN4784. O24 G65 2002

Status: Available

Descript: 232 p.:ill.; 24 cm.

Contents: Introduction: They think you're a traitor—News Mafia—Mugged by the Dan—Emperor is naked—Identity politics—

WHAT A CATALOG TELLS YOU You get a great deal of information from a catalog entry, including basics such as author and title. The following entry came up in a keyword search on "children and television viewing."

Author: Anderson, Daniel R., 1944–
Title: Early childhood television viewing and adolescent behavior: the re-contact study/Daniel R. Anderson . . . [et al.]; with commentary by Reed Larson.

You find out who published the work and what type of source it is—a book, a study, a thesis, or a dissertation, for example.

Imprint: Boston: Blackwell Publishers, 2001.

You get information about the location of the book—in which library, where it is shelved, and whether the book has been checked out.

Location: Mugar
Call No.: LB1103. F35 v. 66 no. 1
Status: Available

The catalog entry will contain other information—length of publication, a brief description of the publication (sometimes with chapter headings or section titles), and subject headings covered in the publication.

Descript: viii, 158 p.; 23 cm.

Series: Monographs of the Society for Research in Child Development; serial no. 264, v. 66, no. 1
Monographs of the Society for Research in Child Development; v. 66, no. 1.

Note: Includes bibliographical references.

Contents: Abstract—[ch.] 1. Introduction—[ch.] 2. Method overview—[ch.] 3. Media use in adolescence—[ch.] 4. Academic achievement—[ch.] 5. Creativity—[ch.] 6. Aggression—[ch.] 7. Extracurricular activities—[ch.] 8. Health behaviors—[ch.] 9. Self-image: role preference and body image—[ch.] 10. Summary and conclusions—References—Acknowledgments—Commentary. **Children** and adolescents in a changing media world/Reed Larson.

Subject: Television and children.
Social interaction in adolescence.
Child development.

Alt author: Larson, Reed, 1950–

EVALUATING BOOKS Use the questions about authorship, scholarship, bias, and currency to help you narrow your book choices (see the box on Criteria for Evaluating Sources). Look at the title, author, and date of publication. The title could provide a good sense of whether the source is right for your purpose.

USING PERIODICALS: ACADEMIC JOURNALS, TRADE JOURNALS, AND POPULAR MAGAZINES

Periodicals of all types are available both online and in print. You can find journal articles by searching through indexes on library databases such as the *Reader's Guide to Periodical Literature*. Academic journals like the *Journal of Finance*; *Social Work: The Journal of the National Association of Social Workers; American Literature*; and *Circulation: The Journal of the American Heart Association* announce and explain new findings in their specialty fields. They are usually not written for the average reader but rather for people with special training or interest in the field. Nevertheless, they can be useful to you because they are reliable and current. Journal articles are juried—that is, they are reviewed and chosen by scholars or experts in the field. Therefore, the articles are usually in-depth, with footnotes and detailed bibliographies. In other words, the conclusions the authors have reached are clearly documented.

Trade journals, too, have specialized audiences, but they can be useful in your research. Trade journals help professionals in specific fields keep up with current trends, new products, and other up-to-date information. Article authors are practitioners in specialty fields, and they are writing for other experts. They are often writing to report trends and new findings, just the information you may be looking for. Studies in the *Journal of the American Medical Association*, for example, often announce new theories or counter conventional medical thinking. Other useful trade and professional publications include *WWD: Women's Wear Daily*, *Nutrition Today*, *Adweek*, and *Editor and Publisher*.

While some popular magazines like *Time*, *Scientific American, Discover*, and *Smithsonian* might not have the authority and depth of academic journals, they are usually reliable, cover a wide range of topics, and are highly readable because they are written for a general audience. Although they quote sources, they do not include bibliographies. They can be good sources for up-to-date news and current reporting on trends and events.

Be especially alert for bias in periodicals because it can be difficult—especially when you search electronically and do not see all the articles in a particular publication—to judge whether an article is fair and reasonably objective. Since popular magazines do not include bibliographic citations or footnotes, you must look carefully at the way the writers cite sources within the text. Their sources might be worth checking. For example, if you find census data that reveal a significant population decrease in a particular state, you might go directly to the most recent census data—through either an online or a library search of government documents—to confirm those figures for yourself before you cite them as factual in your paper.

Sometimes you will consult periodicals that have a distinct point of view. Trade journals, for example, report news from within a certain industry. You will not find criticism of the industry in such publications, but you will find a particular perspective. Being aware of bias proves to your readers that your research is thorough and your writing is trustworthy.

(Continued)

How Bill Clinton cured homelessness—Epidemic of fear—I thought our job was to tell the truth—How about a media that reflects America?—Targeting men—Where thieves and pimps run free—Most important story you never saw on TV—Liberal hate-speech—Ship be sinking—Connecting the dots . . . to terrorism—Newzak.

Isn/music: #0895261901 (alk.paper)

Subject: Journalism—Objectivity.

Television broadcasting of news—United States.

USING NEWSPAPERS

You can search most large daily newspapers through their online archives by going directly to their Web sites; although, the online archives probably will not date back much farther than 1975.

In evaluating news sources, ask:

- Is the news source a well-known paper with an established record of reliability?
- Are the opinion pieces labeled and separated from the news stories, and is advertising set apart from news articles by appearance and by content?
- Does the writer provide attribution following quotations or make clear references to the source in the text ("according to a report released by the NRA today," "according to a company statement released today")?

THE SEARCH: PRIMARY SOURCES

USING SURVEYS AND POLLS

Data gathered from surveys and polls can be useful to writers, especially writers trying to prove a trend in behavior or establish a new wave of current thinking about an issue. In general, though, you should be wary of citing surveys and polls. If you do cite one, carefully evaluate the origin of the study. The U.S. Census Bureau, for example, is a good source. But a quick newspaper opinion poll might not reveal much about public opinion. A poll conducted by a company might be designed to solicit attention for a product rather than to provide information.

Conducting objective and reliable surveys and polls is a job for trained professionals—people who know how to write questions and how to combine them so that the survey solicits clear, valid data from which one can extract meaning. These professionals also know how to administer a survey to a wide variety of people so that the answers represent a cross-section of the group. If a survey or poll is not conducted according to rigorous standards, results can be invalid or twisted to "prove" the point that someone wants to advance.

In evaluating polls and surveys, ask:

- What are the sources of polling and survey data?
- Were the questions written to solicit a certain response? For example, you might ask people on your street if they watch Home Box Office (HBO) at least once a week. Negative replies do not necessarily mean that people do not like the network. What if cable is not available in the area, or if the cost of a premium channel is prohibitive?
- Do the survey responses represent a cross section of the population?
- Did the survey ask enough questions?

USING INTERVIEWS

Many researchers in academia, in the media, and in business do field research. They interview experts for background information and current thinking. Using quotations from these primary sources enlivens writing and makes it convincing and professional. Consider using interviews for news and technical reports, editorials and speeches, proposals, profiles and trend stories, and academic papers.

You may decide to conduct informal interviews, collecting background material to help you understand topics before you start to write about them. You may also conduct more formal interviews, collecting quotations from people who are experts on subjects that you are writing about.

Tips for Conducting Interviews

- **Make a Contact List:** Figure out who the main sources might be: names of experts, organizers, advocates, witnesses, and people central to your writing project.
- **Get Advance Materials before the Interview:** Understand the issues your interview subject represents. Read widely about the issues. Find out if your source has been quoted in writing before, if your source is an expert, or whether he or she has written books or articles. Read all you can to prepare.
- **Set Up the Interview:** Ask for the interview well ahead of your deadline. Identify yourself, how much time you think you will need, and the subject or reason for the interview. Leave your telephone number and your e-mail address in case plans change.
- **Prepare for Your Interview:** Prepare a list questions ahead of time, but do not stick to the script if the conversation takes an interesting turn.
- **Conduct the Interview:** The most productive interviews are conversations, not question-and-answer sessions. Make eye contact. Follow up on brief yes-no type answers. Ask your source to explain or elaborate. Take notes. Jot down observations and descriptive details that might help set a scene or show character. Do not forget to ask your source about other sources: other people to interview, something to read, or a place to visit.
- **Transcribe Your Notes:** As soon as possible after the interview, transcribe or rewrite your notes. Add details of physical appearance or setting that might later be useful. This is a time-consuming process, but do not put it off. The sooner you rewrite your notes, the more you will remember.

The art and craft of interviewing consists of two parts: asking good questions, and listening carefully to the answers. Most people enjoy being interviewed. They like to talk about their work, research, and fields of expertise, and they enjoy expressing their opinions.

CREATING AN ANNOTATED BIBLIOGRAPHY

While gathering your sources for other research projects, you will find it extremely helpful to create an annotated bibliography, an alphabetized list of your sources, put into the documentation style you will be using (MLA, APA, or another; see Chapter 16 on documentation styles). Include in your bibliography notations with summary, evaluation, and/or commentary. Teachers sometimes assign the annotated bibliography as a stand-alone project, a way for you to become knowledgeable about the research in a particular field of study. Professional scholars and researchers often publish annotated bibliographies as major pieces of research, collecting and disseminating the scholarship in a particular field. But, a less formal type of annotated bibliography has also found its way into popular culture and onto many Web sites. The "top ten" or "best of . . ." lists of restaurants, music videos, Web sites, films, and books are variations of the annotated bibliography. The "top ten" or "best" choices in these fields are listed, summarized, evaluated, and often include interesting and quirky personal commentary.

The annotated bibliography can help you with your research in a number of ways:

1. It helps you to read carefully and critically.
2. It helps you sort through the available information and select the material relevant to your topic.
3. It familiarizes you with the issues and perspectives that are being discussed in the area of your research.
4. It helps you develop your line of reasoning and craft your argument.

KINDS OF ANNOTATIONS

Depending on the class and the assignment, you may be asked to provide different kinds of annotations. It is important, as always, to check with your professors about what kind of annotations they want you to do. Most annotations fall into these three categories, and you may be asked to do one or more.

- **Summary**: Write a brief overview of the material. (For more on how to write a summary, see Chapter 4, Reading, Thinking, and Writing Critically) What are the key points? What other topics does it cover?

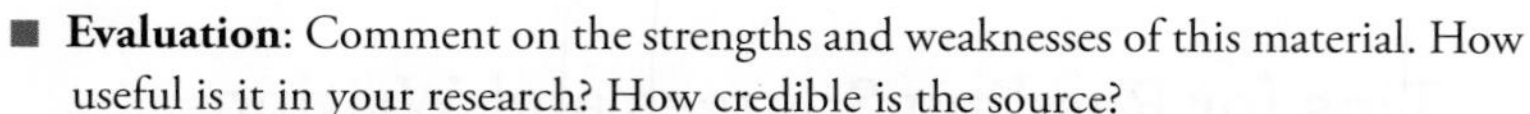

- **Evaluation**: Comment on the strengths and weaknesses of this material. How useful is it in your research? How credible is the source?
- **Personal Commentary**: Note how this material fits into your thinking about the topic. How can you use this material in your argument? Does it support or refute your thesis? Does it open up another topic you might explore?

ORGANIZING YOUR ANNOTATED BIBLIOGRAPHY

The best way to keep track of all your source material is to annotate it as you read it. Annotating as you read helps you remember the key points of each source and not get confused later as to which source made what point. This kind of sequential organization allows you to build your knowledge and understanding of a topic. You will also be able to figure out who the experts are in the field by noting which names are cited most often.

The most common organization for an annotated bibliography follows this sequence:

- A statement of intent. What are the parameters of your bibliography? What topics will you be covering?
- A list of all your sources, alphabetized by last name, and in correct MLA or APA style (See Chapter 16 for correct documentation style guidelines.).
- A concise summary of the material.
- An evaluation of the strengths and weaknesses of the material.
- Your personal commentary on the usefulness of this material to your research.

Tips for Reading Sources and Writing Annotated Bibliographies

- Read your sources carefully to identify their central arguments. You can often find the writer's thesis stated in the introduction and summarized in the conclusion.
- Look at the headings and the topic sentences of paragraphs to understand the scope of the material.
- Write clearly and economically.
- Be consistent in using the correct bibliographic format (MLA, APA, or another format) for all your sources.

(continued)

Tips for Reading Sources and Writing Annotated Bibliographies (continued)

- Be consistent in the format for the annotations. You can use phrases, sentences, or even bullet points, but be sure to use them consistently for each entry.
- Avoid unintentional plagiarism by putting quotation marks around all words you take directly from sources.
- Use the personal commentary section to make connections to your argument but also to raise questions, suggest new paths of inquiry, or clarify your thinking.

ANATOMY OF AN ANNOTATED BIBLIOGRAPHIC ENTRY

This example of an entry for an Annotated Bibliography uses MLA style.

Budiansky, Stephen. "Math Lessons For Locavores." *New York Times*. New York Times, 19 Aug. 2010. Web. 15 October, 2010.

Author's Last Name, First Name. "Title of Article." *Title of Newspaper*.

Publisher, Day Month Year. Medium. Day Month Year of access.

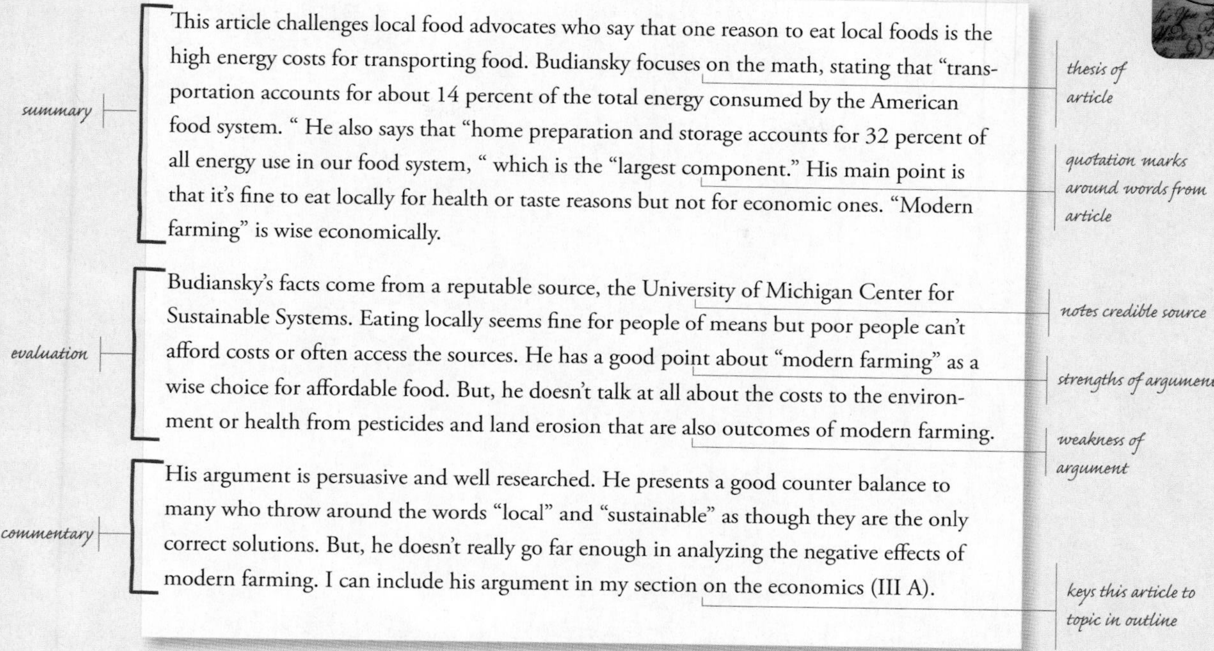

This article challenges local food advocates who say that one reason to eat local foods is the high energy costs for transporting food. Budiansky focuses on the math, stating that "transportation accounts for about 14 percent of the total energy consumed by the American food system. " He also says that "home preparation and storage accounts for 32 percent of all energy use in our food system, " which is the "largest component." His main point is that it's fine to eat locally for health or taste reasons but not for economic ones. "Modern farming" is wise economically.

Budiansky's facts come from a reputable source, the University of Michigan Center for Sustainable Systems. Eating locally seems fine for people of means but poor people can't afford costs or often access the sources. He has a good point about "modern farming" as a wise choice for affordable food. But, he doesn't talk at all about the costs to the environment or health from pesticides and land erosion that are also outcomes of modern farming.

His argument is persuasive and well researched. He presents a good counter balance to many who throw around the words "local" and "sustainable" as though they are the only correct solutions. But, he doesn't really go far enough in analyzing the negative effects of modern farming. I can include his argument in my section on the economics (III A).

ASSIGNMENT Create your own annotated bibliography. Imagine you have been given the task of writing an entry for a "top ten" Web site. Choose an area that interests you (films, books, music videos, restaurants). Or choose a trend you have observed in health, culture, science, technology, politics, entertainment, or consumer habits.

1. You will need to write an entry that summarizes, evaluates, and comments on your choice for the "best" in that top ten category, or create an entry on the trend you have selected.
2. Use the example from "Math Lessons for Locavores" as a model for each entry and create an annotated bibliography with several entries on your "top ten" or on the trend you have selected. Be sure to include summary, evaluation, and personal commentary.

Documentation

16

Heinz Koenig/
Shutterstock.com

The outer surface of truth is not smooth, welling and gathering from paragraph to shapely paragraph, but is encrusted with a rough protective bark of citations.

—Nicholson Baker

DOCUMENTATION

Many of the writing assignments you do in college and at work require you to become knowledgeable about topics that are new to you. Becoming expert enough to write with some authority about a historical era, a scientific discovery, a film theory, or a leading philosopher is one reward of research. To be a credible and reliable researcher, trusted by your readers, you must clearly document all the sources you consulted. The conventions of research writing are specific, and it is important to attend carefully to all the details.

ATTRIBUTING SOURCES

Attributing your sources—an essential part of research writing—means honestly acknowledging the books, periodicals, experts, and Web sites you consulted. Attributing sources gives you credibility. If your points are backed up by reliable and valid research or acknowledged experts in a field, your reader will trust what you have written. Clear attribution also allows readers to find your source and read in more depth about your topic. For each source that you use in your paper, even one you do not quote directly from, you need to provide information that will allow a reader to find and examine the same material that you did.

You have to be scrupulously honest about acknowledging your sources, whether you are using other writers' language or ideas in your work. You must give them credit; if you do not, you have, in effect, plagiarized—stolen from them. The consequences of plagiarism, as you probably know, are serious. Students and professors found guilty of plagiarism are often suspended or dismissed from an institution. In the

WHAT'S TO COME

An Israeli archeologist magnifies the inscription on an ancient Hebrew tablet to document its authenticity.

David Silverman/Getty Images News/Getty Images

professional world, people who plagiarize often lose their jobs. However, most plagiarism in student papers is unintentional, due to lack of knowledge or information rather than a result of dishonesty.

AVOIDING PLAGIARISM

The best way to avoid plagiarism is to keep careful notes as you do your research. Immediately put quotation marks around any words you take from a source, and write down the name of the author, the title of the source, and other publication information. Here is the essential information you need for citing books, articles, and Web sites:

Books	**Articles**	**Web sites**
Author(s) or editor(s)	Authors(s)	Authors(s)
Title	Title	Title
Edition	Periodical	Publisher
Place and date of publication	Volume and issue	Date of electronic publication
Name of publisher	Date	Date you accessed the source
Page numbers	Page numbers	Web address

The ease of cutting and pasting information from Web sites into your notes makes it especially important to be careful when you use Web sources. As you write your notes, be sure to indicate any direct information you have pasted in from Web sites, either by highlighting the information in another color or by inserting quotation marks around it. Follow the material immediately with the information noted in the chart above.

The ethics of research demand absolute honesty in reporting information from your sources. As careful as you are in documenting sources, be equally careful not to twist someone's theories or ideas to fit your thesis. Even adding a word to a quotation without noting that you have added it violates the unspoken contract you have made with your reader to be a reliable and credible researcher.

WHAT TO DOCUMENT

Just as a car or a stereo belongs to you, so does your original thinking. If an author has developed a theory or an insight after studying a subject, that theory or insight is his or her intellectual property, and you cannot use it without giving credit to the source. This rule applies to speech, visuals, music, computer programming code, and mathematical notations as well as to words. If you use someone's original thinking, you have to attribute it to that person by means of a clear citation.

However, you do not have to give a citation for a fact or observation that is general knowledge. If you read in three or four sources that Ronald Reagan was elected

president in 1980, you do not have to provide citations stating where you read that fact. It is considered common knowledge. Common knowledge includes the following:

- Historical facts that you can find in many reference books (George Washington was the first president of the United States)
- Commonly accepted opinions (children should be protected from viewing extreme violence or explicit sex)
- Information that appears in many reference books (the boiling point of water, the colors of the rainbow)
- Commonly known proverbs or quotations (idle hands are the devil's workshop)

On the other hand, if you read a political analyst's theory about the impact of the fall of communism in 1989, you have to attribute that theory to the analyst, even if you do not quote his or her exact words. If you were writing for a history course and using Modern League Association style, you would cite the author's name in the text, giving a brief explanation of his or her expertise.

> **MLA STYLE:** Historian and scholar Timothy Garton Ash, after witnessing the collapse of communism in Eastern Europe, believes that the free market of capitalism will be embraced by Eastern Europeans and regarded as a panacea for economic ills (152).

This in-text reference keys the reader to the full citation on the Works Cited page.

> **MLA STYLE**
> Ash, Timothy Garton. *The Magic Lantern: The Revolution of 89*. New York: Random House, 1990. Print.

INTEGRATING SOURCES: QUOTING, PARAPHRASING, AND SUMMARIZING

When you take material directly from a source, you have three possible ways of using it in your paper: You can quote it, paraphrase it, or summarize it. As you write your paper, you have to make decisions about which and how much material you will use. Too many citations or many long citations make a reader feel as though you have done no original thinking about the topic but have merely strung together the work of others. Choose your quotations on the basis of how authoritative they are and how well they are phrased, and use them to support or illustrate *your* points. Likewise, use summaries sparingly to condense important information, but be assured that your reader does not want to read a whole paper of summaries of other people's ideas. (See Chapter 4 for more discussion of this topic.)

QUOTING

When you quote directly, you copy the words you are citing—carefully and accurately—into your text, and you enclose them in quotation marks. If you are using MLA documentation style and if the material is four or fewer typed lines, enclose it in quotation marks. Be sure to introduce the quotation clearly, attributing the words to the writer. If you quote a passage of five lines or more, indent the material farther than the paragraph indentation (usually another 1/2 inch, or five more spaces), and omit the quotation marks. The indentation and this block format, as well as the page reference at the end, inform your reader that it is quoted material.

IN-TEXT CITATION

> In her interview with Christopher Scanlan, editorial writer Dianne Donovan says, "For an editorial writer, reading is just extremely important because you have to know about so many things" (298).

BLOCK FORM

Different style manuals have different requirements for numbers of spaces to indent and numbers of lines to include in a block quotation. See pages 536–553 for guidelines for quoting material using American Psychological Association style. Here is an example in MLA style.

> In her interview with Christopher Scanlan, editorial writer Dianne Donovan says,
>
>> For an editorial writer, reading is extremely important because you have to know about so many things. You have to have a breadth of knowledge, if not of experience, which most of us don't. That allows you to be able to see a lot of different viewpoints and also to be able to come up with a lot of different things to write about. (298)

PARAPHRASING

When you paraphrase material, you put it into your own words, but you cover all the same material as the original. The length of your paraphrase should be roughly the same as that of the original. Even though you are using your own phrasing and wording, the ideas are not yours, so you still must attribute the passage to the author. You might paraphrase the Christopher Scanlan interview this way:

> In her interview with Christopher Scanlan, Donovan says that because editorial writers have many different topics to write about, they have to read widely and deeply. Most editorial writers cannot know everything about the topics they have to write about, and they have to come up with new topics and be able to see them from multiple perspectives (298).

Using Ellipses, Brackets, and Single Quotation Marks

If YOU INTENTIONALLY leave out some words in a quotation, use ellipses (. . .) to indicate the omission.

> As Dianne Donovan says, "You have to have a breadth of knowledge . . . which most of us don't."

If you add a clarifying word or phrase, put it in brackets to show that it is your language.

> Dianne Donovan says, "[Editorial writers] have to have a breadth of knowledge, if not experience, which most of us don't."

If you incorporate a quotation within your quotation, use single quotation marks to set off the incorporated quotation.

> Discussing how the editorial conference works, Donovan says, "I'll pitch something. 'Here's the issue and here's what I think we should say about it,' and you make your argument."

SUMMARIZING

Summarizing is a way to condense lengthy material. In summarizing, you convey the highlights of someone's ideas, but you do not usually include the details or illustrative examples. One trick in summarizing a long section is to look for the topic sentence in each paragraph. If you put these topic sentences in your own words, you can usually accurately summarize a long piece of writing. Again, if you are summarizing or paraphrasing someone else's ideas, you have to give the person credit in the form of a clear citation.

The first three pages of Dianne Donovan's interview with Christopher Scanlan might be summarized this way:

> In her interview with Christopher Scanlan, Dianne Donovan talks about her craft as an editorial writer. She has always enjoyed writing and began writing editorials in high school. She believes that a good editorial writer has to read widely and deeply. She also believes that writing editorials is a craft, not an art. Her beat originally was family issues, but soon she became interested in welfare reform and juvenile justice. She has written fourteen or fifteen editorials about the juvenile justice system in Chicago (298–312).

DOCUMENTATION GUIDELINES:
MLA AND APA STYLES

Different fields of knowledge have developed different conventions and rules for citing sources within a paper and at the end of a paper in a Works Cited or a References section. Documentation styles vary in terms of where you place the date of publication within a citation, whether to use a comma after the name of an author, and so on. The differences might seem arbitrary, but they provide important information to readers and signal that you have been careful with details. No one expects you to memorize these conventions, but you are expected to consult the appropriate style manual when citing sources and to apply the guidelines accurately.

The two most common documentation styles in academic writing are MLA style and APA style. Modern Language Association (MLA) style is used primarily for writing in the humanities and is described fully in the *MLA Handbook for Writers of Research Papers,* now in its seventh edition (New York: Modern Language Association, 2009). American Psychological Association (APA) style is used primarily for writing in the natural and social sciences and is described fully in *Publication Manual of the American Psychological Association*, currently in its sixth edition (Washington, DC: American Psychological Association, 2009) and updated in the *APA Guidelines to Electronic References*. Some specialized fields use their own documentation forms. A few of these other forms are listed here.

> *The Associated Press Stylebook and Briefing on Media Law*, ed. Norm Goldstein (New York: Associated Press, 2007). This is also called "AP style."
>
> *The Chicago Manual of Style*, 16th ed. (Chicago: University of Chicago Press, 2010). This is also called "Chicago style."
>
> *The Columbia Guide to Online Style*, 2nd ed., Janice Walker and Todd Taylor (New York: Columbia University Press, 2006). This is also called "CGOS style."
>
> *Scientific Style and Format: The CSE Manual for Authors, Editors, and Publishers*, 7th ed. (New York: Cambridge University Press, 2006).

Ask your instructor or editor what style you should use, and then stick to those conventions. Many Web sites, especially sites of university writing centers, contain guides to the major documentation forms. And, of course, each of the listed groups publishes its own manual that gives complete, specific, and clear rules for creating in-text citations and Works Cited or References pages. The following overviews of MLA and APA style will give you the information you need for most of your academic writing assignments.

OVERVIEW OF MLA STYLE

The *MLA Handbook for Writers of Research Papers* is the authoritative source for documenting research papers in English and the humanities. You can consult the handbook or the Modern Language Association Web site at <http://www.mla.org> for more detailed information. The following overview provides information on:

- Formatting the manuscript
- Citing sources in the text
- Creating a Works Cited list

At the end of this section is a student paper in MLA style that you can use as a model.

FORMATTING THE MANUSCRIPT (MLA)

Presentation is important, and the *MLA Handbook* specifies these conventions for preparing a paper for submission. Also see the model paper on pages 532–535.

PAPER Use good quality 8 1/2-by-11-inch paper. Fasten the pages with paper clips; avoid both staples and binders, which make it harder for your professor to read and comment on your work.

TITLE PAGE Title pages are not required in the MLA format, although your professor might require one. If you do not use a title page, set up the first page with your name, the professor's name, the course name and number, and the date in the upper left corner, with all lines double-spaced. Leave a 1-inch margin from the top and the left side. Double-space, center the title, double-space again, and begin typing your paper.

MARGINS, SPACING, FONT, AND INDENTING Leave 1-inch margins on all four sides, and double-space the entire paper. Use an easy-to-read font, for example, 12-point Times or Times New Roman. Times and Times New Roman are the most commonly used. Indent 1/2 inch at the beginning of each paragraph. When you use a quotation of more than four lines of prose or three lines of poetry, indent 1 inch, and do not use quotation marks around the indented quotation. Double-space within the quotation.

PAGING Put your last name and consecutive page numbers in the upper right corner of the paper, about 1/2 inch from the top. Use Arabic numerals (1, 2, 3) for page numbers, and do not use punctuation, the word *page,* or its abbreviation.

HEADINGS Headings are optional in MLA-formatted papers, and MLA does not specify any format in text. However, as this author believes, if the material is

MLA

complicated and would benefit from being subdivided, create headings that are brief and parallel in phrasing, and be consistent in the font you use for them.

VISUALS If you include graphs, tables, maps, charts, illustrations, or photographs, place them as close as possible to your first discussion of them in the text, preferably after they are introduced. Identify a table with a table number and title above the table (Table 1 Album Titles and Release Dates). Label each figure with a number and a caption below the visual (Fig. 1. Album revenues). Cite the source underneath the table or visual.

WORKS CITED The final section of your paper is titled Works Cited. Begin a new page and center the title 1 inch from the top. Use regular type for the title, avoiding quotation marks, boldface, italics, and so on. Alphabetically list all works you cited in the text. Runover lines should be indented 1/2 inch (word processing software calls this a *hanging indent*).

CITING SOURCES IN THE TEXT

The MLA format requires citing sources in the text, usually by placing the author's last name and the page number in parentheses after the quoted or paraphrased material. The citation should be brief but complete enough to lead your reader to the full citation in the works-cited section at the end of the paper. For example, if you mention the author's name in the sentence, you can simply enclose the page number(s) in parentheses after the quotation. The following list shows how to cite sources in the text of your paper.*

DIRECTORY TO IN-TEXT CITATIONS

1. One author: a complete work
2. One author: part of a work
3. Two or more works by the same author(s)
4. Works by authors with the same last name
5. A work by two or three authors
6. A work by four or more authors
7. A work authored by an organization
8. An anonymous work
9. Two or more works included in one citation
10. A series of citations from a single work
11. A work referred to in another work
12. A one-page work
13. A work without page numbers
14. A work in an anthology or a collection

* *Reprinted with permission from* The College Writer's Handbook *by Randall VanderMey, Verne Meyer, John Van Rys, and Pat Sebranek (2006).*

15. An item from a reference work
16. A part of a multivolume work
17. A sacred text or famous literary work
18. Quoting verse
19. Quoting prose

1. **One author: a complete work** You do not need an in-text citation if you identify the author in your text. (See the first entry below.) However, you must give the author's last name in an in-text citation if it is not mentioned in the text. (See the second entry.) When a source is listed in your works-cited page with an editor, a translator, a speaker, or an artist instead of the author, then use that person's name in your citation.

   WITH AUTHOR IN TEXT (preferred for citing a complete work)

   In *No Need for Hunger*, Robert Spitzer recommends that the U.S. government develop a new foreign policy to help Third World countries overcome poverty and hunger.

   WITHOUT AUTHOR IN TEXT

   Do not offer page numbers when citing complete works, articles in alphabetized encyclopedias, one-page articles, or unpaginated sources.

   No Need for Hunger recommends that the U.S. government develop a new foreign policy to help Third World countries overcome poverty and hunger (Spitzer).

2. **One author: part of a work** List the necessary page numbers in parentheses if you borrow words or ideas from a particular source. Leave a space between the author's last name and the page reference. No abbreviation or punctuation is needed.

   WITH AUTHOR IN TEXT

   Bullough writes that genetic engineering was dubbed "eugenics" in 1885 by a cousin of Darwin's, Sir Francis Galton (5).

   WITHOUT AUTHOR IN TEXT

   Genetic engineering was dubbed "eugenics" in 1885 by a cousin of Darwin's, Sir Francis Galton (Bullough 5).

3. **Two or more works by the same author(s)** In addition to the author's last name(s) and page number(s), include a short version of the title of the work when you are citing two or more works by the same author(s). In parentheses, authors and titles are separated by a comma, as in the second example.

   WITH AUTHOR IN TEXT

   Wallerstein and Blakeslee claim that divorce creates an enduring identity for children of the marriage (*Unexpected Legacy* 62).

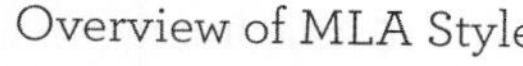

MLA

WITHOUT AUTHOR IN TEXT

They are intensely lonely despite active social lives (Wallerstein and Blakeslee, *Second Chances* 51).

4. **Works by authors with the same last name** When citing different sources by authors with the same last name, it is best to use the authors' full names in the text so as to avoid confusion. However, if circumstances call for parenthetical references, add each author's first initial. If first initials are the same, use each author's full name.

    Some critics think *Titus Andronicus* too abysmally melodramatic to be a work of Shakespeare (A. Parker 73). Others suggest that Shakespeare meant it as black comedy (D. Parker 486).

5. **A work by two or three authors** Give the last names of every author in the same order in which they appear in the works-cited section. (The correct order of the authors' names can be found on the title page of the book.)

    Students learned more than a full year's Spanish in ten days using the complete supermemory method (Ostrander and Schroeder 51).

6. **A work by four or more authors** Give the first author's last name as it appears in the works-cited section followed by *et al.* (meaning "and others").

    Communication on the job is more than talking; it is "inseparable from your total behavior" (Culligan et al. 111).

7. **A work authored by an organization** If a book or other work was written by an organization such as an agency, a committee, or a task force, it is said to have a corporate author. If the corporate name is long, include it in the text (rather than in parentheses) to avoid disrupting the flow of your writing. After the full name has been used at least once, use a shortened form of the name (common abbreviations are acceptable) in subsequent references. For example, *Task Force* may be used for *Task Force on Education for Economic Growth.*

    The Task Force on Education for Economic Growth details a strong connection between education and the depth and breadth of the workforce (105).

    The thesis of the report is that economic success depends on our ability to improve large-scale education and training as quickly as possible (Task Force 113–14).

8. **An anonymous work** When there is no author listed, give the title or a shortened version of the title as it appears in the works-cited section.

    Statistics indicate that drinking tap water can account for up to 20 percent of a person's total exposure to lead (*Information* 572).

9. **Two or more works included in one citation** To cite multiple works within a single parenthetical reference, separate the references with a semicolon.

> In Medieval Europe, Latin translations of the works of Rhazes, a Persian scholar, were a primary source of medical knowledge (Albe 22; Lewis 266).

10. **A series of citations from a single work** If no confusion is possible, it is not necessary to name a source repeatedly when making multiple parenthetical references to that source in a single paragraph. If all references are to the same page, identify that page in a parenthetical note after the last reference. If the references are to different pages within the same work, you need identify the work only once, and then use a parenthetical note with page number alone for the subsequent references.

> Domesticating science meant not only spreading scientific knowledge but also promoting it as a topic of public conversation (Heilbron 2). One way to enhance its charm was by depicting cherubic putti as "angelic research assistants" in book illustrations (5).

11. **A work referred to in another work** If you must cite an indirect source—that is, information from a source that is quoted from another source—use the abbreviation *qtd. in* (quoted in) before the indirect source in your reference.

> Paton improved the conditions in Diepkloof (a prison) by "removing all the more obvious aids to detention. The dormitories [were] open at night: the great barred gate [was] gone" (qtd. in Callan xviii).

12. **A one-page work** Cite a one-page work just as you would a complete work.

> As S. Adams argues in her editorial, it is time for NASA "to fully reevaluate the Space Shuttle's long-term viability for sending humans into space."

13. **A work without page numbers** If a work has no page numbers or other reference numbers, treat it as you would a complete work. This is commonly the case with electronic resources, for example. Do not count pages to create reference numbers of your own; however, if possible, refer to stable divisions within the document, such as sections or paragraphs.

> Antibiotics become ineffective against such organisms through two natural processes: first, genetic mutation; and second, the subsequent transfer of this mutated genetic material to other organisms, which appears to be the main way that bacteria attain a state of resistance (Davies par. 5).

14. **A work in an anthology or a collection** When citing the entirety of a work that is part of an anthology or a collection, if it is identified by the author

MLA

in your list of works cited, treat the citation as you would one for any other complete work.

> In "The Canadian Postmodern," Linda Hutcheon offers a clear analysis of the self-reflexive nature of contemporary Canadian fiction.

Similarly, if you are citing particular pages of such a work, follow the directions for citing part of a work.

> According to Hutcheon, "postmodernism seems to designate cultural practices that are fundamentally self-reflexive, in other words, art that is self-consciously artifice" (18).

15. **An item from a reference work** An entry from a reference work, such as an encyclopedia or a dictionary, should be cited similarly to a work from an anthology or a collection. For a dictionary definition, include the abbreviation *def.* followed by the particular entry designation.

> This message of moral superiority becomes a juggernaut in the truest sense, a belief that "elicits blind devotion or sacrifice" ("Juggernaut," def. 1).

While many such entries are identified only by title (as above), some reference works include an author's name for each entry (as below). Others may identify the author by initials, with a list of full names elsewhere in the work.

> The decisions of the International Court of Justice are "based on principles of international law and cannot be appealed" (Pranger).

16. **A part of a multivolume work** When citing only one volume of a multivolume work, if you identify the volume number in the works-cited list, there is no need to include it in your in-text citation. However, if you cite more than one volume of a work, then each in-text reference must identify the appropriate volume. Give the volume number followed by page number, separated by a colon and a space.

> "A human being asleep," says Spengler, ". . . is leading only a plantlike existence" (2: 4).

When citing a whole volume, however, either identify the volume number in parentheses with the abbreviation *vol.* (using a comma to separate it from the author's name) or use the full word *volume* in your text.

> The land of Wisconsin has shaped its many inhabitants more significantly than they ever shaped that land (Stephens, vol. 1).

17. **A sacred text or famous literary work** Because sacred texts and famous literary works are published in many editions, include sections, parts, or chapters.

If using page numbers, list them first, followed by an abbreviation for the type of division and the division number.

> The more important a person's role in society—the more apparent power an individual has—the more that person is a slave to the forces of history (Tolstoy 690; bk. 9, ch. 1).

Books of the Bible and well-known works may be abbreviated.

> "A generation goes, and a generation comes, but the earth remains forever" (*The New Oxford Annotated Bible*, Eccles. 1.4)

> Hamlet observes, "One may smile . . . and be a villain" (Ham. 1.5.104).

18. **Quoting verse** Cite classic verse plays and poems by division (act, scene, canto, book, part) and line, using Arabic numerals for the various divisions unless your instructor prefers roman numerals. Use periods to separate the various numbers.

    NOTE: A slash, with a space on each side, shows where each new line of verse begins. If you are citing lines only, use the word *line* or *lines* in your first reference and numbers only in additional references.

    > In the first act of the play, Hamlet comments, "How weary, stale, flat and unprofitable, / Seem to me all the uses of this world" (1.2.133–134).
    >
    > In book five of Homer's *Iliad*, the Trojans' fear is evident: "The Trojans were scared when they saw the two sons of Dares, one of them in fright and the other lying dead by his chariot" (lines 22–24).

19. **Quoting prose** To cite prose from fiction, list more than the page number if the work is available in several editions. Give the page reference first, and then add a chapter or section, if appropriate, in abbreviated form after a semicolon.

    > In *The House of the Spirits*, Isabel describes Marcos, "dressed in mechanic's overalls, with huge racer's goggles and an explorer's helmet" (13; ch. 1).

    When you are quoting any sort of prose that takes more than four typed lines, indent each line of the quotation 1 inch (ten spaces) and double-space it; do not add quotation marks. In this case, you put the parenthetical citation (the pages and chapter numbers) outside the end punctuation mark.

    > Allende describes the flying machine that Marcos has assembled:
    >
    > The contraption lay with its stomach on terra firma, heavy and sluggish, looking more like a wounded duck than like one of those newfangled airplanes they were starting to produce in the United States. There was nothing in its appearance to suggest that it could move, much less take flight. (12; ch. 1)

MLA

PLACEMENT AND PUNCTUATION OF PARENTHETICAL DOCUMENTATION

Present and punctuate citations according to these rules: *

- Place the parenthetical reference after the source material.
- Within the parentheses, normally give the author's last name only.
- Do not put a comma between the author's last name and the page reference.
- Cite the page number as a numeral, not a word.
- Don't use the abbreviations *p.*, *pp.*, or *page(s)* before page number(s).
- Place any sentence punctuation after the ending parenthesis.

NOTE: For many of these rules, exceptions exist. For example, classic literary texts could be cited by chapters, books, act, scenes, or lines. Moreover, many electronic sources have no stated authors and no pagination.

CREATING A WORKS-CITED LIST

The last page of your paper will be titled Works Cited. All the parenthetical citations you inserted in your paper refer your reader to the complete entries in this final list. Include each work you have cited in your paper, but do not include works you read but did not cite. Alphabetize your list by the last name of the author or, in the case of an entry without an identified author, the first word of the title, excluding the articles *A*, *An*, and *The*.

DIRECTORY TO MLA WORKS-CITED ENTRIES

Books and other documents

1. A book by one author
2. Two or more books by the same author
3. A work by two or three authors
4. A work by four or more authors
5. A work by a corporate author (an agency, a committee, or other organization)
6. An anonymous book
7. A single work from an anthology
8. A complete anthology
9. Two or more works from the same anthology or collection
10. One volume of a multivolume work
11. An introduction, a preface, a foreword, or an afterword
12. A republished book (reprint)
13. A book with multiple publishers

* *Reprinted with permission from* The College Writer's Handbook *by Randall VanderMey, Verne Meyer, John Van Rys, and Pat Sebranek (2006).*

14. Second and subsequent editions
15. An edition with an author and an editor
16. A translation
17. An article in a familiar reference book
18. An article in an unfamiliar reference book
19. A government publication
20. A book in a series
21. A book with a title within its title
22. A sacred text
23. The published proceedings of a conference
24. A published dissertation
25. A pamphlet, brochure, manual, or other workplace document

Periodicals

26. An article in a weekly or biweekly magazine
27. An article in a monthly or bimonthly magazine
28. An article in a scholarly journal paginated by issue
29. An article in a scholarly journal with continuous pagination
30. A printed interview
31. A newspaper article
32. A newspaper editorial
33. A letter to the editor
34. A review
35. An abstract
36. An anonymous article in a periodical
37. An article with a title or quotation within its title
38. An article reprinted in a loose-leaf collection
39. An article with pagination that is not continuous

Online sources

40. A personal site
41. A professional site
42. A site for a department of a college or university
43. A site for a study course
44. A site with a long URL
45. An online book
46. An article in an online periodical
47. An article in an online reference work
48. An article in an online service
49. A scholarly project or information database
50. An online government publication

51. An online posting in a list server
52. An online posting in a Web forum
53. An online posting in a newsgroup
54. An online posting in a real-time (synchronous) communication forum
55. An online poem
56. An online multimedia resource
57. An online transcript of a broadcast
58. A publication in more than one medium
59. An e-mail communication
60. An online posting

Other sources: Primary, personal, and multimedia

61. A periodically published database on CD-ROM, diskette, or magnetic tape
62. Computer software
63. A television or radio program
64. A film
65. A video recording
66. An audio recording
67. A performance
68. An artwork on display
69. A letter or an e-mail message received by the author (you)
70. An interview by the author (you)
71. A cartoon or comic strip (in print)
72. An advertisement (in print)
73. A lecture, a speech, an address, or a reading
74. A legal or historical document
75. A map or chart

WORKS-CITED ENTRIES: BOOKS AND OTHER DOCUMENTS

The entries that follow illustrate the information needed to cite books, sections of a book, pamphlets, and government publications. The possible components of these entries are listed in order below:

- Author's name
- Title of a part of the book (an article in the book or a foreword)
- Title of the book
- Name of editor or translator
- Edition
- Volume number
- Series name
- Place of publication, publisher, year of publication

- Page numbers, if citation is to only a part (For page spans, use a hyphen or an en dash. If clarity is maintained, you may also drop a digit from the second number: 141–43, but 201–334.)
- Medium of publication (print, Web, CD-ROM; see below for additional media types.)

List only the city for the place of publication if the city is in the United States. For cities outside the United States, add an abbreviation for the country if necessary for clarity. If several cities are listed, give only the first. Publishers' names should be shortened by omitting articles (*a, an, the*), business abbreviations *(Co., Inc.),* and descriptive words *(Books, Press)*. Abbreviate University Press as *UP*. Also use standard abbreviations whenever possible.

NOTE: In general, if any of these components do not apply, they are not included in the works-cited entry. However, in the rare instance that a book does not state publication information, use the following abbreviations in place of information you cannot supply:

n.p.	No place of publication given
n.p.	No publisher given
n.d.	No date of publication given
n. pag.	No pagination given

1. **A book by one author**

   Baghwati, Jagdish. *In Defense of Globalization*. New York: Oxford UP, 2004. Print.

2. **Two or more books by the same author** List the books alphabetically according to title. After the first entry, substitute three hyphens for the author's name.

   Dershowitz, Alan M. *Rights from Wrongs*. New York: Basic, 2005. Print.

   ———. *Supreme Injustice: How the High Court Hijacked Election 2000.* Oxford: Oxford UP, 2001. Print.

3. **A work by two or three authors**

   Bystydzienski, Jill M., and Estelle P. Resnik. *Women in Cross-Cultural Transitions*. Bloomington: Phi Delta Kappa Educational Foundation, 1994. Print.

   NOTE: List the authors in the same order as they appear on the title page. Reverse only the name of the first author.

4. **A work by four or more authors**

   Schulte-Peevers, Andrea, et al. *Germany*. Victoria, Austral.: Lonely Planet, 2000. Print.

   NOTE: You may also choose to give all names in full in the order used on the title page.

MLA

5. **A work by a corporate author**

   Exxon Mobil Corporation. *Great Plains 2000.* Lincolnwood: Publications Intl., 2001. Print.

6. **An anonymous book**

   Chase's Calendar of Events 2002. Chicago: Contemporary, 2002. Print.

7. **A single work from an anthology**

   Mitchell, Joseph. "The Bottom of the Harbor." *American Sea Writing.* Ed. Peter Neill. New York: Library of America, 2000. 584–608. Print.

8. **A complete anthology** If you cite a complete anthology, begin the entry with the editor(s).

   Neill, Peter, ed. *American Sea Writing.* New York: Library of America, 2000.

   Smith, Rochelle, and Sharon L. Jones, eds. *The Prentice Hall Anthology of African American Literature.* Upper Saddle River: Prentice, 2000. Print.

9. **Two or more works from the same anthology or collection** To avoid unnecessary repetition when citing two or more entries from a larger collection, you may cite the collection once with complete publication information (see *Forbes* below). The individual entries (see *Joseph* and *MacNeice* below) can then be cross-referenced by listing the author, title of the piece, editor of the collection, and page numbers.

   Forbes, Peter, ed. *Scanning the Century.* London: Penguin, 2000. Print.

   Joseph, Jenny. "Warning." Forbes 335–36.

   MacNeice, Louis. "Star-Gazer." Forbes 504.

10. **One volume of a multivolume work**

    Cooke, Jacob Ernest, and Milton M. Klein, eds. *North America in Colonial Times.* Vol. 2. New York: Scribner's, 1998. Print.

    NOTE: If you cite two or more volumes in a multivolume work, give the total number of volumes after each title. Offer specific references to volume and page numbers in the parenthetical reference in your text, like this: (8: 112–114).

    Salzman, Jack, David Lionel Smith, and Cornel West. *Encyclopedia of African-American Culture and History.* 5 vols. New York: Simon, 1996. Print.

11. **An introduction, a preface, a foreword, or an afterword** To cite the introduction, preface, foreword, or afterword of a book, list the author of the part first. Then identify the part by type, with no quotation marks or italicizing, followed by the title of the book. Next, identify the author of the work, using the word *By.* (However, if the book author and the part's author are the same person, give just the last name after *By.*) For a book that gives cover credit to an editor instead of an author, identify the editor as usual. Finally, list any page numbers for the part being cited.

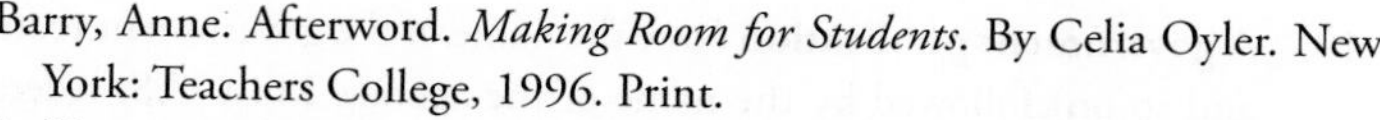

Barry, Anne. Afterword. *Making Room for Students*. By Celia Oyler. New York: Teachers College, 1996. Print.

Lefebvre, Mark. Foreword. *The Journey Home*. Vol. 1. Ed. Jim Stephens. Madison: North Country, 1989. ix. Print.

12. **A republished book (reprint)** Give the original publication date after the title.

Atwood, Margaret. *Surfacing*. 1972. New York: Doubleday, 1998. Print.

NOTE: New material added to the reprint, such as an introduction, should be cited after the original publication facts: Introd. C. Becker.

13. **A book with multiple publishers** When a book lists more than one publisher (not just different offices of the same publisher), include all of them in the order given on the book's title page, separated by a semicolon.

Wells, H. G. *The Complete Short Stories of H. G. Wells*. New York: St. Martin's; London: A. & C. Black, 1987. Print.

14. **Second and subsequent editions** An edition refers to the particular publication you are citing.

Joss, M. *Looking Good in Presentations*. 3rd ed. Scottsdale: Coriolis, 1999. Print.

15. **An edition with an author and an editor** The term *edition* also refers to the work of one person that is prepared by another person, an editor.

Shakespeare, William. *A Midsummer Night's Dream*. Ed. Jane Bachman. Lincolnwood: NTC, 1994. Print.

16. **A translation**

Lebert, Stephan, and Norbert Lebert. *My Father's Keeper*. Trans. Julian Evans. Boston: Little, 2001. Print.

17. **An article in a familiar reference book** It is not necessary to give full publication information for familiar reference works (encyclopedias and dictionaries). For these titles, list only the edition (if available) and the publication year. If an article is initialed, check the index of authors (in the opening section of each volume) for the author's full name.

Lum, P. Andrea. "Computed Tomography." *World Book*. 2000 ed.

When citing a single definition of several listed, add the abbreviation *Def.* and the particular number or letter for that definition.

"Deaf." Def. 2b. *The American Heritage College Dictionary*. 4th ed. 2002. Print.

18. **An article in an unfamiliar reference book** Give full publication information as for any other sort of book.

"S Corporation." *The Portable MBA Desk Reference*. Ed. Paul A. Argenti. New York: Wiley, 1994. Print.

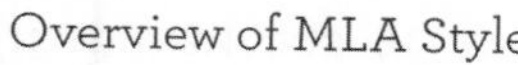

MLA

19. **A government publication** State the name of the government (country, state, and so on) followed by the name of the agency. Most U.S. federal publications are published by the Government Printing Office (GPO).

    United States. Dept. of Labor. Bureau of Labor Statistics. *Occupational Outlook Handbook 2004–2005*. Washington: GPO, 2004. Print.

    When citing the *Congressional Record*, list only the date and page numbers. *Cong. Rec.* 5 Feb. 2002: S311–15. Print.

20. **A book in a series** Give the series name and number (if any) before the publication information.

    Paradis, Adrian A. *Opportunities in Military Careers*. VGM Opportunities Series. Lincolnwood: VGM Career Horizons, 1999. Print.

21. **A book with a title within its title** If the title contains a title normally in quotation marks, keep the quotation marks and italicize the entire title.

    Stuckey-French, Elizabeth. *"The First Paper Girl in Red Oak, Iowa" and Other Stories*. New York: Doubleday, 2000. Print.

    If the title contains a title that is normally italicized, do not italicize that title in your entry:

    Beckwith, Charles E. *Twentieth Century Interpretations of* A Tale of Two Cities: *A Collection of Critical Essays*. Upper Saddle River: Prentice, 1972. Print.

22. **A sacred text** The Bible and other such sacred texts are treated as anonymous books. Documentation should read exactly as it is printed on the title page.

    The Jerusalem Bible. Garden City: Doubleday, 1966. Print.

23. **The published proceedings of a conference** The published proceedings of a conference are treated like a book. However, if the title of the publication does not identify the conference by title, date, and location, add the appropriate information immediately after the title.

    McIlwaine, la C., ed. *Advances in Knowledge Organization*. Vol. 9. Proc. of Eighth Intl. ISKO Conf., 13–16 July 2004, London. Wurzburg: Ergon-Verlag, 2004. Print.

24. **A published dissertation** An entry for a published dissertation contains the same information as a book entry, with a few added details. Add the abbreviation *Diss.* and the name of the degree-granting institution before the publication facts.

    Jansen, James Richard. *Images of Dostoevsky in German Literary Expressionism*. Diss. U of Utah, 2003. Ann Arbor: UMI, 2003. Print.

25. **A pamphlet, brochure, manual, or other workplace document** Treat any such publication as you would a book.

    Grayson, George W. *The North American Free Trade Agreement*. New York: Foreign Policy Assn., 1993. Print.

If publication information is missing, list the country of publication [in brackets] if known. Use the abbreviation *n.p.* (no place) if the country or the publisher is unknown and the abbreviation *n.d.* if the date is unknown.

Pedestrian Safety. [United States]: n.p., n.d. Print.

WORKS-CITED ENTRIES: PERIODICALS The possible components of these entries are listed in order below:

- Author's name, last name first
- Title of article, in quotation marks
- Name of periodical, italicized
- Series number or name, if relevant (not preceded by a period or comma)
- Volume number (for a journal)
- Issue number, separated from volume with a period but no space
- Date of publication (abbreviate all months except May, June, and July)
- Page numbers, preceded by a colon, without *p.* or *pp.*
- Medium of publication consulted
- Supplementary information

NOTE: If any of the components listed above do not apply, they are not listed. The entries that follow illustrate the information needed to cite periodicals.

26. **An article in a weekly or biweekly magazine** List the author (if identified), article title (in quotation marks), publication title (italicized), full date of publication, and page numbers for the article. Do not include volume and issue numbers.

    Goodell, Jeff. "The Uneasy Assimilation." *Rolling Stone* 6–13 Dec. 2001: 63–66. Print.

27. **An article in a monthly or bimonthly magazine** As for a weekly or biweekly magazine, list the author (if identified), article title (in quotation marks), and publication title (italicized). Then identify the month(s) and year of the issue, followed by page numbers for the article. Do not give volume and issue numbers.

    "Patent Pamphleteer." *Scientific American* Dec. 2001: 33. Print.

28. **An article in a scholarly journal paginated by issue** Rather than month or full date of publication, scholarly journals are usually identified by volume number. If there is also an issue number, include that immediately following the volume number, separated by a period. List the year of publication in parentheses, the page numbers of the article, and the medium of publication.

    Chu, Wujin. "Costs and Benefits of Hard-Sell." *Journal of Marketing Research* 32.2 (1995): 97–102. Print.

29. **An article in a scholarly journal with continuous pagination** The new *MLA Handbook* (2009) no longer makes a distinction between separately and

MLA

continuously paginated journals, so include both journal and issue number in your citation.

Tebble, Nicola J., David W. Thomas, and Patricia Price. "Anxiety and Self-Consciousness in Patients with Minor Facial Lacerations." *Journal of Advanced Nursing* 47.2 (2004): 417–26. Print.

30. **A printed interview** Begin with the name of the person interviewed when that is whom you are quoting.

Cantwell, Maria. "The New Technocrat." Interview by Erika Rasmusson. *Working Woman* Apr. 2001: 20–21. Print.

If the interview is untitled and the interviewer is not identified, the word *Interview* (no italics) and a period follow the interviewee's name.

31. **A newspaper article** A signed newspaper article follows the form below:

Bleakley, Fred R. "Companies' Profits Grew 48% Despite Economy." *Wall Street Journal* 1 May 1995, Midwest ed.: 1. Print.

An unsigned newspaper article follows the same format:

"Bombs—Real and Threatened—Keep Northern Ireland Edgy." *Chicago Tribune* 6 Dec. 2001, sec. 1: 20. Print.

NOTE: Cite the edition of a major daily newspaper (if given) after the date (1 May 1995, Midwest ed.: 1). If a local paper's name does not include the city of publication, add it in brackets (not italicized) after the name. To cite an article in a lettered section of the newspaper, list the section and the page number. (For example, A4 would refer to page 4 in section A of the newspaper.) If the sections are numbered, however, use a comma after the year (or the edition). Then indicate sec. 1, 2, 3, and so on, followed by a colon and the page number (sec. 1: 20).

32. **A newspaper editorial** Put *Editorial* (no italics) and a period after the title.

"Hospital Power." Editorial. *Bangor Daily News* 14 Sept. 2004: A6. Print.

33. **A letter to the editor** Put *Letter* (no italics) and a period after the author's name.

Sory, Forrest. Letter. *Discover* July 2001: 10. Print.

34. **A review** Begin with the author (if identified) and title of the review. Use the notation *Rev. of* (no italics) between the title of the review and that of the original work. Identify the author of the original work with the word *by* (no italics). Then follow with publication data for the review.

Olsen, Jack. "Brains and Industry." Rev. of *Land of Opportunity*, by Sarah Marr. *New York Times* 23 Apr. 1995, sec. 3: 28. Print.

35. **An abstract** To cite an abstract, first give the publication information for the original work (if any); then list the publication information for the abstract itself. Add the term *Abstract* and a period between them if the journal title

does not include that word. If the journal identifies abstracts by item number, include the word *item* followed by the number. (Add the section identifier [A, B, or C] for those volumes that have one.) If no item number exists, list the page number(s).

Faber, A. J. "Examining Remarried Couples Through a Bowenian Family System Lens." *Journal of Divorce and Remarriage* 40.3/4 (2004): 121–133. *Social Work Abstracts* 40 (2004): item 1298. Print.

36. **An unsigned article in a periodical** If no author is identified for an article, list the entry alphabetically by title among your works cited (ignoring any initial *A, An,* or *The*).

"Feeding the Hungry." *Economist.* 371.8374 (2004): 74. Print.

37. **An article with a title or quotation within its title** Use single quotation marks around the shorter title if it is normally punctuated with quotation marks.

Morgenstern, Joe. "Sleeper of the Year: 'In the Bedroom' Is Rich Tale of Tragic Love." *Wall Street Journal* 23 Nov. 2001: W1. Print.

38. **An article reprinted in a loose-leaf collection** The entry begins with original publication information and ends with the name of the loose-leaf volume (*Youth*), editor, volume number, publication information including the name of the information service (*SIRS*), the article number, and the medium of publication.

O'Connell, Loraine. "Busy Teens Feel the Beep." *Orlando Sentinel* 7 Jan. 1993: N. pag. *Youth*. Ed. Eleanor Goldstein. Vol. 4. Boca Raton: SIRS, 1993. Art. 41. Print.

39. **An article with pagination that is not continuous** For articles that are continued on a nonconsecutive page, whatever the publication type, add a plus sign (+) after the first page number.

Garrett, Robyne. "Negotiating a Physical Identity: Girls, Bodies and Physical Education." *Sport, Education & Society* 9 (2004): N. pag. Print.

WORKS-CITED ENTRIES: ONLINE SOURCES Citations for online sources follow the strategies used for print sources, with a few additions to reflect the changeable nature of the Internet. After the author's name and the title of the document, include any print publication information; then list the electronic publication details and access information.

- Author's name
- Title of article or Web page (italicized)
- Print publication information
- Title of Internet site (italicized)
- Site sponsor or publisher

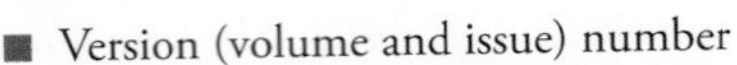

- Version (volume and issue) number
- Date of electronic publication
- Medium (Web)
- Date of access

If any of these components do not apply, they are not listed. For documents with no listed date of electronic publication, use the site's posting date, date of update, or copyright date if available. Date of access means the most recent date on which you viewed the document online. URLs, if needed, are enclosed in angle brackets and should identify the complete address, including the access-mode identifier (http, ftp, telnet, and so on).

40. **A personal site** After the author's name, list the site title (italicized) or the words *Home page* (without italics), whichever is appropriate, followed by a period. Add the date of publication or most recent update and your date of visit. In this case, since it might be difficult for the reader to locate the site without an address, include the URL in brackets.

    Mehuron, Kate. Home page. Web. 30 Sept. 2004. <http://www.emich.edu/public/history/faculty/mehuron.html>.

41. **A professional site** Generally, no author is identified for a professional site, so the entry begins with the site title in italics. Follow with the name of the site sponsor, the date of publication or update of the site; then, include the medium of publication followed by your date of access.

    Latimes.com. Los Angeles Times, 1 Oct. 2004. Web. 1 Oct. 2004.

42. **A site for a department of a college or university** Begin with the name of the department, followed by a description such as *Dept. home page* (without italics), followed by a period. Then list the name of the institution, the medium, and your date of access. No date of publication or latest update is necessary.

    Department of Foreign Languages and Literatures. Dept. home page. Marquette U College of Arts & Sciences. Web. 6 Nov. 2004.

43. **A site for a study course** Start with the instructor's name, reversed as for an author. Then give the course title, without quotation marks, underlining, or italics. Follow with the phrase *Course home page* (without italics), then a period, the course dates, and the department and institution. End with the medium of publication and your date of access.

    Strickland, Ron. Shakespeare on Stage. Course home page. 14 June 2004–4 Aug. 2004. Dept. of English. Illinois State U. Web. 4 Oct. 2004.

44. **A site with a long URL** If the URL is necessary and you must include a line break in it, do so only after a slash (see above), and do not add a hyphen to indicate the break. For a URL that is long and complicated enough to invite errors in transcription, give the URL of the site's search page instead.

MacLeod, Donald. "Shake-Up for Academic Publishing." *Education Guardian.co.uk.* Guardian News and Media Limited, 2004. Web. 10 Nov. 2004. <http://www.guardian.co.uk/Archive/>.

As an alternative or in addition to the URL, a search path may occasionally need to be included.

"Frederica: An Eighteenth-Century Community." National Register of Historic Places. National Parks Service. Web. 27 Feb. 2004. <http://www.cr.nps.gov/nr/>. Path: Education; Hispanic Heritage Month; Frederica.

45. **An online book** In general, follow the format for printed books. Include publication information for the original print version if available. Follow the date of publication with the medium of publication (Web.) and the access date.

Simon, Julian L. *The Ultimate Resource II: People, Materials, and Environment.* College Park: U of Maryland, 1996. Web. 9 Apr. 2001.

When citing part of an online book, the title (or name of the part, such as *Foreword*) follows the author's name; the title of the book (italicized) is followed by its author's name if it is different from the first name listed.

Untermeyer, Louis. "Author's Apology." *The Donkey of God.* 1999. iUniverse. Web. 7 Mar. 2003.

46. **An article in an online periodical** Begin with the author's name; the article title in quotation marks; the italicized name of the periodical, including the volume or issue number for scholarly journals, and the date of publication. Include page numbers (or other sections) if numbered. Close with the medium of publication and the access date.

Dickerson, John. "Nailing Jello." *Time.com* 5 Nov. 2001. Web. 9 Dec. 2001.

47. **An article in an online reference work** Unless the author of the entry is identified, begin with the entry name in quotation marks. Follow with the usual online publication information.

"Eakins, Thomas." *Britannica Concise Encyclopaedia* 2004. Encyclopaedia Britannica. Web. 26 Sept. 2004.

48. **An article in an online service** When you use a library to access a subscription service, add the name of the database if known (italicized), the medium of publication, and the date of access.

Davis, Jerome. "Massacre in Kiev." *Washington Post* 29 Nov. 1999, final ed.: C12. *National Newspapers.* Web. 30 Nov. 1999.

49. **A scholarly project or information database** The title of the site is listed first, then the name of the editor (if given). Follow this information with the version number (if relevant), date of publication or update, name of the sponsor, medium of publication, and the date of access.

Wired Style: Principles of English Usage in the Digital Age. 1994. Wired Digital Inc. Web. 5 Nov. 2001.

If you are citing a book that is part of an online scholarly project, first list information about the printed book, followed by publication information for the project.

Astell, Mary. *Reflections on Marriage*. London: Wilkin, 1706. *Women Writers Project*. Providence: Brown UP, 1999. Web. 7 Feb. 2002.

50. **An online government publication** As with a government publication in print, begin with the name of the government (country, state, and so on), followed by the name of the agency. After the publication title, add the electronic publication information. (When citing the *Congressional Record*, the date and page numbers are all that are required.)

    United States. Dept. of Labor. Women's Bureau. *WB: An Overview*. Web. 12 Aug. 2005.

51. **An online posting in a list server** Begin a citation for a posting distributed by a list server as you would any other e-mail message, with author name and document title (from the subject line). Follow this with the description *Online posting* (without italics) and a period, the date of posting, the name of the group, the medium of publication, and your date of access. Whenever possible, cite an archived version of the posting so that your readers can find the source for themselves.

    Moody, Ellen. "Alternate Persuasions." Online posting. 25 Apr. 1998. The Austen-L Mailing List. Web. 12 Jan. 2005.

52. **An online posting in a web forum** List the author's name and the title of the posting (in quotation marks), followed by *Online posting* (without italics) and a period. Then give the posting date, the forum name, the medium of publication, and your date of access.

    Cubby, J. "Re: Connecting Playwrights and Theatre Companies." Online posting. 27 May 2004. AACT Online Forums: Playwriting & Playwrights. Web. 12 Jan. 2005.

53. **An online posting in a newsgroup** Start a newsgroup message as you would a posting to a list server or Web forum, with the author's name, the posting title, the description *Online posting* (without italics), and a period. Then give the title of the overall Web site in italics, followed by the date of publication, the medium, and your date of access.

    Silverman, Neal. "Re: Perimeter of a Triangle." Online posting *Geometry.com*, 1 Oct. 2004. Web. 12 Dec. 2004.

54. **An online posting in a real-time (synchronous) communication forum** If you are citing a particular speaker, identify that person. Follow with the event description, the date of the event, the communication forum, the medium of publication, and the date of access. Add the Telnet URL, if needed.

Del Rey, Juan Roberto. Online defense of dissertation "Chaos, Cadence, Tonality, Dissonance, and Meaning in the Music of Leonard Bernstein." 18 July 2005. *Connections.* Web. 18 July 2005. <telnet://connections.moo.mud.org:3333/>.

NOTE: If necessary, give readers a link to an archived version of the posting.

Del Rey, Juan Roberto. Online defense of dissertation "Chaos, Cadence, Tonality, Dissonance, and Meaning in the Music of Leonard Bernstein." 18 July 2005. *Connections.* Web. 3 Aug. 2005. <http://web. new.ufl. edu/~tari/connections/archives/delrey_phd_defense.txt>.

55. **An online poem** List the poet's name, the title of the poem, and the print publication information before the electronic publication details.

Nemerov, Howard. "Found Poem." *War Stories.* By Nemerov. U of Chicago P: 1987. *Poets.org.* Web. 5 Oct. 2004.

56. **An online multimedia resource** After the usual information for the type of work (painting, photograph, musical composition, film) being cited, add electronic publication information, including, in this instance, the URL.

Goya, Francisco de. *Saturn Devouring His Children.* 1819–1823. Painting. Museo del Prado, Madrid. Web. 13 Dec. 2003. <http://www.usc.edu/schools/annenberg/asc/projects/comm544/library/>.

57. **An online transcript of a broadcast** Give the original publication information for the broadcast. Then add the description *Transcript* (without italics), followed by a period, the medium of publication, and the date of access.

Lehrer, Jim. "Character above All." *The NewsHour with Jim Lehrer* 29 May 1996. Transcript. Web. 23 Apr. 2004.

58. **A publication in more than one medium** For a work that consists of more than one type of medium, either list all the media that make up the work or cite only the medium that contains the specific material cited in your paper.

CultureGrams. Lindon: Axiom, 2002. Print, CD-ROM.

59. **An e-mail communication** Identify the author of the e-mail; then list the "Subject" line of the e-mail as a title, in quotation marks. Next, include a description of the entry, including the recipient—usually *Message to the author* (no italics), meaning you, the author of the paper. Finally, give the date of the message and the medium (E-mail).

Barzinji, Atman. "Re: Frog Populations in Wisconsin Wetlands." Message to the author. 1 Jan. 2005. E-mail.

60. **An online posting** Follow the author's name and title with *Online posting* (no italics). The posting date is next, followed by the name of the forum, if known; medium of publication; date of access; and, if necessary, the address.

Wilcox, G. "White Gold Finch." Online posting. 7 Nov. 2001. *IN-Bird.* Web. 9 Nov. 2001. <http://www.virtualbirder.com/bmail/inbird/latest.html#1>.

MLA

WORKS-CITED ENTRIES: OTHER SOURCES—PRIMARY, PERSONAL, AND MULTIMEDIA

61. **A periodically published database on CD-ROM, DVD-ROM, diskette, or magnetic tape** Citations for materials published on CD-ROM, DVD-ROM, diskette, or magnetic tape are similar to those for print sources, with these added considerations: (1) The contents of a work may vary from one medium to another; therefore, the citation must always identify the medium. (2) The publisher and vendor of the publication may be different, in which case both must be identified. (3) Multiple versions of the same database may exist, a situation that calls for citation of both the date of the document cited and the date of the database itself.

    Ackley, Patricia. "Jobs of the Twenty-First Century." *New Rochelle Informer* 15 Apr. 1994: A4. *New Rochelle Informer Ondisc*. CD-ROM. Info-Line. Oct. 1994.

62. **Computer software** If you use a reference book recorded on CD-ROM, use the form below. If available, include publication information for the printed source.

    The American Heritage Dictionary of the English Language. 3rd ed. Boston: Houghton, 1992. Cambridge: Softkey Intl., 1994. CD-ROM.

63. **A television or radio program**

    "The Ultimate Road Trip: Traveling in Cyberspace." *48 Hours*. CBS. WBBM, Chicago. 13 Apr. 1995. Television.

64. **A film** The director, distributor, and year of release follow the title. Other information may be included if pertinent.

    Eternal Sunshine of the Spotless Mind. Dir. Michel Gondry. Perf. Jim Carey, Kate Winslet. Focus Features, 2004. Film.

65. **A video recording** Cite a filmstrip, slide program, videocassette, or DVD like a film.

    Monet: Shadow & Light. Devine Productions, 1999. Videocassette.

66. **An audio recording** Indicate *CD, LP, Audiocassette,* or *Audiotape* (without italics), followed by a period. If you are citing a specific song on a musical recording, place its title in quotation marks before the title of the recording.

    Ackroyd, Peter. *Shakespeare*. Random House Audio, 2005. Audiocassette.

67. **A performance** Treat this entry similarly to a film entry, adding the location and date of the performance.

    Chanticleer: An Orchestra of Voices. Young Auditorium, Whitewater, Wisc. 23 Feb. 2003. Performance.

68. **An artwork on display**

Titian. *The Entombment.* 1602–1603. Oil on canvas. The Louvre, Paris.

69. **A letter or memo received by the author (you)** Here, *TS* following the date refers to "typescript." *MS* refers to a handwritten letter ("manuscript").

Thomas, Bob. Letter to the author. 10 Jan. 2005. TS.

70. **An interview by the author (you)**

Brooks, Sarah. Personal interview. 15 Oct. 2004.

71. **A cartoon or comic strip (in print)**

Luckovich, Mike. "The Drawing Board." Cartoon. *Time* 17 Sept. 2001: 18. Print.

72. **An advertisement (in print)** List the subject of the advertisement (product, company, organization, or such), followed by *Advertisement* (without italics) and a period. Then give the usual publication information.

Vaio Professional notebooks. Advertisement. *Campus Technology* Oct. 2004: 45. Print.

73. **A lecture, a speech, an address, or a reading** If there is a title, include it. Conclude with the descriptive label (for example, *Lecture*).

Annan, Kofi. Acceptance of Nobel Peace Prize. Oslo City Hall, Oslo, Norway. 10 Dec. 2001. Lecture.

74. **A legal or historical document** Familiar historical documents such as the U.S. Constitution are typically not included in a works-cited list because they can so easily be abbreviated in a parenthetical note within the text of your paper: "(US Const., art. 4, sec. 1)," for example. (Note that such documents are not italicized.)

To list a legislative act in your works cited, begin with its name, then give its public law number, its date of enactment, and its Statutes-at-Large number.

Do-Not-Call Implementation Act. Pub. L. 108-010. 11 Mar. 2003. Stat. 117-557. Print.

Abbreviate the names of law cases (spelling out the first important word of each party's name). Do not italicize the name in your works cited (although it should be italicized within the body of your paper). Follow with the case number, the name of the court, and the date of decision.

Missouri v. Seibert. No. 02-1371. Supreme Court of the US. 28 June 2004. Print.

75. **A map or chart** Follow the format for an anonymous book, adding the word *Map* or *Chart* (without italics), followed by a period, to conclude the entry.

Wisconsin Territory. Madison: Wisconsin Trails, 1988. Map.

MODEL OF STUDENT PAPER IN MLA STYLE

CASSANDRA LANE'S paper "Paper or Bioplastics?" uses the MLA documentation style that is the preferred style for English courses.

Identifying information should be flush left and double-spaced.

Cassandra Lane

Professor Davis

ENG 201

25 April 2008

The title is centered and double-spaced with no extra space above or below.

Paper or Bioplastic?

The text begins two lines (one double-space) below the title and is double-spaced.

A plastic bag dances in circles, twirling and twisting with the dead leaves on the sidewalk in front of a red brick wall. It is so light that the wind picks it up and tosses it, as if it were one of the leaves.

Spell out the name of the organization and give the abbreviation in parentheses.

Italicize names of films.

This bag is the epitome of beauty for Wes Bentley's character Ricky Fitts in *American Beauty*. The Internet Movie Data Base (IMDb.com) cites a similarly drifting paper bag as screenwriter Alan Ball's inspiration to write the film in the late 1990s. Although many Americans took the film's tagline "look closer . . ." (*American Beauty*) to heart and saw the bag as a symbol for all the little things we miss on a daily basis, isn't it just garbage? After a while, the bag begins to look like a blemish rather than the idyllic image Fitts saw.

This information is general knowledge and requires no citation.

That bag will take up to 1,000 years to break down into small pieces in landfills, and it will never biodegrade. Since plastic bags are polyethylene, a synthetic polymer that comes from petroleum, the microorganisms that consume biodegradable materials do not recognize plastic bags as food. Thus, plastic—a crude-oil-based product—has no place in the natural food chain. In brief, those bags are going to be with us for a long, long time, and the problems that they cause will also be with us. Not only do plastic bags create much of the bulk in landfills, but they also choke wildlife and act as blemishes on the face of otherwise beautiful landscapes. With environmental concerns growing rapidly around the world and movies like Al Gore's *An Inconvenient Truth* winning Oscars, a campaign against that little plastic bag has retailers and consumers changing their behavior, signaling one way that the green movement has real roots.

MLA

The writer's last name appears in every header and is followed by the page number (without a comma).

Citation information appears on the Works Cited page.

Still, about 80 percent of customers choose plastic, according to a May 2007 article by Michael Milstein in *The Oregonian*. He argues that the plastic bags "are often more convenient when walking and sturdier—especially in the rain" than paper alternatives. Michael Jessen, founder of Zero Waste Solutions (a small company in British Columbia that helps corporations reduce overall waste), disagrees. "This is one product that actually does more harm than good. Imagining our lives without plastic bags should be possible," said Jessen ("Bag Beast"). A world without plastic is possible and could become a reality.

The writer gives the author's credentials.

Online source requires no page number.

The international community has already been paying increasing attention to the "floating dump of plastic bigger than the state of Texas in the North Pacific" (Jessen, e-mail). The Environmental Protection Agency says that more than 380 billion plastic bags are used in the United States every year, approximately 100 billion of which are plastic shopping bags (West). Some governments are playing an important role in decreasing the use of the plastic bag. For example, in March 2002, the Irish government levied a fifteen-cent tax on every plastic shopping bag (Jessen, "Bag Beast"). In the first year after the implementation of this Irish "PlusTax," consumption of plastic bags dropped almost instantly, resulting in a nearly five-billion-gallon reduction in the use of crude oil. Government officials and business owners were also pleased: the government gained $9.6 million in revenue, and retailers now were selling reusable totes as well as saving the approximately $50 million per year they were spending on plastic prior to the tax (Jessen, "Bag Beast").

Name the author and source for an author with more than one work cited.

In the United States, the movement is also catching on. The San Francisco Board of Supervisors voted in March 2007 to place an outright ban on plastic bags from large supermarkets and pharmacies, starting discussions of similar bans in many U.S. cities, including Phoenix; Santa Cruz, California; and Portland, Oregon (Viser).

Bans like the one in San Francisco made businesses and consumers look beyond the convenience of plastic, opening the door to viable alternatives. Many are turning to reusable cloth totes, but some (like the small, specialty grocery chain Trader Joe's) have started to use bags make of bioplastics—a compostable cousin to the old classic that is made out of renewable products such as corn or potato starch rather than crude oil (Cody).

Governments are not the only bodies capable of changing the way the world sees the plastic bag; individual firms and consumers are jumping on the green train as well. For example,

Texas-based grocery chain Whole Foods recently promised on its website to rid itself of plastic bags by Earth Day 2008, turning instead to paper bags and reusable cloth totes that sell for 99 cents at most stores.

Some people are even starting to question the viability of the recyclable paper bag. Although some customers might balk at the idea of paying for their grocery bags, paper bags, although they are biodegradable and made from renewable resources, have a relatively short useful life. Cloth bags trump paper bags because their lives are long. Jessen argues that "paper cannot compete [with reusable cloth bags] when life-cycle costs are entered into the equation. The solution is to make people aware that we need to choose the option that can be continued as far as we can see into the future. Whatever choice we make must be viable at least seven generations into the future."

This information is from an online posting.

Firms such as Whole Foods and Trader Joe's have picked up on that idea and are trying to discourage the use of paper in their stores, offering incentives to every customer who brings his or her own bags when grocery shopping. The Whole Foods website offers "a refund of at least 5 cents per bag," and the San Francisco area Trader Joe's stores entered their environmentally friendly consumers in a raffle to win $25 worth of groceries.

The writer cites a work in which a quotation appears.

But waste-reduction efforts across the United States are not all moving at the same pace. In Boston, companies such as CVS Pharmacies still offer only plastic bags. Although Matt Viser described a plastic ban in Boston that would mirror the ban in San Francisco in a *Boston Globe* article in April of 2007, there has been no successful legislation to date limiting Boston's plastic use. In the article, Viser quoted Christopher Flynn, president of the Massachusetts Food Association and an opponent to the proposed legislation, who claimed that legislators were "making the plastic bags a scapegoat for litter and environmental issues, which is not the ultimate problem. The problem is individuals and their own behavior."

Actions taken by stores throughout Boston have successfully created change, though. Several local grocery store chains (including Shaw's and Trader Joe's) are starting to move in similar directions as their West Coast counterparts, away from plastic bags. Colorful signs reminding customers to "Make Beantown a Greentown" hang from cash registers, shelves, and the ceiling throughout the Trader Joe's on Boylston Street in Boston, reminding every person who walks through the sliding doors to use reusable shopping bags. The store sells a variety of bags ranging from simple cloth bags to insulated bags for perishable groceries. For

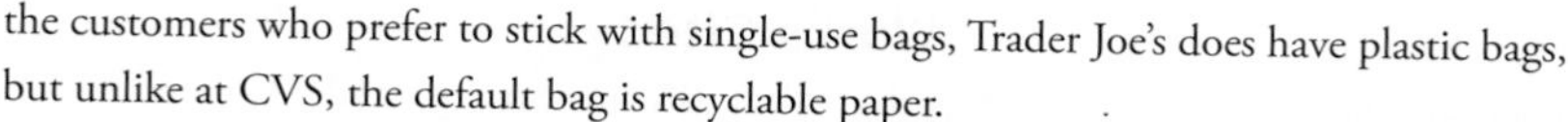

the customers who prefer to stick with single-use bags, Trader Joe's does have plastic bags, but unlike at CVS, the default bag is recyclable paper.

Grocery shopping is not the only place where consumers and suppliers are cutting out plastic: some retailers are also going green. Swedish home decoration store Ikea promises to "bag the plastic bag" in its stores by October 2008, according to an April 2008 article on *The Corporate Social Responsibility Newswire*. Ikea sells cloth bags for fifty-nine cents each and even assigns a five-cent price tag to plastic bags, with the proceeds going to the nonprofit conservation company, American Forests. The success of this experiment led to the proposed plastic bag ban by October 2008.

Raising awareness about banning plastic bags has become popular with fashion designers as well. "High-profile designers have already brought the plastic bag issue needed attention," wrote Michael Jessen in an e-mail to the author. Designers Marc Jacobs and Steve Madden replaced their disposable shopping bags with cloth bags that are reminiscent of the bags on sale in Shaw's and Trader Joe's. Making a fashion statement out of alternatives to single-use plastic bags can also mean profits: "Designers can charge something extra for their bags if they do so in conjunction with an initiative to encourage a ban on plastic," according to Jessen.

The writer cites an e-mail written to her.

Though the movement to rid the world of plastic shopping bags is still in its infancy, the acceptance of the argument in favor of alternatives is growing in popularity and effectiveness. Whether this movement follows the failed path of a similar movement to reduce disposable diaper use remains an open question, but the support of government, retailers, and consumers is beginning to add up to less.

APA

Indent the second line of each entry five spaces or 1/2 inch.

The header is centered.

Works Cited

American Beauty. Dir. Sam Mendes. Perf. Kevin Spacey and Annette Bening. Dreamworks SKG, 1999. Film.

"American Beauty (1999)." Internet Movie Database. Web. 22 Apr. 2008.

Cody. Telephone interview. 29 Apr. 2008.

Jessen, Michael. "Re: Plastic Bag article." Message to the author. 21 Apr. 2008. E-mail.

Jessen, Michael. "The Bag Beast." *Environmentally Speaking: Michael Jessen Speaks Up for the Environment*. Web. 19 Apr. 2008.

Milstein, Michael. "Which Bag Is Best: Paper or Plastic?" *Oregonian* 17 May 2007. Web. 24 Apr. 2008.

"The Results Are in . . . Over 92% of IKEA Customers Bagged the Plastic Bag!" *Corporate Social Responsibility Newswire*. Online posting. 2 Apr. 2008. Web. 24 Apr. 2008.

Viser, Matt. "Plastic Bags May Be Banned in Boston." *Boston Globe* 26 Apr. 2007. Web. 24 Apr. 2008.

"We're going all out for reusable!" Online posting. Web. 26 Apr. 2008.

West, Larry. "Paper, Plastic, or Something Better?" *About.com: Environmental Issues*. Web. 24 Apr. 2008.

OVERVIEW OF APA STYLE

The *Publication Manual of the American Psychological Association* is the authoritative source for documenting research papers in the sciences and social sciences. You can consult the handbook or the Web site at <http://www. apastyle.org> for more detailed information. You will get an overview here of:

- Formatting the manuscript
- Citing sources in the text
- Creating a References page

At the end of this section is a portion of a student paper in APA style that you can use as a model.

FORMATTING THE MANUSCRIPT (APA)

APA style has somewhat different requirements for formatting than MLA style, but presentation is just as important.

PAPER Use good quality 8 1/2-by-11-inch paper. Fasten your manuscript with paper clips; avoid both staples and binders because they make it harder for your professor to read and comment on your work.

TITLE PAGE APA style calls for a separate title page, numbered as page 1. A title—or a shortened title, if yours is long—and page number go against the right margin, about 1/2 inch from the top of the paper. This running head should appear on all the pages of your paper.

Although APA does not specify how to format the title page, the usual format is to center your title about a third of the way down the page. Use regular type and the same font as in the rest of the manuscript (do not use all capital letters, italics, boldface, or the like). Double-space the title if it is longer than one line. Double-spaced and centered under the title, type your name. Double-spaced under your name, type your course number; then, after another double space, type the date.

ABSTRACT The second page of your paper is the abstract, a brief (no more than 120 words) summary of your paper. Center the word *Abstract* about 1 inch from the top of the page, and double-space the text.

MARGINS, SPACING, FONT, AND INDENTING Leave 1-inch margins on all four sides. Double-space your entire manuscript. Use easy-to-read fonts; 10-point to 14-point Times and Times New Roman are most commonly used. Indent 1/2 inch, or between five and seven spaces, at the beginning of each paragraph. For quotations of more than forty words, indent 1/2 inch, or five to seven spaces, and do not use quotation marks. (Some professors will ask you to indent 1 inch or ten spaces in academic papers.) Double-space within the quotation.

PAGING Begin your paper on page 3.

HEADINGS Headings are encouraged in APA-formatted papers. If your material is complicated and would benefit from being subdivided, create headings that are brief, parallel in phrasing, and consistent in the font you use. Use no more than two levels of headings, if possible.

VISUALS If you include graphs, tables, maps, charts, illustrations, or photographs, place them directly after you introduce them in the text. Label the table at the top with the table number and title (Table 1. Album Titles and Release Dates). Label each figure below the image with a number and a caption that identifies it (Figure 1. Album revenues). Cite the source underneath the visual.

REFERENCES The final page of your paper is called References. Center the title about 1 inch from the top of the page. Do not add quotation marks, boldface, italics, and so on. Alphabetically list all works you referred to in the text of your paper, double-spaced with a hanging indent.

APA

CITING SOURCES IN THE TEXT

The APA format requires you to cite at least the author and the date in the parenthetical citations within the text of your paper. Sometimes you will add the page reference as well. A citation should be brief but complete enough to lead your reader to the full citation in the References list at the end of the paper. The following list shows how to cite sources in the text of your paper.*

DIRECTORY TO IN-TEXT CITATIONS

1. One author: a complete work
2. One author: part of a work
3. One author: more than one publication in the same year
4. Works by authors with the same last name
5. Two to five authors
6. Six or more authors
7. A work authored by a committee or other organization
8. A work with no author indicated
9. A work referred to in another work
10. A work in an anthology
11. An electronic or other Internet source
12. An entire Web site
13. Two or more works in a parenthetical reference
14. A sacred text or famous literary work
15. A personal communication

SAMPLE IN-TEXT CITATIONS

1. **One author: a complete work** The correct form for a parenthetical reference to a single source by a single author is opening parenthesis, last name, comma, space, publication year, closing parenthesis. Also note that final punctuation should be placed outside the parentheses.

    The great majority of Venezuelans live near the Caribbean coast (Anderson, 2001).

2. **One author: part of a work** When you cite a specific part of a source, give the page number, chapter, or section, using the appropriate abbreviations (*p.* or *pp., chap.,* or *sec.*). Always give the page number for a direct quotation.

    Bush's 2002 budget, passed by Congress, was based on revenue estimates that "now appear to have been far too optimistic" (Lemann, 2003, p. 48).

3. **One author: more than one publication in the same year** If the same author has published two or more articles in the same year, avoid confusion by placing

* *Reprinted with permission from* The College Writer's Handbook *by Randall VanderMey, Verne Meyer, John Van Rys, and Pat Sebranek (2006).*

a small letter *a* after the first work listed in the references list, *b* after the next one, and so on. The order of such works is determined alphabetically by title.

PARENTHETICAL CITATION

Coral reefs harbor life forms heretofore unknown (Milius, 2001a, 2001b).

REFERENCES

Milius, D. (2001a). Another world hides inside coral reefs. *Science News, 160* (16), 244.

Milius, D. (2001b). Unknown squids—with elbows—tease science. *Science News, 160* (24), 390.

4. **Works by authors with the same last name** When citing different sources by authors with the same last name, it is best to add the authors' initials to avoid confusion, even if the publication dates are different. When possible, mention the author's name in the text the first time material is used. Afterward, including the name in parentheses is appropriate.

   Although J. D. Wallace (2005) argued that privatizing Social Security would benefit only the wealthiest citizens, others such as E. S. Wallace (2006) supported the movement toward greater control for individuals.

5. **Two to five authors** In APA style, all authors—up to as many as five—must be mentioned in the first text citation, like this:

   Love changes not just who we are, but who we can become, as well (Lewis, Amini, & Lannon, 2000).

NOTE: The last two authors' names are always separated by a comma and an ampersand (&) when enclosed in parentheses.

After the first mention, use only the name of the first author followed by *et al.* (the Latin abbreviation for *et alii*, meaning "and others"), like this:

   These discoveries lead to the hypothesis that love actually alters the brain's structure (Lewis et al., 2000).

6. **Six or more authors** If your source has six or more authors, refer to the work by the first author's name followed by *et al.,* for both the first reference in the text and all references after that. However, in your references list, be sure to list the first six authors; any additional authors can be shortened to *et al.*

   According to a recent study, post-traumatic stress disorder (PTSD) continues to dominate the lives of Vietnam veterans, though in modified forms (Trembley et al., 2005).

7. **A work authored by a committee or other organization** Treat the name of the group as if it were the last name of the author. If the name is long and

easily abbreviated, provide the abbreviation in square brackets. Use the abbreviation without brackets in subsequent references, as follows:

FIRST TEXT CITATION

A continuing problem for many veterans is heightened sensitivity to noise (National Institute of Mental Health [NIMH], 2005).

SUBSEQUENT CITATIONS

> In addition, veterans suffering from PTSD continue to have difficulty discussing their experiences and sharing suicidal thoughts with family members or mental health professionals (NIMH, 2005).

8. **A work with no author indicated** If your source lists no author, treat the first two or three words of the title as you would an author's last name. A title of an article or a chapter belongs in quotation marks, whereas the titles of books or reports should be italicized:

   > One key to avoiding serious back injuries and long-term back pain is adopting low-stress postures especially in the workplace ("Diagnosing Back," 2001).

9. **A work referred to in another work** If you need to cite a source that you have found referred to in another source, mention the original source in your text. Then, in your parenthetical citation, cite the secondary source, using the words *as cited in,* like this:

   > A key development in the research on bipolarity was the theorem given by Richards (as cited in McDonald, 1998).

NOTE: In your references list at the end of the paper, you would write out a full citation for McDonald, not Richards.

10. **A work in an anthology** When citing an article or a chapter in an anthology or a collection, use the names of the authors of the specific article, not the names of the anthology's editors. (The article should also be listed by its authors' names in the References section.)

    > Phonological changes can be understood from a variationist perspective (Guy, 2005).

11. **An electronic or other Internet source** As with print sources, cite an electronic source by the author (or by a shortened title if the author is unknown) and the publication date (not the date that you accessed the source). If citing a specific part of the source, use an appropriate abbreviation: *p.* (page), *chap.* (chapter), or *para.* (paragraph).

    > One study compared and contrasted the use of Web and touch screen transaction log files in a hospital setting (Nicholas, Huntington, & Williams, 2001).

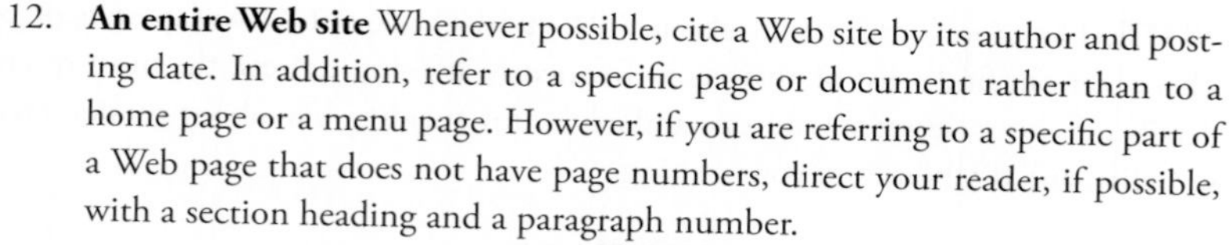

12. **An entire Web site** Whenever possible, cite a Web site by its author and posting date. In addition, refer to a specific page or document rather than to a home page or a menu page. However, if you are referring to a specific part of a Web page that does not have page numbers, direct your reader, if possible, with a section heading and a paragraph number.

    According to the National Multiple Sclerosis Society (2003, "Complexities" section, para. 2), understanding of MS could not start to take shape until the 1920s, when scientists began to research nerve transmission.

13. **Two or more works in a parenthetical reference** Sometimes it is necessary to provide several citations in one parenthetical reference. In that case, cite the sources as you usually would, separating the citations with semicolons. Place the citations in alphabetical order, just as they would be ordered in the References list:

    These near-death experiences are reported with conviction (Rommer, 2000; Sabom, 1998).

14. **A sacred text or famous literary work** Sacred texts and famous literary works are published in many different editions. For that reason, the original date of publication may be unavailable or not pertinent. In these cases, use your edition's year of translation (*trans. 2003*) or indicate your edition's year of publication (*2003 version*). When you are referring to specific sections of the work, it is best to identify parts, chapters, or other divisions instead of your version's page numbers.

    An interesting literary case of such dysfunctional family behavior can be found in Franz Kafka's *The Metamorphosis,* where it becomes the commandment of family duty for Gregor's parents and sister to swallow their disgust and endure him, endure him and nothing more (trans. 1972, part 3).

    Books of the Bible and other well-known literary works may be abbreviated if no misunderstanding is possible.

    "Generations come and generations go, but the earth remains forever" (*The New International Version Study Bible,* 1985 version, Eccles. 1.4).

15. **A personal communication** Personal communications may include personal letters, phone calls, memos, e-mail messages, and so forth. Because they are not published in a permanent form, APA style does not place them among the citations in your references list. Instead, cite them only in the text of your paper in parentheses, like this:

    The manifestation of such kleptomania late in life can be explained by the disintegration of certain inhibitions, according to M. T. Cann (personal communication, April 1, 2005). However, such criminal trespasses are minor compared with the more serious breakdown of mental processes through dementia (M. T. Cann, personal communication, April 1, 2005).

APA

NOTE: For more information about APA style, check out <www.apastyle.org>. There you can find a list of answers to frequently asked questions, the most recent details for citing electronic sources, and advice for avoiding bias about gender, race, sexuality, and disabilities in your writing.

CREATING A REFERENCES PAGE

The last page of your paper will be titled *References.* All the parenthetical citations that you inserted in your paper refer your reader to the complete entry in this final list. Include each work you cited in your paper but not works that you read but did not cite. Alphabetize your list by last name of the author or, in the case of an entry without an identified author, by the first word of the title, excluding the articles *A*, *An*, and *The*.

DIRECTORY TO APA REFERENCES ENTRIES

Books and other documents

1. A book by one author
2. A book by two or more authors
3. An anonymous book
4. A chapter from a book
5. A single work from an anthology
6. One volume of a multivolume edited work
7. A separately titled volume in a multivolume work
8. An edited work, one in a series
9. A group author as publisher
10. An edition other than the first
11. Two or more books by the same author
12. An English translation
13. An article in a reference book
14. A reprint, different form
15. A technical or research report
16. A government publication

Periodicals

17. An article in a scholarly journal, consecutively paginated
18. An abstract of a scholarly article (from a secondary source)
19. A journal article, paginated by issue
20. A journal article, more than six authors
21. A review
22. A magazine article
23. A newspaper article
24. A newsletter article

Online sources

25. A periodical, identical to print version
26. A periodical, different from print version or online only
27. A multipage document created by a private organization
28. A document from an online database
29. Other nonperiodical online document
30. A document or an abstract available on a university Web site
31. A report from a university, available on a private organization Web site
32. A U.S. government report available on a government agency Web site
33. A paper presented at a symposium or other event, abstract retrieved from a university Web site
34. An e-mail message
35. Electronic book

Reference material

36. Online encyclopedia
37. Online dictionary
38. Wiki

Other sources

39. Audio podcast
40. Message posted to a newsgroup, online forum, or discussion group
41. Weblog post
42. Specialized computer software with limited distribution
43. An electronic abstract of a journal article retrieved from a database
44. A television or radio broadcast
45. A television or radio program (episode in a series)
46. An audio recording
47. A music recording
48. A motion picture
49. A published interview, titled, single author
50. An unpublished paper presented at a meeting

APA REFERENCE ENTRIES: BOOKS AND OTHER DOCUMENTS

The general APA form for a book or brochure entry is this:

Author, A. (year). ***Title.*** **Location: Publisher.**

- Author's last name and initial(s) followed by a period
- Year of publication in parentheses followed by a period
- Title lowercased in italics, with only the first word and any proper nouns capitalized, followed by a period

APA

- Publication city (and state, province, or country if the city is not well known for publishing) followed by a colon
- Publisher name followed by a period

1. **A book by one author**

   Guttman, J. (1999). *The gift wrapped in sorrow: A mother's quest for healing.* Palm Springs, CA: JMJ Publishing.

2. **A book by two or more authors** Follow the first author name (or names) with a comma; then join the last and next-to-last names with an ampersand (&) rather than with the word *and.* List up to six authors; abbreviate subsequent authors as *et al.*

   Lynn, J., & Harrold, J. (1999). *Handbook for mortals: Guidance for people facing serious illness.* New York: Oxford University Press.

3. **An anonymous book** If an author is listed as *Anonymous,* treat that word as the author's name. Otherwise, follow this format:

   American Psychological Association. (2001). *The publication manual of the American Psychological Association* (5th ed.). Washington: Author.

NOTE: In this title, the words *American Psychological Association* are capitalized because they are a proper name. The words *publication manual* are not capitalized.

4. **A chapter from a book** List the chapter title after the date of publication, followed by a period or appropriate end punctuation. Use the word *In* before the book title, and follow the book title with the inclusive page numbers of the chapter.

   Tattersall, I. (2002). How did we achieve humanity? In *The monkey in the mirror* (pp. 138–68). New York: Harcourt.

5. **A single work from an anthology** Start with information about the individual work, followed by details about the collection in which it appears, including the page span. When editors' names come in the middle of an entry, follow the usual order: initial first, surname last. Note the placement of the word *Eds.* in parentheses.

   Guy, G. R. (2005). Variationist approaches to phonological change. In B. D. Joseph & R. D. Janda (Eds.), *The handbook of historical linguistics* (pp. 369–400). Malden, MA: Blackwell.

6. **One volume of a multivolume edited work** Indicate the volume in parentheses after the work's title.

   Salzman, J., Smith, D. L., & West, C. (Eds.). (1996). *Encyclopedia of African-American culture and history* (Vol. 4). New York: Simon & Schuster.

7. **A separately titled volume in a multivolume work** When a work is part of a larger series or collection, as with this example, make a two-part title consisting of the series and the particular volume you are citing.

   The Associated Press. (1995). *Twentieth-century America: Vol. 8. The crisis of national confidence: 1974–1980*. Danbury, CT: Grolier Educational Corp.

8. **An edited work, one in a series** Start the entry with the work's author, publication date, and title. Then follow with publication details about the series.

   Marshall, P. G. (2002). The impact of the Cold War on Asia. In T. O'Neill (Ed.), *World history by era: Vol. 9. The nuclear age* (pp. 162–166). San Diego: Greenhaven Press.

9. **A group author as publisher** When the author is also the publisher, simply put the word *Author* in the place where you would list the publisher's name.

   Amnesty International. (2000). *Hidden scandal, secret shame: Torture and ill-treatment of children*. New York: Author.

10. **An edition other than the first** Indicate a second or subsequent edition with that edition's publication date (not the first edition's) plus the edition number in parentheses after the title. Writers accustomed to MLA citations must remember that APA references capitalize only the first word and any proper nouns in a title.

    Trimmer, J. (2001). *Writing with a purpose* (13th ed.). Boston: Houghton Mifflin.

11. **Two or more books by the same author** When you are listing multiple works by the same author, arrange them by the year of publication, earliest first.

    Dershowitz, A. (2000). *The Genesis of justice: Ten stories of biblical injustice that led to the Ten Commandments and modern law*. New York: Warner Books.

    ———. (2002). *Shouting fire: Civil liberties—past, present, and future*. Boston: Little, Brown.

12. **An English translation**

    Setha, R. (1998). *Unarmed* (R. Narasimhan, Trans.). Chennai, India: Macmillan. (Original work published 1995)

13. **An article in a reference book** Start the entry with the author of the article, if identified. If no author is listed, begin the entry with the title of the article.

    Lewer, N. (1999). Non-lethal weapons. In *World encyclopedia of peace* (pp. 279–280). Oxford: Pergamon Press.

NOTE: If you use the original work, cite the original version; the non-English title is followed by its English translation, not italicized, in square brackets.

APA

14. **A reprint, different form**

    Albanov, V. (2000). *In the land of white death: An epic story of survival in the Siberian Arctic.* New York: Modern Library. (Original work published 1917)

NOTE: This work was originally published in Russia in 1917; the 2000 reprint is the first English version. If you are citing a reprint from another source, the parentheses would contain "reprinted from *Title,* pp. 000–000, by A. Author, year, Location: Publisher."

15. **A technical or research report**

    Taylor, B. G., Fitzgerald, N., Hunt, D., Reardon, J. A., & Brownstein, H. H. (2001). *ADAM preliminary 2000 findings on drug use and drug markets: Adult male arrestees.* Washington: National Institute of Justice.

16. **A government publication** Generally, refer to the government agency as the author. When possible, provide an identification number for the document after the title in parentheses.

    National Institute on Drug Abuse. (2000). *Inhalant abuse* (NIH Publication No. 00-3818). Rockville, MD: National Clearinghouse on Alcohol and Drug Information.

APA REFERENCE ENTRIES: PERIODICALS The general form for a periodical entry is this:

> **Author, A. (year). Article title. *Periodical Title, Volume Number,* page numbers.**

- Last name and initial(s) as for a book reference
- Year of publication in parentheses and followed by a period
- Title of article in lowercase, except for the first word and any proper nouns (not italicized or in quotations), followed by a period
- Title and volume number of periodical italicized and capitalized, each followed by a comma
- Inclusive page numbers, with all digits repeated, separated by a dash

Include some other designation with the year (such as a month or season, spelled out in full) if a periodical does not use volume numbers. The entries that follow illustrate the information and arrangement needed to cite periodicals.

17. **An article in a scholarly journal, consecutively paginated** Pay attention to the features of this basic reference to a scholarly journal:

    Epstein, R., & Hundert, E. (2002). Defining and assessing professional competence. *JAMA, 287,* 226–235.

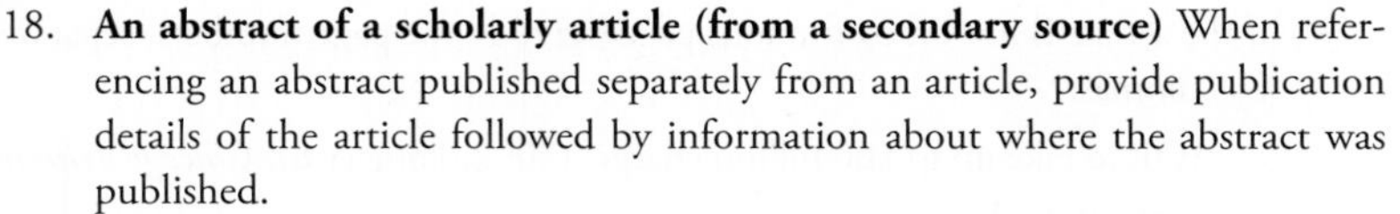

18. **An abstract of a scholarly article (from a secondary source)** When referencing an abstract published separately from an article, provide publication details of the article followed by information about where the abstract was published.

    Shlipak, M. G., Simon, J. A., Grady, O., Lin, F., Wenger, N. K., & Furberg, C. D. (2001, September). Renal insufficiency and cardiovascular events in postmenopausal women with coronary heart disease. *Journal of the American College of Cardiology, 38*, 705–711. Abstract obtained from *Geriatrics,* 2001, *56*(12), Abstract No. 5645351.

When the dates of the article and the secondary-source abstract differ, the reference in your text would cite both dates, the original first, separated by a slash (2001/2002). When the abstract is obtained from the original source, the word *Abstract* is placed in brackets following the title (but before the period).

NOTE: When the page numbering of the issue starts with page 1, the issue number (not italicized) is placed in parentheses after the volume number.

19. **A journal article, paginated by issue**

    Lewer, N. (1999, summer). Nonlethal weapons. *Forum, 14*(2), 39–45.

20. **A journal article, more than six authors**

    Wang, X., Zuckerman, B., Pearson, C., Kaufman, G., Chen, C., Wang, G., et al. (2002, January 9). Maternal cigarette smoking, metabolic gene polymorphism, and infant birth weight. *JAMA, 287*, 195–202.

21. **A review** To reference a book review or a review of another medium (film, exhibit, and so on), indicate the review and the medium in brackets, along with the title of the work being reviewed by the author listed.

    Updike, J. (2001, December 24). Survivor/believer [Review of the book *New and Collected Poems 1931–2001*]. *The New Yorker,* 118–122.

22. **A magazine article**

    Silberman, S. (2001, December). The geek syndrome. *Wired, 9*(12), 174–183.

NOTE: If the article is unsigned, begin the entry with the title of the article:

    Tomatoes target toughest cancer. (2002, February). *Prevention, 54*(2), 53.

23. **A newspaper article** For newspaper articles, include the full publication date, year first followed by a comma, the month (spelled out), and the day. Identify the article's location in the newspaper using page numbers and section letters, as appropriate. If the article is a letter to the editor, identify it as such in brackets following the title. For newspapers, use *p.* or *pp.* before the page numbers;

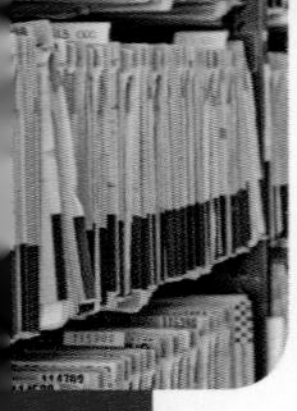

APA

if the article is not on continuous pages, give all the page numbers, separated by commas.

AOL to take up to $60 billion charge. (2002, January 8). *Chicago Tribune,* sec. 3, p. 3.

Stolberg, S. C. (2002, January 4). Breakthrough in pig cloning could aid organ transplants. *The New York Times,* pp. 1A, 17A.

24. **A newsletter article** Newsletter article entries are very similar to newspaper article entries; only a volume number is added, in italics.

Teaching mainstreamed special education students. (2002, February). *The Council Chronicle, 11,* 6–8.

APA REFERENCE ENTRIES: ONLINE SOURCES The 2007 *APA Guidelines to Electronic References* present a few changes to references to materials retrieved electronically. They include the following:

- *For journal articles:* Include both journal issue number and volume number for all journals whether the pagination is separate for each issue or continuous in the volume.
- *Retrieval date:* Include the retrieval date for undated or changeable content retrieved from Web sources, especially from the open Web. Do not include the retrieval date for material with fixed publication dates, such as a journal article or a book.
- *The Digital Object Identifier (DOI):* The Digital Object Identifier (DOI) is a string of numbers and letters often published on the first page of an article. (Sometimes the DOI may be under a button for "article," "Cross-Ref.," or the vendor's name.) When activated, it will link to the content you are referencing. When this DOI is available, substitute it for the URL in the reference.
- *Reference books:* Include the home page or menu page URL for dictionaries and encyclopedias.

25. **A periodical with DOI assigned**

Author, A., & Author, B. (year). Title of article. *Title of Periodical, volume*(issue), inclusive page numbers (if available). doi: letters and numbers

Nelson, G., Aubry, T., & Lafrance, A. (2007). A review of the literature on the effectiveness of housing and support, assertive community treatment, and intensive case management interventions for persons with mental illness who have been homeless. *American Journal of Orthopsychiatry, 77*(3), 350–361. doi: 10:1037/0002–9432.77.3.350

26. **A periodical with no DOI assigned**

Author, A., & Author, B. (year). Title of article. *Title of Periodical, volume*(issue), inclusive page numbers (if available). Retrieved from electronic address

Dyer, J., & Beck, N. (2007). Psychocardiology: Advancing the assessment and treatment of heart patients. *E-Journal of Applied Psychology, 3*(2), 3–12. Retrieved from http://ojs.lib.swin.edu.au/index.php/ejap/issue/view/13

NOTE: Include an issue number in parentheses following the volume number if each issue of a journal begins on page 1. Use the abbreviation *pp.* (page numbers) in newspapers. Page numbers are often not relevant for online sources. End the citation with a period unless it ends with the electronic address.

27. **A multipage document created by a private organization**

National Multiple Sclerosis Society. (n.d.) *About MS: For the newly diagnosed.* Retrieved May 20, 2002, from http://www.nationalmssociety.org

NOTE: Use *n.d.* ("no date") if a date is unavailable. Provide the URL of the home page for an Internet document when its pages have different URLs.

28. **A document from an online database**

Author, A., & Author, B. (year). Title of article or webpage. *Title of Periodical, volume number,* inclusive page numbers. Retrieved Month day, year, from name of database.

Belsie, L. (1999). Progress or peril? *Christian Science Monitor, 91*(85), 15. Retrieved September 15, 1999, from DIALOG online database (#97, IAC Business A.R.T.S., Item 07254533).

NOTE: If the document cited is an abstract, include *Abstract* before the *Retrieved from* statement. The item or accession numbers are optional.

29. **Other nonperiodical online document**

Author, A., & Author, B. (year, Month day). *Title of work.* Retrieved Month day, year, from electronic address

Boyles, S. (2001, November 14). *World Diabetes Day has people pondering their risk.* Retrieved November 16, 2001, from http://my.webmd. com/content/article/1667.51328

Catholic Near East Welfare Association. (2002). Threats to personal security. In *Report on Christian emigration: Palestine* (sect. 5). Retrieved May 20, 2002, from http://www.cnewa.org/news-christemigrat-part1.htm

APA

APA

NOTE: To cite only a chapter or section of an online document, follow the title of the chapter with "In *Title of document* (chap. number)." If the author is not identified, begin with the title of the document. If a date is not identified, put *n.d.* in parentheses following the title.

30. **A document or an abstract available on a university Web site**

Author, A., & Author, B. (year). *Title of work.* Retrieved Month day, year, from name of host: electronic address

Magill, G. (2001). *Ethics of stem cell research.* Retrieved November 23, 2001, from St. Louis University, Center for Health Care Ethics website: http://www.slu.edu/centers/chce/drummond/magill.html

NOTE: Name the university or government agency (and the department or division, if it is named), followed by a colon and the URL.

31. **A report from a university, available on a private organization Web site** List the university and the institute as authors, followed by the publication date, the report's title, and retrieval information.

University, Institute. (year, Month). *Title of work.* Retrieved Month day, year, from electronic address

University of Wisconsin, Sonderegger Research Center and Kaiser Family Foundation. (2000, July). *Prescription drug trends—a chartbook.* Retrieved November 19, 2001, from http://www.kff.org/content/2000/3019/

NOTE: If the private organization is not listed as an author, identify it in the "retrieved from" statement.

32. **A U.S. government report available on a government agency Web site**

Name of government agency. (year, Month day). *Title of report.* Retrieved Month day, year, from electronic address

United States Department of Commerce, Office of the Inspector General. (2001, March). *Internal controls over bankcard program need improvement.* Retrieved July 23, 2001, from http://www.oig.doc. gov/elibrary/reports/recent/recent.html

NOTE: If no publication date is indicated, use *n.d.* in parentheses following the agency name.

33. **A paper presented at a symposium or other event, abstract retrieved from a university Web site**

Author, A. (year, Month day). *Title of paper.* Paper presented at name of event. Abstract retrieved Month day, year, from electronic address

Smale, S. (2001, November 7). *Learning and the evolution of language.* Paper presented at Brains and Machines Seminar Series. Abstract retrieved November 23, 2001, from http://www.ai.mit.edu/ events/talks/brainsMachines/abstracts/F2001/200111071700_StephenSmale.shtml

NOTE: To cite a virtual conference, do not use *Abstract* before the *retrieved from* statement.

34. **An e-mail message** E-mail is cited only in the text of the paper, not in the References list.
35. **Electronic book** Use "available from" when the URL leads you to information about how to get the book. Use "retrieved from" when the URL leads directly to the book.

    Galsworthy, John. (n.d.). *The Forsyte Saga.* Retrieved from http://www.gutenberg.org/catalog/world/readfile?fk_files=101684

APA Reference Material

36. **Online encyclopedia** If no author appears in the article, begin with the title. Include the retrieval date and the home or index page URL.

    Forging, in criminal law. In *The Columbia encyclopedia.* Retrieved May 12, 2008, from http://www.bartleby.com/65/.

37. **Online dictionary**

    Forgery. (n.d.). In *The free dictionary.* Retrieved May 13, 2008, from http://www.thefreedictionary.com/forgery

38. **Wiki** Like *Wikipedia*, all wikis are open to anyone who wishes to write, edit, or change the entry.

    Schizophrenia—developmental factors. (n.d.). Retrieved May 14, 2008, from The Psychology Wiki: http://psychology.wikia.com/wiki/Schizophrenia_Developmental_factors

APA Reference Entries: Other Sources

39. **Audio podcast** Include all the information you can find, including date, title, and identifier.

    Adams, B. (2007, November 12). *The theory of social revolutions.* LibriVox. Podcast retrieved from http://www.archive.org/details/revolutions_librivox

40. **Message posted to a newsgroup, an online forum, or a discussion group** If the author's name is not available, use the screen name. Include the date of posting.

    Howarth, D. (2005, June 6). Intellectual property rights [Meg 6]. Message posted to the information forum, archived at http://www.wipo.int/

roller/comments/ipisforum/Weblog/theme_ seven_how_is_intellectual#comment6

41. **Weblog post**

    Mike, M. (2008, May 12). Re: The [annotated] McCain climate speech. Message posted to http://dotearth.blogs.nytimes.com/2008/05/ 12/the-annotated-mccain-climate-speech/#comments

42. **Specialized computer software with limited distribution** Standard, non-specialized computer software does not require a reference entry. Treat software as an unauthored work unless an individual has property rights to it. Indicate the software version in parentheses after the title, and note the medium in brackets.

    Carreau, S. (2001). Champfoot (Version 3.3) [Computer software]. Saint Mandé, France: Author.

43. **An electronic abstract of a journal article retrieved from a database** The following format applies whether the database is on CD, on a Web site, or on a university server. The item or accession number is not required, but it may be included in parentheses at the end of the retrieval statement.

    Seyler, T. (1994). College-level studies: New memory techniques. *New Century Learners, 30*, 814–822. Abstract retrieved February 1, 1995, from Platinum File: EduPLUS database (40-18421).

44. **A television or radio broadcast** List a broadcast by the show's producer or executive producer, and identify the type of broadcast in brackets after the show's title.

    Crystal, L. (Executive Producer). (2005, February 11). *The NewsHour with Jim Lehrer* [Television broadcast]. New York and Washington: Public Broadcasting Service.

45. **A television or radio program (episode in a series)** When identifying a specific episode in a television or radio series, identify the episode by its writers, if possible. Then follow with the airing date, the episode title, the type of series in brackets, and details about the series itself.

    Berger, C. (Writer). (2001, December 19). Feederwatch [Radio series program]. In D. Byrd & J. Block (Producers), *Earth & Sky.* Austin: The Production Block.

46. **An audio recording** Begin the entry with the speaker's or writer's name, not the producer's. Indicate the type of recording in brackets.

    Kim, E. (Author, speaker). (2000). *Ten thousand sorrows* [CD]. New York: Random House.

47. **A music recording** Give the name and function of the originators or primary contributors. Indicate the recording medium (CD, record, cassette, and so on) in brackets, immediately following the title.

    ARS Femina Ensemble (Performers). (1998). *Musica de la puebla de Los Angeles: Music by women of baroque Mexico, Cuba, & Europe* [CD]. Louisville: Nannerl Recordings.

48. **A motion picture** Give the name and function of the director, producer, or both. If its circulation was limited, provide the distributor's name and complete address in parentheses.

    Jackson, P. (Director). (2001). *The lord of the rings: The fellowship of the ring* [Motion picture]. United States: New Line Productions, Inc.

49. **A published interview, titled, single author** Start the entry with the interviewer's name, followed by the date and the title. Place the interviewee's name in brackets before other publication details.

    Fussman, C. (2002, January). What I've learned [Interview with Robert McNamara]. *Esquire, 137*(1), 85.

50. **An unpublished paper presented at a meeting** Indicate when the paper was presented, at what meeting, in what location.

    Lycan, W. (2002, June). *The plurality of consciousness.* Paper presented at the meeting of the Society for Philosophy and Psychology, New York.

NOTE: Use the abbreviations below in all APA reference entries.

With author's names, shorten first and middle names to initials, leaving a space after the period. For a work with more than one author, use an ampersand (*&*) before the last author's name.

For publisher locations, use the full city name plus the two-letter U.S. Postal Service abbreviation for the state. For international publishers, include a province and country name; for well-known publishing cities such as Boston, you may offer the city only.

Spell out *Press* in full, but for other publishing information, use the abbreviations below:

chap.	Chapter	n.d.	No date
ed.	Edition	No.	Number
Ed.	Editor	Pt.	Part
Eds.	Editors	p. (pp.)	Page (pages)
Rev. ed.	Revised edition	Vol.	Volume
2nd ed.	Second edition	Vols.	Volumes
Trans.	Translator(s)		

MODEL OF A STUDENT PAPER IN APA STYLE

THIS VERSION of Eóin O'Carroll's paper, "Unchained Melodies," uses the APA documentation style that is appropriate for a communication or sociology course. The title page, the abstract, the first page of text, and the References page that are reprinted here illustrate the main points of the APA style of documentation.

The title of the paper appears in the header, followed by five spaces and the page number.

Unchained Melodies 1

Unchained Melodies: Music and Innovation in the Digital Age

Eóin O'Carroll

ENG 201

The title, writer's name, and class go in the center of the title page, double-spaced.

The abstract should be single-spaced and no more than 120 words. It should outline the paper. (See more about writing abstracts on the Writing in the Works Web site.)

Abstract

Record companies are claiming that free mp3 downloads are killing music, but it is really the labels, not the consumers, that are killing music. Even if digital music is hurting album sales—and experts disagree over whether they do—many recording artists are embracing free mp3s for the increased exposure they offer. At the same time, recording artists are complaining that they are being harmed by the labels' business practices. Digital music potentially allows the musician to make a fair wage while providing a broader range of music to the consumer for less money. And they do not need the record labels to do it.

APA

The paper begins on page 3.

The title is centered and double-spaced.

Unchained Melodies: Music and Innovation in the Digital Age

The text begins two lines below the title and is double-spaced.

In the early eighties, the record industry was experiencing a sharp decline in sales. Falling revenues, they claimed, were the fault of the blank audiocassette. "Home taping is killing music" was the industry slogan at the time. Today, with sales slumping again, the record industry is making the same dire predictions. The bugbear of the Recording Industry Association of America (RIAA) this time is not audiocassettes and home tapers, but peer-to-peer networks and mp3 file sharers. On September 8, 2003, the day that the RIAA launched its first round of lawsuits against file sharers, the association issued a press release quoting president Cary Sherman: "We simply cannot allow online piracy to continue destroying the livelihoods of artists, musicians, songwriters, retailers, and everyone in the music industry" (RIAA, 2003, ¶ 4).

Ebin spells out the na of the organization a gives the abbreviation parentheses.

This press release is from a Web page and doesn't have a page number. When citing quotations or facts from Web pages without page numbers in APA style, give the paragraph number.

It is hard to say, however, to what extent digital music is responsible. If file sharing is cutting into album sales, it is not necessarily a bad thing—after all, people who make CD burners have livelihoods, too. Moreover, cutting into album sales is not necessarily the same thing as "killing music." Rather, many of the record industry's practices are killing music. Digital music is more likely to rescue it.

To review some background to present events, in the late 1970s, the record industry saw a looming crisis. After hitting an all-time high in 1978, album sales were declining precipitously. Between 1978 and 1982, sales dropped more than forty percent, with revenues falling from $6 billion to about $3.5 billion (Liebowitz, 2003, p. 7).

This internal text citation gives the author's last name, the year, and the page number. The citation is surrounded by parentheses and followed by a period. No the p. before the page number.

Heading is centered.

Indent the second line of the citation five spaces.

No posting date was available on this site.

If you must break a Web address into two lines, put the break after a period or slash. Never hyphenate a Web URL.

If a page is part of a large and complex website, such as that for a university or a government agency, identify the host organization before the URL. Precede the URL with a colon.

References

Alderman, J. (2001). *Sonic boom: Napster, MP3, and the new pioneers of music.* Cambridge: Perseus.

Berman, D. (2000). Lars Ulrich vs. Chuck D: Facing off over Napster. *Business Week.* May 25, 2000. Retrieved March 11, 2004, from http://www.businessweek.com/ebiz/0005/0525ulrich.htm

Brown, D. (2003). Home taping did not kill music. CBC News Viewpoint. October 23, 2003. Retrieved March 11, 2004, from Canadian Broadcasting Company website: http://www.cbc.ca/ news/viewpoint/vp_browndan/20031023.html

Electronic Frontier Foundation. Making P2P pay artists. (n.d.). Retrieved March 11, 2004, from http://www.eff.org/share/compensation.php

Ian, J. (2002). The Internet debacle: An alternative view. Retrieved March 10, 2004, from http://www.janisian.com/article-internet_debacle.html

Jenkins, M. (2002). Hit charade: The music industry's self-inflicted wounds. *Slate.* August 20, 2002. Retrieved March 11, 2004, from http://slate.msn.com/?id=2069732

Lessig, L. (2001). *The future of ideas.* New York: Random House.

Liebowitz, S. (2003). Will MP3 downloads annihilate the record industry? The evidence so far. Retrieved March 9, 2004, from University of Texas at Dallas website: http://www.pub.utdallas. edu/~liebowit/intprop/records.pdf

Love, C. (2000). Courtney Love does the math. *Salon.* June 14, 2000. Retrieved March 2, 2004, from http://archive.salon.com/tech/ feature/2000/06/14/love

Recording Industry Association of America. (2003). Recording industry begins suing P2P file sharers who illegally offer copyrighted music online. Retrieved March 9, 2004, from the RIAA website: http://www.riaa.com/news/newsletter/090803.asp

Straziuso, J. (2004). Music piracy activity slows. *Detroit Free Press.* February 23, 2004. Retrieved on March 13, 2004, from *Detroit Free Press* website: http://www.freep.com/money/business/bnews23_20040223.htm

Unchained Melodies 5

Figure Captions

Figure 1 Album sales over the past three decades

(Liebowitz, 2003, p. 7)

Unchained Melodies 6

Figure 1

When appropriate, use figures to illustrate your argument.

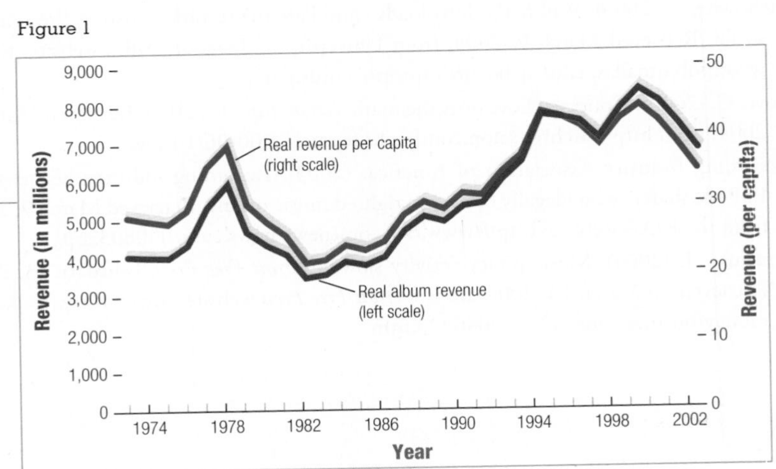

PART VII

Grammar Handbook

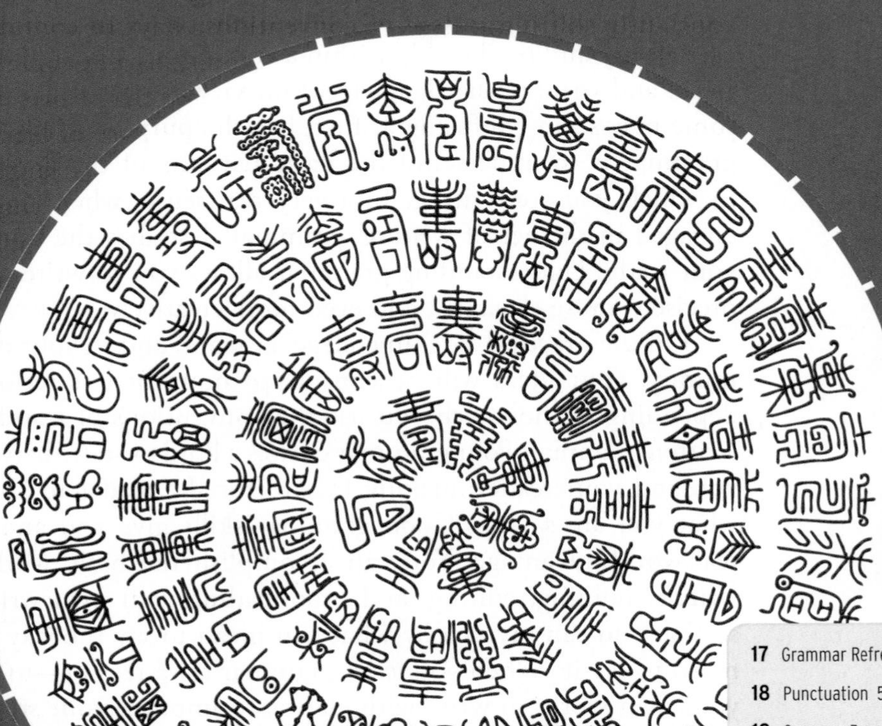

John Lock/Shutterstock.com

Why Study Grammar?

> ...grammar enables us to practice the three behaviors that mark us as literate human beings: it helps us write with power, read with a critical eye, and talk about how meaning is made.
>
> —Roy Peter Clark

Some people believe that grammar is a set of ironclad rules they must memorize. Others believe that grammar describes a constantly shifting system of conventions, ways to communicate clearly and predictably within a community of people who speak and write in that language. Our view is this: Rules exist; some may seem confusing at first, but the purpose of learning grammar is to understand the basic patterns of the language in which you are writing. In a very real sense, when you are engaged in the act of writing, grammar describes the tools of your trade. Understanding grammar allows you to write more precisely, more elegantly, and even more creatively.

On the practical side, in college, at work, and in your community, your ideas will be considered more or less seriously depending on how well you use the conventions of standard, written grammar. Poor grammar creates a kind of static between you and your reader, making it hard for the reader to "hear" what you are saying. Good grammar skills give you another real-world advantage. You can accomplish the basic work of writers: refining, editing, and proofreading your own writing so that you can say exactly what you mean to say the way you mean to say it. When you learn grammar for a reason—to edit your own work, to write with clarity, to improve your style—it may make new sense to you, perhaps in a way it never has before. To ensure that your good ideas will be read with the interest they deserve, learn the rules and play by them. Later on, perhaps, you can break them.

The next four chapters provide an overview of grammar. Chapter 17 will guide you through a review of the basic vocabulary of grammar, and Chapter 18 is a review of punctuation rules. Chapter 19 will help you identify and avoid common grammatical errors. Chapter 20 provides some grammatical tips specific to the challenges of writing English as a second, third, or sometimes fourth language.

You can use these chapters in a number of ways.

- You can read each chapter sequentially, first building a grammar vocabulary, and then using that vocabulary to identify and correct common errors. At the end of each major point is a practice exercise that you can use to test your understanding of that grammatical point and reinforce its concept.
- You can use the chapters as a reference handbook, looking up the conventions of punctuation (18b–f), for example, or the rules governing subject-verb agreement (19b–1).
- Each topic is keyed to one of the numbers and letters in the outline printed at the beginning of each chapter as well as in the index.
- You can use the practices to test your skills in identifying and fixing errors in a text and then to review the points you do not understand.
- You can keep a grammar log of the errors you make in your papers and key them to the sections that address those issues.

THE IMPORTANCE OF PUNCTUATION

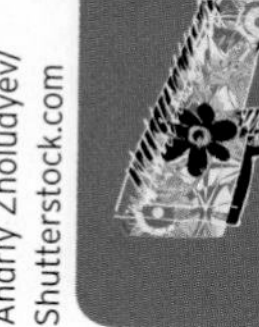

Andriy Zholudyev/
Shutterstock.com

17 Grammar Refresher

This chapter will help you review
- Parts of speech
- Parts of sentences
- Sentence types

17a PARTS OF SPEECH

Knowing the basic parts of speech gives you the vocabulary to talk about grammar and gives you an important understanding of how each part of speech functions. The following is a brief overview of the eight parts of speech.

PRACTICE 17.1

Nouns

Check your understanding of the types of nouns by identifying the boldfaced words in the following sentences as proper nouns (PN), common nouns (CN), or collective nouns (COLL). Circle all noncountable nouns.

1. Ancient **astronomers** saw only twelve **constellations** in the **sky**.
2. A **theory** put forth by **Aristotle** included the **idea** of feeling **pity** and **fear** for the tragic **hero**.
3. In 1988 George **Eastman** invented a **camera** that revolutionized **photography**.
4. A large **community** of Old World **monkeys** sits on the tree **branches** for most of the **day**.
5. **Starfish** live in the shallow **waters** off the **coast**.

17a-1 NOUNS

Nouns name people, places, things, or abstract concepts: *daughter, city, pencil, hope.*

- **Countable Nouns** **Countable nouns** name countable things and have a plural form: *book (books), child (children), friend (friends).*
- **Noncountable Nouns** **Noncountable nouns** name things that you cannot count, so they do not have a plural form: *courage, advice, information* (see 20a).
- **Proper Nouns** **Proper nouns** name specific persons, places, organizations, months, and days of the week. Proper nouns are capitalized: *Mother Jones, Central College, Fridays.*
- **Common Nouns** **Common nouns** name general persons, places, things, or abstract concepts: *parent, school, weekdays.*
- **Collective Nouns** **Collective nouns** name groups but are usually referred to as single entities: *a committee, an audience, a community.*

17a-2 PRONOUNS

Pronouns substitute for or refer to nouns, noun phrases, or other pronouns. The noun that the pronoun refers to is its **antecedent**.

***Professor Garcia* read from *her* new book.** [*Professor Garcia* is the antecedent of *her*.]

***Travel* is *its* own reward.** [*Travel* is the antecedent of *its*.]

- **Personal Pronouns** **Personal pronouns** refer to specific persons, places, or things. Personal pronouns can be subdivided by their function in a sentence, whether they substitute for nouns that function as subjects (see 17b-1), substitute for nouns that function as objects (see 17b-2), or show ownership or possession (see 18e-1).

Subject Pronouns (SP)	Object Pronouns (OP)	Possessive Pronouns (PP)
I	*me*	*my, mine*
you	*you*	*your, yours*
he, she, it	*him, her, it*	*his, her, hers, its*
we	*us*	*our, ours*
they	*them*	*their, theirs*
who/whoever	*whom/whomever*	*whose*

SP PP
She talked about *her* travels in Asia.

SP OP
We gave *her* a standing ovation.

■ **Indefinite Pronouns** **Indefinite pronouns** refer to nonspecific persons, places, or things and do not need antecedents: *all, any, anybody, anyone, anything, both, every, everybody, everyone, everything, few, many, most, none, no one, nothing, somebody, someone, something, several, some.*

Everyone was fascinated by Professor Garcia's adventures.

No one stirred as she talked.

■ **Reflexive Pronouns** A **reflexive pronoun** refers back to the subject or to another noun or pronoun in the sentence.

Singular	Plural
myself	*ourselves*
yourself	*yourselves*
himself	
herself	*themselves*
itself	

Megan traveled for six months by *herself*.

Megan saw the other students starting off by *themselves*.

■ **Intensive Pronouns** **Intensive pronouns** emphasize nouns and use the same forms as reflexive pronouns.

Megan *herself* made all the arrangements.

We *ourselves* decided it was the right time to travel.

■ **Relative Pronouns** **Relative pronouns** introduce dependent clauses (see 17b-4): *who, whom, whose, whoever, whomever, whichever, whatever, that, which, what.*

Professor Garcia was the professor *who* influenced me the most.

Biology class was the one class *that* I never missed.

■ **Interrogative Pronouns** **Interrogative pronouns** begin questions: *who, whom, which, what, whose.*

***Who* went with you?**

***Whose* car did you take?**

■ **Demonstrative Pronouns** **Demonstrative pronouns** point back to their antecedent nouns, noun phrases, or clauses: *this, that, these, those.*

PRACTICE 17.2

Pronouns

Identify the boldfaced words in the following sentences as personal pronouns (PP), indefinite pronouns (IP), reflexive pronouns (REF), intensive pronouns (INT), relative pronouns (REL), interrogative pronouns (INTER), or demonstrative pronouns (DP).

1. Colonel Mustard **himself** put the coded message in **its** secret hiding place.
2. **Anyone** can collect stamps by ordering **them** on the Internet. **Who** wants to order stamps?
3. The architect **who** put the Arts and Crafts detail on **your** front door was a genius.
4. Give the mitten to **whoever** needs warm clothing for the camping trip.
5. Five years ago, **someone** left a mysterious message on **my** phone. **That** was weird.

Amy got an interview with the lead singer of her favorite band. *That* was the highlight of her year.

She wrote these two articles for her school paper. *This* is better than *that*.

17a-3 VERBS

Verbs express action (*read, love, study*) or a state of being (*is, seem, appear*).

■ **Auxiliary Verbs** **Some auxiliary verbs** are forms of *to be, to do*, and *to have* that help the main verbs.

Frida *was* painting in her studio. *(be, am, is, are, was, being, been)*

Frida *does* paint well. *(do, does, did)*

Frida *has* painted beautiful landscapes. *(have, has, had)*

Other auxiliary verbs, called **modals**, express probability, such as *may/might, can/could, will/would, shall/should, must, ought to*, and *have to*.

Frida *ought to* contact a gallery.

She *might* become as famous as her namesake, Frida Kahlo.

■ **Transitive Verbs** **Transitive verbs (VT)** show action and transfer that action from the subject to the receiver of the action, which is called the **direct object (DO)**. The direct object answers the question *what?* or *whom?* after the verb.

Frida *paints* abstract *landscapes*.

She *asked Pablo* to critique her art.

■ **Intransitive Verbs** **Intransitive verbs (VI)** may express an action, but there is no receiver of that action, no direct object. Common intransitive verbs are *lie, sit, sleep, occur, die, fall, walk, go*, and *come*.

Frida *sat* on a stool while she painted.

When she finished her work, Frida *slept* soundly.

■ **Linking Verbs** **Linking verbs (LV),** also known as state-of-being verbs, link the subject to a word after the verb. The word can either describe the subject (an adjective) or rename the subject (a noun). The most common linking verb is the verb *to be* in any of its forms: *am, are, is, was, were*.

Frida *is* lovely. [*Lovely* describes Frida.]

Frida *is* my cousin. [*Cousin* renames Frida.]

Other linking verbs that can express a state of being are *feel, seem, look, taste, smell,* and *appear,* depending on how they are used in the sentence. The verb *feel,* for example, can be either a transitive verb, taking a direct object, or a linking verb, connecting an adjective to the subject.

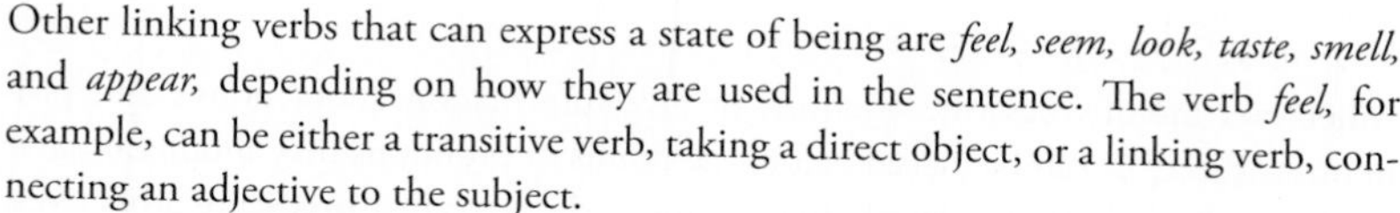

I *feel* the material between my thumb and index finger. [*Feel* is transitive; it takes the direct object *material.*]

I *feel* sad today. [*Feel* is a linking verb, expressing a state of being and linking the adjective *sad* to the subject *I.*]

■ **Verb Tenses** Verb tenses change to indicate the time of an action or process, often relative to the time of the writing.

	Present	**Past**	**Future**
Simple	*I paint*	*I painted*	*I will paint*
Progressive	*I am painting*	*I was painting*	*I will be painting*
Perfect	*I have painted*	*I had painted*	*I will have painted*

Verbs in the **progressive tense** use a form of *to be* plus the *-ing* form of the verb to show actions that continue for a while.

This morning I *am painting* the third in my landscape series.

Yesterday I *was painting* my second landscape.

Verbs in the **perfect tense** express actions completed by the present, past, or future time.

I *have painted* my series, and I am ready for the show.

I *had painted* my second landscape before I fell asleep.

I *will have painted* the entire series when the show opens.

■ **Verb Moods** Verbs express three **moods**. Verbs in the **indicative** mood make statements or ask questions.

I *will paint* today.

***Will* you *join* me?**

Verbs in the **imperative** mood issue commands.

***Come* in here!**

***Do not make* a mess.**

Verbs in the **subjunctive** mood express wishes in conditional terms or hypothetical conditions.

I wish I *were* as good a painter as Frida.

If I *had taken* lessons when I was young, I *might be* an artist today.

PRACTICE 17.3

Verbs

Identify the verbs in the following sentences as transitive verbs (VT), intransitive verbs (VI), or linking verbs (LV).

1. The night sky **seemed** luminous.
2. Joe **slept** past noon every day on his vacation.
3. Leah **ran** the marathon in record time.
4. We **felt** the first stirrings of love that night.
5. Ethan **felt** strong after his workout.

Choose the correct verb tense or mood in the following sentences.

1. Before Zachary (**made/had made**) plans, he (**checked/had checked**) online for the movie times.
2. When Kayla (**ran/ is running**) fast, she always wins the race.
3. If Mac (**was/were**) in charge, things would be different around here.
4. Yoshi made the changes to the proposal that she and Mac (**discussed/had discussed**).
5. When Ben (**was/were**) younger, he was always in trouble.

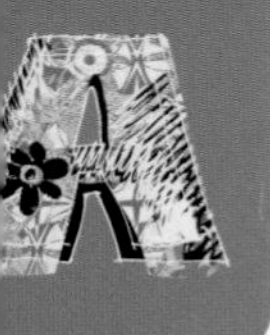

17a-4 ADJECTIVES

Adjectives modify, describe, identify, or give information about nouns and pronouns. Adjectives can be placed before the nouns or pronouns they modify or after linking verbs. Adjectives placed after linking verbs are called **predicate adjectives.** (*Predicate* refers to the part of a sentence or clause that includes the verb and objects or phrases connected to the verb. See 17b-1.)

The *fresh* breeze blew past Joel's head. [*Fresh* modifies *breeze.*]

The breeze felt *fresh*. [*Fresh* is a predicate adjective and modifies *breeze.*]

Adjectives show degree or intensity. The suffix *-er* or the use of the adverb *more* makes an adjective comparative, and the suffix *-est* or the use of the adverb *most* makes the adjective superlative.

Positive	Comparative	Superlative
fresh	*fresher*	*freshest*
independent	*more independent*	*most independent*

■ **Articles** *A, an,* and *the* are types of adjectives that are called **articles**. (See also 20a.) *A* and *an* are **indefinite articles** because they describe one of a number of things.

Give Becca *a* book to read, and she is happy.

***A* library can be *a* sanctuary.**

The is a **definite article** because it describes only one thing or class of things.

Give me *the* book on the shelf.

***The* local library is her sanctuary.**

17a-5 ADVERBS

Adverbs modify or give information about verbs, adjectives, other adverbs, or entire clauses or sentences. They often explain *how*, *when*, *where*, *why*, or *to what extent* something happens. They convey manner, time, frequency, place, direction, and degree.

The thief ran *quickly* down the alley. [The adverb *quickly* modifies the verb *ran*.]

The *very* fast thief jumped the fence. [The adverb *very* modifies the adjective *fast*.]

The thief climbed the ladder *extremely* quickly. [The adverb *extremely* modifies the adverb *quickly*.]

PRACTICE 17.4

Adjectives and Adverbs

Identify the boldfaced words in the following sentences as adjectives (ADJ) or adverbs (ADV). Draw an arrow to what each word modifies.

1. The **fastest** runner was **unfairly** eliminated due to **new** rules about eligibility.
2. The **intense** odor of **noxious** fumes seeped **quickly** from under the **locked** garage door.
3. An **attentive** audience **closely** watched the **unusual** dance program **yesterday**.
4. Although Martin was **picky**, he gave the hotel at the **busy** seaport his **highest** recommendation.
5. Flood water surged **violently** over the **small** bridge; **however**, the bridge held **fast.**

Unfortunately, **the thief escaped.** [The adverb *unfortunately* modifies the entire sentence.]

■ **Conjunctive Adverbs** A **conjunctive adverb** modifies a clause or sentence while helping to connect that clause or sentence to the previous one. Some conjunctive adverbs are *consequently, however, moreover, therefore, thus,* and *for example.*

The thief escaped. *However*, he turned himself in the next day.

He was filled with remorse; *moreover*, he returned the money he stole.

17a-6 PREPOSITIONS AND PREPOSITIONAL PHRASES

Prepositions are often short words like *of, by, for, to, in,* and *around* that begin prepositional phrases. They often show relationships of time and space. Some common prepositions are *about, above, across, after, along, around, before, behind, below, beneath, beside, between, by, except, for, from, in, into, like, near, of, on, through, to, under,* and *with.* (See also 20d-2.)

Around the block

In the air

Down the street

Across the avenue

To the meeting

At one o'clock

A **prepositional phrase** is made up of the preposition and the words that follow it. The noun or pronoun after the preposition is called the *object of the preposition.*

PREPOSITIONAL PHRASE (PREP. … OBJECT) PREPOSITIONAL PHRASE (PREP. … OBJECT)

Ben went *around the neighborhood on his new bicycle.*

PREP. PHRASE (PREP. OBJ.) PREPOSITIONAL PHRASE (PREP. … OBJ.)

At dusk* he went *into his house.

17a-7 CONJUNCTIONS

Conjunctions join two or more similar sentence parts, such as words, phrases, and clauses.

■ **Coordinating Conjunctions** **Coordinating conjunctions (CC)** link two or more parallel words, phrases, or clauses. The seven coordinating conjunctions are *and, but, for, or, nor, so,* and *yet.*

CC

The baker made tarts *and* pies. [The coordinating conjunction *and* connects the two words *tarts* and *pies.*]

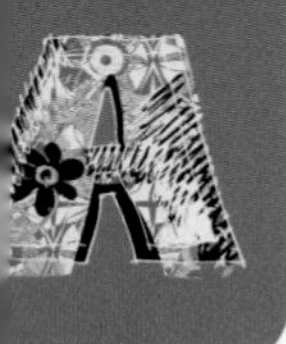

He couldn't decide whether to make a crust *or* to buy one. [The coordinating conjunction *or* connects the two phrases *to make a crust* and *to buy one.*]

He made the pie crust, *but* he bought the tart shell. [The coordinating conjunction *but* connects the two clauses *He made the pie crust* and *he bought the tart shell.*]

■ **Subordinating Conjunctions** **Subordinating conjunctions (SC)** introduce dependent clauses and connect them with independent clauses (see 17b-4). A subordinating conjunction establishes a relationship between dependent and independent clauses, usually telling *when, why,* or *under what conditions.* Some of the many subordinating conjunctions are *after, as, as soon as, because, before, even if, if, since, unless, when, while,* and *why.*

DEPENDENT CLAUSE
SC

***When* he ran out of cherries, the baker started making apple pies.** [*When he ran out of cherries* is a dependent clause. *When* is the subordinating conjunction.]

DEPENDENT CLAUSE
SC

Our mouths watered *while* the pies cooled. [*While the pies cooled* is a dependent clause. *While* is the subordinating conjunction.]

■ **Correlative Conjunctions** **Correlative conjunctions (COR)** appear in different parts of the sentence but work together to join the two sentence parts. Common correlative conjunctions are *both/and, just as/so, either/or, neither/nor, not only/but also,* and *whether/or.*

***Either* cherry pie *or* apple pie is fine with me.**

***Not only* does he love baking them, *but* he *also* loves eating them.**

17a-8 INTERJECTIONS AND EXPLETIVES

Interjections are emotional exclamations and are often punctuated by the exclamation mark if they stand alone.

Eureka!

Ouch!

Wow!

Interjections can also be incorporated into sentences.

I smiled at him, but, *oh*, he made me mad.

***Darn*, he missed the bus.**

PRACTICE 17.5

Prepositions, Conjunctions, Interjections, and Expletives

Identify the boldfaced words in the following sentences as prepositions (P), coordinating conjunctions (CC), subordinating conjunctions (SC), correlative conjunctions (COR), interjections (I), or expletives (EX).

1. The Industrial Revolution began **when** steam-powered machines started spinning cotton thread.
2. The construction crew identified contaminated soil yet failed **to** report it **to** the Environmental Protection Agency.
3. **"Never!"** we answered **after** Coach asked when we would be willing to give up.
4. **Either** I will major in math, **or** I will go into engineering.
5. Bats are scorned and treated as pests, **but** they are useful in controlling mosquito populations.
6. **There** are compelling reasons to study biology, **and there** are equally good ones to specialize in mammals.

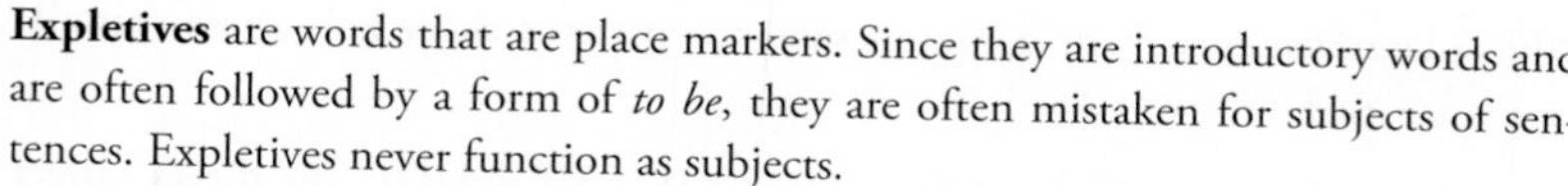

Expletives are words that are place markers. Since they are introductory words and are often followed by a form of *to be*, they are often mistaken for subjects of sentences. Expletives never function as subjects.

There are

Here is

Expletives tend to be overused and can cause confusion with subject-verb agreement. When possible, limit your use of expletives.

USE OF EXPLETIVES: ***There* are two reasons for us to go: economy and efficiency.** [The subject is *reasons*.]

OMITTED EXPLETIVE: Two reasons for us to go are cost and efficiency.

17b PARTS OF SENTENCES

17b-1 SUBJECTS AND PREDICATES

Sentences have two parts: subjects and predicates. The **simple subject** is the agent of the action, *who* or *what* the sentence is about, and the **simple predicate** expresses the action or, in the case of linking verbs, the state of being. (See also 20c.)

SUBJECT PREDICATE

The *senator voted.* [*Senator* is the subject; *voted* is the predicate.]

SUBJECT PREDICATE

The *bill passed.* [*Bill* is the subject; *passed* is the predicate.]

Most sentences are more complicated than a simple subject and predicate and include other words, phrases, and clauses that modify or complement the subject and predicate, forming the complete subject or the complete predicate.

SUBJECT PREDICATE

The angry senator in the first row voted vehemently against the motion. [The complete subject is *The angry senator in the first row*, and the complete predicate is *voted vehemently against the motion*.]

SUBJECT PREDICATE

The appropriation bill passed by a slim margin. [*The appropriation bill* is the complete subject, and the complete predicate is *passed by a slim margin*.]

17b-2 COMPLEMENTS

A word or group of words that completes a predicate is called a **complement**. Complements can be direct objects, indirect objects, object complements, and

PRACTICE 17.6

Parts of Speech

In the passage below, identify each boldfaced word as a noun (N), pronoun (P), verb (V), adjective (ADJ), adverb (ADV), preposition (PR), conjunction (C), interjection (I), or expletive (EX).

Watching a **film** is an experience like no other **that** I have had. **When** the **velvety darkness surrounds** me, I am **literally** transported **to** another **world.** Nothing exists **except** the screen and **me.** The **music** begins, the credits **roll, and** I **am completely hooked. Anyone who** knows me well **knows neither** to offer me a handful of popcorn **nor** to talk to me. I am by **myself in** my own world, apart from **everyday** reality. **Hush! It** is magic.

subject complements. Four common sentence patterns show how these complements are used. (See also 20c-1.)

■ Subject + Transitive Verb + **Direct Object** (S + VT + **DO**): The **direct object** answers the question *what?* or *whom?* after a transitive verb.

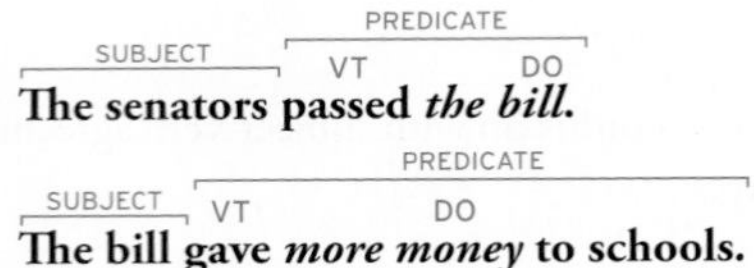

■ Subject + Transitive Verb + **Indirect Object** + Direct Object (S + VT + **IO** + DO): The **indirect object** answers the question *to whom?* or *to what?* after a transitive verb.

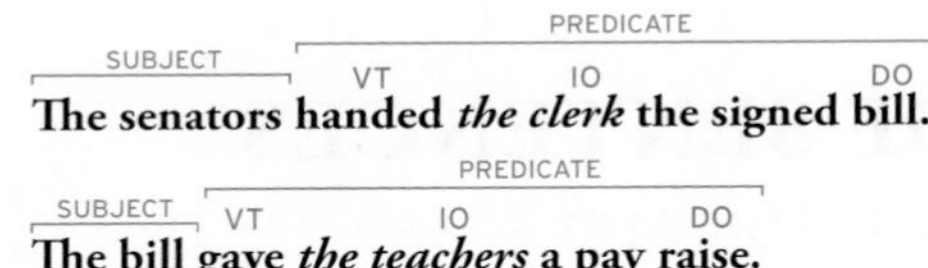

■ Subject + Transitive Verb + Direct Object + **Object Complement** (S + VT + DO + **OC**): The **object complement** describes (adjective) or renames (noun) the direct object.

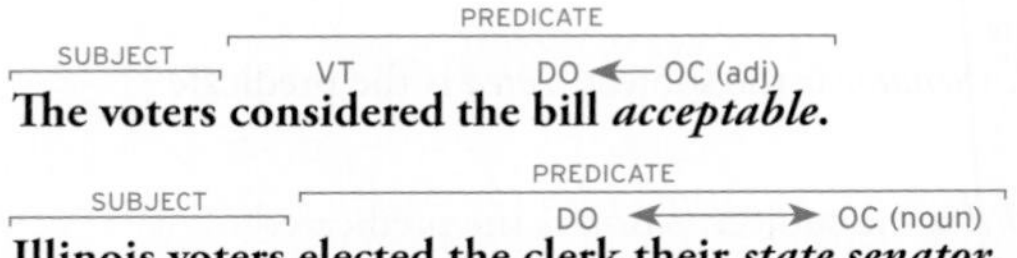

■ Subject + Linking Verb + **Subject Complement** (S + LV + **SC**): The **subject complement** describes or renames the subject after a linking verb (*be, become, appear, feel, seem*). (See 17a-3.)

A complement that describes the subject is called a **predicate adjective (PA).**

A complement that renames the subject is called a **predicate noun (PN).**

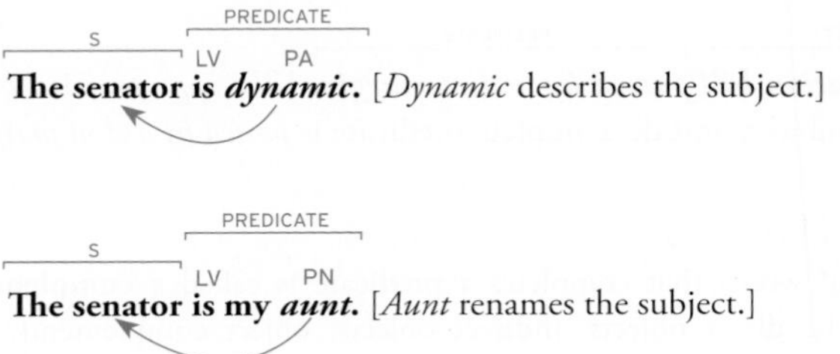

PRACTICE 17.7

Subjects and Predicates

Identify the complete subject and the complete predicate in the following sentences.

1. Life is good.
2. Our lives are sometimes easy and sometimes difficult.
3. I spent an exciting three weeks trekking through the rain forests of Costa Rica.
4. I hiked up mountains and through forests thick with vegetation.
5. Six of us who had taken a course in rock climbing went on a separate adventure.

PRACTICE 17.8

Complements

Show your understanding of complements by writing sentences in the following patterns.

1. Write a sentence with a transitive verb and a direct object.
2. Write a sentence with a transitive verb, an indirect object, and a direct object.

USAGE TIP When you substitute a pronoun for a predicate noun, use the subject form of the pronoun: **The senator is *she*. It is *I*.**

17b-3 PHRASES

A **phrase** is a group of words that lacks a subject or a verb; it never expresses a complete thought by itself but instead modifies a noun or a verb. Four categories of phrases are prepositional phrases, verbal phrases, appositive phrases, and absolute phrases.

■ **Prepositional Phrases** A **prepositional phrase** contains a preposition with its object, which is the noun or pronoun in the phrase.

PREP. PHRASE (PREP. OBJECT) · PREP. PHRASE (PREP. OBJECT) · PREP. PHRASE (PREP. OBJECT)

***Over* the river and *through* the woods, *to* grandmother's house we go.**

■ **Verbal Phrases Verbal phrases** are formed from verbs but function as nouns or modifiers. Three types of verbal phrases are infinitives, gerunds, and participles.

■ **Infinitives Infinitives** are formed by adding *to* in front of the verb (*to pass, to run, to love*). An infinitive phrase includes the infinitive and its modifiers.

> **Jon gave himself a huge party *to celebrate his birthday.*** [infinitive phrase]
>
> **He invited all his family, friends, and colleagues *to dance at a club.*** [infinitive phrase]

■ **Gerunds** A **gerund** is formed by adding *-ing* to a verb, and it functions as a noun in sentences. For example, a gerund could be the subject of a sentence or its direct object. A gerund phrase includes its modifiers.

GERUND AS SUBJECT

> ***Passing the age of twenty* made Jon feel old.** [gerund phrase as subject]

GERUND AS DIRECT OBJECT

> **He loved *celebrating with his friends.*** [gerund phrase as direct object]

■ **Participles Participles** are formed by adding *-ing* in present tense or *-ed* in past tense to verbs, and they function as adjectives that modify nouns or pronouns. A participial phrase includes its modifiers.

> **The boy, *passing Micha on the street,* broke into a run.** [present participle modifying the noun *boy*]
>
> ***Running fast,* he looked back over his shoulder.** [present participle modifying the pronoun *he*]

3. Write a sentence with a linking verb and a predicate adjective.
4. Write a sentence with a linking verb and a predicate noun.
5. Write a sentence with a transitive verb, a direct object, and an object complement.

PRACTICE 17.9

Phrases

Identify the boldfaced phrases as prepositional (P), infinitive (I), gerund (G), participial (PL), appositive (APP), or absolute (ABS).

1. **Shooting a film** is Emma's ambition, but, *Finding Remo*, **her student film,** was terrible.
2. The animation came out jumpy, and no one wanted **to sit through the hour-long film.**
3. **Shooting their film**, Emma and Jesse felt totally confident.
4. **Sweat running down her face**, Jesse yelled, "It's a wrap."
5. **Making films** is truly all they want **to do.**

Exhausted, **Ed slowed to a walk.** [past participle modifying the noun *Ed*]

■ **Appositive Phrases** **Appositive phrases** modify the nouns or pronouns they follow by describing them in different words. An appositive phrase consists of the appositive (the word that describes the noun or pronoun) and its modifiers.

Jack, *my best friend from high school,* broke into a run. [appositive phrase describes *Jack*]

The appositive, *the word that describes the noun or pronoun,* often appears between commas. [appositive phrase describes *appositive*]

■ **Absolute Phrases** An **absolute phrase** modifies a whole sentence or clause and consists of a noun plus a participle with its modifiers or complements. Absolute phrases can be placed anywhere in the sentence.

Noah tiptoed into the room, *his eyes squinting in the sudden light.*

Noah, *his eyes squinting in the sudden light,* tiptoed into the room.

***His eyes squinting in the sudden light,* Noah tiptoed into the room.**

17b-4 CLAUSES

A **clause** is a group of words that includes both a subject and a verb. Clauses may be **independent clauses** or **dependent (subordinate) clauses**.

■ **Independent Clauses** **Independent clauses (IC)** express complete ideas. They can stand alone as complete sentences or be part of longer sentences.

INDEPENDENT CLAUSE
The film was tasteless.

INDEPENDENT CLAUSE
***The film was tasteless* because it showed violence only to gross out the viewer.**

■ **Dependent Clauses** **Dependent clauses (DC)** (also called *subordinate clauses*) cannot stand alone. As all clauses do, a dependent clause has a subject and a verb, but it does not express a complete thought by itself. A dependent clause has to be linked to an independent clause for the meaning to be clear. The signal of a dependent clause is that it begins with a subordinating conjunction (SC), such as *if, when, because,* or *while,* or a relative pronoun (RP), such as *who, whom, which,* or *that.* (See 17a-7.)

INDEPENDENT CLAUSE / SC / DEPENDENT CLAUSE
The film was tasteless *because it showed violence only to gross out the viewer.*

SC / DEPENDENT CLAUSE / INDEPENDENT CLAUSE
***If I could have gotten my money back,* I would have left in the middle.**

PRACTICE 17.10

Clauses

Identify the boldfaced clauses as either dependent or independent. Identify each dependent clause as a noun clause (NC), adjective clause (ADJ), or adverb clause (ADV).

1. Anne Bradstreet was a remarkable poet **who wrote in the seventeenth century.**
2. She came to America **when she was only sixteen.**
3. Even though she was so young, **she was already married to Simon Bradstreet.**
4. **Simon Bradstreet became governor** soon after they arrived from England.
5. **Anne, however, retired to the wilds of Andover and wrote poetry.**

IC / RP / DEPENDENT CLAUSE / IC

My friends, *who do not usually mind violence*, had to cover their eyes.

■ **Noun Clauses** Dependent clauses can function in sentences as nouns, adjectives, or adverbs. **Noun clauses** function as subjects, objects, complements, or appositives, and they begin with relative pronouns such as *that, who, whom*, or *whoever* or with subordinating conjunctions such as *how, why*, or *whatever*.

SUBJECT

***Whatever Jay decides to do* will make him successful.** [noun clause functions as subject]

DIRECT OBJECT

We know *why he works so hard*. [noun clause functions as direct object]

■ **Adjective Clauses Adjective clauses**, sometimes called *relative clauses*, modify nouns or pronouns, and they begin with relative pronouns such as *who, whose, whom, which*, or *that* or subordinating conjunctions such as *how, when*, or *where*.

His father, *whom Jay greatly admires*, set the standard. [adjective clause modifies *father*]

The day *when his father retired* was the day Jay took over the business. [adjective clause modifies *day*]

■ **Adverb Clauses Adverb clauses** modify verbs, adjectives, other adverbs, or whole clauses, and they begin with subordinating conjunctions such as *before, because, if, when*, and *while*.

DEPENDENT CLAUSE / SC / INDEPENDENT CLAUSE

***When he took over the business*, Jay wrote a note to his father.** [adverb clause modifies the independent clause]

INDEPENDENT CLAUSE / SC / DEPENDENT CLAUSE

Jay kept all his father's traditional values *as he updated the business*. [adverb clause modifies the independent clause]

17c SENTENCE TYPES

With an understanding of phrases and clauses, you can build interesting and varied sentences. The three essential types of sentences are simple, compound, and complex. These three types are the patterns on which all sentences are built.

17c-1 SIMPLE SENTENCES

A **simple sentence** has one independent clause (IC). It can be a two-word sentence, with one subject and one verb, or it can be longer, including many modifiers and phrases but no other clauses. Both of the following sentences are simple sentences.

PRACTICE 17.11

Phrases and Clauses

Show your understanding of phrases and clauses by writing the following sentences. Identify each of the elements with a label.

1. Write a sentence that includes a prepositional phrase and an infinitive phrase.
2. Write a sentence that includes a gerund phrase.
3. Write a sentence that includes a participial phrase.
4. Write a sentence that has a subordinate clause that functions as a noun.
5. Write a sentence that has a subordinate clause that functions as an adjective.
6. Write a sentence that has a subordinate clause that functions as an adverb.
7. Write a sentence that has an infinitive phrase, a prepositional phrase, and a subordinate clause. Label each phrase or clause.

INDEPENDENT CLAUSE
SUBJECT VERB
Kim studied.

PREP. PHRASE | PREP. PHRASE | SUBJECT | PARTICIPLE PHRASE

On Tuesday evening between ten and midnight, *Kim*, hoping to ace the

VERB | PREP. PHRASE | PREP. PHRASE | PREP. PHRASE

course, *studied* hard for her midterm exam in history on the causes of the

PREP. PHRASE

Vietnam War.

A simple sentence can have great power. After a long, explanatory paragraph, a simple sentence can emphasize or clarify a point.

> **At that moment I saw my father for what seemed like the first time. He was insecure, jealous, vulnerable, and weary. He was also kind, honest, hard-working, and brilliant. He was a perfect human being.**

17c-2 COMPOUND SENTENCES AND COORDINATION

A **compound sentence** has at least two independent clauses connected by a coordinating conjunction (CC) (*and, but, for, or, nor, so,* or *yet*) that is preceded by a comma. Two independent clauses may also be connected by a semicolon.

INDEPENDENT CLAUSE | CC | INDEPENDENT CLAUSE

***Kim studied for the exam*, and *then she slept soundly*.**

INDEPENDENT CLAUSE | INDEPENDENT CLAUSE

***Kim studied for the exam; then she slept soundly*.**

INDEPENDENT CLAUSE | CC | INDEPENDENT CLAUSE | CC | INDEPENDENT CLAUSE

***Kim studied for the exam*, and *then she went to bed*, but *she slept fitfully*.**

Too many compound sentences can create the rhythm of the breathless narratives of unsophisticated writing *(And then I went to the store, and I saw this man, and he had a big moustache, and I asked him if he saw my pet frog)*.

Avoid too many compound sentences in a row, but a few well-constructed ones can be used to good effect to create a sense of **coordination**. Since compound sentences have independent clauses on either side of the conjunction, they can be used effectively to create a sense of balance in your writing. If you want to show two equally attractive alternatives or give equal emphasis to two ideas, the compound sentence is a good stylistic choice.

> **We had not spoken a word to each other but I knew we were thinking the same thing. Her wide eyes stared into mine, and I could read what was behind them, a plan for her future, exactly what I prayed for, too.**

17c-3 COMPLEX SENTENCES AND SUBORDINATION

A **complex sentence** has one independent clause and at least one dependent clause (DC). The dependent clause begins with a subordinating conjunction such as *although, because, if,* or *when* or a relative pronoun such as *which, who,* or *that.*

DEPENDENT CLAUSE
INDEPENDENT CLAUSE
SC
Although Kim studied hard, she slept fitfully.
DEPENDENT CLAUSE
INDEPENDENT CLAUSE
DEPENDENT CLAUSE
SC
SC
Although Kim studied hard, she slept fitfully because she was nervous.

The idea of one clause being dependent or subordinate should give you a clue about how to use the complex sentence most effectively in your writing. When one idea is less important than another or when one idea depends on another, you can use the structure of the complex sentence to subtly suggest this sense of **subordination**.

> **"Later that evening, *when Thelma insists on stopping at a honky-tonk bar despite Louise's protestations,* the gun comes in handy."**
>
> —Janet Maslin, "On the Run with Two Buddies and a Gun"

PRACTICE 17.12

Sentence Types

Test your understanding of sentence types by identifying the sentences below as simple, compound, or complex.

1. When the stock market crashed, I thought I would not be affected.
2. I knew a few families that had invested their life savings.
3. They had worked hard, and they felt safe.
4. They had made some bad choices, but it was not out of ignorance or greed.
5. Everyone at that time was in the same situation.
6. When classes were over for the semester, Jeff went straight to bed.
7. He slept for two days in a state of complete exhaustion.
8. Jeff had hoped to spend the rest of the break relaxing; however, his empty bank account suggested otherwise.
9. Within a week he had one part-time job at the mall and one at a restaurant.
10. Jeff will finally be able to relax when classes begin again.

Yuri Arcurs/
Shutterstock.com

18 Punctuation

Punctuation is a set of conventions used to clarify your meaning. Punctuation marks have two main purposes: to end sentences and to show grammatical relationships within sentences.

18a PROOFREADING SYMBOLS

Copyeditors, writers, and writing teachers often use a shorthand method to indicate corrections they make while proofreading. Most proofreading symbols are easy to understand, and they give you a convenient way to make corrections when you proofread your own work or a writing partner's work during peer revision. The most common proofreading symbols are in the following chart.

Symbol	Example (change marked)	Example (change made)
⁀o	Correct a typu.	Correct a typo.
⁀r⁀ / m⁀ / ⁀o	Cornect nore than one typu.	Correct more than one typo.
t	Insert a leter.	Insert a letter.
℘	Make a a deletion.	Make a deletion.
℘ (close up)	Delette and close up space.	Delete and close up space.
#	Insertproper spacing.	Insert proper spacing.
# / ⁀	Insertspace and close up.	Insert space and close up.
tr	Transpose letters inidcated.	Transpose letters indicated.
tr	Transpose as words indicated.	Transpose words as indicated.
tr	Reorder shown as words several.	Reorder several words as shown.
⊏	⊏ Move text to left.	Move text to left.
⊐	⊐ Move text to right.	Move text to right.
¶	Indent for paragraph.	Indent for paragraph.
no ¶	⊏ No paragraph indent.	No paragraph indent.
run in	Run back turnover lines.	Run back turnover lines.
⌐	Break line when it runs far too long.	Break line when it runs far too long.
⊙	Insert period here	Insert period here.
^,	Commas commas everywhere.	Commas, commas everywhere.
’	Its in need of an apostrophe.	It's in need of an apostrophe.
“ / ”	Add quotation marks, he begged.	"Add quotation marks," he begged.
;	Add a semicolon don't hesitate.	Add a semicolon; don't hesitate.
:	She advised "You need a colon."	She advised: "You need a colon."
?	How about a question mark	How about a question mark?
⁀=⁀	Add a hyphen to a bill like receipt.	Add a hyphen to a bill-like receipt.
(/)	Add parentheses as they say.	Add parentheses (as they say).
lc	Sometimes you want Lowercase.	Sometimes you want lowercase.
caps	Sometimes you want upperCASE.	Sometimes you want UPPERCASE.
ital	Add italics instantly.	Add italics *instantly*.
rom	But use *roman* in the main.	But use roman in the main.
bf	Add boldface if necessary.	Add **boldface** if necessary.

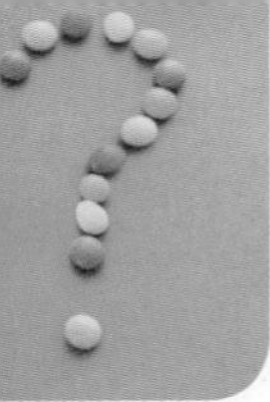

18b PERIODS, QUESTION MARKS, AND EXCLAMATION MARKS

18b-1 PERIODS

Periods (.) are used at the ends of sentences; in abbreviations, decimals, and initials; and inside Internet addresses.

■ **Sentences** A period is placed at the end of a declarative sentence or a mild command or request.

The latest virus disabled my computer.

Show me your paper.

■ **Abbreviations** Periods are also used after most abbreviations: **Dr., Ms., Ph.D., a.m.**

Mr. Carter won the Nobel Peace Prize in 2002.

I will get my B.A. in three years.

Exceptions to this rule are names of organizations, countries, agencies, and U.S. Postal Service abbreviations of state names.

CBS, USA, FBI, ME (Maine)

Usage Tip If you end a sentence with an abbreviation that has a final period, do not add an end period: **In three years I will get my B.A.**

■ **Decimals** Periods are used in decimals and fractional amounts of money.

My GPA is 3.5.

You owe me $3.50.

■ **Initials and Internet Addresses** Periods are used with initials and computer addresses.

You can buy F. Scott Fitzgerald's books on Amazon.com.

18b-2 QUESTION MARKS

A question mark (?) ends an interrogative sentence.

■ **Direct Questions** Place a question mark after a direct question.

Is this lecture confusing?

■ **Direct Quotations** When used in direct quotations, question marks go inside the quotation marks when the quotation asks the question, and outside the quotation marks when the full sentence poses the question.

Who said "Two paths diverged in a yellow wood"?

I asked him, "Who wrote the poem?"

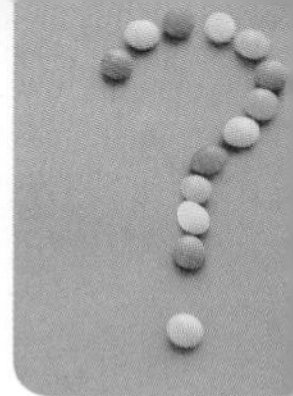

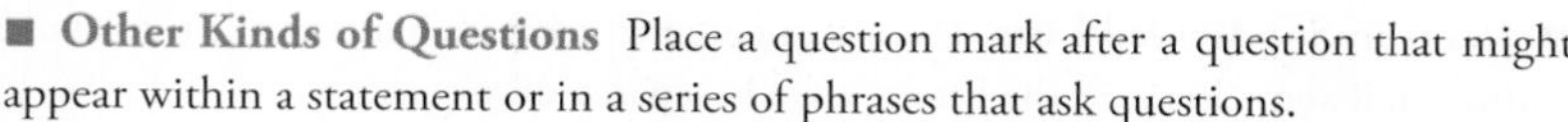

■ **Other Kinds of Questions** Place a question mark after a question that might appear within a statement or in a series of phrases that ask questions.

> **Madame Helen—does anyone remember her?—will be available for consultations after nine o'clock.**
>
> **Do you believe in psychic occurrences? Extrasensory perception? Unidentified flying objects?**

18b-3 EXCLAMATION MARKS

An **exclamation mark (!)** ends an urgent sentence or a sentence that shows emotion or excitement.

> **Bring me a bandage immediately!**
>
> **I won!**

USAGE TIP Limit your use of exclamation marks in formal writing. Try to find a verb that expresses excitement or emphasis rather than using punctuation to signal excitement. **Okay: Schuyler was curious! Better: Schuyler bombarded me with questions.**

18c SEMICOLONS AND COLONS

18c-1 SEMICOLONS

A **semicolon (;)** joins elements in a sentence in specific ways.

■ **Independent Clauses without Conjunctions** Use a semicolon to join two independent clauses that are not joined by coordinating conjunctions. Using a semicolon instead of a period is a stylistic decision that conveys that the ideas in the clauses are closely related.

> **Zoe laughed at his joke; she did not think it was funny.** [closely related]
>
> **Zoe laughed at his joke. Conversation shifted to a new topic.** [not closely related]

■ **Independent Clauses with Conjunctive Adverbs** Use a semicolon to connect independent clauses when the second begins with a conjunctive adverb such as *however, nevertheless, moreover, therefore,* or *thus,* or a transitional phrase such as *for example.* The conjunctive adverb or transitional phrase is followed by a comma.

> **Zoe laughed at his joke; however, she was offended.**
>
> **She tried to change the subject; for example, she asked him where he went to school.**

PRACTICE 18.1

Periods, Question Marks, and Exclamation Marks

Proofread the following short passage. Add periods, question marks, and exclamation marks where necessary. Practice using the appropriate proofreading symbols from the proofreading chart.

Yesterday morning around five a m, two masked men robbed a jewelry store at 51 Main St in St Paul, MN and shot a bystander C B S and N B C had camera crews on the spot within the hour One eyewitness, Maria L Gonzalez, M D, asked the police how she could feel safe going on calls at night knowing she might bump into a thief She exclaimed, "I'm terrified" Then she asked, "How can I protect myself" You can follow the story on CNN com

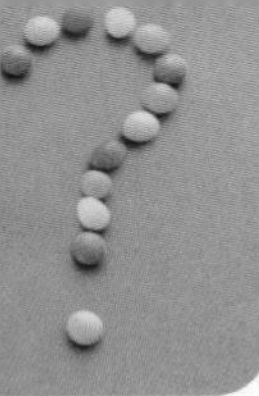

■ **Items in Subdivided Lists** Use a semicolon to separate items in a list, to avoid confusion if some items in the list are already separated by commas.

> **Tamar was at the party with her oldest friends, Marlene and Doug; her twin brothers, Caleb and Jacob; and Cindy and Peter, her coworkers.**

USAGE TIP Always place semicolons outside quotation marks: **At the party he asked, "Do you want to hear this joke?"; I said "No."**

18c-2 COLONS

A **colon (:)** presents specific details.

■ **Before a List, Series, or Quotation** Use a colon to introduce a list, a series, or a formal or long quotation.

> **I did all my work: a history report, an article about cloning, a take-home exam, and math homework.**
>
> **All term my professor repeated this message: "If you manage your time well, you will be able to do all your work and have some time to relax."**

■ **Between Independent Clauses** Use a colon to connect two independent clauses when the second one illustrates or explains the first.

> **Ellen completed her work early and could do the one thing she had wanted to do all term: She slept for twelve hours straight.**

■ **Before an Example** Use a colon after a clause to provide a one-word example.

> **I completed my work early and could do the one thing I have wanted to do all term: sleep.**

■ **Other Uses** Some other common uses of the colon are as follows.

- After a salutation in a formal letter or memorandum

  Dear Professor:

  To: Ben Gould

- In a book title, to separate the subtitle from the title

  The Fourth Genre: Contemporary Writers of/on Creative Nonfiction

- In citations from the Bible or in bibliographic sources

  Judges 11:3

  Hunt, Douglas. *The Dolphin Reader*. 6th ed. Boston: Houghton, 2003.

- In divisions of time

  I get up at 6:05 every day.

PRACTICE 18.2

Semicolons and Colons

Proofread the following short passage, and add semicolons and colons where necessary. Practice using the appropriate proofreading symbols from the proofreading chart.

Dear Town Official

At 530 yesterday evening, I went to return *The Flight of the Iguana A Sidelong View of Science and Nature* to the library on Main Street however, I was unable to cross the street. The traffic was so fierce that I waited for a solid forty minutes then I returned to my home. It is time for this town to take its head out of the sand and install that newfangled modern convenience a traffic light.

18d COMMAS, DASHES, AND PARENTHESES

18d-1 COMMAS

A **comma** (,) clarifies relationships within a sentence.

■ **Lists** Use commas between items in a list.

> **Mia's progress has been slow, steady, and significant.**

USAGE TIP Academic writers use a comma before the conjunction in a list; writers in journalism and media often omit the last comma before the conjunction. Whichever style you choose, be consistent.

■ **Coordinate Adjectives** Use a comma between coordinate adjectives. (Coordinate adjectives each modify the same noun.)

> **Mia has shown a slow, steady improvement.**

■ **Introductory Phrases or Clauses** Use a comma after an introductory phrase or a dependent clause.

> ***To improve over such a short time,* Mia had to have worked hard.** [introductory phrase]

DC IC

> ***Since she had worked so hard,* Mia improved significantly.** [introductory dependent clause]

If the independent clause comes before the dependent clause, do not use a comma.

IC DC

> **Mia improved significantly since she had worked so hard.**

■ **Coordinating Conjunctions** Use a comma before a coordinating conjunction (*and, but, or, for, nor, so, yet*) in a compound sentence.

> **Mia's improvement was significant, but she was still not happy.**

If the conjunction is not followed by an independent clause, do not put a comma before the conjunction.

PA PP

> **Mia's improvement was significant but *unsatisfying* to *her*.** [The expression *unsatisfying to her* is a predicate adjective and a prepositional phrase, not an independent clause]

■ **Inessential Clauses** Use commas around inessential (nonrestrictive) dependent clauses. Do not put commas around essential (restrictive) clauses.

A clause is **inessential** or **nonrestrictive** if it can be taken out of the sentence without changing the basic meaning of the sentence. Commas around the clause signal that the enclosed idea is additional information, not essential to the meaning of the sentence.

An **essential** or **restrictive** clause cannot be taken out of the sentence without altering the meaning of the sentence. The lack of commas signals that the clause is essential to the meaning of the sentence.

> **Mia, *who is almost twenty,* improved significantly in her work.** [provides additional but not essential information]
>
> **The student *who worked so hard* is named Mia.** [provides essential information]

USAGE TIP The relative pronoun *which* always introduces an inessential clause, so commas always go around a *which* clause. The relative pronoun *that* always introduces an essential clause, so commas never go around *that* clauses.

> **The exam, *which I found challenging,* was the final graduation requirement.** [provides additional but not essential information]
>
> **The exam *that I passed* allowed me to graduate.** [provides essential information]

■ **Participial and Appositive Phrases** Use commas around participial phrases (verbal phrases that function like adjectives) and appositive phrases (noun phrases that modify nouns or pronouns by describing them in different words). (See 17b-3.)

Modifies

> **Mia, *having worked as hard as she could,* took a break.** [participial phrase]

Renames

> **Mia, *the most diligent student in the class,* finally earned her A.** [appositive phrase]

■ **Attributions and Interrupters** Use commas around attributions in quotations and around phrases that interrupt a sentence.

> **"I am proud of Mia," *he said,* as he looked over her work.** [attribution]
>
> **Other teachers, *however kind they may be,* do not see her improvement.** [interrupter]
>
> **Show me her scores, *please.*** [interrupter]

■ **Clarity** Use commas to help your reader avoid confusion.

> **To Mia, Anne was the role model of a hard worker.**

■ **Other Uses** Commas are also used in the following situations.

- In addresses and names of geographical places

  Becca lives at 81 Main Street, Madison, Wisconsin.

  Last year she traveled to Florence, Italy.

- In openings and closings of letters

  Dear Professor Lopez,

  Sincerely,

- In direct address

  Michael, do you hear me?

- In inverted names in bibliographies, indexes, and other reference lists

  Lazlo, Ernestine

- To separate a name from a title or degree and with *Jr.* and *Sr.*

  My internist is Ernestine Lazlo, M.D.

  Frank Sinatra, Jr., was never as famous as his dad.

- In dates

  October 22, 1968

- With figures that have more than four digits

  $1, 250

  1, 000,000 burgers sold

18d-2 DASHES

Dashes (— or —) are used in certain situations instead of commas. A dash creates a less formal tone in a piece of writing.

- **Surprise and Irony** Use a dash to create a sense of surprise or signal an ironic comment.

  Professor Tsao told us to read all of Chapter 8, to write out four exercises, to complete our research papers—and to have a good weekend. [sets off an ironic comment]

- **Parenthetical Comments** Use dashes to set off a parenthetical comment in a sentence.

  Professor Tsao—a teacher who loves to challenge students—told us to read all of Chapter 8, to write out four exercises, and to complete our research papers by Monday morning. [sets off a parenthetical comment]

- **Lists and Explanations** Use a dash to introduce a list or explanation at the beginning or end of a sentence.

  Tonight I have a huge amount of homework—all of Chapter 8, four exercises, and a research paper.

18d-3 PARENTHESES

Parentheses—( )—are used in the following cases.

■ **Asides** Use parentheses around asides or incidental information.

Professor Tsao (*my workaholic economics teacher*) piled on the homework.

■ **Explanatory Material** Use parentheses around explanatory material.

I finished all the work (*Chapter 8, four exercises, the research paper*) at midnight on Sunday.

■ **Lists within Sentences** Use parentheses around letters or numbers in a list within a sentence.

I finished the three assignments: *(1) Chapter 8, (2) the exercises, and (3) the research paper.*

> **PRACTICE 18.3**
>
> **Commas, Dashes, and Parentheses**
>
> Proofread the following passage, adding commas, dashes, or parentheses where necessary. Practice using the appropriate proofreading symbols from the proofreading chart.
>
> Lance Armstrong whom some people call the best athlete in America won the Tour de France in 2005. Although fans wondered whether he could come back after his bout with cancer they had no doubts after watching his impressive some even said "superhuman" performance. Armstrong's feats were astonishing sprinting up hills sliding around hairpin curves and crossing the finish line minutes before his closest rival the cyclist from Germany.
>
> "He won" said a long-time fan "and he deserved to win."
>
> This fan who cheered and pumped his fist in the air has been following Armstrong's career for many years.
>
> "Whether or not Armstrong won the race he would be a hero in my book," the jubilant exhausted fan concluded.

18e APOSTROPHES AND HYPHENS

18e-1 APOSTROPHES

Apostrophes (') are used in possessives and contractions.

■ **Possessives** Use an apostrophe to indicate that a noun or an indefinite pronoun is possessive.

Singular Nouns Use *'s* with singular nouns or pronouns.

***Professor Johnson's* class is hard but interesting.**

***Everyone's* workload is lighter than mine.**

Use *'s* with most singular nouns ending in *s*. If the noun ends with a *z* or *eez* sound, use the apostrophe alone.

The *dress's* hem was dragging on the ground.

***Ray Charles'* performance was mesmerizing.** [noun ends with a *z* sound]

■ **Plural Nouns** Use *s'* with plural nouns that form the plural by adding an *s*.

I attended both *professors'* classes.

My workload is heavier than all the *bosses'* workloads put together.

Use *'s* with irregular plural nouns that do not use *s* to form the plural.

Put the cheese next to all the *mice's* holes.

***Children's* games are often more fun than adults' games.**

■ **Compound Nouns** Use *'s* on the last word of a compound noun.

My *sister-in-law's* mother visited yesterday.

■ **Two or More Nouns** Use *'s* on each noun to show individual ownership, but only on the last noun to show joint ownership.

John and Susan's **new house required a huge mortgage.** [joint ownership]

John's and Susan's **studios needed serious renovations.** [individual ownership]

Usage Tip Since possessive pronouns already show possession, they never use apostrophes: *his, hers, its, yours, theirs, whose*: **The line snaked *its* way around the block.**

■ **Contractions** Use an apostrophe to replace the letter or letters deleted in a contraction.

do not	don't
that is	that's
Madam	Ma'am
forecastle	fo'c's'le
it is or it has	it's

(*Continued*)

Armstrong will be signing autographs for fans tomorrow in two locations: 1 the bookstore at 29 Rue d'Orly Cannes and 2 the bookstore on the Champs Élysées Paris.

18e-2 HYPHENS

Hyphens (-) are used as follows.

■ **Compound Modifiers** Use a hyphen to punctuate compound modifiers that work together to modify nouns.

The election was a *hard-fought* battle. [*Hard* modifies *fought*, not *battle*; together *hard* and *fought* modify *battle*.]

Hannah is a *three-year-old* terror. [The words *three, year,* and *old* work together to modify *terror*.]

Generally, when the modifier follows the noun, do not hyphenate it.

The battle was *hard fought*.

When the modifier is preceded by an adverb that ends in *-ly* or by the adverb *very*, omit the hyphen.

Kristen is an *extremely bright* child.

Greg is a *very kindhearted* guy.

■ **Compound Words** Use the hyphen to form a compound word—a word made up of more than one word that functions as a single word.

My *brother-in-law* is a *happy-go-lucky* guy.

Make a compound noun plural by putting *s* at the end of the main noun.

I have two accomplished *brothers-in-law.*

Since conventions vary widely about using compound modifiers, it is a good idea to check your dictionary.

■ **Prefixes and Suffixes** Use the hyphen to link some prefixes and suffixes to words. The most commonly hyphenated prefixes are *ex-, pro-, self-,* and *neo-,* and a common suffix is *-elect.* Do not use a hyphen with the common prefixes *anti, co, non, post, pre,* and *un.*

The *governor-elect* tried to be both *pro-choice* and *pro-life.*

Check a dictionary or style guide to determine whether to hyphenate a word with a prefix or suffix.

■ **Other Uses** Following are additional uses of hyphens.

- At the end of a line to divide a word between syllables
- In written fractions

one-tenth

- In numbers from *twenty-one* to *ninety-nine*
- In numbers and dates that indicate a span

1946-2000

18f ELLIPSES, BRACKETS, AND QUOTATION MARKS

18f-1 ELLIPSES

Ellipses (. . .) have the following uses.

■ **Intentional Omissions** Use ellipses to tell your reader that you have intentionally omitted a word or phrase in quoted material.

In despair Hamlet cries, "O that this too, too sullied flesh would melt . . . How weary, stale, flat, and unprofitable seem to me all the uses of this world!" [The writer has omitted three lines of Hamlet's speech that are not pertinent to her point.]

■ **Hesitancy** Use ellipses to indicate a speaker's hesitation or uncertainty.

Veronica said, "I cannot quite remember . . . well . . . maybe a few lines from *Hamlet* have stayed in my head."

If the ellipses end the sentence, add the period to make four dots.

Veronica said, "I just cannot remember. . . ."

PRACTICE 18.4

Apostrophes and Hyphens

Proofread the following passage, and insert the apostrophes and hyphens where necessary. Practice using the appropriate proofreading symbols from the proofreading chart.

I observed Mrs. Jones fifth grade class yesterday afternoon. In my preobservation conference in the teachers lounge, Mrs. Jones asked if I could help with the antismoking campaign she planned to launch in Mondays assembly. Although Im extremely happy to be useful, I wonder if its an appropriate job for a well intentioned exsmoker like me. I asked my master teacher. She told me that over two thirds of the teachers had been smokers, and she was sure that my expertise would be convincing to the eleven year old children in all the fifth grade classrooms.

18f-2 BRACKETS

Square brackets ([ ]) and **angle brackets** (< >) are used in these situations.

■ **Quotations** Use square brackets to indicate that you have added clarifying material to quoted passages.

> **The governor said, "I will be glad to give her [*his opponent, Senator Reo*] a chance to debate me in a public forum."**

Use square brackets to insert words that are necessary to make a quotation grammatical or comprehensible.

> **The governor said he would be glad to "debate [*Senator Reo*] in a public forum."**

■ **Internet Addresses** Some teachers may ask you to use angle brackets in e-mail addresses and Web URLs.

> **You can find the news at <GHttp://www.cnn.com> or by e-mailing me at <kbaruk@hotmail.com>.**

18f-3 QUOTATION MARKS

Quotation marks (" ") **have the following uses.**

■ **Direct Quotations** Use quotation marks around all material that is directly quoted from other sources or to indicate someone's spoken words in dialogue.

> **Hamlet's most famous speech begins, *"To be or not to be—that is the question."*** [quotation from other source]

> **Senator Reo replied, *"I would love to debate the governor."*** [dialogue]

Do not use quotation marks around indirect quotations.

> **Senator Reo replied that she would love to debate the governor.**

USAGE TIP In a quoted sentence within a sentence, do not use a period: **The line "Show me the money" became popular last year.**

■ **Titles** Use quotation marks to set off titles of magazine articles, television episodes, poems, short stories, songs, and other short works. Titles of longer works such as newspapers, magazines, novels, films, television shows, and anthologies are italicized.

> **I read "The Good Doctor" in the *New Yorker*.**

> **"The Pine Barrens" was my favorite episode of *The Sopranos*.**

■ **Single Quotation Marks** Use **single quotation marks** (' ') to set off quotations inside quotations.

> **The governor announced, "Senator Reo said, 'I accept,' so the debate is on."**

PRACTICE 18.5

Quotation Marks and Accompanying Punctuation

Proofread the following dialogue, adding all necessary commas, periods, question marks, exclamation marks, and quotation marks. Practice using the appropriate proofreading symbols from the proofreading chart.

1. Quiet she commanded
2. What is wrong he asked Do you hear something
3. What I hear is you talking she answered so stop talking
4. I am scared he cried
5. Then go home she growled You asked Can I come and I said Yes you can
6. Well you should have said No way he said and ran home.

■ **Other Punctuation** Follow these rules for using quotation marks with other punctuation marks.

■ **Commas and Periods** Commas and periods always go inside quotation marks.

"Well, then, it is all set,." said the governor, "and I am happy."

■ **Question Marks and Exclamation Marks** Question marks and exclamation marks go inside the quotation marks when the quoted material is a question or an exclamation, and outside the quotation marks when the whole sentence is a question or an exclamation.

Who said, "I accept"? [whole sentence is the question]

The senator asked, "When do you want to debate?" [quoted material is the question]

He said, "Eureka!" [quoted material is the exclamation]

18g CAPITAL LETTERS, NUMBERS, AND ITALICS

18g-1 CAPITAL LETTERS

Capital letters are used at the beginning of sentences, in titles, for proper nouns, and for adjectives derived from proper nouns.

■ **Proper Nouns** Use capital letters to begin specific names of people, races, titles, geographical locations, regions, historical eras, months, seasons, organizations, and institutions, but not general names of the same.

Georgetown High School [specific name] **was the best *high school*** [general name] **in the area.**

I shook *President Zeroff's* [specific title and name] **hand; she was the fifth *president*** [general title] **of *Central College*** [specific institution].

■ **Adjectives from Proper Nouns** Use capital letters to begin adjectives made from proper nouns.

The best ethnic food in London is *Indian* food.

Most Londoners prefer crumpets to *English muffins.*

■ **Sentences and Quotations** Use capital letters to begin sentences and quotations. Do not use a capital letter if the quotation is the continuation of a sentence or an excerpt that is a word, phrase, or dependent clause.

"I tried to run," she said, "but my feet would not move." [quotation is continuation of a sentence]

She felt "awkward, clumsy, and stupid," but it turns out that she was suffering from hypothermia. [quotation is an excerpt]

■ **Titles** Use capital letters to begin all words in titles except for articles (*the/a*), short prepositions, and conjunctions, unless they are the first word in the title: of a book, film, television episode, but do not capitalize for magazines, journals, and newspapers.

"The Pine Barrens" is my favorite episode of *The Sopranos.*

"The Good Doctor" was first published in the *New Yorker*.

■ **Other Uses** Other examples of the use of capital letters include the following.

- Nations: *England, Turkey, Japan*
- Planets: *Mercury, Mars, Venus*
- Stars: *Perseus, Sirius*
- Public places: *Times Square, Fisherman's Wharf, the Chicago Loop*
- Names of streets: *Beacon Street, Oak Lane, Allen Road*
- Days of the week and month: *Friday, November*
- Holidays: *Thanksgiving, Bastille Day, Fourth of July*
- Religions, deities, sacred texts: *Buddhism, Zeus, The Upanishads*
- Languages: *Hindi, Swedish, Vietnamese*
- Names of ships and aircraft: *Queen Mary, Enola Gay*
- The first-person pronoun: *I*

Check a dictionary if you are not sure whether a word or phrase should have an initial capital letter.

18g-2 NUMBERS

Numbers can appear as numerals or as words.

■ **Academic Writing** Spell out numbers from *one* through *ninety-nine* in academic writing.

It rained for forty days and forty nights.

Use numerals for 100 and higher.

Archeologists discovered 5,000 bones at the site.

■ **Media Writing** Spell out numbers from *one* through *ten* for media writing.

The census showed ten single-parent households in this village.

Use numerals for *11* and higher.

The police counted ten members of the clergy and 120 protesters at the sit-in.

■ **Beginning Sentences** Spell out numbers that begin sentences.

Two hundred people attended the council meeting.

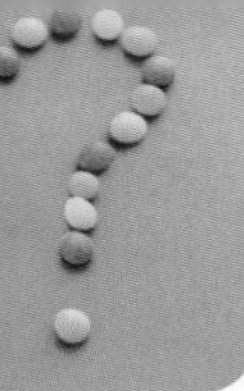

PRACTICE 18.6

Capital Letters, Numbers, and Italics

Proofread the following passage, adding capital letters, numbers in their correct form, and italics where necessary. Practice using the appropriate proofreading symbols from the proofreading chart.

4 years ago I had no idea that college was even in my future. I lived in a small town, population twenty thousand, in the southwest. Only fifty percent of our graduating class went on to college. One day in english class I read a novel by the portuguese writer Jose Saramago. The novel was called blindness, and it is about White Blindness that causes everyone in an unnamed european City to go blind. We discussed the Novel in class, and I realized that I loved talking and thinking about Books and Movies. It was then that I decided that College was indeed what I wanted, and I went to my Guidance Counselor that very day.

- **Page and Chapter Numbers** Use numerals for page and chapter numbers.

  Read pages 3–30 in Chapter 9.

- **Fractions and Percentages** Use numerals for percentages.

  The polls showed a 75 percent approval rating.

- **Addresses and Dates** Use numerals for addresses and dates.

  On January 5, 2006, I will move to 29 Packard Road.

18g-3 ITALICS

Italics (***italics***) or underlining (**underlining**) are used in the following situations.

- **Titles** Use italics (on the computer) or underlining (in handwriting) to set off titles of long works such as books, newspapers, magazines, journals, movies, and plays.

  I read a review of *The Taming of the Shrew* in *Entertainment Magazine*.

  I read a review of The Taming of the Shrew in Entertainment Magazine.

- **Foreign Words** Use italics (on the computer) or underlining (in handwriting) to set off foreign words.

  Jacques called his grandmother "*grand-mére*."

- **Words, Letters, Numbers** Use italics (on the computer) or underlining (in handwriting) to set off words, letters, and numbers when referring to them.

  How many *3*s are in *9*?

  Spell *quick* with a *q* not a *kw*.

19 Common Errors

Shawn Hempel/
Shutterstock.com

Once you understand the parts of speech, parts of sentences, and sentence types reviewed in Chapter 17, you know the basic concepts that will allow you to make sense of grammatical rules. In this section you will learn to identify and avoid making errors in

- Sentence structure
- Agreement
- Verb tense
- Parallelism
- Modification
- Frequently confused words

19a SENTENCE STRUCTURE ERRORS

19a-1 FRAGMENTS

A sentence written in standard English has a subject and a complete predicate (a verb and its modifiers or complements). (See 17b.) A **fragment** is missing one of its parts, either the subject or the verb. Sometimes writers use fragments intentionally for emphasis or to dramatize thinking that is confused.

> **I love you.** ***A lot.*** [emphasis]
>
> **She ran through the corridors.** ***Where to go? In a room? In a closet?*** [confusion]

Using intentional fragments is a stylistic choice. When fragments are unintentional, they are considered sentence structure errors. Learn to identify and correct the following kinds of fragments.

■ **Omitting the Verb** A fragment may be caused by the omission of a verb.

Fragment: ***Isabel running down the corridor into rooms and closets.*** [*Running* (a participle) describes Isabel, and the subject *Isabel* has no true verb.]

Complete Sentence: Isabel ran down the corridor into rooms and closets. [*Ran* is the verb.]

■ **Omitting the Subject** Not including a subject also causes a fragment.

Fragment: Isabel ran down the corridor. ***And looked into rooms and closets.*** [The verb *looked* has no subject.]

Complete Sentence: Isabel ran down the corridor and looked into rooms and closets. [*Isabel* is the subject; *ran* and *looked* are compound verbs describing what she did.]

Complete Sentence: Isabel ran down the corridor. She looked into rooms and closets. [*She* is the subject of the second sentence.]

■ **Using Dependent Clauses Alone** A **dependent (subordinate) clause** contains a subject and a verb, but it cannot stand alone. It must be connected to an independent clause to form a complete sentence.

Dependent clauses begin with subordinating conjunctions such as *although, because, if,* and *when* or relative pronouns such as *who, which,* or *that.* (See 17b-4.)

FRAGMENT: ***Although she was initially scared and confused.*** [Even though this group of words has a subject *she* and a verb *was,* it is a dependent clause and a fragment. It does not express a complete thought and cannot stand alone.]

COMPLETE SENTENCE: Although she was initially scared and confused, Isabel finally figured out where she was. [The dependent clause *Although she was initially scared and confused* is now connected to the independent clause *Isabel finally figured out where she was.*]

COMPLETE SENTENCE: She was initially scared and confused. [Dropping the subordinating conjunction *although* makes this a complete sentence.]

19a-2 FUSED SENTENCES AND COMMA SPLICE ERRORS

Fused sentences and **comma splice errors** occur when two complete sentences are run together. A fused sentence has no punctuation between the two complete sentences.

FUSED: ***Isabel ran down the corridor she did not know where she was going.***

A comma splice error has a comma between the two complete sentences.

COMMA SPLICE: ***Isabel ran down the corridor, she did not know where she was going.***

To correct the errors, first identify the two complete sentences. Then you can fix them in one of four ways.

1. Add a period.

   Isabel ran down the corridor. She did not know where she was going.
2. Add a semicolon.

   Isabel ran down the corridor; she did not know where she was going.
3. Add a comma and a coordinating conjunction.

   Isabel ran down the corridor, but she did not know where she was going.
4. Add a subordinating conjunction to one sentence.

   Although Isabel ran down the corridor, she did not know where she was going. [If you introduce the sentence with a dependent clause, put a comma after the introductory clause.]

19b AGREEMENT ERRORS

In English grammar, subjects agree with their verbs and pronouns with their antecedents.

19b-1 SUBJECT-VERB AGREEMENT

Subjects and verbs agree in number; a singular subject takes a singular verb, and a plural subject takes a plural verb.

PRACTICE 19.1

Fragments, Fused Sentences, and Comma Splice Errors

Identify and correct the sentence structure errors in the following passage. Mark all fragments (frag), fused sentences (FS), and comma splice errors (CS).

> Isabel never forgot her car keys, they were always clipped securely to her belt. Always handy. She was surprised and annoyed that she had lost them, moreover, she was late for her practice. Isabel, not believing she was in such a crunch. She checked the ground near her car, then she bolted for the building. As she ran down the corridor, checking the floors and looking into classrooms. She heard the clanking of metal on metal. In front of her was her little sister Molly, Molly had a grin on her face as she jangled the keys. "I guess you can give me that ride now," Molly said, "Let's go, you don't want to be late for practice."

Singular Subject and Verb: ***Chris runs* three campaigns at the same time.**

A verb agrees with the subject of the sentence, not with the noun in an intervening prepositional phrase.

> ***One* of the boys *runs* the antismoking campaign.** [The subject is *one*, not the noun *boys* in the prepositional phrase *of the boys*.]

Plural Subject and Verb: ***Chris and Jason run* three campaigns together.**

■ **Compound Subject** A verb that agrees with a **compound subject** joined by *and* is usually plural.

> ***Christopher and Jason run* the campaign.** [The compound subject is *Christopher and Jason*.]

A verb agreeing with a compound subject that is preceded by *each* or *every* is singular.

> ***Each* boy and girl *is* a good organizer.**

When a compound subject is joined by *or* or *nor,* the verb agrees with the subject closest to it.

> ***Neither* Christopher *nor* the other *boys run* the campaign in a vacuum.** [*Boys* is the subject closest to the verb, so the verb is plural.]

■ **Collective Noun** A verb agreeing with a **collective noun** (a noun that represents a group but functions as a single entity) is singular. Some examples of collective nouns are *audience, committee, jury, family*, and *group*.

> **The antismoking *committee runs* a fundraiser each year.**

■ **Indefinite Pronoun** Agreement of verbs with **indefinite pronouns** can be confusing. These three rules govern the agreement of indefinite pronouns and verbs.

1. Some indefinite pronouns always take singular verbs; *each, everyone, everybody, everything, either, neither, anyone, anybody, anything, one, no one, nobody, nothing, someone, somebody,* and *something* act as third-person singular pronouns.

   ***Someone has* to run this campaign.**

   ***One* of the boys *is* going to be the high school liaison.**

2. Some indefinite pronouns always take plural verbs; *many, most, both, few*, and *several* are plural in meaning and thus take plural verbs.

   ***Many are* go-getters, but *few are* as enthusiastic as they.**
   ***Several are* extraordinarily talented.**

3. Some indefinite pronouns can be either singular or plural, depending on the context. These indefinite pronouns include *all, any, none,* and *some.*

   S V
   ***All* of the boys *are* qualified to run the campaign.** [In this case, *all* refers to *boys*, which is plural.]

   S V
   ***All* the pie *has* been eaten.** [In this case, *all* refers to *pie*, which is singular.]

19b-2 PRONOUN-ANTECEDENT AGREEMENT

Pronouns must agree in person (first, second, third), gender (male, female), and number (singular, plural) with the nouns or other pronouns they refer to in the sentence. (In pronoun use, **person** refers to the use of *I* or *we* for first person, *you* for second person, and *he, she, it,* or *they* for third person.)

The nouns or pronouns that pronouns refer to are called their **antecedents**. The general rule is that pronouns refer to the closest already-named noun. As a writer, you have to be sure that the pronoun reference is both unambiguous and in agreement.

■ **Ambiguous Pronoun** An **ambiguous pronoun reference** confuses the reader as to whom or what the pronoun refers.

AMBIGUOUS: When Christopher asked Jason to run the campaign, ***he* blushed.** [Since *he* could refer to either man, it is not clear who blushed.]

CLEAR: When Christopher asked Jason to run the campaign, ***Jason* blushed.**

Ambiguity also occurs when pronouns do not refer to anything that has been named in the sentence. Usually the ambiguous pronouns are *it, this, that,* or *which.* In these cases, substitute clear nouns for the ambiguous pronouns.

AMBIGUOUS: The campaign was funny and irreverent. ***They* hung *it* in the student union and put *it* on the campus radio station.**

CLEAR: The campaign was funny and irreverent. ***The committee members* hung *a poster* in the student union and put *an ad* on the campus radio station.**

■ **Agreement in Person** Make sure the pronoun agrees in person (first, second, or third) with its antecedent. Do not, for example, mix a third-person antecedent with a second-person pronoun.

INCORRECT: ***Students* should bring *your* good ideas to the meeting.**

CORRECT: ***Students* should bring *their* good ideas to the meeting.**

■ **Agreement in Gender and Gender-Equal Pronouns** Pronouns and their antecedents have to agree in gender. Male antecedents require *his* as the pronoun referent; female antecedents require *her*. This rule does not usually pose a problem unless you get into the tricky area of deciding whether to refer to a mixed-gender group as male or female. Since you want to be both clear and accurate, the most

PRACTICE 19.2

Agreement

Identify and correct the agreement errors in the following passage. Mark and correct all errors in subject-verb agreement (s-v agr) and pronoun-antecedent agreement (p-a agr).

> Today, a collegewide coalition of student activists meet to launch their anti-smoking campaign. The two organizers, one a sophomore and one a junior, speaks at noon. The event is open to anyone who are students at this college.
>
> Each committee member have created a public awareness poster or radio spot that best expresses his position on the antismoking issue. It should be relevant and appeal to students. Some students have written radio spots; others have drawn posters; someone have even created a television storyboard.
>
> After the presentation, they will vote for the best one. Either one student or two has a chance to win a $50 prize. The best reward, of course, is a heightened awareness of its dangers.

sensible way to solve this problem is either to change the pronoun and its antecedent to their plural forms or to use the slightly longer, but equally acceptable, *his or her*.

PLURAL: ***People brought their* best ideas.**

GENDER EQUAL: ***Each person* brought *his or her* best idea.**

INCORRECT: ***Each person* brought *their* best idea.**

■ **Agreement in Number** Make sure a singular pronoun agrees with a singular antecedent and a plural pronoun with a plural antecedent. If the antecedent is a compound subject joined by *and*, the pronoun will be plural.

> ***Christopher and Jason* did *their* work well.**

If the antecedent is a compound subject joined by *or*, the pronoun will agree with the antecedent closest to the pronoun.

> **Either Christopher or *Jason* did all *his* work.**

If the antecedent is an indefinite pronoun, the pronoun is usually singular. (See the rules for subject-verb agreement in 19b-1 for indefinite pronouns that are singular, plural, or both.)

> ***Either* can do the work as long as *he* is willing.**
>
> **Ask *both* to bring *their* best ideas.**

19c PRONOUN CASE ERRORS

Pronouns change forms depending on whether they are used as subjects or objects in a sentence, or show possession.

Subject Pronouns (SP)	Object Pronouns (OP)	Possessive Pronouns (PP)
I	me	my, mine
you	you	your, yours
he, she, it	him, her, it	his, her, hers, its
we	us	our, ours
they	them	their, theirs
who/whoever	whom/whomever	whose

19c-1 SUBJECT PRONOUNS

Subject pronouns (also known as **nominative pronouns**) substitute for nouns that are subjects in clauses and sentences, are appositives of words in the subject case (17b-3), or are subject complements (nouns that come after linking verbs and rename the subjects). (See 17b-2.) A pronoun can be the subject of the sentence.

> ***He* plays lead guitar in the band.** [*He* is the subject of the verb *plays*.]
>
> ***They* are booked for the next three weekends.** [*They* is the subject of the verb *are*.]

The pronoun can serve as an appositive.

We fans go to all of the shows. [*We* is the appositive of the subject noun *fans.*]

The pronoun can be used as a predicate noun.

The most ardent fan is *she*. [*She* is the subject complement of the noun *fan.*]

It was *they* who began the new sound in popular music. [*They* is the subject complement of the pronoun *it*.]

19c-2 OBJECT PRONOUNS

Object pronouns substitute for nouns that are direct or indirect objects, the objects of prepositions, or appositives of nouns in the objective case. Pronouns can be direct or indirect objects.

IO
The usher gave *us* our programs. [*Us* is the indirect object.]

IO DO
The usher gave *it* to us. [*It* is the direct object.]

A pronoun can serve as the object of a preposition.

My little sister sat *between* my friend and *me*. [*Me* is the object of the preposition *between.*]

An object pronoun can be an appositive.

The lead guitarist sang directly to *us* fans. [*Us* is the appositive of the noun *fans.*]

19c-3 WHO AND WHOM/WHOEVER AND WHOMEVER

Knowing that the pronouns *who* and *whoever* are subject pronouns and *whom* and *whomever* are object pronouns should help you figure out how to use these pronouns correctly.

Greg is the drummer *who* plays with the band. [*Who* is the subject of the verb *plays.*]

The manager hires *whoever* has talent and drive. [*Whoever* is the subject of the verb *has.*]

Greg is the drummer *whom* Tess loves. [*Whom* is the direct object of the verb *loves.*]

Greg is the drummer to *whom* Tess wrote a fan letter. [*Whom* is the object of the preposition *to.*]

Tess contacts *whomever* she admires. [*Whomever* is the direct object of the verb *admires.*]

Sometimes the choice between *who* and *whom* can be confusing when words or phrases come between the subject pronoun *who* and its verb.

PARENTHETICAL
Tess is the fan *who* we all agree is most knowledgeable about the music. [The words *we all agree* form a parenthetical expression that interrupts the sentence. *Who* is the subject of the verb *is.*]

Choosing between *who/whoever* and *whom/whomever* in prepositional phrases can also be tricky. Most of the time, a pronoun in a prepositional phrase takes the object form.

> **To *whom* should Tess give the tickets?** [*Whom* is the object of the preposition *to*.]

However, when the prepositional phrase includes a clause, the rule changes. The pronoun after the preposition becomes the subject of the dependent clause, and the entire clause functions as the object of the preposition. The correct pronoun form should be *who* or *whoever.*

OBJECT OF PREPOSITION
PREP. S V V

> **Tess wanted to speak with *whoever* could get her an autograph.** [*Whoever* becomes the subject of the verb phrase *could get.* The entire noun dependent clause *whoever could get her an autograph* becomes the object of the preposition *with.*]

OBJECT OF PREPOSITION
PREP. S V

> **The band gave autographs to *whoever* waited at the stage door.** [*Whoever* becomes the subject of the verb *waited.* The entire noun dependent clause *whoever waited at the stage door* becomes the object of the preposition *to.*]

19c-4 POSSESSIVE PRONOUNS

Possessive pronouns, like possessive nouns, show ownership.

> **Coach *Brown's* team was not ready for the game.** [*Brown's* is a possessive noun.]
> ***His* team was dispirited because of *its* losses.** [*His* and *its* are possessive pronouns.]

When they show possession, personal pronouns and the relative pronoun *who* do not use apostrophes. *My, mine, our, ours, your, yours, his, her, hers, its, their, theirs,* and *whose* are already in the possessive form. (See 18e-1 for apostrophe use with possessive nouns and indefinite pronouns.) Be careful not to mix up the possessive form of these pronouns with contractions of pronouns and verbs:

it + is = it's   *you + are = you're*
who + is = who's   *they + are = they're*

POSSESSIVE PRONOUN: Give the team ***its* due.**
PRONOUN-VERB CONTRACTION: ***It's* time to look at the bright side.**
POSSESSIVE PRONOUN: This is the team ***whose* efforts have been greatest.**
PRONOUN-VERB CONTRACTION: Jake is the player ***who's* most improved.**
POSSESSIVE PRONOUN: ***Your* hard work has paid off.**
PRONOUN-VERB CONTRACTION: ***You're* to be congratulated.**
POSSESSIVE PRONOUN: ***Their* teamwork has been exemplary.**
PRONOUN-VERB CONTRACTION: ***They're* proud of all the players this season.**

USAGE TIP Be careful not to confuse *their* and *they're* with the expletive *there: There* are many reasons that *they're* proud of *their* efforts.

PRACTICE 19.3

Pronoun Case

Choose the correct pronoun case from the boldfaced words in the following sentences.

1. **(We/Us)** students decided to hike for a week during the break.
2. The seniors gave the job of organizing the equipment to **(we/us)** sophomores.
3. Graham gave us a lecture about **(his/him)** hiking.
4. The most enthusiastic hiker is **(he/him)**.
5. The student **(who/whom)** was the most experienced will be the leader for the first day.
6. Most of us will follow **(whoever/whomever)** we respect.
7. The job of cook will go to **(whoever/whomever)** can boil water.
8. Hikers **(who/whom)** Graham says are fit can begin **(their/they're/ there)** trek tomorrow.
9. Helena will be one of the hikers **(who/whom)** Graham will train tonight.
10. **("Your/ "You're)** ready to start whenever **(your/you're)** group is ready," he said.

Use the possessive case when a pronoun modifies a gerund (a verbal formed by adding *-ing* to a verb that functions as a noun). (See 17b-3.)

***Their* running has been superb.** [*Their* modifies the gerund *running*.]

No one can fault *his* coaching. [*His* modifies the gerund *coaching*.]

19d VERB TENSE ERRORS

Sometimes verbs can trip you up if you are not careful about the time relationships among events in your writing. Two problem areas are maintaining the correct verb tense progression and using the correct verb tense consistently.

19d-1 VERB TENSE PROGRESSION

Verbs change tense in order to show time relationships among events. The principal verb tenses are listed on this chart.

	Present	**Past**	**Future**
Simple	*I run*	*I ran*	*I will run*
Progressive	*I am running*	*I was running*	*I will be running*
Perfect	*I have run*	*I had run*	*I will have run*

Simple tenses show events occurring in the present, the past, and the future.

PRESENT: **Chris *runs* a good campaign.**

PAST: **Chris *ran* a good campaign.**

FUTURE: **Chris *will run* a good campaign.**

Progressive tenses show an action in progress.

PRESENT: **Chris *is running* a good campaign.**

PAST: **Chris *was running* a good campaign.**

FUTURE: **Chris *will be running* a good campaign.**

Perfect tenses show an action completed prior to another action.

PRESENT: **Chris *has run* a good campaign until today.**

PAST: **Chris *had run* a good campaign until he hit a snag yesterday.**

FUTURE: **Chris *will have run* a good campaign when he finally wins an election.**

19d-2 VERB TENSE CONSISTENCY

To maintain verb tense consistency, do not shift verbs from one tense to another unless you are indicating a time change. Once you choose a verb tense in which to report an event or tell a story, be consistent.

INCORRECT: **When the campaign *was* over, they *feel* satisfied.**

PRACTICE 19.4

Verb Tense Progression

Choose the correct verb tense for each sentence below.

1. After the success of the campaign, Chris **(will run/ will have run)** for office in his public relations organization.
2. Jason **(was/had been)** an officer the year before they mounted the campaign.
3. Right now, Chris and Jason **(are speaking/speak)** to students in the Student Union.
4. In high school Chris and Jason **(belonged/had belonged)** to a PR club.
5. Before they **(graduated/ had graduated/were graduating)**, they **(had won/won/were winning)** a prize for creativity.

PRACTICE 19.5

Verb Tense Consistency

Choose the correct verb tense for the boldfaced verbs in the following sentences.

1. Three students **(worked/work)** for Habitat for Humanity over spring break, according to the Office of Student Services.
2. Community service **(is/was)** an important part of an education at our college.
3. Erica **(teaches/had taught/taught)** school kids in Ecuador last year.
4. The plot of the book **(centers/centered)** around three students who wander into the rain forest.
5. When they returned from spring break, they **(write/wrote)** a report to put on file.

PRACTICE 19.6

Parallelism

Correct any errors in parallelism in the following sentences.

1. The benefits of exercise—improved health, you may lose weight, feeling fit, and you look good—are convincing reasons to work out.

CORRECT: When the campaign ***is*** **over, they will** ***feel*** **satisfied.**

CORRECT: When the campaign ***was*** **over, they** ***felt*** **satisfied.**

Three conventions of verb tense use are as follows.

1. In discussing literary works, use present tense.

   Jonathan Franzen *writes* about the Midwest state of mind.
2. In reporting a story for a newspaper, use past tense.

   Jonathan Franzen *explained* his perspective in a reading last night.
3. In making a generalization, use present tense.

   Jonathan Franzen *writes* postmodern fiction.

19e PARALLELISM

To maintain parallelism or parallel structure in your writing, keep words, phrases, and clauses in the same grammatical form when they are in a series or connected by a coordinating conjunction.

PARALLEL NOUNS: Dana does not eat ***candy, cake,*** **or** ***pasta***.

PARALLEL ADJECTIVES: Dana is ***strong, healthy,*** **and** ***athletic***.

PARALLEL VERBS: Dana ***rides*** **horses,** ***plays*** **basketball, and** ***swims***.

PARALLEL PHRASES: Dana loves ***riding horses, playing basketball,*** **and** ***swimming laps in the pool.*** [parallel gerund phrases]

PARALLEL CLAUSES: ***Dana loves to ride horses,*** **and** ***she loves to play basketball.*** [parallel independent clauses]

FAULTY PARALLELISM: Dana loves ***to ride, play,*** **and** ***swimming***. [*to ride* and *play* are infinitives; *swimming* is a gerund]

Maintain parallel structure in comparisons using *as* or *than*.

NONPARALLEL STRUCTURE: ***Eating healthfully*** **is as important as** ***to play sports.***

PARALLEL STRUCTURE: ***Eating healthfully*** **is as important as** ***playing sports.***

NONPARALLEL STRUCTURE: Dana's ***sports equipment*** **is better than** ***Louise***. [comparing sports equipment to Louise]

PARALLEL STRUCTURE: Dana's ***sports equipment*** **is better than** ***Louise's***. [correctly comparing Dana's equipment to Louise's equipment]

Maintain parallel structure with correlative conjunctions (see 17a-7).

NONPARALLEL STRUCTURE: ***Not only*** **does Dana love to swim** ***but*** **she** ***also*** **is running every day.**

PARALLEL STRUCTURE: ***Not only*** **does Dana love to swim** ***but*** **she** ***also*** **runs every day.**

Usage Tip Use parallel structure to achieve a sense of balance and elegance in your writing. Many memorable lines in literature or speech use this kind of parallel structure or balance: *"Ask not what your country can do for you; ask what you can do for your country."*—John F. Kennedy. *"I have nothing to offer but blood, toil, tears and sweat."*—Winston Churchill.

(*Continued*)

2. Either Hank is running every day or he works out three times a week.
3. A penny saved is a penny you are earning.
4. Benjamin Franklin not only wrote aphorisms but he also was becoming the American ambassador to France.
5. Franklin was a statesman, writer, flew kites, and an inventor.

19f MODIFICATION ERRORS

Modifiers are words, phrases, or clauses that qualify or limit. Modifiers function as adjectives or adverbs (see 17a-4 and 17a-5). Errors occur when modifiers are misplaced or positioned so that they do not clearly refer to the word or phrase they modify.

19f-1 MISPLACED MODIFIERS

Modifiers should appear next to the word(s) they modify. Misplaced modifiers often create confusion and sometimes even unintentional humor.

Misplaced: I rented a movie at the video store ***starring Tom Hanks.*** [*starring Tom Hanks* incorrectly refers to the video store, not the movie]

Correctly Placed: At the video store, I rented a movie ***starring Tom Hanks.***

Misplaced: My friend gave me four dollars to rent the movie ***in quarters.*** [*in quarters* incorrectly refers to the movie, not the four dollars]

Correctly Placed: My friend gave me four dollars ***in quarters*** **to rent the movie.**

Modifiers like *only, frequently*, and *sometimes* can be confusing if they are placed in the middle of a sentence; such placement can cause confusion about whether these adverbs are modifying the words that precede them or follow them.

Ambiguous: Tom Hanks plays roles ***frequently*** **portraying a hero.** [*Frequently* can refer to how often Hanks plays roles or to how often he portrays a hero.]

Clear: Tom Hanks ***frequently*** **plays roles portraying a hero.**

Clear: Tom Hanks plays many roles; he portrays a hero ***frequently.***

19f-2 DANGLING MODIFIERS

Dangling modifiers dangle because they have nothing in the sentence to modify. Often, dangling modifiers are introductory participial phrases like *seeing the movie* or infinitive phrases like *to see the movie*. Grammatically, the phrase should modify the noun or pronoun that immediately follows it.

PRACTICE 19.7

Dangling and Misplaced Modifiers

Rewrite the following sentences, identifying and fixing the dangling modifiers (DM) and misplaced modifiers (MM).

1. Seeing the film for the first time, Tom Hanks was perfect in the role.
2. When finding himself alone, a soccer ball became his surrogate friend.
3. Hanks's character dined on fish and coconut milk that he speared in the ocean.
4. After being rescued, raw fish turned his stomach.
5. The camera focused on the lavish buffet of lobster, crabs, and sushi in a tight shot.
6. I eat fish frequently getting an allergic reaction.

DANGLING MODIFIER: ***Seeing the movie,* Tom Hanks was extraordinary.** [*Seeing the movie* dangles. This phrase incorrectly modifies *Tom Hanks.*]

CLEAR: ***Seeing the movie,* Gus thought Tom Hanks was extraordinary.** [*Seeing the movie* modifies *Gus.*]

DANGLING MODIFIER: ***To see the movie clearly,* glasses had to be worn.** [*To see the movie clearly* dangles. The phrase incorrectly modifies *glasses.*]

CLEAR: ***To see the movie clearly,* Gus had to wear his glasses.** [*To see the movie clearly* modifies *Gus.*]

19g FREQUENTLY CONFUSED WORDS

Some pairs of words sound enough alike or have such similar spellings or meanings that they may be confusing. This list explains some word pairs that are frequently confused.

- **advice, advise** *Advice* is a noun, and *advise* is a verb.

My counselor *advised* me to listen to his good *advice.*

- **affect, effect** Most of the time *affect* is a verb meaning "to influence."

How much will that C *affect* my final grade?

Most of the time *effect* is a noun meaning "the result."

What is the *effect* of that C on my final grade?

Used as a verb, *affect* means "to put on a false show."

He *affected* an air of boredom.

Effect can be also a verb, meaning "to cause."

He *effected* the change of mood by laughing loudly.

- **among, between** Generally, use *among* when referring to many things and *between* when referring to two things.

Kenza divided the candy *between* the two kids; they divvied it up *among* their friends.

- **anxious, eager** Use *anxious* to suggest worry and *eager* to suggest anticipation.

Isabella is *eager* to start her new job but *anxious* about making a mistake.

■ **as, like** *As* is a subordinating conjunction. It introduces a subordinate clause.

Jose looks *as if* he saw a ghost.

Like is a preposition. It is followed by the object of a preposition.

He looks *like* a ghost.

■ **bad, badly** *Bad* is an adjective, and *badly* is an adverb. Use the adjective form *bad* after a linking verb.

Scott felt *bad* because he had the flu. [*Bad* describes his state of being.]

Scott played the piano *badly*. [*Badly* describes how he *played* the piano.]

■ **beside, besides** *Beside* means "next to." *Besides* means "also" or "other than."

I put my book *beside* the table.

***Besides*, I wanted to read it before I went to sleep.**

Nothing *besides* a nap would do.

■ **censor, censure** Both words can be nouns or verbs. As a noun, *censor* names the person who deletes objectionable material, and as a verb *censor* is the act of deleting that material.

The *censor censored* my mail.

As a noun, *censure* means "disapproval," and as a verb it means "to disapprove."

The student body *censured* Gene for plagiarism.

Gene took the *censure* seriously.

■ **continual, continuous** *Continual* means "repeated often," while *continuous* means "ongoing."

Shane had *continual* run-ins with his professor.

Their *continuous* argument about grades gave us all headaches.

■ **different from, different than** Generally speaking, use *different from*.

This movie is significantly *different from* the book.

■ **disinterested, uninterested** A *disinterested* person is impartial; an *uninterested* person is bored.

Fatima was *uninterested* in the lecture, but she wanted a *disinterested* person to judge whether the professor was boring.

■ **elicit, illicit** *Elicit* is a verb that means "to draw out"; *illicit* is an adjective that means "illegal."

The detective *elicited* a confession from the crook, but since his words were recorded on an *illicit* wiretap, the confession was inadmissible in court.

■ **farther, further** In formal writing, use *farther* to suggest distance and *further* to suggest degree.

Augie lives *farther* from school than you.

Callie has *further* research to do on her paper.

■ **fewer, less** Use *fewer* with countable items and *less* with quantities or amounts.

The store sold *fewer* quarts of milk this week.

They now have *less* milk in stock.

■ **good, well** Generally speaking, *good* is an adjective and *well* is an adverb.

Lila had a *good* plan that she executed *well*. [*Good* modifies the noun *plan*; *well* modifies the infinitive (a verb form) *executed*.]

After a linking verb, use the predicate adjective *good*.

Although I have attended only one lecture, Professor Bloom seems *good*.

When referring to health, *well* functions as an adjective.

Although she was ill for a while, now Professor Bloom seems *well*.

■ **hanged, hung** Use *hanged* with bodies (executions) and *hung* with objects (curtains).

In old westerns, murderers were *hanged* at dawn.

We *hung* our clothes in the closet.

■ **imply, infer** Both words are verbs, but *imply* means "to suggest" and *infer* means "to deduce" or "to draw a conclusion."

I *implied* that we should be friends, but he *inferred* that I never wanted to see him again.

■ **irregardless, regardless** *Irregardless* is considered nonstandard usage in all situations. Always use *regardless*.

I want to see you *regardless* of the consequences.

■ **its, it's** *Its* is a possessive pronoun, and *it's* is a contraction of *it* and *is*.

The clock had a smudge on *its* face.

***It's* time to go.**

■ **lay, lie** *Lay* is a transitive verb that takes a direct object. It means "to put something down." *Lie* is an intransitive verb that means "to recline."

I *lay* the book on the table.

When I am tired, I *lie* down.

The two verbs use the following forms (see 19d-1).

Present	Past	Perfect	Progressive
Lay	*laid*	*laid*	*laying*
Lie	*lay*	*lain*	*lying*

■ **lend, loan** Use *lend* as a verb and *loan* as a noun.

Jacob had to take out a *loan* because Tony would not *lend* him a dime.

■ **media, medium** *Media* is the plural form of *medium*.

The film *medium* is the most dynamic, but all the visual *media* interest Vassili.

■ **prejudice, prejudiced** *Prejudice* is a noun; *prejudiced* is an adjective.

Jonah had a great deal of *prejudice* against *prejudiced* people.

■ **principal, principle** Use *principal* for a person who is the head of an organization, such as the principal of a school. When used as an adjective, *principal* also means the main or most important element. *Principle* is a truth, a tenet, or a belief.

Mr. Leavy is the *principal* of my sister's high school. [head of school]
The *principal* crop is wheat. [main]

The university's hiring policy is based on the *principles* of diversity and equality. [tenets]

■ **proved, proven** Use *proved* as the past participle form of *prove* and *proven* as the adjective form.

His *proven* [adjective] **record of support for tax cuts *has proved*** [past participle] **that he is the best candidate for mayor.**

■ **quote, quotation** *Quote* is a verb, *quotation* a noun.

Always *quote* accurately from all *quotations.*

Media writers sometimes use *quote* as a noun.

The reporter got some good *quotes* for her article.

■ **raise, rise** *Raise* is a transitive verb, so it always takes a direct object. It means "to cause something to move upward" or "to bring up." *Rise* is an intransitive verb that means "to move upward."

Mama *raised* her kids to *rise* when grownups entered the room.

■ **sit, set** *Sit* is an intransitive verb meaning "to take a seat." *Set* is a transitive verb that takes a direct object and means "to put something down."

PRACTICE 19.8

Frequently Confused Words

To review confusing word pairs, choose the correct word in the following sentences.

1. (To/too/two) often we are so (eager/anxious) to begin a new adventure that we forget to (sit/set) for a while and think about (its/it's) possible outcomes.

(*Continued*)

2. (There/their/they're) are many questions to (rise/raise) before (your/you're) able to choose wisely.
3. For example, (who/whom) do you want to accompany you when you (sit/set) off?
4. (Who/Whom) is your choice of companion when you feel (bad/badly) or when things don't go (well/good)?
5. I would want to be with someone with a (proved, proven) track record, someone (who/whom/that/which) would rather be safe (than/then) take risks (regardless/irregardless) of the consequences.
6. I don't mean to (imply/infer) that I am (prejudice/prejudiced) against risk-takers. I just feel (like/as if) I want to have a cool head around me when I'm about to (lay/lie) my life on the line.
7. My (principal, principle) goals are to experience life, to go (further, farther) than people expect, and to make (fewer/less) mistakes than those who have gone before me.

When you *sit* on your chair, please *set* the teacup on the table.

■ **than, then** Use *than* with comparisons and *then* to indicate time.

She is taller *than* her mother.

She grew as tall as her mother, and *then* she grew taller.

■ **their/there/they're** Each of these homonyms has a different meaning. *Their* is a pronoun that indicates possession. *There* is an adverb that indicates place. *They're* is a contraction of *they* and *are*.

The children have *their* father's eyes.

Put the book down *there*.

***They're* free to leave whenever they desire.**

■ **to, too, two** Each of these homonyms has a different meaning. *To* is a preposition (to the store). *Too* is an adverb meaning "also" or "many." *Two* is the number after *one*.

We went *to* the all-you-can-eat buffet.

We ate *too* much.

***Two* of us had to lie down for an hour.**

■ **who, whom** Use *who* or *whom* when referring to people; use *that* or *which* when referring to objects.

Who functions as a subject in a sentence or clause, and *whom* functions as an object in a sentence or clause.

***Who* is this masked man?** [*Who* is the subject of the sentence.]

He is the masked man *who* saved your life. [*Who* is the subject of the dependent clause.]

***Whom* do you trust?** [*Whom* is the direct object.]

He is the man *whom* I trust with my life. [*Whom* is the direct object in the dependent clause.]

■ **who's, whose** *Who's* is a contraction of *who is*, and *whose* is a possessive pronoun.

***Whose* turn is it to see the man *who's* so ill?**

■ **your, you're** *Your* is a possessive pronoun; *you're* is a contraction of *you are*.

***You're* a person who likes *your* food prepared well.**

20

Martin Lehmann/
Shutterstock.com

Trouble Spots for Nonnative Speakers of English

If you are not a native speaker of English, you have undoubtedly grappled with the thousands of ways English differs from your language in vocabulary, syntax, punctuation, and grammar. Many comprehensive handbooks and Web sites exist for learning English and the rules that govern its grammar. One of the best handbooks is *Keys for Writers*, Sixth Edition, by Ann Raimes *(Cengage, 2011)*. Two good Web sites are <http://www.eslcafe.com> and http://owl.english.purdue.edu

This chapter will help you identify and correct the most common problems that nonnative speakers encounter.

- Nouns and articles
- Verbs and verbals
- Sentence structure
- Idioms

20a NOUNS AND ARTICLES

20a-1 COUNTABLE AND NONCOUNTABLE NOUNS

Countable nouns are specific things that can be counted (one, two, three) and can take a plural form (see 17a-1).

Singular	Plural
one girl	two girls
one room	three rooms
one book	four books

Some quantifiers used with countable nouns are *many, few*, and *a few*.

Noncountable nouns or **mass nouns** cannot be counted and do not have plural forms (see 17a-1).

Correct	Incorrect
advice	advices
gasoline	gasolines
information	informations
wheat	wheats
courage	courages

Some quantifiers used with noncountable nouns are *much, little,* and *a little.* Other noncountable nouns are *furniture, electricity, excitement, jewelry, homework, blood, education, fun, faith, soccer,* and *zoology.*

Some nouns can be either countable or noncountable, depending on their context. When a noun is used in a specific sense, it is countable. The same noun used in a general way is noncountable.

PRACTICE 20.1

Identifying Countable and Noncountable Nouns

Identify the boldfaced words in the following sentences as countable nouns (CN) or noncountable nouns (NCN). Look at the context for nouns that could be either.

1. All my money is in euros.
2. After Josh saw the movie, he decided to major in film.
3. Marie watched the scenery go by as she traveled across the country.
4. The heat on the bus was set far too high.
5. Claudia packed her clothing: dresses, skirts, and sweaters.

Countable	**Noncountable**
The perfume comes in three *fragrances.*	The roses have a lovely *fragrance.*
Three *hairs* turned gray overnight.	Sena's *hair* is short and black.
Boiling and freezing are two specific *temperatures.*	The *temperature* outside is freezing.

20a-2 ARTICLES

To figure out whether to use an **article**—*a, an, the*—in front of a noun, follow these guidelines.

Generally speaking, use *a* or *an* with a nonspecific reference and *the* with specific references.

***A firefighter* has a dangerous job.** [refers to any firefighter]

***The firefighter* suffered from smoke inhalation.** [refers to a specific firefighter]

Use *a* or *an* for nonspecific references to singular countable nouns. Use *a* before words that begin with consonant sounds: *a bird, a dog, a plane.* Use *an* before words that begin with vowel sounds: *an eagle, an insult, an airplane, an hour.*

Kirsten should buy *a dog* to keep her company.

Brendan bought *an angora scarf* to keep him warm.

Use *the* in these cases.

- A specific reference to a noun previously mentioned

Kirsten bought a dog. She named *the dog* Fergie.

- A specific reference to a noun known by the writer and reader

Brendan put *the scarf* around his neck.

- A reference to an entire class of things

***The clothing industry* is suffering from the recession.**

***The boxer* is a noble breed of dog.**

- An adjective in the superlative

That line of clothing is *the warmest.*

My dog Otis was *the best* in the litter.

- A reference to a noun followed by a modifying phrase or clause

***The clothing* that is sold here is made of natural fibers.** [*That is sold here* is a clause modifying *clothing.*]

Holly is *the dog* down the street. [*Down the street* is a prepositional phrase modifying *dog.*]

PRACTICE 20.2

Articles

In the following blanks, put in the correct article: *a, an,* or *the.* If an article is not needed, put an X in the blank.

1. __________ English professor gave me __________ grammar lesson about __________ use of __________ articles.
2. __________ old proverb says, "__________ beauty is in __________ eye of __________ beholder."
3. Rick purchased __________ new notebook for class, but then he discovered that he had bought __________ wrong size.
4. Julie gave __________ ticket to the show to __________ Mother.
5. My adviser gave me __________ useful advice about __________ field I want to study.

- A reference to a plural proper noun (a noun that names a specific person, place, or organization)

  Kirsten memorized *the U.S. presidents*.

  Brendan took Otis hiking in *the Rocky Mountains.*

Use no article at all in these cases.

- A nonspecific reference to a plural countable or noncountable noun

  Susan and Rebecca bought *camping supplies: raisins, protein bars, and freeze-dried apricots.* [All nouns are plural countable nouns.]

  Susan and Rebecca bought *camping equipment: tents, poles, stoves, and sleeping bags.* [*Camping equipment* is a plural noncountable noun.]

- Most proper nouns

  Lettie* gave the book to *Mother.

  Habitat for Humanity* will be building houses in *Central America.

- A generalization about a plural countable noun

  ***Books* are my passion.**

  Trousers* are warmer than *skirts.

20b VERBS AND VERBALS

You might want to review the sections on transitive verbs, intransitive verbs, linking verbs, verb tenses, predicates, verb moods (see 17a-3), and verbal phrases (see 17b-3).

20b-1 VERB COMPLEMENTS

A complete predicate consists of a verb and its complements. **Complements** are nouns or adjectives that can function as direct objects, indirect objects, object complements, or subject complements (see 17b-2 and the discussion in 20c-1).

Hector *recommended going to the theater tonight.* [*Recommended* is the verb; *going to the theater tonight* is the complement of the verb.]

Verb complements can be

- Gerunds (verb + *-ing): running, laughing, jumping*
- Infinitives (*to* + verb): *to run, to laugh, to jump*
- Infinitives with the *to* omitted: *run, laugh, jump*

Gerunds and infinitives are not true verbs but are instead verbals created from parts of verbs that function as other parts of speech (nouns, adjectives, or adverbs). The following guidelines will help you decide when to use each form.

Use the gerund form but not the infinitive form as verb complements after these verbs:

acknowledge	appreciate	can't help	delay
admit	avoid	consider	deny
advise	be	consist of	depend on
detest	imagine	quit	suggest
discuss	insist on	recall	talk about
dislike	keep	recommend	tolerate
enjoy	miss	regret	
escape	postpone	resist	
finish	practice	risk	

CORRECT: **Jean *avoids running* in the dark.**

CORRECT: **She *considers going* to the gym at night.**

INCORRECT: **Jean avoids *to run* in the dark.**

INCORRECT: **She considers *to go* to the gym at night.**

Use the to + verb infinitive form, not the gerund form, as verb complements after these verbs.

afford	demand	need	threaten
agree	expect	offer	venture
ask	fail	plan	wait
attempt	hesitate	prepare	want
beg	hope	pretend	wish
bother	intend	promise	
choose	learn	refuse	
claim	like	seem	
consent	manage	struggle	
decide	mean	tend	

CORRECT: **Max *demanded to go* with his cousins.**

CORRECT: **Jack *begged to join* them also.**

INCORRECT: **Max *demanded going* with his cousins.**

INCORRECT: **Jack *begged joining* them also.**

PRACTICE 20.3

Verb Complements

Fill in the blanks with the correct form of the verb: gerund (*-ing*), infinitive (with *to*), or infinitive (without *to*).

1. When her family arrived for a visit, Maria wanted (take) __________ them to a wonderful restaurant.
2. Traveling by train across the country, Thom appreciated (see) __________ the vastness of the plains.
3. Nicole could not begin (understand) __________ what I was saying until she took off her headphones.
4. Jacques let his sales clerk (take) __________ a day off from work.
5. The dog threatened (bite) __________ José if he did not back off.

Use the to + verb infinitive form or the gerund form as verb complements after these verbs.

begin	continue
cannot stand	dread
hate	start
like	try
love	

CORRECT: **Fwar began *to cook* the dinner.**

CORRECT: **Fwar *began cooking* the dinner.**

CORRECT: **David *tried to help*.**

CORRECT: **David *tried helping*.**

Use the infinitive form without the *to* as a verb complement after these verbs only when the verb is followed by a noun or pronoun.

have	help	let	make

CORRECT: **Lucia *let* all the kids *cook* a dish.**

CORRECT: **Hank *helped* Lucia *set* the table.**

INCORRECT: **Lucia *let* all the kids *to cook* a dish.**

INCORRECT: **Hank *helped* Lucia *to set* the table.**

20b-2 MODAL AUXILIARY VERBS

Modal auxiliary verbs are *will, would, can, could, shall, should, may, might,* and *must.* These verbs are used to show conditions such as possibility, ability, permission, assumption, necessity, and obligation (see 17a-3).

can: ability

could: polite question or conditionality

may: permission or possibility

might: permission or possibility

must: necessity or logical assumption

shall: polite question or intention

should: advisability or expectation

will: intention

would: polite question or conditionality

Modal auxiliary verbs do not change form and are always followed by the simple form of a verb.

CORRECT: **Mac *may go* to the movies.**

INCORRECT: **Mac *may to go* to the movies.**

INCORRECT: **Mac *may going* to the movies.**

Use only one modal at a time. To combine modals with other words that express conditions, use phrases such as *be able to*, *be allowed to*, or *have to*.

INCORRECT: **If they are good, the children *might could* get a treat.**

CORRECT: **If they are good, the children *might be allowed* to get a treat.**

Use *will* or *shall* in the present tense and *would* in the past tense to indicate intention.

We *will* finish our work quickly.

We said that we *would* do it quickly.

Shall is usually used in polite questions.

***Shall* we go?**

Use *can* in the present tense or *could* in the past tense to indicate ability.

If we hurry, we *can* make the show.

We *could* not go because the car had broken down.

Use *may, might, can*, or *could* in the present tense and *could* or *might* in the past tense to indicate permission or possibility.

You *may* go only if the weather holds.

The girls *might* go together, or they might go separately. [present]

The girls *might* have gone if the weather had been good. [past]

Use *would* or *could* to ask a polite question or to indicate conditionality.

***Would* you be able to attend my dinner?** [question]

***Could* you let me know as soon as possible?** [question]

Erin *would* go if Amy went with her. [conditionality]

Sue *could* go also to make it more fun. [conditionality]

Use *should* to indicate advisability or expectation.

John thought that they *should* all go together to save money. [advisability]

They *should* all arrive momentarily. [expectation]

Use *must* to indicate necessity or to make a logical assumption.

John thought that they *must* all go together to save money. [necessity]

They *must* have all left together since they are all here now. [logical assumption]

20b-3 PHRASAL VERBS

Some verbs combine with prepositions or adverbs to create new meanings. When combined in this way, prepositions and adverbs are called **particles**, and they no longer function as prepositions or adverbs. These two- or three-word verbs can be confusing since their meaning is often very different from the meaning of the original

PRACTICE 20.4

Modal Auxiliary Verbs

Rewrite the following sentence using the appropriate modal auxiliary verb for the conditions listed below: Jesse rides horses.

Example: Indicate that Jesse has permission from her mother to go riding this afternoon.

Her mother says that Jesse *may* go riding this afternoon.

1. Indicate that Jesse expects to go riding this afternoon.
2. Indicate that Jesse asked permission to go riding.
3. Indicate that Jesse has the ability to ride horses.
4. Indicate that Jesse's horseback riding depends on whether her mother can take her to the stables.
5. Indicate that it is necessary for Jesse to ride today if she wants to be in the show.

verbs. For example, as an active verb *look* means *to gaze.* However, when you add the preposition *over* to form *look over*, the meaning changes to *review*.

Larry is going to *look over* his notes before the test.

When *for* is added to *look*, it creates *look for*, which means *to seek*.

Larry will *look for* an easy way to memorize the equations.

The following list shows some of these two- and three-word verbs.

Verb	Phrasal Verb	Example
break	break up (separate)	Donald and Daisy *broke up* last night.
	break down (cry)	Daisy tried to be brave, but she *broke down.*
	break down (fail to function)	I guess their communication *broke down.*
bring	bring up (mention)	Fred *brought up* a problem.
come	come across (discover)	Elisa *came across* those old photographs.
	come over (visit)	We plan to *come over* tonight to see them.
	come up with (develop)	They want to *come up with* a way to preserve the photographs.
hang	hang on (persist)	I am sure I can *hang on* until summer.
look	look for (seek)	The police *looked for* a solution to the crime.
	look over (examine)	They *looked over* all the evidence.
	look up to (admire)	The officers *looked up to* their chief.
	look down on (scorn)	They looked *down on* lawbreakers.
put	put on (don)	Izzy *put on* her dancing shoes.
	put off (postpone)	Unfortunately, they *put off* the show.
	put up with (endure)	She *put up with* our teasing.
run	run across (encounter)	Cindy *ran across* her cousin Lionel.
	run out of (use up)	Soon she *ran out of* things to say.

Phrasal verbs can be transitive and take a direct object, or they can be intransitive and not take a direct object (see 17a-3, 17b-2, 17b-3).

Put on is a transitive phrasal verb.

Isabella *put on* a dress. [*Dress* is the direct object of the verb *put on*.]

Come over is an intransitive phrasal verb.

Isabella plans to *come over* tonight. [no direct object]

When a phrasal verb is transitive, the particle can sometimes be placed after the direct object, separated from the verb.

Isabella *put* a dress *on*.

They *looked* all the evidence *over*.

20c SENTENCE STRUCTURE

English sentences have a great deal of variety, but most begin with one of the five basic sentence patterns. By adding words, phrases, and clauses, you can modify these basic patterns.

20c-1 BASIC SENTENCE PATTERNS

English sentences have both subjects and predicates. The subject is the agent of the action, the person or thing acting in the sentence. The subject can be a single word, a phrase, a clause, or a string of these elements. The predicate is an assertion about what that subject does and always includes a verb (See also 17b-1).

SUBJECT PREDICATE
Students study. [The subject is *students*; the predicate is *study*.]

SUBJECT PREDICATE
All the *students* in my class *study* extremely hard for tests. [The complete subject is *all the students in my class*; the complete predicate is *study extremely hard for tests*.]

Subjects and predicates combine to form sentences that fit into a number of predictable patterns (See also 17b-2).

- **Subject + Intransitive Verb** An intransitive verb does not transmit action to an object or a person: *sleep, fall, go.*

S VI
We *went*. [*We* is the subject; *went* is the intransitive verb.]

S VI
Our whole family *slept* at Grandmother's house. [*Family* is the subject; *slept* is the intransitive verb.]

- **Subject + Transitive Verb + Direct Object** A transitive verb transmits the action of the subject to an object or person. The direct object is a noun, pronoun, or noun phrase that receives the action of a transitive verb. It often answers the question *what?* or *whom?* after the verb.

PRACTICE 20.5

Phrasal Verbs

Identify the complete phrasal verbs—the verbs and their particles—in the following sentences. Note whether the phrasal verb is transitive (takes a direct object) or intransitive (does not take a direct object).

1. Although he wanted to study in India, Francisco had to turn the offer down.
2. He looked up the information about the university, but the book had left out some steep costs.
3. Since he hated to call his farewell party off, however, Francisco told all his friends to come over.
4. In the middle of the party, Francisco broke down and told his friends the truth.
5. "I will get over this disappointment," he said, "because I really did not want to give up so many good friendships."

S VT DO
We *brought* a *pie* for dessert. [*Brought* is a transitive verb; *pie* is the direct object that tells *what* we brought.]

S VT DO
Grandmother *put* her best *dishes* on the table. [*Put* is a transitive verb; *dishes* is the direct object that tells *what* Grandmother put on the table.]

- **Subject + Transitive Verb + Indirect Object + Direct Object** The indirect object is a noun, pronoun, or noun phrase that tells *to whom* or *for whom* the verb acts.

S VT IO DO
Uncle Ned gave *me* the biggest piece of pie. [*Me* is the indirect object; it tells *to whom* Uncle Ned gave the piece of pie.]

S VT IO DO
I gave the large brown *dog* the rest of my food. [*Dog* is the indirect object.]

- **Subject + Transitive Verb + Direct Object + Object Complement** The object complement describes or renames the direct object.

S VT DO OC
All that food made the entire family *sleepy*. [*Sleepy* is the object complement; it describes the direct object, *family*.]

S VT DO OC
Grandmother called us *couch potatoes*. [*Couch potatoes* is the object complement; it renames the direct object, *us*.]

- **Subject + Linking Verb + Subject Complement** The subject complement describes or renames the subject after a linking verb. Linking verbs connect subjects to complements. The most common linking verbs are *be, became, appear, feel,* and *seem.*

S LV SC
Uncle Ned became *cranky*. [*Cranky* is the subject complement; it describes Uncle Ned after the linking verb, *became*.]

S LV SC
My brother Don is *his favorite nephew*. [*Nephew* is the subject complement; it renames *Don* after the linking verb, *is*.]

Usage Tip The verb comes before the subject in a question or when a sentence begins with *there* or *here*:

S LV
Gina *is* a good athlete. [subject + verb]

LV S
Is Gina a good athlete? [verb + subject]

V S
There *are many good athletes* on the team. [verb + subject]

PRACTICE 20.6

Basic Sentence Patterns

Identify the sentences below as one of these patterns:

S + VI (subject + intransitive verb)

S + VT + DO (subject + transitive verb + direct object)

S + VT + IO + DO (subject + transitive verb + indirect object + direct object)

S + VT + DO + OC (subject + transitive verb + direct object + object complement)

S + LV + SC (subject + linking verb + subject complement)

1. John rode his new motorcycle carefully in the traffic.
2. He is a very cautious rider.
3. John gave Fritzi a ride on the back of the motorcycle.
4. Fritzi fell off.
5. Luckily, Fritzi was unhurt.

20c-2 MODIFYING SENTENCE PATTERNS

Once you know these five sentence patterns, you can modify the sentences by adding words, phrases, and clauses. A few guidelines will help you modify the sentences clearly. Since adverbs can be placed in different parts of sentences, they can cause some confusion.

■ **Adverbs** Adverbs and adverb phrases that express time (*today, next week, at four o'clock*) and place (*in the room, outside, in the country*) are placed at the beginning or end of a sentence but not between a verb and a direct object (See also 17a-5).

CORRECT: **The blues singer gave a wonderful performance *yesterday.***

CORRECT: ***Yesterday* the blues singer gave a wonderful performance.**

INCORRECT: **The blues singer gave *yesterday* a wonderful performance.**

CORRECT: **The fans bought her CDs *at the performance.***

CORRECT: ***At the performance,* the fans bought her CDs.**

INCORRECT: **The fans bought *at the performance* her CDs.**

Adverbs of frequency (*always, sometimes, never*) are placed right before the verb they modify.

CORRECT: **We *always* go directly home after the concert.**

INCORRECT: ***Always* we go directly home after the concert.**

Some adverbs of frequency (*often, many times*) can be placed at the end of a sentence.

CORRECT: **We have been to the concert hall *often.***

CORRECT: **We have been to the concert hall *many times.***

Adverbs that modify adjectives or adverbs are placed directly before those adjectives or adverbs. Adverbs that modify sentences or clauses are placed directly before those sentences or clauses.

CORRECT: **Marlene is *extremely* interested in child-care issues.** [modifies the adjective *interested*]

CORRECT: **She works *very* intensely at her job.** [modifies the adverb *intensely*]

CORRECT: ***Fortunately,* she manages her time well.** [modifies the entire sentence]

Some adverbs that modify sentences can be placed after the subject or at the end of the sentence.

Marlene, *fortunately,* manages her time well.
Marlene manages her time well, *fortunately.*

PRACTICE 20.7

Modifying Sentence Patterns

Using the guidelines for modifying sentence patterns, write the following sentences.

1. State when you went to bed last night. Use an adverb of time.
2. State how often you phone your friends. Use an adverb of frequency.
3. Describe your room. Use an adjective phrase.
4. State to whom you gave a gift. Use direct and indirect objects.
5. Explain when you will visit home. Use a subordinate clause.

■ **Adjective Phrases** Adjective phrases are placed after the nouns they modify.

CORRECT: **The museum *recommended by my friend* had a fascinating exhibit.**

INCORRECT: **The *recommended by my friend* museum had a fascinating exhibit.**

CORRECT: **The dinosaurs, *extinct for centuries,* seemed real.**

INCORRECT: **The *extinct for centuries* dinosaurs seemed real.**

■ **Indirect Objects** Indirect objects are placed after the verbs and before the direct objects.

CORRECT: **The guide gave *me* a wonderful tour.** [The indirect object *me* goes after the verb *gave* and before the direct object *wonderful tour*.]

CORRECT: **The audio guide showed *visitors* the major exhibits.** [The indirect object *visitors* goes after the verb *showed* and before the direct object *major exhibits*.]

■ **Pronouns** Pronouns that restate the subject should be omitted (See 17a-2).

CORRECT: **Doug and Alex love baseball.**

INCORRECT: **Doug and Alex *they* love baseball.**

CORRECT: **Erica is a football fan.**

INCORRECT: **Erica *she* is a football fan.**

■ **Subordinating Conjunctions** Subordinating conjunctions (*although, after, since, if*) are not used with coordinating conjunctions (*and, but, for, nor*) (See 17a-7).

CORRECT: Although the storm was over, the waters were still rising.

INCORRECT: ***Although*** the storm was over, ***but*** the waters were still rising.

CORRECT: Since the streets were flooded, the rescue workers rode in boats.

INCORRECT: ***Since*** the streets were flooded, ***and*** the rescue workers rode in boats.

20c-3 REPORTED QUESTIONS AND QUOTATIONS

Questions and quotations can be direct (reported firsthand) or indirect (reported secondhand). The sentence structure changes in these two modes. (See 18f-3 on the punctuation of quotations.)

■ **Quotations** Direct quotations report a speaker's exact words. The words are enclosed in quotation marks. Indirect quotations do not use quotation marks, and the pronouns, verb tense, and time markers shift.

DIRECT QUOTATION: **Joe asked me, *"Are you* ready to party?"**

INDIRECT QUOTATION: **Joe asked me if *I was* ready to party.** [The pronoun shifts from *you* to *I*; the tense shifts from *are* to *was*.]

DIRECT QUOTATION: **The bandleader said, "*We will give* a great show *tomorrow night.*"**

INDIRECT QUOTATION: **The bandleader said that *they would give* a great show *the next night.*** [The pronoun shifts from *we* to *they*; the tense shifts from *will give* to *would give*; the time marker shifts from *tomorrow night* to *the next night.*]

■ **Questions** Reported direct questions use the inverted pattern, verb + subject. Reported indirect questions use the standard subject + verb pattern but omit the question mark.

DIRECT QUESTION: **Ingrid asked Carlos, "Are your parents coming to visit this winter?"**

INDIRECT QUESTION: **Ingrid asked Carlos whether his parents were coming to visit this winter.**

DIRECT QUESTION: **My parents asked me, "Will we stay with you?"**

INDIRECT QUESTION: **My parents asked me if they would stay with me.**

20d IDIOMS

An *idiom* is a common expression whose meaning cannot be understood from the meaning of its individual words. Expressions like *watch your back,* which means "be careful," and *keep an eye on,* which means "watch something," cannot be figured out by looking up each word. Many phrasal verbs (see 20b-3) and prepositional phrases (see 17b-3) are idiomatic expressions.

To master the idioms of English, you have to learn them in context. As you talk with people, listen to the radio, watch films and television, or read, be alert for these expressions and write them down. Many Web sites and handbooks contain lengthy lists of English idioms, and you can look up their meanings or add them to your personal list. A few Web sites you might want to visit are <http://www.eslcafe.com>, and <http://www.comenius.com/idiom/index>.

20d-1 SOME COMMON IDIOMS

This list explains a few of the hundreds of idiomatic expressions in English.

Idiom	Definition	Example
at this point	at this time	*At this point,* he stopped his lecture.
be broke	lack money	Gail could not go to the movies because she *was broke.*
brush up on	review	Steve will *brush up on* verbs before the test.
cut down on	decrease	Hector has to *cut down on* sweets.

PRACTICE 20.8

Reported Questions and Quotations

Change the following direct questions and quotations to indirect questions and quotations.

1. Senator Lopez asked us, "How many of you will vote for me?"
2. The reporter from the *Daily News* said, "The crowd went wild."
3. The police officer told the crowd, "Settle down, or we will ask you to disperse."

Change the following indirect questions and quotations to direct questions and quotations.

4. We told the police that we had just come to see Senator Lopez that evening.
5. The reporter said that he had never seen such an unruly crowd.

drop off	deliver	Kris *dropped off* the sweater you left in her car.
foot the bill	pay	Mike got a raise and will *foot the bill* at the restaurant.
go to pieces	lose emotional control	Olivia *went to pieces* when she lost her wallet.
lose one's temper	get angry	Bad drivers make me *lose my temper.*
mixes up	confuses	Petey always *mixes up* the twins.
on second thought	thinking again	*On second thought,* Rebecca decided to go.
out of the question	not possible	Going out on a school night is *out of the question*.
take turns	alternate	Lily and Cate *took turns* crying.

PRACTICE 20.9

Idiomatic Prepositional Phrases

Fill in the blanks with the correct preposition: *at, in, on,* or *to.*

1. Yesterday ___________ noon, I met my friend Anne ___________ a restaurant ___________ the new mall.
2. We did not like anything ___________ the menu, so we called the server ___________ the table.
3. One of the cooks ___________ the kitchen said she could make us a special meal ___________ one o'clock.
4. We left the restaurant and went ___________ some of the stores ___________ Elm Street. ___________ one o'clock we returned ___________ the restaurant and ate ___________ style.

20d-2 IDIOMATIC PREPOSITIONAL PHRASES

Prepositional phrases are difficult to learn because the same preposition can have different meanings. The phrases *on the boat, on time*, and *on the menu* all use the preposition *on,* but in slightly different ways. It is best to learn prepositional phrases as you learn all idiomatic expressions: as a whole and in context. A few common prepositional phrases will give you a sense of their usage (See also 17b-3).

at	at noon, at the dance, at home, at a glance, at peace
in	in the box, in April, in Asia, in love, in time, in the airplane
on	on top of, on time, on Sunday, on the bed, on Main Street
to	to the store, to bed, to the bottom, to the city, face to face

Credits

TEXT CREDITS

Chapter 1

Pages 18-20: JON PARELES, "Lavish Worlds, and the Headwear to Match" from http://www.nytimes.com/2010/01/22/arts/music/22gaga.html. Reprinted with the permission of PARS International.

Chapter 2

Page 24: Nathan Welton (Student), "I react with a few instinctive ideas."

Page 24: Reprinted by permission of Matt Sato.

Page 24: Reprinted by permission of Arielle Greenleaf.

Page 30: Anne Lamott, "Shitty First Drafts," from Bird by Bird: Some Instructions on Writing and Life, copyright (c) 1994 by Anne Lamott. Used by permission of Pantheon Books, a division of Random House, Inc.

Pages 32-33: Charles Fishman, "Bar None" from "Agenda Items," Fast Company, June 2001, p. 147. Reprinted with permission.

Pages 32-33: Carol Stocker, "House Styles of New England," The Boston Globe, Life at Home, June 5, 2003. Reprinted with permission.

Pages 33-34: Noreen P. Browne, "Anatomy of an Autopsy," Biography Magazine (August 2002): 76. Copyright © 2002 A&E Television Networks. All rights reserved.

Pages 42-44: Simon & Schuster, Inc. Reprinted with the permission of Scribner, an imprint of Simon & Schuster, Inc., from ON WRITING: A MEMOIR OF THE CRAFT by Stephen King. Copyright (c) 2000 by Stephen King. All rights reserved.

Chapter 3

Pages 61-63: Andrew Waite, "Recovery Is Not Something You Get Over," New York Nurse (February 2007). Reprinted with permission from the New York State Nurses Association.

Chapter 4

Pages 75-77: Joel Preston Smith, "Hardscrabble Salvation," from In Good Tilth - November-December 2010. Reprinted with permission.

Chapter 5

Page 117. Reprinted by permission of Yoshi Makishima.

Pages 118-120. Tess Langan, "Looking for Students Like Me!" from The New York Times, November 7, 2010. Reprinted with permission of PARS International.

Pages 122-123: Anny Chih, "The Best Job in the World: In 500 Words or Less," Posted by Anny Chih on annychih.com. Reprinted with permission.

Chapter 6

Pages 130-132: Frederick Hill & Associates. Antonya Nelson, "All Washed Up," as appeared in The New Yorker, April 21 & 28, 2003, p. 152. Reprinted by permission of Frederick Hill Associates.

Page 140: Carolyn T. Hughes, "A Thinking Life: A Conversation With Pete Hamill," Poets & Writers Magazine, September/October 1999. Reprinted by permission of the publisher, Poets & Writers Inc., 90 Broad Street, Suite 2100, New York, NY 10004. www.pw.org.

Page 147: From Bernard Cooper, "Dream House," Harper's Magazine, July 1990.

Pages 154158: Reprinted by permission of David Tankelfsky.

Pages 159-162: Reprinted by permission of Melissa Hochman.

Pages 163-165: From HOLIDAYS ON ICE by David Sedaris. Copyright (c) 1997, 2008 by David Sedaris. Reprinted by permission.

Chapter 7

Pages 175-178: Cynthia Anderson, "Of Carpenters and Scrabble Kings," from Christian Science Monitor November 11, 2006. Reprinted with permission.

Page 187: Reprinted by permission of Yoonie Park.

Page 190: Judith Newman, "Running for Life" from SELF. Reprinted with permission.

Pages 193-196: Jack Falla, "The Top Drill Instructor in Boot Camp," adapted from Campus Voice, August/September 1984. Reprinted with permission.

Pages 197-201: Reprinted by permission of Thanos Matthai.

Pages 201-208: J.R. Moehringer, "A Hidden and Solitary Soldier," from LA Times, January 20, 2002. Reprinted with permission.

Page 191: David Maloof, "Notes for Pan Music," a profile published in the Hampshire Life Magazine section of the Daily Hampshire Gazette, June 27, 1997. Reprinted by permission of the author.

Page 210: Mike Sager, The Marine, Esquire 136, no. 6 (December 2001). Reprinted by permission of the author.

Chapter 8

Pages 218-219: Charles Fishman, "The Scoop on Disney's Dirty Laundry" from The Orlando Sentinal Sunday Magazine, February 4, 1990. Reprinted with permission.

Pages 229-230: Janet Rae-Dupree, "How Bullets Tell a Tale," from US News & World Report, October 21, 2002. Reprinted with permission.

Pages 230-233: Reprinted by permission of Katie Koch.

Pages 233-234: Gunjan Sinha, "Listening to Earwax," from Popular Science, September 2002, p. 31. Reprinted with permission.

Pages 234-236: Lauren Wilcox, "Going with the Grain," from Smithsonian Magazine, September 2007. Reprinted with permission.

Pages 236-237: Charles Fishman, "Mighty Mice," from "Agenda Items," Fast Company, June 2001, p. 147. Reprinted with permission.

Chapter 9

Pages 244-246: Reprinted by permission of Katherine Donnelly.

Pages 258-259: Institute of Medicine, Report Brief of September 2009, "Local Government Actions to Prevent Childhood Obesity." Reprinted with permission.

Pages 264-265: Feiner, Lee. "Strode chases Open dream in qualifying draw." Open Source. 24 August 2010. Reprinted with permission.

Pages 266-268: From Xu, Zeyu, Jane Hannaway, and Colin Taylor. Making a Difference? The Effects of Teach for America in High School. The Urban Institute. 27 March 2008. Reprinted with permission.

Pages 269-272: Lauren McKown, "Bearing the Burden," from The State News, September 23, 2010. Reprinted with permission.

Chapter 10

Pages 282-285: Ty Burr, "Avatar," from The Boston Globe, December 17, 2009. Reprinted with permission of PARS International.

Page 300: Tom McCarthy, excerpt from "The Visitor." Reprinted by permission of Tom McCarthy.

Pages 301-304: From Janet Maslin, "Such a Very Long Way from Duvets to Danger," New York Times, October 15, 1999. Reprinted by permission of PARS International.

From Roger Ebert, Fight Club movie review, from the Roger Ebert column by Pages 304-307: Roger Ebert, copyright © 1999 The Ebert Company, distributed. by Universal Press Syndicate.

Pages 307-309: Reprinted by permission of Ryan Conrath.

Chapter 11

Pages 316-318: Vivian Ho, "The New Trend in College Admissins: Using Social Media."

Pages 335-341: Susan Saulny, "Race Remixed," from New York Times, January 29, 2011. Reprinted by permission of PARS International.

Reprinted by permission of Meredith Jeffries.

Pages 341-347: Reprinted by permission of Meredith Jeffries.

Pages 347-349: Copyright © 2010, NPR®, News report by NPR's Anthony Kuhn was originally broadcast on NPR's All Things Considered® on April 13, 2010, and is used with the permission of NPR. Any unauthorized duplication is strictly prohibited.

Pages 349-357: From MATT RICHTEL, "Growing Up Digital, Wired for Distraction," from The New York Times. Reprinted by permission of PARS International.

Chapter 12

Pages 366-368: Stephen Budiansky, "Math Lessons for Locavores," from The New York Times, August 19, 2010. Reprinted by permission of the author.

Pages 388-390: David Brooks, "Gangsta, in French" from The New York Times, November 10, 2005. Reprinted by permission of PARS International.

Pages 390-393: Jody Rosen, "David Brooks, Playa Hater," from Slate, posted November 10, 2005. Reprinted by permission of PARS International.

Page 394: Philip Babcock, "Falling Standards in Universities," from New York Times Room for Debate, October 11, 2010. Reprinted by permission of the author.

Page 395: Raphael Pope-Sussman, "We Are Not Lazy," from New York Times Room for Debate, October 11, 2010. Reprinted by permission of the author.

Page 395-397: Anya Kamanetz, "With a Job on the Side," from New York Times Room for Debate, October 11, 2010. Reprinted by permission of the author.

Pages 397-401: From Caryl Rivers and Rosalind Chait Barnett, "The Difference Myth," The Boston Globe, October 28, 2007. Reprinted with permission.

Chapter 14

Pages 446-448: Reprinted by permission of Garland Waller.

Pages 466-468: Jessica Hollander (student), "Stopping Teen Dating Violence," Boston Globe, October 3, 2003. Reprinted with permission.

Pages 468-473: Reprinted by permission of Dana Benjamin, Joanna Mayhew, Alexandra Mayer-Hohadahl, and Peter Myers.

Chapter 16

Pages 532-536: Reprinted by permission of Cassandra Lane.

Pages 554-558: Reprinted by permission of Eoin O'Carroll.

PHOTO CREDITS

Front matter: Page v: Segretain/Getty Images; page v: Enrique's Journey © 2002 Los Angles Times. Photos by Don Barletti; page v: TAO Images/SuperStock; page v: Image Source/Aurora Photos; page vi: Luba Lukova; page vi: Tony Law/Redux Pictures; page vi: John Lock/Shutterstock.com.

Chapter 1: Page 1: Segretain/Getty Images; page 2: Arman Zender/Shutterstock.com; page 3 all: Réunion des Musées Nationaux/Art Resource, NY; page 10: Calvin and Hobbes © 1993 Watterson, distributed by Universal Press Syndicate. Reprinted with permission. All rights reserved.; page 17: The Saul Steinberg Foundation/Artists Rights Society (ARS), New York; page 18: Newscom.

Chapter 2: Page 21: Tischenko Irina/Shutterstock.com; page 22: George Booth/Cartoonbank.com; page 25: AP Photo/Carson Walker; page 39: Lebrecht Music and Arts Photo Library/Alamy.

Chapter 3: Page 45: godrick/Shutterstock.com; page 46 all: Winslow Homer, Breezing Up (A Fair Wind), gift of the W.L. and May T. Mellon Foundation, image © 2004 Board of Trustees National Gallery of Art, Washington, DC.; page 48: Solar Photographers.

Chapter 4: Page 65: Nataliya Hora/Shutterstock.com; page 66: david pearson/Alamy; page 68: Roger Cicala; page 75: Joel Preston Smith; page 76: Joel Preston Smith; page 77: Joel Preston Smith; page 82: Harper Collins Publishers; page 83: Harper Collins Publishers; page 84 all: Ryan Alexiev.

Chapter 5: Page 93: Enrique's Journey © 2002 Los Angles Times. Photos by Don Barletti; page 94: The Saul Steinberg Foundation/Artists Rights Society (ARS), New York; page 95: Lynn Watson/Shutterstock.com; page 97: Thinkstock/Getty Images; page 102: Ken Andreyo/Carnegie Mellon; page 107: Gavriel Jecan/Encyclopedia/CORBIS; page 110: Bernard Schoenbaum/Cartoonbank.com; page 123: David Koscheck/ shutterstock.com.

Chapter 6: Pages 126, 138: ©unshovelingthepast.blogspot. com/Sarah Ambrose, page 127: Kate Burak; page 129: Nora Tejada /Getty Images; page 133: Scott S. Warren/National Geographic Society/Corbis; page 137: Kate Burak; page 138: Elizabeth "Yoshi" Makishima; pages 138, 142: 007 by Smith Magazine. Reprinted by permission of HarerCollins Publisher, photo Elliott David; page 139: Author photo; page 139: Kate Burak; pages 139, 149: Photo by Marc F. Henning; page 151: PERSEPOLIS: The Story of a Childhood by Marjane Satrapi, translated by Mattias Ripa & Blake Ferris, translation Copyright © 2003 by L'Association, Paris, France. Used by permission of Pantheon Books, a division of Random House, Inc. page 3; page 152: PERSEPOLIS: The Story of a Childhood by Marjane Satrapi, translated by Mattias Ripa & Blake Ferris, translation Copyright © 2003 by L'Association, Paris, France. Used by permission of Pantheon Books, a division of Random House, Inc.; page 153: PERSEPOLIS: The Story of a Childhood by Marjane Satrapi, translated by Mattias Ripa & Blake Ferris, translation Copyright © 2003 by L'Association, Paris, France. Used by permission of Pantheon Books, a division of Random House, Inc.

Chapter 7: Page 170: 2011 The Andy Warhol Foundation for the Visual Arts, Inc./Artists Rights Society (ARS), New York. Photo:Art Resource; page 171: Vaclav Taus/ Shutterstock.com; page 173: Shanna Baker/Getty Images; page 174: Library of Congress; page 179: Cynthia Anderson; page 180: Pam Berry; page 184: Jamie Wyeth/Collection of Cheekwood Botanical Garden and Museum of Art; page 185: Photo by Hans Namuth Courtesy Center for Creative Photography, University of Arizona © 1991 Hans Namuth Estate; page 189: Peter Doyle; page 190: Scala/ Art Resource, NY.

Chapter 8: Page 213: TAO Images/SuperStock; page 214: Photo by John Moore/Getty Images; page 215: Frontpage, 2009/Used under license from Shutterstock.com; page 217: Thinkstock/Getty Images; page 220: Charles Fishman; page 224: John Kepsimelis/U.S.Coast Guard via Bloomberg; page 224: Joe Raedle/Getty Images; page 225 all: John Moore/Getty Images; page 228: Sage Stossel/Boston Globe Magazine January 16,2011.

Chapter 9: Page 240: Janis Krums; page 241: EmiliaU/ Shutterstock.com; page 243: Nora Tejada /Getty Images; page 247: Joseph Lee; page 248: John Tlumacki/Globe Staff/ Getty Images; page 249: Suzanne Kreiter/Globe Staff/Getty Images; page 250: Bill Greene/Globe Staff/Getty Images; page 251: Jim Davis/Globe Staff/Getty Images; page 252: The Smoking Gun; page 254: Jonathan Wiggs/Globe Staff/Getty Images; page 255: Boston Globe via Getty Images; page 265: Nick Laham/Staff/Getty Images; page 269: The State News/ statenews.com.

Chapter 10: Page 277: Image Source/Aurora Photos; page 278: 20th Century Fox/Everett Collection; page 279: akva/ Shutterstock.com; page 281: Shanna Baker/Getty Images; page 283: Photos 12/Alamy; page 286: Ty Burr; page 288: WARNER BROS./THE KOBAL COLLECTION/ART RESOURCE; page 294: Focus Films/Zuma Press; page 295: 20TH CENTURY FOX / THE KOBAL COLLECTION / ADLER, SUE/ Picture Desk; page 295: FOX SEARCHLIGHT/THE KOBAL COLLECTION/GREGORY, DOANE/ART RESOURCE; page 296: FILM 4/CELADOR FILMS/PATHE INTERNATIONAL/THE KOBAL COLLECTION/ART RESOURCE; page 300: OVERTURE FILMS/THE KOBAL COLLECTION/ART RESOURCE; page 302: 20TH CENTURY FOX/THE KOBAL COLLECTION/ART RESOURCE; page 304: Michel Bourquard/PACHA/Corbis Entertainment/CORBIS.

Chapter 11: Page 312: Celeste Pille (www.celeste-doodleordie. blogspot.com); page 313: ildogesto/Shutterstock.com; page 315: Thinkstock/Getty Images; page 319: Robin Berghaus; page 326: Kate Burak; page 328: Courtesy of Randy Krum/www.coolinfographics.com; page 330: Reprinted from The Lancet, Volume 376, No. 9752, David J Nutt, Leslie A King, Lawrence D Phillips, Drug harms in the UK: a multicriteria decision analysis, p. 1513-1616, Nov 6, 2010, with permission from Elsevier; page 331: www.creditloan.com; page 334: ©Infographic World/www. infographicworld.com; page 335 all: Stephen Crowley/The New York Times/Redux Pictures.

Chapter 12: Page 361: Luba Lukova; page 362: Ankush Trakru "Lord Q"; page 363: Complot/Shutterstock.com; page 365: Nora Tejada/Getty Images; page 369: Stephen Budiansky; page 371: Courtesy of Martin C. Hansen (designer), Amanda Abramson, Michael McCarthy; page 371: Time & Life Pictures/Getty Images; page 373: Indiana University-Purdue University Indianapolis; page 376: Universal Press Syndicate; page 377: CORBIS; page 378: www.politicalcartoons.com; page 379: Eric Allie/www. politicalcartoons.com; page 380: Clay Bennett c 2002 The Christian Science Monitor; page 381: Christo Komarnitski/ www.politicalcartoons.com; page 387: Craig Ruttle/Alamy.

Chapter 13: Page 406: SPCA-Singapore; page 407: Yuliyan Velchev/Shutterstock.com; page 409: Shanna Baker/Getty Images; page 410: The Ad Council; page 411: Tom Fauls; page 415 all: Image Courtesy of The Advertising Archives; page 416: Kansas Department of Transportation Safety & Technology; page 417: Terry Harris/Alamy; page 423: Image Courtesy of The Advertising Archives; page 424: Image Courtesy of The Advertising Archives; page 426: Image Courtesy of The Advertising Archives; page 431: Screening for Mental Health, Inc.; page 432: Clarity Coverdale Fury; page 433 all: Clarity Coverdale Fury; page 435: Image Courtesy of The Advertising Archives; page 436: Image Courtesy of The Advertising Archives; page 437: Kate Burak.

Chapter 14: Page 442: Image Courtesy of The Advertising Archives; page 443: alterfalter/shutterstock.com; page 445: Thinkstock/Getty Images; page 449: Photo by Peter Smith; page 453: Bill Heinsohn/Alamy; page 453: Enigma/Alamy; page 453: Vibe Images/Alamy; page 461: Courtesy, David Tranter, School of Social Work, Lakehead University. Photo: New Line Skateparks, Inc.; page 462 all: Courtesy, David Tranter, School of Social Work, Lakehead University. Photo: New Line Skateparks, Inc.; page 463 all: Courtesy, David Tranter, School of Social Work, Lakehead University. Photo: New Line Skateparks, Inc.; page 464 all: Courtesy, David Tranter, School of Social Work, Lakehead University. Photo: New Line Skateparks, Inc.; page 469: Cengage Learning; page 469: Picture Contact BV/Alamy; page 469: Kate Burak; page 471: Photos courtesy, Christian Solidarity International.

Chapter 15: Page 477: Tony Law/Redux Pictures; page 478: Cartoon by Peter Steiner/Cartoonbank.com; page 479: Nejron Photo/Shutterstock.com; page 482: Mugar Memorial Library, Boston University; page 483: Encyclopedia Britannica; page 488: Cengage Learning; page 489: Cengage Learning.

Chapter 16: Page 502: David Silverman/Getty Images News/Getty Images; page 503: Heinz Koenig/Shutterstock.com.

Chapter 17: Page 559: John Lock/Shutterstock.com; page 562: Bizarro (News) c Dam Piraro 2002/King Features Syndicate; page 563: Andriy Zholudyev/Shutterstock.com.

Chapter 18: Page 578: Yuri Arcurs/Shutterstock.com.

Chapter 19: Page 593: Shawn Hempel/Shutterstock.com.

Chapter 20: Page 609: Martin Lehmann/Shutterstock.com

Index